Principles of
Services Marketing
4th edition

Principles of Services Marketing
4th edition

Adrian Palmer

The **McGraw·Hill** Companies

London   Boston   Burr Ridge, IL   Dubuque, IA   Madison, WI   New York   San Francisco
St Louis   Bangkok   Bogotá   Caracas   Kuala Lumpur   Lisbon   Madrid   Mexico City
Milan   Montreal   New Delhi   Santiago   Seoul   Singapore   Sydney   Taipei   Toronto

Principles of Services Marketing 4/e
Adrian Palmer
ISBN 0-07-710794-2

 Education

Published by McGraw-Hill Education
Shoppenhangers Road
Maidenhead
Berkshire
SL6 2QL
Telephone: 44 (0) 1628 502 500
Fax: 44 (0) 1628 770 224
Website: www.mcgraw-hill.co.uk

British Library Cataloguing in Publication Data
A catalogue record for this book is available from the British Library

Library of Congress Cataloguing in Publication Data
The Library of Congress data for this book has been applied for from the Library of Congress

Acquisitions Editor: Mark Kavanagh
Associate Development Editor: Rachel Crookes
Senior Marketing Manager: Marca Wosoba
Senior Production Editor: Jennifer Harvey

Text Design by Jonathan Coleclough
Cover design by Ego Creative
Printed and bound in Finland by WS Bookwell

Contents

1

What is services marketing?

Learning objectives

This chapter will explain:

- what is meant by the term services
- how national economies have become dominated by services
- the distinguishing characteristics of intangibility, perishability, inseparability and variability
- differences between the marketing of goods and services
- the extended marketing mix for services
- special requirements of not-for-profit services marketing.

1.1 **Introduction**

Citizens of the western world are living in increasingly service-based economies. Services are no longer a minor or superficial part of economies, but go to the heart of value creation within the economy. Of course, the service sector is nothing new, as evidenced by biblical references to innkeepers and money lenders, among others. Today most products that we buy include some element of service in them. We can readily identify activities such as accountancy, banking and hairdressing as being service based. In addition to these, a wide range of goods relies on service-based activities to give them a competitive advantage. A car buyer now typically buys a comprehensive bundle of service benefits, such as financing, maintenance and insurance, in addition to the tangible components of the car. Many apparently 'pure' goods such as television sets and washing machines usually come with service offers based on delivery, financing, insurance and maintenance benefits.

Although there has been a big growth in interest in the service sector in recent years, the academic literature has not always recognized the value of services. Early economists paid little attention to services, considering them to be totally unproductive, adding nothing of value to an economy. Adam Smith, writing in the mid-18th century, distinguished between production that had a tangible output – such as agriculture and manufacture – and production for which there was no tangible output. The latter, which included the efforts of intermediaries, doctors, lawyers and the armed forces, he described as 'unproductive of any value' (Smith, 1977, p. 430). This remained the dominant attitude towards services until the latter part of the 19th century when Alfred Marshall argued that a person providing a service was just as capable of giving utility to the recipient as a person producing a tangible product. Indeed, Marshall recognized that tangible products may not exist at all were it not for a series of services performed in order to produce them and to make them available to consumers. To Marshall, an agent distributing agricultural produce performed as valuable a task as the farmer himself. Without the provision of transport and intermediary services, agricultural products produced in areas of surplus would be of no value. Today, despite some lingering beliefs that the service sector is an insubstantial and relatively inferior sector of the economy, considerable attention is paid to its direct and indirect economic consequences. Indeed, in one recent article which talked about the 'service-centric' organization, services were seen as the driving force behind all value creation in the economy (Vargo and Lusch, 2004).

There are many definitions of what constitutes a service. Modern definitions of services focus on the fact that a service in itself produces no tangible output, although it may be instrumental in producing some tangible output. Perhaps one of the simplest definitions of a service was given by *The Economist*, which described services as 'anything that cannot be dropped on your foot'.

The definition of **services** that will be used to define the scope of this book is:
The production of an essentially intangible benefit, either in its own right or as a

significant element of a tangible product, which through some form of exchange, satisfies an identified need.

This definition recognizes that most products are in fact a combination of goods elements and services elements. In some cases, the service element will be the essential element of the service (e.g. hairdressing and management consultancy), while in other cases the service will simply support the provision of a tangible good (e.g. a loan facility provided to support the sale of a new car).

In the evolution of the services marketing literature, there has been argument about the extent to which services should be considered a distinctive area of study in marketing. On the one hand, some have argued that a service contains many important elements common to goods, which makes services marketing obsolete as a separate discipline. Thus Levitt (1972) observed:

... there is no such thing as service industries. There are only industries where service components are greater or less than those of other industries.

On the other hand, many have pointed to the limitations of traditional marketing principles when applied to the marketing of services. Grönroos (1978), Lovelock (1981), Shostack (1977), Berry (1980) and Rathmell (1966) were among the early critics who argued that the differences that exist between goods and services mean that the marketing tools used for goods marketing cannot easily be translated to services marketing.

In reality, services marketing is about refining the basic philosophy of marketing to allow the principles to be operationalized more effectively in the service sector. Many of these principles will be familiar to those involved in the marketing of goods and can be applied to services with relatively little refinement. In some cases – such as the analysis of **service encounters** – a new area of marketing thought needs to be opened up.

In addition to the grey area between a pure good and a pure service, some marketing activities do not fit easily on this scale. The first of these which has attracted growing interest is the marketing of ideas, whether these be the ideas of a political party, a religious sect or an idea on a specific subject, such as road safety. The second – and related area – is the marketing of a cause, such as famine relief in Africa or a campaign to prevent the construction of a new road. Both of these types of activity are distinguished from normal goods and services marketing as there is no exchange of value between the producer and the individuals or organizations at whom the marketing effort is aimed. To take an example, the consumer of transport services enters into an exchange and pays for a transport service, either directly and willingly – as in the case of a train fare – or indirectly, and possibly unwillingly, through general taxation – as is the case for the use of roads. By contrast, when a pressure group mounts a campaign to bring about the building of a new road, the concept of exchange of value becomes extremely tenuous, only really occurring where, for example, a member of the public subsequently contributes to a cause, either financially or by actions. Generally, however, the concept of services does not offer an appropriate framework for analysing the marketing of ideas and causes where these do not form part of a service process. Of course, in many cases, consumers of a service are buying into an idea promoted by the service provider, or may identify with a cause that the provider promotes. Many customers of Fairtrade products, for example, choose that supplier for their coffee or tea because of its identification with the cause of producers in the developing world. In this case, there is a market-based transaction (the purchase of the coffee) to support the idea. At other times, a service exchange may be based almost entirely on an idea. Copywriters and consultants may be selling little more than an idea, but again, there is an exchange between the parties (a payment in return for a creative idea). We will return to the idea of ideas, or knowledge-based services, in Chapter 2.

1.1.1 The growth of service-based economies

There is little doubt that the service sector has become a dominant force in many national economies. According to Euromonitor, services accounted for 68% of GDP in the EU in 2000 (Euromonitor, 2001). Between 1970 and 1997, it is reported that about one and a half million new jobs per year were created in the service sectors within the EU – twice the average for the rest of the economy (Eurostat, 1998).

There appears to be a close correlation between the level of economic development in an economy (as expressed by its GDP per capita) and the strength of its service sector. The more highly developed economies are associated with a high proportion of employees accounted for by the service sector. According to the International Labor Organization (ILO, 2004), over three-quarters of workers in most western developed economies are employed in the service sector (e.g. United States, 75%; Canada, 75%; Australia, 74%; and the United Kingdom, 73%). Those western countries that are considered to be less developed have proportionately fewer employed in their service sector – for example, Spain (59%), Portugal (53%), Ireland (53%) and Greece (49%). The lowest levels of services employment are found in the less-developed countries such as Mexico (30%), Bangladesh (28%) and Ethiopia (9%). Figure 1.1 indicates the close correlation between GDP per head and service sector employment.

While there is undoubtedly a close correlation between the level of a country's economic development, and the level of services activity within its economy, which is cause and which is effect? Does the existence of a service sector result in growth, or are services an outcome of that growth? To answer this question, we need to distinguish between *producer services* and *consumer services*. Producer services, which help a country by providing inputs to production processes, have often had a major impact on national economies and many service industries have facilitated improved **productivity** elsewhere in the manufacturing and agricultural sectors. As an example, transport and distribution services have often had the effect of stimulating economic

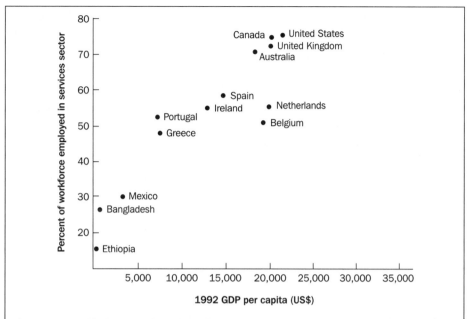

Figure 1.1 Graph showing, for selected countries, the association between GDP per head and the percentage of employment in the service sector (compiled from OECD and ILO data). (Based on OECD and ILO data for 2000, or the most recent available)

development at local and national levels (e.g. following the improvement of rail or road services). One reason for Russian agriculture not having been fully exploited has been the ineffective service-based distribution systems available to food producers. Consumer services, on the other hand, consume wealth rather than create it. As national economies become more prosperous, we have a tendency to increase our consumption of a wide range of consumer services, such as holidays, entertainment and eating out.

Although it is conventional wisdom that the service sectors have grown strongly in recent years, we need to hedge this with a few caveats.

■ The level of accuracy with which service sector statistics have been recorded is generally less than for manufacturing and primary sectors. For many years the system of Standard Industrial Classifications (SICs) did not disaggregate the service sector in the same level of detail as manufacture or agriculture. Many service sectors do not fall neatly into one of the classifications, making it difficult to get an overall picture of them.

■ The intangible nature of services can make them relatively difficult to measure, especially in the case of overseas trade. While flows of tangible goods through ports can usually be measured quite easily, trade flows associated with services are much more difficult to identify and measure. Furthermore, cutbacks in government statistical collection have increased the inaccuracy of many series. As an example, the UK trade figures relating to tourism and financial services frequently have to be revised after initial publication.

■ Part of the apparent growth in the service sector may reflect the method by which statistics are collected, rather than indicating an increase in overall service level activity. Within many manufacturing organizations, people are employed to produce service-type activities, such as cleaning, catering, transport and distribution. Where a cook is employed by a manufacturing company, output and employment are attributed to the manufacturing sector. However, a common occurrence during the past two decades has been for manufacturing industries to contract out many of these service activities to external contractors. Where such contracts are performed by contract catering, office cleaning or transport companies, say, the output becomes counted within the service sector, making the sector look larger, even though no additional services have been produced – they have merely been switched from internally produced to externally produced and traded.

Services can have a **multiplier effect** on local and national economies in that initial spending with a service producer triggers further expenditure. The **services multiplier** works like this. The first producer spends money buying in supplies from outside (including labour) and these outside suppliers in turn purchase more inputs. The multiplier effect of this initial expenditure can result in the total increase in household incomes being much greater than the original expenditure. A good example of the multiplier effect was used to argue the case for the development of London's Millennium Dome on a derelict site at Greenwich. Internationally, many governments have supported bids to host major sporting events such as the Olympic Games in order to gain the resulting multiplier benefits. While these events initially create direct employment within themselves, demand ripples out to other service sectors, such as hotels and transport. This in turn can generate additional demand for local manufacturing industry; for example, visitors require food, which may be produced locally, the producers of which may in turn require additional building materials to increase production facilities. The multiplier effects of additional service activity will depend on the proportion of the subsequent spending that is kept within the local area.

One approach to understanding the contribution of services to other aspects of economic activity is to analyse input–output tables of production and data on labour and capital inputs. Wood (1987) used these to estimate the effects that productivity improvements in all of the direct and indirect supply sectors had on the productivity levels of all other sectors. Some apparently high-productivity sectors were shown to be held back by the low productivity of some of their inputs, including service inputs. On the other hand, efficiency improvements in some services such as transport and distribution were shown to have had widespread beneficial effects on the productivity contribution of other sectors.

Should western developed economies focus on becoming service-based economies, even at the expense of the manufacturing sector? This may sound appealing, but the logic of this argument can be pushed too far, in particular:

1. A large part of the growth in the service sector during recent years has reflected the prosperity of the manufacturing sector. As manufacturing industry increases its level of activity, the demand for producer services such as accountancy, legal services and business travel increases. The sudden decline of many UK financial service sectors in the early 1990s reflected the downturn in manufacturing activity, resulting in lower demand for business loans, export credits, etc.

2. In the UK, the assumption that the country has a comparative cost advantage in the production of services needs to be examined closely. In the same way that many sectors of the UK manufacturing industry lost their **competitive advantage** to developing nations during the 1960s and 1970s, there is evidence that a once unquestioned supremacy in certain service sectors is now being challenged. Financial services markets that achieved prominence in London when Britain was the world's most important trading nation are increasingly following world trade to its new centres such as Tokyo and Frankfurt. High levels of training in competing nations have allowed those countries to develop their own indigenous services and then to develop them for export. Banking services, which were once a net import of Japan, are now exported by the Japanese throughout the world.

Figure 1.2 Plant growing has traditionally been associated primarily with the agricultural sector. However, crocus.co.uk has shown how even such a basic agricultural activity can be transformed into a service. The company doesn't just grow and sell plants, but offers a complete service to the buyer which includes delivery and planting, as well as continuing to give advice about caring for the plant. (Reproduced with permission of crocus.co.uk Ltd)

Improved telecommunications have offered an opportunity for Indian-based call centre providers to challenge British-based call centres.

3. Over-reliance on the service sector could pose strategic problems for the UK. A diverse economic base allows a national economy to be more resilient to changes in world trading conditions.

All steam and service?

The textbooks have described what happened in Britain during the early part of the 19th century as the Industrial Revolution. Visions of new technologies involving steam power, factory systems and metal production have led to the dominant view that Britain advanced economically primarily as a result of progress in the manufacturing sector. But could the industrial revolution have happened without the service sector? The period saw the development of many services whose presence was vital to economic development. Without the development of railways, goods would not have been distributed from centralized factories to geographically dispersed consumers and many people would not have been able to get to work. Investment in new factories called for a banking system that could circulate funds at a national rather than a purely local level. A whole new service sector emerged to meet the needs of manufacturing, including intermediaries who were essential to get manufacturers' goods to increasingly dispersed markets. Today, we continue to rely on services to exploit developments in the manufacturing sector. Should we rewrite history and talk about the 'Service Revolution' rather than the industrial revolution of 19th-century England?

1.2 Defining marketing in a services context

A traditional definition of **marketing** is provided by the Chartered Institute of Marketing:

The management process which identifies, anticipates and supplies customer requirements efficiently and profitably.

Marketing orientation first emerged in the relatively affluent countries for goods where competition between suppliers had become the fiercest. Adoption of marketing by the service sector generally came later, largely due to the effects of significant public-sector monopolies and the existence of professional codes of practice which, until recently, have restrained many service organizations' marketing activities.

Many people have tried to define just what is meant by marketing orientation. Work by Narver and Slater (1990) has sought to define and measure the extent of marketing orientation, and their analysis identified three important components:

1. *Customer orientation,* meaning that an organization has a sufficient understanding of its target buyers that allows it to create superior value for them. This comes about through increasing the benefits to the buyer in relation to the buyer's costs or by decreasing the buyer's costs in relation to the buyer's benefits. A customer orientation requires that the organization understands value to the customer not only as it is today, but also as it will evolve over time.

2. *Competitor orientation,* defined as an organization's understanding of the short-term strengths and weaknesses and long-term capabilities and strategies of current and potential competitors.

3. *Interfunctional co-ordination,* referring to the manner in which an organization uses its resources in creating superior value for target customers. Many individuals within an organization have responsibility for creating value, not just marketing staff, and a marketing orientation requires that the organization draws upon and integrates its human and physical resources effectively and adapts them to meet the **customer's needs**. There has been extensive research into the internal barriers that prevent companies developing a marketing orientation (e.g. Harris, 2002; Morgan, 2002).This aspect of marketing is crucial to the service sector, where production and consumption are inseparable. Later chapters will emphasize the importance to a company of satisfying customer needs through the integration of marketing, human resource management and operations management.

   Marketing orientation is used to describe both the basic philosophy of an organization as well as the techniques it uses.

■ As a business philosophy, marketing puts the customer at the centre of all the organization's considerations. Basic values such as the requirement to identify the changing needs of existing customers and the necessity to constantly search for new market opportunities are instilled in all members of a truly marketing-oriented organization, covering all aspects of the organization's activities. For a fast-food retailer, the training of serving staff would emphasize those items – such as the standard of dress and speed of service – which research had found to be particularly valued by existing and potential customers. The personnel manager would have a selection policy that sought to recruit staff who fulfilled the needs of customers rather than simply minimize the wage bill. The accountant would investigate the effects on customers before deciding to save money by cutting stock-holding levels, thereby possibly reducing customers' choice. It is not sufficient for an organization to merely appoint a marketing manager or set up a marketing department – viewed as a philosophy, marketing is an attitude of mind that pervades the whole organization.

■ Marketing orientation is associated with a range of techniques. For example, market research is a technique for finding out about customer needs and advertising is a technique to communicate the service offer to potential customers. However, these techniques lose a lot of their value if they are conducted by an organization that has not fully embraced the philosophy of marketing. The techniques of marketing also include, among other things, pricing, the design of channels of distribution, and new product development. Application of these techniques to the service sector is described in later chapters.

Of course, there are many service organizations that operate in an environment with very little competitive pressure, so they can afford to pursue a production orientation rather than a marketing orientation. Sometimes, local or temporary shortages of service providers may bring this about. During the boom in property prices that occurred in the UK during 2000–2004, the services of builders were in short supply, especially in south-east England. Stories abounded of builders 'selecting' customers and delaying the completion of jobs because they knew that customers had very little choice.

Can you spot the marketing-oriented company?

It is easy for a service organization to say that it is marketing oriented and puts customers first. But, all too often, it is very easy to spot tell-tale signs that marketing is only skin deep. Consider some of the following give-away signs:

- opening hours that are designed to suit the interests of staff rather than customers (very common among many public-sector services)
- administrative procedures that make life easier for the company rather than its customers (e.g. expecting customers to contact several sections of the organization, rather than offering a 'one-stop' facility)
- reserving prime car-parking spaces for staff rather than customers
- advertising that is aimed at the egos of company managers rather than the needs and aspirations of potential buyers.

Can you think of any further give-aways?

1.2.1 The marketing mix for services

The **marketing mix** is the set of tools available to an organization to shape the nature of its offer to customers. Goods marketers are familiar with the 4Ps of product, price, promotion and place. Early analysis by Borden (1965) of marketing mix elements was based on a study of manufacturing industry at a time when the importance of services to the economy was considered to be relatively unimportant. More recently, the 4Ps of the marketing mix have been found to be too limited in their application to services. Particular problems that limit their usefulness to services are as follows.

- The intangible nature of services is overlooked in most analyses of the mix – for example, the product mix is frequently analysed in terms of tangible design properties that may not be relevant to a service. Likewise, physical distribution management may not be an important element of place mix decisions.

■ The price element overlooks the fact that many services are produced by the public sector without a price being charged to the final consumer.

■ The promotion mix of the traditional 4Ps fails to recognize the promotion of services which takes place at the point of consumption by the production personnel, unlike the situation with most fast-moving consumer goods which are normally produced away from the consumer and therefore the producer has no direct involvement in promoting the good to the final consumer. For a bank clerk, hairdresser or singer, the manner in which the service is produced is an important element of the total promotion of the service.

As well as throwing up ambiguities about the meaning of some of these four elements of the marketing mix, this simple list also fails to recognize a number of key factors which marketing managers in the service sector use to design their service output. Particular problems focus on:

■ defining the concept of quality for intangible services, and identifying and measuring the mix elements that can be managed in order to create a quality service

■ the importance of people as an element within the service product, both as producers and co-consumers

■ the over-simplification of the elements of distribution which are of relevance to intangible services.

These weaknesses have resulted in a number of attempts to redefine the marketing mix in a manner that is more applicable to the service sector. While many have sought to refine the marketing mix for general application, the expansions by Booms and Bitner (1981) and Christopher *et al.* (1991) provide useful frameworks for analysis, although they are not empirically proven theories of services marketing. In addition to the four traditional elements of the marketing mix, both frameworks add the additional elements of people and process. In addition, Booms and Bitner talk about physical evidence making up a seventh 'P' while Christopher *et al.* add customer service as an additional element.

The principle of the **extended marketing mix** (as indeed with the traditional marketing mix) is to break a service offering down into a number of component parts and to arrange them into manageable subject areas for making strategic and tactical decisions. Decisions on one element of the mix can be made only by reference to other elements of the mix in order to give a sustainable product positioning. The importance attached to each element of the extended marketing mix will vary between services. In a highly automated service such as vending machine dispensing, people will be a less important element of the mix than in a people-intensive business, such as a restaurant.

A brief overview of these marketing mix ingredients is given below, with fuller discussion following in subsequent chapters.

Products

Products are the means by which organizations seek to satisfy consumer needs. A product in this sense is anything that the organization offers to potential customers, whether it be tangible or intangible. After initial hesitation, most marketing managers are now happy to talk about an intangible service as a product. Thus bank accounts, insurance policies and holidays are frequently referred to as products, sometimes to the amusement of non-marketers, while pop stars or even politicians are referred to as a product to be marketed.

Product mix decisions facing a services marketer can be very different from those dealing with goods. Most fundamentally, **pure services** are best defined using process descriptions rather than tangible descriptions of outcomes. Elements of the product mix such as design, reliability, brand image, and product range may sound familiar to a goods marketer, but assume different roles, as discussed in Chapter 2. There is also a significant difference with goods in that new service developments cannot be protected by patent.

Pricing

Price mix decisions include strategic and tactical decisions about the average level of prices to be charged, discount structures, terms of payment and the extent to which price discrimination between different groups of customers is to take place. These are very similar to the issues facing a goods marketer. Differences do, however, occur where the intangible nature of a service can mean that price in itself can become a very significant indicator of quality. The personal and non-transferable nature of many services presents additional opportunities for price discrimination within service markets, while the fact that many services are marketed by the public sector at a subsidized or no price can complicate price setting.

Promotion

The traditional promotion mix includes various methods of communicating the benefits of a service to potential consumers. The mix is traditionally broken down into four main elements: advertising, sales promotion, public relations and personal selling. The promotion of services often needs to place particular emphasis on increasing the apparent tangibility of a service. Also, in the case of services marketing, production personnel can themselves become an important element of the promotion mix.

Place

Place decisions refer to the ease of access that potential customers have to a service. Place decisions can therefore involve physical location decisions (as in deciding where to place a hotel), decisions about which intermediaries to use in making a service accessible to a consumer (e.g. whether a tour operator uses travel agents or sells its holidays direct to customers) and non-locational decisions which are used to make services available (e.g. the use of Internet-based delivery systems). For pure services, decisions about how to physically move a good are of little strategic relevance. However, most services involve movement of goods of some form. These can either be materials necessary to produce a service (such as travel brochures and fast-food packaging material) or the service can have, as its whole purpose, the movement of goods (e.g. road haulage, plant hire).

People

For most services, people are a vital element of the marketing mix. Where production can be separated from consumption – as is the case with most manufactured goods – management can usually take measures to reduce the direct effect of people on the final output as received by customers. Therefore the buyer of a car is not concerned whether a production worker dresses untidily, uses bad language at work or turns up for work late, as long as there are quality control measures that reject the results of lax behaviour before they reach the customer. In service industries, everyone is what Gummesson (2001) calls a 'part-time marketer' in that their actions have a much more direct effect on the output received by customers.

While the importance attached to people management in improving quality within manufacturing companies is increasing – for example, through the development of quality circles – people planning assumes much greater importance within the service sector. This is especially true in those services where staff have a high level of contact with customers. For this reason, it is essential that service organizations clearly specify what is expected from personnel in their interaction with customers. To achieve the specified standard, methods of recruiting, training, motivating and rewarding staff cannot be regarded as purely personnel decisions – they are important marketing mix decisions.

People planning within the marketing mix also involves developing a pattern of interaction between customers themselves, which can be very important where service consumption takes place in public. An important way in which drinkers judge a pub might be the kind of people who frequent the pub. An empty pub may convey no atmosphere while a rowdy one may convey the wrong impression to important segments. As well as planning the human input to its own production, marketing management must also develop strategies for producing favourable interaction between its customers – for example, by excluding certain groups and developing a physical environment which affects customers' behaviour.

Physical evidence

The intangible nature of a service means that potential customers are unable to judge that service before it is consumed, thereby increasing the riskiness inherent in a purchase decision. An important element of marketing planning is therefore to reduce this level of risk by offering tangible evidence of the nature of the service. This evidence can take a number of forms. At its simplest, a brochure can describe and give pictures of important elements of the service product – a holiday brochure gives pictorial evidence of hotels and resorts for this purpose. The appearance of staff can give evidence about the nature of a service – a tidily dressed ticket clerk for an airline gives some evidence that the airline operation as a whole is run with care and attention. Buildings are frequently used to give evidence of service nature. Towards the end of the 19th century, railway companies outbid each other to produce the most elaborate station buildings. For people wishing to travel from London to Scotland, a comparison of the grandeur of the three terminals in London's Euston Road could give some clue to the ability of the railway to provide a substantial service. Today, a clean, bright environment used in a service outlet can help to reassure potential customers at the point where they make a service purchase decision. For this reason, fast-food and photo-processing outlets often use red and yellow colour schemes to convey an image of speedy service.

Processes

'A service firm has no products, only *interactive* processes' (Grönroos, 2001). Production processes are usually of little concern to consumers of manufactured goods, but can be of critical concern to consumers of 'high contact' services where consumers can be seen as a co-producer of the service. Visitors to a restaurant are deeply affected by the manner in which staff serve them and the amount of waiting that is involved during the production process. Issues arise as to the boundary between the producer and consumer in terms of the allocation of production functions – for example, a restaurant might require customers to collect their meals from a counter, or expect them to deposit their own rubbish. With services, a clear distinction cannot be made between marketing and operations management.

Customer service

The meaning of customer service varies from one organization to another. Within the service sector, it can best be described as the total quality of the service as perceived by the customer. As such, responsibility for this element of the marketing mix cannot be isolated within a narrowly defined customer services department, but becomes a concern of all production personnel, both those directly employed by the organization and those employed by suppliers. Managing the quality of the service offered to the customer becomes closely identified with policy on the related marketing mix elements of product design and personnel.

1.2.2 The use of metaphors in the services literature

The literature on services marketing evolved after the literature on goods marketing. In evolving, many metaphors have been used to describe services (Goodwin, 1996). Factory metaphors have frequently been applied to services, using such terms as inputs, processing, outputs and productivity. The early phases of service research deliberately drew parallels between production of a tangible good and delivery of an intangible service. Early articles placed consumers in the factory, as contributors to production processes (Lovelock and Young, 1979) or as potential bottlenecks to be processed as quickly as possible (Chase, 1978). However, factory metaphors fail when marketers are forced to recognize the unique aspects of human consumers as inputs to a service production process, as compared to inanimate inputs. The latter can be inventoried in a warehouse for months at a time, whereas customers can become dissatisfied after waiting for just a few minutes in a queue.

As we will explore in Chapter 3, discussion of services has drawn heavily on metaphors associated with the theatre. Services have been compared to theatrical productions, complete with script, actors, props, a stage, director and audience. Service processes have been differentiated into front stage and back stage. The drama metaphor incorporates experiential, hedonistic elements of service consumption and, as in the theatre, there may be a desire of the audience (customers) to temporarily suspend their belief in the reality of the act.

1.3 **Marketing in transition?**

In recent years, marketing has matured as a discipline. One sign of this maturity is an increasing willingness of marketing academics and practitioners to look inwardly and become more self-critical of their discipline. An abundance of scholarly research and practitioner proclamations has suggested that marketing is undergoing a fundamental, epoch-breaking change (e.g. Brady and Davis, 1993; Grönroos, 1997). Talk about new paradigms has been interspersed with gloomy predictions about the future of the marketing department and the triumph of chaos where previously there was order (Gummesson, 1997; Murray and O'Driscoll, 1997).

The scientific approach to marketing, based on the management of the marketing mix has been held by some to be too constraining in a world where consumers increasingly break the 'rules' of consumption. Grönroos (1997) stated that 'the major problem with the marketing mix and its 4Ps has been their position as the major, and in many situations as the only acceptable marketing paradigm'. He asked why the marketing mix management paradigm and the 4Ps model have become such a straitjacket for marketers and suggested that the 'main reason is for pedagogical virtues'. The marketing mix is atheoretical and has formed the basis for the overwhelming majority of texts on marketing. A more creative, holistic approach to solving customers' problems has been called for, in place of company-focused marketing plans. '**Postmodern marketing**' and 'new marketing manifestos' typify recent debate (Brown, 1995; Grant, 1999). Wilson and Gilligan (1997, p. 25) declared that 'there has been an increasing recognition over the past few years that marketing is, or may be facing what is loosely referred to as a mid-life crisis' due to the widespread concern that 'something is amiss'. In addition, Brown (1995, p. 42) proclaimed that the 'marketing concept is deeply, perhaps irredeemably flawed, that its seemingly solid theoretical foundations are by no means secure and that the specialism is teetering on the brink of serious intellectual crisis'.

It is possible that the domination of economies by services has led to the final breakdown of the traditional marketing models that have been developed for goods-based economies. Trying to stretch goods-based models of buyer behaviour to fit services may not work, given the different search processes and credence qualities of services, for example. There has been discussion that developed countries are moving to an 'experience'-based economy in which hedonistic values of consumption predominate (Pine and Gilmore, 1999). But despite talk of marketing being in 'crisis' and the need for new paradigms, the case for change is somewhat ambiguous. Consider the following anecdotal evidence from the service sector. In the UK grocery retail sector, 'new' marketing ideas stress the importance of individual one-to-one dialogue between a retailer and its customers, yet research has shown that the most profitable retailers are not those with personalized loyalty programmes, but those which offer standardized, low prices for all (Knox, 1998; Murphy, 1998). Similarly, in the airline sector, new marketing paradigms might have expected operators who finely tailor their operations to the needs of multiple small segments to win out over airlines that offer one standard of service to all. However, the fastest-growing sector of the civil aviation **market** has been the low-cost, low-frills sector, while many full-service airlines have either made heavy losses, or gone out of business (*The Independent*, 2004).

1.4 **Distinguishing features of services**

Services have a number of distinctive characteristics that differentiate them from goods and have implications for the manner in which they are marketed. These characteristics are often described as intangibility, inseparability, variability, perishability and the inability to own a service. These characteristics will be a recurrent theme throughout this book, and their nature is introduced below.

1.4.1 **Intangibility**

A pure service cannot be assessed using any of the physical senses – it is an abstraction which cannot be directly examined before it is purchased. A prospective purchaser of most goods is able to examine the goods for physical integrity, aesthetic appearance, taste, smell, etc. Many advertising claims relating to these tangible properties can be verified by inspection prior to purchase. On the other hand, pure services have no tangible properties that can be used by consumers to verify advertising claims before the purchase is made. The intangible process characteristics that define services, such as reliability, personal care, attentiveness of staff, their friendliness, etc., can only be verified once a service has been purchased and consumed.

The level of tangibility present in the service offer derives from three principal sources:

1. tangible goods, which are included in the service offer and consumed by the user

2. the physical environment in which the service production/consumption process takes place, and

3. tangible evidence of service performance.

Where goods form an important component of a service offer, many of the practices associated with conventional goods marketing can be applied to this part of the service offer. Restaurants represent a mix of tangibles and intangibles and, in respect of the food element, few of the particular characteristics of services marketing are encountered. Therefore, production of the food can be separated from its consumption and the perishability of food is less significant than the perishability of an empty table. Furthermore, the presence of a tangible component gives customers a visible basis on which to judge quality.

The tangible elements of the service offer comprise not just those goods that are exchanged but also the physical environment in which a service encounter takes place. Within this environment, the design of buildings, their cleanliness and the appearance of staff present important tangible evidence that may be the only basis on which a buyer is able to differentiate one service provider from another. While some services are rich in such tangible cues (e.g. restaurants, shops), other services provide relatively little tangible evidence (e.g. life insurance).

Tangibility is further provided by evidence of service production methods. Some services provide many opportunities for customers to see the process of production, indeed the whole purpose of the service may be to see the production process (e.g. a pop concert). Often this tangible evidence can be seen before a decision to purchase a service is made, either by direct observation of a service being performed on somebody else (e.g. watching the work of a builder) or indirectly through a description of the service production process (a role played by brochures that specify and illustrate the service production process). On the other hand, some services provide very few tangible clues about the nature of the service production process. Portfolio management services are not only produced largely out of sight of the consumer, it is also difficult to specify in advance in a brochure what the service outcomes will be.

Intangibility has a number of important marketing implications (Figure 1.3) that will be examined in more detail in later chapters. The lack of physical evidence that intangibility implies increases the level of uncertainty that a consumer faces when choosing between competing services. An important part of a services marketing programme will therefore involve reducing consumers' perceived risk by such means as adding physical evidence and the development of strong brands.

It is interesting to note that pure goods and pure services tend to move in opposite directions in terms of their general approach to the issue of tangibility. While service marketers seek to add tangible evidence to their product (Figure 1.4), pure goods marketers often seek to augment their products by adding intangible elements such as after-sales service and improved distribution.

1.4.2 Inseparability

The production and consumption of a tangible good are two discrete activities. Companies usually produce goods in one central location and then transport them to the place where customers most want to buy them. In this way, manufacturing

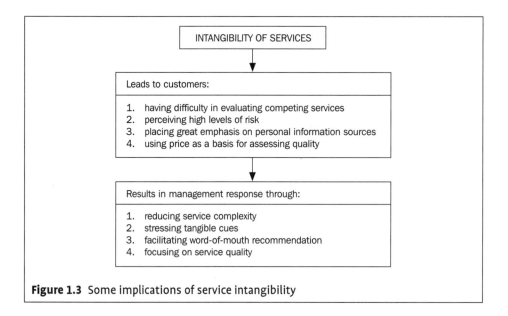

Figure 1.3 Some implications of service intangibility

companies can achieve economies of scale through centralized production and have centralized quality control checks. The manufacturer is also able to make goods at a time that is convenient to itself, then make them available to customers at times that are convenient to customers. Production and consumption are said to be separable. On the other hand, the consumption of a service is said to be inseparable from its means of production. Producer and consumer must interact in order for the benefits of the service to be realized – both must normally meet at a time and place that is mutually convenient in order that the producer can directly pass on service benefits. In the extreme case of personal care services, the customer must be present during the entire production process – a surgeon cannot provide a service without the involvement of a patient. For services, marketing becomes a means of facilitating complex producer–consumer interaction, rather than being merely an exchange medium.

Inseparability occurs whether the producer is human – as in the case of healthcare services – or a machine (e.g. a bank ATM). The service of the ATM can only be realized if the producer and consumer interact. In some cases, it has been possible to separate service production and consumption, especially where there is a low level of personal contact.

Inseparability has a number of important marketing implications for services (Figure 1.5). Firstly, whereas goods are generally first produced, then offered for sale and finally sold and consumed, inseparability causes this process to be modified for services. They are generally sold first, then produced and consumed simultaneously. Secondly, while the method of goods production is to a large extent (though by no means always) of little importance to the consumer, production processes are critical to the enjoyment of services.

Figure 1.4 Services are often promoted as inspirational products whose characteristics cannot be fully evaluated at the time of purchase, and may only become apparent some time later at the time of consumption. This advert from the Orlando Tourism Bureau illustrates how customers may buy into a dream without much opportunity for actual assessment at the time of purchase. In these situations, service buyers typically seek to reduce their risk by consulting multiple sources of information, especially word-of-mouth recommendation from friends who have previously used the service. Orlando's many tourist facilities have a long history of providing high-quality attractions and customer service, giving rise to widespread word-of-mouth recommendation. However, it should not be forgotten that if any service company fails to deliver its promised dream, it would not be able to rely on future word-of-mouth recommendation. (Reproduced with permission of the Orlando Tourism Bureau)

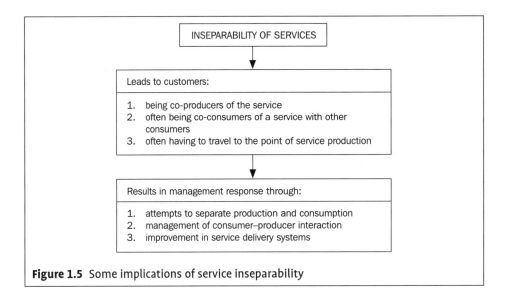

Figure 1.5 Some implications of service inseparability

In the case of goods, the consumer is not usually a part of the process of production and in general, as long as the product he or she takes delivery of meets their expectations, they are satisfied (although there are exceptions, for example, where the **ethics** of production methods cause concern (Figure 1.6), or where quality can only be assessed with a knowledge of production stages that are hidden from the consumer's view). With services, the active participation of the customer in the production process often makes this process as important as defining the outcome of the service process. In some cases, an apparently slight change in service production methods may totally destroy the value of the service being provided. A person buying a ticket for a concert by Cliff Richard may derive no benefit at all from the concert if it is subsequently produced by Boy George instead.

1.4.3 **Variability**

For services, **variability** impacts upon customers not just in terms of outcomes but also in terms of processes of production. It is the latter point that causes variability to pose a much greater problem for services, compared to goods. Because customers are usually involved in the production process for a service at the same time as they consume it, it can be difficult to carry out monitoring and control to ensure consistent standards. The opportunity for pre-delivery inspection and rejection which is open to the goods manufacturer is not normally possible with services – the service must normally be produced in the presence of the customer without the possibility of intervening quality control. Particular problems can occur where personnel are involved in providing services on a one-to-one basis – such as hairdressing – where no easy method of monitoring or control is possible.

There are two aspects of variability that are relevant to services:

Figure 1.6 Manufacturers of goods are able to separate the production of the goods they make from the consumers who buy them, hence the success of clothing and electrical goods manufacturers in China who have successfully exploited their low cost base and exported their goods to prosperous western markets. For most services, this separation of production and consumption is not possible, as the producer must interact with the consumer in order for the service benefits to be produced and passed on. However, the development of telecommunications is allowing new opportunities to lessen the effects of service inseparability. Many service companies have located call centres in low-cost countries such as India, and customers may be quite unaware that their call is being answered several thousand miles away. (Reproduced with permission of Iserve Systems Ltd)

1. the extent to which production standards vary from a norm, both in terms of outcomes and of production processes

2. the extent to which a service can deliberately be varied to meet the specific needs of individual customers.

Variability in production standards is of greatest concern to service organizations where customers are highly involved in the production process, especially where production methods make it impractical to monitor service production. This is true of many labour-intensive personal services provided in a one-to-one situation, such as healthcare. Some services allow greater scope for quality control checks to be undertaken during the production process, allowing an organization to provide a consistently high level of service. This is especially true of machine-based services, for example telecommunication services can typically operate with very low failure rates (British Telecom claims that in over 99% of all attempts to obtain service, customers are able to make a connection to their dialled number at the first attempt).

The tendency today is for equipment-based services to be regarded as less variable than those which involve a high degree of personal intervention in the production process. Many service organizations have sought to reduce variability – and hence to build strong brands – by adopting equipment-based production methods. Replacing human telephone operators with computerized voice systems and the automation of many banking services are typical of this trend. Sometimes reduced personnel variability has been achieved by passing on part of the production process to consumers, in the way that self-service petrol filling stations are no longer dependent on the variability of forecourt serving staff.

The second dimension of variability is the extent to which a service can deliberately be customized to meet the specific needs of individual customers. Because services are created as they are consumed, and because consumers are often a part of the production process, the potential for customization of services is generally greater than for manufactured goods. The extent to which a service can be customized is dependent upon the production methods employed. Services that are produced for large numbers of customers simultaneously may offer little scope for individual customization. The production methods of a railway do not allow the individual customer's needs to be met in the way that the simpler production methods of a taxi operator may be able to.

The extent to which services can be customized is partly a function of management decisions on the level of authority to be delegated to front-line service personnel. While some service operations seek to give discretion to front-line staff, the tendency is for service firms to 'industrialize' their encounter with customers. This implies following clearly specified standardized procedures in each encounter. While industrialization often reduces the flexibility of producers to meet customers' needs, it also has the effect of reducing the variability of processes and outcomes.

The variability of service output can pose problems for brand-building in services compared to tangible goods. For the latter it is usually relatively easy to incorporate monitoring and quality control procedures into production processes in order to ensure that a brand stands for a consistency of output. The service sector's attempts to reduce variability concentrate on methods used to select, train, motivate and control personnel – issues that are examined in Chapter 12. In some cases, service offers have been simplified, jobs have been 'deskilled' and personnel replaced with machines in order to reduce human variability (Figure 1.7).

1.4.4 **Perishability**

Services differ from goods in that they cannot be stored (Figure 1.8). A producer of cars that is unable to sell all its output in the current period can carry forward stocks to sell in a subsequent period. The only significant expenses are storage costs, financing costs and the possibility of loss through obsolescence. By contrast, the producer of a service that cannot sell all of its output produced in the current period gets no chance to carry it forward for sale in a subsequent period. An airline that offers seats

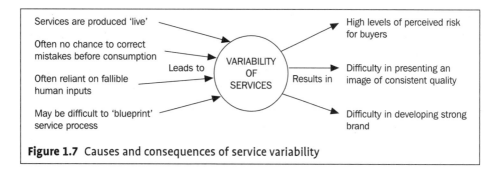

Figure 1.7 Causes and consequences of service variability

on a 9.00 am flight from London to Paris cannot sell any empty seats once the aircraft has left at 9.00 am. The service offer disappears and spare seats cannot be stored to meet a surge in demand that may occur at 10.00 am.

Very few services face a constant pattern of demand through time. Many show considerable variation, which could be daily (city-centre sandwich bars at lunchtime), weekly (the Friday-evening peak in demand for railway travel), seasonal (hotels, stores at Christmas), cyclical (mortgages) or an unpredictable pattern of demand (e.g. emergency building repair services following heavy storms).

The **perishability** of services results in greater attention having to be paid to the management of demand by evening out peaks and troughs in demand and in scheduling service production to follow this pattern as far as possible. Pricing and promotion are two of the tools commonly adopted to tackle this problem; these are discussed in Chapter 13.

1.4.5 **Ownership**

The inability to own a service is related to the characteristics of intangibility and perishability. In purchasing goods, buyers generally acquire title to the goods in question and can subsequently do as they wish with them. On the other hand, when a service is performed, no ownership is transferred from the seller to the buyer. The buyer is merely buying the right to a service process such as the use of a car park or

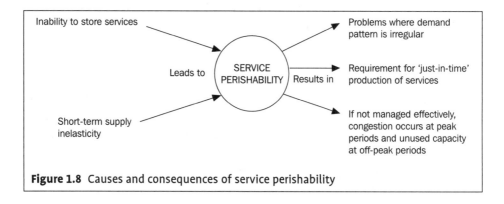

Figure 1.8 Causes and consequences of service perishability

a solicitor's time. A distinction should be drawn between the inability to own the service act, and the rights that a buyer may acquire to have a service carried out at some time in the future (a theatre ticket, for example).

The inability to own a service has implications for the design of distribution channels, so a wholesaler or retailer cannot take title, as is the case with goods. Instead, direct distribution methods are more common and where intermediaries are used they generally act as a co-producer with the service provider.

1.5 Analysis of the service offer

In practice, it can be very difficult to distinguish services from goods, for when a good is purchased, there is nearly always an element of service included. Similarly, a service is frequently augmented by a tangible product attached to the service. In this way, a car may be considered to be a good rather than a service, yet cars are usually sold with the benefit of considerable intangible service elements, such as a warranty or a financing facility. On the other hand, a seemingly intangible service such as a package holiday includes tangible elements in the purchase – use of an aeroplane, the hotel room and transfer coach, for example. In between is a wide range of products which are a combination of tangible good and intangible service. A meal in a restaurant is a combination of tangible goods (the food and physical surroundings) and intangible service (the preparation and delivery of the food, reservation service, etc.). Figure 1.9 shows schematically that considerable diversity exists within the service sector. In fact, rather than talking about the service sector as a homogeneous group of activities, it would be more appropriate to talk about degrees of service orientation. All productive activities can be placed on a scale somewhere between being a pure service (no tangible output) and a pure good (no intangible service added to the tangible good). In practice, most products fall between the two extremes by being a combination of goods and services.

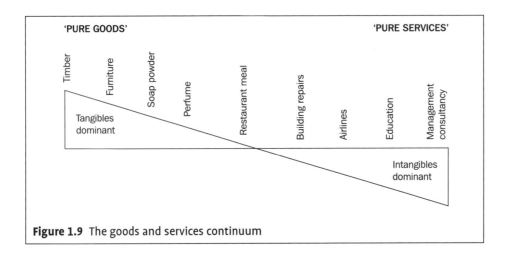

Figure 1.9 The goods and services continuum

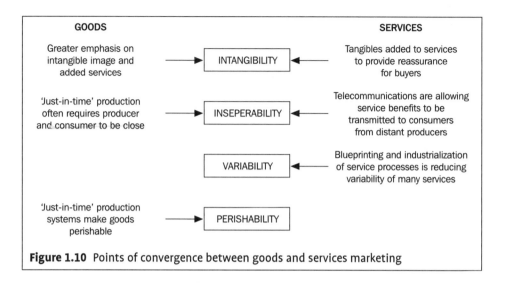

Figure 1.10 Points of convergence between goods and services marketing

The extent to which the five features of services described above can be used to distinguish between goods and services marketing has been questioned by many. For example, on the subject of variability, there are some non-service industries – such as tropical fruits – which have difficulty in achieving high levels of consistent output, whereas some service industries such as car parks can achieve a consistent standard of service in terms of availability and cleanliness, etc. Similarly, many tangible goods share the problem of intangible services in being incapable of full examination before consumption. It is not normally possible, for instance, to judge the taste of a bottle of wine in a supermarket before it has been purchased and (at least partially) consumed. Services marketers have learnt a lot from the marketing activities in the goods sectors, and vice versa. Some of the points of convergence are illustrated in Figure 1.10.

An attempt was made by Shostack (1977) to analyse the elements of a service using a 'molecular model' of interrelated services and goods components. Using this approach, an airline offers an essentially intangible service – transport. Yet the total service offer includes tangible elements such as the aeroplane as well as intangible elements such as the frequency of flights, their reliability and the quality of in-flight services. When many of these intangibles are broken down into their component parts, they too include tangible elements, so that in-flight service includes tangible elements such as food and drink. The principles of services marketing have most relevance where the molecular structure is weighted towards intangible elements. A hypothetical application of the molecular model approach to the analysis of the complex output of a theatre is shown in Figure 1.11.

1.5.1 Goods as 'self-services'

A distinction can be drawn between a service that is delivered directly by an organization to consumers, and services that are delivered by means of the goods they have

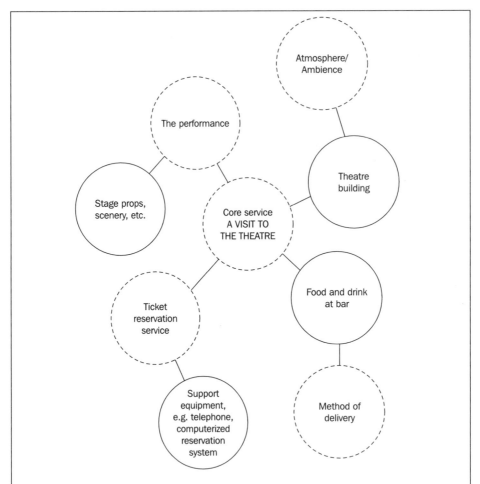

Figure 1.11 An application of Shostack's molecular model of service components to the output of a theatre. Tangible elements of the service offer are shown with solid lines; intangible elements with broken lines

purchased. Conceptually, many goods purchases effectively result in a consumer buying a stream of internally produced services. Consider the following examples of goods and the service-type benefits that they produce:

- a washing machine provides indirect service benefits that may otherwise have been provided directly by a launderette
- a car provides benefits otherwise provided by taxis and public transport
- an espresso coffee maker provides cups of coffee that might otherwise have been provided by a take-away coffee shop.

Substitutions have been made in economies as the relative costs of goods and services have changed. In general, the cost of goods has tended over the past decade to fall, as production and distribution efficiencies have increased. The ability of goods manufacturers to transfer production to low-cost countries has hastened this trend. On the other hand, the cost of services has tended to rise, especially for labour-intensive services, which have faced the need to pay rising levels of wages and to comply with growing levels of employment legislation (although some newly deregulated and equipment-intensive service sectors, such as telecommunications, have experienced rapidly falling costs).

While the rising real costs of some types of services may have led to substitution with goods-producing services, this has been offset by rising real incomes. Greater wealth has resulted in an increase in the consumption of most services. Where this increased demand is channelled into labour-intensive service industries (e.g. restaurants, personal healthcare), one result is often an acute labour shortage in these sectors.

1.6 Services marketing and SMEs

Many service sectors are dominated by small and medium-sized enterprises (SMEs). Even in a sector such as UK retailing where the perception is often of a few large organizations, the reality is that nearly two-thirds of retail outlets are single-branch businesses. The relevance of much marketing theory to SMEs has often been queried. Managers of SMEs have been criticized in the past for their lack of commitment to strategic planning and their resistance to prescribed marketing tools and techniques (e.g. Lancaster and Waddelow, 1998). Their mere survival has sometimes surprised academics who consider their theories and practices vital to improving business performance.

Mitchell (1998) noted that, for SMEs that typically work with a small number of customers and operate locally or with few distribution outlets, marketing's essential task of winning and keeping customers necessarily takes a very different form and may not even be seen as marketing at all. For example, in his study of 'hidden champions' – smaller firms which quietly excel – Simon noted that most do not have marketing departments or staff with 'marketing' job titles. Yet, he notes, proportionately more employees in these firms regularly spend more time with their customers than their larger rivals. While the hidden champions are not marketing professionals, they can be described as 'closeness-to-customer professionals' (Simon, 1996).

In SMEs, one person is typically involved in a wide range of decisions – from everyday issues such as customer enquiries, financial control and production matters, to less recurrent problems such as employee recruitment and rent reviews. Stanworth and Gray (1991) noted that small business owner-managers are 'generalists' and it would be wrong to suggest that they should become 'marketing specialists'. This observation seems quite consistent with recent thinking that all individuals within an organization – large or small – should be boundary-spanners and perform the role of 'part-time marketers' (Gummesson, 2001).

SMEs within the service sector have long been practising many of the techniques that are considered novel by a number of their larger competitors. For example, methods of developing customer loyalty are quite familiar to many SMEs, but a revelation to many larger corporations who have recently developed customer loyalty programmes. A small retailer, for example, is likely to have had direct contact with customers, knowing them personally so that it could anticipate their needs. The pattern of relationships which SMEs have traditionally developed with customers and suppliers is now being emulated by many larger organizations.

1.7 Distinctive characteristics of public and not-for-profit sector marketing

The marketing of public and not-for-profit sector services is even further removed from goods marketing and there have been many attempts to operationalize marketing concepts to this sector (Sargeant *el al.*, 2002). The range of not-for-profit organizations covers local authorities, charities and various non-departmental public bodies (sometimes referred to as 'QUANGOs') that have been set up to run health services, schools and museums, among others. Here, marketing managers' financial objectives and the requirement to meet customers' needs must be further constrained by wider social objectives. In this way a public reference library may be set an objective of providing the public with a range of materials that help to develop the knowledge and skills of the population it serves. Therefore the 'quality press' may be the only newspapers purchased, although customer preferences may call for the purchase of popular tabloids. This apparently centrally planned approach is not incompatible with a marketing philosophy – the library may work within its objectives of developing knowledge and skills by seeking to maximize the number of people reading its quality newspapers. Marketing strategies that might be employed to achieve this could include a promotional campaign, the development of a friendly, welcoming attitude and accessible opening hours.

Many not-for-profit sector services such as museums and leisure services are increasingly being given clearly defined business objectives, which makes it much more difficult for officers to continue doing what they like doing rather than what the public they serve wants. Marketing orientation has been most rapidly adopted by those public-sector services that provide marketable goods and services, such as swimming pools and municipal bus services. It is much more difficult to adopt marketing orientation where the public sector is a monopoly provider of a statutory service. In the provision of school places, the UK government has moved away from the traditional basis of centralized resource allocation to a quasi-market-based system where funding – in principle – follows parents' choices. The schools that are popular with parents, and provide their service at a competitive cost to local and central government funding providers, will grow, while the schools that don't will gradually lose resources. While developing a marketing framework for public services may sound fine in principle, new problems may be created. If consumers of services express their preferences for a provider, there is no guarantee that additional government funding will be provided to make available the additional capacity which consumers have demanded. And to what extent can government funding agencies take a view of long-term capital commitments based on possibly short-term changes in consumer preferences?

In other public services, it may be even more difficult to introduce a marketing discipline. The core of the work carried out by the police force, fire brigade and the armed services cannot easily be subjected to the test of market forces. It is difficult for the consumer to exercise any choice over who polices their town and equally difficult in practice for local authorities to subcontract provision via a competitive tender.

The previous discussion indicates that it is difficult to generalize and talk about not-for-profit and public-sector services as though they comprised a homogeneous range of activities sharing similar marketing needs. There is in fact a range of activities from the pure public service to the pure private service, and the marketing needs of 'pure' public services can differ quite markedly from those of the private sector. Some of the more important differences are summarized below.

1. Traditional definitions of marketing are based on an assumption that a market exists in which buyers and sellers are free to choose with whom they wish to do business. In effect, public-sector marketing can imply marketing without markets. In the public sector, choice is often neither available nor possible in practical terms. Consumers of social services cannot normally choose to receive their services from a provider other than the one that has been designated. Similarly, many public-sector service providers are constrained in the choice of clients they are able to target. While government policy has often aimed to create markets to replace central planning, there are limits to the extent to which this can be achieved in practice.

2. The aim of most private-sector organizations is to earn profits for the owners of the organization. By contrast to these quantifiable objectives, many not-for-profit-sector services operate with relatively diverse and unquantified objectives – for example, a museum may have scholarly objectives in addition to a more quantifiable objective of maximizing revenue.

3. The private sector is usually able to monitor the results of its marketing activity as the benefits are usually internal to the organization. By contrast, many of the aims that not-for-profit organizations seek to achieve are external and a profit and loss statement or balance sheet cannot be produced in the way that is possible with a private-sector organization operating to narrow internal financial goals.

4. The degree of discretion given to a public-sector marketing manager is usually less than that given to a counterpart in the private sector. It could be argued that statutorily determined standards affect public-sector organizations to a greater extent than the private sector – for example, the marketing of schools in the UK is constrained by the need to adhere to the national curriculum. Even where a local authority has a significant area of discretion, the checks and balances imposed on

many public-sector marketing managers reflect the fact that local authorities are accountable to a wider constituency of interests than the typical private-sector organization.

5. Many of the marketing mix elements which private-sector organizations can tailor to meet the needs of specific groups of users are often not open to the not-for-profit marketer. For non-traded public services, price – if it is used at all – is a reflection of centrally determined social values rather than the value placed on a service by the consumer.

6. It can be difficult in marketing non-traded public services to identify who the customer is. It could be argued that unlike most private-sector services, the recipient is very often not the customer. In the case of publicly provided school education, the customer could be viewed either as the child undertaking the education, or the parents of the children, or society as a whole, which is investing in a trained workforce of tomorrow.

1.8 Services marketing and ethics

The intangibility of services and the fact that services cannot be examined before they are consumed implies that customers must trust a service provider to deliver the service that they promised. In some cases, the superior knowledge of the supplier relative to the customers may result in the customers not really being able to verbalize what they want (for example, a car owner may have no idea about the nature of the fault in his or her car nor the service that needs to be carried out to repair it). Ethics, therefore, becomes an important element of services marketing.

Ethics is essentially about the definition of what is right and wrong. However, a difficulty occurs in trying to agree just what is right and wrong. It can also be difficult to distinguish between ethics and legality – for example, it may not be strictly illegal to recommend unnecessary repairs to a car, but it may nevertheless be unethical. Ethics are very much culturally bound and what is considered unethical in one society may be considered perfectly acceptable in another.

In western societies, ethical considerations confront services marketers on many occasions. Consider the following scenarios.

■ The operator of a solarium may advertise its service and provide information which is technically correct, but omit to provide vital information about side-effects associated with using the service. Should service suppliers be required to spell out the drawbacks of using their services, as well as the benefits?

■ A dentist is short of money and diagnoses fillings which may need renewing. How does he reconcile his need to maximize his earning potential with the need to provide what is best for his patient?

■ In order to secure a major new construction contract, a sales person must entertain the client's buying manager with a weekend all-expenses-paid holiday. Should this be considered normal business practice in Britain? Or in South America?

Ethical judgements about services are made by consumers at a number of levels.

- At an *instrumental* level, customers take a view of a service supplier's ethics and judge whether it will be a good organization with which to do business. Patients of a dentist will form a view about whether the dentist will act in their own best interests – for example, by not recommending unnecessary treatments for their teeth. Clients of a financial services intermediary will judge whether they believe the adviser will give fair and impartial advice which does not put pressure on them to buy services that are not in their long-term best interest. The high credence qualities of many services makes this type of ethical evaluation very important for service providers. An individual is likely to be guided by the word-of-mouth recommendation of friends and by general media reports about the ethics of a service provider.

- At a *product* level, buyers may evaluate an individual product's acceptability to society at large. Initial interest in the social acceptability of products focused on the manufactured goods sector, with environmentalism emerging as a major factor affecting consumer purchases during the 1980s. Because of the intangible nature of services, social costs and benefits of services can be less easy to identify than for goods. Nevertheless, there is evidence that some segments of the population are widening their evaluatory criteria to include the benefits that a service brings to society (or the social cost they cause). Within the financial service sector, there is now a wide range of fund management services available to investors who are concerned about the ethics of their investments. Within the travel and tourism sector, many tour operators now make claims about their fair treatment of host country populations. Some customers of package holidays – admittedly a small niche group – choose their package holiday destination on the basis of tourism's environmental impact at a resort, and choose their services provider – the tour operator – on the basis of their policies towards environmentally benign development of resorts.

- At a *corporate* level, buyers evaluate the overall ethics of a company. It is argued in later chapters that the promotion of service organizations' corporate brands is generally more important than the promotion of specific product brands. For this reason, many service organizations are keen to promote their ethical standards and to link themselves to good social causes (see the vignette overleaf). The Co-operative Bank, for example, has taken a distinctive position within the crowded financial services marketplace by agreeing to run its business in accordance with a set of ethical guidelines.

Clean and green services?

Services have traditionally been seen as relatively 'clean' activities which have not attracted public criticism for the harm they cause, in contrast to manufacturing and mining industries, for example, where harmful effects can easily be identified. However, in recent years service organizations have attracted increasing levels of criticism from some sectors of the population for the alleged harm that they cause to society. Many multinational household-name service companies, such as McDonald's, have become symbols to some people of an economic system which exploits employees and suppliers, while also exploiting the gullibility of consumers with products which are not in the customers' best interests. Many people have become disillusioned with specific service sectors following revelations of unethical practices, for example mis-selling of pensions by banks and insurance companies. It is to overcome such allegations that many service organizations have gone out of their way to show that they are good citizens, and give back to the communities which they serve. The supermarket operator Sainsbury's seeks to position itself as a socially responsible company. Like many UK supermarket operators, Sainsbury's has attracted some criticism for a number of alleged socially bad practices – for example, using its power to squeeze prices paid to small farmers, and causing traffic congestion and pollution by transporting its goods unnecessarily long distances by road. For the segment of shoppers that is concerned with these issues, Sainsbury's advertising seeks to present a more socially responsible image of the company.

Case study

Old MacDonald had a farm – and a services business too?

By Paul Custance, Harper Adams University College

The children's nursery rhyme about Old MacDonald's farm tells about the cow, the pig, the horse and the sheep which the farmer kept, but says nothing about farm services. Farming has shifted from an overwhelming emphasis on commodity products to adding value to these products, and providing an increasing array of services.

Being a farmer in Britain was not generally a happy experience during the last years of the 20th century. The salmonella in chickens scare of the mid-1980s, 'mad cow' disease of the mid-1990s, and the foot and mouth disease outbreak of 2001 left farmers burdened with additional costs, and an increasingly sceptical public. Moreover, farmers found themselves squeezed between the rising costs of running their businesses, complying with health and safety and minimum wage legislation, and the seemingly unceasing pressure from the big grocery retailers for lower prices to match those that they could obtain from low-cost countries in eastern Europe, Africa and elsewhere.

The troubled times of farmers were reflected in falling farm incomes, and a sharp decrease in the numbers of people working in agriculture – down from 12% of all employment in 1901 to just 1.3% in 2003.

It seemed that customers were not prepared to pay high enough prices to make it attractive for farmers to grow crops, raise animals and produce milk and eggs. Admittedly, there had been some bright spots in the quest to improve profit margins, with farming becoming ever more intensive from the 1960s onwards, with larger, more efficient farms using land, machinery and chemicals intensively. By 2000, the public was growing concerned with this approach because of the environmental and health implications. Even organic farming – seen as a hope of the 1990s – has lost some of its glamour as competition forced down farmers' margins.

By 2002, 58.3% of farmers were engaged in some form of diversified activity, to the extent that nearly one in five diversified holdings now had no conventional agricultural production (Centre for Rural Research, 2003). The idea of adding value was nothing new to farmers; after all, many had undertaken some processing of the food that they had produced, such as turning milk into cheese. Many more had ventured into services by selling the produce that they had grown through their own farm shops. These had developed from simple roadside stalls that operated only at harvest time, to become fully fledged service activities in their own right. It was no longer good enough to simply have the right fruit and vegetables, but also opening hours, car parking and customer facilities that met buyers' rising expectations. Some farm shops have even developed into mini out-of-town visitor centres which families visit to eat, go shopping and provide entertainment for children.

Getting closer to customers is also achieved by selling produce from the farm at the farmers' markets which have sprung up in many towns and cities since the late 1990s. Little Common Farm, which produces jams, preserves and pickles that are sold at farmers' markets in Cambridgeshire, provides an example of small-scale direct marketing activity – the business is traditional and customer focused, and no one offers customers a plastic loyalty card.

In an attempt to get a higher price for their produce, some farmers have developed innovative service-based methods of delivery. Vegetable box schemes have become very popular with some segments of food buyers who prefer to pay a premium price for freshly delivered local produce. Barcombe Organic Nurseries, in Lewes, Sussex, is typical of many farms that have developed a vegetable box scheme by offering buyers Internet-based ordering, home delivery and food preparation advice.

Increasingly, farmers have diversified into even more wide-ranging services sectors, reflecting the nature of consumer demand. Many farms have diversified into various aspects of tourism, ranging from caravan parks, paintball competitions, and bed and breakfast accommodation, to 4×4 driving courses and pop concert venues. Some have opened their doors as visitor centres, giving urban visitors an insight into life on a farm. Most farm attractions offer a standard range of 'unthemed' activities such as: animals, countryside access, museum/exhibition events, arts and crafts, children's entertainment and retail and catering. Some are linked to the activity on the farm, such as cider farms and vineyards. Nearly one-quarter of diversified farms provide accommodation and catering services to the general public. These days, Old MacDonald's spouse might well be running these service businesses and be a member of Women in Rural Enterprise (WiRE).

The British Equestrian Trade Association's 2003 National Equestrian Survey found that the £2.5 billion equestrian industry is now the second largest employer in the rural economy, and is rapidly expanding. In 2003 there were approximately 900 000 horses and ponies in the UK with over 2 million riders, buying riding lessons worth over £500 million.

It is not only consumers who have seen the results of farmers' diversification into services. Behind the scenes, a wide range of new business-to-business services have developed. The days when a farmer would retain staff and equipment to undertake all farming tasks himself are disappearing, as specialist service suppliers are brought in. True, farmers have always relied on bought-in administrative services, such as those provided by accountants and solicitors. Today, even basic agricultural operations such as crop spraying and harvesting are likely to be bought in from a specialist service supplier. Many farmers have come to realize that it is more cost-effective to get a contractor to harvest their wheat and barley, rather than keep a combine harvester for their own use. Farm labour has been increasingly casualized as many farmers rely on the services of employment agencies to source gangs of workers to cope with the harvesting of fruit and vegetables.

Even the business of applying fertilizer and pesticides has been turned into a service activity. Some pesticide manufacturers, for example, offer farmers an 'integrated pest management' service. They claim to save up to 50% of pesticide costs and at the same time increase yields by the timely application of pesticides. In a more developed version the pesticide provider could even offer a crop insurance service, guaranteeing the farmer that certain pests and diseases will not affect yield. The whole pesticide application would be carried out by the services provider. For a few farmers, all of the farm operations are now undertaken by contract service providers.

Old MacDonald might not recognize today's farm, but services suppliers have certainly spotted the opportunities.

Case study review questions

1. To what extent is the presence of a well-developed agricultural service sector a prerequisite for an efficient and profitable agricultural sector? Or is the development of the agricultural service sector a consequence of advanced farming methods?

2. What are the principal challenges that a farmer is likely to face as he or she develops new consumer services to supplement the basic agricultural output?

3. What business are modern western farmers in? What business could or should they be in?

Chapter summary and links to other chapters

Services are becoming an increasingly important element of developed economies, and this chapter has traced their development and the thinking that has been associated with their marketing. An important message of this chapter is that services are not a homogeneous group of activities, but rather we should see a continuum of products from pure goods to pure services. Intangibility, inseparability, perishability and variability have been introduced as key defining characteristics of a service. The effects on marketing activities of these characteristics have been noted. While the general principles of marketing may apply to all products, an extended marketing mix for services has been suggested which takes account of the staff interaction and intangible process characteristics of services. In the case of not-for-profit-sector services, further constraints on marketing management have been noted.

This chapter has set the scene for subsequent chapters. Definitions of services introduced here will be elaborated later, for example **Chapter 2** defines what is meant by the service product offer and **Chapter 3** analyses services in terms of customer–provider encounters. Buyer behaviour and relationship development are considered further in **Chapters 4 and 5**. Information management (**Chapter 6**) is becoming increasingly crucial to achieving a marketing orientation and to developing sustainable competitive positions (**Chapter 7**). The concept of service quality in **Chapter 8** brings together various elements of marketing activity. The extended marketing mix of management tools is considered in **Chapters 8 to 12**. The final chapter offers an integrated perspective on how service firms might replicate their success in overseas markets.

Chapter review questions

1. To what extent do you consider that the principles of marketing that have traditionally been applied to the goods sector are appropriate for the service sector?

2. Of what use is the concept of a marketing mix for the development of marketing strategies for services?

3. What is meant by inseparability? Suggest why its existence might pose problems to service organizations and methods by which its impact may be reduced.

4. Analyse the nature of the needs that may be satisfied by a household mortgage.

5. What problems might be associated with an over-enthusiastic adoption of marketing within the public service sector?

6. To what extent do you consider that purchasers of services have concern for the ethics of how a service is produced? How would you assess firms' responses to such concerns?

Activity

Develop a checklist of points that you consider to be important indicators of whether a service organization is marketing oriented. Why did you choose these indicators? Now select two or three services organizations from the following: a fast-food retailer; a bank; a college or university; a hotel. Use your checklist to evaluate whether your chosen organizations are truly marketing oriented. If not, analyse the reasons why this may be. What, if anything, could or should the organization do to become more marketing oriented?

Key terms

Competitive advantage A firm has a marketing mix that the target market sees as meeting its needs better than the competitors' marketing mix.

Customer's needs The underlying forces that drive an individual to make a purchase and thereby satisfy his or her needs.

Ethics A set of principles based on moral judgement.

Extended marketing mix An extension of the 4Ps marketing mix framework to make it relevant to services. Usually includes people, processes and physical evidence.

Inseparability The production of most services cannot be spatially or temporally separated from their consumption.

Intangibility Pure services present no tangible cues that allow them to be assessed by the senses of sight, smell, sound, taste or touch.

Market A group of potential customers with similar needs who are willing to exchange something of value with sellers offering products that satisfy their needs.

Marketing The management process which identifies, anticipates and supplies customer requirements efficiently and profitably.

Marketing mix The aspects of marketing strategy and tactics that marketing management use to gain a competitive advantage over its competitors. A conceptual framework which for services usually includes elements labelled the 'product offer', 'price', 'promotion', 'accessibility', 'people', 'physical evidence' and 'processes'.

Multiplier effect The addition to total income and expenditure within an area resulting from an initial injection of expenditure.

Perishability Describes the way in which service capacity cannot be stored for sale in a future period. If capacity is not sold when it is produced, the chance to sell it is lost for ever.

Postmodern marketing An alternative to the traditional scientific, rules-based approach to marketing.

Product mix The total range of services offered by an organization.

Productivity The efficiency with which inputs are turned into outputs. Difficult to measure for services as inseparability means that changes in production inputs often affect consumers' perceptions of the value of service outcomes.

Pure services Services which have none of the characteristics associated with goods, i.e. are intangible, inseparable, instantly perishable and incapable of ownership.

Service encounters The period during which an organization's human and physical resources interact with a customer in order to create service benefits.

Services Products which are essentially intangible, inseparable, perishable and cannot be owned.

Variability The extent to which service processes or outcomes vary from a norm.

Selected further reading

The first article is a classic one which explores the idea of a continuum between pure goods and pure services marketing, and introduces a 'molecular model' of all products being composed of elements of goods and services.

Shostack, G.L. (1977) 'Breaking free from product marketing', *Journal of Marketing*, 41 (April), 73–80.

The following five references are typical of the early debate about whether services marketing should be considered to be a separate subject in its own right. They are useful for identifying the key characteristics of services.

Bateson, J. (1977) 'Do we need service marketing?', in *Marketing Consumer Services: New Insights*, Report 77–115, Marketing Science Institute, Boston.

Berry, L.L. (1980) 'Services marketing is different', *Business*, 30 (3), 24–9.

Levitt, T. (1981) 'Marketing intangible products and product tangibles', *Harvard Business Review*, 59 (May–June), 95–102.

Lovelock, C. (1981) 'Why marketing needs to be different for services', in J.H. Donnelly and W.R. George (eds), *Marketing of Services*, American Marketing Association, Chicago, IL.

Rathmell, J.M. (1966) 'What is meant by services?', *Journal of Marketing*, 30 (October), 32–6.

This debate is brought up to date in the following article, which places services as the driving force for all economic activity.

Vargo, S.L. and Lusch. R.F. (2004) 'Evolving to a new dominant logic for marketing', *Journal of Marketing*, 68 (1), 1–17.

For a review of the distinctive aspects of the public and not-for-profit sectors and how they impact on marketing, the following articles are useful.
Sargeant, A., Foreman, S. and Liao, Mei-Na (2002) 'Operationalizing the marketing concept in the nonprofit sector', *Journal of Nonprofit and Public Sector Marketing*, 10 (2), 41–64.
Butler, P. and Collins, N. (1995) 'Marketing public sector services: Concepts and characteristics', *Journal of Marketing Management*, 11 (1), 83–96.

For a general introduction to the principles of marketing, numerous texts are available, including the following.
Baker, M. (2003) *The Marketing Book*, 5th edn, Butterworth-Heinemann.
Kotler, P., Armstrong, G., Saunders, J. and Wong, V. (2002) *Principles of Marketing*, 3rd European edn, FT Prentice Hall, London.

References

Berry, L.L. (1980) 'Services marketing is different', *Business*, 30 (3), 24–9.
Booms, B.H. and Bitner, M.J. (1981) 'Marketing strategies and organization structures for service firms', in J.H. Donnelly and W.R. George (eds), *Marketing of Services* American Marketing Association, Chicago, IL, 51–67.
Borden, N.H. (1965) 'The concept of the marketing mix', in G. Schwartz, *Science in Marketing*, J Wiley & Sons, New York, 386–97.
Brady, J. and Davis, I. (1993) 'Marketing's mid-life crisis', *The McKinsey Quarterly*, 2, 17–28.
Brown, S. (1995) *Postmodern Marketing*, Routledge, London.
Centre for Rural Research (2003) *Farm Diversification Activities: Benchmarking Study 2002*. Final Report to DEFRA. CRR Research Report 4. Centre for Rural Research, University of Exeter and Rural and Tourism Research Group, University of Plymouth.
Chase, R.B. (1978) 'Where does the customer fit in a service operation?', *Harvard Business Review*, November/December, 137–42.
Christopher, M., Payne, A. and Ballantyne, D. (1991) *Relationship Marketing*, Heinemann, London.
Euromonitor (2001) *European Marketing Data and Statistics 2001*, 36th edn, Euromonitor, London.
Eurostat (1998) *Services in Europe – Key Figures*, Office for Official Publications of the European Communities, Luxembourg.
Goodwin, C. (1996) 'Moving the drama into the factory: The contribution of metaphors to services research', *European Journal of Marketing*, 30 (9), 13–36.
Grant, J. (1999) *The New Marketing Manifesto; The 12 Rules for Building Successful Brands in the 21st Century*, Orion Business.
Grönroos, C. (1978) 'A service oriented approach to marketing of services', *European Journal of Marketing*, 12 (8), 588–601.
Grönroos, C. (1997) 'From marketing mix to relationship marketing – towards a paradigm shift in marketing', *Management Decision*, 35 (3; March–April), 322–40.
Grönroos, C. (2001), 'Guru's view: The perceived service quality concept – a mistake?', *Managing Service Quality*, 11 (3), 150–2.
Gummesson, E. (1997) 'Relationship marketing as a paradigm shift: Some conclusions from the 30R approach', *Management Decision*, 35 (3–40), 267–73.
Gummesson, E. (2001) *Total Relationship Marketing*, Butterworth-Heinemann.

Harris, L.C. (2002) 'Developing market orientation: An exploration of differences in management approaches', *Journal of Marketing Management*, 18 (7/8), 603–32.

ILO (2004) Bureau of Statistics, International Labor Organization, http://laborsta. ilo.org/, accessed 17 April 2004.

Independent (2004) 'Budget airline easyJet rises after broker boost', *Independent*, 1 April.

Knox, S. (1998) 'Loyal to the core', *Campaign*, 3 July, 30–2.

Lancaster, G. and Waddelow, I. (1998) 'An empirical investigation into the process of strategic marketing planning in SMEs: Its attendant problems and proposals towards a new practical paradigm', *Journal of Marketing Management*, 14, 835–78.

Levitt, T. (1972) 'Production line approach to service', *Harvard Business Review*, 50, September/October), 41–52.

Lovelock, C. (1981) 'Why marketing needs to be different for services', in J.H. Donnelly and W.R. George (eds), *Marketing of Services* American Marketing Association, Chicago, IL.

Lovelock, C.H. and Young, R.F. (1979) 'Look to consumers to increase productivity', *Harvard Business Review*, May/June, 168–78.

Mitchell, A. (1998) 'Concentrate on how to serve your existing customers better', *Management Today*, January, 84–6.

Morgan, N.A. (2002) Antecedents and consequences of market orientation in chartered surveying firms', *Construction Management and Economics*, 20 (4), 331–41.

Murphy, C. (1998) 'Tesco customer numbers rocket', *Marketing*, 29 October, 6.

Murray, J.A. and O'Driscoll, A. (1997) 'Messianic eschatology: Some redemptive reflections on marketing and the benefits of a process approach', *European Journal of Marketing*, 31 (9–10), 706–20.

Narver, J.C. and Slater, S.F. (1990) 'The effect of a market orientation on business profitability', *Journal of Marketing*, October, 20–35.

Pine, B.J. and Gilmore, J.H. (1999) *The Experience Economy*, Harvard Business School Press.

Rathmell, J.M. (1966) 'What is meant by services?', *Journal of Marketing*, 30 (October), 32–6.

Sargeant, A., Foreman, S. and Liao, Mei-Na (2002) 'Operationalizing the marketing concept in the nonprofit sector', *Journal of Nonprofit and Public Sector Marketing*, 10 (2), 41–64.

Shostack, G.L. (1977) 'Breaking free from product marketing', *Journal of Marketing*, 41, 73–80.

Simon, H. (1996) 'You don't have to be German to be a hidden champion', *Business Strategy Review*, 7 (92), 1–13.

Smith, A. (1977) *The Wealth of Nations*, Penguin, Middlesex (first published 1776).

Stanworth, J. and Gray, C. (eds) (1991) *Bolton 20 Years On: The Small Firm in the 1990s*, Paul Chapman Publishing, London.

Vargo, S.L. and Lusch, R.F. (2004) 'Evolving to a new dominant logic for marketing', *Journal of Marketing*, 68 (1), 1–17.

Wilson, R. and Gilligan, C. (1997) *Strategic Marketing Management*, Butterworth-Heinemann, London.

Wood, P.A. (1987) 'Producer services and economic change, some Canadian evidence', in K. Chapman and G. Humphreys (eds), *Technological Change and Economic Policy*, Blackwell, London.

The service offer

Learning objectives

This chapter will explain:

- the essential elements that make up a service offer

- the effects of intangibility on buyers' perception of service benefits

- the diversity of services that comprise the service sector

- bases for classifying services according to their marketing requirements.

2.1 **Introduction**

Products form the focal point for an organization's effort in satisfying its customers' needs. The features, design, styling and ranges of the product – among other things – help the organization to gain competitive advantage in meeting its customers' needs more effectively than its competitors. Product decisions form just one set of decisions which an organization makes in order to satisfy customers' needs. They must be related to decisions in respect of the other elements of the marketing mix in order to give a coherent market position for a service.

It was noted in Chapter 1 that the traditional marketing mix formulation that has been applied to goods might not be appropriate for the marketing of services. However, most reformulations of the marketing mix continue to place great emphasis on product decisions, although the concept of a product and the nature of product decisions for services can be quite different compared to goods. The purpose of this chapter is to consider conceptual frameworks for understanding the nature of service product offers.

2.2 **The service offer**

The term 'product' is used to describe both tangible goods offerings and relatively intangible service offerings. A starting point for understanding the nature of products is to take a generic definition provided by Dibb *et al.* (2002), who define a product as:

… a complexity of tangible and intangible attributes, including functional, social and psychological utilities or benefits. A product can be an idea, a service, a good or any combination of these three.

While this definition is intended to be universal in its coverage, Kotler (1997) recognized that significant differences occur between different product offerings and proposed four categories of product offers:

1. pure tangibles

2. tangibles with accompanying services

3. major services with accompanying minor goods and services

4. pure services.

The fact that most products are usually a combination of goods and services has been highlighted in the evolution of the services marketing literature. Rathmell (1966) distinguished between support goods and facilitating goods in the service offer. The former are tangible aspects of a service that aid the service provision (a textbook in education, for example), whereas facilitating goods must exist for the service to be provided in the first place (for example, a car is a prerequisite for the provision of a car hire service). In reality, customers do not buy products as such, but buy the benefits that a product offers. The most important element of any organization's marketing mix therefore can be considered to be its 'offer', and what is being considered in this chapter is the organization's 'service offer'.

An understanding of just what constitutes the service offer from both buyers' and sellers' points of view is imperative. Sasser *et al.* (1978) defined purchase bundles, or the 'service concept', in terms of three elements.

1. Firstly, the physical items are the tangible/material elements that are the facilitating or support goods – for example, the food or drink served in a restaurant.

2. Secondly, there are the sensual benefits, which can be defined by one or more of the five senses, such as the taste and aroma of a restaurant meal or the ambience of a restaurant.

3. Finally, Sasser *et al.* identify the psychological benefits of a service purchase bundle. These are the benefits which cannot be clearly defined and are determined by the customer subjectively. The existence of this type of benefit makes the management of the service offer very difficult.

Service offers can be distinguished from goods offers by their inseparability. The fact that a service cannot usually be separated from the person who provides it, nor from the place at which it is provided, results in services being 'consumed' as soon as they are produced and this, therefore, means a high degree of buyer/supplier interaction. The concept of value added in the product also takes on new meaning. In both production and marketing, the concept of value added is the difference between input and output at various levels on the supply side. Since services are not resold, Rathmell has argued that there can only be one level of value added, with the concept of input being redefined to mean only supplies consumed and the depreciation of capital goods used up in the production of a service.

2.2.1 Analysis of the service offer

A number of elements within the service offer can be identified, some of which are fundamental to the nature of the product, while others refine or differentiate it. For products in general, an analysis by Kotler *et al.* (2002) distinguishes between three different levels of an individual product.

1. The first level is known as the *core* product. This is defined in terms of the underlying need which a product satisfies.

2. The second level is known as the *tangible* product. The core product is made available to consumers in some tangible form, which is expressed in terms of the product's features, styling, packaging, brand name and quality level.

3. The third level of product defined by Kotler *et al.* is the *augmented* product. This is the tangible product plus additional services and benefits, included to satisfy the additional needs of consumers and/or to further differentiate a product from its competitors. Many of these additional features tend to be services such as pre-sales and after-sales service, guarantees, etc.

An application of this multi-level approach to the analysis of the product offering of a car is shown in Figure 2.1.

While this analysis is held to be true of products in general, doubts have been expressed about whether it can be applied to the service offer. Is it possible to identify a **core service** representing the essence of a consumer's perceived need that requires satisfying? If such a core service exists, can it be made available in a form that is 'consumer friendly', and, if so, what elements are included in this form? Finally, is there a level of service corresponding to the augmented product that allows a service provider to differentiate its service offer from its competitors in the same way that a car manufacturer differentiates its augmented product from its competitors?

A number of writers have sought to revise this basic framework to identify different levels of the service offer. Sasser *et al.* (1978) distinguished between the substantive service and peripheral services. Grönroos (1984) distinguished between the service concept and elements of what he calls the 'interactive marketing function'.

Most contemporary analyses of the service offer recognize that the problems of inseparability and intangibility make application of the three generic levels of product offer less meaningful to the service offer. Instead, the service offer is analysed here in terms of two components:

1. The core service, which represents the core benefit

2. The secondary service, which represents both the tangible and augmented product levels.

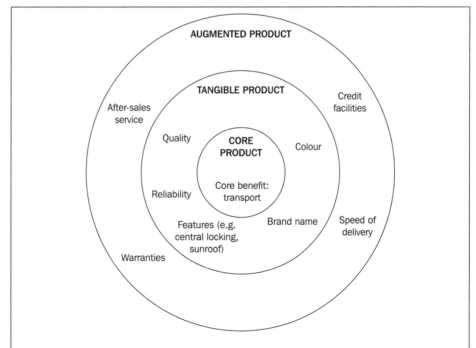

Figure 2.1 Analysis of the product offering of a car into core, tangible and augmented components

2.3 **The core service level**

Sasser *et al.* (1978) called this the *substantive* service, which is best understood as the essential function of a service. Grönroos (1984) used the term 'service concept' to denote the core of a service offering. Grönroos stated that it could be general, such as offering a solution to transport problems, e.g. car hire, or it could be more specific, such as offering Chinese cuisine in a restaurant.

In any event, there seems to be little difference between services and material goods when considering this fundamental level of a firm's offer. All customers' needs and wants are intangible – they cannot be seen or touched. The offer should be developed, produced and managed with consumers' benefit in mind in such a way that they perceive it as being successful in satisfying their needs and wants. The offer can be a tangible good, a service, or a combination of both.

It follows that an understanding of customers' needs and wants is vital if a service provider wishes to be successful, requiring a 'common view' or 'perceptual congruence' between itself and service users. This in turn requires 'soft' data of a behavioural nature which allow an understanding of what benefits the customer derives from a service. This highlights the importance of appropriate marketing research, in particular qualitative research and its attempts to measure consumers' perceptions, beliefs and attitudes. In formulating service design, market research should place great emphasis on customer perceptions of the service itself.

2.4 **The secondary service level**

It was noted above that the secondary level of a service offering could be seen as representing both the tangible level of a product and the augmented level. At the augmented level, service suppliers offer additional benefits to consumers that go beyond the tangible evidence. This is done either to meet additional consumer wants and/or to further differentiate the product from the competition.

As there is no 'tangible' level of a service in the manner that the term is understood in a goods context, it could be argued that it is not possible to define an augmented service. However, many of the elements normally considered to be part of the augmented product relate to *how* the product is distributed/delivered, e.g. installation, delivery, credit availability and after-sales service. The idea of intangibility implies that when a consumer decides to purchase a service there is no guarantee that he or she will be able to experience (feel, see, hear, taste or smell) the service before it is purchased. Rushton and Carson (1985) also noted that in many cases, services can also be mentally intangible in that they are concepts that are difficult to grasp.

Shostack (1977) looked at the issue of intangibility in more depth. She saw services as being more than just products that are intangible:

… it is wrong to imply that services are just like products except for intangibility. By such logic apples are just like oranges, except for their 'appleness'. Intangibility is not a modifier, it is a state.

Shostack's molecular model (discussed in Chapter 1) is merely her way of making the point that there is a product continuum. A service-dominant offer concerned primarily with intangible elements is at one extreme, and a product-dominant offer consisting predominantly of tangible elements is at the other. For Shostack, the greater the weight of intangible elements in an offer, the greater the divergence from the approach of goods marketing. Services knowledge and goods knowledge are not gained in the same way. Customers of physical products can 'know' their product through physical examination and/or quantitative measurement. Service reality must be defined experientially by the user and there are many versions of this reality.

For services, therefore, the secondary level of a service offer involves a combination of both tangible and intangible elements in order that the core benefit is realized by the customer. There are, however, a number of specific difficulties involved in determining the particular combination of these tangibles and intangibles. One major difficulty is the actual articulation of the elements, for it is far easier to articulate the tangible aspects than it is to produce and display the intangibles. In addition, the intangible elements are relatively difficult to control and therefore there is a tendency for service managers to emphasize the controllable, i.e. tangible, elements rather than the more difficult intangibles. Shostack (1977) believed that the more intangible the service, the greater the need for tangible evidence and, more importantly, for managing tangible evidence.

Another major conceptual problem in defining the service offer is that because of the inseparability of production and consumption, some elements of the secondary service level are not actually provided by the service provider but by the customers – themselves – for example, the student who 'reads around' a subject before attending a seminar.

Notwithstanding the above difficulties, the secondary level of the service offer can be analysed in terms of a number of elements, some of which bear comparison with the elements used in analysing the offering of a tangible good. The principal elements are discussed below and some of these are illustrated in Figure 2.2, where an insurance product is used as an example.

2.4.1 Features

In the tangible product, features represent specific components of the product that could be added or subtracted without changing its essential characteristics. Features can be added to or subtracted from the product so that an organization produces a range of products that appeal to a variety of different market segments, each with the same core needs but with each segment requiring marginally different products to satisfy slightly differing secondary needs.

In much the same way, most service offers can be analysed in terms of differentiating features; for example, banks usually offer different types of current account to appeal to segments of the population with slightly differing needs. Features may include ease of access (e.g. by telephone, Internet or through local branches); paying-in/withdrawal facilities; the use of an ATM card and overdraft facilities.

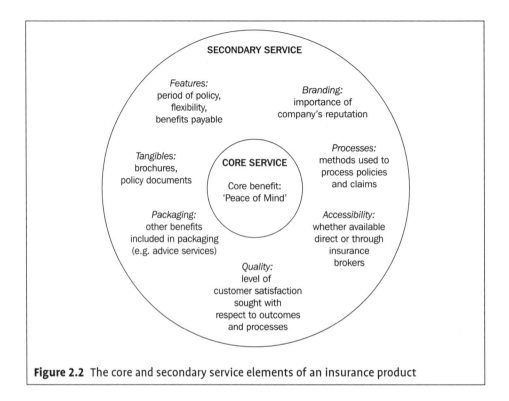

Figure 2.2 The core and secondary service elements of an insurance product

2.4.2 **Styling**

Styling means giving the product a distinctive feel or look. Is this a possibility with a service? It would seem at first glance easier to do this in relation to the tangible elements of the service offer than for the intangible elements. However, if a broader definition of style is considered to comprise an external manner, mode or approach rather than merely a physical quality, there is little difficulty in applying this concept to the service offer. In this instance, the customer gains the 'sensual benefits' that were described earlier.

The inseparability of the service offer makes the relationship between customer and service provider of paramount importance and it is through this relationship that a service manager can develop a distinctive style. For example, there is a difference between the style of a McDonald's restaurant and that of a Little Chef restaurant although they are both in the business of selling relatively low-value, high-speed food and drink. The style of a service is a result of the combination of features, including tangible decor and the intangible manner in which front-line staff interact with customers. The overall service style can be established either before or after the target market is identified.

2.4.3 **Packaging**

The intangible nature of services prevent them being packaged in the traditional sense of providing physical wrapping which can both protect the product and help to develop a distinctive identity. However, the tangible elements of a service can be packaged, performing much the same function as the packaging of goods. Good packaging can make service consumption easier – for example, the design of take-away containers can ease the handling of take-away food as well as conveying messages which distinguish the provider of the service from its competitors.

In a wider sense, service packaging can refer to the way in which tangible and intangible elements are bundled together to provide a comprehensive service offer – for example, a mortgage offer may be packaged to include buildings insurance and a surveyor's report, or a restaurant may include a home delivery service in its service package.

2.4.4 Branding

The purpose of **branding** is to identify products as belonging to a particular organization and to enable differentiation of its products from those of its competitors. While most tangible product offerings are branded in some form, the service offer itself is less likely to be branded. Instead of the individual service offering being branded, it is more likely that the process of branding will focus on the service provider's corporate image. In this way, both fast-food restaurants and accountants are usually differentiated on the basis of their corporate name and reputation rather than the specific services they offer.

There are, however, instances where the service itself is branded, or there is a hierarchy of brands and sub-brands representing both corporate identity and service-specific identity. Often, service-specific branding has a tangible basis (e.g. a 'Big Mac' offered by McDonald's) although at other times the product brand is based largely on intangibles (e.g. where a bank applies specific brand names to types of account). The role of a brand in developing a market position for a service offer is considered further in Chapter 7.

2.4.5 Physical evidence

While manufacturers of goods tend to introduce additional services into their augmented product, service marketers are more likely to differentiate their services from the competition by adding tangible features – for example, distinctive designs of brochures, staff uniforms and service outlets.

2.4.6 Service delivery

Just as delivery can be an important differentiator for goods, it can also be equally important for a service. According to Grönroos, service marketers should use the concept of accessibility rather than see service provision in terms of distribution/delivery as with goods. A number of resources affect this accessibility, e.g. human resources (especially contact personnel), machines, buildings and other physical infrastructure, as well as supplementary services. These resources can be managed by a service organization to enhance the accessibility of its service to consumers. The service itself may be intangible but these resources make the delivery of the service a reality.

A brand new university, or just a new brand?

Brands seem to be encroaching into product areas where the language of brand management has until now appeared alien. But what about promoting a university as a brand? 'Good' universities have known for some time that they have their reputation to preserve, but the language today in many universities is about managing brand values. Research among applicants to UK universities has often shown a low level of knowledge about the standards of provision of such items as accommodation, library facilities and the quality of teaching. However, certain universities have come to be rated more highly than others, often on the basis of quite incidental information such as their sports teams or the nightlife in town. For many 'modern' universities, developing a strong brand image with which to challenge the established universities has been seen as a priority. Even students felt it was important to belong to a university which had a 'good' name, however irrational the basis for it. De Montfort University has been one of the pioneers in university brand-building, supporting its efforts with television advertising. It undertook research among current students which showed, perhaps surprisingly, that many preferred limited university funds to be spent on a brand-building advertising campaign, rather than improvements to the library facilities. Going to a known rather than an unknown university was seen as an important part of a university education. Cynics have been quick to criticize such efforts. How can a brand be sustained over the long term if the fabric of a university is crumbling all around?

2.4.7 Process

Most services are evaluated as much by their production process as by their final outcomes. Grönroos noted that '… a service firm has no products, only *interactive* processes' (Grönroos, 2001). Service design should therefore pay attention to processes and the manner in which service personnel interact with customers during this process. There have been many attempts to define and to classify service processes (e.g. Mayer *et al.*, 2003), to which we will return in Chapter 3. One approach to designing the process is to use Shostack's 'Blueprinting' approach (discussed in Chapter 3).

2.4.8 People

It was noted above that the people involved in the process of delivering a service can be crucial in defining that service and customers' perceptions of it. Personnel therefore become an important element of the service offer and management must define the role expectations of employees and support this with training where necessary. In addition to managing the interaction between customers and service producers' own personnel, other consumers who use or buy the service may influence the perception of the service where it is consumed in public. Many service industries therefore employ methods to control the behaviour of their customers where they are likely to influence other customers' enjoyment or image of a service.

2.4.9 **Quality**

The level of quality to which a service is designed is a crucial element in the total service offering. Quality is an important factor used by customers to evaluate the services of one organization in comparison to the offerings of others. In fact, customers may judge not so much the **quality of service** of an individual offer, but rather the quality of the service provider.

In goods marketing, quality can be understood as the level of performance of a product. In services marketing, quality is the perceived level of performance of a service, but with the major difficulty that measuring service quality can be much more difficult than measuring the quality of goods. Not only can it be difficult to measure quality parameters, it can also be difficult to identify the quality factors to which customers attach importance. A service that may be seen by the producer as having high technical quality may in fact be perceived very differently by a consumer who has a different set of quality evaluation criteria.

The intangible nature of service quality standards is reflected in the difficulty which services companies have in designing quality standards that will be readily accepted by potential customers. Customer expectations form an important element of quality. A service that fails to meet the expectations of one customer may be considered by him or her to be of poor quality, while another customer receiving an identical service, but not holding such high expectations, may consider the service to be of a high quality. In this way, someone who has won a holiday on board a first-class cruise ship such as *Queen Mary 2* may consider that all aspects of the service experience exceeded expectations if he or she has never travelled on a cruise ship before. On the other hand, a regular cruise passenger with relatively exacting expectations may rate the same service as being of low quality on account of niggling problems such as the speed of check-in facilities and the range of drinks available in the bar.

There is great interest in the concept of service quality, both among academics and practitioners, who see superior quality levels as a way of gaining competitive advantage. For this reason, considerable research has been undertaken to understand the processes by which customers evaluate quality. A sound understanding of these processes can allow service companies to be clearer in their specification of the quality levels they incorporate in their offering, as well as allowing a clearer communication to potential customers of the service level on offer.

In general, tangible goods can be designed and produced to a predetermined standard, and because such standards can generally be quantified, it is relatively easy to monitor and maintain them. With intangible services, the difficulties associated with quantification of standards makes it much more difficult for an organization to monitor and maintain a consistently high standard of service. Furthermore, the intangibility and inseparability of most services results in a series of unique buyer–seller exchanges with no two services being provided in exactly the same way. It is in an attempt to reduce the problems of uniqueness that many service providers have sought to 'industrialize' their output by offering a limited range of machine-assisted services with lower variability in output.

Because of the importance of quality in the total service offer, the subject of defining, measuring, planning, implementing and monitoring quality standards is considered in more detail in Chapter 8.

2.4.10 Ongoing buyer–seller relationships

Finally, an increasingly important feature of many services is the level of support provided by a company to customers after the initial service process has been completed. A company offering a guarantee to speedily rectify any results of faulty service delivery offers additional benefits compared to a company that leaves customers to sort out the results of failures by themselves. An ongoing relationship could be based on a contractual agreement or the reputation of the service provider. Companies also add an ongoing relationship to the service offer where this makes it easier for customers to request service. An ongoing maintenance contract and breakdown service for a central heating system offers benefits to customers compared to a series of one-off transactions for maintenance and repair. The subject of ongoing relationships is discussed further in Chapter 5.

2.5 Customers' perception of service attributes

From the previous discussion it should become clear that it is much more difficult to describe services objectively than it is to describe goods. Services, or at least the benefits from consuming them, can only really be described in the minds of their consumers. It is therefore important for service organizations to understand the processes by which customers evaluate the total service offer. In the early literature on services, Sasser *et al.* (1978) suggested that buyers initially assess the core service for its ability to satisfy their substantive need for a service, such as a basic need for transport. There are, however, a number of other secondary needs such as the need for a sense of control, trust, self-fulfilment and status which are translated into a number of sought service attributes. These are translated into desired attributes which Sasser *et al.* have labelled:

- *security* (the consumer's desire for the safety of themselves and/or his/her property)
- *consistency* (reducing mental anguish associated with unpredictable patterns of service delivery)
- *attitude* (of the service provider, e.g. was service provided with a smile?)
- *completeness* (the comprehensiveness of the service range)
- *condition* (the environment in which the service is provided)
- *availability* (whether the service is available at the time and place that it is of most value)
- *timing* (length of time required for, and pace of performance of the service).

Service providers compete by producing service offers that contain a permutation of these attributes which meet customers' secondary needs better than their competitors.

An indication of the relationship between core and secondary service levels and their relationship to customer product evaluation processes is shown in Figure 2.3.

Faced with an array of service attributes, some understanding of the processes by which customers evaluate each bundle of attributes is desirable. Three basic approaches can be identified (we will return to these in more detail in Chapter 4 on services buying behaviour).

1. Firstly, a consumer may make a judgement based on an overpowering attribute, which for that particular individual is of great importance in a given situation.

2. Secondly, judgement may be made on the basis of minimum levels of certain attributes but final judgement is based on the existence of a single specific attribute.

3. Thirdly, the consumer may decide upon alternatives using a weighted average of attributes.

A major difficulty with this model, however, is that customers are often not consciously aware of what their needs are. Rathmell (1966) noted that in some respects, the service product is an *idea*, and as such, the need for a service is often unrecognized by the buyer until he/she becomes aware of its availability. Many people, for example, are not aware of their need for life insurance until advertising makes them aware of it. Even if consumers are aware of their needs, they often have difficulty in expressing their desires to service providers. In addition, customers' needs are unlikely to remain constant as individual customers and their marketing environment change.

A service offer cannot be defined without the consumer benefit concept being considered. Although the understanding of customer service requirements can be a difficult task, it is essential that service firms do not fall into the trap of being production oriented.

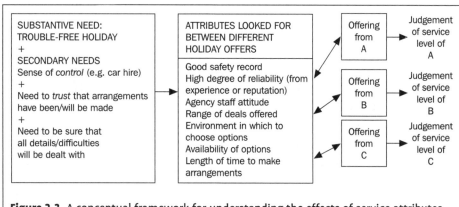

Figure 2.3 A conceptual framework for understanding the effects of service attributes on consumers' judgement of the total service offering

2.6 **Classification of services**

In the previous chapter it was noted that most products lie on a continuum from a pure good to a pure service. This chapter has so far suggested that service offers can be very complex, satisfying a diverse range of consumers' needs. The contrast between a simple local window cleaning service and a complex international banking corporation illustrates this diversity. Because of this diversity, any analysis of the service sector will prove to be very weak unless smaller categories of services can be identified and subjected to an analytical framework which is particularly appropriate to that category of service.

The most common basis for classifying services has been the type of activity that is performed. Statistics record service activities under headings such as banking, shipping and hotels, based largely on similarity of production methods. In this way, shipping is defined in terms of organizations who are largely engaged in movement by sea, even though freight movement between Dover and Calais is quite different from the operation of a cruise ship in the Caribbean.

Such simple classification systems are not particularly helpful to marketers. In the first place, a single production sector can cover a very diverse range of activities with quite different marketing needs. Small guest houses and international hotels may fall within the same sector, but their marketing needs are likely to be quite different. Secondly, most services are in fact a combination of services. Retail stores, for example, often go beyond their traditional sectoral boundaries by offering banking facilities. Thirdly, the marketing needs of a particular production-based sub-sector may share more in common with another unrelated sub-sector rather than other areas within its own sector.

Marketers should be more interested in identifying sub-sectors in terms of similarity of marketing requirements. In this way, the provision of hotel services may have quite a lot in common with some shipping operations in terms of the processes by which customers make purchase decisions, methods of pricing and promotional strategies, for example.

Defining categories of services is arguably more complex than for manufactured goods, where terms such as fast-moving consumer goods, shopping goods, speciality goods, white goods, brown goods, etc., are widely used and convey a lot of information about the marketing requirements of products within a category. The great diversity of services has made attempts to reduce services to a small number of categories difficult to achieve. Instead, many analysts have sought to classify services along a number of continua, reflecting the fact that products cannot be classified into dichotomous goods and services categories to begin with.

Many of the bases for classifying services derive from the five fundamental characteristics of services described in Chapter 1. Thus, groups of services as diverse as merchant banking and psychoanalysis show similar levels of intangibility which results in, among other things, high levels of uncertainty in the buying process. The following sections discuss further bases on which marketers can classify groups of services in order to identify common marketing needs.

2.6.1 **Marketable v unmarketable services**

This first classification distinguishes between those services that are considered marketable and those where the social and economic environment of the time considers it desirable that benefits should be distributed by non-market-based mechanisms. Among the latter group, many government services are provided for the public benefit but no attempt is made to charge users of the service. This can arise where it is impossible to exclude individuals or groups of individuals from benefiting from a service. For example, it is not possible in practice for a local authority to charge individuals for the use of local footpaths. The benefits are essentially external in that it is not possible to restrict the distribution of the benefit to those who have entered into some form of exchange relationship. Furthermore, many public services are said to result in no 'rivalry' in consumption in that one person's enjoyment of a service does not prevent another person enjoying the same service. One person using a footpath does not generally prevent another person from using the same path.

A second major group of services which many cultures do not consider to be marketable are those commonly provided within household units, such as cooking, cleaning and the bringing up of children. While many of these services are now commonly marketed within western societies (e.g. child-minding services), many societies – and segments within societies – would regard the internal provision of such services as central to the functioning of family units (Figure 2.4). Attempts by western companies to launch family-based services in cultures with strong family traditions may result in failure because no market exists.

As with all service classifications, a whole range of services lie between these two extremes and the classification of any service is dynamic, reflecting changes in the political, economic, social and technological environments. Attempts are often made to internalize many of the **external benefits** of public services, turning them into marketable services. The provision of road facilities in the UK may have been considered until recently to be totally unmarketable, for the reasons described above. More recently, however, marketing principles have been introduced, with users of roads in central London now charged a 'congestion charge' for the use of scarce peak-time road capacity. Similarly, users of the M6 motorway in the West Midlands now have a choice of roads, and some road users prefer to pay a fee to use a relatively uncongested alternative motorway. Similarly, attitudes towards which household-produced services should be considered marketable have changed over time and government social policy has had the effect of forcing trade-offs between home-produced services and bought-in services, for example in relation to the buying in of care services for elderly relatives.

2.6.2 **Producer v consumer services**

Consumer services are provided for individuals who use the service for their own enjoyment or benefit. No further economic benefit results from the consumption of the service. In this way, the services of a hairdresser can be defined as consumer services. On the other hand, **producer services** are those that are bought by a business

Figure 2.4 Childcare services have emerged as an important new service sector in many western countries. Changing family structures and growing career orientation among women has led many people to seek outside childcare services, rather than caring for children entirely within the family unit. Some cultures may regard childcare as central to family life, and so the abhorrence of the idea of putting children out for their care would render commercial childcare services essentially unmarketable. Attitudes in western countries have changed, and a growing proportion of people would regard it as quite normal to buy in professional help to look after their children. Many service providers, such as this one, have emerged to satisfy this new market.

to enable it to produce something else of economic benefit. A road haulage company sells services to its industrial customers in order that they can add value to the goods they produce, by allowing their goods to be made available where customers want them.

Many services are provided simultaneously to both consumer and producer markets. Here, the challenge is to adapt the marketing programme to meet the differing needs of each group of users. In this way, airlines provide a basically similar service to both consumer and producer markets, but the marketing programme may emphasize a low price for the former, and quality and greater short-notice availability for the latter.

While this is a very common basis for classifying service sectors, it could be argued that a private household may act as a production unit in which services are bought not for their own intrinsic value, but in order to allow some other benefit to be produced. Thus a mortgage is not so much consumed, but rather used to produce the benefit of homemaking. There is also evidence that commercial buyers of services do not simply judge a service on its ability to profitably add value to their own production process, but the personal, non-organizational goals of individuals within an organization may cause some decisions to be based on personal consumption criteria. A mobile telephone service may be judged for its personal status value as well as for its productive value.

2.6.3 **The status of the service in the total product offer**

It was stated above that most products are a combination of a goods and a service element. Services can be classified according to the role of the service in that total offering, and three principal roles can be identified.

1. A pure service exists where there is little if any evidence of tangible goods, for example an insurance policy or a management consultancy service. With this group, where tangible elements do exist, their primary function is to support an intangible service, in the way that a tangible aircraft supports the essentially intangible service of transport.

2. A second group of services exists in order to add value to a tangible product. This can occur where a goods manufacturer augments its core tangible product with additional service benefits, such as after-sales warranties. In other cases, the service is sold as a separate product which customers purchase to add value to their own goods – in this way, a car-valeting service is purchased to add to the resale value of a used car.

3. A further group of services may add value to a product more fundamentally by making it available in the first place. Such services can facilitate delivery of a tangible good from the point of production to the place where it is required by the consumer, or can provide the means through credit arrangements which allow tangible goods to be bought. In this way, mortgages facilitate house purchase and road haulage services facilitate delivery of goods.

2.6.4 **Extent of customer involvement**

Involvement is a well-established marketing concept, referring to the level of attachment that an individual has with a product. For high-involvement products, buyers have a close relationship with the product, and the manner in which the product is used has the capacity to deeply affect their happiness. Many personal medical services fall into this category. Low-involvement products have less consequence for an individual's psychological well-being. If a mistake is made in choosing an unsuitable product, we would not worry about it unduly. We can normally live with the consequences of parking our car in an inconvenient car park, but choosing the wrong hairstyle at the hairdresser may significantly affect our self-image.

Involvement is closely associated with risk. High-involvement purchase decisions are seen as being more risky in terms of their outcomes, so we are likely to spend more time and effort in trying to avoid a bad purchase for such services.

In the service sector, involvement also refers to the extent to which a customer personally interacts with the service production process. Some services can only be provided with the complete involvement of customers, whereas others require them to do little more than initiate the service process. In the first category, personal care services, almost by definition, require the complete involvement of customers during the service production and delivery process. This is often of an interactive nature, such as clients of a hairdresser answering a continuous series of questions about the emerging length and style of their hair. For such a customer, the quality of the service production process, as well as of outcomes, are important. For other services, it is not necessary for the customer to be so fully involved in the production process. Customers listening to music on a radio do not need to be actively involved in the production process to receive the benefit – they can receive the service quite passively.

Customer involvement is generally lower where the service is carried out not on the mind or body directly, but on customers' possessions. The transport of goods, cleaning of a car or the operation of a bank account do not involve a service being carried out directly on the customer, whose main task is to initiate the service and to monitor performance of it. Monitoring can take the form of examining tangible evidence of service performance, such as examining whether a carpet has been cleaned to the required standard, or examining intangible evidence of performance, such as a statement about an investment that has been made on the customer's behalf.

Because it is relatively difficult to maintain consistent production standards for services, many service organizations have sought to reduce the level of customer involvement in the production process. Simplification of the service production process and distant communication by mail or telephone – among other things – have been used to achieve this. We will return to some of the methods used to achieve this in the following chapter.

2.6.5 The pattern of service delivery

Two aspects of service delivery are distinguished here:

1. whether a service is supplied on a continuous basis or as a series of separate transactions, and

2. whether it is supplied quite casually or within an ongoing relationship between buyer and seller.

With respect to the continuity of supply, a first group of services can be identified which are purchased only when they are needed as a series of one-off transactions. This is typical of low-value, undifferentiated services which may be bought on impulse or with little conscious search activity (e.g. taxis and cafés). It can also be true of specialized, high-value services which are purchased only as required (e.g. funeral services are generally bought casually only when needed).

By contrast, other services can be identified where it is impractical to supply the service casually. This can occur where production methods make it difficult to supply a service only when it is needed (e.g. it is impractical to provide a telephone line to a house only when it is needed – the line itself is therefore supplied continuously) or where the benefits of a service are required continuously (e.g. insurance policies).

Continuous service supply is associated with a relationship – formal or informal – existing between buyer and seller. A long-term relationship with a supplier can be important to customers in a number of situations: where the production/consumption process takes place over a long period of time (e.g. a programme of medical treatment); where the benefits will be received only after a long period of time (many financial services); and in cases where the purchaser faces a high level of perceived risk. Supply through an ongoing relationship rather than by a series of separate transactions can also reduce the transaction costs of having to search and order a service afresh on each occasion (e.g. an annual maintenance contract on domestic equipment avoids the need to find an engineer on each occasion that a failure occurs).

Sometimes, it is sensible to supply the central element of a service through an ongoing relationship, but to supply additional service benefits casually as and when required. In this way, a telephone line is supplied within an ongoing relationship, whereas individual calls are supplied casually as and when needed.

Services are classified according to the nature of their supply in Figure 2.5.

Service marketers generally try to move customers into the category where the service is provided continuously rather than through separate, discrete transactions, and also by an ongoing relationship rather than casually. The former can be achieved by offering incentives for the purchase of a continuous stream of service benefit (e.g. offering attractively priced annual travel insurance policies rather than selling individual short-term policies as and when required). The latter can be achieved by a number of strategies which are discussed more fully in Chapter 5. At its simplest, relationships could be developed through a communication programme to regularly inform existing customers of new service developments. It could develop into methods to tie customers to a single service provider by offering a long-term supply contract. In this way a bus company may seek regular custom from individuals by offering season tickets which restrict the consumer's choice to one particular service provider.

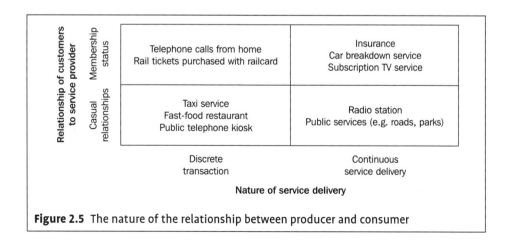

Figure 2.5 The nature of the relationship between producer and consumer

2.6.6 **People-based v equipment-based services**

Some services involve very labour-intensive production methods. A fortune teller employs a production method which is almost wholly based on human actions. At the other extreme, many services can be delivered with very little human involvement – a pay-and-display car park involves minimal human input in the form of checking tickets and keeping the car park clean.

The management of people-based services can be very different from those based on equipment. While equipment can generally be programmed to perform consistently, personnel need to be recruited, trained and monitored carefully. People-based services can usually allow greater customization of services to meet the individual customer's needs. These issues are considered further in Chapter 3.

2.6.7 **Process-based v outcome-based services**

It has already been noted that services are essentially about processes. However, in some cases, the outcome of the process is more important than the process itself. This applies particularly to services that maintain an individual's tangible or intangible assets. For a car repair garage, many invisible processes may be involved in repairing a customer's car. However, other than the brief encounter which occurs at the time of delivering the car and picking it up, the customer sees very little of the service process. He or she is more likely to be concerned with whether the car that he or she collects performs satisfactorily. Similarly, with the maintenance of an intangible financial portfolio, the customer is more likely to be concerned with the performance of his or her portfolio, rather than the many investment management processes that the service provider may have undertaken invisibly on his or her behalf.

Contrast a high outcome-oriented service with one that is high in process considerations. A visit to a cinema has no clear outcome (except possibly the outcome of gaining knowledge about the film and the ability to give an opinion to friends). It follows that the evaluation criteria for the cinema will be quite different compared with the financial portfolio management service.

2.6.8 **Knowledge base of the service**

Sometimes, a service provider has to take very few actions, other than providing knowledge to the buyer. Where a particular type of knowledge is in scarce supply, the credibility of that knowledge may overshadow all the service activities that surround it – for example, the way in which the knowledge is delivered, pre-sales diagnosis of needs and after-sales enquiries.

Examples of highly knowledge-based services include top barristers who give their knowledge on a specialist area of the law, and medical consultants who have specialized in a narrow field of medicine and give a diagnosis based on symptoms presented. If there are only a handful of consultants specializing in rare forms of tropical diseases, their knowledge of a condition is likely to comprise the most important element of the service offer. Evaluation of the claimed knowledge of the specialist may be the primary basis for evaluating the service offer. Very little by way of traditional services activities, such as methods of service delivery, may be important in consumers' evaluation. In the case of many medical services, there may be an information asymmetry that can put considerable power in the hands of a doctor (Hogg *et al.*, 2003). As Neuberger (2000, p. 7) noted, the traditional relationship between doctor and patient is one of 'deference, obedience and instruction'.

Of course, all services comprise a knowledge element to some extent. A restaurant offers the knowledge of its chefs and waiting staff which are applied to make a good meal served in the appropriate environment. An accountant carrying out a client's routine financial audit brings his or her knowledge of tax law to the service process, which might include extensive analysis of the client's books and producing a report at the end of the process. In both of these cases, knowledge is an implicit element of the service offer, which is used to evaluate competing services, along with their outcomes and processes.

In extreme knowledge-based services, many of the frameworks developed in this book will have relatively little meaning. The concept of a service encounter (Chapter 3) is reduced in significance where the only encounter is an exchange of expert opinion.

2.6.9 **The significance of the service to the purchaser**

Some services are purchased frequently, are of low value, are consumed very rapidly by the recipient and are likely to be purchased on impulse with very little pre-purchase activity. Such services may represent a very small proportion of the purchaser's total expenditure and correspond to the goods marketer's definition of fast-moving consumer goods (fmcg). A casual game on a slot machine would fit into this category. At the other end of the scale, long-lasting services may be purchased infrequently and, when they are, the decision-making process takes longer and involves more people. Life insurance and package holidays fit into this category.

2.6.10 **Multiple classification**

A number of overlapping bases for classifying services have now been presented. In practice, services need to be classified by a number of criteria simultaneously in order that groups of similar service types can be identified. A number of researchers have sought to use a multidimensional approach to identify clusters of similar services. One example is provided by Solomon and Gould (1991) who researched consumers' perceptions of 16 different personal and household services. A cluster analysis revealed two statistically significant bases for grouping services. The first – called the service locus – was defined along a scale from personal (e.g. doctors' services) to environmental (services performed on a person's possessions rather than his or her body). The second – service instigation – referred to the underlying reason for a service being purchased. At one extreme, a service could be purchased for basic maintenance purposes (e.g. regular visits to a dentist) while, at the other, it is purchased for enhancement (e.g. health and fitness clubs).

If the clustering of service types has been carried out in an appropriate manner, it could be deduced that all services within that cluster will benefit from a broadly similar approach to marketing strategy. In Figure 2.6, a simple and hypothetical clustering has placed services along three classificatory scales: the extent of customer involvement; the extent to which the pattern of demand is peaked; and the degree of variability in production from the norm. Within the sector defined by high customer involvement, a constant pattern of demand and middling variability in production, three service offers can be identified: language tuition in a language laboratory; eye-testing services; and dry-cleaning services. On the basis of this analysis, each of these services could be expected to benefit from broadly similar marketing programmes. These may include stressing the benefit to potential customers of the service's equipment base for reducing variability, developing a strong brand and encouraging word-of-mouth recommendation. In fact, the marketing programmes of three large UK operators in each field – Linguaphone, Dollond & Aitchison and Sketchley – would appear to converge on these points.

Finally, it is worth noting that while classification of services on the basis of their underlying marketing needs is desirable, very little data is published on this basis.

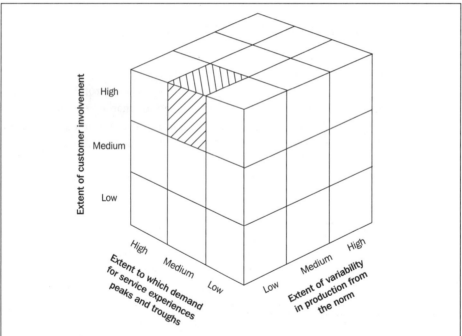

Figure 2.6 This chapter has identified a number of bases for classifying services, and in reality, services can usually be classified according to a large number of criteria simultaneously. This three-dimensional classification of services shows three criteria: extent of customer involvement; extent to which demand for services experiences peaks and troughs; and the extent of variability in production. The shaded cell shows a service that is characterized by a high level of customer involvement, a low level of production variability, and a moderately peaked pattern of demand (for example, video mobile phone services).

Where marketers seek to establish the size and characteristics of services markets, they must generally rely on data that is collected on the basis of production-oriented measures. To give some indication of the nature of a published classification system, Table 2.1 shows the diversity of Standard Industrial Classifications (SICs) used for just one sector – tourism. While this system is widely used, marketers must question whether there is sometimes more similarity between the groups than within them.

Table 2.1 **Standard Industrial Classifications (SICs) used for the tourism sector**

SIC	Description	SIC	Description
661	Restaurants, cafés, etc.	7500	Air transport
6620	Public houses and bars	7700	Travel agents
6630	Nightclubs and licensed clubs	8150	Credit card companies
6650	Hotels	8490	Car hire firms
6670	Other tourist or short-stay accommodation	9690	Tourist offices, etc.
7100	Railways	9770	Libraries, museums, etc.
7210	Urban railways, buses, etc.	9791	Sport and other recreational services
7400	Sea transport		

Case study

New line in marketing mobile phones

By Tony Conway, University of Salford

One of the oldest principles of marketing is that sellers may sell features, but buyers essentially buy benefits. This is a distinction sometimes lost on technology-led organizations, and the service sector is no exception. Recent experience of the UK's largest telecommunications company, Vodafone, illustrates how crucial it is to see service offers in terms of the benefits they bring to customers.

By 2004 Vodafone had become the UK's largest mobile phone operator, with over 12 million UK customers, who made 50 million calls and sent 10 million text messages per day. It had opened the UK's first cellular network in January 1985 and had been the market leader since 1986. Such was the rate of growth that it took Vodafone more than 13 years to connect its first three million subscribers but only 12 months to connect the next three million. Vodafone had the largest share of the UK cellular market (33%) and, with equity interests in 28 overseas mobile networks and international roaming agreements with 220 networks in 104 countries, it claimed that 1 in 100 people throughout the world was connected to Vodafone.

But what benefit does an individual derive from a mobile phone? To what extent do users seek emotional, as distinct from practical, benefits?

Researchers at the University of Surrey's Incite programme used ethnographic research methods to learn that the notion of place is key in understanding young people's use of mobile devices (Cooper *et al.*, 2002). Place is extremely important in the cultural worlds of young people, who experience place, both its opportunities and constraints, in different ways than do adults. An example of this practice in the United Kingdom is the typical initial answer given by a mobile user, which may be something like 'Hello, I'm on the train' or 'I'm just leaving home'. In a study of young mobile phone users travelling on London's 73 bus route, the researchers drew spatial meaning out of everyday use of mobile phones. They pointed out how individual users experience the space of the bus as a site of encounter, watching fellow passengers board and disembark. At the same time individual passengers drew their own connections with other spaces in and out of the city. They noted that many bus travellers might have been thinking about the activity connected with their destination (e.g. shopping in Oxford Street, meeting friends in a bar, going to work, etc.).

Meanwhile, research by Vodafone had indicated that personal buyers bought its phone services for essentially rational reasons rather than having any emotional attachment to the brand. The success of the competing Orange network, which had developed a very strong brand image, was a lesson to Vodafone that a significant proportion of personal buyers did not understand many of the product features on offer, but instead identified with a brand whose values they could share. Vodafone recognized that it needed to be perceived as contributing to a consumer's lifestyle. Given the increasing complexity of product features, positioning on technical features alone was likely to make life even more confusing for personal customers. An alternative approach was needed which focused on image and lifestyle benefits. How could the company connect with the real benefit that individuals derived from a mobile phone?

The company hired the consultancy Identica to revamp its brand communications and advertising strategy in an effort to make Vodafone more appealing to personal customers. Identica created a new 'visual language' for the Vodafone brand, and the company embarked on the biggest TV, press, poster and radio advertising campaign in its 15-year history. Employing a completely new style, the advertising centred on the theme, 'You are now truly mobile. Let the world come to you', and featured a new end-line: Vodafone YOU ARE HERE. The campaign demonstrated how Vodafone's services were designed to make life easier for its customers.

The campaign, created by BMP DDB, was worth £20 million over the first two months alone and ran through 2000. In an attempt to bring meaning to the Vodafone brand and what it represented, a series of advertisements showed how Vodafone let the world come to its customers, enabling them to be truly mobile. This portrayed how Vodafone always pioneered to make things possible for its customers in a wire-free world.

In press and poster executions, Vodafone used arrows photographed in various real-life situations to depict its flagship services, e.g. a weather vane was used to illustrate the Vodafone interactive weather service, showing how weather information could be brought to customers through their mobile. Each advertisement again had the Vodafone YOU ARE HERE end-line. The arrows indicated the directional approach of Vodafone, letting the world come to the customer. Other executions illustrated cinema-listing information, sports updates, share price information, international roaming and the Vodafone Personal Roadwatch 1800 service.

Like the University of Surrey researchers, Vodafone had recognized in its advertising campaign the importance that individuals attach to place. This was good positioning for the future, as new developments in global positioning systems (GPS) allow the full benefits of place identity to be exploited.

Source: adapted from 'Vodafone Image Shift', *Marketing*, 4 May 2000, and Vodafone home page, http://www.vodafone.co.uk

Case study review questions

1. Identify the principal benefits that customers derive from a mobile phone. What differences exist between market segments?

2. Is a strong brand identity on its own a source of sustainable competitive advantage? To what extent must this be backed up by real product features?

3. Are goods different to services in the way that a distinction is made between features and benefits?

Chapter summary and links to other chapters

Services are intangible and can only be defined in the minds of consumers in terms of the benefits received. Services as a category of activities is very broad and some form of sub-division is useful to allow further analysis of the marketing needs of services. A number of bases for classifying services have been suggested. Above all, services are generally concerned with a process rather than a tangible outcome, and where the production process comes into contact with consumers, a service encounter occurs. The nature of service encounters is discussed in the following chapter. How the components of a complex service offer can influence the buying decision process is discussed further in **Chapter 4**. The idea of an ongoing relationship to provide support to customers is being seen as an increasingly important component of a service and this is an aspect we will return to in **Chapter 5**. Quality is an important attribute of a service which many people have sought to conceptualize and measure. The task is particularly difficult for intangible services and these issues are discussed further in **Chapter 8**. There are many approaches to the positioning of services relative to competitors and the concept of competitive advantage – which positioning contributes to, is discussed further in **Chapter 7**. Finally, this chapter has emphasized that service providers' employees are an integral part of the service offer, and this subject will be returned to in **Chapter 12**.

Chapter review questions

1. Identify the key differences between the service product offering and the tangible goods offering.

2. Consider the various elements of a higher education course. Having identified the core service and the secondary service elements, could these be modified to be more customer oriented?

3. 'Services can only be defined in the minds of consumers.' What is meant by this statement and to what extent is this a unique characteristic of services rather than goods?

4. What is the role of a brand name within the total service offer?

5. Outline the reasons why it is useful – from a marketing perspective – to classify services. Identify the most important bases for classification.

6. Is the process of classifying services a science or an art?

Activity

Go through a business directory such as *Yellow Pages* and randomly select 20 business classification headings from the service sectors. Critically analyse the nature of the service offer provided by organizations in each of these sectors. Then try grouping your selected service sectors, according to the similarity in their marketing needs. On what basis did you arrive at similarity? What lessons can be learnt by sectors that may appear outwardly quite different, but share many underlying similarities?

Key terms

Branding The process of creating a distinctive identity for a product which differentiates it from its competitors.

Consumer services Services that are finally used up in consumption by individuals and give rise to no further economic benefits.

Core service The essential nature of a service, expressed in terms of the underlying need which it is designed to satisfy.

External benefits Service benefits for which the producer cannot appropriate value from recipients.

Producer services Services that are sold to other businesses in order to assist them in producing something else of value. Often referred to as 'business-to-business services'.

Quality of service The standard of service delivery, expressed in terms of the extent to which customers' expectations are met.

Selected further reading

A good starting point for studying the service product offer is the classic article by G. Lyn Shostack which sees all products as being made up of a combination of tangibles and intangibles.
Shostack, G.L. (1977) 'Breaking free from product marketing', *Journal of Marketing*, 41 (April) 73–80.

One service sector can learn a lot about its marketing by looking to other sectors with similar marketing needs. The following papers discuss various bases for classifying services.
Lovelock, C.H. (1983) 'Classifying services to gain strategic marketing insights', *Journal of Marketing*, 47 (Summer), 9–20.
Clemes, M., Mollenkopf, D. and Burn, D. (2000), 'An investigation of marketing problems across service typologies', *Journal of Services Marketing*, 14 (7), 573–94.

To put services into perspective, the following paper explores how service has become a dominant element of most products.
Vargo, S.L. and Lusch, R.F. (2004) 'Evolving to a new dominant logic for marketing', *Journal of Marketing*, 68 (1), 1–17.

For a discussion of involvement, the following papers provide application to the service sector.
McColl-Kennedy, J.R. Fetter, R.E. (2001) 'An empirical examination of the involvement to external search relationship in services marketing', *Journal of Services Marketing*, 15 (2), 82–98.
Abdullah, H.A. and Buttle, F. (2001) 'Consumer involvement in financial services: An empirical test of two measures', *International Journal of Bank Marketing*, 19 (6), 232–45.

References

Dibb, S., Simkin, L., Pride, W.M. and Ferrell, O.C. (2000) *Marketing: Concepts and Strategies*, 4th European edn, Houghton Mifflin.
Grönroos C. (1984) 'A service quality model and its marketing implications', *European Journal of Marketing*, 18 (4), 36–43.
Grönroos, C. (2001) 'Guru's view: The perceived service quality concept – a mistake?', *Managing Service Quality*, 11 (3), 150–2.
Hogg, G., Laing, A. and Winkelman, D. (2003) 'The professional service encounter in the age of the Internet: An exploratory study', *Journal of Services Marketing*, 17 (5), 476–94.
Kotler, P. (1997) *Marketing Management: Analysis, Planning, Implementation and Control*, 9th edn, Prentice Hall, Englewood Cliffs.
Kotler, P., Armstrong, G., Saunders, J. and Wong, V. (2002) *Principles of Marketing*, European edn, FT Prentice Hall.
Mayer, K.J., Bowen, J.T. and Moulton, M.R. (2003) 'A proposed model of the descriptors of service process', *Journal of Services Marketing*, 17 (6/7), 621–39.
Neuberger, J. (2000), 'The educated patient: New challenges for the medical profession', *Journal of Internal Medicine*, 247, 6–10.
Rathmell, J.M. (1966) 'What is meant by services?', *Journal of Marketing*, 30 (October), 32–6.
Rushton, A.M. and Carson, D.J. (1985) 'The marketing of services: Managing the intangibles', *European Journal of Marketing*, 19 (3), 19–41.
Sasser, W.E., Olsen, R.P. and Wyckoff, D.D. (1978) *Management of Service Operations: Texts, Cases, Readings*, Allyn & Bacon, Boston, Mass.

Shostack, G.L (1977) 'Breaking free from product marketing', *Journal of Marketing*, 41 (April), 73–80.

Solomon, M.R. and Gould, S.J. (1991) 'Benefiting from structural similarities among personal services', *Journal of Services Marketing*, 5 (2; Spring), 23–32.

The service encounter

Learning objectives

This chapter will explain:

- issues and problems created for the services marketer which arise from having to produce a service 'live' in front of customers

- the nature of the producer–consumer encounter

- critical incidents and their impact on consumers

- conceptual frameworks for analysing the service encounter

- services failures and methods by which service firms seek to recover from failure

- the role of other customers in the service encounter

- methods used to industrialize the service encounter

- challenges of computer-mediated service encounters.

3.1 **Introduction**

Inseparability was introduced in Chapter 1 as a defining characteristic of services. The fact that the production of services cannot normally be separated from their consumption results in producer–consumer interaction assuming great importance within the service offer. The service process can itself define the benefit received by the customer – for example, the way in which customers are handled by a tour guide forms a very large part of the benefit that customers receive. By contrast, a company producing manufactured goods generally only comes into contact with its customers very briefly at the point where goods are exchanged for payment. In many cases, the manufacturer doesn't even make direct contact with its customers, acting instead through intermediaries. Furthermore, the processes by which goods are manufactured are usually of little concern to the consumer.

This chapter begins by considering the basic nature of the interaction that occurs between producer and consumer, and some of the implications of this interaction which are reflected in marketing strategy.

3.2 **The service encounter**

Service encounters occur where it is necessary for consumer and producer to meet in order for the former to receive the benefits which the latter has the resources to provide. The concept has been defined broadly by Shostack (1985) as 'a period of time during which a consumer directly interacts with a service'. This definition includes all aspects of the service firm with which a consumer may interact, including its personnel and physical assets. In some cases, the entire service is produced and consumed during the course of this encounter. Such services can be described as 'high contact' services and the encounter becomes the dominant means by which consumers assess service quality. At other times, the encounter is just one element of the total production and consumption process. For such 'low contact' services, a part of the production process can be performed without the direct involvement of the consumer.

Some measure of the importance of the multiplicity of contacts between the organization and its customers can be found by counting the total number of interactions that customers have with a particular organization's employees – both marketing and non-marketing. These are sometimes referred to as 'moments of truth', and in a study of Scandinavian Airline Systems, Carlzon (1987) estimated them to be in the order of 50 million per annum.

From the consumer's perspective, interaction can take a number of forms, dependent upon two principal factors.

1. Firstly, the importance of the encounter is influenced by whether it is the customer who is the recipient of the service, or whether it is the customer's possessions.

2. Secondly, the nature of the encounter is influenced by the extent to which tangible elements are present within the service offer.

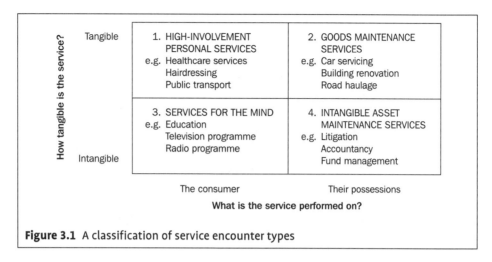

Figure 3.1 A classification of service encounter types

These two dimensions of the service encounter are shown diagrammatically in matrix form in Figure 3.1 and some of the implications flowing from this categorization are discussed below.

1. High-involvement personal services

The most significant types of service encounter occur in the upper-left quadrant of Figure 3.1 where the consumer is the direct recipient of a service and the service offer provides a high level of tangibility. These can be described as high-contact encounters. Examples are provided by most types of healthcare where the physical presence of a customer's body is a prerequisite for a series of quite tangible surgical operations being carried out. Public transport offers further examples within this category. The benefits of a passenger train service are fundamentally to move customers, and without their presence the benefit cannot be received. Services in this quadrant represent the most intense type of service encounters. Customer and producer must physically meet in order for the service to be performed, and this has a number of implications for the service delivery process.

- Quality control becomes a major issue, for the consumer is often as much concerned with the processes of service production as with the end result (not only 'Will the surgery make me better?', but also 'Will I feel comfortable during the surgery?'). Furthermore, because many services in this category are produced in a one-on-one situation where judgement by the service provider is called for, it can be difficult to implement quality control checks before the service is consumed.

- Because the consumer must attend during the production process, the location of the service encounter assumes importance. An inconveniently located doctor, or one who refuses to make home visits, might fail to achieve any interaction at all.

- The problem of managing the pattern of demand is most critical with this group of services, as delays in service production have an adverse consequence not only for the service outcome, but for consumers' judgement of the service process.

2. Goods maintenance services

Here, services are performed on customers' objects rather than their person, an example being the repair of electrical appliances or the transport of goods. A large part of the production process can go unseen without any involvement of the customer, who can be reduced to initiating the service process (e.g. delivering a car to a garage for repair) and collecting the results (picking up the car once a repair has been completed). The process by which a car is repaired – the substantive service – may be of little concern to the customer, so long as the end result is satisfactory. However, the manner in which they are handled during the pre-service and after-service stages assumes great importance. It follows that while technical skills may be essential for staff engaged in the substantive service production process, skills in dealing with customers assume great importance for those involved in customer encounters. Because the customer is not physically present during the substantive service production process, the timing and location of this part of the process allows the service organization a much greater degree of flexibility. In this way, the car repairer can collect a car at a customer's home (which is most convenient to the customer) and process it at its central workshops (which is most convenient to the service producer). As long as a service job is completed on time, delays during the substantive production process are of less importance to the customer than would be the case if the customer was personally delayed during the production of the service.

3. Services for the mind

Here, the consumer is the direct recipient of a service, but does not need to be physically present in order to receive an essentially intangible benefit. The intangibility of the benefit means that the service production process can in many cases be separated spatially from the consumption of the service. In this way, viewers of an intangible television channel do not need to interact with staff from the television company in order to receive the benefits. Similarly, recipients of educational services often do not need to be physically present during an encounter with the education provider. Open University courses and other Internet-based distance learning programmes can include little direct contact.

4. Intangible asset maintenance services

The final category of service encounters is made up of intangible services performed on a customer's assets. For these services, there is little tangible evidence in the production process. It follows that the customer does not normally need to be physically present during the production process, as is the case with most services provided by fund managers and solicitors. Here, a large part of the substantive service production process (such as the preparation of house transfer deeds) can be undertaken with very little direct contact between customer and organization. The service encounter becomes less critical to the customer and can take place at a distance without any need to physically meet. Customers judge transactions not just on the quality of their encounter, but also to a much greater extent on outcomes (e.g. the performance of a financial portfolio).

3.2.1 **Critical incidents**

Incidents occur each time producers and consumers come together in an encounter. While many incidents will be quite trivial in terms of their consequences to the consumer, some of these incidents will be so important that they become critical to a successful encounter. Bitner *et al.* (1990) define **critical incidents** as specific interactions between customers and service firm employees that are especially satisfying or especially dissatisfying. While their definition focuses on the role of personnel in creating critical incidents, they can also arise as a result of interaction with the service provider's equipment.

At each critical incident, customers have an opportunity to evaluate the service provider and form an opinion of service quality. The processes involved in producing services can be quite complex, resulting in a large number of critical incidents, many of which involve non-front-line staff. The complexity of service encounters – and the resultant quality control problems – can be judged by examining how many critical incidents are present. A simple analysis of the interaction between an airline and its customers may reveal the following pattern of potentially critical incidents.

Pre-sales:	Initial telephone enquiry
	Making reservation
	Issue of ticket
Post-sales/pre-consumption:	Check-in of baggage
	Inspection of ticket
	Issue of boarding pass
	Advice of departure gate
	Quality of airport announcements
	Quality of waiting conditions
Consumption:	Welcome on boarding aircraft
	Assistance in finding seat
	Assistance in stowing baggage
	Reliability of departure time
	Attentiveness of in-flight service
	Quality of food service
	Quality of in-flight entertainment
	Quality of announcements
	Safe/comfortable operation of aircraft
	Fast transfer from aircraft to terminal
Post-consumption:	Baggage reclaim
	Information available at arrival airport
	Queries regarding lost baggage, etc.

This list of critical stages of interaction is by no means exhaustive. Indeed, the extent to which any point is critical should be determined by customers' judgements, rather than relying on a technical definition by the producer. Where there is a high level of involvement on the part of the consumer, an incident may be considered to be particularly critical. At each critical point in the service process, customers judge the quality of their service encounter.

Successful accomplishment of many of the critical incidents identified above can be dependent upon satisfactory performance by support staff who do not directly interact with customers – for example, the actions of unseen baggage handlers can be critical in ensuring that baggage is reclaimed in the right place, at the right time and intact. This emphasizes the need to treat everyone within a service organization as a 'part-time marketer' (Gummesson, 2001).

3.2.2 **Identifying critical incidents**

It can be quite easy to say that companies should pay attention to critical incidents, but much more difficult to identify just how a customer defines a critical incident. It can be even more difficult to determine when a company has failed in a critical incident. In the academic literature, critical incidents have most often been based on analyses of customers' spontaneous statements following a short interview (Edvardsson and Strandvik, 2000). Such an approach represents top-of-the-mind memories of service interactions that are socially acceptable to report to an unknown interviewer. Often, no probing has been done and respondents have not been asked to elaborate about how negative or positive such an incident has been. More importantly, within the context of buyer–seller relationships, it can be unrealistic to look at critical incidents in isolation from previous incidents and the whole context of the relationship. There is some evidence that the length of a customer relationship may moderate the effects of failure of a critical incident (Palmer *et al.*, 2000). To overcome the problems of series of critical incidents, Stauss and Weinlich (1995) have suggested the sequential incident technique (SIT). This technique considers the whole history of a relationship and the incidents that have occurred within it. SIT is also useful in the context of 'blueprinting' a service design (described later in this chapter).

Many services companies have tried to facilitate complaining behaviour by customers in order that they can more precisely identify failed critical incidents. The increasing use of freefone helplines and customer comment cards is evidence of this. There is a suggestion that complaining may in itself lead to a feeling of satisfaction, simply because the complainants have managed to get the matter off their chests. In one study of members of a fitness centre in the USA, it was found that the greater increase in satisfaction from customers who had been asked for their views came from the most dissatisfied customers (Nyer, 2000). Providing the opportunity to express feelings about a service can prove beneficial to satisfaction levels but must be seen in the context of the business's willingness to correct errors or offences. Against this, it must also be noted that many companies have experienced an increase in 'bogus complaints'. With such encouragement to complain, some customers may be tempted to push their luck in the hope of getting some form of compensation for quite spurious complaints.

Not enough complaints?

Nipping complaints in the bud is an important part of service recovery strategy. But how far should companies go in actively encouraging customers to complain? There have been suggestions that Britain – well known for its traditional reserve – has developed a breed of professional complainers who abuse systems set up by companies to invite complaints and feedback about their products. Restaurants, rail operators and hotels have handed out thousands of pounds in vouchers and compensation to bogus complainants who are exploiting firms' fear of losing their loyal customers. Companies seem to be victims of importing the American philosophy that once a customer has had a complaint successfully dealt with, he/she will stay loyal for life. It is commonly accepted that the cost of recruiting a new customer can be around five times the cost of keeping an existing one. But how do companies reconcile the need to satisfy complaining customers with the need to stem the tide of bogus complaints? One company, Sainsbury's, now logs all of its complaints centrally in order to try to identify frequent complainers.

There appears to be variation in different types of consumers' propensity to complain. Heung and Lam (2003) found that female, young and well-educated customers tend to complain more, and confirmed earlier findings that an individual's level of educational achievement is a good predictor of that person's propensity to complain.

3.2.3 **The customer–producer boundary**

The inseparability of services means that consumers will invariably be an important part of the production process, especially in the case of 'high contact' services. Customers are not passive consumers of a service (as they may be in the case of goods), but are instead active co-producers of the service. But to what extent should they be 'designed into' this production process, rather than leaving the bulk of the inputs to the service provider? The customer–producer boundary is a movable interface whose position can be central to the design and positioning of a service offer. Should the service provider position itself as a premium service in which it takes a lot of **co-production** responsibility away from the consumer (as in the case of home delivery of groceries), or should it offer a more basic service in which consumers are expected to put in more of their own effort, usually in return for a lower price?

Services are, in general, very labour intensive and have not witnessed the major productivity increases seen in many manufacturing industries. Sometimes, mechanization can be used to improve productivity (see below), but for many personal services, this remains a difficult possibility. An alternative way to increase the service provider's productivity is to involve the consumer more fully in the production process.

73

As real labour costs have increased and service markets become more competitive, many services organizations have sought to pass on a greater part of the production process to their customers in order to try to retain price competitiveness. At first, customers' expectations may hinder this process, but productivity savings often result from one segment taking on additional responsibilities in return for lower prices. This, then, becomes the norm for other follower segments. Examples where the boundary has been redefined to include greater production by the customer include:

■ petrol stations, which have replaced attendant service with self-service

■ the Royal Mail, which gives discounts to bulk mail users who do some pre-sorting of mail themselves

■ train operators, which have replaced porters with self-service luggage trolleys

■ television repair companies, which require equipment for repair to be taken to them, rather than collecting it themselves

■ restaurants, which replace waiter service with a self-service buffet.

While service production boundaries have often been pushed out to involve consumers more fully in the production process, some service organizations have identified segments that are prepared to pay higher prices in order to relieve themselves of parts of their co-production responsibilities. Examples include:

■ tour operators, who arrange a taxi service from customers' homes, avoiding the need for customers to get themselves to the airport

■ car repairers, who collect and deliver cars to the owner's home

■ fast-food firms, who avoid the need for customers to come to their outlet by offering a delivery service.

A number of commentators have used the term *service convenience* to describe the extent to which the producer adapts to consumers' needs, by relieving consumers of the need to perform part of the service production process themselves (Figure 3.2). Berry *et al.* (2002) identified five types of service convenience: decision convenience, access convenience, transaction convenience, benefit convenience and post-benefit convenience. *Decision convenience* refers to consumers' perception of the time and effort needed to choose a service (has the service provider guided me through the options that are best for me?); *access convenience* refers to perceptions of the time and effort needed to gain access to a service (how far is the nearest outlet of a restaurant?); *transaction convenience* is consumers' time and effort needed to complete a transaction (do I have to go to a bank branch to open an account?); *benefit convenience* is consumers' time and effort expenditure to experience a service's core benefits (does the train go directly to my destination, or do I have to wait for a connecting train?) and *post-benefit convenience*, which relates to consumers' time and effort expenditure following consumption (e.g. in respect of service failures).

Figure 3.2 As consumers' incomes rise, they are likely to purchase more 'luxury' services. This often means that consumers do less of the production process themselves and the service provider does more. This effect can be clearly seen in the market for convenience food. The UK in recent years has seen a growth in the number of convenience food outlets, which have capitalized on consumers' desire to buy ready-cooked food. With increasing wealth, consumers have been able to purchase cooked food routinely, and not just for special occasions. With increasing wealth, many consumers have decided that they would rather not have to go to collect their food, but would rather have the service provider bring it to them. The delivery of cooked food, such as the service provided by this pizza company, has become a growth area and it effectively represents a shift in the consumer–producer boundary which reduces the input from the consumer. (Reproduced with permission of Domino's Pizza)

3.3 Conceptual frameworks for analysing the service encounter

Services are essentially about processes and cannot be as easily reduced to objective descriptions as in the case of most tangible goods. A fairly precise description of a confectionery bar is usually possible, thus enabling a buyer to judge it and a manufacturer to replicate it. Such a description is much more difficult in the case of a service encounter such as a restaurant meal where a large part of the outcome can only be judged subjectively by the consumer and it is difficult to define the service process in such a way that it can easily be replicated. This problem in defining the service encounter has given rise to a number of methodologies, which essentially 'map out' the service process. In this section we will begin with the basic process of 'blueprinting' a service, which has been elaborated into the development of 'servicescapes' and 'servuction' methodologies. We will also consider dramaturgical approaches to the service encounter which define the service encounter in terms of role-playing.

3.3.1 Blueprinting

Where service production processes are complex, it is important for an organization to gain a holistic view of how the elements of the service relate to each other. **'Blueprinting'** is a graphical approach proposed by Kingman-Brundage (1989) to overcome problems that occur where a new service is launched without adequate identification of the necessary support functions. The approach essentially attempts to draw a map of the service process.

A customer blueprint has three main elements:

1. all the principal functions required to make and distribute a service are identified, along with the responsible company unit or personnel

2. timing and sequencing relationships among the functions are depicted graphically

3. for each function, acceptable tolerances are identified in terms of the variation from standard, which can be tolerated without adversely affecting customers' perception of quality.

The essence of a blueprint is to show how customers, possessions and information are processed, an implication being that customers are inputs that can be viewed as sources of uncertainty. The principles of a service blueprint are illustrated in Figure 3.3 with a very simple application of the framework to the purchase of a cup of tea in a café.

A customer blueprint must clearly identify all steps in a service process – that is, all contacts or interactions with customers. These are shown in time-sequential order from left to right. The blueprint is further divided into two 'zones': a zone of visibility (processes that are visible to the customer and in which the customer is likely to participate) and a zone of invisibility (processes and interactions that, although necessary to the proper servicing of a customer, may be hidden from his or her view).

The blueprint also identifies points where consumers may potentially perceive failure in the service production process – the critical incidents on which customers base their perception of quality. Identifying specific interaction points as potential failure points can help marketers focus their management and quality control attentions on those steps most likely to cause poor judgements of service quality.

Finally, the blueprint indicates the level of tolerance for each event in the service process and indicates action to be taken in the event of failure, such as repeating the event until a satisfactory outcome is obtained.

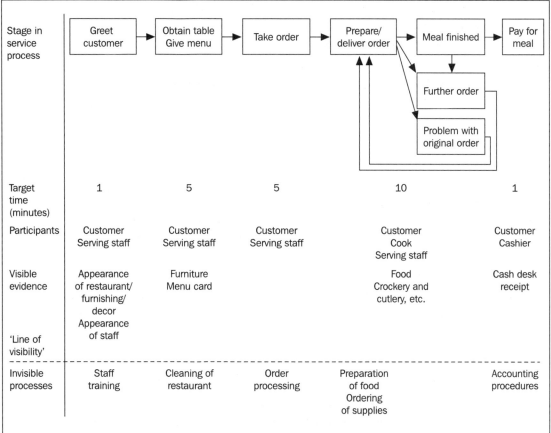

Figure 3.3 Customer service blueprint: a simplified application to the purchase of a cup of tea in a café

Blueprinting is not a new idea; it has many precedents in methods of critical path analysis. What is important here is that marketing, operations management and human resource management focus on processes that deliver benefits that are effective to customers and efficient for the company. High-involvement personal services can only be sensibly understood in terms of their production processes rather than outcomes, so blueprinting assumes particular significance.

The example of a blueprint shown in Figure 3.3 is, of course, very simplistic. In practice, firms with complex service processes produce lengthy manuals describing procedures for the different components of their processes. By way of example, a blueprint can be used to identify what employees should do in any of the following circumstances.

■ When a dentist has to cancel appointments due to illness, who should inform his patients? When and by whom should alternative arrangements be made? Should some patients be regarded as higher priority than others for rescheduling of appointments?

- A restaurant customer complains of a badly cooked meal. Who should have the authority to decide whether any recompense should be given to the complainant? On what basis should replacement or compensation be assessed?

- A hotel overbooks its accommodation. Which alternative hotels should the duty manager approach first to try to obtain alternative accommodation for its guests? Should it actively try to 'buy off' intending guests with free vouchers for use on future occasions? If so, who will authorize them and how will their value be calculated?

It doesn't matter how a blueprint is expressed, whether it is in the form of a diagrammatic portrayal of processes or simply in words. The important point is that it should form a shared and agreed basis for action which is focused on meeting customers' needs effectively and efficiently. Of course a blueprint cannot anticipate all contingencies for which a response will be required, for example a bomb explosion in a restaurant or the kidnapping of a bank clerk. Risk management techniques are sometimes used to estimate the likelihood of certain types of events occurring. Nevertheless, if the general nature of a process problem is identified, the outline of possible next steps can be developed.

3.3.2 Dramaturgical approaches

The concept of **role-playing** has been used to apply the principles of social psychology to explain the interaction between service producer and service consumer (e.g. Solomon *et al.*, 1985). It sees people as actors who act out roles that can be distinguished from their own personality. In the sociological literature, roles are assumed as a result of conditioning by the society and **culture** of which a person is a member. Individuals typically play multiple roles in life – as family members, workers, members of football teams, etc. – each of which comes with a set of socially conditioned role expectations. A person playing the role of worker is typically conditioned to act with reliability, loyalty and trustworthiness. An analysis of the expectations associated with each role becomes a central part of role analysis. The many roles that an individual plays may result in conflicting role expectations, as where the family role of a father leads to a series of role expectations which are incompatible with his role expectations as a business manager. Each role might be associated with competing expectations about the allocation of leisure time.

The service encounter can be seen as a theatrical drama. The stage is the location where the encounter takes place and can itself affect the role behaviour of both buyer and seller. A scruffy service outlet may result in lowered expectations by the customer and in turn a lower level of service delivery by service personnel (see Bitner, 1990). Both parties work to a script which is determined by their respective role expectations – an air stewardess is acting out a script in the manner in which she attends to passengers' needs. The script might include precise details about what actions should be performed, when and by whom, including the words to be used in verbal communication. In reality, there may be occasions when the stewardess would like to do anything but wish their awkward customers a nice day. The theatrical analogy extends to the costumes which service personnel wear. When a doctor wears a white coat or a bank manager a suit, they are emphasizing to customers the role they are playing. Like the actor who uses costumes to convince his audience that he is in fact Henry VIII, the bank manager uses a suit to convince customers that he is capable of taking the types of decision that a competent bank manager takes.

In a service encounter, both customers and service personnel are playing roles that can be separated from their underlying personality. Organizations often employ staff not to act in accordance with this personality, but to act out a specified role (although, of course, personality characteristics can contribute to effective role performance). It follows that employees of banks are socialized to play the role of cautious and prudent advisers and to represent the values of the bank in their dealings with customers. Similarly, customers play roles when dealing with service providers. A customer of a bank may try to act the role of prudent borrower when approaching a bank manager for a small business loan, even though this might be in contrast to his fun-loving role as a family member.

Buyers and sellers both bring role expectations into their interaction. From an individual customer's point of view, there may be clear expectations of the role that a service provider should play. Most people would expect a bank manager to be dressed appropriately to play his or her role effectively, or a store assistant to be courteous and attentive. Of interest to marketers are the specific role expectations held by particular segments within society. As an example, a significant segment of young people might be happy to be given a train timetable by an enquiry office assistant and expect to read it themselves. On the other hand, the role expectations of many older people might be that the assistant should go through the timetable and read it out for them. Similarly, differences in role expectations can be identified between different countries. While a customer of a supermarket in the United States would expect the checkout operator to pack their bags for them, this is not normally part of the role expectation held by UK shoppers.

It is not just customers who bring role expectations to the interaction process. Service producers also have their idea of the role which their customers should perform within the co-production process. In the case of hairdressers, there may be an expectation of customers' roles which includes giving clear instructions at the outset, arriving for the appointment on time and (in some countries) giving an adequate tip. Failure of customers to perform their role expectations can have a demotivating effect on front-line personnel. Retail sales staff who have been well trained to act in their role may be able to withstand abusive customers who are acting out of role – others may resort to shouting back at their customers.

The service encounter can be seen as a process of simultaneous role-playing in which a dynamic relationship is developed. In this process, each party can adapt to the role expectations held by the other. The quality of the service encounter is a reflection of the extent to which each party's role expectations are met. An airline which casts its cabin crew as the most caring in the business may raise customers' expectations of their role in a manner which the crew cannot deliver. The result would be that customers perceive a poor-quality service. By contrast, the same standard of service may be perceived as high quality by a customer travelling on another airline which had made no attempt to try and project such a caring role on its crew. The quality of the service encounter can be seen as the difference between service expectations and perceived delivery. Where the service delivery surpasses these expectations, a high quality of service is perceived (although sometimes, exceeding role expectations can be perceived poorly, as where a waiter in a restaurant offers incessant gratuitous advice to clients who simply want to be left alone).

Over time, role expectations change on the part of both service staff and their customers. In some cases, customer expectations of service staff have been raised, as in the case of standards expected from many public services. In other instances, expectations have progressively been lowered, as where customers of petrol stations no longer expect staff to attend to their car, but are prepared to fill their tank and to clean their windscreen themselves. Change in customers' expectations usually begins with an innovative early adopter group and subsequently trickles through to other groups. It was mainly young people who were prepared to accept the simple, inflexible and impersonal role played by staff of fast-food restaurants which many older segments have subsequently accepted as a role model for restaurant staff.

Goodwin (1996) has described how a service encounter drama can involve game-based strategies to outwit an opponent. Service providers sometimes manipulate customers' perceptions of reality, for example by concealing queues to make them appear shorter than they actually are. Some customers also play games, by trying to obtain a higher level of service than the one to which they are entitled (e.g. airline customers seeking an upgrade). Customers may seek reward by abusing guarantees and complaint-handling policies, complaining about non-existent problems and demanding refunds.

3.3.3 Servicescapes

The concept of a 'Servicescape' was developed by Booms and Bitner to emphasize the impact of the environment in which a service process takes place. If you were to try to describe the differences a customer encountered when entering a branch of McDonald's, compared with a small family-owned restaurant, the concept of Servicescapes may be useful. Booms and Bitner defined a Servicescape as 'The environment in which the service is assembled and in which seller and customer interact, combined with tangible commodities that facilitate performance or communication of the service' (Booms and Bitner, 1981, p. 36). In the service encounter the customer is in the 'factory' and is part of the process. Production and consumption of the service are simultaneous.

The design of a suitable service environment should explicitly consider the likely emotional states and expectations of target customers (Figure 3.4). Booms and Bitner

Figure 3.4 Many consumers regard a service outlet not so much as a functional place where a service can be delivered efficiently, but rather as an experience to be enjoyed in its own right. Hard Rock Cafes provide food and drink, but this is only a small part of the total service offer. At Hard Rock Cafes throughout the world, consumers are not just buying a cup of coffee, but an experience in an imaginatively themed bar.

distinguished between 'high-load' and 'low-load' environments, both of which can be used to suit particular emotional states and customer types. They noted that:

A high-load signifies a high information rate; a low-load represents a low information rate. Uncertainty, novelty, and complexity are associated with high-load environments; conversely a low-load environment communicates assurance, homogeneity, and simplicity. Bright colours, bright lights, loud noises, crowds, and movement are typical elements of a high-load environment, while their opposites are characteristic of a low-load environment. People's emotional needs and reactions at a given time determine whether they will be attracted to a high- or a low-load environment.

(Booms and Bitner, 1981, p. 39)

81

The Servicescape must encourage target customers to enter the service environment in the first place, and to retain them subsequently. Booms and Bitner discuss 'approach behaviour' as involving such responses as physically moving customers towards exploring an unfamiliar environment, affiliating with others in the environment through eye contact, and performing a large number of tasks within the environment. Avoidance behaviour includes an opposite set of responses. The likelihood of approach behaviour is directly linked to the two dimensions of pleasure and arousal, with a stimulating and pleasing environment being most likely to attract custom. Brightly lit window displays, a prominent and open front door and front-of-house greeting staff are typical actions designed to induce approach. A door which is difficult to find or difficult to open is more likely to achieve the opposite effect.

After entering the service production system, the Servicescape must be efficient and effective for the service provider in securing customers' co-operation in the production system. Clearly explained roles for the customer, expressed in a friendly way, will facilitate this process of compliance. The ambience of the environment, such as lighting, floor plan and signposting, contribute to the Servicescape. The physical aspects of the environment are brought to life by the actions of employees – for example, staff could be on hand to help a customer who gets lost in the service process. Ultimately, the Servicescape should encourage customers to repeat their visit. The environment should leave no reminders of poor service (such as unpleasant queuing conditions) which will cause negative feelings about the service provider. The Servicescape may include **tangible cues** to facilitate repeat business, for example a schedule of forthcoming events may be given to patrons of a theatre.

3.3.4 **Servuction**

The **servuction** model, developed by Eiglier and Langeard (1987), emphasizes experiential aspects of service consumption and is based on the idea of organizations providing consumers with complex bundles of benefits. The service features provided by an organization providing the service are divided into two parts – visible and invisible. The visible part consists of the physical environment within which the service experience occurs, and the service providers or contact personnel who interact with the consumer during the service experience. The visible part of the organization is supported by the invisible part, comprising the support infrastructure which enables the visible part of the organization to function. The model is completed by the introduction of other consumers, with whom the original consumer may interact within the system. This is important, because in many service encounters, such as tourism and shopping, the actions of fellow consumers can contribute greatly to the overall encounter.

Everyone and everything that comes into contact with the consumer is effectively delivering the service. Bateson has noted that identifying the Servuction system can be difficult because of the often large number of contacts between the service provider and the customers, which may be significantly underestimated (Bateson, 1989).

The Servuction approach is particularly relevant to services which involve high levels of input from fellow consumers or third-party producers. Consumers essentially create their own bundle of benefits from the contributory elements of the **service offer**. The Servuction model has been applied to the marketing of towns as tourism and shopping destinations (Warnaby and Davies, 1997) in which consumers must essentially define their own bundle of benefits from the complexity of facilities provided by multiple organizations within the town.

3.4 The role of other customers in the service encounter

It is implicit from the above that many service offers can only sensibly be produced in large batches, while the consumers who use the service buy only individual units of the service. It follows therefore that a significant proportion of the service is consumed in public – train journeys, meals in a restaurant and visits to the theatre, for example, are consumed in the presence of other customers. In such circumstances, there is said to be an element of joint consumption of service benefits. A play cannot be produced just for one patron and a train cannot run for just one passenger – a number of customers jointly consume one unit of service output. An environment is created in which the behaviour pattern of any one customer during the service process can directly affect other customers' enjoyment of their service. In the theatre, the visitor who talks during the performance spoils the enjoyment of the performance for others.

The actions of fellow consumers are often therefore an important element of the service encounter, and service companies seek to manage customer–customer interaction. By various methods, organizations seek to remove adverse elements of these encounters and to strengthen those elements that add to all customers' enjoyment. Some commonly used methods of managing encounters between customers include the following.

■ *Selecting customers on the basis of their ability to interact positively with other customers.* Where the enjoyment of a service is significantly influenced by the nature of other customers, formal or informal selection criteria can be used to try to ensure that only those customers who are likely to contribute positively to service encounters are accepted. Examples of formal selection criteria include tour companies who set age limits for certain holidays – people booking an 18–30 holiday can be assured that they will not be holidaying with children or elderly people whose attitudes towards loud music may prevent enjoyment of their own lifestyle. Formal selection criteria can include inspecting the physical appearance of potential customers – many nightclubs and restaurants set dress standards in order to preserve a high-quality environment in which service encounters take place. Informal selection criteria are aimed at encouraging some groups who add to customers' satisfaction with the service environment, while discouraging those who detract from it. Colour schemes, service ranges, advertising and pricing can be used to discourage certain types of customer. Bars which charge high prices for drinks and offer a comfortable environment will be informally excluding the segment of the population whose aim is to get drunk as cheaply as possible.

- *Determining rules of behaviour expected from customers*. The behaviour of one customer can significantly affect other customers' enjoyment of a service. Examples include smoking in a restaurant, talking during a cinema show and playing loud music on public transport. The simplest strategy for influencing behaviour is to make known the standards of expected behaviour and to rely on customers' good-will to act in accordance with these expectations. With increasing recognition by most people in society that smoking can be unpleasant for others, social pressures alone may result in most smokers observing no-smoking signs. Where rules are not obeyed, the intervention of service personnel may be called for. Failure to intervene can result in a negative service encounter continuing for the affected party and, moreover, the service organization may be perceived as not caring by its failure to enforce rules. Against this, intervention that is too heavy handed may alienate the offender, especially if the rule is perceived as one that has little popular support. The most positive service encounter results from intervention that is perceived as a gentle reminder by the offender and as valuable corrective action by other customers.

- *Facilitating positive customer–customer interaction*. For many services, an important part of the overall benefit is derived from positive interaction with other customers. Holidaymakers, people attending a conference and students of a college can all derive significant benefit from the interaction with their peer group (Figure 3.5). A holiday group where nobody talks to each other may restrict the opportunities for shared enjoyment. The service providers can seek to develop bonds between customers by, for example, introducing customers to one another or arranging events where they can meet socially.

3.4.1 **Service security**

Service marketers must increasingly be aware of the possibilities for terrorism to disrupt their service encounters. Terrorism can impact on marketing in a number of ways, as described below.

- The need to take security measures may make a service process unattractive to some consumers, who no longer buy the service. (For example, there has been a suggestion that increased delays at airports due to security screening have led some people to believe that the hassle of flying is too great, and so they have chosen other means of transport, or not travelled at all.)

- The fear of terrorism itself may deter some people from buying a service. (For example, few people ventured into the restaurants and bars of central Belfast

Figure 3.5 Services are often produced and consumed in public; indeed one of the benefits of a service may be the ambience which is provided by a crowd of fellow customers. One reason for the continuing high attendance at horse race meetings, in the face of increasing levels of televised racing, is the atmosphere which is generated by thousands of people simultaneously cheering their horse on. But this atmosphere needs to be carefully managed if it is not to detract from the overall service offer. The horse racing authorities are keen to avoid problems that have been experienced in the past by football clubs. Football clubs increasingly manage the expected behaviour of supporters, mindful of the fact that live football increasingly targets women and family groups, rather than being the traditional all-male preserve. Football clubs have become more vigilant in curbing anti-social behaviour, such as racially insensitive chanting, the use of flags and banners which obscures fellow fans' view of the game, as well as controlling drunken and disorderly behaviour. Racing in the UK has not traditionally suffered from the past problems of football fans' anti-social behaviour, but the owners of the country's race tracks are mindful of the potential harm that could be caused by bad behaviour between customers. (Copyright Cheltenham Tourism/David Sellman)

during the periods of the 'troubles' in Northern Ireland. With the return of peace, restaurants in Belfast's 'Golden Mile' are busy once more.)

■ By contrast, rigorous security measures may be perceived by many customers as a price worth paying in order to ensure that they can be consumers of the service without fear or interruption. (For example, the Israeli airline El Al is acknowledged to have the strictest security of any airline, and this has been used by the airline to promote reassurance to consumers.)

Although terrorism has become a much more important item on the agenda of many service organizations since the events of 11 September 2001, it is of course nothing new. Companies operating in Northern Ireland and Israel have long experience of designing the threat of terrorism into their service blueprint.

Terrorist attacks can affect manufacturers as well as services organizations, but their effects on services organizations can be very much greater. Manufacturing companies can take steps to protect the security of their production facility by controlling access only to employees. Cases of deliberate damage to manufactured goods are rare, and manufacturers have taken steps to reduce this risk throughout its distribution channels, for example by introducing tamper-evident packaging. This is in contrast to services organizations, where customers typically enter the production process and cannot easily be screened out in the way that unauthorized entry to a factory can be prevented. Indeed, the whole point of most services is for customers to enter the service 'factory', so with relatively open access risks are so much greater.

Services organizations have become targets for terrorist groups. Sometimes, the group may be campaigning against a particular company. This has been the case, for example, with the direct action that has been taken against the companies who supplied services to Huntingdon Life Sciences, a company that undertakes experiments on live animals and has been targeted by numerous groups. At other times, a services company may simply represent the values of a group which terrorists are opposed to, and an attack is a means of making this point publicly and with maximum impact. When a group bombed a branch of the British-owned HSBC Bank in Istanbul in January 2004, it probably did not have any particular grudge against the bank, but the bank symbolized a set of western values and intervention in the world to which the group was opposed. Whatever the reason, services offer relatively easy opportunities for terrorist groups to have great impact through the publicity and disruption that their actions cause. Attacks on underground trains, aircraft and shopping centres can attract considerable publicity for a cause.

How should service organizations handle the possibilities of terrorism? One view is that it may be almost impossible to prevent disruption from a determined terrorist without causing even greater disruption through security processes. If terrorism didn't result in the disruption of a plane being blown up, it may nevertheless have caused disruption through the lengthy security checking of all passengers.

What lengths should an organization go to in order to reduce the possibilities of a terrorist attack? There are a number of issues here.

- What is the best estimate of the probability of a terrorist attack actually occurring? Many service organizations use risk-assessment methodologies, often employing specialist risk assessors

- What will be the downside cost of an attack actually occurring, in terms of physical damage and damage to an organization's reputation?

- What is the public's perception of the probability of an attack and its likely consequences? Consumers often make apparently irrational choices – for example, over the past few decades it has been estimated that the probability of being injured or killed in a terrorist aircraft hijacking is much less than the probability of being injured or killed in a road traffic accident. Despite this, it is quite common for the fear of flying to be much greater than a fear of driving.

■ What is the public's perception of measures taken to reduce the threat of terrorism? Are consumers likely to be deterred by extensive security measures, such as body searches and identity checking, or do these provide a source of reassurance?

■ What security measures are operationally feasible? Would it, for example, be feasible to search all passengers entering a busy commuter train station during the peak period?

Am I a comedian, or are you serious?

'Security' has become a blanket excuse used by many service companies to explain why they cannot fulfil a customer's request. Of course, there are often good security reasons which explain the response, but there are many instances where apparently silly 'security' responses are made. Consider the case of the entertainer and TV presenter Jeremy Beadle, who was reportedly prevented from boarding an aircraft bound from London to Glasgow in January 2004 because he did not have any formal identity papers. The check-in staff appeared to be in doubt that he was actually the entertainer who had been seen by millions of people each week on television. Many nearby fans were apparently able to vouch for his identity. But without the right piece of paper to prove that he was in fact the well-known entertainer, he could not proceed.

In many service industries, empowered staff would use their common sense and would weigh up the situation and come to a decision. But the security industry is labour intensive and there can be fierce competition between security service providers who operate on low margins. Staff tend to be paid the minimum wage level and opportunities for choosing top-quality staff and training them in judgement skills are limited. So, in order to comply with government requirements, it is easier for companies to rely on strict rules-based blueprint approaches to security checking.

Fans of Jeremy Beadle who were waiting in Glasgow for him to perform may have been disappointed when he did not turn up. Disappointment may also have been experienced by the thousands of frail little old ladies who have innocently tried to take nail scissors on board an aircraft, but have had them confiscated because 'those are the rules'. Despite the 'rules', a smart and determined terrorist might have developed a much more ingenious method of smuggling harmful objects on board an aircraft.

Often, the appearance of a strictly enforced security policy may give some reassurance to customers that management is taking measures to avoid a terrorist attack. But sometimes the visible appearance of security may be a front for much deeper flaws. While there may have been few reported cases of little old ladies using their nail scissors as weapons to overpower cabin crew, it may be easier to imagine a determined terrorist breaking a glass bottle to use as a much more lethal weapon. Little old ladies with nail scissors may be an easy and visible sign that security is being treated seriously by an airline, but would airlines voluntarily enforce a bottle ban, thereby annoying even more passengers, and causing a loss of valuable duty-free sales in airport shops?

3.5 The role of third-party producers in the service encounter

Service personnel who are not employed by a service organization may nevertheless be responsible for many of the critical incidents which affect the quality of service encounters perceived by its customers. Three categories of such personnel can be identified, as discussed below.

1. A service company's intermediaries can become involved in critical incidents before, during or after consumption of a service. The first contact that many people have with an organization is through its sales outlets. In the case of the airline above, the manner in which a customer is handled by a travel agent is a highly critical incident, the outcome of which can affect the enjoyment of the rest of the service, for example where the ticket agent gives incorrect information about departure times or the ticket is ordered wrongly. The incidents in which intermediaries are involved can continue through the consumption and post-consumption phases. Where services are delivered through intermediaries, as is the case with franchisees, they can become the dominant source of critical incidents. In such cases, quality control becomes an issue of controlling intermediaries.

2. Service providers themselves buy in services from other subcontracting organizations. Service organizations buying subcontracted services must ensure that quality control procedures apply to many of their subcontractor processes, as well as to their outcomes. Airlines buy in many services from subcontractors. In some cases these generate very little potential for critical incidents with the airline's passengers. Where in-flight meals are bought in from an outside caterer, the subcontractor has few if any encounters with the airline's customers and quality can be assessed by the tangible evidence being delivered on time. On the other hand, some services involve a wide range of critical incidents. Airlines often subcontract their passenger checking-in procedures to a specialist handling company, for whom quality cannot simply be assessed by quantifiable factors such as length of queues or numbers of lost bags. The manner in which the subcontractor's personnel handle customers and resolve such problems as over-booked aircraft, lost tickets and general enquiries assumes critical importance.

3. Sometimes staff who are not employed by the services organization or its direct subcontractors can contribute towards critical incidents in the service encounter. This occurs, for example, at airports where airport employees, air traffic controllers and staff working in shops within the airport contribute to airline passengers' perception of the total service. In many cases, the airline might have little – if any – effective control over the actions of these personnel. Sometimes, it may be possible to relocate the environment of its service encounters – such as changing departure airports – but it may still be difficult to gain control over some critical publicly provided services, such as immigration and passport control. The best that a service organization can do in these circumstances is to show empathy with its customers. An airline may gain some sympathy for delays caused by air traffic controllers if it explains the reason for delays to customers and does everything within its power to overcome resulting problems.

3.6 **Service failure and recovery**

Almost inevitably, service companies will fail at some critical incidents. The inseparable and intangible nature of services gives rise to the high probability of failures occurring. From a customer's perspective, a **service failure** is any situation where something has gone wrong, irrespective of responsibility. The inseparability of **high-contact services** has a consequence that service failure usually cannot be disguised from the customer. Service failures may vary in gravity from being very serious, such as a food poisoning incident, to something trivial, such as a short delay. The service failure literature has produced many typologies characterizing the general nature of service failures (e.g. Bitner *et al.*, 1990; Kelley and Davis, 1994). It has been suggested by Halstead *et al.* (1993) that a single service failure may have two effects. Firstly, a 'halo' effect may negatively colour a customer's perceptions (for example, if an airline loses a passenger's bag, the passenger may subsequently associate any communication from the airline with failure). Secondly, a 'domino' effect may engender service failures in other attributes or areas of a service process. This can occur where a failure in an early stage of a service process puts a customer in a bad mood where he or she becomes more critical of minor failures in subsequent stages. A diner who has been unreasonably delayed in obtaining a pre-booked table may become more ready to complain about minor problems with the subsequent delivery of his or her food.

Service providers should have systems for identifying, tracking and analysing service failures. This allows management to identify common failure situations (Hoffman *et al.*, 1995). More importantly, it allows management to develop strategies for preventing failures occurring in the first place, and for designing appropriate recovery strategies where failure is unavoidable. Firms with formal service recovery programmes supplement the bundle of benefits provided by the core product and enhance the service component of the firm's value chain (Hoffman and Kelley, 2000).

It is often suggested that a happy customer will go away and tell two or three people about the good service, but a dissatisfied customer will tell probably a dozen about a failure (Figure 3.6). Businesses commonly lose 15 to 20% of their customer base each year (Reichheld and Sasser, 1990). Although customers may defect to the competition for a number of reasons (e.g. better prices, better products, change of market locations, etc.), minimizing the number of customers who defect due to poor customer service is largely controllable. However, there is plenty of evidence that firms do not take complaining customers seriously and that unresolved complaints actually strengthen the customer's negative feelings towards the company and its representatives (Hart *et al.*, 1990). Organizations need to have in place a strategy by which they can seek to recover from failure.

There is a growing body of literature on the methods used by service organizations to recover from an adverse critical incident and to build up a strong relationship once again. **Service recovery** processes are those activities in which a company engages to address a customer complaint regarding a service failure. A good recovery can turn angry, frustrated customers into loyal ones and may create more goodwill than if things had gone smoothly in the first place (Hart *et al.*, 1990).

BUTLER'S RESTAURANT

We hope you enjoyed your meal with us today.
If you were unhappy with anything, please tell us so we can put it right.
If you are happy, please tell others.

Jane Deakin

Jane Deakin
Restaurant Manager

Figure 3.6 Like many service providers, this restaurant encourages dissatisfied customers to make their dissatisfaction known, rather than going away with an unresolved problem and passing on negative word-of-mouth. Estimates vary, but it is often thought that a happy customer may typically tell two or three friends about their good experience, but an unhappy customer may tell a dozen or so.

The study of service failure and recovery has built on a number of theoretical frameworks. These include: attribution theory (Heider, 1958; Maxham and Netemeyer, 2002); justice theory (Adams, 1965; Tax *et al.*, 1998); disconfirmation theory (Oliver, 1980; Churchill and Surprenant, 1982; Parasuraman *et al.*, 1985); social exchange theory (Kelley and Thibaut, 1978; Homans, 1961) and fairness theory (Spreng *et al.*, 1995; Folger and Cropanzano, 1998; McColl-Kennedy and Sparks, 2003).

Justice theory offers the most comprehensive framework for understanding the complaint resolution process from initial service failure to final resolution. Justice theory has evolved to incorporate three dimensions:

1. distributive justice (the fairness of the outcome of the complaint resolution process)

2. procedural justice (whether the procedures for resolving the failure were considered to be fair)

3. interactional justice (which concerns interpersonal behaviour employed in the complaint resolution procedures and delivery of outcomes).

Complaint handling can be viewed as a sequence of events, beginning with communicating a complaint about the service failure, and generating a process of interaction leading to a decision and an outcome. Justice literature suggests that each part of the sequence is subject to a fairness consideration and that each aspect of a complaint resolution creates a justice episode (Bies, 1987; Tax *et al.,* 1998).

A successful recovery is accomplished when the aggrieved consumer is provided with an appropriate blend of the three justice dimensions (Maxham and Netemeyer, 2002). The importance of the three dimensions depends on several factors, including: the type and magnitude of the service failure (Smith *et al.,* 1999; McColl-Kennedy and Sparks, 2003), the service context (Mattila, 2001), the extent of any prior relationship (Hoffman and Kelley, 2000), and customer psychographics (McCole and Herwadkar, 2003).

The most important step in service recovery is to find out as soon as possible when a service has failed to meet customers' expectations. A customer who is dissatisfied and does not report this dissatisfaction to the service provider may never come back and, worse still, may tell friends about the bad experience. Services companies are therefore going to increasing lengths to facilitate feedback of customers' comments in the hope that they are given an opportunity to make amends. Service recovery after the event might include financial compensation which is considered by the recipient to be fair, or the offer of additional services without charge, giving the company the opportunity to show itself in a better light. If service recovery is to be achieved after the event, it is important that appropriate offers of compensation are made speedily and fairly. If a long dispute ensues, aggrieved customers could increasingly rationalize reasons for never using that service organization again and tell others not only of their bad service encounter, but also of the bad post-service behaviour encountered.

Rather than wait until long after a critical incident has failed, service companies should think more about service recovery during the service delivery process. It can be possible for service organizations to turn a failed critical incident into a positive advantage with its customers. In the face of adverse circumstances, a service organization's ability to empathize with its customers can create stronger bonds than if no service failure had occurred. As an example, a coach tour operator could arrive at a hotel with a party of customers only to find that the hotel has over-booked, potentially resulting in great inconvenience to its customers. The failure to swiftly check its guests into their designated hotel could represent failure of a critical incident which results in long-term harm for the relationship between the coach tour operator and its customers. However, the situation may be recovered by a tour leader who shows determination to sort things out to the best advantage. This could involve the tour leader demonstrating to the customers that he or she is determined to confront the hotel manager and get the room allocation restored. There could also be negotiation with the hotel management to secure alternative hotel accommodation of a higher standard at no additional charge, which customers would appreciate. If the process of rearranging accommodation looked like taking time, the tour leader could avoid the need for customers to be kept waiting in a coach by arranging an alternative enjoyable activity in the interim, such as a visit to a local tourist attraction.

The extent to which service recovery is possible depends upon two principal factors. Firstly, front-line service personnel must have the ability to empathize with customers. Empathy can be demonstrated initially in the ability to spot service failure as it is perceived by customers, rather than some technical, production-oriented definition of failure. Empathy can also be shown in the manner of front-line staff's ability to take action which best meets the needs of customers. Secondly, services organizations should empower front-line staff to take remedial action at the time and place which is most critical. This may entail authorizing – and expecting – staff to deviate from the scheduled service programme and, where necessary, empower staff to use resources at their discretion in order to achieve service recovery. In the case of the tour leader facing an over-booked hotel, taking customers away for a complimentary drink may make the difference between service failure and service recovery. If the tour leader is not authorized to spend money in this way, or approval is so difficult that it comes too late to be useful, the chance of service recovery may be lost for ever.

The role of blueprinting service processes can be emphasized again here. While it may not be possible to anticipate the precise nature of every service failure, a blueprint can indicate what to do in the event of certain general types of failure occurring.

Consider the case of the cancellation of an airline flight which causes great inconvenience to passengers. A blueprint should be able to immediately show:

- who is responsible for informing intending passengers of the cancellation
- which passengers will have priority in being rescheduled to alternative services
- what compensation choices will be offered to passengers
- who will handle unresolved claims for compensation.

In too many organizations, poor blueprinting of recovery processes merely compounds the problem of the original service failure, as customers gain further evidence that the company is not organized effectively and does not have their best interest at heart. However, although blueprinting may provide a basis for service recovery, it may not be sufficient to turn failed customers into advocates. Understanding the emotional state of the customer can be critical, requiring the service provider's response to be carefully tailored to individual customers' emotional states (see Smith and Bolton, 2002). In one study, it was noted that the warmth shown by employees, their ability to deal with customers' emotions and to demonstrate empathic behaviours had a significant effect on customer loyalty following a service failure (Lemmink and Mattsson, 2002).

Wrong kind of excuse put on the line

Train operators in the UK have a long tradition of giving excuses for service failures which have become stock-in-trade for stand-up comedians. 'Leaves on the line' is a problem which perplexes commuters each autumn, amazed that a few small leaves can halt a 100-tonne train. The greatest ridicule was reserved for British Rail in 1987 when 'the wrong kind of snow' grounded the latest Sprinter trains, which had supposedly been tested in the Arctic.

There are signs that the privatized train operating companies have improved their standards of communication with passengers. Many companies have instructed their train crews that blaming delays on 'operating problems' or 'technical difficulties' is just not good enough for intelligent customers who, with a bit of careful thought, could be brought to empathize with the train company and its problems. Crews have also made greater efforts to keep passengers updated on progress towards resolving a problem, helped by improved two-way communications between trains and central control rooms.

At first sight, the strategy might appear to be paying off. During the first five years of privatization, total passengers carried by train companies increased, despite a general worsening of reliability indicators (although, of course, other factors, such as road traffic congestion could have explained the increase in passenger numbers). The media remains highly sceptical about train companies' excuses, and running down the railways remains a national pastime. As an example, in 2000 the media ran stories about Connex South Central blaming delays on 'atmospheric conditions affecting adhesion of rolling stock'. Had the company gone back to insulting the intelligence of its customers with gobbledegook excuses? Rather than still having to make excuses, shouldn't it be addressing the underlying problems? One company which fully acknowledged the intelligence of its customers was Virgin Railways. Richard Branson wrote in the company's customer magazine that its service standards just weren't good enough, but pleaded with customers to be patient while the company invested money to reverse decades of government neglect.

3.7 **Industrializing the service encounter**

Services organizations face a dilemma, for while most seek to maximize the choice and flexibility of services available to customers, they need to reduce the variability of service outcomes in order that consistent brand values can be established. They also need to pursue methods for increasing productivity, and in particular reducing the amount and cost of skilled labour involved in production processes.

Complex and diverse service offers can result in personnel being required to use their judgement and to be knowledgeable about a wide range of services. In many service sectors, giving too much judgement to staff results in a level of variability which is incompatible with consistent brand development. The existence of multiple choices in the service offer can make training staff to become familiar with all of the options very expensive, often matched by a minimal level of income which some services generate. For these reasons, service organizations often seek to simplify their service offerings and to 'deskill' many of the tasks performed by front-line service staff. By offering a limited range of services at a high standard of consistency, the process follows the pattern of the early development of factory production of goods. The process has sometimes been described as the **industrialization of services** and can take a number of forms.

- *Simplifying the range of services available.* Organizations may find themselves offering services which are purchased by relatively few customers. The effort put into providing these services may not be justified by the financial return. Worse still, the lack of familiarity of many staff with little-used services could make them less than proficient at handling service requests, resulting in a poor service encounter which reflects badly on the organization as a whole. Where peripheral services do not produce significant net revenue, but offer a lot of scope for the organization to make mistakes, a case can often be made for dropping them. As an example, retailers have sometimes offered a home delivery service at an additional charge, only to experience minimal demand from a small segment of customers. Moreover, the lack of training often given to sales staff (e.g. on details of delivery areas, etc.) and the general complexity of delivery operations (such as ensuring that there is someone at home to receive the goods) could justify a company in dropping the service. Simplification of the service range to just offering basic retail services allows a wide range of negative service encounters to be avoided, while driving relatively few customers to competitors. It also allows service personnel to concentrate their activities on doing what they are best at – in this case, shop-floor encounters.

- *Providing 'scripts' for role performance.* It was noted above that service personnel act out their role expectations in an informally scripted manner. More formal **scripting** allows service staff to follow the expectations of their role more precisely. Formal scripting can include a precise specification of the actions to be taken by service staff in particular situations, often with the help of machine-based systems. In this way, a telephone sales person can be prompted what to say next by messages on a computer screen. Insurance companies have long experience of simplifying the task of telephone sales personnel so that calculations of premiums are based entirely on data provided by customers, and the sales assistant does not need to use his or her own judgement. Scripting specifies welcoming and closing messages.

■ *Tightly specifying operating procedures.* In some instances, it may be difficult to set out operating procedures which specify in detail how service personnel should handle each encounter. Personal services such as hairdressing rely heavily on the creativity of individual staff and operating procedures can go no further than describe general conduct. However, many service operations can be specified in much greater detail. At a managerial level, many jobs have been deskilled by instituting formalized procedures, which replace much of the judgement previously made by managers. In this way, bank managers use much less judgement in deciding whether to advance credit to a client – the task is decided by a computer-based credit-scoring system. Similarly, local managers in sectors such as retailing and hotels are often given little discretion over such matters as the appearance of their outlets and the type of facilities provided – these are specified in detail from head office and the branch manager is expected to follow them closely. In this way, organizations can ensure that many aspects of the service encounter will be identical, regardless of the time or place.

■ *Replacing human inputs with machine-based inputs.* Machines are generally more predictable in delivering services than humans. They also increasingly offer cost savings, which may give a company a competitive price advantage. Although machines may break down, when they are functioning they tend to be much less variable than humans, who may suffer from tiredness, momentary inattentiveness or periodic boredom. In addition to reducing the variability of service outcomes, machine-based encounters offer a number of other advantages over human-based encounters. We will turn to these in the next section.

Mayo may not be served this way

A student visited her local branch of McDonald's in Northern Ireland. After she had received her burger and fries she asked the serving assistant for some mayonnaise to accompany her food. No sachets of mayonnaise were available, so the server obliged, with typical Irish hospitality, by taking some mayonnaise from a bulk container and putting it on a coffee cup lid for the student. This seemed a pragmatic solution which the customer was more than happy with. But for the serving assistant, it brought a sharp reprimand from her supervisor. This was evidently not allowed by the service blueprint. Perhaps handing over mayonnaise on a cup lid didn't present an image of consistently high professional standards. There may even have been food safety issues involved. But on this occasion at least the customer had been pleased that the server had thought for herself and resolved the problem. How does a company like McDonald's strike a balance between rigid procedures and the need for flexibility to meet the individual customer's requirements?

3.7.1 **Computer-mediated encounters**

There has been a lot of excitement about how computer-based systems are likely to change the way consumers interact with service providers. The vision has been presented of consumers sitting at home behind a computer terminal communicating with another computer at the other end, as a result of which services are provided. There is nothing new, of course, in the use of technology to intervene in a producer–consumer encounter. Banks, for example, have for some time reduced the amount of contact that their staff have with customers through the use of ATMs, so Internet banking could be seen as an extension of this technological development.

The extent to which computers are able to intervene in service encounters is influenced by the type of service in question. Chapter 2 discussed bases for classification and it should be quite clear that the role of direct human encounters will always be crucial to some types of services. Where the services process requires direct contact with the customer's body (as in the case of many medical services), the possibilities for computer-based intervention are likely to be small (although it could nevertheless be used to provide support services such as booking facilities for a doctor or a simplified diagnostic facility). Where services involve processes being carried out on the customer's physical assets (e.g. car repairs), there is still likely to be a point of contact where the assets are collected/delivered, although reservation and accounting facilities may be undertaken without direct human encounters. It is in the area of pure services with few tangible components that computer mediated service delivery has had greatest impact. Many 'pure' information services, such as the provision of bank savings accounts and share price information, can be done with very little, if any, face-to-face contact between a customer and a company's employees.

Computer-mediated encounters can impact on traditional face-to-face encounters in a number of ways, as described below.

- Computer mediation can completely replace the need for a face-to-face encounter. For example, the airline easyJet uses its website to remove the need for face-to-face contact for customers booking a ticket with the company.

- Computer mediation may facilitate face-to-face encounters. For example, Thetrainline.com sells train tickets through its website, which can be collected from a customer's local rail station, reducing the amount of queuing at a booking office

- Sometimes, a website can be used to 'educate' a customer prior to a face-to-face encounter. For example, one study of medical practitioners showed patients engaged in Internet-based information search that changed the nature of the primary encounter and presented challenges to medical professionals both in terms of doctor–patient relationships and their professional judgement (Hogg *et al.*, 2003).

- The service provider may be able to offer a much wider range of encounter possibilities. For example, Internet banking and ATMs allow many bank transactions to be undertaken at a time which is convenient to the customer, and also at a place which is convenient.

■ It is often possible to programme machinery to provide a range of services reliably in a manner that would not have been possible if the encounter was based on a human service producer. Many telephone companies now offer a wide range of automated telephone services (e.g. call interception services) which can be delivered at lower cost and with higher levels of reliability than if human operators had to be used.

■ Automated encounters can give some customers a feeling of greater control over an encounter. A bank customer phoning the local branch to ask for the balance of his or her account may feel that he or she is having to work hard to get the information out of a bank employee and may feel intimidated by asking additional questions. By calling an automated banking information system or using an Internet banking service, some customers may feel they have greater control over their dealings with the bank. (Although, against this, many services users may feel uncomfortable with computer-mediated services and would feel much happier with face-to-face encounters.)

By designing service processes around customers' needs and the opportunities provided by the new technology, more efficient and effective service processes can be designed. As an example, many airlines have developed web-based electronic ticketing systems, which remove all need for direct intervention by the service provider's employees until the point where the customer is about to board the aircraft (Figure 3.7).

Figure 3.7 easyJet claims to be the 'web's favourite airline' and has used the Internet effectively to simplify encounters between the company and its customers. By 2004, the company claimed that about 80% of its customers used the Internet for booking their tickets, saving administrative costs for the airline which are passed on in lower prices to customers. The company has refused to pay the 10–15% commission traditionally paid by airlines to travel agents. But to make sure that it doesn't miss out on business from individuals or companies who would prefer to book through an agent, easyJet nevertheless welcomes bookings through travel agents. However, it makes clear that travel agents should pass on their handling costs to the final customer, in recognition of the fact that a travel agent's customer is buying a different kind of encounter. Despite the additional service charge, some customers still prefer the convenience and reassurance that dealing face to face with a travel agent may provide. (Reproduced with permission of easyJet Airline Company Ltd)

Computer-mediated interaction needs to take account of all the stages involved in an encounter. Building on the discussion earlier in this chapter, classification of the service delivery process to online encounters can be described as follows.

- *Access phase.* This may involve consumers gaining access to a functioning ATM or an Internet-connected computer.

- *Check-in phase.* In this phase, consumers identify themselves to the service organization – for example, by supplying a user name and PIN number. How does a service provider balance the sometimes conflicting need of ease of checking in with the need for security and privacy?

- *Diagnosis stage.* When the consumer is presented, the system must identify his or her needs as quickly as possible. For example, an ATM terminal should be able to diagnose quickly whether a consumer who has checked in wishes to withdraw cash, obtain a statement, pay a bill or deposit a cheque.

- *Delivery.* The consumer's needs are fulfilled (e.g. cash dispensed by an ATM, copy of statement printed).

- *Check-out stage.* During this stage, the consumer is securely disengaged from the service delivery system – for example, by the return of a bank ATM card, or logging off a website.

Of course, service encounters that are computer-mediated need to be designed with the same care and attention to detail as those that involve human encounters. It is not uncommon to find websites that are slow and confusing in their layout and operation or that fail to bring about the desired service. Just as in the failure of a human-based critical incident, failure during a web-based encounter may result in defection of the customer to a competitor. The study of **Human–computer interaction** (HCI) has become an important area of study in its own right.

Some segments of consumers may be slow to embrace computer-mediated exchanges, as we shall see in the next chapter. However, it is not only service users who may be slow to adapt to new self-service technologies. Research has found that designing, updating and maintaining websites proves particularly difficult for small firms (Blackburn and Athayde, 2000).

3.7.2 **Measuring service productivity**

Productivity can be defined as the efficiency with which an organization's inputs are turned into outputs. The Industrial Revolution that took place in England in the 18th and 19th centuries was characterized by dramatic improvements in the productivity of human, equipment and financial resources. Many have pointed to a 'service revolution' during the past few decades when productivity in many services sectors has shown a significant improvement. Processes of service industrialization, described in this chapter, have contributed to this improvement in productivity. However, services are still a relatively low-productivity sector of the economy. Using a measure of 'gross value added' (GVA), the UK Office for National Statistics has calculated that although the services sector provides around three times as many jobs as the production sector, it manages only to deliver less than twice as much approximate GVA. Consequently, services-sector labour productivity is about two-thirds that of the production sector. During the two decades 1981–2000, real productivity growth in services was lower than in the manufacturing sector, except for a brief period in 1995–98 (Lau, 2002).

The whole concept of productivity is much more complex for services than for goods. For goods, production can generally be separated from consumption, and consumers are not generally affected by the way in which the item has been manufactured. Provided it performs to standard, a car buyer is not too concerned whether the car has been produced with automated or manual methods of production. However, for the service consumer the nature of production methods can be crucial, because the inseparability of production and consumption means that the whole nature and benefit of the service can change when production methods change. A bank replacing its counter staff with ATMs and telephone banking may appear to have improved its productivity when assessed by such measures as customer transactions per employee or cost per transaction. However, the automated service may be perceived as something quite different from that which went before it. Because of the problem of inseparability, it can be difficult to gain a clear picture of what is happening to the true productivity of the service sector. More efficient does not necessarily mean more effective in meeting consumers' needs.

Case study

Creating a drama at TGI Friday's

Is it a pub? Is it a restaurant? Or is it theatre? The operators of TGI Friday's would hope that their customers see it as all three. For diners who tire of the scripted industrialized service processes of many fast-food chains, the service encounter at a branch of TGI Friday's may come as welcome relief.

TGI Friday's is a themed American restaurant and bar group started in 1965 in the USA and which has been operated as a franchise since 1986 in the UK by Whitbread plc. By 2004, TGI Friday's had 42 restaurants in the UK, and a worldwide total of 735 in 55 countries.

The credo of TGI Friday's – according to Richard Snead, president and CEO of Carlson Restaurants Worldwide, parent company of TGI Friday's – is 'to treat every customer as we would an honoured guest in our home, and it is reflected in everything we do'.

There are four crucial components of the company philosophy which contribute to successful service encounters at its restaurants:

1. *employees* – these are seen as the key to service quality; this applies not only to front-line staff who visibly contribute to guests' experience, but also back-room staff

2. *product* – a meal is a focal point of a customer's visit and consistency of standards is important

3. *package* – this comprises the building and furnishings, which must be well maintained.

4. *ambience* – this is an important part of the meal experience that is difficult to specify, but memorable to customers.

The first TGI Friday's was opened at First Avenue and 63rd Street in New York City in 1965 and featured the now familiar red and white stripes. Inside were wooden floors, Tiffany lamps, bentwood chairs and striped tablecloths. Decor has become a key element in the TGI Friday's experience, transforming an otherwise bland and boring industrial-type building into a theatrical stage. For TGI Friday's interior decor, a full-time antique 'picker' travels extensively to auctions and flea markets. Memorabilia has to be authentic and, if possible, unique to the area where a new restaurant would be located.

TGI Friday's offers '**mass customization**' in which the company offers a basically standard service to all customers, but the customers can personalize their meal through an extensive range of menu permutations. The company's approach to managing the service encounter distinguishes between 'hard' and 'soft' elements. Hard elements include core service processes and tangible elements of the product offer, such as car-parking facilities, the menu offered and target service times. The fundamental design of TGI restaurants is remarkably similar throughout the world, with a large central bar area with dining facilities surrounding the bar and authentic American decorative memorabilia. Even the location of the toilets is standard, and an American guest visiting the TGI Friday's restaurant in Coventry would immediately know where to look for them. Red and white striped awnings, wooden floors, Tiffany lampshades, cane chairs, and striped tablecloths create an aura of the American bar/diner. Each restaurant offers a range of approximately 100 American/Mexican food menu items and approximately the same number of cocktails. Service target times form part of the 'hard' element of the service encounter and the company requires that starters should be served within seven minutes of receipt of a customer's order. A computer program helps managers to monitor the achievement of these service times. The 'hard' elements of the service encounter tend to be specified by head office, and branch managers are expected to achieve specified standards. Menus and the product range are designed and priced centrally at head office.

However, it is the 'soft' elements of the service encounter that distinguish TGI Fridays from its competitors. Crucial to this is the empowering of employees to take whatever actions they see fit in order to improve customers' experience. Employee performance requires, therefore, more than the traditional acts of greeting, seating and serving customers. Employees have to be able to provide both the behaviours, and the emotional displays, to match with customers' feelings. Getting serving staff to join in a chorus of 'Happy Birthday' may not be easy to script, but spontaneous singing when a meal is served to a group of diners celebrating a birthday can make all the difference in customers' experience of their meal. Of course, recruitment of the right kind of people becomes crucial, and prospective candidates are selected as much for their sense of fun as on the strength of their CV. Initial interviews take the form of 'auditions' in which potential recruits are set individual and group tasks to test their personality type. Opportunities are given for trained staff to express their personality and individuality – for example, by wearing outlandish clothes that make a statement about their personality.

TGI Friday's has become a preferred place of employment for restaurant staff, who have enjoyed relatively good working conditions, above-average earnings for the sector – especially when tips are taken into account – and a sense of fun while at work. The chain has won numerous awards as a good employer, including the UK's 15th best workplace according to the *Financial Times* 2004 Survey of Best UK Places to Work, and the only restaurant chain to be included on the list for a second year running. It was also the fourth most fun place to work according to the *FT*.

Is the pattern of service encounters developed by TGI Friday's a sustainable business model? Among the portfolio of restaurant formats operated by Whitbread plc, TGI Friday's has been a star performer, in contrast to some of its more traditional formats, such as Beefeater, which have become less popular with consumers. A glance at the customer review site www.ciao.co.uk provides an insight to customers' experience of the service encounter. Overall, contributors seem to be happy with the format, although a number of people observed that service standards could decline when a restaurant becomes very busy. It may be fine for serving staff to sing to customers when times are quiet, but how can they do this and still meet their service delivery time targets when the restaurant is busy? A number of customers also commented on very high prices charged by TGI Friday's, with more than one person describing them as 'rip-off prices'. But in order to get the best staff who can create a memorable experience, is it a good business model paying them a little more and passing this on to customers as higher prices?

Case study review questions

1. What are the connections between theatre and TGI Friday's? Is the dramaturgical analogy a good one?

2. What is meant by a critical incident? How can TGI Friday's identify what constitutes a critical incident and assess whether it has achieved customer satisfaction?

3. Discuss the relative merits of 'blueprinting', 'Servicescapes' and 'Servuction' as conceptual frameworks for analysing the service encounter at TGI Friday's.

Chapter summary and links to other chapters

This chapter has built on the previous chapter by defining a service in terms of its processes. For high-contact services, consumers can be very closely involved in these processes, posing problems of quality control which are not present in the manufactured goods sector where goods can be produced out of sight and stockpiled during periods of low demand. Because they are produced 'live' in the presence of consumers, services have a high chance of failing to meet consumers' expectations, therefore firms must have a strategy for recovering from such failures.

Attempts to measure the quality of a service encounter are considered in more detail in **Chapter 8**. The quality of the service encounter contributes towards consumers' decision on whether to repurchase from a particular supplier, to the extent that an ongoing relationship is developed (**Chapters 4 and 5**).

A critical factor in service encounters which relies on staff inputs by the provider is the quality and consistency of staff. This chapter has highlighted the preoccupation of many service providers with simplifying and deskilling staff tasks. There is a limit to which this can go and staff will need to be appropriately selected, trained and monitored for most service encounters. These issues are returned to in **Chapter 12**. Delays during a service process can impact directly upon consumers, therefore service providers aim to avoid bottlenecks by carefully matching their capacity with the level of demand. The issue of demand management is considered further in **Chapter 13**.

Chapter review questions

1. What distinguishes 'high contact' services from 'low contact' ones?

2. Choose one high-contact services sector with which you are familiar and identify the critical incidents that occur during the service production–consumption process.

3. What is meant by service failure? Suggest strategies that a fast-food restaurant can employ to recover from service failure most effectively.

4. What is meant by the industrialization of services? What are the limits to the industrialization process within the restaurant sector?

5. Many analyses of the service encounter have drawn analogies with the theatre. To what extent is this comparison valid?

6. The service encounter usually involves customers as active participants in the production process. To what extent is it desirable, or possible for a service provider to 'train' customers to be efficient co-producers of a service?

Activity

Choose one of the following service processes: taking a car to a garage to have its exhaust system renewed; minor building repairs to a house; hair styling and colouring. Draw a service blueprint which describes the service processes involved. Your blueprint should identify the different stages involved in the service production process; target times for each stage to be undertaken; the participants involved in each stage; visible evidence of the service process; and the invisible processes involved.

Key terms

Blueprinting A method of visually portraying the processes and participants involved in the production of a service.

Co-production A service benefit can be realized only if more than one party contributes to its production, e.g. customer–producer co-production implies that customers take a role in producing service benefits.

Critical incidents Encounters between customers and service producers that can be especially satisfying or dissatisfying.

Culture The whole set of beliefs, attitudes and customs common to a group of people.

High-contact services Services in which the production process involves a high level of contact between an organization's employees and its customers.

Human–computer interaction The study of how people use computers.

Industrialization of services The process of deskilling and simplifying service production processes with the aim of reducing variability in outcomes and processes.

Mass customization The use of mass-production techniques that allow customization of output to the individual customer's preferences.

Role-playing Behaviour of an individual which is a result of his or her social conditioning, as distinct from innate predispositions.

Scripting Pursuing a pattern of behaviour that is tightly specified by another party.

Service failure Failure to meet customers' expectations about the standard of service delivery.

Service offer The complexity of tangible and intangible benefits that make up the total functional, psychological and social benefits of a service.

Service recovery Processes used by a company to recover from a service failure.

Servicescape A description of the environment in which service delivery takes place.

Servuction A description of the producer–consumer service production system.

Tangible cues Physical elements of the service offer, brochures and adverts which provide tangible stimuli in the buying decision-making process.

Selected further reading

The central role of the encounter between an organization's staff and its customers has led to a considerable literature in defining service encounters and prescribing methods for improving the quality of encounters. The following are important papers in the development of this stream of literature.

Carlzon, J. (1987) *Moments of Truth*, Ballinger Books, Cambridge, MA.

Bitner, M. (1990) 'Evaluating service encounters: The effects of physical surroundings and employee responses', *Journal of Marketing*, 51 (April), 69–82.

Bitner, M.J., Booms, B.H. and Tetreault, M.S. (1990) 'The service encounter: Diagnosing favorable and unfavorable incidents', *Journal of Marketing*, 54 (January), 71–84.

Shostack, G.L. (1985) 'Planning the service encounter', in J.A. Czepiel, M.R. Solomon and C.F. Suprenant (eds) *The Service Encounter*, Lexington Books, Lexington, MA, 243–54.

Shostack, G.L. (1984) 'Designing services that deliver', *Harvard Business Review*, January/February, 133–319.

The following articles update discussion on service encounters in the context of technology-mediated encounters.

Dabholkar, P.A. and Bagozzi, R.P. (2002) 'An attitudinal model of technology-based self service: Moderating effects of consumer traits and situational factors', *Journal of the Academy of Marketing Science*, 30 (3), 184–201.

Bitner, M.J., Brown, S.W. and Meuter, M.L. (2000) 'Technology infusion in service encounters', *Journal of the Academy of Marketing Science*, 28 (1), 138–49.

Meuter, M.L., Ostrom, A.L., Roundtree, R.I. and Bitner, M.J. (2000) 'Self-service technologies: Understanding customer satisfaction with technology-based service encounters', *Journal of Marketing*, 64 (3), 50–64.

Hogg, G., Laing, A. and Winkelman, D. (2003) 'The professional service encounter in the age of the Internet: An exploratory study', *Journal of Services Marketing*, 17 (5), 476–94.

The following papers offer a further discussion of role-playing and scripting, which is an important aspect of industrialized service encounters.

Goodwin, C. (1996) 'Moving the drama into the factory: The contribution of metaphors to services research', *European Journal of Marketing*, 30 (9), 13–36.

Gabbott, M. and Hogg, G. (1996) 'The glory of stories: Using critical incidents to understand service evaluation in the primary health care context', *Journal of Marketing Management*, 12 (6), 493–503.

Parker, C. and Ward, P. (2000) 'An analysis of role adaptations and scripts during customer-to-customer encounters', *European Journal of Marketing*, 34 (3/4), 341–58.

The literature on failed service encounters and the ways in which companies recover from service failure has been growing in recent times. The following papers are relevant.

McColl-Kennedy, J.R. and Sparks, B.A. (2003) 'Application of fairness theory to service failures and service recovery', *Journal of Service Research*, 5 (3), 251–66.

Maxham, J.G. and Netemeyer, R.G. (2002) 'A longitudinal study of complaining customers' evaluations of multiple service failures and recovery efforts', *Journal of Marketing*, 66 (October), 57–71.

Lewis, B.R. and Clacher, E. (2001) 'Service failure and recovery in UK theme parks: The employees' perspective', *International Journal of Contemporary Hospitality Management*, 13 (4), 166–75.

Hart, C.W.L., Sasser, W.E. Jr and Heskett, J.L. (1990) 'The profitable art of service recovery', *Harvard Business Review*, July–August, 148–56.

Hoffman, D.K. and Scott, W.K. (2000) 'Perceived justice needs and recovery evaluation: A contingency approach', *European Journal of Marketing*, 34 (3/4), 418–32.

Andreassen, T.W. (2000) 'Antecedents to satisfaction with service recovery', *European Journal of Marketing*, 34 (1/2), 156–75.

de Ruyter, K. and Wetzels, M. (2000) 'Customer equity considerations in service recovery: A cross-industry perspective', *International Journal of Service Industry Management*, 11 (1), 91–108.

Mattila, A.S. (2001) 'The effectiveness of service recovery in a multi-industry setting', *Journal of Services Marketing*, 15 (7), 583–96.

References

Adam, J.S. (1965) 'Inequality in social exchange', in L. Berkowitz, *Advances in Experimental Social Psychology*, vol. 2, Academic Press, New York, 267–99.

Bateson, J.E.G. (1989) *Managing Services Marketing – Text and Readings*, 2nd edn, Dryden Press, Forth Worth, USA.

Berry, L.L., Seiders, K. and Grewal, D. (2002) 'Understanding service convenience', *Journal of Marketing*, 66 (3), 1–17.

Bies, R. (1987) 'The predicament of injustice: The management of moral outrage', *Research in Organizational Behavior*, 9, 289–319.

Bitner, M. (1990) 'Evaluating service encounters: The effects of physical surroundings and employee responses', *Journal of Marketing*, 51 (April), 69–82.

Bitner, M.J., Booms, B.H. and Tetreault, M.S. (1990) 'The service encounter: Diagnosing favourable and unfavourable incidents', *Journal of Marketing*, 54 (January), 71–84.

Blackburn, R. and Athayde, R. (2000) 'Making the connection: The effectiveness of Internet training in small businesses', *Education and Training*, 42 (4/5).

Booms, B.H. and Bitner, M.J. (1981) 'Marketing strategies and organization structures for service firms', in J. Donnelly and W.R. George (eds), *Marketing of Services*, American Marketing Association, Chicago, 51–67.

Carlzon, J. (1987) *Moments of Truth*, Ballinger Books, Cambridge, MA.

Churchill, G.A. and Surprenant, C. (1982) 'An investigation into the determinants of customer satisfaction', *Journal of Marketing Research*, 19 (November), 491–504.

Edvardsson, B. and Strandvik, T. (2000) 'Is a critical incident critical for a customer relationship?', *Managing Service Quality*, 10 (2), 82–91.

Eiglier, P. and Langeard, P. (1987) *Servuction*, McGraw-Hill, New York.

Folger, R. and Cropanzano, R. (1998) *Organizational Justice and Human Resource Management*, Sage, Thousand Oaks, CA.

Goodwin, C. (1996) 'Moving the drama into the factory: The contribution of metaphors to services research', *European Journal of Marketing*, 30 (9), 13–36.

Halstead, D., Drogue, C. and Cooper, M.B. (1993) 'Product warranties and post purchase service: A model of consumer satisfaction without complaint resolution', *Journal of Services Marketing*, 7 (1), 33–40.

Hart, C.W.L., Sasser, W.E. Jr and Heskett, J.L. (1990) 'The profitable art of service recovery', *Harvard Business Review*, July–August, 148–56.

Heung, V.C. and Lam, T. (2003) 'Customer complaint behaviour towards hotel restaurant services', *International Journal of Contemporary Hospitality Management*, 15 (5), 283–9.

Hoffman, K.D. and Kelley, S.W. (2000) 'Perceived justice needs and recovery evaluation: A contingency approach', *European Journal of Marketing*, 34 (3/4), 296–304.

Hoffman, K.D., Kelley, S.W. and Rotalsky, H.M. (1995) 'Tracking service failures and employee recovery efforts', *Journal of Services Marketing*, 2, 49–61.

Hogg, G., Laing, A. and Winkelman, D. (2003) 'The professional service encounter in the age of the Internet: An exploratory study', *Journal of Services Marketing*, 17 (5), 476–94.

Homans, G.C. (1961) *Social Behavior*, Harcourt Brace and World, New York.

Kelley, S.W. and Davis, M.A. (1994) 'Antecedents to customer expectations for service recovery', *Journal of the Academy of Marketing Science*, 22 (1), 52–61.

Kelley, H.H. and Thibaut, J. (1978) *Interpersonal Relations: A Theory of Interdependence*. Wiley, New York.

Kingman-Brundage, J. (1989) 'The ABCs of service system blueprinting', in M.J. Bitner and L.A. Crosby (eds), *Designing a Winning Service Strategy*, American Marketing Association, Chicago, IL.

Lau, E. (2002) 'Productivity measures: ONS strategy', *Economic Trends*, 581, 20–5.

Lemmink, J. and Mattsson, J. (2002) 'Employee behavior, feelings of warmth and customer perception in service encounters', *International Journal of Retail and Distribution Management*, 30 (1), 18–33.

Mattila, A.S. (2001) 'The effectiveness of service recovery in a multi-industry setting', *Journal of Services Marketing*, 15 (7), 583–96.

Maxham, J.G. and Netemeyer, R.G. (2002) 'A longitudinal study of complaining customers' evaluations of multiple service failures and recovery efforts', *Journal of Marketing*, 66 (October), 57–71.

McCole, P. and Herwadkar, A. (2003) 'Towards a more inclusive model for understanding service failure and service recovery', Proceedings of ANZMAC 2003, Adelaide, Australia.

McColl-Kennedy, J.R. and Sparks, B. (2003) 'Application of fairness theory to service failures and service recovery', *Journal of Service Research*, 5 (3), 251–66.

Nyer, P.U. (2000) 'An investigation into whether complaining can cause increased consumer satisfaction', *Journal of Consumer Marketing*, 17 (1), 9–19.

Oliver, R. (1980) 'A cognitive model of the antecedents and consequences of satisfaction decisions', *Journal of Market Research*, 17 (November), 460–9.

Palmer, A., Beggs, R. and Keown-McMullan, C. (2000) 'Equity and repurchase intention following service failure', *Journal of Services Marketing*, 14 (6), 513–28.

Parasuraman, A., Zeithaml, V. and Berry, L.L. (1985) 'A conceptual model of service quality and its implications for future research', *Journal of Marketing*, 49 (Fall), 41–50.

Reichheld, F.E. and Sasser, W. (1990) 'Zero defections: Quality comes to services, *Harvard Business Review*, 68 (5), 105–11.

Shostack, G.L. (1985) 'Planning the service encounter', in J.A. Czepiel, M.R. Solomon and C.F. Suprenant (eds) *The Service Encounter*, Lexington Books, Lexington, MA, 243–54.

Smith, A. and Bolton, R. (2002) 'The effect of customers' emotional response to service failures on their recovery effort evaluations and satisfaction judgements', *Journal of the Academy of Marketing Science*, 30 (1), 5–23.

Smith, A.K., Bolton, R.N. and Wagner, J. (1999) 'A model of customer satisfaction with service encounters involving failure and recovery', *Journal of Marketing Research*, 36 (3), 356–72.

Solomon, M.R., Surprenant, C., Czepiel, J.A. and Gutman, E.G. (1985) 'A role theory perspective on dyadic interactions: The service encounter', *Journal of Marketing*, 49 (Winter), 99–111.

Spreng, R.A., Harrell, G.D. and Mackoy, R.D. (1995) 'Service recovery: Impact on satisfaction and intentions', *Journal of Services Marketing*, 9 (1), 15–23.

Stauss, B. and Weinlich, B. (1985) 'Process oriented measurement of service quality by applying the sequential incident method', Proceedings of the Workshop on Quality Management, University of Tilburg.

Tax, S.S., Brown, S. and Chandrashekaran, M. (1998) 'Customer evaluation of service complaint experiences: Implication for relationship marketing', *Journal of Marketing*, 62 (April), 60–76.

Warnaby, G. and Davies, B.J.J. (1997) 'Cities as service factories? Using the Servuction system for marketing cities as shopping destinations', *International Journal of Retail and Distribution Management*, 25 (6–7), 204–10.

Services buying processes

Learning objectives

This chapter will explain:

- processes by which consumers initiate, carry out and conclude the purchase of services

- the effects of service intangibility on perceptions of riskiness in the buying process

- the effects on behaviour of post-consumption dissonance

- decision-making units and their effects on services buying

- differences between personal and business buying of services

- the effects of computer mediation on consumer services buying processes

- bases for segmenting services markets

- the role of service providers' ethical standards in consumer choice.

4.1 **Introduction**

A company can put years of effort into developing a new service, but find it rejected by buyers in the few minutes, or sometimes even seconds, that it may take them to choose between the alternatives available. The company may have made false assumptions about the processes by which purchase decisions are made, for example by under-estimating the role played by key influencers in the decision process. Although the chapters of this book break the elements of the extended marketing mix into separate sections for discussion, it should never be forgotten that buyers judge the service offer much more holistically.

This chapter explores the effects of intangibility on the service buying decision process and notes that choosing between competing services is often perceived as being more difficult and risky than is the case with goods. The lack of physical evidence means that sellers' claims about a product can often only be taken on trust and verified after consumption. The chapter will begin by discussing ways in which buyers make decisions and these will be integrated into models of buyer behaviour. An important theme of buying processes is the evident need of buyers to simplify their decision-making when faced with a sometimes seemingly endless array of choices.

This chapter concentrates on decision processes involved in the purchase of *consumer services*. However, differences occur with *producer services* and these will be noted.

4.2 **Risk and services buying decisions**

Consumers experience pre-purchase uncertainty during the purchase of most products. However, because the amount and quality of information available is generally less in the case of an intangible service, compared with goods, the amount of perceived risk can be expected to be higher. Intangibility often leads to a consumer's evaluaton of a service being based on tangible evidence and price rather than the core service offer (Zeithaml, 1981). A number of factors influence the level of risk experienced by a consumer when approaching a service purchase.

- *The level of tangible evidence which is available to support evidence of the service process and outcomes.* Service providers often go to great lengths to demonstrate service benefits using tangible cues, e.g. an airline which seeks to charge a premium price for its business-class seats may demonstrate the benefits of its seats with a replica seat in travel agents' offices.

- *The level of the buyer's involvement in the service.* Going back to our classification of services in Chapter 2, it will be recalled that services can be defined in terms of their level of consumer involvement. Where involvement levels are high (as in the case of many personal healthcare services), the perceived risk of a decision is likely to be greater than a low-involvement service such as the rental of a video.

■ *The novelty of the purchase.* If a particular type of purchase is new to us, we are more likely to experience high levels of risk than if we are a repeat buyer. A first-time mortgage buyer will most likely perceive much higher levels of risk than someone who has arranged many mortgages during his or her life.

■ *The purchaser's individual risk threshold.* Just as some people are more prepared to take risks in the way they gamble money or drive their car, so some buyers will be more prepared to take risks when choosing between competing services (Figure 4.1). A cheap holiday with an unknown foreign airline may appeal to some, but be perceived as too risky by others.

■ *Situational factors affect perceptions of risk.* If we are desperate to use a service we may lower our risk threshold. If we have just missed the last bus home, we may be more prepared to risk a taxi ride in a 'dubious' car, which is perceived as being more risky than the taxi that we might choose in more relaxed conditions.

■ *There may be a perception of safeguards available to consumers which reduces perceptions of risk.* In many cases, legislation protects consumers from non-delivery of a service, so consumers may be more prepared to take a risk. Within the financial services sector, for example, there is an extensive protection mechanism which prevents small savers losing deposits paid to regulated banks. Most UK investors do not therefore perceive the risk of losing their money when putting their savings in

Figure 4.1 The market for Internet Service Providers (ISPs) in the UK is fiercely competitive, but buyers have few bases for evaluating competing service providers. If I sign up for a 12-month contract for this provider, can I be sure of a reliable connection? Will it be fast? How good are the information sources provided by the site? If I have a technical problem, will I get good advice speedily? The possibility of failure in any of these areas may pose a risk to purchasers, who may just prefer to carry on with their existing ISP, or not bother buying at all. Freeserve (now known as Wanadoo) established itself as a leading UK ISP but appreciated the risks its potential customers may have perceived. Like many of its competitors, it has offered a free trial period, during which customers can test the company's service claims with little or no risk to themselves. The company's experience is that a high proportion of trial users go on to sign up for a one-year service contract. (Reproduced with permission of Freeserve, now part of Wanadoo)

a domestic bank, but perceptions of risk would be much higher if the bank was offshore and unregulated.

The whole subject of risk and its link to service expectations is relatively unexplored. One study found that uncertainty was negatively associated with pre-purchase expectations in industrial buying situations, in other words we expect better outcomes where risks are lowest (Paterson *et al.*, 1997). As expectations play a major role in determining consumers' post-consumption service quality evaluations (see Chapter 8), it follows that an understanding of perceived risk is important to comprehending consumers' assessments of quality.

4.3 **The buying process**

It is important for services marketers to gain an insight into the processes and critical factors involved in an individual's purchase decision. Organizations must develop a thorough understanding of a number of aspects of their customers' buying processes; in particular, answering the following questions.

■ Who is involved in making the purchase decision?

■ How long does the process of making a decision take?

■ What is the set of competing services from which consumers make their choice?

■ What is the relative importance attached by decision-makers to each of the elements of the service offer?

■ What sources of information are used in evaluating competing service offers?

The basic processes involved in purchase decisions are illustrated in Figure 4.2. Simple models of buyer behaviour usually see some underlying need triggering a search for need-satisfying solutions. When possible solutions have been identified, these are evaluated according to some criteria. The eventual purchase decision is a consequence of the interaction between the final decision-maker and a range of

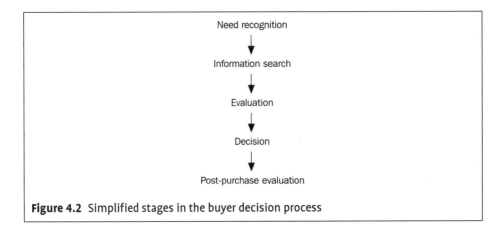

Figure 4.2 Simplified stages in the buyer decision process

influencers. Finally, after purchase and consumption, the consumer develops feelings about his or her purchase which influence future decisions. In reality, service purchase decision processes can be complex iterative processes involving large numbers of influencers and diverse decision criteria. **Needs** can themselves be difficult to understand and should be distinguished from expectations. The intangible nature of services and the general inability of buyers to check the quality or nature of a service until after it has been consumed adds to the importance of understanding the sources of information which are used in the process of evaluation.

4.3.1 **Need recognition**

The buying process is triggered by an underlying need. That need motivates us to seek a solution which will restore a sense of physiological and psychological balance which was previously absent. Needs can be extremely complex and are no longer dominated by basic physiological needs. The service industry sector has benefited from the tendency for societies to climb to higher levels of Maslow's 'hierarchy of needs' (Maslow, 1943). Among consumer services, a high proportion of high growth sectors would appear to be catering to individuals' 'higher order' social and self-actualization needs. Multi-channel television services, flower delivery services and long-haul travel are all a long way from satisfying our basic needs but are typical of the sectors that expanded rapidly in recent years by satisfying consumers' higher order needs. Figure 4.3 offers an illustration of how changing needs have influenced the type of food we buy. In less-developed societies, consumers are driven primarily by the basic nutritional content of food in order to satisfy a basic need for body maintenance. In more developed societies

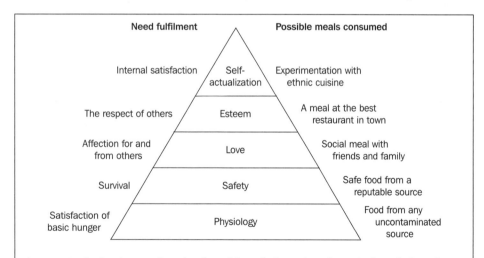

Figure 4.3 The food sector has developed from being primarily agriculturally based to being increasingly service based. Affluent societies no longer just satisfy a basic need for safe, wholesome food, but are motivated by higher-order needs for sociality and self-actualization. This diagram, based on Maslow's hierarchy of needs model, illustrates some of the effects of changing needs on the way in which we buy food-related services.

we are increasingly likely to base our search for food on the basis of a need for social togetherness or curiosity. Hence the great growth in social eating out, and in particular the variety of ethnic restaurants which can now be found in most towns.

Maslow's hierarchy provides a basis for understanding the needs which underlie demand for services, but the hierarchy is no more than a conceptual model. In practice, it is difficult to measure where an individual actually is on the hierarchy of needs. Furthermore, it is essentially based on western values of motivation and there is a lot of evidence of cultural influences on needs (e.g. Jai-Ok *et al.*, 2002). How, for example, would you explain religious sacrifice and penance which are an important motivator for many services associated with religious rituals, especially in non-western consumers?

In addition to our inherent physiological and psychological needs, our needs are influenced by the situation in which we currently find ourselves. The subjects of age and socio-economic status can have profound effects on buying behaviour. The stage that an individual has reached in the 'family life cycle' also has a significant influence on needs (Figure 4.4).

So far, needs have been discussed in the context of a stimulus–response model in which the stimulus of a need leads to action being taken. However, it has been suggested that stimulus–response models are too simplistic in the way that needs are portrayed as being something conscious. While this criticism may be true of products in general, it has particular relevance to services. As well as being physically intangible, many services may be mentally intangible. Few young people, for example, recognize an underlying need for the security in old age which a pension will provide. Such people may only purchase a pension policy if they become aware of the product. Prior to this, they may not have been aware of the underlying need which a pension policy seeks to satisfy.

4.3.2 **Information search**

In the classic model of buyer behaviour, the next stage in the process is to collect information about services which are capable of satisfying the underlying need. These can be derived from a combination of service provider and other extraneous sources (e.g. **word-of-mouth** recommendation from friends).

Once a need has triggered the search for need-satisfying solutions, a search for information will begin. But where do buyers look for information when making purchases? In the case of the routine repurchase of a familiar service, probably very little information is sought about the product; but where there is a greater element of risk, buyers are likely to seek out more comprehensive information about the alternative ways in which they can satisfy their needs. The following information sources are likely to be used.

■ Personal experience will be a starting point, so if a buyer has already used a company's products, the suitability of the proposed purchase may be assessed in the light of the previous purchases.

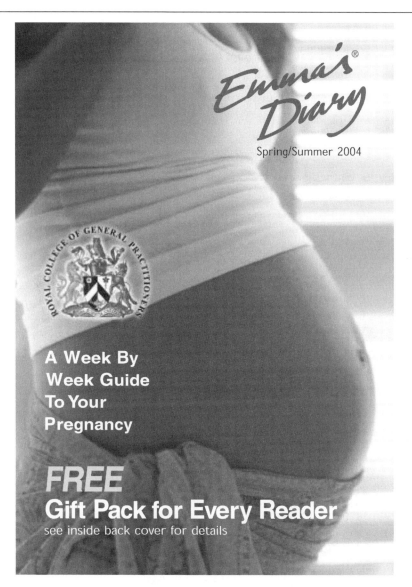

Figure 4.4 An individual's needs for different types of service typically change through his or her lifetime, and certain 'trigger' events may bring about a new set of needs. Lifecycle Marketing Services Limited has understood the radically changed needs of mothers-to-be and publishes the magazine *Emma's Diary* and website www.emmasdiary.co.uk to guide them through the stages of pregnancy and childbirth. By registering with the company, individuals receive further information and offers appropriate to their needs at the different stages of their pregnancy. The company has built up a valuable database of customers who have come to trust the advice given by *Emma's Diary*. Advertisers in the magazine and on the website realize that the birth of a child, especially the first one, is a significant trigger to new patterns of expenditure. Targeted individuals are likely to be highly receptive to the firms' messages. (Reproduced with permission of Lifecycle Marketing Ltd)

- Word-of-mouth recommendation from friends is important for many categories of services where an individual may have had no previous need to make a purchase. When looking for a plumber or a solicitor, for example, many people will initially seek the advice of friends.

- Rather than referring to individuals on a face-to-face basis, we may use various other reference groups to guide us. What restaurant is it considered fashionable to eat in at the moment? What bar in town is currently the coolest place to be seen in by your peer group?

- Newspaper editorial content and directories such as those published by the Consumers' Association may be consulted as a relatively objective source of information.

- Advertising and promotion in all of its forms is studied, sometimes being specifically sought and at other times being casually seen without any search activity involved.

- Increasingly, consumers are using the Internet to find information about alternatives available. There is evidence that, within the travel sector, consumers undertake extensive surfing of the web to establish information about a resort and the alternative means of getting there, even if the Internet is not subsequently used as the medium for booking the holiday.

The greater the perceived risk of a purchase, the longer and more widespread the search for information. Of course, individuals differ in the extent to which they are prepared to methodically collect information. Some may make a purchase more impulsively than more calculating individuals, reflecting their lower risk threshold, lower level of involvement or greater familiarity with that type of purchase.

4.3.3 Evaluation and decision

A lot of effort has gone in to trying to understand the processes which consumers use to evaluate competing services. By the time that all possible competing alternatives have been reduced to a smaller shortlist (or 'choice set'), many possibilities will have been discarded along the way. This may simply be due to poor awareness of a product's existence, or an inability to acquire sufficient information about it. Even allowing for services which a consumer has not become aware of, they will probably be left with too many choices to evaluate each one individually in detail. It is usual, therefore, to base evaluation on a 'choice set' of a small number of alternatives, which will be subjected to a more detailed comparative analysis.

There is increasing interest in the role of a consumer's emotional states in the evaluation process (Bagozzi *et al.*, 1999; Mattila, 1999). Many low-involvement service purchasers can be evaluated in a fairly rational way using methods such as those described below. However, high-involvement services may involve strong emotions which are more difficult to model. As an example, the evaluation process for selecting

From word-of-mouth to word-of-mouse

Word-of-mouth recommendation can be an important way of influencing buyers' choices, but it has traditionally been a fairly slow means of spreading recommendation about a product. Now, the Internet has allowed the whole process to be speeded up and has widened its impact. From word-of-mouth, companies now talk about word-of-mouse, leading to 'viral marketing' in which a purchase recommendation can spread very quickly as one person passes on a message to half a dozen friends, each of whom in turn passes on the message to another half dozen friends. Chat rooms and websites devoted to customer complaints and comments (e.g. www.complaints.com; www.dooyou.com) allow happy or complaining customers to spread their message very quickly. Some companies have attracted unauthorized websites devoted to criticism of the company (e.g. the McSpotlight site, www.mcspotlight.org, which carries information critical of McDonald's Restaurants and the Boycott Shell site at www.essential.org/action/shell. News now crosses geographical frontiers quicker than a blink of the eye and corporate reputations can be savaged as disgruntled customers and shareholders swap comments on the World Wide Web.

How reliable are websites for buyers who seek information about a proposed purchase? Inevitably there is a trade-off between moderated, paid-for services (such as the Consumers' Association's *Which?* Site (www.which.net) and unmoderated sites which may not be representative of real buyers' opinions (and indeed competitors may have submitted negative reports to spoil their rivals). And the blur between customers' views and advertisers' messages adds further reason for caution for buyers seeking advice from the Internet. But then, even the process of deciding what is a useful site can be the result of word-of-mouth recommendation from friends.

a garage to carry out a planned and routine replacement of a tyre is likely to be quite different to the evaluation process to repair a broken-down car which is urgently needed to get the person to an important appointment. The emotional significance of having a car to get to that appointment is likely to impact on the evaluation process and a final decision.

A private buyer seeking to buy a low-involvement service such as a car insurance policy may have narrowed down the set to a choice of four. Analysts of buyer behaviour have developed a number of frameworks for trying to understand how a consumer chooses between these competing alternatives. One approach is for the consumer to use a sense of intuition as to what feels best. Such non-systematic methods of evaluation may be quite appropriate where the service in question involves low levels of cost, risk and involvement.

Even apparently intuitive bases of evaluation can be reduced to a series of rules, implying some systematic basis. One framework is a multiple attribute choice matrix which holds that consumers refer to a number of component attributes of a product to evaluate the overall suitability of that product. Figure 4.5 shows a typical matrix where four competing mortgage loans are compared in terms of five important attributes. In this matrix, the four shortlisted alternatives in the choice set are shown by the column headings A, B, C and D. The left-hand column shows five attributes on which buyers base their purchase decision. The second column shows the importance which the consumer attaches to each attribute of the service (with maximum importance being given a score of 10 and a completely unimportant attribute a score of zero). The following four columns show how each service scores against each of the five evaluation attributes. Consumers' perceptions of attributes and the importance they attach to them can only be found out through a programme of market research. Conjoint analysis has been widely used in the analysis of components of service offers.

If it is assumed that a consumer evaluates each service provider without weighting each attribute, service provider B will be the preferred supplier, as it has the highest overall rating. It is more realistic to expect that some factors will be weighted as being more important than others, therefore the alternative *linear compensatory* approach is based on consumers creating weighted scores for each service provider. The importance of each attribute is multiplied by the score for each attribute, so in this case provider A is preferred as the attributes which consumers rank most highly are also those which are considered to be the most important. A third approach to evaluation is sometimes described as a *lexicographic approach*. This involves the buyer in starting their evaluation by looking at the most important attribute and ruling out those suppliers which do not meet a minimum standard. Evaluation is then based on the second most important attribute, with service providers being eliminated who do not meet their standard. This continues until only one option is left. In Figure 4.5, branch location is given as the most important attribute, so the initial evaluation may have reduced the choice set to A and D (these score highest on location). In the second round, friendliness of staff becomes the most important decision criterion. Only A and D remain in the choice set, and as A has the highest score for friendliness of staff, it will be chosen in preference to A.

	Importance weights	A	B	C	D
Location of branch	10	10	7	8	10
Friendliness of staff	9	10	9	8	8
Reputation of lender	8	10	10	9	9
Overall cost	7	10	10	10	5
Short-term incentives	6	4	10	10	4
Overall rating		44	46	45	36
Weighted rating		7.3	7.2	7.0	6.1

Figure 4.5 A hypothetical choice set for motor insurance: a multiple attribute matrix

However, it can be one thing for buyers to express a preference for a particular service, or even an intention to purchase it, but they may nevertheless make their purchase with another service provider. In a study of restaurant patrons, it was found that those who expressed strong purchase intent and made a subsequent purchase demonstrated distinct attitude differences when compared to those who also expressed strong purchase intent but failed to make a subsequent purchase. The results suggest that the service manager could be misled, and therefore could make costly service mix mistakes, if purchase intent is used solely to model purchase behaviour (Newberry *et al.*, 2003).

Can we have too much choice? Making decisions involves effort and the psychological anxiety that we might have made the wrong decision. Limiting the range of services that we choose from is therefore a natural reaction. Ideally, we would like to be presented with just one choice that reflects our needs perfectly. Good sales personnel realize that most buyers cannot handle more than a shortlist of five or six alternatives and have developed the skill of probing a buyer's key preferences and

A confusing design or designed to confuse?

The term 'confusion marketing' has been used by some commentators to describe the practices of some service providers. Even staff working for services companies have been heard to use the term, off the record. In an ideal world, we would all be able to evaluate the options open to us and make a rational choice from the available options. Classical economic theory is based on an assumption of informed decision-making. But how do you go about the task of evaluation when there is enormous choice and service providers appear to go out of their way to confuse buyers with excessive, missing or inappropriate information?

Many buyers of mobile phone services have been overwhelmed at the choices available to them – in the UK the final purchase decision has to be made from a permutation of four basic network operators, dozens of different tariffs for each network, hundreds of different handsets and thousands of retail outlets. To many people, the tariff plans offered by the phone companies seem unbelievably complex, with an array of peak/off peak price plans, 'free' inclusive minutes and discounts for loyalty. Comparing a few 'headline' prices may be difficult enough, but the task becomes even harder when account is taken of extras which are often hidden in the small print – for example, the charges made for itemized billing and multi-media messages, or for using a phone abroad. One professor of mathematics calculated that it would take a UK buyer over a year to evaluate the costs and benefits of all permutations of networks, tariffs and handsets.

Is the approach of mobile phone companies an attempt to confuse buyers with low 'headline' prices, but a confusing range of supplementary prices? Or does the approach reflect a genuine concern to segment markets so finely that every buyer's preferences are catered for?

then presenting a simple choice set of just three or four alternatives. More than this and the buyer may just walk away confused and defer a purchase. But if the three or four alternatives offered are poorly selected, the buyer may walk away anyway.

Increasingly, with the use of databases, companies are able to understand the preferences of customers and present choices based on this understanding (Figure 4.6). An ongoing buyer–seller relationship (discussed in more detail in the next chapter) is often used to provide a better-informed choice set. Indeed, summing up developments in relationship marketing, Sheth and Parvatiyar (2002) have described firms' motivation to develop ongoing relationships as being based primarily on 'choice reduction'.

The more choice that is offered to buyers, the greater the probability that they will regret the choices they have actually made. We will return to the notion of regret in the next section.

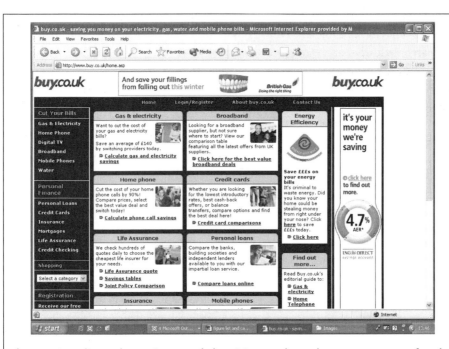

Figure 4.6 In the UK domestic gas and electricity supply market, consumers are faced with a sometimes bewildering and confusing choice of suppliers, all offering a basic commodity product, which by law cannot be differentiated. Evaluation is made more difficult because the different companies choose different bases for pricing, with many offering several different price plans. Some give introductory discounts, some give high-user or low-user discounts and many give discounts for payment by direct debit. The website www.buy.co.uk has become a popular choice for many consumers seeking comparative information on a novel purchase. This calculator for gas and electricity guides consumers through all the choices available and identifies which supplier and price plan is best for them. It is claimed that an average family that switches suppliers on buy.co.uk or uSwitch.com saves £140 on its annual energy bills. (Reproduced with permission of buy.co.uk)

4.3.4 **Post-purchase evaluation**

The buying process does not end once a service has been purchased and consumed (see Figure 4.7). Completion of consumption often marks the beginning of the process of making a follow-up purchase. We can only truly evaluate a service after we have consumed it, and at this point we develop attitudes towards the service. If we are entirely happy with the service, we may become an advocate of it, and tell our friends about it, as well as putting the service provider at the top of our shortlist the next time that we seek that type of service. Where we are unhappy with some aspect of the service, we may experience **cognitive dissonance**. Festinger (1957) first defined dissonance as the psychologically uncomfortable state following the act of choosing between a set of alternatives, which motivates an individual to do something to eliminate the inconsistency between thoughts and behaviour, thereby reducing the dissonant state. It has been noted that dissonance may result when 'an opinion is formed or a decision taken when cognition and opinions direct us in different directions' (Sweeney *et al.*, 2000, p. 369).

We can reduce dissonance in a number of ways, including: trying to filter out of our minds bad aspects of the service and concentrating on the good aspects so that we believe we have made the right choice; downplaying the expectations that we thought we had about the service; and initiating some form of complaining behaviour. For

Figure 4.7 The buying process does not end with a purchase. In this advertisement, BT encourages its UK phone customers who have recently switched to a rival company to reflect on their feelings towards their new supplier. As well as encouraging former customers to return, this advertisement makes current BT customers feel more comfortable with their current supplier, by reducing the temptation to search for alternatives. (Reproduced with the permission of British Telecommunications plc. Photography by Chris Frazer-Smith)

goods which had caused us dissonance, we might return the goods to the seller. However, this is not possible in the case of service processes which have already been consumed. We may be able to claim against a service provider's guarantee of satisfaction, and it is to reduce the prospect of dissonance that some service providers offer to refund the cost of a service if the customer is not completely satisfied.

It was noted in the previous section that too much choice can result in a psychologically costly decision-making process. Too much choice can also increase postpurchase levels of dissonance. 'Regret theory' contends that the more choices we have forgone, the greater the likelihood that we will regret the choice that we actually make (Herrmann *et al.*, 1999). If there was only one hotel in a resort where we could stay, we couldn't be unhappy when we subsequently saw another hotel which looked better. If we had in fact been offered a choice of hotels in the resort, we may subsequently regret not choosing those hotels which were not our first choice.

4.3.5 **The decision-making unit**

Few service purchase decisions are made by an individual in total isolation from other people. Usually other people are involved in some role and have a bearing on the final decision. It is important to recognize the key players in this process, in order that the service format can be configured to meet the needs of these people, and that promotional messages can be adapted and directed at the key individuals involved in the purchase decision. A number of roles can be identified among people involved in the decision process.

- *Influencers* are people or groups of people who the decision-maker refers to in the process of making a decision. Reference groups can be primary (e.g. friends, acquaintances and work colleagues), or secondary, in the form of remote personalities with whom there is no two-way interaction. Where research indicates that the primary reference group exerts major influence on purchase decisions, this could indicate the need to facilitate word-of-mouth communication, for example, giving established customers rewards in return for the introduction of new customers. An analysis of secondary reference groups used by consumers in the decision process can be used in a number of ways. It will indicate possible personalities to be approached who may be used to endorse a product in the company's advertising. It will also indicate which opinion leaders an organization should target as part of its communication programme in order to achieve the maximum 'trickle down' effect. The media can be included within this secondary reference group – what a newspaper writes in its columns can have an important influence on purchase decisions.

- *Gatekeepers* are most commonly found among commercial buyers. Their main effect is to act as a filter on the range of services which enter the decision choice set. Gatekeepers can take a number of forms – a secretary barring calls from sales representatives to the decision-maker has the effect of screening out a number of possible choices. In many organizations, it can be difficult to establish just who is acting as gatekeeper. Identifying a marketing strategy which gains acceptance by the gatekeeper, or bypasses the gatekeeper completely, is therefore made difficult. In larger organizations, and the public sector in particular, a select list of suppliers who are invited to submit tenders for work may exist. If not on this list, a provider of services is unable to enter the decision set.

■ Although gatekeepers are most commonly associated with the purchase of services by business organizations, they can also have application to private consumer purchases. In the case of many household services, an early part of the decision process may be the collection of information or telephoning to invite quotations for a service. While the final decision may be the subject of joint discussion and action, the initial stage of collecting information is more likely to be left to one person. In this way, a family member picking up holiday brochures acts as a gatekeeper for that family, restricting subsequent choice to the holidays of those companies whose brochures appealed to him or her.

Profiting from pester power?

What role do children play in the purchase of the services they consume? There has been a lot of debate about the extent of 'pester power', where parents apparently give in to the demands of their children. Increasingly, advertisers are aiming their promotional messages over the heads of adults and straight at children. The ethics of doing this have been questioned by many, and some countries have imposed restrictions on television advertising of children's products. However, even with advertising restrictions, companies have managed to get through to children in more subtle ways, for example by sponsoring educational materials used in schools and paying celebrities to endorse their products.

For fast-food restaurants, winning the minds of children can be crucial to getting parents along. In the minds of many young children, having a birthday party at the local McDonald's has become highly desirable. How has this come about? There is little doubt that the basic service format appeals to young children – brightly coloured internal decor, play facilities and the food itself are clearly attractive to the young consumer. In addition, like many fast-food restaurants, McDonald's has developed a programme of educational support materials which it takes to schools. Its materials promote the identity of McDonald's in an apparently educational manner, while at the same time generating desire among pupils.

Having access to these materials may help cash-strapped teachers by providing much needed resources, but is it ethical to target young children in this way? Does it make it harder for parents to encourage their children to eat a healthy diet?

- In some cases, ordering a service may be reduced to a routine task and be delegated to a *buyer*. In the case of business-to-business services, low-budget items which are not novel may be left to the discretion of a buyer. In this way, casual window cleaning may be contracted by a buying clerk within the organization without immediate reference to anyone else. In the case of modified rebuys, or novel purchases, the decision-making unit is likely to be larger.

- The *users* of a service may not be the people responsible for making the actual purchase decision. This is particularly the case with many business-to-business service purchases. Nevertheless, research should be undertaken to reveal the extent to which users are important influencers in the decision process. In the case of the business air travel market, it is important to understand the pressure which the actual traveller can exert on their choice of airline, as opposed to the influence of a company buyer (who might have arranged a long-term contract with one particular airline), a gatekeeper (who may discard promotional material relating to new airlines) or other influencers within the organization (e.g. cost centre managers who might be more concerned with the cost of using a service, in contrast to the user's overriding concerning with its quality).

- The *decision-maker* is the person (or group of individuals) who makes the final decision to purchase, whether the purchase is executed by one person or that person instructs others to do so. With many family-based consumer services, it can be difficult to identify just who within the family carries most weight in making the final decision. Research into family service purchases which are purchased jointly has suggested that in the case of package holidays, wives dominate in making the final decision, whereas in the case of joint mortgages, it is the husband who

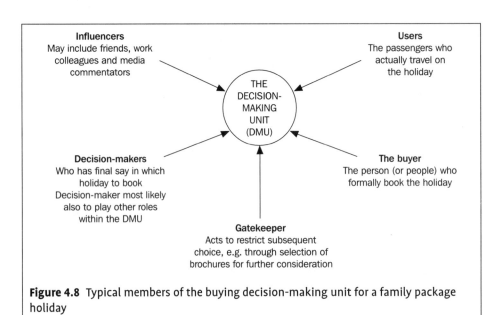

Figure 4.8 Typical members of the buying decision-making unit for a family package holiday

Any excuse for a pint?

Companies are able to capture ever-increasing amounts of information in order to build up a better picture of their customers' buying behaviour. The retailer Tesco is one of many companies that gather large volumes of data from till receipts, loyalty card data and other bought-in data, to give previously unimaginable insights into consumer behaviour. Using data-mining techniques, one discovery that is reported to have intrigued the company's analysts was the apparent correlation between sales of beer and sales of nappies. The two products were not in any way complementary to each other, so why should their sales appear to be associated? Was this just another spurious correlation, to be binned along with other gems of information such as a previously reported correlation between an individual's shoe size and his or her propensity to use a gym? The company didn't give up, and refined its analysis to study the correlation for different categories of store and by different times of day. Where it also had details of customers' demographic characteristics (gathered through its Clubcard loyalty programme) it was able to probe for further insights. The company was edging towards a better understanding of why the sales of these two products should be closely correlated, but it took further qualitative analysis techniques to provide a fuller explanation. It appeared that men were offering to run a household errand to the shops in order to buy babies' nappies. This was an excuse to leave the family home in order to buy more beer for their own consumption. The company learnt from this exercise and subsequently positioned the two products closer together in selected stores.

But should it take data mining to reveal these insights to consumer behaviour? The landlord of the traditional Irish pub spotted this type of behaviour long ago, with pubs doubling up as the local post office, bookseller or grocer, giving the Irish drinker plenty of good reasons to visit.

dominates. Within any particular service sector, an analysis of how a decision is made can only realistically be achieved by means of qualitative in-depth research. In the case of decisions made by commercial buyers, the task of identifying the individuals responsible for making a final decision – and their level within the organizational hierarchy – becomes even more difficult.

In reality, people play multiple roles in this process, sometimes switching between roles. An illustration of the roles with reference to the purchase of a package holiday is shown in Figure 4.8.

4.4 Models of buyer behaviour

The very basic model of buyer behaviour, which was described in Figure 4.2, provides a useful starting point and conceptual framework for analysing buying processes. If a model is to have value to marketing managers, it should be capable of predicting actual buying behaviour, given the set of conditions on which the model was based. For this reason, a number of researchers have sought to develop models which explain how buying decisions are made in specified situations, and from this to predict the likely consequences of changes to marketing strategy. Modelling buyer decision processes poses many problems. At one extreme, simple models such as that presented in Figure 4.2 may help in very general terms in developing marketing strategies, but are too general to be of use in any specific situation. At the other extreme, models of buyer behaviour based on narrowly defined sectors may lose much of their explanatory and predictive power if applied to another sector where assumptions on which the original model was calibrated no longer apply. In any event, most models of buyer behaviour provide normative rather than strictly quantitative explanations of buyer behaviour and there can be no guarantee that the assumptions on which the model was originally based continue to be valid.

The earliest models of buyer behaviour focused attention on explaining the decision processes involved in goods purchases. One widely used framework which has been applied to consumer service purchase decisions is that developed by Howard and Sheth (1969), illustrated in Figure 4.9.

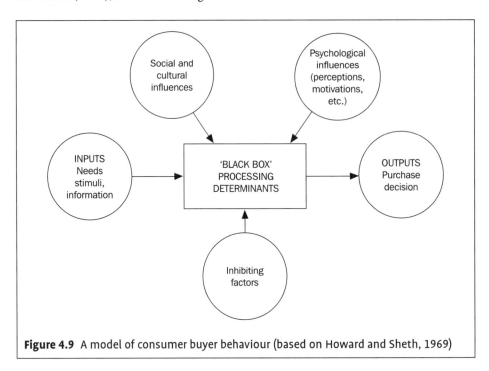

Figure 4.9 A model of consumer buyer behaviour (based on Howard and Sheth, 1969)

The framework incorporates a number of elements, as follows.

■ *Inputs*. This element comprises information about the range of competing services which may satisfy a consumer's need. Information may be obtained from personal or published sources.

- *Behavioural determinants.* Individuals bring to the purchase decision a predisposition to act in a particular way. This predisposition is influenced by the culture in which they live, and family and personality factors, among others.

- *Perceptual reaction.* Inputs are likely to be interpreted in different ways by different individuals, based on their unique personality make-up and conditioning which results from previous purchase experiences. While one person might readily accept the advertising messages of a holiday company, another might have been disappointed by that company in the past, or by holiday companies' advertising in general. They are therefore less likely to perceive such inputs as credible.

- *Processing determinants.* This part of the model focuses attention on the way in which a decision is made. Important determinants include the motivation of the individual to satisfy a particular need, the individual's past experience of a particular service or organization, and the weight attached to each of the factors which are used in the evaluation. For some consumers for some services, critical product requirements may exist which must be present if a product is to be included in the decision set. At other times, consumers attach weights to each of its attributes and select the product with the highest weighted 'score' (see above). Some models have identified changes in process and outcome variables which will influence consumer behaviour in only one direction (for example, an increase in price may reduce demand, but a reduction in price may have no effect on the level of demand), while others assume that the effect of changes in a variable will be reversible, influencing consumer behaviour in both directions.

- *Inhibitors.* A number of factors might prevent an individual moving towards making a decision to purchase a particular service, such as the difficulty of gaining access to the service, the price of the service and the terms and conditions for service delivery.

- *Outputs.* The outcome of the decision process may be: to go ahead and purchase; or not to buy; or to defer a decision to a later date.

The Howard–Sheth model was developed as a general framework to explain both goods and services decision processes. There has been more recent recognition that this type of model does not fully address the issue of producer/seller interaction which occurs during the evaluation process. The intangibility of services and the inability of consumers to evaluate a service before consumption can also result in a much more complex process of information collection and evaluation than is the case with goods.

An example of a model which is based specifically on the service sector was developed by Fisk (1981) and is shown diagrammatically in Figure 4.10. The model sees the purchase process as being divided into three stages: pre-consumption, consumption and post-consumption. The pre-consumption stage comprises the range of activities that commonly take place before a purchase decision is made, beginning with the initial problem recognition, collection of information and identification

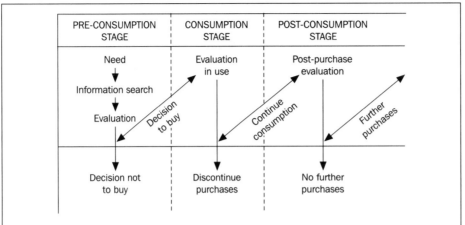

Figure 4.10 The consumption/evaluation process for services (based on Fisk, 1981, pp. 191–5)

of the choice set. At this stage, consumers identify what they *expect* to be the best solution. In the following consumption stage, the consumer actually decides, through experience, what in considered to be the best choice. During this phase, expectations raised during the pre-consumption phase are compared with actual service delivery. A gap between the two results in attempts to reduce dissonance – for example, dissatisfaction resulting from failure to meet expectations may be resolved by complaining. In the post-consumption phase, the whole service encounter is evaluated and this determines whether the consumer will be motivated to purchase the service again.

The literature on services buyer behaviour models can be linked with that on service quality. Service quality is commonly defined as the difference between an individual's expectations of a service and his or her perceptions of service delivery (Chapter 8). Where expectations have been met, the behavioural intention to repurchase is increased. One model which integrates service quality with buyer behaviour was developed by Davies *et al.* (1999). Their model encompasses measurable standards capable of being examined prior to undergoing the service experience (search qualities); consideration of experience during the service (performance qualities), and consideration of outcomes after service delivery (credence qualities). Behavioural intention is influenced by whether a purchase is novel to the buyer (in which case the emphasis will be on search qualities) or whether they have prior experience of that type of purchase (in which case performance and credence qualities become more important).

So far, models of services buying behaviour have been discussed at a general level. Marketers are particularly concerned with the factors that influence consumer behaviour in their own specific sector and therefore more specific models of buyer behaviour have been developed as a result of research into specific service sectors. Many of these have sought to rank, in order of importance, the factors that contribute towards the purchase decision and to identify critical factors, the absence of which will exclude a possibility from a choice set. As an example, a study of rail passengers disaggregated a service into pre-core and core service performances, and used these elements to create a model of the effects on relevant service attitudes and intentions. Based on a sample of 2529 passengers, the research found that the core service elements of on-board conditions, buffet facilities and on-time performance were most strongly related to attitude towards the service provider (Tripp and Drea, 2002).

4.4.1 **Computer-mediated buying behaviour**

Service companies are often very keen to migrate their customers from face-to-face encounters to computer-mediated encounters. Financial incentives and additional benefits online have been used by banks, among others, to get more of their transactions undertaken online. However, while service providers may try to move customers to the new self-service technology, they often face resistance from some segments of consumers. Why do buyers of services differ in their readiness to use computer-mediated methods?

Several models of technology acceptance have emerged which seek to explain the processes by which consumers come to accept self-service technologies (e.g. Dabholkar and Bagozzi, 2002; Curran *et al.*, 2003). Parasuraman (2000) developed a 'Technology Readiness' Index designed to assess consumers' likelihood of adopting new technologies on the basis of four dimensions: their optimism; innovativeness, discomfort and insecurity. It has been noted that consumers' adoption of self-service technologies is likely to be facilitated where the technology fits in with their existing lifestyle (Walker *et al.*, 2002) and they have a low perception of risk (Bobbit and Dabholkar, 2001).

Models of technology adoption have their origins in the disciplines of psychology, information systems and sociology (Venkatesh *et al.*, 2003). The Technology Acceptance Model (TAM; Davis *et al.*, 1989), based on the Theory of Reasoned Action (Fishbein and Ajzen, 1975; Ajzen and Fishbein, 1980) has become well established as a model for predicting acceptance of new IT-based services (Venkatesh and Davis, 2000). The model (Figure 4.11) introduces two specific beliefs that are relevant for technology usage, namely perceived usefulness (U) and perceived ease of use (E). Actual behaviour is determined by behaviour intention (BI), however behavioural intention is jointly determined by the individual's attitude towards a technology (A) and perceived usefulness (U). Finally, perceived ease of use (E) is a direct determinant of attitude (A) and perceived usefulness (U). In the case of less sophisticated bank customers, where there is often little benefit to be gained by switching to computer-mediated banking because other banking methods are available, it is likely that perceived ease of use would have a stronger influence on behavioural intentions than would perceived usefulness. However, in a business banking context, perceived usefulness is likely to be a stronger predictor of behavioural intention than attitude.

It has been noted that consumers who use computer-mediated service delivery may

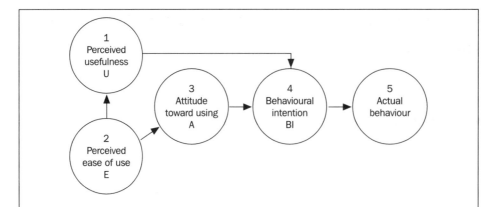

Figure 4.11 Services companies often encourage their customers to adopt new self-service technologies, thereby reducing their costs, especially staffing costs. They may also promote the fact that service users can obtain additional benefits by using an automated form of service delivery. However, many service users may remain deeply sceptical, failing to see the benefits to themselves, and influenced by horror stories in the media of how the new technology has previously let customers down (for example, many people remain cautious about giving their credit card details over the Internet, although, rationally, this is safer than giving details over the telephone). When planning the expansion of self-service facilities, companies need to be able to estimate the take-up rate, so that queues do not form or capacity remains unused. This model has been developed to explain the influences of perceived usefulness and attitude on consumers' intention to use, and actual use of new technology. (Based on Davis, Bogazzi and Warshaw, 1989, p. 985)

experience a number of post-purchase paradoxes, which a service provider should seek to address (Mick and Fournier, 1998).

■ *Freedom/enslavement.* Consumers are likely to experience feelings of freedom when their use of new technology gives them new levels of independence, but on the other hand are likely to experience enslavement when they become dependent on the technology.

■ *Control/chaos.* A feeling of control arises when consumers can use new technology, and use it to direct their activities, but chaos results when the technology inhibits their activities and causes turmoil.

■ *Engaging/disengaging.* Technology can be engaging when customers enjoy the facilities and activities it brings. But disengagement can occur where it results in distraction and inhibits activities.

■ *Fulfils/creates needs.* While technology may fulfil one set of needs, it may merely serve to emphasize others which are not fulfilled.

■ *Competence/incompetence.* A feeling of competence may arise out of the successful use of new technology, but incompetence when the technology either fails or is not understood fully.

4.5 **Personal and organizational buyer behaviour compared**

The processes by which private consumers purchase services can differ from the way in which organizations buy services. A number of reasons can be identified for this.

- Two sets of needs are being met when an organization buys services – the formal needs of the organization and the needs of the individuals who make up the organization. While the former might be thought of as being the more economically rational, the needs which individuals in an organization seek to satisfy are influenced by their own perceptual and behavioural environment, very much in the same way as would be the case with private consumer purchases. Individuals may be more risk averse when buying on behalf of their organization. It is often said that 'nobody got fired for buying IBM' – an acknowledged manufacturer of reliable computer systems. Would an individual within an organization want to run the risk of being blamed for hiring an unknown firm of management consultants rather than a firm with a good international reputation?

- More people are typically involved in organizational purchases. High-value service purchases may require evaluation and approval at a number of levels of an organization's management hierarchy. An attempt should be made to find out whereabouts in an organization the final decision-making power lies. An analysis of the decision-making unit (see above) might also reveal a wide range of influencers who are present in the decision-making process (Figure 4.12).

- Organizational purchases are more likely to be made according to formalized routines. At its simplest, this may involve delegating to a junior buyer the task of making repeat orders for services which have previously been evaluated. At the other extreme, many high-value service purchases may only be made after a formal process of bidding and evaluation has been undertaken.

- The greater number of people involved in organizational buying often results in the whole process taking longer. A desire to minimize risk is inherent in many formal organizational motives and informally present in many individuals' motives, often resulting in lengthy feasibility studies being undertaken. In some new markets, especially overseas markets, trust in service suppliers might be an important factor used by purchasers when evaluating competing suppliers and it may take time to build up a trusting relationship before any purchase commitment is secured.

- The elements of the service offer which are considered critical in the evaluation process are likely to differ. For many services, the emphasis placed on price by many private buyers is replaced by reliability and performance characteristics by the organizational buyer. In many cases, poor performance of a service can have direct financial consequences for an organization – a poor parcel delivery service might merely cause annoyance to a private buyer, but might lead to lost production output or lost sales for an organizational buyer.

Figure 4.12 In the fixed-line phone market, the differing needs of business and domestic users lead to differences in buying behaviour. For the domestic consumer, lowest perceived price, ease of signing up and promotional incentives for signing up may be the most important evaluation criteria. However, for the business buyer, reliability and flexibility may be much more important. If a domestic telephone breaks down, it may cause no more than annoyance and inconvenience to the members of the household. But, for business users, the consequences of a failure can be much more serious, possibly leading to lost sales, delayed orders and missed production. Few members of the organizational decision-making unit would want to carry the blame for selecting a phone service provider which subsequently lets the company down. For business customers, telephone companies must appeal to all members of the decision-making unit by stressing that their services are reliable and have benefits in use, which will be good value to the company. This advertisement from BT, the largest provider in the UK telecoms market, stresses a particular concern of business buyers – the need to get a faulty phone repaired quickly so that business is not interrupted. (Reproduced with permission of British Telecom plc)

■ The need for organizational buyers' risks to be reduced and their desire to seek the active co-operation of suppliers in tackling shared problems has resulted in greater attention being paid to the development of organizational buyer–seller relationships over time, rather than seeing individual purchases in isolation. The importance of mutual trust in the relationship between a service organization and its commercial buyers has been shown in a number of studies. It has been pointed out by Grönroos (1990) that as the complexity of service offerings increases, the organizational buying unit perceives a greater need for confidence and trust in its services suppliers. The subject of ongoing buyer–seller relationships is considered in more detail in the following chapter.

4.6 **Market segmentation and buyer behaviour**

The purpose of studying buyer behaviour is to develop a company's marketing mix so that a desired response is achieved from targeted buyers. Naturally, individuals differ in the way they respond to marketing stimuli, implying differences in individuals' processing determinants. Service providers need to understand these individual differences and fine-tune their marketing mix so that it achieves a desired response from each member of the target market. In a diverse society, it is unlikely that one formulation of the marketing mix will bring about a desired response from everyone. Just as a carpenter needs to adjust his hammers and drills to suit the job in hand, so too the marketer needs to adjust the marketing mix to the needs of individual buyers.

Market segmentation is a fundamental principle of marketing and its advantages are well documented, as are the conditions which are necessary for its successful implementation. This section provides a brief overview of segmentation issues relevant to the service sector, and further information on segmentation theory and practice can be found in the suggested further reading. In the service industries there is a clear understanding of the benefits that may accrue from successful market segmentation and it is therefore used extensively throughout the sector. Many service organizations are at the forefront of the development of segmentation methods within the UK with banks, building societies, insurance companies, the travel and hospitality sectors, among others, having well-defined approaches to the segmentation of their markets.

It can be argued that segmentation is a much more important tool for the services marketer than for the goods marketer. The inseparability of services production and consumption results in service suppliers being able to define their segments in such a way that only individuals within a specified segment benefit from a particular marketing mix. This is an advantage not available to most goods marketers. Because the production of goods can be separated from their consumption, it is usually possible for a consumer to buy in one market and then to sell on to another market segment. It is very difficult for the manufacturer of soft drinks or training shoes, for example, to ensure that only a targeted segment of, say, students or citizens of a particular country, can buy its product at a concessionary price. It is quite likely that goods will be transferred from the market with a low price to a segment which is charged a higher price. This is seen routinely in the way that cheap alcohol and tobacco products are transported around the world from low-cost to high-cost countries. By contrast, service organizations can generally insist on proof of an individual's membership of a segment in order to benefit from a preferential marketing mix. So, a train company can ensure that only students, who may be considered to be a more price-sensitive segment, can benefit from a lower price offer.

The development of segmentation and target marketing reflects the movement away from production orientation towards marketing orientation. When the supply of services is scarce relative to demand, organizations may seek to minimize production costs by producing one homogeneous product which satisfies the needs of the whole population. Over time, increasing affluence has increased buyers' expectations. Affluent customers are no longer satisfied with the basic package holiday, but instead are able to demand one which satisfies an increasingly wide range of needs – not just for relaxation, but for activity, adventure and status associations. Furthermore, society has become much more fragmented. The 'average' consumer has become much more of a myth, as incomes, attitudes and lifestyles have diverged.

Alongside the greater fragmentation of society, technology is increasingly allowing highly specialized services to be tailored to ever-smaller market segments. Using computerized databases, package holidays need no longer be aimed at broad market segments, but can cater to very small groups who have distinctive needs and buying processes.

Different buyers within a market can behave very differently when evaluating alternative services. To be fully marketing oriented, a company would have to adapt its offer to meet the needs of each individual. In fact, very few firms can justify aiming to meet the needs of each specific individual – instead, they aim to meet the needs of small sub-groups within the market. With developments in technology and the fragmentation of society, these segments have tended to become smaller over time.

Segmentation or discrimination?

Segmentation and targeting are central to the marketer's task of meeting consumers' needs at a profit to their organization. But to other social commentators, the practices of segmentation and targeting may appear to be more like discrimination, with all the connotations of social divisiveness that have been associated with various forms of social discrimination. Admittedly, marketers seldom find themselves practising the kind of discrimination that typified South Africa during its years of apartheid, but there can be a thin line between the desirable aims of segmentation and the undesirable consequences of discrimination. The issue is particularly great for services marketers, because the inseparability of services allows segmentation strategies to be implemented much more effectively than for goods, which can generally be traded freely between segments.

Legislation in most western countries is gradually squeezing out the opportunities for marketers to blatantly sell their services to one group but not to another. The days when the owner of a bar could admit customers on the basis of their colour are now long gone. Nightclubs in the UK which once advertised different prices for men and women would now most likely find themselves breaking the Sex Discrimination Act. However, marketers have sometimes found subtle ways of pursuing their segmentation strategies anyway. A bar may subtly make its atmosphere more conducive to one ethnic group and seemingly inaccessible to others. Nightclubs have learnt that discriminating on the basis of gender may be illegal, but a differential pricing policy based on whether a customer is wearing trousers or a skirt may come close to achieving the nightclub's objectives legally.

Despite a growing volume of legislation in developed countries to protect clearly identifiable groups based on sex, race, disability and increasingly on age, many people remain concerned that the processes of segmentation and targeting are leaving pockets of individuals who are denied access to many basic services. This is seen in the way that mainstream banks in most western countries have targeted relatively affluent individuals with a steady source of income. In the UK, a sizeable group of people find it difficult to borrow money from these banks, or even to open a basic bank account. Without a bank account, many life opportunities are closed to individuals. In the United States, banks have been suspected of 'redlining' certain areas of towns, from which the banks will not take new customers. Many states have responded with legislation making illegal such geographically generalized basis for selection. In the UK, **geodemographic analysis** remains an important basis for banks' segmentation and targeting, but although there is no legislation to prevent geodemographic targeting, the government has shown its impatience with banks' reluctance to target poorer groups, even with basic bank accounts. One initiative in response to this apparent problem was the proposed creation of a 'Universal Bank' based on collaboration between the main banks and local post offices, making a basic bank account facility available to poorer people with a bad credit history. In many service sectors providing essential public services, such as electricity, water and telephones, regulatory agencies ensure that private-sector companies do not unduly disadvantage poorer groups in their pursuit of profits.

When does segmentation become discrimination? To what extent should commercial organizations be expected to do business with individuals who on a narrow commercial basis are unlikely to be profitable? How far will companies' shrewd analysis of their social and political environment – and a visible response to problems of emerging discrimination – allow these issues to be resolved? Or will it take further government legislation to protect the interests of disadvantaged groups who may be further marginalized in society by commercial firms' segmentation and targeting policies?

4.6.1 Bases for market segmentation

If the segmentation methods used by service organizations are examined more closely, it becomes apparent that demographic variables tend to be the most widely used segmentation bases. In this respect service industries are no exception – the same tends to be true in goods marketing. Age, sex and socio-economic analysis, along with geographic location provide useful information for building up a profile of users of a service. This can be used for targeting purposes in media planning, assisting in new service development, and can contribute to pricing policy and service outlet location. Some indication of the importance of demographic bases for segmentation can be seen in the choice of magazines in which American Express advertises, the range of accounts offered by NatWest Bank, the pricing practices of British Airways, and the location of Lunn Poly Holiday Shops.

In all of these applications of segmentation methods there is a heavy reliance upon the availability of accurate and timely market data. Geodemographic methods of segmentation, for example, require sources of information which provide details of customers' demographics and their geographical location, and can involve secondary data acquisition or primary investigations undertaken on behalf of an organization. The sophistication with which segmentation is being approached has moved forward immensely as advances in the capabilities of information technology have occurred. Two relatively recent developments should be mentioned.

1. A number of firms offer a geodemographic segmentation analysis which allows the identification of small geographical pockets of households according to a combination of their demographic characteristics and their buying behaviour. These computerized data systems – such as MOSAIC (Figure 4.13) are of considerable value in the planning of direct mail campaigns, store location and merchandising.

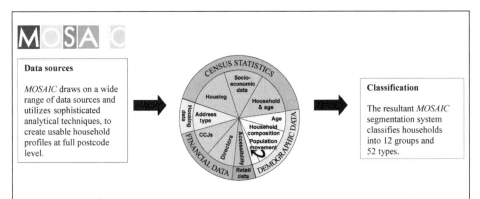

Figure 4.13 MOSAIC is a widely used method of geodemographic segmentation. From an individual postcode, MOSAIC can predict the spending characteristics of the occupants of an address and is widely used by firms for targeting direct mailshots and for identifying the best locations for proposed new service outlets.

2. The wealth of data provided by the operation of electronic point of sale (EPoS) systems means that service firms can study in detail the buying behaviour of individuals or groups of individuals. How often does an individual visit their store? What goods and services tend to be bought as complementary products to each other? How responsive are individuals to price reductions or coupon offers? EPoS offers new insights into buying behaviour.

For most practical marketing purposes, service organizations tend to rely upon demographic and geographic data. Yet there is a real conflict between the theoretical and practical aspects of market segmentation. In practice, the established bases are employed, at least in part, because the data readily available in this format and targeting is therefore reasonably straightforward. However, although they do have this practical value they do not really explain *why* there are differences in the buying behaviour of consumers. There are therefore a number of other approaches to segmentation which are seen to be more theoretically sound, such as psychographics (based upon personality, attitudes, opinions and interests) and self-concept (how customers perceive themselves). Many companies in the tourism sector, for example, have been observed to base their segmentation and targeting on lifestyle factors (e.g. Gonzalez and Bello, 2002). Such approaches rely on attitude measurement techniques including Likert scales and semantic differentials in order to elicit the necessary information from customers. These segmentation bases provide a useful supplementary set of tools for the sub-division of markets in practice, although they are generally used in conjunction with demographic profiles for targeting purposes.

An alternative qualitative approach to identifying clusters of customers is based around the analysis of the components of a particular service offering. This is effectively a benefit-based technique for distinguishing market segments. Cluster analysis of responses is commonly applied after the qualitative stage of a study. The segments derived from this type of investigation, based upon a combination of factors, may then be targeted by a service firm with specific product offers which have been designed in accordance with the observed buying processes of the segments.

4.7 **Business ethics and the purchase decision**

Finally in this chapter we will consider the role that ethical evaluations play in buyer behaviour.

Increasing numbers of services buyers are bringing ethical issues into their decision-making process. If two competing services are judged to be basically similar in all other respects, why not choose the service provider whose contribution to society's welfare is believed to be the greatest? Consider the following cases.

■ Hundreds of thousands of customers of Shell throughout Europe boycotted the company's petrol service stations during 1995 in protest against the ethics of dumping an obsolete oil-drilling platform in the North Sea. For most customers, visiting one petrol station rather than another incurred little, if any, cost, yet allowed them to express their feelings about Shell's ethics.

■ The UK retailer The Body Shop has attracted a loyal following of customers who share the company's attitudes towards human and animal welfare issues, and buy its products in preference to functionally similar competitors. Such is the importance of customers' perceptions of the company's ethics that its share price has fallen following allegations of poor ethical conduct.

■ Many financial services companies now offer investment products but refuse to invest in companies whose business is considered to be unethical. In the UK, the Co-operative Bank offers unit trusts which appeal to many market segments because of their refusal to invest in companies involved with animal experiments, tobacco manufacture and arms manufacture, among others.

Many have argued that, today, when a consumer buys a product, he or she is inclined to think not just of the benefit which it will bring to him or her directly, but also the benefit which it will bring to society more widely. Research undertaken in the UK during 2002 by the organization Business in the Community suggested that 89% of the British public had specifically purchased a product or service associated with a cause or charity they care about in the past year (Business in the Community, 2002).

Ethical judgements involve the evaluation of an individual product's acceptability to society at large, and the overall ethics of a company. Initial interest in marketing ethics has focused on the manufactured goods sector, with environmentalism emerging as a major factor affecting consumer purchases during the 1980s. As with the development of a general marketing orientation, issues of marketing ethics have since found application within the service sector. Because of the intangible nature of services, the social costs and benefits of services can be less easy to identify than for goods. Nevertheless, there is evidence that some segments of the population are widening their evaluatory criteria to include the benefits which they bring to society (or the social cost which they avoid). Within the financial services sector, there is now a wide range of fund management services available to investors who are concerned about the ethics of their investments. Within the travel and tourism sector, it is now recognized that intensive tourism development can create significant environmental problems, for example the threat to the breeding habits of the loggerhead turtle on the Greek island of Zakynthos which has resulted from the intensive development of beaches for recreational purposes. Some customers of package holidays – admittedly a small niche group at the moment – choose their package holiday destination on the basis of tourism's environmental impact at a resort, and choose their service provider – the tour operator – on the basis of their policies towards the environmentally benign development of resorts.

It is argued in later chapters that the promotion of service organizations' corporate brands is generally more important than the promotion of specific product brands. For this reason, many service organizations are keen to link themselves to good social causes (Figure 4.14). The Tesco supermarket group's support for unleaded petrol and

Figure 4.14 After a series of widely publicized corporate scandals, many segments of consumers have become increasingly sceptical about the behaviour of organizations they buy from, and are likely to be attracted by a company's ethical reputation. This may be important in services markets where there is otherwise little to distinguish one company's service offer from others. Many people would regard the major coffee shop chains as being essentially similar in what they offer, and many customers may challenge the disparity between the seemingly high price charged to consumers for a cup of coffee and the low price that producers in the developing world receive for raw coffee beans. Starbucks has developed a loyal following of customers for whom the atmosphere of its stores warrants a premium price. However, the company is conscious of critics who point to low prices paid to producers, and addresses this by offering Fairtrade-certified coffee. In 2003, Starbucks purchased 6.7 million pounds (3.1 million Kg) of Fairtrade-certified coffee, certified organic and shade-grown coffees. It also rewards farmers who provide independent verification that they are producing high-quality coffee in an environmentally sustainable and socially responsible manner. Oxfam noted that, 'It is a welcome relief to see Starbucks taking a lead amongst the major coffee companies in addressing the crisis in the coffee market.' Many western consumers of coffee feel happier drinking their cappuccino knowing that they have helped, rather than exploited, coffee growers in poor countries. Starbucks makes this source of competitive differentiation clear in its advertising, and backs it up with a full report about its coffee sourcing practices on its website (http://starbucks.co.uk/NR/rdonlyres/49305FD2-2037-47DD-A19C-5C70FAF41B4D/0/CSR04_Final.pdf). (Reproduced with permission of Starbucks Coffee Company)

Snooping or learning?

Finding out about how people actually go about choosing and using a service can be a daunting task because there are so many barriers that get in the way between what people actually do, what they say they do, and what researchers subsequently interpret they do. Where researchers are far removed from the subjects in which they are interested, a very false picture of consumer behaviour can be the basis for marketing decisions. Observing behaviour is not new to marketers who have often preferred to know about the reality of what people actually do rather than individuals' expressed attitudes, which may never be manifested in actual purchasing behaviour.

In a nation which has been gripped by voyeuristic 'reality' television programmes such as *Big Brother*, it is not surprising that marketers should also try to gain a better insight into behaviour that might previously have been considered private. How far should marketers legitimately be able to go in their pursuit of these better insights? And at what point does it become intrusive?

In recent years, researchers have paid increasing attention to the use of ethnography in the study of consumer behaviour. A typical study might involve asking participants to use a service, and watching their interactions with it and with their friends. But what if consumers are observed in a non-consensual manner? In one widely reported study, ethnographic researchers travelled on London's number 73 bus to observe how passengers used their mobile phones, and revealed a variety of behaviours which were not affected by respondents' need to conform. A mobile phone is more than a mere technology-based service, and it became quite apparent that the pattern of needs satisfied by a mobile phone was very complex.

More recently, marketers have used technology to probe individuals' behaviour, but critics have argued that 'big brother' techniques may be exploiting consumers without their agreement. Many users of the Internet may be unaware that cookies lodged in their computer are spying on them, trying to understand their buying behaviour. So when an Internet Service Provider flashes a banner advert for car rental on your screen, it may not have been by chance, but an analysis of your previous search behaviour that led the system to deduce that you were in the process of looking for a car rental service. Closed-circuit television (CCTV) has been used by researchers to study how people move around a supermarket and the processes used in searching for products. Would you be happy in the knowledge that all of your indecision, strained facial expressions and bad temper were being recorded to be replayed over and over again by researchers?

recycling schemes helped to give it a distinctive **positioning** as an environmentally friendly store during the late 1980s. The opposite – linking a corporate brand to a bad cause – can have long-term harmful effects on an organization, for example the Royal Bank of Scotland faced a boycott in 2000 when the bank became identified with anti-libertarian views publicly pronounced by one of its American investors.

With increasing levels of media availability and an increasingly marketing-literate audience, it is becoming easier to expose examples of unethical business practice. Furthermore, competition in many service sectors has become more intense, so ethics can become a differentiating factor for many buyers.

Case study

Coffee to go is no go for Israeli consumers

By Michael Etgar, College of Management, Tel Aviv, Israel

The ways in which people from different countries buy cups of tea or coffee are steeped in tradition. The English tearoom is quintessentially English, usually providing homely surroundings in a very traditional atmosphere. Other regions, by contrast, have traditionally drunk coffee, and have taken great delight in pavement cafés. The Viennese coffeehouse has become a cultural institution in itself. With growing globalization of service industries and evidence of cultural convergence, these traditional drinking places have been facing challenges and opportunities. So, many British people are now quite happy to patronize trendy coffee bars in preference to a traditional English tearoom. Café culture has spread from the warm climates of the Mediterranean to the streets of Watford and Woking.

Many service companies have spotted changing habits in a nation's pattern of drinking, and have extended their established service format to new markets where they are considered novel. But, this can be a very risky process and a good understanding of buyer behaviour is essential to ensure success. Who will be the early adopters for the new service format? What factors will it take for there to be a trickle-down effect to other groups who are maybe more traditional in their buying behaviour? How can a company avoid being ridiculed as being totally alien to the culture it seeks custom from?

Starbucks has become a household name among coffee drinkers in the 22 countries where it operates. It was established in 1971 and by 2003 had a worldwide network of over 5900 branches. But the failure of its launch in Israel illustrates how important it is to understand the processes by which people buy and consume coffee.

Starbucks joined a long list of foreign services companies that have entered the Israeli market. In the 1995–2000 period, over 30 different global retailing chains entered the country, among them Burger King, McDonald's, Zara, Max Mara, Ace,

Mothercare, Blockbuster, Toys 'Я' Us, etc. With just a few exceptions, foreign chains failed to understand buyer behaviour, lost money and stopped operating, with heavy losses. During this period, the coffeehouse sector grew rapidly and, despite Starbucks' failure, several coffeehouse chains, both local and international, survived and prospered.

Starbucks decided not to set up its own branches in Israel but to operate through a local company, Israel Coffee Partners (ICP). Starbucks International had a 20% stake in the venture. ICP received a master franchisee licence to open and operate Starbucks branches in Israel. The first Starbucks coffee shop opened in Israel in 2000 and the company aimed to establish 80 branches within five years. Yet within three years it had opened just six branches in urban areas in and around Tel Aviv and Herzeliya Pituach. In 2003, Starbucks' Israeli venture had accumulated debts of over US$6 million and it was closed. At the same time, another US-based coffeehouse chain – Coffee Bean – entered the Israeli market and appeared to prosper. What went wrong for Starbucks?

One possible reason for the company's failure may be its insistence on standardizing its service offer, which required that all the components of the retailing format in the USA were copied identically in Israel. A major innovation of Starbucks to the Israeli market was the concept of 'coffee to go', whereby customers bought their coffee in order to drink it elsewhere. The original US-based Starbucks concept was coffee only, without any fresh foods, while local tradition demanded to have a light snack with coffee. As a result, consumers had to queue up, pay and then receive their cups of coffee in Styrofoam cups before carrying them out in the streets. Customers were expected to leave, not to delay and consume their coffee on the premises. All on-the-premises consumption was expected to be fast and efficient. Places for sitting down were limited and the decor was simple.

However, this type of coffee consumption did not fit the local style of consumption. While the Starbucks concept provided a real added value to consumers in countries without a tradition of good-quality coffee (such as Canada and Japan), its value proposition was lost on the Israelis. Unlike the USA or Japan, when Starbucks arrived in Israel, the country had already been exposed to quality espresso coffee Italian style, and several local chains serving quality coffee had already been operating in this market. The Israelis, like other Mediterranean people, liked to sit down in their coffeehouses for discussions, meals and even business meetings. The concept of buying coffee in Styrofoam cups and taking it somewhere else was not part of the local culture. A factor which contributed to the failure of the chain was faulty or insufficient market intelligence about local culture, customer behaviour and the competitive situation. A better understanding of the local coffeehouse scene and the directions of its development may have avoided some of these pitfalls.

The company had also underestimated the price premium that customers were prepared to pay for a globally promoted brand. In many markets that Starbucks had entered, such as South Korea and Turkey, drinking a skinny latté at Starbucks became a symbol of new found middle-class status for some socially mobile groups.

Starbucks had greatly under-estimated the power of established operators to keep their custom, and greatly over-estimated the power of its brand to attract customers. This belief led the local operator to set high prices (relative to the market prices in corresponding coffeehouse chains). Similarly, the entrance of the chain was not supported by advertising, nor was the brand maintained by advertising effort. In reality, brand awareness was not as high as expected and it did not translate into usage rates. The Starbucks brand equity was greatly reduced in the fight with other brands and consumers were not willing to pay premium prices.

Case study review questions

1. What programme of research into buyer behaviour would you recommend that a company such as Starbucks should undertake when it considers entering a new foreign market?

2. If you were opening a coffeehouse, what aspects of buyer behaviour would you seek to understand before proceeding?

3. What is the effect of peer-group influence on the process of choosing between competing coffeehouses?

Chapter summary and links to other chapters

The intangibility of services and their perceived riskiness makes buyers' task of choosing between competing products more complex than is the case for manufactured goods. Consumers cannot properly evaluate a service until after it has been consumed, therefore the bases for prior evaluation are limited. Tangible cues can be vital to give some indication of subsequent service quality. Brands and ongoing relationships with a service provider can help to reduce the riskiness of a service purchase. Very often, the image of the service provider is more important in evaluation than the **service image** of individual offers, and this image is increasingly being influenced by its perceived ethical standards.

The development of ongoing buyer–seller relationships as a means of simplifying service purchase decisions is discussed further in the following chapter. The role of brands in appealing to specific target markets is discussed further in **Chapter 7**. Methods of judging the quality of a service, and hence influencing repurchase intention, are discussed in **Chapter 8**. Attempts to influence buyer behaviour through promotional activities are discussed in **Chapter 11**. The importance of gathering information about customers' evaluation and purchasing processes is discussed in **Chapter 6** in the context of information management.

Chapter review questions

1. What are the causes and consequences of risk in the services purchasing process? What can service providers do to overcome problems of buyers' perceived risk?

2. In what ways do models of buyer behaviour differ between goods and services purchases?

3. In what ways do buying processes for airline travel typically differ between private buyers and business buyers? How should airlines respond to these differences?

4. With growing choice available to consumers of many types of service, to what extent do you consider that models of buyer behaviour are essentially about 'choice reduction'?

5. In what ways does the practice of market segmentation differ between a seller of pre-recorded videos and the operator of a cinema?

6. To what extent are considerations of a service provider's ethics important in evaluating alternative service offers? Would you expect differences to exist between private and organizational buyers?

Activity

Consider a recent case where you took part in some type of service activity with a group of friends. This might include going out for a meal at a restaurant, going to a bar or going to the cinema. Critically examine the processes involved in deciding between the alternatives available. Ask yourself: How long did the whole process take from having the initial idea to making the final decision? Who initiated the process? Who were involved as influencers? What sources of information did you consult? How important was word-of-mouth recommendation? How was the final decision arrived at? After you had made your decision and consumed the service, what thoughts did you have? Did these subsequently affect your repurchase intention? Did you subsequently make any recommendation to friends?

Key terms

Cognitive dissonance Mental discomfort that occurs following a purchase decision which the buyer may subsequently believe to have been a poor decision.

Geodemographic analysis The analysis of markets using a combination of geographic and demographic information.

Market segmentation A process of identifying groups of customers within a broad product market who share similar needs and respond similarly to a given marketing mix formulation.

Needs The underlying forces that drive an individual to make a purchase and thereby satisfy their needs.

Positioning Decisions about how the marketing mix for a company's service offer should be developed in comparison to the marketing mix of competing services.

Service image The way consumers picture a service offer, based on their set of beliefs and previous experience of the service.

Word-of-mouth The act of recommendation by existing customers to their friends and colleagues.

Selected further reading

For a general review of buyer behaviour, numerous books are available which deal with products in general, including:

Solomon, M., Bamossy, G. and Askegaard, S. (2001) *Consumer Behaviour: A European Perspective*, 2nd edn, FT Prentice Hall.

Blackwell, R.D., Miniard, P.W. and Engel, J.F. (2000) *Consumer Behaviour*, 9th edn, Thomson Learning.

The following two papers review the general differences between goods and services in the way consumers make purchase decisions.

Zeithaml, V.A. (1981) 'How consumers' evaluation processes differ between goods and services', in J.H. Donnelly and W.R. George (eds), *Marketing of Services*, American Marketing Association, Chicago, pp. 186–90.

Gabbott, M. and Hogg, G. (1994) 'Consumer behaviour and services: A review', *Journal of Marketing Management*, 10 (4), 311–24.

For an update of services buying behaviour in the context of the Internet, consult the following.

Bobbit, L. and Dabholkar, P.A. (2001) 'Integrating attitudinal theories to understand and predict use of technology-based self-service: The internet as an illustration', *International Journal of Service Industry Management*, 12 (5), 423–50.

Walker, R.H., Craig-Lees, M., Hecker, R. and Francis, H. (2002) 'Technology-enabled service delivery: An investigation of reasons affecting customer adoption and rejection', *The International Journal of Service Industry Management*, 13 (1), 91–106.

Curran, J.M., Meuter, M.L. and Surprenant, C.F. (2003) 'Intentions to use self-service technologies: A confluence of multiple attitude', *Journal of Service Research*, 5 (3), 209–24.

The following provide an overview of segmentation methods.

Ehrenberg, A. (2002) 'More on modeling and segmentation', *Marketing Research*, 14 (3), 42.

Gonzalez, A.M. and Bello, L. (2002) 'The construct lifestyle in market segmentation: The behaviour of tourist consumers', *European Journal of Marketing*, 36 (1/2), 51–85.

McDonald, M. and Dunbar, I. (1998) *Market Segmentation*, Palgrave, Basingstoke.

References

Ajzen, I. and Fishbein, M. (1980) *Understanding Attitudes and Predicting Social Behaviour*, Prentice Hall, Englewood Cliffs, NJ.

Bagozzi, R.P., Gopinath, M. and Nyer, P.U. (1999) 'The role of emotions in marketing', *Journal of the Academy of Marketing Science*, 27 (2), 184–206.

Bobbit, L. and Dabholkar, P.A. (2001) 'Integrating attitudinal theories to understand and predict use of technology-based self-service: The internet as an illustration', *International Journal of Service Industry Management*, 12 (5), 423–50.

Business in the Community (2002) *Cause Related Marketing Tracker – 21st Century Giving*. London, Business in the Community.

Curran, J.M., Meuter, M.L. and Surprenant, C.F. (2003) 'Intentions to use self-service technologies: A confluence of multiple attitude', *Journal of Service Research*, 5 (3), 209–24.

Dabholkar, P.A. and Bagozzi, R.P. (2002) 'An attitudinal model of technology-based self service: Moderating effects of consumer traits and situational factors', *Journal of the Academy of Marketing Science*, 30 (3), 184–201.

Davies, B., Baron, S., Gear, T. and Read, M. (1999) 'Measuring and managing service quality', *Marketing Intelligence and Planning*, 17 (1), 33–40.

Davis, F.D., Bagozzi, R.P. and Warshaw, P.R. (1989) 'User acceptance of computer technology: A comparison of two theoretical models', *Management Science*, 35 (8), 982–1003.

Festinger, L. (1957) *A Theory of Cognitive Dissonance*, Stanford University Press, Stanford.

Fishbein, M. and Ajzen, I. (1975) *Belief, Attitude, Intention and Behaviour: An Introduction to Theory and Research*, Addison-Wesley, Reading, Mass.

Fisk, R.P. (1981) 'Toward a consumption/evaluation process model for services', in J.H. Donnelly and W.R. George (eds), *Marketing of Services*, American Marketing Association, Chicago.

Future Foundation (2003) *Complicated Lives*, The Future Foundation, London.

Gonzalez, A.M. and Bello, L. (2002) 'The construct lifestyle in market segmentation: The behaviour of tourist consumers', *European Journal of Marketing*, 36 (1/2), 51–85.

Grönroos, C. (1990) 'Relationship approach to marketing in service contexts: The marketing and organizational interface', *Journal of Business Research*, 20, 3-11.

Herrmann, A., Huber, F. and Braunstein, C. (1999) 'A regret theory approach to assessing customer satisfaction when alternatives are considered', *European Advances in Consumer Research*, 82–8.

Howard, J.A. and Sheth, J.N. (1969) *The Theory of Buyer Behaviour*, John Wiley, New York.

Insight Research (2002) *Store Formats*, Insight Research, London.

Jai-Ok, K., Forsythe, S., Qingliang, G. and Sook, J.M. (2002) 'Cross-cultural values, needs and purchase behavior', *Journal of Consumer Marketing*, 19 (6), 481–502.

Maslow, A. (1943) 'A theory of human motivation', *Psychological Review*, 50 (4), 370–96.

Mattila, A. (1999) 'Do emotional appeals work for services?', *International Journal of Service Industry Management*, 10 (3), 292–307.

Mick, G.D. and Fournier, S. (1998) 'Paradoxes of technology: Consumer cognizances, emotions and coping strategies', *Journal of Marketing*, 64 (3), 50–64.

Newberry, C.R.F., Klemz, B.R. and Boshoff, C. (2003) 'Managerial implications of predicting purchase behavior from purchase intentions: A retail patronage case study', *Journal of Services Marketing*, 17 (6), 609–20.

Parasuraman, A. (2000) 'Technology readiness index (TRI): A multiple-item scale to measure readiness to embrace new technologies', *Journal of Service Research*, 2 (4), 307–20.

Paterson, P., Johnson, L. and Spreng, R. (1997) 'Modeling the determinants of customer satisfaction for business-to-business professional services', *Journal of the Academy of Marketing Science*, 25 (Winter), 4–17.

Sheth, J. and Parvatiyar, A. (2002) 'Evolving relationship marketing into a discipline', *Journal of Relationship Marketing*, 1 (1), 3–16.

Sweeney, J.C., Hausknecht, D. and Soutar, G.N. (2000) 'Measuring cognitive dissonance: A multidimensional scale', *Psychology and Marketing*, 17 (5), 369–86.

Tripp, C. and Drea, J. (2002) 'Selecting and promoting service encounter elements in passenger rail transportation', *Journal of Services Marketing*, 16 (5), 432–42.

Venkatesh, V. and Davis, F.D. (2000) 'A theoretical extension of the technology acceptance model: Four longitudinal field studies', *Management Science*, 46 (2), 186–204.

Venkatesh, V., Morris, M.G., Davis, G.B. and Davis, F.D. (2003) 'User acceptance of information technology: Towards a unified view', *MIS Quarterly*, 27 (3), 425–78.

Walker, R.H., Craig-Lees, M., Hecker, R. and Francis, H. (2002) 'Technology-enabled service delivery: An investigation of reasons affecting customer adoption and rejection', *The International Journal of Service Industry Management*, 13 (1), 91–106.

Zeithaml, V.A. (1981) 'How consumers' evaluation processes differ between goods and services', in J.H. Donnelly and W.R. George (eds), *Marketing of Services*, American Marketing Association, Chicago, 186–90.

Relationship marketing and customer loyalty

Learning objectives

This chapter will explain:

- alternative definitions of relationship marketing

- reasons for the development of relationship marketing

- the role of relationships as an additional service benefit

- theoretical underpinnings of buyer–seller relationship development

- methods used by companies to turn casual transactions into ongoing relationships

- customer loyalty and reasons for the development of customer loyalty programmes

- limitations to the development of relationship marketing

- stakeholder approaches to multiple relationship markets.

5.1 **Introduction**

The term **relationship marketing** has become very widely used in recent years. However, as with many new ideas in business which come along, confusion sets in as to just what the term means. There has been a lot of debate about what is meant by relationship marketing, with the strongest advocates claiming that it represents a paradigm shift in marketing, while some sceptics have argued that it is really all about well-established business practices dressed up as something new.

Conceptually, relationship marketing has been positioned variously between being a set of marketing tactics, in which any interaction between buyers and sellers is described as a relationship, and a fundamental marketing philosophy which goes to the core of the marketing concept through its customer lifetime focus. Many have pointed to the central role played by the concepts of commitment, interdependence and trust (e.g. Crosby *et al.*, 1990; Morgan and Hunt, 1994).

Building on Berry's conceptualization of three levels of relationship marketing (Berry, 2002), the published literature on relationship marketing can be classified into three broad approaches.

1. At a *tactical* level, relationship marketing is used as a sales promotion tool. Developments in information technology have spawned many short-term **loyalty** schemes. However, the implementation of such schemes has often been opportunistic, leading to expensive loyalty schemes which create loyalty to the incentive rather than to the supplier (Barnes, 1994).

2. At a more *strategic* level, relationship marketing has been seen as a process by which suppliers seek to 'tie in' customers through legal, economic, technological, geographical and time bonds (Perry *et al.*, 2002). Again, it has been pointed out that such bonds may lead to customer *detention* rather than *retention* (Dick and Basu, 1994) and that a company which has not achieved a more deep-seated affective relationship with its customers may be unable to sustain those relationships if the legal or technological environment changes. What often passes as a relationship, therefore, is an asymmetric association based on inequalities of knowledge, power and resources, rather than mutual trust and empathy. Where tying in is achieved through mutually rewarding co-operation, mutual dependence and shared risk, the relationship is likely to show greater stability and endurance.

3. At a more *philosophical* level, relationship marketing goes to the heart of the marketing philosophy. Traditional definitions of marketing focus on the primacy of customer needs, and relationship marketing as a philosophy refocuses marketing strategy away from products and their life cycles and towards customer relationship life cycles. Recent conceptualizations of marketing as being the integration of a customer orientation, competitor orientation and inter-functional co-ordination (Narver and Slater, 1990) stress the key features of a relationship marketing philosophy; using all employees of an organization to profitably meet the lifetime needs of targeted customers better than competitors.

The language of relationship marketing can be misleading. In the service sector, many organizations are simplifying and 'industrializing' their processes, usually in an attempt to improve their operational efficiency and consistency of performance. Such companies may talk about relationship development with customers, based on a dialogue which is driven by information technology. But such relationships can be qualitatively quite different from those based on social bonds and trust. While UK clearing banks have become vigorous in their development of customer databases and named personal banking advisers, many customers would feel that the relationship with their bank is qualitatively worse than when a branch manager was able to enter into a more holistic dialogue with customers.

Managers of firms seeking to develop relationships with their customers should avoid the arrogant belief that customers seek such relationships. Surveys have indicated that many categories of buyers are becoming increasingly confident in venturing outside of a business relationship and reluctant to enter into an ongoing relationship. Relationship marketing strategies may fail where buyers' perception is of reduced choice and less freedom to act opportunistically rather than the added value which can derive from a relationship. Added value must be defined by sellers in terms of buyers' needs, rather than focusing on customers as captives who can be cross-sold other products from a firm's portfolio.

Transactional and relational marketing are compared in Figure 5.1.

Traditional transaction-oriented marketing	Relationship marketing
Focus on a single sale	Focus on customer retention
Short-term orientation	Long-term orientation
Sales to anonymous buyers	Tracking of named buyers
Sales person is the main interface between buyer and seller	Multiple levels of relationships between buyer and seller
Limited customer commitment	High customer commitment
Quality is the responsibility of production department	Quality is the responsibility of all

Figure 5.1 The components of transactional and relational exchange compared

5.2 **Reasons for the development of relationship marketing**

There is nothing new in the way that firms have sought to develop ongoing relationships with their customers. In simple economies where the production of goods and services took place on a small scale, it was possible for the owners of businesses to know each customer personally and to come to understand their individual characteristics. They could therefore adapt service delivery to the needs of individuals on the basis of knowledge gained during previous transactions, and could suggest appropriate new product offers. They would also be able to form an opinion about customers' credit-worthiness. Networks of relationships between buyers and sellers are still the norm in many Far Eastern countries and many western exporters have found it difficult to break into these long-standing, closed networks.

With the growth in size of western organizations, the personal contact which an organization can have with its customers has been diluted. Instead of being able to reassure customers on the basis of close relationships, organizations in many cases sought to provide this reassurance through the development of strong brands.

Recent resurgence of interest in relationship marketing has occurred for a number of reasons, as described in the following sections.

5.2.1 Product differentiation through relationships

In many markets, relationships have become a new source of differentiation, adding to services as a point of differentiation for many manufactured products. In increasingly competitive markets, good products alone are insufficient to differentiate an organization's products from those of its competitors. For example, in the car sector, manufacturers traditionally differentiated their cars on the basis of superior design features such as styling, speed and reliability. Once most companies had reached a common standard of design, attention switched to differentiation through superior added service facilities, such as warranties and finance. Once these service standards became the norm for the sector, many car manufacturers sought to differentiate their cars on the basis of superior relationships. So most major car manufactures now offer customers complete packages which keep a car financed, insured, maintained and renewed after a specified period. Instead of a three-yearly one-off purchase of a new car, many customers enter an ongoing relationship with a car manufacturer and its dealers which gives the customer the support they need to keep their car on the road and have it renewed when this falls due (Figure 5.2).

Figure 5.2 The changing focus of marketing from product emphasis to relationship emphasis – an illustration of the car sector

5.2.2 **Retain existing customers**

A second major reason why firms pursue ongoing relationships is because it is generally more profitable to retain existing customers than continually seeking to recruit new customers to replaced lapsed ones. A 'leaky bucket' has often been used as an analogy to illustrate the effects of high levels of customer 'churn' (Figure 5.3). A bucket which has holes in its sides and bottom will leak water, so if a stable level is required, this can only be achieved by topping up the bucket with fresh water. This may be an expensive process, so it would make more sense to prevent water escaping in the first place, perhaps by investing in a better-quality bucket which did not leak. So too for businesses that 'lose' customers. There have been many exercises to calculate the effects on a company's profits of even a modest improvement in the rate at which customers defect to competitors (e.g. Reichheld and Sasser, 1990; Reichheld, 1993). Fewer defections mean less expenditure on recruiting new customers to replace lost ones. The example in Figure 5.4 illustrates the principles of profitable customer retention.

Of course, customers are not all equally profitable, and there may be some categories of customer that a company would rather lose than pursue a relationship with. Being able to identify these segments is therefore also an important part of a relationship marketing strategy. Many companies use past records to develop a profile of the most promising groups to target and do less to encourage those inherently disloyal groups who are likely to leave the company as quickly as they were attracted to it. Sometimes, companies go through their customer list and actively seek to terminate their relationship with groups who are unprofitable. Many UK building societies have attracted media criticism when they have closed the accounts of customers who kept only minimal account balances and did not buy any other services offered by the

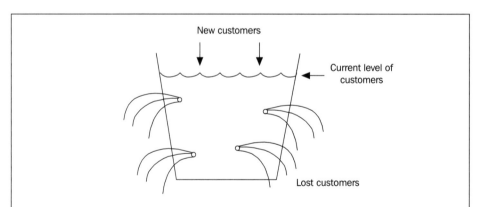

Figure 5.3 The 'leaky bucket' model of customer retention and defection. A leaky bucket is costly to maintain, because in order to maintain a constant level of water, new water must be acquired to replace the water that has been lost through wastage. Similarly, if a company seeks to maintain a constant number of customers, it is generally easier to avoid wastage of existing customers, so that it does not have to go to the expense of recruiting new ones.

1. Before the development of relationship marketing

   - Assume that the bank has 500 000 customers and loses 10% of these each year, for one reason or another.
   - This implies that the average length of relationship between the company and its customers is 10 years.
   - It costs £100 to recruit a new customer (in advertising, incentives and processing costs). In order to replace its lapsed customers, it spends £5 000 000 a year (50 000 lapsed customers to replace × £100) on advertising and customer recruitment.
   - The company makes an average profit of £50 per year from each of its customers.

2. After the introduction of a relationship marketing programme

   - A customer care programme is introduced which costs £20 per customer (this may include the cost of sending a magazine to all customers, setting up an improved customer service centre or offering rewards for loyalty, etc.).
   - The customer defection rate falls from 10% p.a. to 5%.
   - The average relationship duration is therefore extended from 10 to 20 years.

Financial effects on the company

   - Each new customer now represents a profit potential of 20 years × £50 p.a. = £1000, rather than 10 years × £50 = £500, a gain of £500.
   - The net effect, after taking into account the additional expenditure of £20 per customer p.a. for a customer care programme is to increase the lifetime profitability of each new customer by £100 (previously 10 years × £50 per year profit = £500 lifetime value; now 20 years × £50 per year profit (less £20 per year customer care programme) = £600).
   - If the company was content to maintain a stable volume of business, it could cut by half the number of new customers it needs to recruit each year, from 50 000 to 25 000. At a recruitment cost of £100 per new customer, this saves the company £2 500 000 p.a.

In summary, on the basis of these very simplistic assumptions, revenues (in terms of customer lifetime value) have been increased and costs (recruitment of new customers) have fallen.

Figure 5.4 An illustrative example of the financial effects for a bank of developing customer retention strategies

society. Like many banks and financial services companies, they had recognized that relationship marketing needs to focus on profitable customers and that an exit strategy may be needed for unprofitable ones. Naturally, one bank's target customers for relationship development may be the same as its competitors' targets, so intense competition can occur for key types of customer. This competition can create a dynamic tension in which customers' loyalty is continually challenged by the efforts of competitors to undermine it.

5.2.3 The use of information technology

Developments in information technology have had dramatic effects in developing relationship marketing activities. The development of powerful user-friendly databases has allowed organizations to recreate in a computer what the individual small business owner knew in his or her head. Large businesses are now able to tell very quickly the status of a particular customer, for example their previous ordering pattern, product preferences and profitability. Developments in information technology have also allowed companies to enter individual dialogues with their customers through direct mail and increasingly through electronic means (although, we shall

Orange hello call costs £256

The mobile phone operator Orange has been much admired in the UK for its successful launch and rapid growth based on a strong brand. Key to its continuing success will be tackling the problem of 'churn' which affects all mobile phone operators. It has been estimated that about a quarter of all mobile phone users change service provider during the course of a year, attracted by competitors' special offers and introductory discounts. In 1996, Orange had a better than average defection rate of 20% a year, and according to the company's flotation prospectus it was costing £256 to recruit each new customer, reflecting the cost of introductory offers, subsidized phones, advertising and processing costs. With 13.3 million active customers at the end of 2002, reducing the churn rate from 20% to 10% would have brought about annual savings of over £300 million in recruitment costs alone. But how can mobile phone companies stem their rates of defection? Orange's research had suggested that the quality and range of services (especially the coverage area), not price, were the main reason behind defections. Its response was to double the speed of its network expansion programme, with an investment of £800 million for the three-year period up to the end of 2000. It also invested heavily in customer services, to such an extent that in 2003 Orange was ranked No. 1 mobile telephone service for customer satisfaction in the UK for the fourth year running, according to the annual J.D. Power & Associates mobile telephone customer satisfaction study.

As another approach, could UK operators shake themselves out of the habit of giving such big discounts to sign up customers for a year, then charging prices which, by European standards, are high? Such attempts have been made in the past, for example in 2002 mobile phone companies cut back on the incentives they gave to attract new business in the relatively unprofitable 'pay as you go' market. However, with continuing competitive pressure, these incentives gradually reappeared.

Challenges to customer loyalty have also come from number portability, which from 2000 has allowed customers to take their existing phone number when they switch phone supplier. In theory, this cuts the transaction costs of switching supplier for an individual who no longer has to inform friends and colleagues of his or her new telephone number. On the other hand, another surprise challenge to customer loyalty has come from the growth in spam text messages, with some customers finding that the easiest way to stop such messages is to get a new phone, at the same time taking advantage of the best deals on offer.

How else can mobile phone companies improve their ongoing relationships with customers so that competitors are perceived as being inferior and a transfer would involve too much cost and disruption?

see in the following chapter that managing databases effectively can present many challenges for service organizations). Increased production flexibility based on improved technology allows many manufacturers and service organizations to design unique products which meet the needs of individual customers, rather than broad segments of customers.

5.2.4 The use of JIT

Just-in-time (JIT) production methods have become very widespread in western countries, thanks to the lead given by Japanese manufacturing companies. It often makes sense for a manufacturer to keep its holdings of component parts down to an absolute minimum. This way, it ties up less capital, needs less storage space and suffers less risk of stocks becoming obsolete. So instead of keeping large stocks of components 'just in case' they are needed, manufacturers arrange for them to be delivered 'just in time' for them to be used in their production process. It is not uncommon to find car manufacturers receiving batches of components which, within an hour, are incorporated into a car. JIT systems demand a lot of co-operation between supplier and customer which cannot easily be achieved if each transaction is to be individually bargained. Some form of ongoing relationship between the two is essential. While just-in-time is essentially a concept of the manufacturing sector, its effects have been to draw the manufacturing and service sectors closer together. JIT implies a system of production in which manufacturing capacity becomes instantly perishable if component parts are not delivered at the right time. Service industries face a very similar problem of perishable output. JIT within the manufacturing sector has also given many opportunities to service firms who organize the logistics for just-in-time delivery of materials.

5.2.5 Male and female approaches to relationships

Finally, it has been commented that an emphasis on one-off transactions in which each transaction is bargained is very much associated with masculine values of conquest and victory. There is an extensive body of literature on differences in personality traits which exist between males and females. One important area of difference is in the way that males and females develop relationships with others, with masculine gender traits being characterized as aggressive and instrumental, while feminine traits are more commonly associated with showing empathy and resolving conflicts through reconciliation (Barry *et al.*, 1957; Meyers-Levy and Sternthal, 1991; Palmer and Bejou, 1995). Recent moves from warfare approaches to business exchange towards collaborative approaches may appear novel when judged by the stereotypical value system of males, but may be considered normal by the value system of females. In recent years, females have taken on increasingly important roles in business, both as buyers and sellers of goods and services. Although there is the possibility of role conflict, women as buyers and sellers are likely to bring values to commercial exchanges which are more relational than transactional.

> ### A lifetime of eating?
>
> What is the lifetime value of a restaurant customer? First-time customers may only be spending £20 on this occasion, but if they like what they get, how much are they likely to spend in the future? A typical diner eating out just once a month could be worth £1200 in just five years. If they are happy, they are likely to tell their friends. If they're not, they are likely to tell even more of their friends. It follows that customers should be seen as investments, to be carefully nurtured over time. When things go wrong (for example, through overbooking) it would probably be to the restaurant's advantage to spend heavily on putting things right for the customer (e.g. by offering money off a future meal). Judged on the basis of the current transaction, the restaurant may make a loss, but it has protected its investment in a future income stream. Like all investments, some customers are worth more than others. Some attempts have been made to develop predictive models to calculate the likely lifetime value of a customer (e.g. Reinartz and Kumar, 2003), but these have often proved difficult to operationalize. How should a company decide which customers are priority relationships to invest in? And what level of investment can be justified in terms of the expected future profitability from the relationship?

5.3 Theoretical paradigms underlying buyer–seller relationships

Before we look at the methods and practices of relationship marketing, we will briefly consider some of the theory which underlies the creation of buyer–seller relationships. Two streams of literature are particularly relevant here: transaction cost economics and resource dependence theory. In addition, models of consumer choice help to explain why relationships are sought. This is not an exhaustive list of the theoretical roots of relationship marketing, but the ideas contained in these theories have made significant contributions to the subject.

Transaction cost economics, given prominence by Williamson (1985), is based on the notion that there are costs of doing business which are in addition to readily identifiable resource costs. These costs can cover administrative costs and the cost of insuring against contingencies when dealing with unknown customers and suppliers.

Williamson noted that the primary objective of economic organizations is to 'economize in both transaction and neo-classical production costs' (Williamson, 1985, p. 28). Transaction costs are affected by information availability and uncertainty. Hybrid forms of organization, such as strategic alliances, networks, equity joint ventures, etc., can be attributed to the search for efficiency in transaction costs

(Williamson, 1993). In the theoretical model, all transactions lie somewhere on a continuum from being purely market based to being internal to an organization. According to Williamson, firms exist as a means of reducing the risk (and hence transaction costs) of dealing with the uncertainties of a market, thereby reducing transaction costs. On the other hand, market forces can stimulate competition and hence bring down production costs. Firms seek to reduce their total costs and in reality, 'hybrid' types of organization emerge. Networks of buyer–seller relationships represent a hybrid type of organization which reduces the uncertainty of pure market-mediated exchanges, while overcoming the inefficiencies of internal (hierarchical) systems of exchange.

Co-operation between firms which creates value through lowering transaction costs and/or increasing benefits to each party may result in one or both parties giving preferential treatment to the other. Within a transaction cost framework, this could come about as a result of growing levels of trust, which reduces the need for contingencies against risk and uncertainty in transactions. It can also arise where scale benefits encourage preference being given to one partner who is capable of delivering increasing levels of benefits relative to costs.

Resource dependency theory approaches commercial relationships by conceptualizing them as a strategic response by firms to conditions of uncertainty (Pfeffer and Salanick, 1978). Firms have been conceptualized as bundles of competencies such as tacit knowledge, skills, etc., and this framework has been extended to the study of inter-organizational relationships. Through co-operation, partners can exchange core competencies and thereby avoid the risk of tackling novel products or markets alone. In the discussion on strategic relationships between organizations, the ability of member organizations to exchange their technical and marketing competencies has been noted (Hamel *et al.*, 1989). As an example, many alliances between airlines and hotels are formed where individual companies calculate that there will be benefits in sharing access to each other's customers who are mutually exclusive in terms of their geographical representation and/or product requirements. The value of networks of relationships has been shown to be particularly valuable where 'strategic holes' exist in the connectivity between members, and the network can create social capital by bringing together disparate individuals and organizations (Burt, 1992; Baker, 1994).

A further school of thought based on models of buyer behaviour sees buyer–seller relationships as being essentially about a process of *choice reduction* (Sheth and Parvatiyar, 2002) From the buyer's perspective, having excessive choice involves spending time and effort evaluating the competing alternatives. Models of buyer behaviour have been developed to show how consumers reduce the total available set of products to a more manageable 'choice set', which typically may involve just five or six products which are evaluated in greater detail. A relationship is one way of managing this process of choice reduction – in other words, a buyer will initially confine the search to those suppliers with whom he or she has already established a satisfactory relationship.

5.4 **Methods of developing buyer–seller relationships**

A number of attempts have been made to analyse the development of relationships, often using the principles of life cycle theories. A theoretical model of relationships proposed by Dwyer *et al.* (1987) identified five stages of relationship development: awareness, exploration, expansion, commitment and dissolution. The model proposed that a relationship begins to develop significance in the exploration stage when it is characterized by attempts of the seller to attract the attention of the other party. The exploration stage includes attempts by each party to bargain and to understand the nature of the power, norms and expectations held by the other. If this stage is concluded satisfactorily, an expansion phase follows. Exchange outcomes in the exploratory stage provide evidence as to the suitability of long-term exchange relationships. The commitment phase of a relationship implies some degree of exclusivity between the parties and results in the information search for alternatives – if it occurs at all – being much reduced. The dissolution stage marks the point where buyer and seller recognize that they would be better able to achieve their respective aims outside the relationship (Figure 5.5). Subsequent studies have validated the existence of a relationship life cycle (Palmer and Bejou, 1994).

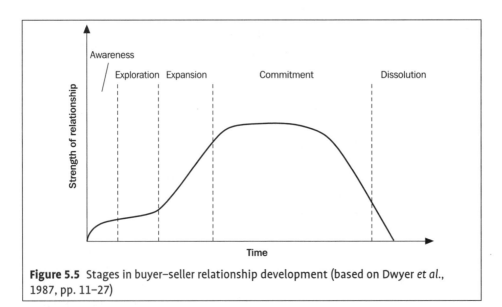

Figure 5.5 Stages in buyer–seller relationship development (based on Dwyer *et al.*, 1987, pp. 11–27)

Organizations use a number of strategies to move their customers through the stages of relationship development.

- The possibility of relationships developing can only occur where the parties are aware of each other and of their mutual desire to enter into exchange transactions. At this stage, the parties may have diverging views about the possibility of forming a long-term relationship. The supplier must be able to offer potential customers reasons why they should show disloyalty to their existing supplier. In some cases, low introductory prices are offered by organizations which provide a sufficient incentive for disloyal customers of other companies to switch supplier. Non-price-related means of gaining attention include advertising and direct mail aimed at the market segments with whom relationships are sought. Over time, the supplier would seek to build value into the relationship so that customers would have little incentive for seeking lower price solutions elsewhere. Inevitably, sellers face risks in adopting this strategy. It may be difficult to identify and exclude from a relationship invitation those segments of the population who are likely to show most disloyalty by withdrawing from the relationship at the point when it is just beginning to become profitable to the supplier.

- On entering into a relationship, buyers and sellers make a series of promises to each other (Grönroos, 1989). In the early stages of a relationship, suppliers' promises result in expectations being held by buyers as to the standard of service that will actually be delivered. Many studies into service quality have highlighted the way in which the gap between expected performance and actual performance determines customers' perception of quality. Quality in perceived service delivery is a prerequisite for a quality relationship being developed.
- Many organizations record information about customers which will be useful in assessing their future needs (Figure 5.6). This can be used to build up a database from which customers are kept in touch with new product developments of specific

In order to keep our records up to date please fill in all the following details and tick all relevant boxes. (Please use block capitals.)

Are you the travel arranger? Yes ☐ No ☐
Are you the traveller? Yes ☐ No ☐
What is the purpose of your trip? Business ☐ Leisure ☐

PLEASE FILL IN YOUR 3 MOST FREQUENT JOURNEYS AND TICK THE RELEVANT BOXES

UK DEPARTURE AIRPORT	DESTINATION AIRPORT	FREQUENCY	CLASS
1.		☐ 1–5 times ☐ 5–15 times ☐ above 15	☐ Economy ☐ Business ☐ First Class
2.		☐ 1–5 times ☐ 5–15 times ☐ above 15	☐ Economy ☐ Business ☐ First Class
3.		☐ 1–5 times ☐ 5–15 times ☐ above 15	☐ Economy ☐ Business ☐ First Class

NAME: ______
POSITION: ______
COMPANY: ______
ADDRESS: HOME/WORK* ______
______ POSTCODE ______
TELEPHONE NO. ______
*PLEASE DELETE AS APPROPRIATE

OCCASIONALLY WE MAY PASS YOUR DETAILS ON TO OTHER COMPANIES IN THE TRAVEL INDUSTRY. PLEASE TICK THIS BOX IF YOU DO NOT WISH TO BE INCLUDED IN THESE MAILERS ☐

Birmingham International Airport

BIA 11.97

Figure 5.6 Birmingham International Airport uses the opportunity of an information request to build up a profile of its customers. Like all companies operating in the EU, the airport is required to obtain the consent of respondents before it can use their details for other purposes. Those who consent to receiving further information have received, among other things, a quarterly magazine containing information about new services offered by the airport. The airport has used reader surveys and competitions to further build up a picture of airport users. (Reproduced with permission of Birmingham International Airport Ltd)

interest to them. We will return to customer information management in the following chapter.

■ Financial incentives are often given to customers as a reward for maintaining the relationship. These can range from a simple money-off voucher valid for a reduction in the price of a future purchase, to a club-type scheme which allows a standard level of discount for club members. Incentives which are purely financially based have a problem in that they can defeat the service supplier's central objective of getting greater value out of a relationship. It is often expensive to initiate a relationship and organizations therefore seek to achieve profits at later stages by raising price levels to reflect the value which customers attach to the relationship. There is a danger of buyers becoming loyal to the financial incentive, rather than the brand it is designed to promote. Once the financial incentive comes to an end, loyalty may soon disappear. In some cases, greater bonding between customer and supplier can be achieved by selling membership plans to customers which allow subsequent discount, as is the case with many gym membership plans. Having invested in a membership plan, customers are likely to rationalize their reasons for taking advantage of it, rather than taking their business elsewhere.

■ Rather than offer price discounts, companies can add to the value of a relationship by offering other non-financial incentives. Companies must ask 'Why should a customer want a relationship with us?' The answer is that a relationship, to be sustainable, must add value in the eyes of customers. This value can come about in a number of ways, including the following.

– *Making reordering of services easier*. Information about the preferences of individual customers can be retained in order that future requests for service can be closely tailored to their needs. In this way a travel agent booking accommodation for a corporate client can select hotels on the basis of preferences expressed during previous transactions. By offering a more personalized service, the travel agent is adding value to the relationship, increasing the transaction costs of transferring to another travel agent. Similarly, many hotels record guests' details and preferences to speed up the checking-in process.

– *Offering privileges to customers who wish to enter into some type of formal relationship* (for example, many retailers hold special preview events for card holders, and send them a free copy of the store's magazine).

– *Developing an ability to jointly solve problems*. As an example, a car repair garage may try to identify exactly what the problem is that a customer seeks to have fixed, rather than leave it to the customer to have to specify the work that he or she wishes to be carried out. Such joint problem-solving requires a considerable level of trust to have been developed between the parties.

■ A strategy used by some companies is to create relationships by trying to turn one-off service delivery into continuous delivery. In this way, companies offering travel insurance often encourage customers to buy all-year-round coverage rather than purchase a policy each time they travel abroad.

- A more intensive relationship can develop where customers assign considerable responsibility to another company for identifying their needs. In this way a car repairer may attempt to move away from offering a series of one-off services initiated by customers, to a situation where it takes total responsibility for maintaining a customer's car, including diagnosing problems and initiating routine service appointments.

- In a competitive marketplace, customer satisfaction is the surest way to ensure that buyers return repeatedly. To achieve high levels of satisfaction requires the effort of all functions within an organization. Relationship development cannot simply be left to a relationship manager. There are many notable cases of companies that have not developed any explicit relationship marketing programme, but nevertheless achieve very high levels of customer loyalty.

- Even companies which have an apparently poor standard of service can achieve high levels of repeat business by charging low prices. Airlines such as easyJet and Ryanair have developed strong loyalty from price-sensitive customers who consider that the total service offer (ease of booking, flight times, range of destinations and reliability, etc.) are acceptable in return for the price they have paid. The danger here is that competitors may enter the market with similarly low prices, but offering higher levels of service. Would customers still remain loyal?

Although there has been much recent interest in relationship marketing – for goods as well as for services – this has tended to emphasize the producer's perspective on a relationship. It can be argued that with increasing knowledge and confidence, consumers are increasingly happy to venture outside a long-term relationship with a service provider. This is reflected, for example, in the observation by the Consumers' Association that about 20% of the population changes bank account or credit card in a year, something which runs counter to earlier anecdotal observations that a relationship which individuals have with their bank is more enduring than the relationship with their spouse. With increased knowledge of financial services, consumers are more willing today to venture to another bank which offers the best personal loan for them, or the most attractive credit card. Also, a long-term relationship often begins with attractive introductory discounts and a significant segment of many service markets is prepared to move its business regularly to the service provider which is offering the most attractive discount. The motorist who reviews his or her car insurance each year, for example, may not allow an insurance company to develop a long-term profitable relationship. In the case of many business-to-business services contracts, these may be reviewed regularly as a matter of course, as in the 'best value' tendering which is required for many government purchases of services. In such circumstances, it is often not possible to add value and higher prices to a long-term relationship.

5.5 Customer loyalty

Many services companies have developed customer loyalty programmes as part of their relationship development activities. As with the concept of relationship marketing itself, there is much debate and confusion about just what is meant by customer loyalty.

The *Oxford English Dictionary* defines loyalty as the state of 'being faithful . . . true to allegiance'. However, too frequently, mere repetitious behaviour by customers has been confused with loyalty as defined above. Repetitious purchasing behaviour may be a result of a market structure in which buyers find themselves with few alternatives, or where available alternatives can only be obtained at a high cost in terms of breaking current ties with a supplier. In many markets, some segments are likely to purchase repetitively out of inertia or lack of awareness of the alternatives available. The loyalty of customers who are influenced by such inertia is likely to be very different to that of a customer who strongly advocates a product and feels emotionally attached to it. Becoming an advocate of a company is the peak of a 'ladder of loyalty' (Figure 5.7).

Dick and Basu developed the notion of relative attitude as a theoretical grounding to the loyalty construct. Relative attitude refers to 'a favourable attitude that is high compared to potential alternatives' (Dick and Basu, 1994, p. 100). They suggest that loyalty is evidenced both by a more favourable attitude towards a brand (compared to other alternatives) and repeat buying behaviour. By their analysis, low relative attitude with low repeat purchase indicates an absence of loyalty, while low relative attitude with high repeat purchase indicates 'spurious' loyalty. Satisfaction with a service provider is seen as an antecedent of relative attitude because, without satisfaction, consumers will not hold a favourable attitude towards the service provider, compared to other alternatives available.

Many loyalty schemes can be seen as classical sales promotion activity in that they offer a short-term incentive to disloyal brand switchers. It has been noted that much sales promotion activity is very short term in effect and can actually undermine the

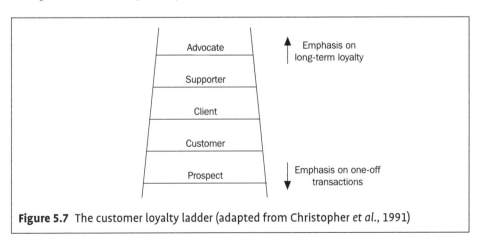

Figure 5.7 The customer loyalty ladder (adapted from Christopher *et al.*, 1991)

Is there loyalty in a traffic jam?

Just because customers repeatedly come back to a company does not necessarily mean that they are loyal to that company. This point was made, tongue in cheek, during the continuing war of words between British Airways and Virgin Atlantic Airways. The latter had objected to BA's use of the advertising slogan 'The world's favourite airline'. Statistically, it was true that more passengers travelled internationally with British Airways than with any other airline, but surveys of airline users had consistently put Virgin ahead of BA in terms of perceived quality of service. Virgin's Richard Branson claimed that on BA's logic, the M25, London's notorious orbital motorway, could be described as the world's favourite motorway. Despite coming back to the motorway day after day, few motorists could claim to be loyal to it – they simply have no other choice.

The spat between BA and Virgin serves to underline the point that loyalty is about more than repetitious buying. True loyalty involves customers becoming enthusiastic advocates of a company.

long-term task of developing a strong brand (O'Brien and Jones, 1995). There is evidence to suggest that sales promotion activity, by encouraging brand switching, can bring about a short-term increase in sales for a company. In the case of manufactured goods companies, this may simply bring forward consumers' purchases, resulting in a subsequent fall as stockpiles are used up. In the case of services, the problem of carrying forward stockpiles does not exist, but disloyal brand switchers who were attracted by one company's offer may be just as easily attracted away by a competitor's incentive.

A medium-term attempt to create loyalty from customers is sometimes made through the creation of structural bonds whereby buyers are tied to a seller (Figure 5.8). Structural bonds have been defined by Turnbull and Wilson (1989) in terms of investments that cannot be retrieved when a relationship ends, or when it is difficult to end the relationship due to the complexity and cost of changing relational partners. A structural bond between buyer and seller has the effect of tying one to the other, through the creation of barriers to exit, although such ties may be asymmetric. One way in which buyers can become tied to sellers is by designing services in such a way that transferring to another supplier involves significant switching costs. Within the commercial banking sector, one means by which banks increase their retention rate is to increase switching costs by such means as long-term mortgages with penalties for early closure. Airlines' frequent-flyer programmes have a similar effect in seeking to make the cost of competitor airlines appear more expensive by virtue of the opportunity cost of forgoing loyalty rewards.

Where the process of tying in is achieved through a process of mutually rewarding co-operation, mutual dependence and shared risk, the relationship is likely to show greater stability and endurance (Han *et al.*, 1993).

Figure 5.8 Boots is one of many retailers offering benefits to customers who sign up for their loyalty programmes. One of the challenges of Boots is to encourage the large number of people who visit it stores each day to spend more during their visit. So instead of just buying a tube of toothpaste or bottle of shampoo, customers could be tempted to buy a new camera, kitchen equipment, or one of the company's range of services which include insurance, dentistry and eye care. A loyalty card offers an inducement to customers to place a larger part of their total expenditure with the company, rather than going to competitors, especially where the rewards are seen as significant. However, the biggest benefit of a loyalty programme to a company such as Boots is to get a much deeper insight into the shopping behaviour of its customers. No longer does it have to base its marketing planning simply on till receipt analysis, it can now understand individuals pattern of buying over time. It can also link data collected at the point of sale with other demographic data provided by card holders. Although some retailers have dismissed loyalty programmes as an expensive gimmick which adds to a company's operating costs, many others have taken the view that the additional operating costs involved are a low price to pay for the rich data that is provided. (Reproduced with permission of Boots the Chemists)

5.5.1 Loyalty programmes and profitability

An important aim of loyalty programmes is to extend a customer's life with a company so that their lifetime profitability is increased. Unfortunately, it can be very difficult to measure the effectiveness of a loyalty programme. The conceptual difficulties in measuring the performance of loyalty programmes stem from the difficulty of comparing the performance of a marketing plan which includes a loyalty programme, with a plan which does not include one. Some companies have experimented

Card wars in store

During the mid-1990s, the UK grocery retail sector seemed to be going the way of the international airline industry in its development of store loyalty cards. The 'card wars' were initiated by Tesco Stores, which launched its Clubcard in 1993. The card was initially launched as a means of getting information about the shopping habits of its customers. Previously, the company had no way of routinely disaggregating its revenues between different groups of shoppers and was unable to track the spending habits of individuals. Information collected with each purchase allowed the company to target promotions at individuals whose spending pattern suggested that they would be particularly receptive to a specific promotion. To encourage use of the card, Tesco offered an effective rebate to customers of 1% of their bill, which was forwarded in the form of vouchers. Tesco's Clubcard undoubtedly gave it a significant competitive advantage, helping it to beat Sainsbury's to the spot of largest UK grocery retailer. Meanwhile, Tesco's competitors had been researching their own loyalty cards and eventually joined the battle, and loyalty bonuses eventually became part of many customers' expectations. The pitch of the battle was upped when the supermarkets started adding financial services to their loyalty cards, so that they became debit/credit cards. From here, the way was open to developing a very broad relationship with customers – from baked beans to banking and potatoes to pensions. In 2003 a significant development in loyalty programmes occurred when a consortium of non-competing companies – including Barclaycard, Sainsbury's, Debenhams and Vodafone – got together to launch the Nectar loyalty programme. For customers, there was an incentive to spend more with consortium members in order to accrue rewards more rapidly. For the companies, they gained valuable new insights into consumer behaviour across a range of product categories.

Now that loyalty rewards had become the expectation of many customers, was the retail sector as a whole really any better off? Had it got to the situation of American Airlines, whose chairman was once quoted as saying that he wished he could 'disinvent' the loyalty programmes which had cost the airline sector so much? If customer loyalty cards are here to stay, how can individual supermarkets position their card to give them a continuing competitive advantage? Had the supermarkets now got their hands on more customer information than they could realistically handle? Two of the other top four UK supermarkets, Asda and Safeway (now owned by Morrisons) evidently thought so and withdrew their loyalty card programmes in favour of an 'every day low price' policy. Meanwhile a new breed of 'no frills' discount grocers, such as Aldi, Netto and Lidl had been steadily growing in the UK and proudly proclaimed that they gave their customers low prices and not loyalty points. If Tesco and Sainsbury's believed that loyalty cards were so important for learning about their customers, how did this new generation of retailers manage to learn about *their* customers?

with cross-sectional data by comparing sales performance at outlets which are similar, except for the existence of a loyalty programme. There are few published long-term studies of the effectiveness of loyalty programmes.

In any given industry sector, there are usually significant benefits of being the first company to offer a loyalty programme. However, while pioneers in a sector may introduce incentive schemes and gain additional profitable business from competitors, incentives can rapidly become a sector norm which buyers expect (Gilbert and Karabeyekian, 1995). Loyalty schemes may fail to give a long-term strategic advantage to a company because they are easy for competitors to copy. There is evidence that once one innovator in a sector introduces a loyalty scheme, competitors soon follow.

For firms, the most rewarding relationships with customers result from continued investment to create affective loyalty, rather than financially based incentives (Barnes, 1994; Kanter, 1994). The excessive use of financial incentives to create loyalty may put a firm at cost disadvantage in a market where cost leadership is important, while securing little underlying loyalty.

A further reason why it is very difficult to evaluate the effectiveness of a loyalty programme is because one of the main benefits to a company is the data which programmes can give them. To many companies, a loyalty programme represents a cost-effective way of gathering longitudinal data about customers' behaviour, and also being able to link this to customers' demographic information. The example was given in the previous chapter of the retailer Tesco, which used data-mining techniques to identify a link between the sale of beer and the sale of nappies. This insight could not have been provided very easily by an analysis of till receipts alone, but by analysing data over time, for different stores, and for different categories of customers.

Against these benefits to companies, is an increasing realization by some customers of the privacy implications of allowing so much data to be collected about them. While it is probably true that the majority of customers are quite happy to simply collect rewards – maybe they are unconcerned about the privacy issues, or are simply unaware of the amount of data which is collected about them – there are nevertheless some customers who decline to use loyalty programmes and to give information about themselves.

5.6 Is relationship marketing universally applicable within the service sector?

Should relationship marketing be viewed as a blueprint which is of universal applicability to business, or a special case of limited applicability? The arguments in favour of pursuing strategies designed to obtain a greater share of customers' total expenditure have been well developed in terms of the effects on companies' profitability (e.g. Reichheld and Sasser, 1990; Reichheld, 1993). Initial interest in relational exchange focused on industrial marketing (e.g. Ford, 1981; Cunningham and Turnbull, 1982) where transactions are typically large in value and limited in number. More recently, the concepts of relationship marketing have been applied to lower-value consumer sales. In extending the application of relational exchange, proponents may be following a trend in circumstances where theory and practice suggest that one-off transactional exchanges may be a more appropriate method of securing profitability. Relational exchange may be an unrealistic pursuit in any of the following circumstances: where there is no reason why a buyer would ever wish to return to a seller; where buyers seek to avoid an asymmetric relationship in which they become dependent upon a seller; where buying processes become formalized in a way that prevents a seller developing relationships based on social bonds; where buyers' confidence lowers the need for risk reduction which is an outcome of relationship development; and where the costs associated with relationship development put a firm at a cost disadvantage in a price-sensitive market. Finally, from a social welfare perspective, relationships have been associated with anti-competitive practices which restrict buyers' choice.

These limitations to the concept of relational exchange are considered below.

5.6.1 Parties to an exchange may have no expectation of ongoing relationships

One of the defining characteristics of relational exchange is a time orientation within which exchange takes place (Macneil, 1980). However, it may be naive to assume that parties to an exchange have expectations that a relationship will develop beyond the current transaction. The frequency of transactions between a buyer and seller does not necessarily imply any long-term loyalty from one to the other (O'Brien and Jones, 1995). The use of technological, economic and legal bonds between buyers and sellers may lead to a feeling of involuntary customer detention rather than willing customer retention. There is evidence that companies' loyalty schemes in fact have little effect on underlying affective commitment (e.g. Uncles *et al.*, 2003).

In some cases, businesses serve market segments where customers have no underlying need to make further purchases of a category of product that a company is able to supply. In an extreme case, a small-scale company may appeal to the curiosity of buyers for whom a second-time purchase will have little of its original value – curiosity. This phenomenon is present in many tourism-related businesses in destinations of symbolic rather than aesthetic quality (for example, many people make a religious pilgrimage once in their lifetime with little incentive to return again). While firms with a diverse product and geographical coverage may be able to build on their initial curiosity contact, opportunities for relationship development by smaller companies in such circumstances are limited.

5.6.2 Relationships may be created in an asymmetric manner leading to a desire by one party to reduce their dependence

It was noted in Chapter 1 that the traditional marketing mix has been criticized for being production oriented in the way in which the 4Ps provide a framework for things to be 'done' to buyers (Grönroos, 1994). Attempts to create ongoing relationships are similarly frequently initiated in a non-consensual manner. It has been suggested that buyers frequently have no wish to enter into a relationship with a company, despite the efforts of companies to use information from customers to build databases.

A non-consensual relationship, where one superior party is able to exercise authority over a subordinate party, has been seen as qualitatively inferior to a relationship based on bilateral governance mechanisms (Heide, 1994). In the absence of symmetrical dependence, an individual party will have little incentive to show flexibility, because no guarantee exists that such actions will be reciprocated. In fact, short-term disturbances might represent opportunities for individual parties to pursue opportunistically short-term advantages.

Recent conceptualizations of commercial exchange consider reciprocity to be a fundamental virtue which builds solidarity and contributes to the creation and maintenance of balance in social relations (Becker, 1990; Bagozzi, 1995). Equity theory has been used to argue that customers who feel that they are getting a better ratio of benefits to costs than their exchange partner will feel a greater sense of commitment to their exchange partner (Goodwin and Ross, 1992; Kelley and Davis, 1994) and are likely to show greater forbearance in the event of a failure by the supplier.

How deep is our relationship?

It is all too easy for marketers to believe that their customers want a relationship with them. In fact, customers are often quite fickle and the mere fact that they come back to a company for repeat purchases does not necessarily mean that they have any degree of emotional attachment to the company.

Research undertaken by The Henley Centre for Christian Brann indicated the fickleness of buyers. Respondents were asked about their feelings towards a brand which they had recently purchased. One question asked whether they felt they had a relationship with the company. Only 9% claimed to have a relationship with a tour operator, 11% with a travel agent and 44% with a personal loan provider. Very little loyalty was shown, with only 10% saying they were loyal to a tour operator, 20% to a travel agent and 35% to a personal loan provider. As marketers increasingly focus on customer loyalty, is their excitement an illusion when customers in fact focus on much more short-term issues about a purchase?

5.6.3 Formalized buying processes may prevent the development of ongoing relationships based on social bonds

Much of the literature on buyer–seller relationship development, especially in the business-to-business sector, has highlighted the importance of developing social bonds between buyers and sellers (Ford, 1981; Liljander and Strandvik, 1995). Social bonds have been observed to reduce buyers' perceived levels of risk and to simplify the reordering process.

An alternative view is that social bonds can become too pervasive, to the point where they allow economic inefficiencies to develop. In the extreme case, corrupt networks of buyers and sellers may acquire sufficient market power to result in an overall loss of economic welfare. Counterbalances are needed to offset such possible relationship-based inefficiencies.

Measures to suppress buyer–seller relationships based on social bonds have been most evident in the formalized ordering procedures for government contracts. In the UK, 'best value' legislation requiring the review and tendering of a wide range of local government services has transferred many services from being internally produced to being bought in from outside contractors. Previous deficiencies in accountability have been replaced by clearly specified contracts for which all parties are accountable. Where services continue to be provided by internal direct labour organizations, the extent to which there has been a formal split between client and contractor roles has varied between local authorities. A relatively distinct client–contractor split is the norm (Shaw, *et al.*, 1993).

Tightly specified supplier–buyer relationships, and a requirement for contracts to be re-submitted for tender after a specified period, reduce the scope for ongoing socially based relationships to be developed. It has been argued that the emphasis on obtaining value for money has often stressed cost reduction at the expense of more qualitative measures of efficiency and effectiveness.

5.6.4 Buyers' increasing level of confidence reduces their need for an ongoing relationship

Much of the literature on relationship marketing has focused on *suppliers'* needs to develop relationships (e.g. Day and Wensley, 1983; Webster, 1992), overlooking the perspective of buyers' need, or lack of need, to develop ongoing relationships. Commitment by a customer to one supplier relationship can imply foregoing alternative opportunities when they present themselves. Buyers may deliberately seek to minimize risk of dependency by developing a portfolio of suppliers.

In many consumer markets, buyers' need for ongoing trusting relationships has been reduced by legislation, which has had the effect of reducing the risk associated with buying goods and services from previously unknown sources. In the UK, for example, statutory provision for investors' compensation funds has lessened the need for investors to rely on an intermediary they have come to trust. Legislation has reduced the chances of a poor relationship being developed and provided means for compensating investors who suffer loss as a result of failure by an intermediary, thereby encouraging greater transactional orientation.

Recent developments in information technology (IT) have emphasized the benefits to producers of being able to gain an asymmetrical position of power in private buyer–seller relationships. With further development, IT is strengthening the willingness and ability of private consumers to engage in multiple sourcing of purchases at the expense of ongoing relationships. For example, the Internet is increasingly allowing consumers to search quickly and easily for the cheapest quotation when their car insurance is due for renewal, reducing the chances of renewal through inertia.

5.6.5 Relationship marketing can add to costs, as well as to revenues

For firms, the most rewarding relationships with customers generally result from investment to create affective loyalty, rather than short-term financially based incentives. The excessive use of financial incentives to create loyalty may put a firm at a cost disadvantage in a market where cost leadership is important, while securing little underlying loyalty. While pioneers in a sector may introduce incentive schemes and gain additional profitable business from competitors, incentives for loyalty can rapidly become a sector norm which customers expect. In the case of airlines' frequent-flyer programmes, a cycle of development has been described which began in the 1980s where the first companies to launch achieved revenue benefits. By the end of the 1980s, the use of frequent-flyer programmes had become more widespread and their revenue benefits marginal. By the 1990s, most major airlines had developed programmes, yielding little advantage from this tool (Gilbert and Karabeyekian, 1995). Frequent-flyer programmes, had become part of travellers' expectations, resulting in heavy losses of revenue for airlines. It should also be noted that many service sectors are characterized by a variety of firms which range from full service with a customer loyalty programme through to no frills and no loyalty programme. Within the airline sector, it has been noted that in 1999 British Airways, with its comprehensive customer loyalty programme, made a loss, while the no-frills competitor Ryanair made substantial profits without a loyalty programme. At the same time, within the retail sector, the poorest-performing stores were those such as Sainsbury's and Marks & Spencer which had invested in its customer relationships, while stores without a customer loyalty programme, including Asdá, Matalan and Morrisons, had out-performed the market.

5.6.6 Networks of relationships can have anti-competitive implications

Finally, the economic benefits of relationship marketing have been questioned because of the anti-competitive implications that can be present in close relationships between businesses. Karl Marx observed that capitalists were more concerned with *avoiding* risks rather than *taking* risks. The development of networks of buyer–seller relationships may be seen as a means of reducing entrepreneurs' exposure to risk, thereby reducing some of the presumed benefits of a competitive market environment.

More fundamentally, relationship marketing activities can be seen as a process by which a seller seeks to restrict the choice set of buyers. Restriction can come about consensually where buyers limit their choice set as a result of a history of satisfaction with their current supplier, or more non-consensually where bonds unwittingly lead to restricted access to alternative sources of need-satisfying products. Summing up current developments in relationship marketing, Sheth and Parvatiyar have described firms' motivation to develop ongoing relationships as being based primarily on 'choice reduction' (Sheth and Parvatiyar, 2002).

Evidence of the abuse of preferential relationships by firms who are dominant in their markets has been seen in a number of cases. In July 1999, the European Commission fined British Airways €6.8 million for providing excessive loyalty rewards to its travel agents, thereby abusing its dominant position in the market (Mortished, 1999). British Airways had developed a loyalty programme for its travel agents which rewarded high volumes of business by granting loyalty bonuses to preferred agents. It was argued by the Commission that such action made it unacceptably difficult for smaller airline competitors to compete for distribution coverage within travel agents.

Regulatory bodies are increasingly recognizing that structural bonds can become anti-competitive. In 1996, British Telecom, which had a dominant position in the UK telephone market, sought to develop a strategic alliance with BSkyB, the dominant player in the cable television sector. BT customers would gain preferential pricing for BSkyB's services and would become committed to taking their telephone service from BT rather than one of its competitors. This relationship was held by the regulatory body Oftel to be against the public interest, despite the benefits that it would appear to bring to the parties involved.

It has been observed that the pattern of doing business in many countries may be based on a tightly knit network of relationships between buyers, sellers, suppliers and distributors, typified by Japan's manufacturing and distribution *keiretsus* (Ohmae, 1989; Cutts, 1992). It may seem ironic that while companies in western countries seek to develop closer relationships between businesses, many of those same companies have been applying pressure through their governments for such practices to be curtailed in Japan. Businesses in the latter country are characterized by networks of supply and distribution chains which have had the effect – intentional or not – of making it difficult for a new entrant to break into the market.

5.7 Relationship breakdown

Buyer–seller relationships may break down for a variety of reasons. It was noted earlier that in some cases the service supplier may actively seek to break off a relationship where a customer is judged to offer no long-term profit potential. At other times, it is the customer who drifts away. Sometimes there are good extraneous reasons for this defection. For example, a customer of an airline may break off their relationship if the airline ceases to serve their local airport, or if the customer moves their residence to an area not served by the airline. For some categories of product, relationships may end when a customer no longer needs that product and the supplier does not have any new service propositions which might satisfy the customer's changing needs. Many relationships fail when a customer dies or a company goes out of business.

Of more concern to marketers is where a breakdown in a buyer's commitment to a relationship is associated with greater competition and the availability of alternative suppliers. Competition tests the true loyalty of a customer. A further challenge to loyalty arises from service failures. Service encounters can result in failure as perceived by customers in a number of ways, including the unavailability of a service, slow service and errors in delivery (Bitner *et al.*, 1990). By failing to deliver on its promises, the trust which goes to the foundation of a relationship is undermined. Through a recovery process, service failure can be transformed into a positive act which creates increasingly strong attitudes of customers towards a supplier (Hart *et al.*, 1990). A service failure can occur at any stage of a customer's relationship with a supplier. It has been argued that a failure occurring early in the customer's relationship with a supplier will be perceived more adversely than one which occurs later in a relationship because the customer has less experience of successful service experiences to counterbalance the failure (Boulding *et al.*, 1993). Drawing on literature of conflict resolution, the existence of a relationship has been shown to moderate the effects of disputes on attitudes towards relationship partners (Kaufmann and Stern, 1992).

Companies often put a lot of effort into finding out the reasons why customers defect, but getting to the real reasons for defection calls for a wide range of research methods. In a study of bank customers in Australia and New Zealand, the reasons for switching banks were classified into three main problem areas: service failures, pricing problems and denied services. Results indicated that problems with pricing had the most important impact on switching behaviour. In contrast, customers tended to complain more often about service failures prior to exiting the firm. This finding suggested that customers were staying silent about the problems that were most important in their decision to leave the bank (Colgate and Hedge, 2001). This highlights the point made in the previous chapter that service organizations should pay a lot of attention to gathering complaints about service delivery while they are still in a position to rectify the situation, rather than wait until the customer leaves.

5.8 The multiple relationship markets of firms

Finally, it must be recognized that an organization's relationships can be very complex, especially in the case of business-to-business relationships. A company may see another organization as a co-operative relational partner in some aspects of its business, but competitive in others. An airline, for example, may compete fiercely with another airline for customers, yet have co-operative relationships in respect of aircraft maintenance. This has led to exchanges between organizations being seen increasingly as multi-faceted, rather than being based on contact solely through their respective buyers and sellers (Figure 5.9).

This chapter has taken a largely dyadic perspective on buyer–seller relationships, but in reality, what might appear a simple one-to-one relationship may involve many partners. A service principal may deliver its service through subcontractors, result-

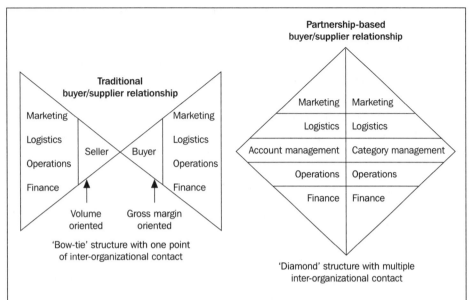

Figure 5.9 Relational exchange between organizations should occur between all of each organization's main functions. The traditional 'bow-tie' approach, in which communications between firms is focused on firms' buyers and sellers, is increasingly being replaced by the 'diamond' approach, in which communication is dispersed through all of their main functions.

ing in possibly multiple relationships with each customer. This has led some to talk about multiple stakeholders in a relationship (e.g. Malhotra, 2002) and to move the analysis of relationships from a 'one-to-one' to a 'many-to-many' basis (Gummesson, 2003).

The question has often been raised whether there should be a consistency in organizations' pattern of relationships with the different groups with whom they do business. Can an organization pursue a strategy of relationship marketing with its customers while it pursues one of 'hire and fire' with its employees and suppliers? A useful analytic framework for considering the consistency between an organization's multiple relationships is the 'six markets' model proposed by Christopher *et al.* (1991). The six markets comprise:

1. customers

2. suppliers

3. employees

4. other internal departments within the organization

5. referral markets, comprising advocates for the organization (e.g. intermediaries)

6. influence markets, comprising bodies such as regulatory agencies which can significantly affect the organization.

Some organizations are notable for the way in which they have managed to create consistency in their dealings with each of their markets. The retailer Marks & Spencer has a long-standing policy of creating long-term relationships with its suppliers, and its employment practices have emphasized the development and retention of personnel. In recent years, the company has taken a number of measures to improve the quality of ongoing relationships with its customers. The quality of its goods and customer service has always encouraged buyers to return, and this has been supplemented in recent years by the development of its charge card and related financial services. At the opposite end of the retailing spectrum, some chains of discount shops position themselves as price leaders with little attempt to reward customer loyalty, other than continuing low prices. Negotiations with suppliers are likely to be based on bargaining of individual consignments. Staff may be paid little more than the minimum wage.

While consistency between the six markets may seem intuitively attractive, questions are asked where companies try to impose different patterns in each of their markets. British Airways has prided itself on the quality of its service and the benefits that customers receive from belonging to its Executive Club frequent-flyer programme. During a cabin crew strike in the summer of 1997, many commentators expressed concern at the strongarm tactics used by the company to try to get its staff back to work. Could a company which prided itself on its customer loyalty expect loyalty from its staff when they had been treated in this way?

Case study

Is there credit in a relationship?

By Steve Worthington, Monash University, Melbourne

As in human life generally, buyer–seller relationships are often not straightforward and simple. This point is well illustrated in the credit card market where a whole network of relationships can lie behind a seemingly simple-looking credit card. The emergence of 'affinity' credit cards illustrates the importance of multi-lateral relationships.

Financial institutions issue affinity credit cards to members or supporters of a specific organisation or cause. Since their launch in the UK in the mid-1980s, affinity cards have proliferated and now cover a wide range of organizations as diverse as universities, football clubs, charities and political parties.

Affinity credit cards work on the basis of an agreement between a card-issuing bank and a membership-based organization. Most agreements include both an initial donation by the card issuer to the affinity group, and also a turnover-related donation. The aim is to encourage the affinity organization to promote the card and for its members to use it in preference to other credit cards.

The concept of affinity marketing would appear to satisfy a number of parties' interests. The card-issuing bank gets access to a new customer base, who may be predisposed to take out the bank's card because of the links it has with the association of which it is a member. The association benefits from payments made by the bank to the association, both through the initial sign-up fee and ongoing turnover-related payments, which are typically in the region of 25p per £100 spent. This is funded out of the 'interchange fee' that merchants make to the credit card issuer every time a customer uses a credit card to buy goods or services, and is typically in the range of £1–£2 per £100 spent. The individual cardholder may gain pride and status from holding an affinity card that may help him or her to identify more fully with an organization. Manchester United supporters, for example, may see their club-endorsed card as a proxy for the support that they give their team. The University of Edinburgh Platinum MasterCard, issued by the Bank of Scotland is a simple way for an individual to show a link to their university and also, when they use the credit card, the university benefits through the turnover-related payments.

With 63% of affinity groups currently in a relationship with a credit card issuer, personal lender or mortgage lender, affinity marketing in retail banking is now a relatively mature market. According to Datamonitor (2003), there were 2.2 million affinity credit cards in circulation in the UK in 2003. Cardweb.com (www.cardweb.com) estimated that 250 million affinity cards were in circulation worldwide, accounting for a third of all credit cards.

The Co-operative Bank has one of the longest-running affinity credit card relationships in the UK with the Royal Society for the Protection of Birds (RSPB). The bank first linked up with Europe's largest nature conservation charity in 1988 with the launch of the RSPB affinity card. By 2003, the card had raised in excess of £5million for RSPB conservation work. The Co-operative Bank's relationship with the RSPB goes even further in support of conservation work. The bank has been the official species sponsor of the bittern, one of the UK's rarest birds, with the RSPB receiving £10,000 per year towards its bittern habitat work, helping UK bittern numbers increase from 11 males in 1997 to 42 in 2003.

But how generous are affinity cards in supporting membership organizations? A survey in 2004 by www.moneysupermarket.com of charity affinity cards found that the meanest payers were the Childline and Breakthrough Breast Cancer cards, both run by MBNA, where the charities receive £3 and £4 respectively when the cards are first used, and then just 0.15% of spending. Nationwide's Comic Relief card was the most generous, donating £5.50 on the first purchase, then 0.5% of spending thereafter.

'Cashback' cards, where the money goes directly into cardholders' pockets, were found to be much more generous. The moneysupermarket.com survey highlighted a number of conventional cashback cards that pay 1% directly to the cardholder, double the best amount paid to a charity by an affinity card. Some campaigning groups, such as the Consumers 'Association, have suggested that it would be better for consumers to shop around for the best cashback credit card, and then send their end-of-the-year cashback payment as a donation to their chosen charity. Of course, few people are likely to make a conscious effort to do this, so the card issuers rely on the large number of credit card users who typically do not make detailed evaluations about which card is best for them.

Further complexity to the relationships behind affinity credit cards lies with the major credit card systems, notably Visa, MasterCard and American Express. These are payment processing systems, each of which has developed relationships with millions of shops, goods and services suppliers throughout the world, so that cards issued with their logo will be accepted almost anywhere. Without this network of relationships, a Blackburn Rovers affinity credit card would not be of much value to an individual.

Faced with a confusing variety of credit card offers, an individual's relationship with a club, association or charity may provide a basis for choice simplification. Quite apart from the quantifiable product characteristics (e.g. interest rate charged, length of interest-free period, whether Internet access to the account is available), are a series of more qualitative relationships that an individual uses to evaluate possible credit cards. Loyalty to a card system such as Visa or MasterCard may be very low. Loyalty to an issuing bank such as MNBA or Bank of Scotland may also be fairly low. However, it is the emotional relationship that an individual has with a club, association or cause that may finally lead them to sign up for a new credit card. This may explain why the big card issuers have been so keen to pursue these triadic relationships.

Case study review questions

1. Summarize the network of relationships which lies behind an affinity credit card.

2. What are the reasons for the growth of affinity credit cards? Which other services might benefit from relationship-based marketing in the same manner as affinity credit cards?

3. What does an analysis of affinity credit card marketing say about relationship marketing being essentially about a process of 'choice reduction'?

Chapter summary and links to other chapters

An ongoing relationship between a service provider and its customers is very often a key feature of a firm's service offering. Indeed, many suppliers of manufactured goods have developed service-based relationships to differentiate themselves from their competitors. Developing ongoing relationships with customers is not a new idea, but has become popular as a result of changes in the business environment. By improving customer retention rates, the lifetime profitability of customers can be increased.

An ongoing relationship is one basis on which the service offer can be defined and distinguished from its competitors (**Chapter 2**). A relationship can improve the quality of the service encounter (**Chapter 3**) – for example, by configuring the service to meet the recorded preferences of each customer. The process of choosing between competing suppliers is facilitated by an ongoing relationship which can reduce perceived risk (**Chapter 4**). Service quality is a prerequisite for the development of an ongoing buyer–seller relationship (**Chapter 8**) and can often only be provided with appropriate selection, training and monitoring of employees (**Chapter 12**). To be effective, relationship marketing needs to embrace intermediaries (**Chapter 9**) and be given a high priority by management (**Chapter 12**). The timely collection, analysis and dissemination of information is an important part of customer relationship development (**Chapter 6**).

Chapter review questions

1. Is relationship marketing a new business idea or just traditional practices applied in a new context?

2. Critically assess methods used by banks to develop ongoing relationships with their personal customers.

3. To what extent should a service organization ensure that the style of exchange adopted with respect to its customers is similar to that adopted in relation to its employees?

4. If relationship marketing is a natural evolution from services marketing, what do you think may be the next basis on which firms develop a competitive advantage?

5. Critically define what is meant by customer loyalty in a services context.

6. Using a service company's loyalty scheme of your choice, critically assess its overall value to the company in developing profitable business.

Activity

Log on to the Internet or pick up brochures for mobile phone service providers. Compare the service offer for a 'pay as you go' phone, with a monthly contract phone. What benefits does a monthly contract give to the consumer and to the company compared to a 'pay as you go' phone? Why do you think a large market still exists for 'pay as you go' phones? What evidence do you see of mobile phone service providers seeking to move 'pay as you go' customers to an ongoing relationship with the company?

Key terms

Just-in-time (JIT) Reliably getting products to the customer just before they are needed. An essential aspect of perishable service production processes.

Loyalty Non-random repeat purchasing from a seller, with behavioural and attitudinal dimensions.

Relationship marketing A means by which an organization seeks to maintain an ongoing relationship between itself and its customers, based on continuous patterns of service delivery, rather than isolated and discrete transactions.

Selected further reading

For an introduction to the general principles of relationship marketing and its role in turning buyers into regular customers, the following are useful.
Varey, R.J. (2002) *Relationship Marketing: Dialogue and Networks in the e-Commerce Era*, Wiley, Chichester.
Christopher, M., Payne, A. and Ballantyne, D. (2001) *Relationship Marketing: Creating Stakeholder Value*, Butterworth-Heinemann, London
Sheth, J.N. and Parvatiyar, A. (2000) *Handbook of Relationship Marketing*, Sage, USA.
Arias, J.T.G. (1998) 'A relationship marketing approach to Guanxi', *European Journal of Marketing*, 32 (1–2), 145–55.

For a more thorough understanding of the theoretical underpinnings of buyer–seller relationships, the following are useful.
Morgan, R.M. and Hunt, S.D. (1994) 'The commitment–trust theory of relationship marketing', *Journal of Marketing*, 58 (July), 20–38.
Duncan, T. and Moriarty, S.E. (1998) 'A communication-based marketing model for managing relationships', *Journal of Marketing*, 62 (2), 1–14.
Healy, M., Hastings, K., Brown, L. and Gardiner, M. (2001), 'The old, the new and the complicated – A trilogy of marketing relationships', *European Journal of Marketing*, 35 (1), 182–93.

Grönroos, C. (1989) 'Defining marketing: A market-oriented approach, *European Journal of Marketing*, 23 (1), 52–60.

Palmer, A. (2000) 'Relationship marketing: A Darwinian synthesis', *European Journal of Marketing*, 35 (5), 687–704.

The processes of relationship development and dissolution have been explored in a number of papers, including the following.

Dwyer, F.R., Schurr, P.H. and Oh, S. (1987) 'Developing buyer and seller relationships', *Journal of Marketing*, 51 (April), 11–27.

Palmer, A. and Bejou, D. (1994) 'Buyer–seller relationships: A conceptual model and empirical investigation', *Journal of Marketing Management*, 6 (10), 495–512.

Rizal, A. and Buttle, F. (2002) 'Customer retention management: A reflection of theory and practice', *Marketing Intelligence and Planning*, 20 (3), 149–61.

The inter-organizational issues involved in developing relationship marketing are discussed in the following.

Ryals, L. and Knox, S. (2001) 'Cross-functional issues in the implementation of relationship marketing through customer relationship management', *European Management Journal*, 19 (5), 534–42.

Gummesson, E. (2001) *Total Relationship Marketing*, Butterworth Heinemann, London.

Malhotra, N. (2002) 'A stakeholder perspective on relationship marketing: Framework and propositions', *Journal of Relationship Marketing*, 1 (2), 3–37.

Batonda, G. and Perry, C. (2003) 'Approaches to relationship development processes in inter-firm networks', *European Journal of Marketing*, 37 (10), 1457–84.

A number of papers have sought to identify limits to the concepts of relationship marketing, highlighting the fact that it is often adopted cynically by many companies at the same time as the quality of relationships deteriorate.

O'Malley, L. and Tynan, C. (2000) 'Relationship marketing in consumer markets – Rhetoric or reality?', *European Journal of Marketing*, 34 (7), 797–815.

Zolkiewski, J. (2004) 'Relationships are not ubiquitous in marketing', *European Journal of Marketing*, 38 (1), 24–9.

Tzokas, N. and Saren, M.J. (1997) 'Some dangerous axioms of relationship marketing', *Journal of Strategic Marketing*, 6 (3), 187–96.

Palmer, A. (1996) 'Relationship marketing: A universal paradigm or management fad?', *The Learning Organization*, 3 (3), 19–26.

Finally, customer loyalty has emerged as a sub-set of the literature on relationship marketing, and the following provide useful references and a caution that loyalty to a service provider is about more than merely repetitious purchasing.

Newell, F. (2000) *Loyalty.com: Customer Relationship Management in the New Era of Internet Marketing*, McGraw-Hill, New York.

Dick, A.S. and Basu, K. (1994) 'Customer loyalty: Toward an integrated conceptual framework', *Journal of the Academy of Marketing Science*, 22, (2), 99–113.

O'Brien, L. and Charles, J. (1995) 'Do rewards really create loyalty?', *Harvard Business Review*, May–June, 75–82.

Palmer, A., McMahon-Beattie, U. and Beggs, R. (2000) 'A structural analysis of hotel sector loyalty programmes', *Journal of Strategic Marketing*, 12 (1), 54–60.

O'Malley, L. (1998) 'Can loyalty schemes really build loyalty?', *Marketing Intelligence and Planning*, 6 (1), 47–56.

References

Bagozzi, R.P. (1995) 'Reflections on relationship marketing in consumer markets', *Journal of the Academy of Marketing Science*, 23 (4), 272–7.

Baker, W.E. (1994), *Networking Smart: How to Build Relationships for Personal and Organizational Success,* McGraw-Hill, New York.

Barnes, J.G. (1994) 'Close to the customer: But is it really a relationship?', *Journal of Marketing Management*, 10 (7), 561–70.

Barry, H., Bacon, M.K. and Child, K.L., (1957) 'A cross-cultural survey of some sex differences in socialization', *Journal of Abnormal and Social Psychology*, 55, 327–32.

Becker, L.C., (1990) *Reciprocity*, University of Chicago Press, Chicago.

Berry, L.L. (2002) 'Relationship marketing of services: Perspectives from 1983 and 2000', *Journal of Relationship Marketing*, 1 (1), 59–77.

Bitner, M.J, Booms B.H. and Tetreault, M.S. (1990) 'The service encounter: Diagnosing favorable and unfavorable incidents', *Journal of Marketing*, 54 (January), 71–84.

Boulding, W., Kalra, A., Staelin, R. and Zeithaml, V.A. (1993). 'A dynamic process model of service quality: From expectations to behavioral intentions', *Journal of Marketing Research*, 30 (February), 7–27.

Burt, R. (1992) *Structural Holes: The Social Structure of Competition*, Harvard University Press.

Chrisopher, M., Payne, A. and Ballantyne, D. (1991) *Relationship Marketing*, Butterworth-Heinemann.

Colgate, M. and Hedge, R. (2001) 'An investigation into the switching process in retail banking services', *International Journal of Bank Marketing*, 19 (5), 201–12.

Copulsky, J.R. and Wolf, M.J. (1990) 'Relationship marketing: Positioning for the future', *Journal of Business Strategy* (July/August), 16–20.

Crosby, L.A., Evans, K.R. and Cowles, D. (1990) 'Relationship quality in services selling: An interpersonal influence perspective', *Journal of Marketing*, 54 (July), 68–81.

Cunningham, M.T. and Turnbull, P.W. (1982) 'Inter-organizational personal contact patterns', in H. Hakansson (ed.), *International Marketing and Purchasing of Industrial Goods*, John Wiley, New York.

Cutts, L. (1992) 'Capitalism in Japan: Cartels and Keiretsu', *Harvard Business Review* 70 (July/August), 48–55.

Datamonitor (2003) *Affinity Marketing in UK Retail Banking*, Datamonitor, London.

Day, G.S. and Wensley, R. (1983) 'Marketing theory with a strategic orientation', *Journal of Marketing*, 47 (Fall), 79–89.

Dick, A.S. and Basu K. (1994) 'Customer loyalty: Toward an integrated conceptual framework', *Journal of the Academy of Marketing Science*, 22 (2), 99–113.

Dwyer, F.R, Schurr, P.H. and Oh, S. (1987) 'Developing buyer and seller relationships', *Journal of Marketing*, 51 (April), 11–27.

Ford, D. (1981) 'The development of buyer–seller relationships in industrial markets', *European Journal of Marketing*, 14, 339–53.

Gilbert, D.C. and Karabeyekian, V. (1995) 'The frequent flyer mess – A comparison of programmes in the USA and Europe', *Journal of Vacation Marketing*, 1 (3), 248–56.

Goodwin, C. and Ross, I. (1992) 'Consumer responses to service failures: Influence of procedural and interactional fairness perceptions', *Journal of Business Research*, 25 (September), 149–63.

Grönroos, C. (1989) Defining marketing: A market-oriented approach, *European Journal of Marketing*, 23 (1), 52–60.

Grönroos, C. (1994) 'From marketing mix to relationship marketing', *Management Decision*, 32 (1), 4–20.

Gummesson, E. (2003) 'Many-to-many marketing in the new network economy', paper presented at the 11th International Colloquium in International Marketing, University of Gloucestershire, Cheltenham.

Hamel, G., Doz, Y. and Prahalad, C.K. (1989), 'Collaborate with your competitors – and win', *Harvard Business Review*, 67 (January/February), 133–9.

Han, S.L., Wilson, D.T. and Dant, S.P. (1993) 'Buyer–supplier relationships today', *Industrial Marketing Management*, 22, 331–8.

Hart, C.W.L., Sasser, W.E. Jr and Heskett, J.L. (1990) 'The profitable art of service recovery', *Harvard Business Review*, (July–August), 148–56.

Heide, J.B. (1994) 'Interorganizational governance in marketing channels', *Journal of Marketing*, 58 (January), 71–85.

Kanter, R.M. (1994) 'Collaborative advantage', *Harvard Business Review*, 72 (July– August), 96–108.

Kaufmann, C.F. and Stern, L.W. (1992) 'Relational exchange, contracting norms and conflict in industrial exchange', in G.L.C Frazier (ed.), *Advances in Distribution Channel Research*, Vol. 1, 135–59.

Kelley, S.W. and Davis, M.A. (1994) 'Antecedents to customer expectations for service recovery', *Journal of the Academy of Marketing Science*, 22 (1), 52–61.

Liljander, V. and Strandvik, T. (1995) 'The nature of customer relationships in services', in T.A. Swartz, D.E. Bowen and S.W. Brown (eds), *Advances in Services Marketing and Management*, Vol. 4, JAI Press, London.

Macneil, I.R. (1980) *The New Social Contract: An Inquiry into Modern Contractual Relations*, Yale University Press, New Haven, CT.

Malhotra, N. (2002) 'A stakeholder perspective on relationship marketing: Framework and propositions', *Journal of Relationship Marketing*, 1 (2), 3–37.

Meyers-Levy, J. and Sternthal, B. (1991) 'Gender differences in the use of message cues and judgements', *Journal of Marketing Research*, 28 (February), 84–96.

Morgan, R. and Hunt, S. (1994) 'The commitment–trust theory of relationship marketing', *Journal of Marketing* 58 (3), 20–38.

Mortished, C. (1999) 'BA fined £4m over illegal sweeteners', *The Times*, 15 July, 2.

Mowlana, H. and Smith, G. (1993) 'Tourism in a global context: The case of frequent traveller programmes', *Journal of Travel Research*, Winter, 7–20.

Narver, J.C. and Slater, S.F. (1990) 'The effect of a market orientation on business profitability', *Journal of Marketing* (October), 20–35.

O'Brien, L. and Jones, C. (1995) 'Do rewards really create loyalty?', *Harvard Business Review* (May–June), 75–82.

Oliver R. (1996) 'Equity: how consumers interpret fairness', in R. Oliver (ed.), *Satisfaction: A Behavioral Perspective on the Consumer*, McGraw-Hill Series in Marketing, McGraw-Hill, USA, 193–215.

Palmer, A. and Bejou, D. (1994) 'Buyer–seller relationships: A conceptual model and empirical investigation', *Journal of Marketing Management*, 6 (10), 495–512.

Palmer, A. and Bejou, D. (1995) 'The role of gender in the development of buyer–seller relationships', *International Journal of Bank Marketing*, 13 (3), 18–27.

Perry, C., Cavaye, A. and Coote, L. (2002) 'Technical and social bonds within business-to-business relationships', *Journal of Business and Industrial Marketing*, 17 (1), 75–88.

Pfeffer, J. and Salanick, G.R. (1978) *The External Control of Organizations*, Harper & Row, New York.

Reichheld, F.F. (1993) 'Loyalty based management', *Harvard Business Review*, 71 (2), 64–73.

Reichheld, F.F. and Sasser, W.E. (1990), 'Zero defections', *Harvard Business Review*, 68 (5), 105–11.

Reinartz, W. and Kumar, V. (2003) 'The impact of customer relationship characteristics on profitable lifetime duration', *Journal of Marketing*, 67 (1), 77–99.

Shaw, K., Fenwick J. and Foreman, A. (1993) 'Client and contractor roles in local government: Some observations in managing the split', *Local Government Policy Making*, 20 (2), 22–7.

Sheth, J. and Parvatiyar, A. (2002) 'Evolving relationship marketing into a discipline', *Journal of Relationship Marketing*, 1 (1), 3–16.

Turnbull, P.W. and Wilson, D.T. (1989) 'Developing and protecting profitable customer relationships', *Industrial Marketing Management*, 18, 233–8.

Uncles, M.D., Dowling, G.R. and Hammond, K. (2003) 'Customer loyalty and customer loyalty programs', *Journal of Consumer Marketing*, 20 (4), 294–316.

Webster, F.E. (1992) 'The changing role of marketing in the corporation', *Journal of Marketing*, 56 (October), 1–17.

Williamson, O.E. (1985) *The Economic Institutions of Capitalism*, The Free Press, New York.

Williamson, O. (1993) 'Calculativeness, trust, and economic organization', *Journal of Law and Economics*, 34, 453–500.

Managing knowledge

Learning objectives

This chapter will explain:

- knowledge as a core competence of service organizations

- the role of information in allowing service organizations to make better-informed plans for the future

- methods of effectively managing customer relationships

- customer analysis and profiling

- the effects of service intangibility on market research processes

- methods used to forecast demand for services

- performance monitoring and control.

6.1 **Introduction**

Knowledge management permeates many activities of a service organization and should cut across departmental boundaries. These are some of the more common benefits which result from effective knowledge management.

- *Customer information management.* Most companies need to assess what information they have on their customers and how individuals within the organization can use that information most effectively. For example, salespeople should know when they last talked with a customer, what issues that customer is facing and what he or she is thinking about buying six months from now. Without capturing that knowledge, a company can lose valuable information when this salesperson leaves. Even if he or she stays, there might be other people within the organization who could use this information – for example, service support staff.

- *Demand forecasting.* A company should have superior knowledge not just about demand conditions as they are today, but as they are likely to develop over the next few months or years. By being better informed, a company can downsize or expand capacity more effectively.

- *New service development.* By looking at historical trends and retaining knowledge about competitors and changes in the marketing environment, a company can stay ahead in new service development. Very often, someone within an organization would already have information relevant to a new service proposal, so an effective knowledge management system can prevent the company wasting time in 're-inventing the wheel'.

- *Performance monitoring.* A company should have knowledge about which of its human and physical assets are performing effectively so that future procurement can reflect proven performance. Staff recruiters, for example, should have full knowledge about the performance patterns of different types of employees.

The transition from individuals' information to corporate knowledge requires sharing of knowledge by all concerned. This raises problems where employees perceive that knowledge is a powerful asset which they can use in their negotiations with senior management or other functional departments. A knowledge management programme is needed to break down a *laissez-faire* attitude, and would typically include the following elements:

- a strong knowledge-sharing culture, which can only emerge over time with the development of trust

- measures to monitor that sharing, which may be reflected in individuals' performance reviews

- technology to facilitate knowledge transfer, which should be as user-friendly as possible

- established practices for the capture and sharing of knowledge – without clearly defined procedures, the technology is of only limited value

■ leadership and senior management commitment to sharing information – if senior management doesn't share information, why should anyone else bother?

Marketing information cannot in itself produce decisions – it merely provides data which must be interpreted by marketing managers. As an inter-functional integrator, marketing information draws data from all functional areas of an organization, which in turn use data to focus on meeting customers' needs more effectively. Increasingly, information technology is allowing firms to deal with their customers on a one-to-one basis. Research involving employees, both as sources of information and recipients of research findings, assumes importance as an integrating device.

As information collection, processing, transmission and storage technologies improve, information is becoming more accessible not just to one particular organization, but also to its competitors. Attention is therefore moving away from how information is collected, to who is best able to make use of the information. It is too simple to say that marketing managers commission data collection by technical experts and make decisions on the basis of this data.

Recent technological innovations – for example, electronic point of sale (EPoS) systems and web-based services – have enabled service companies to greatly enhance the quality of their core services in terms of speed, accuracy and consistency. In turn, the resulting increase in operational efficiency, combined with the additional information which it is now possible to generate, has allowed service organizations to improve other areas of their service offering – such as the development of customer loyalty programmes – as a means of gaining competitive advantage. At the same time, the increasing ease with which data can be collected and disseminated has made it easier for services companies to manage service quality by setting quantifiable objectives that can be monitored effectively.

Organizations must also understand the effects of other environmental factors such as the state of the local or national economy. Without this broader environmental information, routine pieces of marketing research information – such as the market share held by a company's brands over the past year – cannot be interpreted meaningfully. Marketing information allows management to improve its strategic planning, tactical implementation of programmes and its monitoring and control. A practical problem is that information is typically much more difficult to obtain to meet strategic planning needs than it is to meet operational and control needs. There can be a danger of marketing managers focusing too heavily on information which is easily available at the expense of that which is needed.

6.1.1 **What is meant by the knowledge-based organization?**

Knowledge is one of the greatest assets of most service organizations and its contribution to sustainable competitive advantage has been noted by many (e.g. Quinn, 1992; Drucker, 1999). For some professional service providers, such as lawyers and medical consultants, specialist knowledge held by staff can be the service provider's principal source of competitive advantage. In a broader sense, information represents a bridge between the organization and its environment and is the means by which a picture of the changing environment is built up within the organization. Marketing management is responsible for turning information-based knowledge into specific marketing plans.

Ikujiro Nonaka began an article in the *Harvard Business Review* with a simple statement: 'In an economy where the only certainty is uncertainty, the one sure source of lasting competitive advantage is knowledge' (Nonaka, 1991). A firm's knowledge base is likely to include, among other things, an understanding of the precise needs of customers; how those needs are likely to change over time; how those needs are satisfied in terms of efficient and effective production systems and an understanding of competitors' activities. We are probably all familiar with service organizations where knowledge seems to be very poor – the reservation which is mixed up, the delivery which does not happen as specified, or junk mail which is of no interest at all. On the other hand, customers may revel in a company which delivers the right service at the right time and clearly demonstrates that it is knowledgeable about all aspects of the transaction. The small business owner may have been able to achieve all of this in his or her head, but in large organizations, the task of managing knowledge becomes much more complex. Where it is done well, it can be a significant contributor to a firm's sustainable competitive advantage.

Let us begin by defining the terms 'knowledge' and 'information'. Even though in some senses they may be used interchangeably, many writers have suggested that the two concepts are quite distinct. In fact, knowledge is a much more all-encompassing term which incorporates the concept of beliefs that are based on information. It also depends on the commitment and understanding of the individual holding these beliefs, which are affected by interaction and the development of judgement, behaviour and attitude (Berger and Luckmann, 1966). Knowledge only has meaning in the context of a process or capacity to act. Drucker noted that, 'There is no such thing as knowledge management, there are only knowledgeable people. Information only becomes knowledge in the hands of someone who knows what to do with it' (Drucker, 1999). Knowledge, then, is evidenced by its association with actions, and its source can be found in a combination of information, social interaction and contextual situations which affect the knowledge accumulation process at an individual level.

Here we need to distinguish between knowledge at the level of the individual and at the level of the organization. Organizational knowledge comprises shared understandings and is created within the company by means of information and social interaction and provides potential for development. It is this form of knowledge that is at the heart of **knowledge management**. Organizational progress is made when knowledge moves from the domain of the individual to that of the organization.

Two different types of knowledge can be identified. First, there is knowledge which is easily definable and is accessible, often referred to as 'explicit' knowledge. This type of knowledge can be readily quantified and passed between individuals in the form of words and numbers. Because it is easily communicated it is relatively easy to manage.

Knowledge management is concerned with ensuring that the explicit knowledge of individuals becomes a part of the organizational knowledge base and that it is used efficiently and contributes where necessary to changes in work practices, processes and products. This, however, is not the limit of knowledge management. The second type of knowledge comprises the accumulated knowledge of individuals which is not explicit, but which can still be important to the successful operation of an organization. This type of knowledge, often known as 'tacit' knowledge is not easy to see or express, it is highly personal and is rooted in an individual's experiences, attitudes, values and behaviour patterns. This type of 'tacit knowledge' can be much more difficult to formalize and disseminate within an organization. If tacit knowledge can be captured, mobilized and turned into explicit knowledge it would then be accessible to others in the organization and would enable the organization to progress rather than have individuals within it having to continually relearn from the same point. The owner of a small service business could have all of this information readily available to him in his head. The challenge taken on by many large corporations is to emulate the knowledge management of the small business owner. One outcome of a knowledge-based organization has often been referred to as the 'learning organization' in which the challenge is to learn at the corporate level from what is known by the individuals that make up the organization.

Finding true knowledge on the shop floor?

Information is often described as management's window on the world. But what happens if management staff work in a large corporate head office, far removed from customers and day-to-day operations? It is sadly all too familiar for senior management staff to become cut off from the service operations they manage. A recent BBC television series, *Back to the Floor*, invited chief executives to spend a few days changing their role to that of a front-line employee. In one case, the chief executive of the grocery retailer Sainsbury's seemed to be oblivious to customers' annoyance with shopping trolley design and availability, and, in another, the chief executive of Pickfords Removals couldn't understand why the company was so inflexible when minor changes in customers' requirements occurred. Of course, the managers of small businesses do not generally have such problems as they are in regular contact with their customers and do not need structured information management systems to give them a window on the world. Their success in keeping in touch with customers has led many larger businesses to emulate some of their practices. 'Management by walking about' has become a popular way in which senior executives try to gain information about their marketing environment which is not immediately apparent from structured reporting systems. Some companies have adopted a formal system of role exchanges where senior executives spend a period at the sharp end of their business.

6.2 **Marketing information systems**

Many analyses of organizations' information collection and dissemination activities take a systems perspective. The collection of marketing information can be seen as one sub-system of a much larger knowledge management system, which was discussed earlier. Other component information systems typically include production, financial and human resource management systems. In a well-designed knowledge management system, the barriers between these component systems should be conceptual rather than real – for example, sales information is of value to all of these sub-systems to a greater or lesser extent (see Figure 6.1).

In so far as a marketing information sub-system can be identified, it can conceptually be seen as comprising four principal components, although in practice they are operationally interrelated:

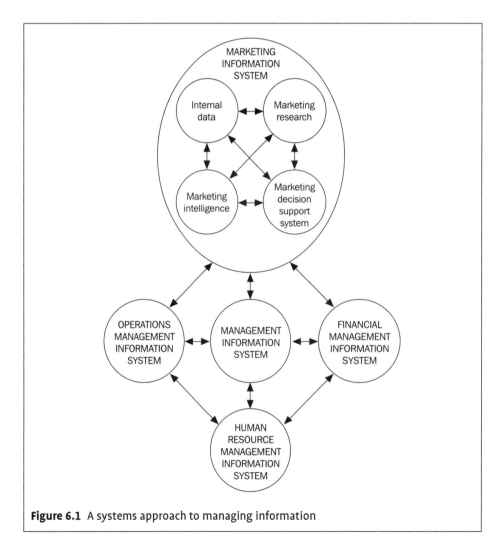

Figure 6.1 A systems approach to managing information

1. Much information is generated internally within organizations, particularly in respect of customer orders and operations. By carefully arranging its collection and dissemination, internal data can provide a constant and up-to-date flow of information at relatively little cost, useful for both planning and control functions.

2. Marketing research is that part of the system concerned with the structured collection of marketing information. This can provide both routine information about marketing effectiveness – such as brand awareness levels or delivery performance – and one-off studies, such as changing attitudes towards diet or the pattern of income distribution.

3. Marketing intelligence comprises the procedures and sources used by marketing management to obtain pertinent information about developments in their marketing environment. It complements the marketing research system; whereas the latter tends to focus on structured and largely quantifiable data collection procedures, intelligence gathering concentrates on picking up relatively intangible ideas and trends. Marketing management can gather this intelligence from a number of sources, such as newspapers, specialized cutting services, employees who are in regular contact with market developments, intermediaries and suppliers to the company, as well as specialized consultants. It has been noted by Carson *et al.* (2001) that for many small business owners, this form of research is inseparable from daily business. According to their study, research by networking is 'informal, often discreet, interactive, interchangeable, integrated, habitual, reactive, individualistic, and highly focused on the enterprise' (2001, p. 56).

4. Marketing decision support systems comprise a set of models that allow forecasts to be made. Information is not only an input to such models, in that data are needed to calibrate a model, but also an output, in that models provide information on which decisions can be based. Models are frequently used in service outlet location decisions (see Chapter 9), where historical data may have established a relationship between one variable (e.g. the level of sales achieved by a particular service outlet) and other variables (e.g. pedestrian traffic in a street). Predicting the sales level of a proposed new outlet then becomes a matter of measuring pedestrian traffic at a proposed site, feeding this information into the model and calculating the predicted sales level.

For those organizations that have set up **marketing information systems**, a number of factors will determine their effectiveness, as outlined below.

- *The accuracy with which the information needs of the organization have been defined.* Needs can themselves be difficult to identify and it can be very difficult to identify the boundaries of the firm's environments and to separate relevance from irrelevance. This is a particular problem for large multi-service firms. The mission statement of an organization may give some indication of the boundaries for its environmental search – for example, many banks have mission statements which talk about becoming a dominant provider of financial services in their domestic market. The information needs therefore include anything related to the broader environment of financial services rather than the narrower field of banking.

- *The extensiveness of the search for information.* A balance has to be struck between the need for information and the cost of collecting it. The most critical elements of the marketing environment must be identified and the cost of collecting relevant information weighed against the cost which would result from inaccurate information.

- *The appropriateness of the sources of information.* Information for decision-making can typically be obtained from numerous sources, for example quality perceptions can be measured using a variety of quantitative and qualitative techniques. Companies often rely on the former when only the latter can give a depth of understanding which makes for better management decisions. Successful services companies use a variety of appropriate sources of information.

- *The speed of communication.* The marketing information system will only be effective if information is communicated quickly and to the people capable of acting on it. Deciding what information to withhold from an individual and the concise reporting of relevant information can be as important as deciding what information to include if information overload is to be avoided.

Paralysis by analysis?

Is marketing an art or a science? This age-old debate has been given new impetus in recent times by developments in information technology which allow marketing managers to make supposedly scientific decisions, rather than relying on gut instinct. But when all marketing managers have access to the same data analysis packages, might this not result in a series of 'me-too' decisions being made? A survey carried out in 1997 by Taylor Nelson found that 59% of 105 marketers who were interviewed believed that marketing is more of an art than a science. Many marketing managers seemed to be sheltering behind their piles of numbers and used research merely as a justification for their earlier decisions.

Another picture was painted by research commissioned for the decision support software specialist Business Objectives into the way managers use information to make decisions. Of 100 senior managers from the *Times* Top 1000 companies, more than three-quarters claimed to rely mainly on gut instinct rather than hard facts when making decisions. A total of 60% of managers claimed not to receive the right quality or quantity of information to make a decision, even though most of them had access to a personal computer. More worryingly, a majority of sales and marketing managers surveyed claimed that they rely on other people for information which they are dubious about, or which is out of date. The picture emerged of an information underclass that relies on instinctive decision-making processes.

Many of the great marketing developments of recent times have come about from individuals taking inspired decisions which might have seemed irrational when assessed by scientific processes. It must be remembered that information cannot in itself give answers. Indeed too much information can lead to 'paralysis by analysis'. In a turbulent marketing environment, it is the quality of interpretation of data which gives a firm a competitive advantage. Would Virgin Atlantic ever have taken to the air had the entrepreneur Richard Branson not had the courage of his convictions by ignoring the so-called experts' research advice?

These reported studies seem to be consistent with Smith and Dexter's (2001) observation that 'All knowledge starts with prejudice' in which information-gathering is punctuated by a constant 'shuttling between the initial pet theory and the available evidence', as a fit between the two is sought. Together, the reported research leaves unanswered the question of whether managers should be criticized for their failure to use hard information, or applauded for being bold and creative in their decision-making.

6.3 **Managing customer information**

It has been noted in previous chapters that ongoing buyer–seller relationships have become a source of competitive advantage. The quality of the relationship can become a defining characteristic of a service. Many customers choose to go back to the same hotel chain or airline because of the quality of the relationship on offer. This can refer to the ability of the customer to rapidly reorder a service without having to explain their details again; the ability of the service provider to configure the service offer to the customer's changing needs; or it could be that a customer finds the rewards offered by a service provider's loyalty programme sufficiently attractive to justify going back to a company.

Whatever the reason for a relationship developing, an important part in creating and sustaining that relationship is likely to be made by information held about customers. A small business owner, such as a small shopkeeper or guest house owner may have the ability to keep in their head all the information that they need in order to deliver a high quality of relationship, but in a large service organization, information about individual customers needs to be shared, so that, for example, a customer of a hotel chain will find their personal details readily on hand every time they deal with the chain's hotels or reservations office. They should not need to explain each time that their preference is for a non-smoking room, or be asked for details of their loyalty programme each time.

Managing information about customers has become an increasingly complex task as service organizations have grown in size and customers' expectations of seamless service delivery have become greater. Unfortunately, it is not uncommon to find firms that have invested heavily in IT systems to handle customer information, only to discover that the information may actually hinder rather than help the task of creating more effective customer relationships. In too many organizations, numerous databases and customer service systems exist which are not linked to each other. A customer may make an initial enquiry to a freefone telephone line and make a subsequent order from another system within the company which is not connected to the initial enquiry line. The rapid growth of some companies, changes in corporate information technology policy and mergers and demergers have, sadly, resulted in disconnected information systems being a not uncommon phenomenon.

Customer relationship management (CRM) has become a generic term to describe processes that essentially seek to join up a company's customer-focused information systems and to track dealings with individual customers throughout the relationship life cycle. Many companies offer technological solutions which promise integrated information management. However, this is of little value if management does not give the leadership and create a culture which is conducive to integrated systems.

There are many definitions of customer relationship management which reflect the varying scope of CRM within different companies. It is defined here as:

The systems and processes used by an organization to integrate all sources of information about a customer so that the organization can meet individual customers' needs more effectively and efficiently.

One reason for variation in definitions is that organizations may pay differing levels of attention to the components of CRM (Figure 6.2). The basic components can be described as:

- data collection and management

- customer analysis and profiling

- computer-aided sales support

- customer information and service.

Of course, these are not mutually exclusive components, but form the basis for the following discussion.

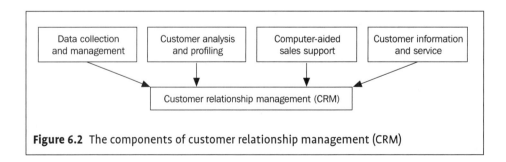

Figure 6.2 The components of customer relationship management (CRM)

6.3.1 **Data collection and management**

During the 1990s a whole new industry based on managing customer information emerged. A company's database is likely to be constructed from a number of sources, including its own trading records, bought-in lists and bought-in database services from specialized service providers.

A customer is likely to have started life with an organization as a *prospect*. Although CRM is essentially about maintaining ongoing relationships with customers, it must be remembered that customers have to be acquired in the first place. To build up a database of prospects, a company would often buy in the services of specialist companies that offer database management services. One supplier of database management services is Experian, which has compiled a database of consumers and businesses from, among other sources:

■ the Electoral Roll, listing 42 million adults

■ investor data from 630 company share registers, comprising 8.5 million individuals

■ lifestyle data from ongoing and ad hoc surveys, which establish lifestyle and product purchasing data and hold one million records

■ home data, including details on commercial and residential properties such as value, location, size, etc.

■ telephone data, matching telephone numbers and addresses for 14 million individuals

■ County Court judgments.

A client company can purge and merge these lists to form its own database. It is crucial for a company to maintain its list by removing duplicated names and the names of those who do not want to, or should not, be contacted.

From this acquired data, a company will select certain prospects to target with a service offer (see below). The next task is to collect and record information about those prospects who have gone on to become customers. At first, it may be quite easy to capture the response to an initial sales offer, but a good database will go on to capture information from all of the 'touchpoints' that a customer has with the organization. Information may typically come from:

■ orders received via mail, telephone or Internet

■ payments received by cheque, standing order or credit card

■ enquiries made by mail, phone and Internet for further services

■ comments and complaints received from the customer

■ information from survey questionnaires that the customer may have completed.

At the same time as the company is collecting information directly from its customers, it may also be buying in supplementary data about them. At the least it would hope to acquire additional demographic data (for example, the customers might not have stated at the time of first order their age and whether they had children – this information may be obtained either directly from the customers, or bought in from another company). The company is also likely to periodically buy in credit-worthiness data and other lifestyle data.

How much data should a company collect about its customers? A trade-off has to be made between the cost and inconvenience of collecting information and the benefits obtained. Is it really worthwhile for a company to ask questions to prospective customers the first time they call? Will this be regarded as too intrusive? Will it add to costs by slowing up the process of taking customers' orders? Will the information actually be used to profitably improve sales and service delivery?

Merging and updating databases can be a very complex task, especially where a company has multiple points of access by customers. It is quite common to find telephone sales and Internet sales databases, for example, not linked to each other. The problem of linkages is particularly great where companies have merged or been acquired, and the resulting 'legacy' systems do not interface easily with each other. It is reported that when Lloyds Bank merged with Trustee Savings Bank (TSB), it took over two years for both banks' customer databases to be integrated effectively.

6.3.2 Customer analysis and profiling

A clear understanding of the needs of individual customers is essential if their needs are to be catered for effectively and efficiently. A key to successful customer relationship management is the analysis of data to produce models of buyer behaviour. A well-developed database can have a huge number of pieces of information available about each customer – for example, it has been estimated that Royal Bank of Canada has an average of 1200 data points on each of its customers (Thompson, 2001). Having amassed a lot of data from previous sales, a company can identify the variables which are associated with sales success. Analysts are no longer constrained by simple correlation and regression techniques to identify causative factors. Data mining using techniques such as 'fuzzy logic' can look for patterns in the data which might not have been expected at the outset. You will recall from Chapter 4 that Tesco used data-mining techniques, based on shopping basket analysis and loyalty card information, to identify a link between beer and nappy sales. Initial correlations became more apparent when a model was developed which looked at specific stores at specific times of the day and week.

Where a company has a large database of customers, it could further refine its model by conducting experiments. It would typically offer a number of different service propositions to two or more sub-samples of the database, who are otherwise similar in terms of demographics etc. The company would monitor the response to each offer which was put to the groups. It would typically measure a number of response indicators, from short term to long term. At the very least, it would record whether the customer made an enquiry in response to the service offer. It would then record whether an order was made, and may, as part of its experimental framework, go on to record whether the customer went on to buy further services from the company. On the basis of an experiment with a sub-sample of its database, the company may then roll out the most successful service offer to everyone in its database who satisfies some specified criteria.

Profiling is about more than just generating sales leads or cross-selling additional services to existing customers. Analysis is commonly used to analyse the following.

■ *The current profitability of individual customers, or groups of customers.* Many service companies divide their customers into categories based on their profitability (e.g. UK banks have been known to refer to segments of 'lemons' who are of little long-term value, and 'peaches' and 'plums' who offer better prospects for profit).

■ *The expected lifetime value of each customer, based on models developed of customer longevity.* Models can sometimes only build up a very general picture of future profitability, for example in the way that banks have identified that student customers in general, and medical students in particular, are likely to go on to become their most profitable customers. Where there is evidence of future lifetime profits, a service company may consider it worthwhile incurring a loss in the short term (as banks frequently do with student bank accounts).

■ *Sources of service failure can be identified* and an analysis undertaken to see whether failures are associated with particular types of customer.

■ *A model can be developed to identify early warning signs that a customer is about to defect from the company.* Has a bank customer suddenly started using a rival bank's ATMs? Have they initiated new direct debits to a rival financial service provider? These may be signals that a customer is likely to defect, and if they are spotted in time, the bank might take action (e.g. a promotional offer to reward loyalty) which might reduce the chances of defection actually occurring.

■ *Based on a profitability analysis, a company can identify which customers should be 'exited'.* Many companies have a segment of customers who incur costs to service, but may generate insufficient revenue to allow a profit. However, care must be taken to avoid exiting customers who have the potential to become profitable, but which has not been realized yet. Again, a well-developed model should allow improved multi-variate predictions of which customers have long-term profit potential.

6.3.3 **Computer-aided sales support**

When the customer database is made accessible to sales teams (through a modem), it has the potential to enhance their performance substantially. For companies involved in business-to-business services, the database may hold company information such as product listings, specifications, availability and pricing details. Customer and potential customer details may include buyer details, contact details, quotations outstanding, order status, previous purchases, installed equipment and purchases from competitors. It is also possible to store information about competitors on the database, thereby making it directly available to the field salesforce where it is most needed, rather than being hidden away in inaccessible, centrally held files. As well as improving the productivity of sales personnel, a database can improve the quality of sales leads generated.

6.3.4 Customer information and service (CIS)

There are many reasons why customers and potential customers may wish to contact a supplier of services direct. Companies may need to respond to enquiries about the bill (public utilities), statements (banks), amount outstanding on a loan (finance company), adjusting monthly investment (pension company), technical questions (Internet service providers), availability (package holidays) or schedules (flights).

Provision of advice and information is now expected by customers immediately, either via the phone, fax, e-mail or Internet. Increasingly, customers expect a supplier to have all of the information available at one contact point, without being passed around from department to department and from one nameless person to another only to be left with a vague promise of a call back.

Customer helplines are an important feature offered by a growing number of companies. The database and computerized telephone systems now provide the opportunity for companies to deal directly with their customers in a speedy and informed manner. Companies often use helplines to understand the causes of service failure and to enable them to put things right before a dissatisfied customer tells friends about it.

A 'Wild West' for data?

The Internet has spawned a new generation of service organizations who seemingly have boundless amounts of data. But how valuable is this data to researchers in the service sector?

One of the big advantages of doing business through the Internet is that all transactions are recorded in a form that is immediately available for analysis. No more transcribing the newspaper enquiry coupon into a database or recording the essence of a customer's telephone call in a series of codes to be saved in a database. In both cases, creating a database can be time consuming, costly and subject to human transcription error – better to let customers enter the data themselves. Where a prospective customer approaches a company's website with an enquiry, the fact can be recorded automatically. Fairly simple software will allow a company to record how the visitor got to its site; how long was spent at each page, the results of the visit (e.g. a request for further information; quotation request, purchase order); and where he or she went after leaving the site. More sophisticated data is provided by companies such as doubleclick.com which insert 'cookies' into users' PCs – often without their knowledge – which are then used to send back to the company information about all of the sites that the user has visited. This can be very valuable information that third-party companies buy to improve their targeting. Of course, collecting information through use of such 'spyware' raises ethical questions.

Faced with such a huge amount of research data, just how valuable is it to marketers? Inevitably, there are some gems amidst a mass of debris. The ability to measure response rates to different page designs and/or different links to a company's site can sharpen marketers' analytic skills and improve their accountability for their actions. It is no longer good enough to just have a hunch that a website is effective when there is copious information to measure its performance.

How useful are the statistics that marketers routinely collect from the web? Simple records of visitors to a website are prone to many errors, including the problem of identifying 'unique' visitors from those who might repeatedly enter and leave a site in quick succession. Many apparent visits are actually hits recorded by 'spiders' – search engines that routinely seek out websites for indexing. A bigger problem of Internet data is the difficulty that often prevents Internet-based databases being integrated with existing records of consumer behaviour, lifestyle and attitudes. With concerns over Internet security remaining high, individuals may be reluctant to divulge personal information through the Internet which would allow a company to build up a full picture. Unfortunately, the people with the greatest concerns about privacy are often the same groups as those that many companies are most interested in learning more about (see Graeff and Harmon, 2002).

In its early days of development, the Internet has been described as the new 'Wild West', in which rules are few and far between and anything goes. Unfortunately, this description can also be applied to many of the statistics circulating about website usage, with potential advertisers unsure about the true value of advertising on a particular site. More recently, the development of audit schemes (e.g. VeriSign) have helped to provide some reassurance to users about the validity of web statistics.

The development of the Internet as a marketing research tool has not been helped by the sometimes confused communications between marketing and IT departments within a company, highlighted in a report published by the Chartered Institute of Marketing in 2000. IT systems often fail to meet marketers' expectations because needs have not been defined accurately. As in other aspects of marketing, getting the inter-functional dynamics of a company right can be crucial in the quest for competitive advantage, and may explain the success of, among others, Direct Line Insurance and First Direct.

The creation of call centres has become a major service activity in its own right, with banks, airlines, insurance companies and telephone companies, among others, establishing large centres which can handle all incoming calls efficiently using the latest technology. As an example, American Airlines decided to locate its new European reservation centre in Ireland, which was predicted to result in savings of £20 million as it phased out five regional offices throughout Europe. The teleservicing centre was expected to handle 2.5 million calls a year, employing 220 multi-lingual staff.

6.3.5 Assessing the effectiveness of customer relationship management

Customer relationship management (CRM) is a good idea in theory, but unfortunately it too often fails to be effective in practice. There have been reports suggesting that, typically, three-quarters of CRM systems fail to deliver the promised integration of customer information (Hellweg, 2002). In a study by Bligh and Turk (2004) of chief executives in Ireland, a majority of respondents claimed to be disappointed with the results of their CRM system, and 20% reported that their CRM initiatives had not only failed to deliver profitable growth but had actually damaged customer relationships. A large number of firms thought that the large volume of data gathered in their CRM did not improve relationships with their customers.

The evident failings of many CRM systems remind us that CRM is not just a technological solution provided by installing software in the company (Peppard, 2001). CRM is really about an entire change of mindset in which the organization as a whole becomes customer oriented and focuses on the ongoing needs of customers, just as the small shopkeeper is able to do. Even integration of the technology of customer relationship management fails in many companies, with a failure to bring together otherwise free-standing applications such as sales automation, data-mining tools and business applications. Without such integration, CRM is likely to be ineffective (not providing what customers want) and inefficient (providing a given level of customer service at a higher cost to the company than is necessary). In one study of Australian financial services companies, no significant and positive relationship was found between companies' increased use of information technology and the productivity of their customer relationship management activities (Terziovski et al., 2003).

The activities of CRM have been increasingly constrained by legislation. In the UK, the Data Protection Act 1998, based on an EU directive, limits the ability of a company to use information which it has collected in a different area of business. So if a solicitor had built up a database of clients buying its legal services, that data could not then be used to try to sell unrelated financial services, unless the client had specifically agreed. This has limited the database-building activities of many large service organizations whose ability to cross-sell services is made difficult. Furthermore, the Competition Commission makes it difficult for companies who are dominant in one market to use customer information collected in that market to promote services in other markets, even if they are related. In the UK, British Telecom is a dominant provider of domestic telephone services. It has been held against the public interest that the company should use its database to cross-sell security alarm systems which are connected through the telephone network.

For some companies, the focus of information management is not so much the *customers*, but their *assets*. In the case of high-value, long-life assets, such as industrial machinery and cars, companies may keep a record of all services performed on that asset. The benefit of this approach becomes apparent when an asset changes hands and the new owner can gain access to its complete service history. Value is added in the form of the higher resale values which customers achieve.

A challenge to customer relationship management comes from the opposite perspective of *customer managed relationships*. So far, CRM has been presented as something which is done by sellers to manipulate buyers, even if the use of the word 'relationship' might suggest some sense of mutuality or equality in the relationship. The idea of buyers managing their suppliers is nothing new in business-to-business markets. The relationship between UK grocery supermarket buyers and grocery manufacturers has not in recent times been generally described as one where the supplier manages the relationship. The size of the top five retailers has given them considerable power to determine the nature of the relationships that they have with their suppliers, including terms of delivery, the range of products bought, and returned goods policy. In business-to-consumer markets, there is some evidence that customers are taking an increasingly active role in managing their relationships. Of course, in highly competitive markets, customers can effectively control a relationship by deciding whether to continue with it or to defect. In addition to this, the facilities open to private consumers to manage their suppliers appear to be increasing. One financial services website, www.blueyonder.co.uk, for example, permits customers to place their entire bank and savings accounts on one website, allowing apparently seamless management of a large number of suppliers' financial services from one site.

6.4 **Forward planning with marketing research**

Marketing research is an important source of a company's knowledge. As a planning tool, marketing research provides management with market- and product-specific information, which allows it to minimize the degree of uncertainty in planning its future marketing effort. This risk minimization function can apply to the whole of the marketing operation, or to any of its constituent parts, such as advertising.

It is difficult to define precisely the exact functions of marketing research within a marketing information system, as organizations differ widely in size and structure. However, in Figure 6.3, an attempt has been made to show, by means of shaded boxes the areas inside which the marketing research function normally operates.

Information sources can be divided into those that are available internally within an organization and those collected from external data sources. It is in the area of

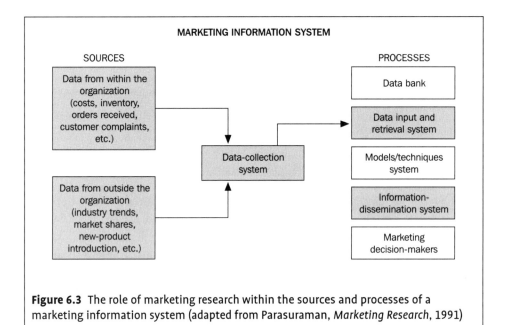

Figure 6.3 The role of marketing research within the sources and processes of a marketing information system (adapted from Parasuraman, *Marketing Research*, 1991)

internal data collection that the line between marketing research and other marketing information system functions is most difficult to define neatly. Much depends on the size, scope and structure of the marketing information system itself. In many large organizations the collation of regularly generated information, such as costs and sales figures, will not be central to the research activity. However, marketing research may well generate new information from within the organization – for example, by collecting information on a more ad hoc basis from key groups such as management, the sales staff and front-line service personnel. In practice, the main focus for marketing research activity within most service organizations is external data collection.

6.4.1 Major services research activities

A market research problem almost always results from a gap in the market information already available to management. For example, a company may have comprehensive and up-to-date information on the market for its current products, but may wish to discover what – if any – market needs remain unsatisfied, in order to develop new products.

The range of tasks which marketing research contributes to the services marketing planning process is growing. Some of the more important specific marketing research activities are listed below, many of which are in fact associated with service quality issues and are covered in greater detail in Chapter 8.

- *Research into customer needs*. Research is undertaken to learn what underlying needs individuals seek to satisfy when they buy services. Identifying needs which are currently unmet by service offerings spurs new service development.

■ *Research into customer expectations.* Needs should be distinguished from expectations and a variety of qualitative techniques are used to study the standards of service that customers expect when consuming a service – for example, with respect to delays, friendliness of staff, etc.

■ *Customer perception studies.* Perception studies can be undertaken during or after consumption to test the perceived level of quality delivery. Research can also be undertaken to test the extent to which external factors might have influenced the way an individual perceives an organization or its specific service offers.

■ *Customer surveys.* Ad hoc or regular programmes of survey research carried out among customers provide information about customers' behaviour, attitudes, perceptions and expectations. These can have the dual functions of providing the service organization with much-needed information as well as providing a public relations tool by allowing customers to feel that they have made their feelings known in a way which may allow them to be acted upon.

■ *Similar industry studies.* Many services industries can learn from research undertaken in what at first sight appear to be totally unrelated industries. By learning about operating practices and customer reactions to their service offering, marketing managers in one sector, such as shipping, can learn a lot from studies carried out within the hotel sector. Through a process often referred to as 'benchmarking', an organization can set itself targets based on best practice in its own, or a related, industry.

■ *Research into service intermediaries.* Agents, dealers and other intermediaries are close to consumers and therefore form a valuable conduit for gathering marketing research. In addition, intermediaries are customers of service principals, therefore research is undertaken to establish – among other things – their perceptions of the standard of service that they are receiving from the service principal.

■ *Key client studies.* Most organizations see some customers as being more important than others, on account of the volume and/or the profitability of the custom they generate. Where a company derives the majority of its income from one customer, it may make particular effort to ensure that this customer is totally satisfied with its standards of service and prices. The loss of the business as a result of shortcomings of which it is unaware could otherwise be catastrophic. In some cases, the relationship with key customers may be of such mutual importance that each partner may spend considerable time jointly researching shared problems. For example, an airport operator with two or three key airline customers may jointly develop a programme of research to judge passengers' perception of the total experience that they perceive as they pass through the airport. Sometimes, **key clients** with whom a sound relationship has been built up can be used as a basis for researching new service ideas before they are released more widely.

■ *Employee research.* As part of a programme of internal marketing, research into employees is often undertaken by service organizations. This can focus on employees as internal customers of services within an internal market as well as their thoughts on the methods of service delivery. Employee suggestion schemes can form an important part of research into employees.

The variability of services makes research into them very different compared to manufactured goods, which may be used over and over again without any significant variance. Therefore the constant or intermittent interaction between customers and the service provider, which occurs as a stream of service encounters, must be evaluated as an ongoing process in order to ascertain the degree of customer satisfaction, which may fluctuate from one encounter to another. Some aspects of the service may be perceived as good on one occasion and bad on another. For instance, a customer may be satisfied with the time spent waiting in a queue at a bank one week and dissatisfied the next. Loyalty comes from developing a good long-term relationship with customers, and feedback should be solicited on a regular basis in order to determine the level of satisfaction that is being achieved. There should be some means by which the bank knows when a customer is dissatisfied and the reasons why.

In addition, goods marketing does not normally involve any face-to-face interaction with production staff, unlike services, where employees usually perform the service on, or in conjunction with, the customer. The crucial importance of staff in making the service offer a satisfactory one increases the necessity to examine their perceptions. Because employees contribute greatly to service quality in so many service industries it is important to consider their views about how well a service is being received by customers and how it may be improved. After all, it is the front-line staff within an organization who have regular and close contact with the users of a service, so the information that they provide can be of enormous value.

Organizations should also undertake employee research because they can be seen as internal recipients of marketing efforts. A successful service company should be just as proficient at managing the management/staff interface as it is at managing the staff/customer interface – feedback from these internal customers should be treated as an important aspect of services marketing research.

6.4.2 **The marketing research process**

Most definitions of marketing research activity focus on its role as a means by which those who provide goods and services keep themselves in touch with the needs and wants of those who consume their products. Within the context of services industries, this could be extended to include the means by which management keeps in touch with the motivation and behaviour of its staff. In either case, the key phrase which encompasses all marketing research activity is *keeping in touch*. Data collected should be as up to date and relevant to a problem as time and cost constraints allow.

A simplified model of the research process, which begins with the definition of the research problem and ends with the presentation of the findings is shown in Figure 6.4. It can be seen that this process follows the same basic pattern as for other forms of research activity, such as scientific or academic research. To be useful,

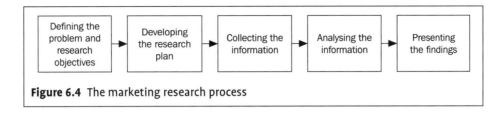

Figure 6.4 The marketing research process

keeping in touch needs to be conducted objectively and accurately. Casual, unstructured research is at best wasteful and at worst misleading.

Market research is itself a service industry, with its own functions and specialists. In order to explain the way in which the process illustrated in Figure 6.4 works, it is useful to briefly describe the structure of the industry. Essentially, market researchers fall into two groups:

1. those employed by services companies themselves, for example banks, retailers and airlines (often referred to as 'client' companies); these researchers provide information for internal use and generally have specific product and market knowledge of their sector

2. a second group of researchers are employed by marketing research organizations whose specific purpose is the supply of information to other users; these supply companies are often referred to as agencies, something of a misnomer as they are paid on a fee rather than a commission basis; staff employed by these companies can generally achieve a high level of expertise in particular research techniques, some of which were described above.

The research process allows for the expertise of both groups to be incorporated at different stages. Client company researchers define a research problem, after discussion with marketing and other management. This is usually communicated to potential suppliers in the form of a research brief. The objectives of the study are set by matching management information needs with what can realistically be obtained from the marketplace, particularly in the light of time and budgetary constraints (Figure 6.5), and may well be defined after initial discussions with possible suppliers.

The area in which marketing research agencies dominate is that of information collection. The degree to which the client company will be involved in developing the research plan and analysing and presenting the findings varies; to a large extent this depends on the size and expertise of its research department. Before deciding on the final plan, however, most client companies approach several possible suppliers and ask for their suggestions in the form of a research proposal.

6.4.3 **Sources of information**

Data sources are traditionally divided into two categories according to the methods by which they were collected. These are known as secondary and primary data sources – often referred to as desk and field research, respectively. Most organizations

A larger sample and longer survey improves the confidence level of the results

A short, quick survey may contribute to a firm's cost advantage and allow it to get to market early

Figure 6.5 Balancing the costs and benefits of undertaking marketing research. There is no limit to the amount of money that a company could potentially spend on conducting marketing research. However, it is likely that, beyond a certain point, further research will not be cost-effective, as it will not contribute significantly to better-quality decisions, and may put a company at a competitive disadvantage by delaying the introduction of revised or new services.

would approach a research exercise by examining the available sources of secondary data.

Secondary data refers to information which in some sense is second-hand to the current research project. Data could be second-hand because it has already been collected internally by the organization, although for a different primary purpose. Alternatively, the information could be acquired second-hand from external sources.

Internal information, on products, costs, sales, etc., may be accessed through an organization's marketing information system. Where such a system does not exist formally, the information may still be available in relevant departmental records, though it would probably need to be reworked into a form that market researchers can use. Despite modern data-processing technology, the task of going manually through stacks of back-invoices in order to quantify annual sales by product and customer is still not unknown.

There are numerous external sources of secondary data, in both document and electronic format. These cover government statistics, trade associations and specialist research reports. A good starting point for a review of these is still the business section of a good library. Some examples of secondary data sources are shown in Table 6.1.

Traditionally, it has been much easier to find external secondary information on goods than services. However, there has been a considerable increase in services marketing intelligence reports in recent years. Data is also often obtainable from special interest panels, for example information on attitudes towards airlines is obtainable from a regular airline users' panel. It is also worth checking on whether other organizations, possibly even competitors, have conducted similar studies to the one which is proposed. Although secondary information will not be as up to date or relevant as that obtained by commissioning a new survey, it will normally be available at a fraction of the cost.

Table 6.1 **Some examples of secondary data used in services marketing research**

- National media – e.g. *Financial Times* industry surveys
- Trade, technical and professional media – e.g. *Travel Trade Gazette, Marketing Week*
- Government departments and official publications – e.g. General Household Survey, transport statistics
- Local chambers of trade and commerce
- Professional and trade associations – e.g. Association of British Travel Agents, Law Society
- Yearbooks and directories – e.g. *Dataquest*
- Subscription services, providing periodic sector reports on market intelligence and financial analyses, such as Keynote, MEAL, Mintel, etc.
- Subscription electronic databases – e.g. Mintel OnLine, FT.com

While secondary or desk research, as the name implies, is not the most exciting activity in the world, it is very worthwhile although the research objectives may not be achieved by this method alone. It can, however, be conducted by company employees, and provides a useful starting point for further investigation. Undertaking unnecessary primary research which is available through secondary sources is an expensive and time-consuming exercise.

Primary, or 'field', research is concerned with generating new information direct from the target population. The phrase *keeping in touch* was highlighted earlier, and marketing research professionals spend most of their time designing and implementing such studies, either on an ad hoc (one-off) or a continuous (monitoring) basis.

6.4.4 **Research methods**

One important decision that needs to be made when developing a primary research plan is whether to conduct a qualitative or quantitative survey, or a combination of both.

Qualitative research

Qualitative research is the exploration and interpretation of the perceptions and behaviour of small samples of target consumers, and the study of the motivators involved in purchasing choices. It is highly focused, exploring in depth, for example, the relationship between respondents' motives and their behaviour. The techniques used to encourage respondents to speak and behave honestly and unselfconsciously are derived from the social sciences, in particular psychology.

When definitions and descriptions are needed – in other words, when no one knows exactly where to start – qualitative research is at its most useful. It can define the parameters for future studies, and identify key criteria among consumers that can then be measured by quantitative research. For example, if a bank observed that older consumers were not using Internet banking, it might conduct some focus groups with older consumers in order to explore why this particular group was reluctant to use this technology. It is important, however, that the consumers are asked in as objective and sympathetic a form as possible. Qualitative research plans generally incorporate a discussion outline for those collecting the information, but are essentially unstructured and respondent-led.

Quantitative research

Quantitative research is used to measure consumers' attitudes and choices where the nature of the research has been defined and described. These studies are designed to gather information from statistically representative samples of the target population. In order to achieve total accuracy it would be necessary to take a complete census of everyone in the target group. The scale and cost of the UK census, however, illustrates the impracticality of this in most cases. Therefore, samples of respondents are selected for interview, the sample size being related to the size of the total population and degree of statistical reliability required, balanced against time and cost constraints. In order to achieve margins of error small enough to make the final measurements useful, however, quantitative research is usually conducted among several hundred, sometimes thousands, of respondents. For this reason, information is generally obtained using standardized structured questionnaires.

A penny for your thoughts ...

Like many well-run companies, the UK retailer Asda provides comment cards and a freefone telephone number that customers can use to pass on their suggestions, complaints and praise about the company's operations. But the company goes one step further by offering rewards and recognition for the valuable information that customers provide it with. In one particular campaign the company promised to make a donation to the BBC 'Children in Need' charity for each call that it received on its freefone number. The company has also provided feedback for customers, in an attempt to overcome many customers' attitude that their views 'won't make any difference'. It has placed notice boards in its stores that identify a selection of customers' recent comments and, alongside these, the company notes its response. As an example, a comment 'There are too few disabled parking spaces close to the store' may be matched with a response 'We have relocated 5 disabled parking spaces to be closer to the main entrance'. Of course, life for any services company is never as easy as simply saying yes to all customers' suggestions, and the costs and benefits of each suggestion have to be assessed. If the company always said yes to suggestions that it should provide more convenient disabled parking spaces, might this upset its other, able-bodied, customers who would now have to walk further from their cars?

6.4.5 **Data collection**

Data can be collected either indirectly by observation or through direct interaction with the person being researched.

Observational techniques claim objectivity – being relatively free of respondent bias – but are limited to descriptions of behaviour. They find a number of uses within the service sector for planning purposes, for example site location decisions which are often based on observation of pedestrian or vehicle flows past a site, as well as the routine monitoring of competitor price levels.

A survey, a direct interaction data collection method, would normally request some attitudinal, personal or historical information about respondents. Questions in a survey can be asked face to face, by telephone, through the Internet, or distributed by mail for self-completion. While considerably cheaper than face-to-face interviews, the refusal rate for telephone surveys can be up to three times higher than for personal interviews. The increased used of computer-assisted information collection for telephone (CATI) and personal (CAPI) interviews has speeded up the whole survey process dramatically, with responses being processed as they are received. Immediately prior to the 2001 UK general election these systems were used in the next-day publication of survey results from total sample sizes extending into thousands.

In the case of self-completion surveys, respondents obviously self-select, so no matter how carefully the original sample to be contacted is chosen, the possibility of bias is highest. Furthermore, the response rate may be less than 5%, particularly where a postal survey is used. However some service-sector companies, in particular airlines and hotels, have used self-completion questionnaires for a number of years to obtain customer feedback.

In qualitative research, the open-ended nature of the questions, and the need to establish the confidence of respondents, precludes the use of telephone and self-completion interviews. Face-to-face (or personal) depth interviews are used particularly in business-to-business research, where confidentiality is especially important, and it is usually most convenient for respondents to be interviewed at their place of work.

In consumer markets, group discussions are frequently used. Groups normally consist of about eight people, plus a trained moderator – quite often a psychologist – who leads the discussion. Respondents are recruited by interviewers, who use recruitment questionnaires to ensure that those invited to attend reflect the demography of the target market, and to filter out unsuitable respondents. In national markets, groups are arranged at central points throughout the country, the number of groups in each region once more reflecting the regional breakdown of the target population.

It was noted earlier that the collection of market information is the part of the research process most dominated by research agencies rather than client companies. There are two main reasons for this. Firstly, very few client companies, however large or diverse their range of services, can generate sufficient research to warrant the full-time employment of armies of interviewers throughout the nation. Secondly, respondents are more likely to give honest answers to third parties than when reply-ing directly to representatives of the organization providing the service being discussed.

6.4.6 **Effects on research methods of service inseparability**

For manufactured goods, it is usually possible within the research process to separate the technical characteristics of a product from the identity and image of the company producing them. For example, in testing a drinks product, such as tea or beer, it is possible to isolate reactions to the core product by presenting it to respondents in blind format, i.e. in a plain (usually white) container with no clue as to the brand or manufacturing company. The respondent is then asked to rate the product along a number of dimensions, e.g. strength–weakness or light–dark colour. The extent to which perceptions are influenced by brand or company connotations can be meas-ured by presenting an identically constructed sample with the same product, fully branded and packaged, and measuring the differences in response along the same dimensions.

It is not always possible to make this kind of neat separation when researching services – respondents cannot rate the level of satisfaction provided by a financial service, for example, unless they have actually experienced it, which may be difficult to achieve in a laboratory type of setting. Furthermore, interviewees' responses to proposed new services cannot be isolated from their perceptions of the service provider. An insurance policy cannot be seen in isolation from the reputation of the insurance company that will be responsible for delivering the service benefits at some time in the future. Indeed, some providers of services marketing research argue that attempting such a separation is undesirable and that it is essential to look at all aspects of the company/customer relationship – attitudinal and perceptual, as well as factual and transactional.

6.5 **Demand forecasting**

Forecasting the future is one of the most difficult aspects of knowledge management. There have been many examples of failures to accurately forecast demand.

- When the Prudential Assurance company launched its new Egg credit card, it experienced an unexpectedly high level of take-up, resulting in delays and frustration for potential customers.

- Many people in the industry expected the launch of 'Freeview' digital television services in 2002 to be a flop, following the previous low levels of take-up of ITV digital services. In fact, Freeview quickly became very popular, with reports of shortages of set-top adapter boxes.

It is often inadequate to assume that market conditions will continue on present trends, but what other knowledge can be used to predict the future? A stark indication of the rewards of looking forwards rather than backwards is provided by an analyst who studied stock market performance. If a cumulative investment of $1 had been invested from 1900 on 1 January each year in the stock which had performed best in the *previous* year, and then reinvested the following year, the accumulated value in 2000 would be £250. However, if it had been invested each year in the stock which went on to perform best in the *year ahead*, the accumulated value would be over $1 billion. Similarly for service provision, successful companies have often been those who correctly forecast the market and were able to satisfy customers' needs more cost-effectively than competitors. Being first to market when trends are changing can be much more profitable than simply reacting to a market trend. However, predicting future trends can be very difficult and can involve a lot of risk.

The amount of effort which an organization puts into refining its demand forecasting techniques will depend on a number of factors.

- The level of turbulence in the marketing environment will vary between firms operating in different markets. For example, the marketing environment of an undertaker has been – and will probably continue to be – less turbulent than that of a commercial radio station. An extrapolation of recent trends might be adequate for the former, but the latter must seek to understand a diverse range of changing forces if it is to accurately predict the likely future nature of its operating environment.

- The cost associated with an inaccurate forecast will reflect the capital commitment to a project. A window cleaner with only limited investment and transferable skills can afford to pay only limited attention to understanding its environment. On the other hand, the cost of developing a new rapid transit system will call for relatively sophisticated techniques if expensive failure is to be avoided.

- More sophisticated analytic techniques are needed for long-term projects where there is a long time lag between the planning of the project and the time when it begins to yield its stream of service output. The problem of inaccurate forecasting will be even more acute where an asset has a long life span with few alternative uses (see Figure 6.6).

- Qualitative and quantitative techniques may be used as appropriate. In looking at the future, facts are hard to come by. What matters is that senior management is in a position to make better-informed judgements about the future in order to aid strategic marketing planning.

A number of approaches to demand forecasting are considered below. While trend extrapolation should be possible with routine output from a marketing information system, expert opinion and scenario building are usually associated with more irregular activity by larger organizations operating in more turbulent markets.

Figure 6.6 It is easy with hindsight to explain demand levels for new service facilities, but it can be very difficult to predict demand for large-scale, completely new services. One case where demand forecasting proved to be extremely difficult was London's Millennium Dome, open to the public for just one year in 2000. The business plan had forecast an attendance of 12 million paying guests, but in the event, only about half this number actually came. Forecasts were made difficult because of the absence of comparable previous projects that might give some idea of the likely take-up. The earlier Festival of Britain was held by many to be a valid comparator, but too many other factors had changed since the time of the Festival to allow reliable extrapolation. Many uncertainties remained during the forecasting process, including the effects of competing millennium attractions, the impact of press reviews, the state of the national economy and the capacity of the local transport infrastructure. By contrast, another of London's millennium attractions – the London Eye – beat its forecasts of demand.

6.5.1 Trend extrapolation

At its simplest, a firm identifies a historic and consistent long-term change in demand for a product over time and seeks to explain this in terms of change in some underlying variables. Marketing planning then seeks to predict changes in these underlying variables and therefore – on the basis of the long-term relationship between variables – the likely future size and nature of a market.

While correlation techniques can be used to identify the significance of historical relationships between a number of variables, extrapolation methods suffer from a number of shortcomings. Firstly, one variable is seldom adequate to predict future demand for a product, yet it can be difficult to identify the full set of variables which have an influence. Secondly, there can be no certainty that the trends identified from historic data are likely to continue in the future. Trend extrapolation takes no account of discontinuous environmental change, as was brought about by the sudden increase in oil prices in 1973 and the effect this had on demand for air travel. Thirdly, trend extrapolation is of diminishing value as the length of time which it is used to forecast increases – the longer the time horizon, the more chance there is of historic relationships changing and new variables emerging. Fourthly, it can be difficult to gather information on which to base an analysis of trends – indeed, a large part of the problem in designing a marketing information system is in identifying the type of information which may be of relevance at some time in the future.

At best, trend extrapolation can be used where planning horizons are short, the number of dependent variables are relatively limited and the risk level is relatively low.

6.5.2 Expert opinion

Trend analysis is commonly used to predict demand where the state of the dependent variables is given. In practice, it can be very difficult to predict what will happen to these variables. One solution is to consult expert opinion to obtain the best possible forecast of what will happen to them.

In Diffenbach's (1983) study of US corporations, 86% of all firms said they used expert opinion as an input to their planning process. Expert opinion can vary in the level of its speciality, from an economist being consulted for a general forecast about the state of the national economy, to industry-specific experts. Expert opinion may be unstructured and come from a few individuals either inside the organization, or from external advisers or consultants. The most senior managers in organizations of any significant size tend to keep in touch with developments by a number of means. Paid and unpaid advisers may be used to keep abreast of a whole range of issues such as technological developments, environmental issues, government thinking and intended legislation. Large companies may employ Members of Parliament as advisers as well as retired civil servants. Consultancy firms may be employed to brief the company on specific issues or to monitor the environment on a more general basis.

Relying on individuals may give an incomplete or distorted picture of the future. There are, however, more structured methods of gaining expert opinion. One of the best known is probably the Delphi method. This involves a number of experts, usually from outside the organization, who preferably do not know each other and who do not meet or confer while the process is in play. A scenario or number of scenarios about the future are drawn up by the company. These are then posted out to the experts. Comments are returned and the scenario(s) modified according to the comments received. The process is run through a number of times with the scenario being amended on each occasion. Eventually a consensus of the most likely scenario is arrived at. It is believed that this is more accurate than relying on any one individual, because it involves the collected wisdom of a number of experts who have not been influenced by dominant personalities.

6.5.3 **Scenario-building**

Scenario-building is an attempt to paint a picture of the future by building a small number of alternative scenarios based on differing assumptions. This qualitative approach is a means of handling environmental issues which are hard to quantify because they are less structured, more uncertain and may involve very complex relationships.

In the real world, many unpredictable environmental factors can interact with each other, resulting in a seemingly endless permutation of scenarios. One method of analysing the relationship between environmental factors is a cross-impact analysis, which presents a framework within which the combined effects of changes in a number of factors can be assessed. A number of permutations are shown in Figure 6.7, where the interaction of the distinct possibility of oil prices rising to $80 per barrel with the 'wildcard' event of cancer being linked to flying can be noted. For an airline, a development option if this scenario came true might be to rapidly downsize its passenger-carrying capacity and concentrate on business and freight traffic.

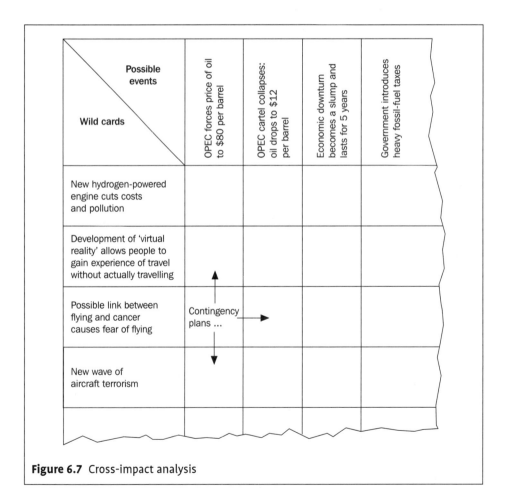

Figure 6.7 Cross-impact analysis

The use of scenarios can allow a company to come to a view as to which is the most likely outcome, and plan accordingly, while still being able to develop contingency plans which could be rapidly implemented if any of the alternative foreseen scenarios came true.

6.6 **Information and control systems**

Many service organizations have developed elaborate planning systems but have failed because implementation of the plan was not appropriately monitored and controlled. It is important therefore that a marketing information system recognizes the key elements of the plan which need to be monitored and provides information which will allow control action to be taken where a variance from the plan is observed. These are some of the things on which most service organizations will need information if they are to monitor implementation adequately:

- *financial targets* – sales turnover/contribution/profit margin, disaggregated by product/business unit
- *market analysis* – e.g. market share
- *effectiveness of communication* – productivity of sales personnel, effectiveness of advertising, effectiveness of sales promotion
- *pricing* – level of discounts given, price position
- *personnel* – level of skills achieved by employees, survey of customer comments on staff performance
- *quality levels achieved* – e.g. reliability, complaint level.

Where performance is below target, the reasons may not be immediately obvious. A comprehensive marketing information system can allow an organization to analyse variance. A uniform fall in sales performance across the organization, combined with intelligence gained about the state of the market, would suggest that remedial action aimed at improving the performance of individual sales personnel may not be as effective as a reassessment of targets or strategies in the light of the changed sales environment.

Successful control mechanisms require three underlying components to be in place:

1. the setting of targets or standards of expected performance
2. the measurement and evaluation of actual performance
3. taking corrective action where necessary.

6.6.1 **Setting targets**

A clear statement of objectives at the start of the planning process provides a vital foundation for comparing targets with actual performance. In general, the greater the level of disaggregation of targets, the greater the degree of control which will be possible. To be effective in a control process, targets should be specified and communicated which:

- give individual managers a clear indication of the standards of performance that are expected of them
- distinguish between controllable variables that can be managed by an individual manager and those that are uncontrollable and should therefore be excluded from their standards for performance
- allocate targets to the right person – ultimately, all costs and revenues are someone's responsibility and should be monitored and controlled at the appropriate point within an organization, and even a relatively fixed and uncontrollable element such as rent can become controllable by senior management over the longer term
- show which targets are to take priority – in any event, targets should not be mutually incompatible
- are sufficiently flexible to allow for changes in the organization's environment which were not foreseen at the time the targets were set.

For control purposes, quantitative targets are generally preferred to qualitative ones. Many apparently qualitative targets, such as customer satisfaction and attentiveness of front-line service personnel, can often be reduced to quantifiable indices – for example, by setting targets for the number of complaints received or the percentage of customers booking a repeat service, or by using an analytic technique such as **SERVQUAL** (see Chapter 8). There is a danger, however, in setting purely quantified targets that complex phenomena may be represented by a series of relatively simple indicators. Staff seeking to achieve these targets may concentrate their attention on meeting them, possibly at the expense of other more important qualitative aspects of their performance. A telephone enquiry office set with a target of answering calls within a specified time may lose sight of the quality of information given during the call if its attention is primarily focused on responding within the target time. There is also an argument that marketing managers should not be assessed solely on the basis of their ability to meet quantifiable targets. A more realistic appraisal system might also examine the quality of the decisions which a manager made during the previous period, taking account of the fact that the operating environment posed numerous problems and opportunities which may not have been apparent at the time targets were initially set.

6.6.2 **Performance monitoring**

So far, information collection and analysis have focused on understanding the current marketing environment and planning for the future. But information also has a vital role to play in monitoring performance. Marketers have sometimes been accused of being good at planning, but not so good at evaluating how well their plan has actually performed.

Information is needed to measure two aspects of performance: efficiency and effectiveness. Efficiency can be defined in terms of an organization's success in turning inputs into outputs, while effectiveness is the level of success in producing a desired result. An efficient business in a competitive market cannot succeed if it is efficient at doing the wrong things – that is, it is ineffective.

Where an organization competes in a market on the basis of its cost leadership, efficiency may be a key measure for evaluating management performance. Within the service sector, important efficiency measures can include the number of services performed per employee, value of sales achieved per salesperson, the cost of advertising per 1000 valued impressions and the level of utilization of assets (e.g. load factors on aircraft).

In contrast to planning information, much of the information needed for control is derived from internal sources and can be collected routinely. Examples include:

- technical measures of service quality, for example failure rates of ATMs, percentage of flights delayed by more than 10 minutes, time taken to answer a telephone

- sales figures should be routinely analysed and actual values compared with budget under headings such as regional distribution, customer type, size of purchase. invoicing should not be seen narrowly as an accounting function, but an opportunity to collate marketing data

- routine analysis of invoices will indicate whether an organization has been able to maintain its price level

- expenditure budgets should give an up-to-date summary of actual against target expenditure under headings such as advertising, salesforce cost, intermediaries' expenses

- sales personnel's performance records are routinely maintained.

These regular sources of information may need to be supplemented with external sources of data and ad hoc studies. These are likely to include the following.

- Up-to-date information about the size of a market (collected through syndicated research, trade associations and government agencies) will allow an organization to monitor its market share.

- While technical quality can often be measured by an organization on a continuous basis, the measurement of functional quality (see Chapter 8) frequently calls for marketing research to be commissioned. This can include periodic questionnaire surveys of customers, or less frequent and more in-depth diagnostic research sessions. For control purposes, a service organization may set its managers an objective that at least 90% of customers surveyed in such surveys should state that their service experience is 'good' or better.

- Observational research is becoming increasingly popular as a means of controlling the quality of the service delivery process. A trained **mystery customer** is now employed by many restaurants, banks and transport companies to check that the service format as specified is actually being delivered. Findings from this form of research are often linked to employees' pay.

- Transaction analysis – many organizations track the progress of services provided to clients, both during and after delivery. This can provide valuable information about customers' perceptions of service quality compared to their expectations. It can also be used to internally monitor the attainment of performance targets.

- Analysis of complaints – service organizations often see complaints as a positive source of information from customers, and analyse their content (see Friman and Edvardsson, 2003). If complaints are communicated, management is in a better position to prevent future repeats of the factors that gave rise to them, than would be the case if the aggrieved customer remained silent and quietly took his or her custom elsewhere. For this reason, many service organizations try to make it easy for their customers to communicate grievances to them, and carefully analyse their responses.

- Research is often commissioned to monitor the effectiveness of an organization's advertising, for example by monitoring awareness levels or enquiry response rates.

Traditionally, service organizations have focused their monitoring and control information on balance sheet items, or at least those items which can easily be quantified in monetary terms. Technical measures of performance are the most frequently collected non-financial type of information, for example a bank may record the percentage availability of its ATMs. It is the qualitative aspects of service delivery that have been less likely to be measured. While the bank may have a daily report of its ATM availability across its entire network, it may rely on a small annual survey of customers to measure customers' attitudes to the bank.

There have been a number of attempts to develop improved performance measures. These have ranged from improved financial metrics (e.g. measures of economic value) to multi-dimensional frameworks for strategic performance measurement which combine financial and non-financial measures (Ittner and Larcker, 1998). One approach that has attracted considerable interest from academics and practitioners in recent years is the **Balanced Scorecard** (BSC) approach.

The Balanced Scorecard is a framework for describing value-creating strategies that link tangible and intangible assets (Speckbacher *et al.*, 2003). This is done by formulating strategic objectives with respect to four types of assets: financial, customer, internal business process, and learning and growth (see Kaplan and Norton, 2001a; Malmi, 2001). However, it has been noted that organizations using the BSC often start with only a very simple scorecard, and subsequently enhance its functions and its scope step by step (see Kaplan and Norton, 2001b). It is claimed that the true potential of the BSC approach can only be achieved if its measures are linked to employees' reward systems (Kaplan and Norton, 1996; Otley, 1999; Malmi, 2001). In this sense, the value created by the internal value chain (discussed in Chapter 12) is recognized and rewarded.

Several surveys have indicated that the BSC concept is widely used in large companies in the United States and throughout Europe (Speckbacher *et al.*, 2003).

A good marketing information system can generate a lot of information. The key to effective control is to give the right information to the right people at the right time. Providing too much information can be costly in terms of the effort required to assemble and disseminate it, and can also reduce effective control where the valuable information is hidden among information of secondary importance. Also, the level of reporting will be determined by the level of tolerance allowed for compliance to target.

Many control systems fail because employees within an organization have been given inappropriate or unrealistic targets. Even where targets are set, and appropriate data is collected, control systems may still fail because of a failure by management to act on the information available. Control information should identify variances from target and should be able to indicate whether the variance is within or beyond the control of the person responsible for meeting the target. If it is beyond their control, the issue should become one of revising the target so that it becomes once more achievable. If the variance is the result of factors which are subject to a manager's control, a number of measures can be taken to try to revise their behaviour.

- Bureaucratic controls can be used where instructions are sent to subordinates, failing which disciplinary action is taken.

- Incentive schemes can be used as a control mechanism. Incentives are often linked directly to performance: for example, performance-related pay and sales commission.

- The allocation of resources (including personnel) offers an important form of organizational control as this has the effect of facilitating some actions and inhibiting others (for example, a branch manager of a bank which has missed its targets may be denied an increase in staff levels).

- Informal controls can often be exercised by an employees' peer group in an attempt to bring about conformity.

Case study

Click here for visitors to Carmarthenshire

Tourism destinations are probably some of the most difficult products to market. What is on offer at a typical tourist destination combines the services of hundreds or thousands of individual hotels, restaurants, transport and tourist attraction operators. Their target customers may be very widely dispersed throughout the world. Furthermore, the tourism destination may mean quite different things to different people. To some people, London as a tourism destination may primarily be about historic buildings and culture. To others, it may be about the theatre and culture, while to others still it may primarily be a shopping destination or a place to go to visit friends and relatives.

It has long been recognized that tourism destinations can be promoted much more effectively through co-operative action by all of the companies involved in providing services at a destination, rather than each of them acting alone. Some destination marketing organizations have achieved notable success in developing tourism destinations as brands in their own right. Notable among successes have been the Viva Espana campaign and the 'I Love New York' campaign, and more recently one of the priority tasks of the Mayor of London has been to promote London as a global tourism brand.

But promoting a tourism destination is about more than simply building a strong brand, important though that is. Destinations are increasingly recognizing that it is important to get the right information to the right people at the right time. This can involve multi-directional flows of information, with tourism suppliers not only providing information to tourists, but also collecting information from tourists and disseminating this to members of a destination marketing organization in order to improve their forward planning and operational performance. Tourists choosing between competing destinations are becoming increasingly information rich and real-time information is increasingly expected to be available through a growing range of Internet-enabled devices, hand-held PDAs, kiosks, computer games consoles, etc.

The benefits of having the right information available are increasingly being seen as a source of a destination's competitive advantage and many have invested in sophisticated destination management systems to handle this multi-directional flow of information. How easily can a potential visitor find out about availability of accommodation in the area? About a forthcoming music festival? Or about the best places to eat?

Destination management systems (DMSs) take the development of an online destination brand beyond the stages of merely offering an online brochure, or a standalone accommodation reservation service. A DMS provides a suite of tools for managing a destination's tourism activities. This includes systems for managing information for all of the constituent tourism organizations' websites as well as sales offices, call centres, literature fulfilment and marketing functions. Also included are systems to manage communications services and online reservation systems.

There are now a number of software companies that offer destination management systems, usually on a modular basis, which allows users to add on facilities depending on their specific requirements. A typical destination marketing system is illustrated in Figure 6.8.

The modules which make up a DMS are a combination of those which are immediately visible to the public, and a range of 'back office' functions. The following are typical functions of a DMS.

- *Website server.* This provides templates allowing users of the DMS to easily create and maintain websites for different regions, in specific languages.

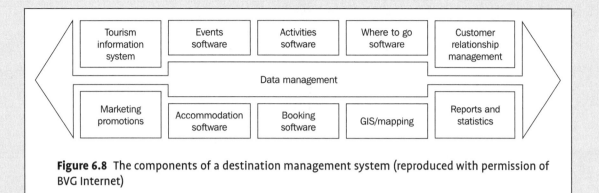

Figure 6.8 The components of a destination management system (reproduced with permission of BVG Internet)

- *An online reservation system.* This can either be provided as a self-managed system with its own inventory, or linked to a global distribution system. The system would be linked to an electronic payment system.

- *E-mail management.* This includes newsletter subscriber forms, mailing list manager, multiple respondent accounts, automatic responders and online mail administration for POP accounts.

- *Search facility.* This allows users to quickly find information on a subject which may otherwise be difficult to find in a large website.

- *Personal web brochure.* This allows visitors to the system to pick their options and have them provided with a personal view of the destination relevant to their needs.

- *Programme tracking.* This gives an ability to establish and monitor Internet pages for integrated marketing promotions and campaigns. From this, the destination can evaluate the effectiveness of a campaign in real time.

- *Online shopping.* This is typically for guide books.

- *Promotional services.* For example, e-postcards, visitors journals, guest books, newsgroups, special promotions, screensaver downloads, etc.

- *Media relations system.* This includes copies of recently produced press releases.

- *Calendar.* The item through which participating organizations can add events and festivals, and classify them for multiple listings.

- *Integrated databases.* These can be used to provide tourist information through CD multi-media productions, kiosks, call centres, visitor information bureaux and corporate information systems.

- *Archives system.* This allows partners to add items to a user-searchable archive and to upload files and graphics directly using their browser.

- *Client profile and survey system.* This provides a record of details of people who have made contact with the DMS (e.g. by e-mail, telephone, personal visit to a TIC or by post). Profiles can be developed and selected to meet the needs of specific marketing campaigns.

- *Mobile targeting.* Developments in global positioning systems are allowing systems which can target customers through mobile phones depending upon their location.

Because of the high cost of developing a DMS, a system will typically offer some of these services, but few offer all of them. The World Travel Organization has estimated that a major DMS may cost between $500 000 and $8 000 000 to develop and typically over $250 000 annually to operate (World Travel Organization, 1999). Fortunately, destination management organizations do not have to develop these systems themselves and can configure standard systems from suppliers such as AXSES SCI, Travelinx and BVG Internet.

It is not, however, just major tourism destinations such as London and New York that develop destination management systems. There are many examples of successful systems being implemented for much smaller destinations. An example of the application of a DMS in a rural, secondary tourism area is provided in Carmarthenshire, Wales. The local tourism sector comprises around 520 principal tourism businesses and 475 secondary businesses in a diverse range of activities which include accommodation, catering, trekking and golf courses.

The Carmarthenshire Tourist Association (CTA) developed a key partnership with the local authority and other agencies in the county and from this developed its first basic website in 1997. In 2001, in conjunction with Carmarthenshire Enterprises, the local enterprise agency CTA sought to go one stage further with a DMS. The key requirements for a DMS were that it should have a proven track record and be:

- sustainable and self-financing
- capable of future growth
- administratively easy to operate
- automated
- quickly implemented
- comprehensible.

For an association which drew support from many non-computer specialists, it was particularly important that the system was quick to use, easily administered, and empowered individual businesses to provide information in a style and form that reflected their own businesses. Developing a style which can span from large corporate hospitality sites through to one-man trekking businesses can be a challenge.

The BVG–Internet Tourist Information System (TIS) met the requirements of the Association and in under eight weeks from going live over 350 businesses had added their information to the site, many of which claimed they had never used a computer before. A small team of two staff administered the site on a part-time basis and provided the local networking hub. The site, which can be found at http://www.tourlink. co.uk/indexframenoflash.cfm is now at the centre of communications within the Carmarthenshire tourism sector.

Destination management systems can be applied at a number of geographic levels, from small town, through regions and whole counties or groups of countries. Good systems should integrate these levels, in the way that the Visit England (www.visitengland.com) site links to regional tourism sites. In some cases, groups of towns or regions which share a common tourism interest have joined together to offer a system which has many of the characteristics of a DMS. One example is BookTownNet (www.booktown.net), a five-nation, 75-strong SME consortium of second-hand and antiquarian book dealers located in rural areas of Europe who combined to form an IT network to attract visitors to 'book towns' (Skogseid and Jansen, 2001).

Case study review questions

1. Summarize the benefits of an integrated destination-wide approach to data management, rather than individual service providers relying solely on their own internal data management.

2. What practical problems may prevent the full benefits of a destination management system being achieved?

3. What objectives might be appropriate to set for a destination management system? How could the operators of the system monitor its performance?

Chapter summary and links to other chapters

Information is becoming increasingly important as a means by which service organizations gain competitive advantage. With recent advances in the ability of firms to collect data, greater attention is now placed on the effective integration of individual employees' information into corporate knowledge. This chapter has reviewed the planning and control uses of information. A number of effects of service intangibility and inseparability on research processes have been noted. It is often difficult to separate research into the characteristics of a service from the characteristics of the service provider. The interaction between employees and customers presents additional opportunities for data collection.

Information is vital for effective strategic management of a service organization (**Chapter 12**) and in managing capacity (**Chapter 13**). The importance of information is noted in a number of other chapters, particularly in respect of quality (**Chapter 8**), segmentation and buyer decision processes (**Chapter 4**), targeting (**Chapter 7**), promotional effectiveness (**Chapter 11**) and pricing (**Chapter 10**). Current interest in relationship marketing programmes (**Chapter 5**) rests on the availability of information about customers.

Chapter review questions

1. Are there any major distinctions between the processes and practices of marketing research in services and goods markets?

2. To what extent do you agree that the intangibility of services creates a researchability problem?

3. How important is it to have a structured approach to marketing research?

4. Identify the most likely marketing research objectives for a hotel chain.

5. Explain how information on consumer buying processes may be important for a cinema chain seeking to enhance its service offer.

6. Choosing a service industry of your choice, identify the ways in which information can be used for control purposes.

Activity

Choose one of the following consumer service activities: a student refectory; a local bus service; a public library. Design an ongoing programme of research which will be cost-effective in identifying consumers' needs. You should also seek to identify competitors and you should develop a system which is able to monitor change over time. Critically assess your proposed programme of research for cost-effectiveness.

Key terms

Balanced Scorecard A method of evaluating the performance of an organization using financial and non-financial data.

Customer relationship management (CRM) A process of integrating the multiple contacts which a customer may have with an organization to create shared knowledge about the customer's history, preferences and likely future needs.

Key clients Customers who are particularly important to an organization.

Knowledge management The collection and analysis of relevant information for the benefit of the organization as a whole.

Marketing information system Structured systems and processes for collecting, analysing and disseminating marketing information.

Mystery customer A person employed by an organization to systematically record the standard of its service delivery.

Profiling Building up a picture of customers, typically based on their social, economic, demographic and lifestyle characteristics.

SERVQUAL A method of researching service quality, and the gaps between the expectations of customers and their perceptions of actual service delivery.

Selected further reading

For a general discussion of the principles of marketing research, the following texts are recommended.
Wright, L.T. and Crimp, M. (2000) *Marketing Research*, 5th edn, FT Prentice Hall, Hemel Hempstead.
Malhotra, N. and Birks, D. (2000) *Marketing Research: European Edition*, Prentice Hall International Editions.
Churchill, G.A. (2001) *Marketing Research: Methodological Foundations*, Thomson Learning.

The subject of turning research information into corporate knowledge is addressed in the following texts.
Davenport, T.H. and Prusak, L. (2000) *Working Knowledge: How Organizations Manage What They Know*, Harvard Business School Press.
Pfeffer, J. and Sutton, R. (2000) *Knowing–Doing Gap: How Smart Companies Turn Knowledge into Action*, Harvard Business School Press.
Gamble, P. and Blackwell, J. (2001) *Knowledge Management: A State of the Art Guide*, Kogan Page.

The subject of managing customer information and customer relationship management (CRM) is covered in the following.
Buttle, F. (2004) *Customer Relationship Management: Concepts and Tools*, Elsevier Butterworth-Heinemann.
Lee-Kelley, L., Gilbert, D. and Mannicom, R. (2003) 'How e-CRM can enhance customer loyalty', *Marketing Intelligence & Planning*, 21 (4) 239–48.
Ryals, L. and Knox, S. (2001) 'Cross-functional issues in the implementation of relationship marketing through customer relationship management', *European Management Journal*, 19 (5), 534–42.

The following regularly updated UK government statistics are frequently used as a basis for marketing research within the service sector.
Family Expenditure Survey. A sample survey of consumer spending habits, providing a snapshot of household spending. Published annually.
Social Trends. Statistics combined with text, tables and charts which present a narrative of life and lifestyles in the UK. Published annually.
Regional Trends. A comprehensive source of statistics about the regions of the UK allowing regional comparisons.
Population Trends. Statistics on population, including population change, births and deaths, life expectancy and migration.

References

Berger, P.L. and Luckmann, T. (1966) *The Social Construction of Reality,* Doubleday, Garden City, NY.

Bligh, P. and Turk, D. (2004) *CRM Unplugged: Releasing CRM's Strategic Value*, Wiley, New York.

Carson, D., Gilmore, A., Perry, C. and Gronhaug, K. (2001) *Qualitative Marketing Research*, Sage, London.

Diffenbach, J. (1983) 'Corporate environmental analysis in US corporations', *Long Range Planning*, 16 (3), 107–16.

Drucker, P. (1999) *Management Challenges for the 21st Century*, Harper Business, New York.

Friman, M. and Edvardsson, B. (2003) 'A content analysis of complaints and compliments', *Managing Service Quality*, 13 (1), 20–6.

Graeff, T.R. and Harmon, S. (2002) 'Collecting and using personal data: Consumers' awareness and concerns', *Journal of Consumer Marketing*, 19 (4/5), 302–16.

Hellweg, E. (2002) 10 July 2002, online at http://www.business2.com/b2/web/articles/0,17863,514879,00.html

Ittner, C. and Larcker, D. (1998) 'Innovations in performance measurement: Trends and research implications', *Journal of Management Accounting Research*, 10, 205–38.

Kaplan, R.S. and Norton, D.P. (1996) *The Balanced Scorecard: Translating Strategy into Action*, Harvard Business School Press, Boston.

Kaplan, R.S. and Norton, D.P. (2001a) 'Transforming the Balanced Scorecard from performance measurement to strategic management', *Accounting Horizons*, 15 (1), 87–104.

Kaplan, R.S. and Norton, D.P. (2001b) *The Strategy-Focused Organization*, Harvard Business School Press, Harvard.

Malmi, T. (2001) 'Balanced Scorecards in Finnish companies: A research note', *Management Accounting Research*, 12 (2), 207–20.

Nonaka, I. (1991) 'The knowledge-creating company', *Harvard Business Review,* 69 (November–December), 96–104.

Otley, D. (1999) 'Performance management: A framework for management control systems research', *Management Accounting Research*, 10 (4), 363–82.

Peppard, J. (2001) *Customer Relationship Management (CRM) in Financial Services*, FINEOS Corporation Paper.

Quinn, J.B. (1992) *Intelligent Enterprise: A Knowledge and Service Based Paradigm for Industry*, The Free Press, New York.

Skogseid, I. and Jansen, A. (2001) 'Booktown.net – A cultural heritage or a technical artefact?' Proceedings of the NOKOBIT Conference, Norway, Agder University College.

Smith, D. and Dexter, A. (2001) 'Whenever I hear the word paradigm I reach for my gun: How to stop talking and start walking', *International Journal of Market Research*, 43 (3), 321–40.

Speckbacher, G., Bischof, J. and Pfeiffer, T. (2003) 'A descriptive analysis on the implementation of Balanced Scorecards in German-speaking countries', *Management Accounting Research*, 14, 361–87.

Terziovski, M., Fitzpatrick, P. and O'Neill, P. (2003) 'Successful predictors of business process reengineering (BPR) in financial services', *International Journal of Production Economics*, 84 (1), 35.

Thompson, E. (2001) 'CRM: The Gartner perspective', Paper presented at the Gartner CRM Conference, Paris, June.

World Tourism Organization (1999) *Marketing the Destination Online*, Madrid.

Service positioning and targeting

Learning objectives

This chapter will explain:

- positioning strategies for service providers and individual service offers

- direct and indirect competitor analysis

- brand development as an element of the service positioning process

- service life cycles and the need to develop a portfolio of service offers

- how new service ideas are generated, developed and launched

- deletion strategies for services that have reached the end of their life cycle.

7.1 **Introduction**

So far, the focus of attention in this book has been on understanding consumers' needs. This chapter marks a transition point because the following chapters will focus on how companies manage the extended marketing mix in order to satisfy identified consumer needs. An important link between consumer needs and service development is provided by the concepts of positioning and targeting. Which groups of buyers should a service provider target? What products should be offered to these groups? How should it differentiate its services from those of its competitors?

An important aspect of developing a market position is the development of a brand image that concisely states and reinforces the adopted market position. This chapter will examine the problems and opportunities for developing brands where the service offer is highly variable and intangible.

Finally, service organizations, like all organizations, cannot afford to stand still with their existing **service portfolio**. As services approach the end of their life cycle, it is important to develop new services and to eliminate those which absorb more management effort than is justified by the contribution they make. The chapter will conclude with a review of new service development processes and relate this back to the need to develop a clear position in the marketplace.

7.2 **Service positioning**

Imagine that you were considering starting a chain of restaurants in the UK. You look around at what is available to consumers already and you find a bewildering variety of service formats, ranging from low-cost, fast-food outlets, through to gourmet restaurants. You would probably find enormous variation in the size of restaurant, type of location, choice offered to customers and average price charged. What would be the distinguishing features and benefits of your proposed restaurant in relation to the existing competitors? This is the essence of positioning strategy.

Positioning strategy distinguishes a company's service offers from those of its competitors in order to give it a competitive advantage within the market. Positioning puts a firm in a sub-segment of its chosen market, so a firm which adopts a product positioning based on 'high reliability/high cost' will appeal to a sub-segment which has a desire for reliability and a willingness to pay for it. For some marketers positioning has been seen essentially as a communications issue where the nature of a service is given and the objective is to manipulate consumer perceptions of it. But we need to bear in mind that positioning is more than merely advertising and promotion, and involves considerations of pricing, distribution and the nature of the product offer itself, the core around which all positioning strategies revolve.

Organizations must examine their opportunities and take a position within a marketplace. A position can be defined by reference to a number of scales. The level of service quality provided to customers and the price that is charged are two very basic dimensions of positioning strategy which are relevant to service industries. Figure 7.1 shows these two dimensions applied to UK supermarket retailing in which both the price and quality scales are conceptualized as running from high to low. Quality in this case can be considered as a composite of product range, speed of service, quality of personnel, quality of the shopping environment, etc. Price can be a general indication of price levels charged relative to competitors. The position of a number of UK retailers is shown. This illustrates clearly that most supermarkets lie on a diagonal line between the high-quality/high-price position adopted by Marks & Spencer and the low-price/low-quality position adopted by KwikSave. Points along this diagonal represent feasible positioning strategies for supermarket operators. A strategy in the upper-left quadrant (high price/low quality) can be described as a 'cowboy' strategy and generally is not sustainable, although it may be an attractive position in some instances – for example, some tourism-related activities where tourists are unlikely to return to the area. A position in the lower-right quadrant (high quality/low price) may indicate that an organization is failing to achieve a fair exchange of value for itself.

An analysis of competitors relative to market size can indicate the attractiveness of alternative positioning strategies. An analysis of UK clothing retailers towards the early 1990s indicated that while there was an abundance of stores in the upper-right quadrant, there were relatively few in the lower-left quadrant in relation to the numbers of people who sought this type of store. The result during the 1990s was the expansion of a number of low-cost/no-frills operators such as Matalan and Peacocks to take this position.

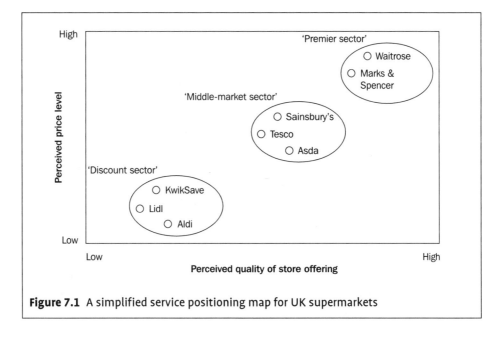

Figure 7.1 A simplified service positioning map for UK supermarkets

7.2.1 **Competitor analysis**

Any plan to develop a competitive advantage must be based on a sound analysis of just who a company's competitors are. At first, it may seem obvious who the competitors are, but as Theodore Levitt pointed out, a myopic view may focus on the immediate and direct competitors while overlooking the more serious threat posed by indirect and less obvious sources of competition. When railway companies in the 1930s saw their main competitors as other railway companies, they overlooked the fact that the most serious competition would derive from road-based transport operators. More recently, banks have been made to realize that their competitors are not just other banks, or even other organizations providing financial services, but any organization that has a strong brand reputation and customer base. Through these, supermarkets, airlines and car companies have all developed banking services that now compete with mainstream banks.

Even without considering the possibility of new market entrants appearing, it is possible to identify direct and indirect competitors. Direct competitors are generally similar in form and satisfy customers' needs in a similar way. Indirect competitors may appear different in form, but satisfy a fundamentally similar need. Consider the examples of services in Figure 7.2, the underlying needs which they satisfy and their direct and indirect competitors.

Taking this bigger picture to consider indirect competitors is important because consumers essentially seek to satisfy the underlying need that can be met in a number of ways. Most customers do not need a bank – they may simply need a cash withdrawal service that can be provided just as well by a supermarket or a petrol station. The precise form of a new competitor may appear quite unlike the established service format, but in terms of positioning within consumers' minds the **new service** could be quite similar. If customers only need a bank to withdraw cash, a supermarket may have a superior position in their mind in terms of accessibility and ease of use.

Michael Porter's model of industry competitiveness identified sources of turbulence in a market that can affect the positioning of a company's products in relation to the competition. Five forces require evaluation:

Product	Typical underlying need	Direct competitors	Indirect competitors
Overseas holiday	Relaxation	Rival tour operators	Garden conservatories
Restaurant meal	Social gathering	Other restaurants	Ready-prepared gourmet meals for home entertaining
Television programme	Entertainment	Other television programmes	Internet service provider

Figure 7.2 Examples of services, the needs they satisfy, and their direct and indirect competitors

1. the threat of new entrants

2. the threat of substitute products

3. the intensity of rivalry between competing firms

4. the power of suppliers

5. the power of buyers.

With many services being easy to copy, it is not surprising that positioning strategy has become much more complex in many markets. In recent years, the UK has seen the example of banks moving into car leasing, a gas supply company moving into car breakdown assistance, and grocery retailers becoming Internet service providers.

7.2.2 **Positioning criteria**

Although price and quality were used in the example above, these are generally too simplistic in themselves as criteria for positioning. Wind (1982, pp. 79–81) suggested six generic scales along which all products can be positioned. These are examined below by reference to the possible positioning of a leisure centre.

1. *Specific product features.* A leisure centre can promote the fact that it has the largest swimming pool in the area, or the most advanced solarium.

2. *Benefits or needs satisfied.* The leisure centre could position itself somewhere between meeting pure physical recreation needs and pure social needs. In practice, positioning will make trade-offs between the two sets of needs, for example by giving up gym space to allow the construction of a bar.

3. *Usage occasions.* The centre could be positioned primarily for the occasional user, or the service offer could be adapted to aim at the more serious user who wishes to enter a long-term programme of sports training.

4. *User categories.* A choice could be made between a position aimed at satisfying the needs of individual users and one aimed at meeting the needs of institutional users such as sports clubs and schools.

5. *Positioning against another product.* The leisure centre could promote the fact that it has more facilities than its neighbouring competition.

6. *Positioning by product class.* Management could position the centre as an educational facility rather than a centre of leisure, thus positioning it in a different product class.

Selecting a position for a service involves three basic steps, as follows.

1. *Identifying the organization's strengths and the opportunities of the marketplace to be exploited.* An organization that is already established in a particular product position will normally have the advantage of customer familiarity to support any new service launch. A holiday tour operator that has positioned itself as a high-quality/high-price operator can use this as a strength to persuade customers to pay

relatively high prices for a new range of value-added holidays. Sometimes a weakness can be turned into a strength for positioning purposes – for example, the Avis car rental chain has stressed in its advertising that by being the number two operator, it has to try harder than its competitors. Against internal strengths must be considered the attractiveness of a sub-segment. For the tour operator seeking to build upon its strong reputation for offering high-quality/high-cost holidays, an analysis of the market may reveal greater opportunities in a segment that seeks a basic budget range of holidays. Should the organization decide to enter this market, it must avoid tarnishing its established brand values by association with a lower-quality product. One solution is to adopt a separate identity for a new service that assumes a different position.

2. *Evaluating the position possibilities and selecting the most appropriate.* An organization may discover a number of potential positions but many may have to be discarded if they result in uneconomically small market segments, or are too costly to develop. Other positions may be rejected as being inconsistent with an organization's image. Selection from the remaining possibilities should be on the basis of the organization's greatest differential advantage in areas which are most valued by target customers. When it entered the Indonesian market, the UK retailer Marks & Spencer realized that its UK positioning would be unsustainable against low-cost local competition. It therefore adopted a much more exclusive position with small shops, limited product ranges and relatively high prices.

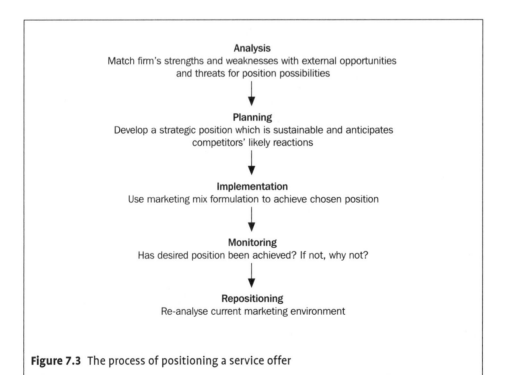

Figure 7.3 The process of positioning a service offer

3. *Developing the marketing mix and establishing in the eyes of target customers the position that has been adopted.* Organizations must develop programmes to implement and promote the position that they have adopted. In this way an airline such as British Airways which positions itself as providing superior in-flight cabin crew services must develop a programme for recruiting, training, motivating and retaining appropriate crews who can deliver the desired service. It must also develop a creative platform for its promotional programme that makes clear in the minds of target customers just what a brand stands for. Positioning for a service industry differs from manufacturing industry in that the method of producing the service is an important element of the positioning process (Figure 7.3).

7.2.3 **Positioning the service provider**

Services can be positioned either on a standalone basis or as part of a service organization's total service range – in effect, the service organization adopts a position, rather than the individual service. The fact that consumers are likely to evaluate the service provider at least as much as a particular service makes this approach to position analysis attractive. Shostack (1987) suggested that within a range of services provided by an organization (or 'service family'), a marketer can consider positioning strategies based on structural complexity and structural diversity. Structural complexity comprises the number of steps that make up a service production process, and diversity the extent to which service output is variable. In this way, a doctor's service is highly complex in terms of the number of processes involved in a consultation or operation. It is also highly variable, for service outcomes can be diverse in terms of both planned and unplanned deviations in outcomes. Some processes can be high in complexity but low in diversity. Hotels, for example offer a complete range of processes but are generally able to establish relatively low levels of diversity. A singer provides an example of a service that is low in complexity but high in diversity.

Shostack sees positioning as a process of deciding how the service provider wishes to position its total range of services in relation to its customers – complexity and diversity are two key dimensions by which an organization can be positioned. Positioning decisions have implications for the overall image of the provider, and hence of individual services within its range. As an example, a dentist could take a more divergent position by adding general counselling on health matters, or reduce it by undertaking only diagnostic work. Complexity could be increased by adding retailing of supplies, or reduced by offering only a limited range of dental treatments. These options are shown diagrammatically in Figure 7.4. The position adopted by an organization will be influenced by its strengths and weaknesses relative to the market that it seeks to address. A large dental practice may be better placed to position itself as a provider of complex services, but would need to ensure that diversity in outcomes was minimized in order not to adversely affect its image. A small dentist may find the most appropriate service position to be the provision of relatively simple services with divergent outcomes.

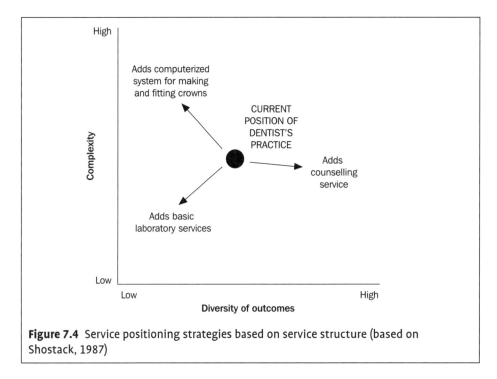

Figure 7.4 Service positioning strategies based on service structure (based on Shostack, 1987)

Many service organizations have found a low-complexity/low-diversity position to offer great opportunities for exploiting niche markets. In this way, solicitors have set up as specialist will-writing businesses, offering one **product line** with little scope for variability. By developing expertise and reducing overheads, such companies can satisfy customers who do not have the need for the more complex, but also more divergent, services of full-service solicitors.

7.2.4 **Repositioning**

Over time, an organization may need to reposition its service offer. This could come about for a number of reasons.

■ The original positioning strategy was inappropriate: over-estimation of an organization's competitive advantage or of the size of the sub-segment to whom the positioning was intended to appeal could force a re-evaluation of positioning strategy.

■ Where the nature of customer demand has changed: for example, it is argued that UK customers' attitudes towards package holidays changed during the 1990s away from an emphasis on low price and towards greater emphasis on high quality standards. Many tour operators accordingly repositioned their offering to provide higher standards at higher prices.

■ Service providers seek to build upon their growing strengths to reposition towards meeting the needs of more profitable sub-segments. In many service industries, organizations start life as simple, no-frills, low-price operations, subsequently gaining a favourable image that they use to 'trade up' to relatively high-quality/high-price positions. This phenomenon is well established in the field of retailing in which McNair (1958) identified what has become known as the 'Wheel of Retailing'. This contends that retail businesses start life as cut-price, low-cost, narrow-margin operations which subsequently 'trade up' with improvements in display, more prestigious premises, increased advertising, delivery and the provision of many other customer services which serve to drive up expenses, prices and margins. Eventually, retailers mature as high-cost, conservative and 'top-heavy' institutions with a sales policy based on quality goods and services rather than price appeal. This in turn opens the way for the next generation of low-cost innovatory retailers to find a position which maturing firms have vacated.

7.3 Developing the brand

A brand identity provides a shorthand reference to the position adopted by a service offer or service provider. Brands are important in guiding buyers when choosing between otherwise seemingly similar competing services. Consider the following cases.

- Buyers of pension plans are typically not very knowledgeable about pensions, yet several tens of thousands of British people have entrusted their pension provision to the Virgin Group, largely on the strength of its brand reputation and despite the company being a newcomer to the pensions industry with no proven track record.

- When booking an overseas hotel, many travellers would chose from a shortlist of hotel brand names with which they are familiar, despite the existence of locally run hotels which would probably offer better quality at a lower price.

- Buyers of package holidays in the UK are often prepared to pay a premium for the Thomson brand name, in preference to less well-known competitor brands that offer lower prices for an apparently identical holiday.

Brands are frequently used by companies to provide evidence of consistent standards and are particularly important where a company has not had an opportunity to develop an ongoing relationship with its customers. The use of brands in the service sector is becoming increasingly important as a means of limiting the search activities of potential buyers. Rather than considering all possible options, a brand encourages buyers to refuse other products that do not come with the statement of values that a brand stands for.

Historically, branding assumed significance when economies of scale meant that producers were no longer able to have a direct and individual relationship with their growing number of customers, and therefore could not provide personal reassurance of product quality. A brand acted as a substitute for a personal relationship in managing buyers' exposure to risk. Branding has been found to simplify the decision-making process by providing a sense of security and consistency which may be absent outside of a relationship with a supplier (Barwise and Roberston, 1992). Risk levels are perceived as being higher for products that fulfil important needs and values, so in these situations the value of brands can be higher.

There have been many conceptualizations of the unique attributes of a brand and how these affect buying decision processes. These usually distinguish between elements that can be objectively measured (such as the reported reliability of an airline) and the subjective values that can only be defined in the minds of consumers (such as the perceived personality of the Virgin airline brand). Gardner and Levy (1955) distinguished between the 'functional' dimensions of a brand and its 'personality', while other dimensions have been identified as utilitarianism versus value expressive (Munson and Spivey, 1981), need satisfaction versus impression management (Solomon, 1983), and functional versus representational (de Chernatony and McDonald, 2003). The functional dimensions of a brand serve to reassure buyers that important elements of a service offer will be delivered as promised, for example an airline can be trusted to operate safely, a tour operator not to overbook its hotels and a savings institution to return its investors' money promptly when required.

With increasing affluence, the non-functional expectations of brands have become more important positioning tools. For services which offer very little tangible evidence, the emotional dimensions of a brand can be particularly important in guiding buyers' evaluation. A number of dimensions of a brand's emotional appeal have been identified, including trust, liking and sophistication. As consumers buy products, they learn to appreciate their added value and begin to form an emotional preference for them. While there are many companies offering bank accounts and credit cards, individual companies such as Virgin and American Express have created emotional brands that guide customers in a market dominated by otherwise generic products.

There is an extensive literature on the emotional relationship consumers develop between a brand and their own perceived or sought personality. Brands are chosen when the image that they create matches the needs, values and lifestyles of customers. Through socialization processes, individuals form perceptions of themselves, which they attempt to reinforce or alter by relating to specific groups, products and brands (Solomon and Buchanan, 1991). There is evidence that branding plays a particularly important role in purchase decisions where the product is conspicuous in its use and purchase, and in situations where group social acceptance is a strong motivator (Moschis, 1976; Miniard and Cohen, 1983). While conspicuous consumption is most commonly associated with manufactured goods (for example, brands of training shoes, designer clothes labels and makes of car), the concept of a conspicuous brand also has meaning in a services context. An individual may use their membership of an upmarket gym or their possession of a 'gold' credit card to make statements about themselves in much the same way as a Rolex watch or Nike trainers.

There has been a lot of recent discussion about the role of brands in influencing purchasing decisions. The growth in 'own-label' products sold by many retailers has led some to suggest that we are becoming less conscious of brands in our buying decision process. With greater education, maybe consumers are 'seeing through' the efforts of brand-building marketers? Own-brands first achieved prominence among low-value, low-involvement manufactured goods but have since become popular with many buyers of services. Retailers such as Tesco and Marks & Spencer have recently introduced 'own-brand' bank accounts, savings schemes and personal loans to sell alongside their 'own-brand' baked beans and underwear. Is this a challenge to the traditional role of branding, or merely a reorientation to meet changes in the business environment?

The traditional role of branding has been to differentiate products, but brands have been increasingly applied to **organizational image** too. This has occurred particularly with services where the intangibility of the product causes the credentials of the provider to be an important choice criterion. The notion of an emotional relationship to a product has been extended to develop an emotional relationship between an organization and its customers. In this way, Tesco and Marks & Spencer have become strong brands in their own right that command the respect and trust of buyers.

Service intermediaries such as Tesco and Marks & Spencer have developed strong functional attributes of their brand through consistent delivery of high service standards. This has been supplemented by their portrayal as caring service

---

BILL THACKERY

24 Brinton Way, Leckhampton, Cheltenham

Quality decorator, personal service – no job too small

Tel: 01242 612018
Mobile: 07973 043526
Phone for an estimate

Figure 7.5 Many service sectors are dominated by large numbers of small businesses. For many, such as this decorator, marketers' language of brand development may be quite alien, but nevertheless such businesses have often developed a loyal customer following based on quality of service and word-of-mouth recommendation. Small businesses co-exist alongside much larger ones in service sectors as diverse as catering, accountancy, travel retailing and legal services. Small and large-sized competitors have successfully developed a position for themselves, with the smaller competitors typically positioning themselves on the basis of personal, friendly service; lower overhead costs and greater flexibility to meet customers' needs. Larger competitors in these sectors have typically used their economies of scale, economies of scope and a strong brand that simplifies the decision process for buyers who are inexperienced in buying a category of service.

organizations that develop strong preference at an emotional level. The brand position must be consistent throughout even when it is extended to diverse ranges of services. For example, the Virgin brand has traditionally been positioned as reliable, slightly offbeat and honest. This has been sufficient for customers to make the leap from trusting Virgin's CDs and cola to entrusting their savings and investments to the company. The brand needs to be carefully protected when it is extended to new products. Many came to question the Virgin position on reliability following the company's acquisition of the West Coast Main Line rail franchise. If the company's trains were consistently at the bottom of the league tables for performance, what did this say about the company's pension schemes?

It has been argued that a further challenge to the role of brands has emerged from the increasing importance of consumer legislation. Characteristics such as reliability and consistency may have traditionally added value to a brand, but these are increasingly enshrined in legislation and therefore less capable of being used to differentiate one organization's services from another. A good example of this is to be found in the

---

Taxis in any colour, including black

How do people choose a taxi? An example of the effects of legislation on brand choice can be observed by contrasting buyer behaviour in areas with strict licensing (e.g. London) and areas where a relatively unregulated market exists (common in many UK provincial cities). In London, the famous black cabs are highly regulated in terms of the standards of drivers, the vehicles themselves and prices charged. Drivers must pass a 'knowledge' test before being allowed to operate, and cannot refuse to carry a passenger, except in clearly specified cases. Few people would bother spending much effort in selecting one cab from another – they have been reduced to a commodity whose consistent standards are rigorously maintained by the licensing body, the Public Carriage Office.

Contrast this with the situation in towns where regulations are minimal and buyers may have little idea about the integrity of the car they are getting into or the reliability of its driver. This is the classic opportunity for the development of brands by taxi operators to give them a distinctive position in the marketplace, and thereby simplifying buyers' choice processes. While many local authorities control the fares which all taxi operators must charge, it is open to individual operators to develop a brand which is associated with reliability, safety and courteousness. Next time a customer seeks a taxi, he or she may know which taxi companies to avoid and which to go for out of preference.

Debate has taken place between those who would like to see a free market in taxis and those who see regulation as vital to the public interest. What is the experience in your area? Of what value are brands in guiding the choices of taxi users?

financial services sector, where most countries have strict regulations which protect investors from being sold investment schemes which are of dubious security or are inappropriate for their needs. There is less need to trust a financial services company with a strong brand name when legislation guarantees similar standards from all companies, and a compensation system if those standards are not met. Many financial services companies have recognized the limits on the development of functional aspects of branding by concentrating on the emotional aspects. The Virgin Group has been successful in this respect by appealing to groups who value its 'no-nonsense' approach to doing business, while Schroders has stressed its long-established history and comprehensive range of facilities.

7.3.1 **Branding and buyer–seller relationships**

There has been a lot of recent interest in the methods that companies use to develop ongoing relationships with their customers, including the use of databases, loyalty programmes and added-value benefits for members. The subject of relationship marketing was considered in Chapter 5, and similarities between brand-building and relationship development should be noted. Both seek to simplify buyers' decision processes by reducing the inherent riskiness of a purchase. Branding appeals to buyers' sense of trust in a product whose characteristics become familiar through reputation and promotion, such that the purchase of any other product is seen as highly risky. The presence of a brand simplifies buyers' decision processes, because it avoids the need to evaluate a wide range of competing sources of supply each time a decision has to be made. Of course, a brand is only as good as its reputation, and a brand which fails to deliver its promises will not maintain its position in its marketplace.

Services have traditionally focused on relationship development and manufactured goods on brand development. Typical of the former are one-to-one relationships that buyers have developed with their bank managers, doctors, hairdressers and car repairers. In the goods sector, branding has been used extensively to position the functional and emotional attributes of a product. However, as the distinction between goods and services becomes blurred, so the roles of relationship and brand development have come to overlap. In the case of services, the industrialization and deskilling of many service processes renders the service provider relatively anonymous and incapable of having a personal relationship with its customers. Personal banking is a good example of a sector in which personal relationships have become much weaker as a result of the automation of bank branches and deskilling of bank managers' tasks. At the same time, all of the major UK banks have spent considerable effort in developing strong brand images in an attempt to develop an identifiable market position and to simplify the choice process of customers. By contrast, many manufactured goods have augmented their offering with services – for example, cars are now frequently sold with the benefit of long-term service support. This implies an ongoing relationship that may exert very great influence on the next purchase decision (for example, a car buyer may gain preferential treatment by trading in his or her car for a new one provided by the current provider).

Flying the global flag for Britain?

In the 1990s the world airline industry underwent major changes as a result of deregulation, privatization and the creation of strategic alliances. In the early 1990s, British Airways – one of the first state-owned airlines to be privatized – had been a trailblazer with rapid expansion and enviable profitability. But by the end of the 1990s research had shown that the company was perceived by its customers as boring, stuffy and lacking in creativity. Furthermore, its Britishness was seen as a contributor to this stuffiness. In an increasingly global market for airline services, it needed to shed this image, yet at the same time still needed to recognize that over half its business came from British people. Companies who have faced this positioning dilemma have resorted to the traditional maxim of 'think global, act locally'. The solution adopted by British Airways was to position itself as a global airline that recognized ethnic differences from around the world. A visible manifestation of this was provided by developing multiple liveries for the company's aircraft and publicity material from around the world. The theory was that the Japanese, for example, might be more able to identify with the airline if its tail fins carried examples of Japanese art. The company thought long and hard about whether to drop the title 'British' from its title, following the example set by other previously state-owned organizations such as British Telecom, British Gas and British Airports Authority, who had dropped the British title as part of their global positioning. Did the ethnic positioning strategy work for British Airways? The strategy may have made life more interesting for plane spotters, but subsequent research showed that many British business-class passengers felt alienated by the repositioning. This was not helped when arch-rival Virgin Atlantic restored a Union Flag to its aircraft, positioning itself as the natural choice of British travellers. Worse still, by 2002, the whole idea of global coverage was being questioned by British Airways, after it failed to turn around US Air and Deutsch BA, and minority holdings in a number of other airlines which it had acquired earlier. After just under two years, British Airways realized that the global positioning may have harmed its core British market and restored a stylized Union Flag to the majority of aircraft in its fleet.

7.4 Developing the portfolio of services

Few service organizations can survive by offering just one specialized service. Instead, a mix of services is usually offered. This section considers the issues involved in managing a portfolio of services.

To begin, the services range offered by an organization can be disaggregated for analysis. The most basic unit of output is often referred to as an *item* – this is a specific version of a service. Such an item would normally be part of a service line that is a group of related service items. The service mix is the combination of services that an organization offers to customers. A distinction can be made between the depth of the service mix and its width. Product depth refers to the number of different services in a service line. Service width refers to the number of service lines offered by an organization.

An example of an individual service item offered by a bank is a young person's card-based savings account. This in turn will form part of a line of savings accounts. The depth of this line may be indicated by the presence of a wide range of savings accounts to meet the needs of customers who require ease of access, high interest, flexibility, etc. Savings accounts represent just one line of service offering for most banks – other lines would typically include personal loans, mortgages, credit cards, etc.

To go where the organization has never gone before?

Should a company 'stick to its knitting' and do what it is good at, or search continually for new products and new markets? Countless companies have reported disastrous results after going into areas they knew very little about. The rapid growth of Next from its core of fashion retailing to newsagents and home furnishings contributed to its near collapse in the late 1980s. WHSmith went through bad years in the mid-1990s when the newsagent's diversification into DIY retailing and television failed to work. Abbey National diversified in the late 1990s from its core household mortgage business into wholesale banking, acquiring on the way train- and aircraft-leasing companies. But by 2003 it had realized the error of its ways and reported an annual loss of nearly £1 billion, mainly attributable to its new ventures.

But isn't change essential for companies, especially those facing static or declining markets? One of the UK's leading grocery retailers, Asda, would not be where it is today had not the Associated Dairy company taken a risk and set up a retailing operation. The security service company Securicor knew that it was taking a risk when it invested in a joint venture with British Telecom to create the successful Cellnet (now O_2) mobile phone network. And a small manufacturing company called WPP (standing for Wire Plastic Products) took huge risks on its way to becoming the owner of one of the world's leading advertising agencies.

It is fine, with hindsight, to criticize a firm's decisions about which direction its product portfolio should take. But in an uncertain world, risks have to be taken. A sound analysis of a company's strengths and weaknesses, and of its external environment certainly helps, but success also depends upon an element of luck.

Decisions about an organization's service mix are of strategic importance. In order to remain competitive in the face of declining demand for its principal service line, a service company may need to widen its product mix. For example, the increasing diversity in food tastes has forced many specialized fast-food outlets to widen their range. In the UK, for example, traditional fish and chip shops have often had to introduce new lines such as kebabs or home delivery services. On the other hand, decisions may need to be made to delete services from the mix in cases where consumer tastes have changed or competitive pressures have made the continuing provision of a service uneconomic. Service mix extension and deletion decisions are continually made in order that organizations can provide services more effectively (providing the right services in response to consumers' changing needs) and more efficiently (providing those services for which the organization is able to make most efficient use of its resources).

For any service organization, its service offering will be constrained by the capabilities, facilities and resources at its disposal. It is therefore important for service firms to constantly examine their capabilities and their objectives to ensure that the range of services provided meets the needs of the consumer as well as the organization. Through a process sometimes referred to as a service product audit, an organization can get an understanding of whether it is continuing to provide the right services to the right target groups. Key questions for an audit are as follows.

- What benefits do customers seek from the service?
- What is the current and continuing availability of the resources required to provide the service?
- What skills and technical know-how are required?
- What benefits are offered over and above the competition?
- Are competitor advantages causing the organization to lose revenue?
- Does each service provided still earn sufficient financial return?
- Do services meet the targets which justify continued funding?

The answers to these questions form the basis of service mix development strategy.

7.5 Product/service life-cycle concept

It was noted earlier that the position adopted by a service offer needs to be continually reviewed. Repositioning may be needed because new competitors have entered a market, forcing a company to consider whether it wants to meet the new entrants head on, or to find a position in the market which is less accessible to the new competitors. More importantly, most services go through some form of life cycle, necessitating changes in marketing strategy as the service passes from one stage in the cycle to the next. There is evidence that service life cycles are becoming shorter, especially where the service offer has a high-technology base. Within the mobile phone sector, for example, analogue phone services were soon replaced by GSM and PCN services, which by 2000 were being challenged by new WAP and third-generation (3G) phone services. The cyclical nature of many services offers calls for continued scanning of the environment for new service opportunities, which are discussed in the following section.

The product/service life cycle graphically depicts the changing fortunes of a service, or groups of services within an organization's portfolio. Services typically go through a number of stages between entering the portfolio and leaving, each calling for adjustments to marketing activities. Five stages are identified in Figure 7.6.

- Phase 1: *Introduction* – new services are often costly to develop and launch, and may have teething problems. People may be wary of trying something new, especially a new service whose intangibility prevents prior evaluation. Sales, therefore, tend to be slow and are restricted to those who like trying out new products or who believe they can gain status or benefit by having them.

- Phase 2: *Growth* – by this time, the service has been tested and any problems have been resolved. The service is now more reliable and more readily available. Buyers now start to see the benefits that can be gained by using the service. Sales start to increase greatly and this is a signal for competitors to start entering the market.

- Phase 3: *Maturity* – almost everyone who wants to buy the service has now done so, which is a particular problem for services that are bought as a one-off rather than a recurrent purchase. The number of competitors in the market has risen.

- Phase 4: *Saturation* – there are now too many competitors and no further growth in the market. Competitors tend to compete with each other on the basis of price.

- Phase 5: *Decline* – with falling demand and new substitute products appearing, organizations drop out of the market.

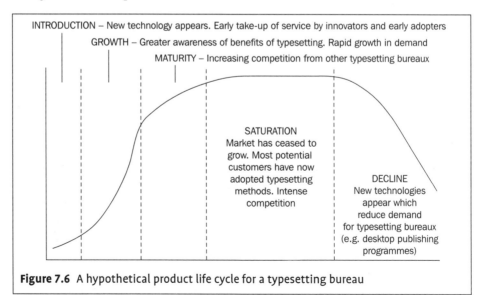

Figure 7.6 A hypothetical product life cycle for a typesetting bureau

The usefulness of the life-cycle concept lies in the recognition that marketing activity for a service is closely related to the stage in the life cycle that a service has reached. In this way, promotional planning is closely related to the life cycle, with emphasis placed in the launch phase on raising awareness through public relations activity, building on this through the growth phase with advertising, resorting to sales promotion incentives as the market matures and becomes more competitive, and finally possibly allowing promotional activity to fall as the service is allowed to go into decline. The message used at each stage may position the service offer quite differently, beginning for example as a 'latest technology' message, through 'most reliable', and perhaps to 'lowest cost'. In a similar way, distribution and pricing decisions can also often be related to the stage which a service has reached in its life cycle.

Of course, the **product life cycle** presented above is a conceptual abstraction. Different products move through the life cycle at different paces. Some products have been in the maturity/saturation stage for many years (e.g. bank current accounts), whereas others disappear very soon after introduction (e.g. some trendy clothing retailers). Empirical evidence also seems to imply a variety of life-cycle modifications and mutations.

7.5.1 Difficulties in applying the life-cycle concept

Although the idea of product life cycles is appealing and seems to be validated by research, it is important to be aware of the possible failings with this conceptual approach in terms of both goods and services. It can be argued that the product/ service life cycle concept is probably more useful for strategic planning and control purposes than for developing short-term forecasts and costed marketing programmes. In reality, life-cycle patterns are far too variable in both shape and duration for any realistic predictions to be made. A further difficulty in applying the life-cycle concept lies in the inability of marketers to accurately ascertain where in the life cycle a service actually is at any time. A stabilization of sales may be a movement into maturity or simply a temporary plateau due to external causes, for example. In fact, it is possible that the shape of the life cycle is a result of an organization's marketing activity rather than being an indication of environmental factors which the organization should respond to – in other words, it could in fact lead to a self-fulfilling prophesy.

Another criticism of the concept is that the duration of the stages will depend upon whether it is a product class, form or brand that is being considered. For example, the life cycle for holidays is probably quite flat, whereas life cycles for particular formulations of holidays and for specific holiday operators' brands become progressively more cyclical. Carman and Langeard (1979) noted that most service organizations have only a very small number of core services and, consequently, they suggest a degree of caution in using the life-cycle concept for services, particularly as the basis for portfolio approaches to service product planning.

Taking these points into consideration, the life-cycle concept may still be helpful in guiding a firm in its service mix decisions. Although life cycles may be unpredictable for services in terms of the length of time a service may remain at a particular stage, the understanding that services are likely to change in their sales and profit performance over a period of time implies a need for proactive service mix management.

7.6 **New service development**

As a result of analysis and evaluation of its product mix, an organization may consider the need to add to its service portfolio in response to the changing nature of its operating environment. The following are typical circumstances when new services may be necessary.

■ If a major service has reached the maturity stage of its cycle and may be moving towards decline, new services may be sought to preserve sales levels.

■ New services may be developed as a means of utilizing spare capacity, for example unoccupied rooms during off-peak periods may lead a hotel operator to develop new service offers designed to fill the empty rooms.

A typing service in cyberspace?

Putting the spoken word into print has seen a quickening pace in the technologies available that can do the job speedily and accurately. The typewriter eventually gave way to the word processor and keyboard. But what about the likely fortunes of a new speech recognition service launched at the end of the 1990s?

A UK company called Speech Machines (www.speechmachines.co.uk) uses computers to receive dictation over the telephone or as voice messages sent through the internet by e-mail. The dictation is transcribed automatically by computer with a claimed 95% accuracy. Specially written software manages the incoming dictation and automatically sends the transcribed document to one of the contract typists the company uses for checking and correction of the final manuscript. It is then sent back to the customer through the internet. The service has found a useful niche in the USA with the legal and medical professions, offering a speedy and efficient alternative to employing a secretary in-house. But how long a life can this service expect before it is overtaken by increasingly sophisticated and user-friendly voice-recognition software that allows users to complete the task in-house? If it is to maintain its business, how can the company offering this new service continue to develop its service offer so that it meets customers' changing needs better than any of the alternatives currently available? The benefits of the company's services were recognized by the American company MedQuist, which acquired Speech Machines in 2001. The company had already built a niche in the medical profession and added the Speech Machines service to its portfolio of document management solutions.

■ New services can help to balance an organization's existing sales portfolio and thereby reduce risks of dependency on only a few services offered within a range.

■ In order to retain and develop a relationship with its customers, an organization may be forced to introduce new products to allow it to cater to customers' diverse needs.

■ An opportunity may arise for an organization to satisfy unmet needs with a new service as a result of a competitor leaving the market.

Although the task of new product development within the service sector shows many elements in common with the manufacturing sector, a number of differences between the two have been noted, including differences in key success factors (Johne and Storey, 1998; Henard and Szymanski, 2001); the range of activities undertaken (Edgett, 1994; Johne and Storey, 1998); managerial pressures, and they types of strategies pursued (Venkatraman and Prescott, 1990).

7.6.1 **What is meant by a 'new service'?**

The intangible nature of services means that it is often quite easy to produce slight variants of an existing service, with the result that the term 'new service' can mean anything from a minor style change to a major innovation (Figure 7.7). In fact, the term 'new service' could be applied to any of the following.

■ *Process changes.* These include redesign of the service encounter, for example a sandwich bar offering a new ordering facility via its website.

■ *Outcome changes.* These may be considered important where a service is evaluated primarily on the basis of outcomes, for example a financial services company may offer a new form of equity-based investment which guarantees a specified return at the end of a five-year period.

■ *Changes to associated tangibles.* The use of new tangible materials can create the impression of a new service, for example an airline's website may be redesigned, but nevertheless offer very much the same processes and outcomes as previously.

■ *Service line extensions.* These are additions to the existing service product range – a university offering a new part-time version of its MBA programme, for example. However, although the programme may be new to the university, it is not genuinely a new service if it is already offered by other universities.

■ *Major innovations.* These are entirely new services for new markets – the provision of diagnostic tele-medicine services, for example.

The distinctive characteristics of services would imply that there are some special issues that need to be considered in new service development, when compared to the development of new tangible products.

Figure 7.7 Fast-food restaurants have become adept at adapting their service offer to suit the needs of a changing marketing environment. During the 1980s and 1990s, fast-food chains capitalized on changing patterns of family meal eating, growing levels of disposable income (especially among younger adults), a growing desire for variety seeking and increasing concern with value for money. The rise of McDonald's to pre-eminence in the sector can partly be explained by its ability to innovate with new menus and new service formats for new target markets. By the end of the 1990s, the company faced growing concern in many western countries over problems of obesity caused by eating too much high-fat food. McDonald's has continued its pattern of innovation with products which address the changed health concerns of the early 21st century, including McCafés and, as here, a fruit bag which is aimed at making fresh fruit more appealing to children (and their parents). (Reproduced with permission of McDonald's Corporation)

- The very intangibility of services has tended to lead to a proliferation of slightly different service products. Because of their intangibility, new services can be relatively easy to develop and the variety of different services can cause confusion. As an example, banks frequently introduce 'new' mortgage offers which are only slightly differentiated from existing offers – e.g. by offering a lower rate for the first two years of the mortgage.

- The characteristic of inseparability between service production and consumption means that front-line operational staff have greater opportunity to identify new service ideas which are likely to be successful.

■ As services are more likely than goods to be customized to the needs of individual customers, there could be greater opportunities for marginally different new services, each having its own unique selling proposition.

Will they return to the Rovers?

When Granada Television announced plans to develop a tourist attraction at its Manchester studios, the sceptics were out in force. What tourists would want to visit a run-down part of inner-city Manchester? But following its opening in 1985, the Granada Studios Tour seemed to be a great success, with numbers steadily rising to around 300 000 visitors a year. Furthermore, a strong price position was maintained, with admission ticket prices rising from £5.99 to £12.99 over a 10-year period. But by the mid-1990s, visitor numbers had stabilized and then actually fell, despite buoyancy elsewhere within the tourism industry. Had the attraction reached the downward stage of its life cycle? The attraction appealed to the curiosity of the 17 million *Coronation Street* viewers, especially those who lived within easy travelling distance of Manchester. Once they had visited the studios, their curiosity at visiting the 'Rovers Return' had been satisfied and the number of new customers who had not previously visited the attraction was diminishing. The challenge facing Granada was to reinvent the product to appeal to new markets and to bring previous visitors back for repeat visits. A number of new markets were identified, including the weekend break market. By linking with local hotels, the market for Granada Studios was extended beyond the original local day-trip market. Corporate hospitality groups were identified as another important market segment. To get previous visitors back, investment was made in major new attractions including an interactive exhibition of futuristic technology and a footballing 'Hall of Fame'. An extensive programme of research among visitors and non-visitors was undertaken to try to understand the attraction's perceived image. One result was to drop the word 'Tour' from the title and just call it 'Granada Studios'. This reflected the high level of involvement which visitors felt during their visit.

7.6.2 The new service development processes

Research has indicated that a systematic process of development helps to reduce the risk of failure when new products are launched. In reality, there is evidence that most firms do not have a formal NSD strategy. A study by Kelly and Storey (2000) showed that only half of a sample of firms in banking, telecommunications, insurance and transportation had a formal NSD strategy; that only a quarter had a culture in which ideas were continually generated; and only a third had an idea search methodology.

Although a variety of different procedures have been proposed and implemented, they all tend to have the common themes of beginning with as many new ideas as possible and having the end objective of producing a tested service idea ready for launch. One common sequence is shown in Figure 7.8, although in practice, many of the sequential stages shown are compressed so that their timing overlaps with other stages.

Although, in principle, the new product development process is similar for goods and services, differences arise because of the intangibility, inseparability, variability and perishability of services. The differences are discussed below in the context of each stage of the development process.

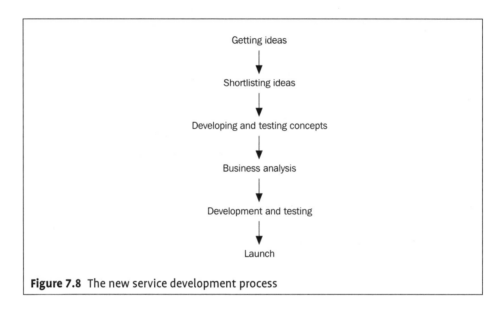

Figure 7.8 The new service development process

Getting ideas

Ideas can be generated from within an organization and also from outside, either formally or informally. Easingwood, in his study of new service development, found that generating new ideas is not a problem for most service firms (Easingwood, 1986). Inseparability means that front-line staff have a closer understanding of both service operations and customer needs, and therefore it would seem logical that a large number of new ideas would come from the operating staff. Perhaps surprisingly, Easingwood found that the most common internal source of new service ideas was the marketing function rather than the operational function. The marketing function had constant contact with both customers and competitors and thus had market information 'on-tap'. He found that a much smaller proportion of new ideas came from the operations function because 'new' services were perceived by them as a further burden which would complicate their operations. Cowell (1988) noted that although the generation of ideas is relatively easy for service organizations, the degree of novelty of idea tends to be slight. Many ideas tend to be conservative, focusing on minor modifications, geographical extensions or 'me-too' ideas.

Customers can be an important source of ideas for new service and, for this purpose, a study of the interaction between service provider and customer may be worthwhile. MacKay and Conway (1992) considered the variety of potential influences on new services idea generation within the corporate financial services sector and indicated that the application of a network perspective could be useful in identifying the various influences on the generation of new financial services ideas.

Shortlisting ideas

This stage involves evaluating the ideas generated and rejection of those that do not justify the organization's resources. Criteria are usually established so that comparisons between ideas can be made, but because each firm exists in its own particular environment, there is no standard set of evaluative criteria that fits all. Easingwood found a variety of screening practices, all with differing degrees of formality, noting that screening processes for financial services were particularly rigorous. Within this sector, each new idea would be evaluated by customer discussion groups, feedback on proposed features and advertising would be collected, and financial projections calculated with some detail. It was suggested that this rigour is partly due to the difficulties in withdrawing a financial service once it is being provided.

Intangibility makes services difficult to assess and therefore 'image' is an important means by which customers reassure themselves about the credibility of a service provider. Easingwood found that enhancement or support of an organization's image was an important criteria used by firms in the screening process.

Developing and testing concepts

Ideas that survive the shortlisting stage need to be translated into service concepts. These concepts are then tested with a sample of target users to assess their reactions to them. A challenge for pure services is to convey the concepts without the help of diagrams or artists' impressions which are available when trying to portray a new concept for a manufactured product. It may be very difficult to build up a mental picture of a new service concept when nothing similar could have been experienced previously.

Business analysis

The proposed idea is now translated into a business proposal. The likelihood of success/failure is analysed including resource requirements in terms of manpower, extra physical resources, etc. At this stage, many of the factors that will determine the financial success of the proposed new service remain speculative. The activities of competitors' new product development processes could have a crucial effect on the firm's eventual market share, as well as the price which it is able to sustain for its service.

Developing and testing

This is the translation of the idea into an actual service which is capable of delivery to customers. The tangible elements as well as the service delivery systems which make up the whole service offering all have to be designed and tested. Unfortunately, testing may not always be possible, and evidence from Easingwood implies that test marketing generally among service firms is limited. One possibility is to test a new service with a sample of existing customers with no external promotion. Many UK banks tested their new online banking facilities on existing customers who were invited to try the new service and give their feedback, ahead of a full launch.

Launch

The organization now makes decisions on when to introduce the new service, where, to whom and how. Time is a key issue. The longer a new service goes through the various developmental stages, the greater the chance that competitors will enter the market beforehand. The firm can be a pioneer and enter the market first or be a follower and reduce the risks considerably. In the UK, there was a race in 2003 to launch the first 'third generation' mobile phone network. The new operator, '3', created some publicity for being the first to launch a network (on 3 March 2003), despite the fact that no handsets were available until some time afterwards (Fagan, 2003).

Where there are still some uncertainties about how the service will work, or if there are doubts about whether there is capacity to cope, a service provider may go for a 'soft launch'. This involves opening the service to selected customers, who are advised that some aspects of the **service process** may not be completely finalized. In return for a special price, customers can obtain a bargain and the company obtains feedback which it can use to fine-tune the service before a full public launch. The hotel and cruise ship industries frequently use soft launches – for example, in December 2003, the Cunard Line invited employees' families on the inaugural cruise of its new flagship *Queen Mary 2*, prior to the ship's first advertised trans-Atlantic crossing. For companies operating globally, timing of the launch in different national markets can be critical, as markets are likely to be at different stages of development and a global roll-out may be inefficient for a company to manage (Wong, 2002). A staggered roll-out allows a company to exploit profits from one market before moving on to progressively less attractive markets, thereby maintaining a portfolio of products at different stages of market development.

So far, the stages of new product development have been presented as if they are steps which necessarily have to be tackled in a sequential order. In fact, the time taken to go through this process can be considerable, allowing competitors to gain a lead. There have therefore been many attempts to carry out some of the steps simultaneously. Virtual-reality systems, for example, are allowing customers to get a feel for the final service process at a very early stage, allowing this to take place at the same time as concept testing and avoiding the need to wait while all steps of the process are progressed (Dahan and Hauser, 2002).

The new service development process can be extremely complex, with many examples of cost overruns and delayed results (Kim and Wilemon, 2003). A key to more effective new service development activity is close working relationships between marketing and operational functions. Even simple administrative matters

How long will the queue be at the e-bank?

The online bank Egg has now established itself as one of Europe's leading online financial services providers, with over 2.1 million customers by the end of 2002. Egg had attained brand awareness with 88% of adults in the UK, which is impressive for such a young company, and acquired 600 000 new customers in 2001 alone – 100 000 more than the total number of customers for its nearest UK internet rival (ABA, 2002). But despite careful planning, the launch of Egg got off to a bumpy start.

When ATMs first appeared a couple of decades earlier, many people thought they would never work because people like to go into a branch and deal with a human being. Would people have the same fears about Internet banking? In 1998, the Internet was only beginning to catch the public's imagination and there were still major concerns about privacy, security, download speed and access to the Internet. Would Internet banking be a runaway success, or just another over-hyped new service development, of which there were many at the height of the dotcom boom?

Egg targeted busy people with neither the time nor the inclination to shop around for financial services. But how many customers should the company have geared itself up to handle when it launched its new product? Launching a new product often involves a lot of guesswork. If the number is under-estimated and the company does not have the capacity to cope with large numbers, frustration and harm to the brand reputation can soon build up.

Egg's then parent company – Prudential – undertook testing of its new banking service among a small group of customers. This allowed it to understand more about demand when it eventually went for a full public launch in 1998, backed by heavy online and offline advertising. Despite this, it soon became apparent that its servers could not cope, as potential customers complained of spending hours trying to log on to the bank's website. Egg's call centre was similarly overwhelmed, despite being available 24 hours a day, 7 days a week. It seemed that the bank had inadequately understood the peaked nature of demand which meant that call centre operators might be rushed during the early evening, but idle during much of the night and early morning.

Taking a longer-term perspective, the launch of Egg was a success. It had managed to gain 'first mover' advantage in the emerging market for an online banking service, something that might have been lost had it spent more time researching its market. Since launch, it has learnt a lot more about its customers and has embraced emerging technology to launch Egg TV in April 2000, which was the first interactive digital TV service from a financial services provider in Britain. But would Egg face a challenge from the high-street banks who set about reinvigorating their branches by removing glass panels and wooing customers with a coffee shop culture?

such as rapid communication following the results of one stage can help to speed up the new product development process. The complexity of the new service development process has often led to companies outsourcing the whole process to specialist companies who have developed an expertise in product development and market testing (Howley, 2002). The use of an outside consultancy can also be beneficial where a company's ethos is production oriented and it seeks to bring on board broader marketing skills. It has been noted that brilliant inventors do not necessarily make good marketers of a new product (Little, 2002).

Alternative forms of organization structures and their impact on new service development will be discussed in Chapter 12.

7.7 **Service deletion**

Good product management depends upon reliable marketing information to show when a product is failing to achieve its objectives. As well as maintaining successful services and investing in new ones, service organizations must also have the courage to eliminate services which are no longer likely to be of benefit to the organization as a whole. This implies a need for the following:

- establishment of targets for each service

- periodic reviews of each service's performance

- modification of existing services where necessary

- elimination of services where necessary

- development of new services.

In general, there is a tendency to 'add on' rather than subtract, and thus many service offers do not die but merely fade away, consuming the resources of an organization which could be better used elsewhere. 'Old' products may not even cover overheads. In addition there are a number of 'hidden' costs of supporting dying services that need to be taken into consideration:

- a disproportionate amount of management time is spent on them

- short and relatively uneconomic 'production' runs may be required where a service has not been deleted and there is irregular demand for it

- they often require frequent price adjustments (and stock adjustments where tangible goods are involved).

- the search for new products and services is delayed, as so much time is spent on existing products/services that the desired allocation of time to consider new ones is inadequate.

Firms should therefore have a marketing planning system that incorporates service deletion decisions. It would be naive, however, to assume that deletion is a simple process. In reality, there are a number of reasons why logical deletion procedures are not readily followed, as outlined below.

- Firms often do not have the information which they need to identify whether a service needs to be considered for elimination. Even if an organization is aware of a potential deletion candidate, the reasons for its failure may not be known and management may just leave things as they are and hope that the problem will go away by itself.

- Managers often become sentimental about services, hoping that sales will pick up when the market improves. Sometimes, particular elements of marketing strategy will be blamed for lack of success and there is the belief that a change in advertising or pricing, for example, will improve the situation.

- Within organizations, there may be political difficulties in seeking to delete a service. Some individuals will have vested interests in a service and may fight elimination efforts. In fact, some individuals may hide the true facts of a service's performance to ensure that deletion is not considered at all.

- Finally, there is sometimes the fear that the sales of other products and services are tied into the service being deleted. As an example, a car dealer which closes down its new car sales department may subsequently lose business in its servicing and repairs department. Furthermore, some candidates for elimination may be sold to a small number of important customers, leading to fears that deletion would cause all of their business to go elsewhere.

In fact, many companies tackle service elimination in a piecemeal fashion, only considering the matter once a service is seen to be losing money, or when there is some crisis leading to a cut-back. There is clearly, therefore, a need for a systematic approach. At regular intervals, every service should be reviewed in terms of its sales, profitability, average cost, market share, competitor share, competitor prices, etc. Today, information technology allows firms to calculate important ratios that can indicate how a service is performing in its marketplace.

Having acquired the relevant information, an organization can identify 'weak' elements of its service portfolio using a number of warning signals. Some of these relate to poor sales performance, some to poor profit performance and others to more general danger signals such as new competitor introductions or increasing amounts of executive time being spent on one service. The presence of these warning signals merely indicates a need for further consideration and the possibilities of either service modification or total elimination. Identification of a 'weak' service does not automatically mean that deletion is required.

One possible method of deciding which products to eliminate is the development and implementation of a product/service retention index. This can include a number of factors, each of these being individually weighted according to the importance attached to them by a particular firm. Each service is then ranked according to each factor, the product retention index thus being equal to the sum of the products of the weighted index. An illustration of a product retention index is shown in Figure 7.9.

Factor weighting (FWi)	Factor	Product/service score (SRi)
7	Future market potential for product/service?	4
7	How much could be gained from modification?	6
6	How much could be gained from marketing strategy modification?	5
6	How much useful executive time could be released by abandoning product/service?	8
5	How good are the firm's alternative opportunities?	7
4	How much is the product/service contributing beyond its direct costs?	3
4	How much is the product/service contributing to the sale of other products/services?	5
	The product/service retention index SRI = the sum of FWi × SRi	

Figure 7.9 Production retention index

Two of the product retention factors relate to potential modification approaches either in terms of the service itself or of the whole marketing strategy. A number of non-deletion alternatives for poorly performing services can be identified – that is, attempts can be made to reverse the decline stage of the product life cycle. In many cases, a potential deletion candidate can be saved by adjusting its marketing programme, including:

- modifying the product or service
- increasing the price (may be a good idea if demand is fairly inelastic)
- decreasing the price (may be useful if demand is elastic)
- increasing promotional expenditure to stimulate sales
- decreasing promotional expenditure to cut costs
- revising the promotional mix
- increasing salesforce effort to boost sales
- decreasing salesforce effort to reduce costs
- changing the channels of distribution
- changing the physical distribution system (where there is a significant tangible element)
- undertaking additional marketing research to identify possible new markets for the service; additionally, information relating to why success has declined may also be forthcoming
- licensing agreements to another firm.

If, on the other hand, deletion is the chosen alternative, decisions must be made as to how this is to be implemented. This is not always a simple task and a number of options can be identified, as follows.

- *Ruthlessly eliminate 'overnight'*. The potential problem here is that there are still likely to be customers of the service. How will they respond? Will they take their business to other competitors? Will they take their business for other services in the mix with them?

- *Increase the price and let demand fade away*. This could mean that the firm makes good profits on the service while demand lasts.

- *Reduce promotion or even stop it altogether*. Again this could increase profitability while demand lasts.

Whichever decision is made, an organization has to consider the timing of such a decision. In determining a time for deletion, the following factors need to be taken into account.

- *Inventory level.* Although pure services cannot be inventoried, the tangible elements of the service offer can be. Where these are an important element of a service offer, they should be taken into account in deciding when to delete the service.

- *Notification of consumers.* It is generally better for firms to inform consumers that service deletion is imminent. Such a policy at least allows people time to make alternative arrangements and this may also have the added advantage of promoting the firm's 'caring' image. Some announcements of deletion have even had the effect of raising awareness of the service, which has helped to build a long-term sustainable demand (e.g. announcement of the proposed withdrawal of London–Scotland sleeper trains led to a surge in demand).

- *Resources.* Management should move freed-up resources, particularly labour, to other appropriate services as soon as possible. This not only eliminates the possibility of idle resources, and lay-offs of manpower, but is also an essential part of internal marketing, which is important for service firms.

- *Legal implications.* Service elimination may bring with it legal liabilities. In the case of suppliers, an organization may be committed to take supplies regardless of a deletion strategy (for example, a holiday tour operator may be contractually committed to buying aircraft seats for the remainder of a season). In the case of customers, it may not be possible to delete services provided under a long-term contract until that contract comes to an end. This can be particularly important for the financial services sector where mortgages and pension plans usually allow no facility for a unilateral withdrawal of supply by the service producer, even though a pension policy may still have over 30 years to run.

The above implies that firms have a choice in deciding whether a service needs to be deleted from the mix. In fact, a study by Hart (1988) on product deletion in British companies found that deletion decisions were generally forced on management by circumstances beyond its control. Hart noted that by the time managers are contemplating deletion, the circumstances may well be outside management control. She doesn't, however, say that circumstances are unavoidable. In fact, by reading the market climate, monitoring the quality of their products and assessing the fit between their current offering, the market and future possibilities, managers are afforded greater time to consider, plan and execute the deletion for minimum disruption to revenue.

Case study

Will 3G phone company learn from a Rabbit?

The mobile telephone sector hardly existed just 20 years ago, but during its short history it has grown phenomenally to the point where, in 2004, over two-thirds of the UK population own a mobile phone. The pace of growth posed enormous risks for the companies involved, especially where new technologies displace the technology which went before them, calling for ever-increasing capital investment and no chance of a return from consumers until long after the initial investment has been made in new capacity.

Many commentators saw third-generation (or '3G') technology as the key to a whole new world of mobile telephony in which the mobile phone would be positioned not just as a device for voice communication, but a vital business and information tool. In 2000 the UK government held an auction for five new 3G mobile telephone licences, and the mobile phone companies paid a total of £22 billion for licences. Would they get back their huge investment, not only in licences, but in the infrastructure that was needed to support the new 3G networks?

During 2003, the Hong Kong-based Hutchison Whampoa became the first company to launch a 3G service in the UK, with its '3' network. The launch was accompanied by endless hype about the wireless Internet and video links. The world was going to be transformed by streaming of video and football clips live to customers' mobile phones, and a whole new world of mobile advertising media would open up. Location-based services (LBS) had been a small but growing sector of the mobile phone industry. A report by Concise Insight (2004) noted that Vodafone UK's mobile content reached 1.9% of total service revenue for March 2004, almost double the 1.0% the previous year. It seemed that location technology was underpinning value-added data services. Even the emergency services stood to benefit from 3G's ability to pinpoint precisely a caller's location. By 2004, 60% of calls to the UK emergency services were made from mobiles, but in many instances callers didn't know exactly where they were, and ambulances and fire brigades only had very approximate locations.

But after long delays in rolling out the new phones and networks, followed by sluggish uptake of the early services, 3 found itself in 2004 focusing on more mundane marketing issues, such as the cost of old-fashioned voice calls. The costs of recruiting new customers were high, with Mark James, telecoms analyst at Japanese investment bank Nomura, estimating that 3's customer acquisition costs in its first year were £600 per customer – around four times the European average.

Initially, technical glitches, the high price of handsets and poor customer service were compounded by a phone shortage. But 3 was on a mission to grab market share ahead of the launch of its rivals' 3G services, seemingly almost regardless of the cost. During 2003 its 'land grab' programme received a boost with the launch of a highly desirable lightweight silver clam-shell-style phone manufactured by LG. Just a year previously, one of these cost more than £400, but now 3 was giving them away free of charge on the back of generous tariffs that offered consumers 500 or 750 voice minutes to any network for £25 or £35 a month, respectively.

Analysts estimated that Hutchison, which had placed a US$22 billion bet on the fledgling technology, was seeing a worldwide 3G cash-burn of about HK$100 million ($12.8 million) per day, and market concern about its 3G exposure was beginning to depress the group's share price. By June 2004, the company had already lost one of its key shareholders – Japanese heavyweight NTT DoCoMo – which sold its 20% stake in 3 UK back to Hutchison at a 90% loss on its initial investment. However, Hutchison Whampoa had deep pockets to fund an expensive launch – although it had net borrowings, most of those were long-term debts, and disposals during 2003/4 meant it had HK$111 billion (£8 billion) of cash on its balance sheet.

More worrying to many commentators were the effects of Hutchison's tactics on the fledgling 3G industry. At the time of launch, 3 emphasized its 'gee-whiz' features. But after only a year, it was increasingly emphasizing the more mundane affordability of its calling plans. Rival operators that were preparing their own 3G launches would aim to start by pricing the technology at a premium. But their problem was that 3 was already pricing its phones and services – which offered ITN news and premiership football clips among other features – at cut-throat prices. Their best hope was that 3's model would prove unsustainable. After all, anyone can get customers if they effectively give their product away.

Hutchison is not new to taking big risks in the mobile phone market. It was behind the 'Rabbit' network of semi-mobile Telepoint phones launched in the UK in the 1980s. These allowed callers to use a compact handset to make outgoing calls only, when they were within 150 metres of a base station, these being located in public places such as railway stations, shops, petrol stations, etc. As in the case of many new markets that suddenly emerge, operators saw the advantages of having an early market share lead. Customers who perceived that one network was more readily available than any other would – all other things being equal – be more likely to subscribe to that network. Operators saw that a bandwagon effect could be set up – to gain entry to the market at a later stage could become a much more expensive market challenger exercise.

Such was the speed of development that the Telepoint concept was not rigorously test-marketed. To many, the development was too much product led, with insufficient understanding of buyer behaviour and competitive pressures. Each of the four companies forced through their own technologies, with little inclination or time available to discuss industry-standard handsets which could eventually have caused the market to grow at a faster rate and allowed the operators to cut their costs.

The final straw for the Rabbit network came with the announcement by the UK government of its proposal to issue licences for a new generation of personal communications networks – these would have the additional benefit of allowing both incoming and outgoing calls, and would not be tied to a limited base station range. While this in itself might not have put people off buying new Rabbit handsets, it did have the effect of bringing new investment in the network to a halt, leaving the existing networks in a state of limbo.

Could the point about leapfrogging technology – which had wiped out Hutchison's Rabbit network – happen again with 3G technology? By 2004 the next generation of mobile phone services was under development, with Japanese trials of 4G well under way and already promising even greater functionality and transfer rates. The International Telecommunication Union (ITU) defined 4G as providing a minimum stationary data rate of 1 Gbps and a moving (say in a car or a train) data rate of around 100 Mbps. In field tests held in Kanagawa, the Japanese telephone company NTT achieved up to 300 Mbps at 30 km and an average moving transfer rate of 135 Mbps up to 1 kilometre from the base station.

Could 3G become old hat before it had even had a successful and profitable launch? Or should Hutchison point to its record with another of its previous ventures – the launch of the UK Orange network in the early 1990s, which critics initially dismissed as a costly failure, but which went on to become one of the UK's strongest mobile phone brands?

Case study review questions

1. Critically assess the methods used by mobile phone companies in general – and 3 in particular – to launch their new 3G services.

2. What, if anything, can 3G operators learn from the previous launch of Telepoint services such as Rabbit?

3. How would the launch of 3G services differ in a less-developed country with a less-sophisticated telecommunications infrastructure?

Chapter summary and links to other chapters

In competitive markets, service providers must select a position which builds on their strengths and profitably caters for the identified needs of consumers. This chapter has argued that the task of positioning services is more complex than for goods. The positioning of the service provider can be just as important as the positioning of individual service offers. Most services go through some form of life cycle and service providers should have strategies for developing new services and deleting mature services which are no longer profitable.

An important element of service positioning is based on the configuration of the service offer and service encounter, which were discussed in **Chapters 2 and 3**. Positioning must take account of differences in individuals' buying processes and their desire to seek ongoing relationships (**Chapters 4 and 5**). Positioning, new service development and deletion decisions call for adequate information (**Chapter 7**). The perceived quality of the service offer can affect its position (**Chapter 8**). The marketing mix elements of accessibility, price and promotion (**Chapters 8–11**) help to define a position, while effective employees and management (**Chapter 12**) are essential for implementing and sustaining it.

Chapter review questions

1. Critically discuss the idea that positioning is much more difficult for a service provider than a goods manufacturer.

2. Using examples, discuss the problems that are likely to result from a firm seeking to reposition its service offer.

3. To what extent can the various stages in the new service development process be distinguished? To what extent should they be integrated more fully?

4. What possible problems could be encountered by a service firm trying to develop new services?

5. What is the relationship between innovation and profitability? Can a service-based firm succeed without being an innovator?

6. With reference to specific examples, examine the practical problems of deleting items from a company's service mix.

Activity

Go through your local *Yellow Pages* directory for one of the following business classifications: restaurants, grocery retailers, hotels. Develop the outline of positioning maps which can be used to position all of the companies listed in your chosen classification. Justify the bases for your positioning criteria. Then try drawing on the positioning map those organizations from your classification with which you are familiar.

Key terms

New service An additional service offered by a company, ranging from a completely new service which is unlike anything previously offered in the market, to minor modification of existing services.

Organizational image The way consumers see the organization providing a service, based on the consumers' set of beliefs and previous exposure to the organization.

Product life cycle A hypothetical description of the stages that a product passes through between its development and deletion.

Product line A range of service offers that are related to each other.

Service portfolio The total range of services offered by an organization.

Service process The activities involved in producing a service which can be specified in the form of a blueprint.

Selected further reading

The following is a classic paper which argues that the inseparability of services leads to positioning being more relevant to service providers than individual service offers.
Shostack, G.L. (1987) 'Service positioning through structural change', *Journal of Marketing*, 51, 34–43.

For a more general insight into how positioning contributes to a firm's competitive advantage, refer to the following.
Bharadwaj, S.G., Rajan, P. and Fahy, J. (1993) 'Sustainable competitive advantage in service industries: A conceptual model and research propositions', *Journal of Marketing*, 57, 83–99.
Trout, J. and Rivkin, S. (1996) *The New Positioning*, McGraw-Hill, New York.

For a general overview of brand development processes, refer to the following.
De Chernatony, L. and McDonald, M. (2003) *Creating Powerful Brands*, Butterworth-Heinemann.
Moorthi, Y.L.R. (2002) 'An approach to branding services', *Journal of Services Marketing*, 16 (3) 259–74.
Aaker, D. (1996) *Building Strong Brands*, Free Press, New York.

For an insight into new service development processes, the following articles offer useful insights.
Kelly, D. and Storey, C. (2000) 'New service development: Initiation strategies', *International Journal of Service Industry Management*, 11 (1), 45–65.
Johne, A. and Storey, C. (1998) 'New service development: A review of the literature and annotated bibliography', *European Journal of Marketing*, 32, 184–251.
Ekdahl, F., Gustafsson, A. and Edvardsson, B. (1999) 'Customer-oriented service development at SAS', *Managing Service Quality*, 9 (6), 403–10.

References

ABA (2002) 'What's Egg?', *ABA Banking Journal*, 94 (9), 60–1.

Barwise, P. and Roberston, T. (1992) 'Brand portfolios', *European Management Journal*, 10 (3; September), 277–85.

Carman, J.M. and Langeard, E. (1979) 'Growth strategies for service firms', *Proceedings of the 8th Annual Meeting of the European Academy for Advanced Research in Marketing*, Groningen.

Concise Insight (2004) *European Location-Based Services*, Concise Insight, London.

Cowell, D. (1988) 'New service development', *Journal of Marketing Management*, 3 (3), 296–312.

Dahan, E. and Hauser, J.R. (2002) 'The virtual customer', *Journal of Product Innovation Management*, 19 (5), 332–51.

De Chernatony, L. and McDonald, M. (2003) *Creating Powerful Brands*, Butterworth-Heinemann.

Easingwood, C.J. (1986) 'New product development for service companies', *Journal of Product Innovation Management*, 4, 264–275.

Edgett, S. (1994) 'The traits of successful new service development', *Journal of Services Marketing*, 8, 40–9.

Fagan, M. (2003) 'Three launches 3G services – But without handsets', *Sunday Telegraph*, 2 March.

Gardner, B. and Levy, S. (1955) 'The product and the brand', *Harvard Business Review*, 33 (March–April), 33–9.

Hart, S. (1988) 'The causes of product deletion in British manufacturing companies', *Journal of Marketing Management*, 3 (3) 6–17.

Henard, D.H. and Szymanski, D.M. (2001) 'Why some new products are more successful than others', *Journal of Marketing Research*, 38, 362–75.

Howley, M. (2002) 'The role of consultancies in new product development', *Journal of Product and Brand Management*, 11 (6/7), 447–58.

Johne, A. and Storey, C. (1998) 'New service development: A review of the literature and annotated bibliography', *European Journal of Marketing*, 32, 184–251.

Kelly, D. and Storey, C. (2000) 'New service development: Initiation strategies', *International Journal of Service Industry Management*, 11 (1), 45–65.

Kim, J. and Wilemon, D. (2003) 'Sources and assessment of complexity in NPD projects', *R & D Management*, 33 (1), 16–30.

Little, G. (2002) 'Inventors don't always make great marketers', *Design Week*, 17 (27), 15.

MacKay, S. and Conway, A.(1992) *A Network Approach to New Service Development*, Working Paper for the Marketing Education Group Conference, Salford University.

McNair, M.P. (1958) 'Significant trends and developments in the post-war period', in Smith, A.B. (ed.), *Competitive Distribution in a Free High Level Economy and its Implications for the University*, University of Pittsburgh Press, Pittsburgh, 1–25.

Miniard, P.W. and Cohen, J.E. (1983) 'Modelling personal and normative influences on behavior', *Journal of Consumer Research*, 10 (September), 169–80.

Moschis, G.P. (1976) 'Social comparison and informal group influence', *Journal of Marketing Research*, 13 (August), 237–44.

Munson, M. and Spivey, W. (1981) 'Products and brand users stereotypes among social classes', in K. Monroe (ed.), *Advances in Consumer Research*, Ann Arbor, ACR.

Shostack, G.L. (1987) 'Service positioning through structural change', *Journal of Marketing*, 51, 34–43.

Solomon, M. (1983) 'The role of products in social stimuli: A symbolic interactionism perspective', *Journal of Consumer Research*, 10 (December) 319–29.

Solomon, M. and Buchanan, B. (1991) 'A role theoretic approach to product symbolism: Mapping of consumption constellation', *Journal of Business Research*, 22 (2), 95–109.

Venkatraman, N. and Prescott, J. (1990) 'Environment–strategy coalignment: An empirical test of its performance implications', *Strategy Management Journal*, 11, 1–23.

Wind, Y.J. (1982) *Product Policy: Concepts, Methods and Strategy*, Addison-Wesley, Reading, Mass.

Wong, V. (2002) 'Antecedents of international new product rollout timeliness', *International Marketing Review*, 19 (2/3), 120–32.

Service quality

Learning objectives

This chapter will explain:

- linkages between the concepts of service quality, satisfaction and value

- the importance of service quality in the service–profit chain

- major paradigms for the study of service quality–performance only measures, disconfirmation models and importance–performance analysis

- methods used to set standards of service quality

- methods used to research consumers' expectations of service quality and to monitor firms' performance

- managing approaches for ensuring delivery of specified quality standards.

8.1 **Introduction**

The subject of service quality has aroused considerable recent interest among business people and academics. Of course, buyers have always been concerned with quality, but the increasingly competitive market for many services has led consumers to become more selective in the services they choose. Conceptualizing the quality of services is more complex than for goods, and this chapter will review conceptual frameworks for evaluating service quality. Because of the absence of tangible manifestations, measuring service quality can be difficult and this chapter discusses possible research approaches. Comprehensive models of service quality are discussed and their limitations noted. Understanding just what dimensions of quality are of importance to customers in their evaluation process can be more difficult than is usually the case with goods. It is not sufficient for companies to set quality standards in accordance with misguided assumptions of **customers' expectations**. A further problem in defining service quality lies in the importance which customers often attach to the quality of the service provider as distinct from its service offers – the two cannot be separated as easily as in the case of goods. As well as discussing conceptual issues about the measurement of service quality, this chapter will explore how companies set quality standards and implement programmes of quality management.

8.2 **Defining service quality**

Quality is an extremely difficult concept to define in a few words. At its most basic, quality has been defined as 'conforming to requirements' (Crosby, 1984). This implies that organizations must establish requirements and specifications; once established, the quality goal of the various functions of an organization is to comply strictly with these specifications. However, the questions remain: whose requirements and whose specifications? A second series of definitions therefore state that quality is all about fitness for use (Juran, 1982) – a definition based primarily on satisfying customers' needs. These two definitions can be united in the concept of customer perceived quality – quality can only be defined by customers and occurs where an organization supplies goods or services to a specification that satisfies their needs.

Many analyses of service quality have attempted to distinguish between objective measures of quality and measures which are based on the more subjective perceptions of customers. A definition from Swan and Comb (1976) identified two important dimensions of service quality: 'instrumental' quality describes the physical aspects of the service while the 'expressive' dimension relates to the intangible or psychological aspects. A development of this idea by Grönroos (1984) identified 'technical' and 'functional' quality as being the two principal components of quality. **Technical quality** refers to the relatively quantifiable aspects of a service which consumers receive in their interactions with a service firm. Because it can easily be measured by both customer and supplier, it often forms an important basis for judging service quality. Examples of technical quality include the waiting time at a supermarket checkout and the reliability of train services. This, however, is not the only element that makes up perceived service quality. Because services involve direct consumer–producer interaction, consumers are also influenced by *how* the technical quality is delivered to them. This is what Grönroos describes as **functional quality** and cannot be measured as objectively as the elements of technical quality (see Mels *et al.*, 1997). In the case of the queue at a supermarket checkout, functional quality is influenced by such factors as the environment in which queuing takes place and consumers' perceptions of the manner in which queues are handled by the supermarket's staff. Grönroos also sees an important role for a services firm's corporate image in defining customers' perceptions of quality, with corporate image being based on both technical and functional quality. Figure 8.1 illustrates diagrammatically Grönroos's conceptualization of service quality, as applied to an optician's practice.

If quality is defined as the extent to which a service meets customers' requirements, the problem remains of identifying just what those requirements are. The general absence of easily understood criteria for assessing quality makes articulation of customers' requirements and communication of the quality level on offer much more difficult than is the case for goods. Service quality is a highly abstract construct, in contrast to goods, where technical aspects of quality predominate. Many conceptualizations of service quality therefore begin by addressing the abstract expectations that consumers hold in respect of quality. Consumers subsequently judge service quality as the extent to which perceived service delivery matches up to these initial expectations. In this way, a service which is perceived as being of mediocre standard may be

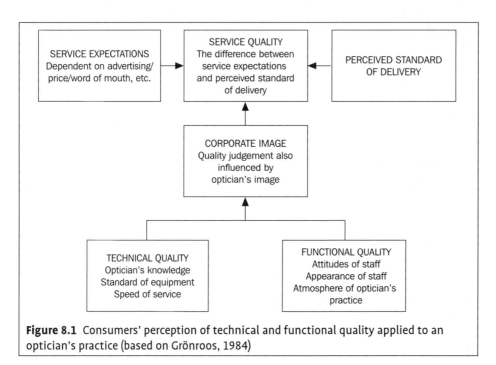

Figure 8.1 Consumers' perception of technical and functional quality applied to an optician's practice (based on Grönroos, 1984)

considered of high quality when compared against low expectations, but of low quality when assessed against high expectations. Much research remains to be done to understand the processes by which expectations of service quality are formed, and this is discussed later in this chapter.

Analysis of service quality is complicated by the fact that production and consumption of a service generally occur simultaneously, with the process of service production often being just as important as the service outcomes. Grönroos (1984) pointed out that a buyer of manufactured goods only encounters the traditional marketing mix variables of a manufacturer, i.e. the product, its price, its distribution and how these are communicated to him or her. Usually, production processes are unseen by consumers and therefore cannot be used as a basis for quality assessment. By contrast, service inseparability results in the production process being an important basis for assessing quality.

A further problem in understanding and managing service quality flows from the intangibility, variability and inseparability of most services, which results in a series of unique buyer/seller exchanges with no two services being provided in exactly the same way. It has been noted that intangibility and perceived riskiness affect expectations and in one study of a long-distance phone service, a bookstore and a pizza shop service, it was concluded that intangibility had some role in service quality expectations (Bebko, 2000). Managing customers' expectations can be facilitated by means of managing the risks a consumer perceives when buying a particular service.

8.2.1 Quality and satisfaction

The effects of service quality on consumer decision-making appear to be largely indirect and mediated by value and satisfaction (Brady and Cronin, 2001). A review of the literature will reveal that the terms quality and satisfaction are quite often used interchangeably. While both concepts are related and appear to be merging there are still gaps in the understanding of the two constructs, their relationship to each other and their antecedents and consequences (Gwynne et al., 1999). A distinction has often been made between the two constructs. According to Cronin and Taylor (1992):

this distinction is important to both managers and researchers alike, because service providers need to know whether their objective should be to have consumers who are satisfied with their performance or to deliver the maximum level of perceived service quality.

Oliver (1997) takes the view that satisfaction is 'the emotional reaction following a disconfirmation experience'. Getty and Thompson (1994) defined satisfaction as a 'summary psychological state experienced by the consumer when confirmed or disconfirmed expectations exist with respect to a specific service transaction or experience'. Rust and Oliver suggested that customer satisfaction or dissatisfaction – a 'cognitive or affective reaction' – emerges as a response to a single or prolonged set of service encounters. Satisfaction is a 'post-consumption' experience which compares perceived quality with expected quality, whereas service quality refers to a global evaluation of a firm's service delivery system (Parasuraman *et al.*, 1985; Anderson and Fornell, 1994). Perceived quality, on the other hand, may be viewed as a global attitudinal judgement associated with the superiority of the service experience over time (Getty and Thompson, 1994). As such, it is dynamic in nature and less transaction specific (Parasuraman *et al.*, 1988).

Not surprisingly there has been considerable debate concerning the nature of the relationship between the constructs of satisfaction and quality. While much research suggests that service quality is a vital antecedent to customer satisfaction (Parasuraman *et al.*, 1985; Cronin and Taylor, 1992) there is also strong evidence to suggest that satisfaction may be a vital antecedent of service quality (Bitner, 1990). Regardless of which view is taken, the relationship between satisfaction and service quality is strong when examined from either direction. Satisfaction affects assessments of service quality, and assessments of service quality affect satisfaction (McAlexander *et al.*, 1994). In turn both are vital in helping buyers develop their future purchase intentions. In one of the few empirical studies of the relationship between quality and satisfaction, Iacobucci *et al.* (1995) concluded that the key difference between the two constructs is that quality relates to managerial delivery of the service while satisfaction reflects customers' experiences with that service. They argued that quality improvements that are not based on customer needs will not lead to improved customer satisfaction.

There is a suggestion that consumers are indifferent to levels of service that fall within their zone of tolerance and are motivated by unexpectedly high levels of service quality that in turn produce 'delight'. There is also evidence that satisfied customers may nevertheless not return to a service provider (Brady and Cronin, 2001). There has been discussion over the issue of whether some characteristics of a service generate satisfaction in customers while others generate dissatisfaction (Galloway, 1999). The general argument is that the achievement of some standard, or improvement in an element, will generate satisfaction, but its absence, or reduction, will not generate dissatisfaction. Conversely, the failure to achieve a standard in another element may generate dissatisfaction in the customer, though its presence will not necessarily generate satisfaction and repeat purchase. Traditional survey methodologies are linear based – that is, they assume consistent returns across all responses. There is, however, some research evidence which indicates that the impact of poor performance may carry a greater consequence than the benefit of performance excellence (i.e. delight). Suggestions that word-of-mouth effects from poor performance are many times greater than those resulting from positive performance represent evidence of a possible non-linear effect (Cronin, 2003).

Swan and Comb (1976) noted that 'consumers judge products on a limited set of attributes, some of which are relatively important in determining satisfaction, while others are not critical to consumer satisfaction but are related to dissatisfaction when performance on them is unsatisfactory' (1976, p. 27). For a bank, increasing the number of branches may not be a satisfier which encourages a customer to spend more of their budget with that bank. However, a reduction in the number of branches may be a dissatisfier which reduces behavioural intention. In one study of the UK retail banking sector, it was found that integrity and, to a lesser extent, reliability, were dissatisfiers. Consumers behaved as if these were assumed standards which all banks will achieve, and were dissatisfied where a bank failed to achieve them (Johnston, 2001).

8.3 **The service–profit chain**

What is the effect on a company's profitability of providing a high quality of service? This is an important question, and has led to extensive research into the financial returns from improving all aspects of an organization's value-creating processes. The idea of improvements in service quality feeding through to increased profitability is best portrayed through the concept of a **service–profit chain** (Figure 8.2). A number of studies have sought to establish the contribution to profitability made by groups of employees, who trade services internally between each other during the process of delivering a service to external customers (e.g. Paraskevas, 2001).

There is considerable support for a link between improvements in service quality and improvements in financial performance. Grant (1998) reported that the American Customer Satisfaction Index studies found a positive correlation between customer satisfaction and stock market returns. In a large and wide-ranging empirical study

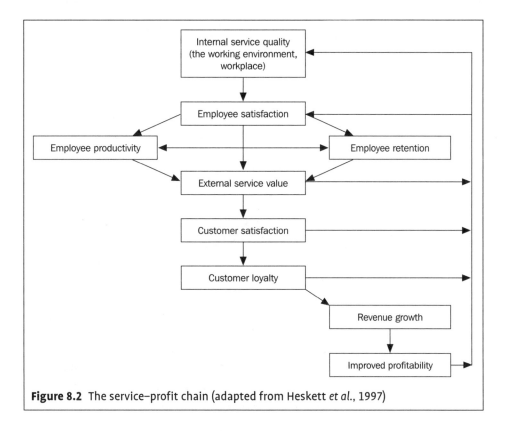

Figure 8.2 The service–profit chain (adapted from Heskett *et al.*, 1997)

undertaken in the UK, it was found that better service providers had a significantly better return on equity than the poorer providers, and this appeared to apply to both small and large organizations (Bates *et al.*, 2003).

A number of studies have sought to establish a link between satisfaction and loyalty. Dick and Basu, in a conceptual paper on loyalty, viewed satisfaction as an antecedent of relative attitude because, without satisfaction, consumers will not hold a favourable attitude towards a brand as compared to other alternatives available, and will therefore not be predisposed to repurchase (Dick and Basu, 1994). The link between customer satisfaction and loyalty has been widely replicated (e.g. Fornell *et al.*, 1996). It was noted in Chapter 5 that it can be much more profitable for companies to retain loyal customers than to recruit new ones to replace lapsed customers.

The opposite of satisfaction – dissatisfaction – has been seen as a primary reason for customer defection or discontinuation of purchase. Zeithaml *et al.* (1996) suggested that a customer's relationship with a company is strengthened when a customer makes a favourable assessment about the company's service quality and weakened when a customer makes negative assessments. They argued that favourable assessment of service quality will lead to favourable behavioural intentions like 'praise for the company' and expressions of preference for the company over other companies. In an earlier study, Zeithaml *et al.* had reported a positive relationship between service quality and willingness to pay a premium price and to remain loyal even when prices go up (Zeithaml *et al.*, 1990).

Much of the research into the outcomes of satisfaction has measured behavioural intentions – for example, the likelihood of recommending a service or repurchasing it. However, the dangers of predicting actual behaviour on the basis of intention have been noted (e.g. Newberry *et al.*, 2003). In the light of increasing levels of competition in most services markets, behavioural intention based on loyalty generated through good service can easily be broken. This has been attributed to a number of factors, including: greater choice and information available to customers; the 'commoditization' of many categories of services; and increased levels of competition. Customers may be 'captive' and therefore repeat purchasing behaviour is unlikely to be influenced in the short term by levels of satisfaction. Any observed loyalty may be what Dick and Basu have described as 'spurious' loyalty. For many buyers, the psychological cost of switching may be perceived as too high and they may therefore be prepared to tolerate high levels of dissatisfaction before a trigger point is reached and they switch. Individuals' perceptions of equity in service encounters has been shown to influence repeat service purchase (Bolton and Lemon, 1999).

Against this, some researchers have pointed out that much of the evidence to support a link between quality and financial performance is anecdotal in nature and refuted by analysis of corporate performance. It is suggested that there is widespread evidence of managers' frustration with the inability of quality improvements to improve organizational performance (Anderson *et al.*, 1994). For example, within the airline sector many companies (e.g. British Airways) that score well on customer satisfaction have performed poorly financially, compared to relatively low-quality carriers such as Ryanair.

In a study by Cronin and Taylor (1992) service quality did not appear to have a significant positive effect on intentions to purchase again. Passikoff (1997) cites a Juran Institute study which indicated that less than a third of top managers of America's largest corporations believed that their customer satisfaction programmes yield any economic benefit. Anderson *et al.* (1994) expressed the fear that if firms are not able to demonstrate a link between customer satisfaction and economic performance, then firms may abandon the focus on customer satisfaction measurement.

In the context of online service quality, recent research has found no relationship between e-service quality and commercial online retail success (Feinberg *et al.*, 2002; Muhanna and Wolf, 2002; Zeithaml *et al.*, 2002; Thornton and Marche, 2003).

Developments in information technology are offering new insights into the link between quality and financial performance. Large multiple outlet services organizations are increasingly able to experiment with elements of service quality in test sites and to judge economic performance over time. A fast-food restaurant, for example, may implement a new staff payment system or training programme in a number of 'experimental' sites and will be able to identify changes in performance relative to other 'control' branches. Some service providers have disaggregated their information even further by linking service quality questionnaires to features of the service which a respondent actually received. In this way, individual employees or groups of employees can be linked to measures of quality. While information technology, and the use of 'Balanced Scorecards' is opening up new possibilities for correlating data about inputs and perceived outcomes, the problem of analysing cross-sectional data remains. It is very difficult within a research framework to isolate all of the contributors to customers' perceptions of quality, except those in which the researcher is interested. We will return to the issue of rewarding staff for performance in Chapter 12.

8.4 Paradigms for understanding and measuring service quality

Given the complex nature of service quality, it is not surprising that there have been divergent views about the best way to conceptualize and measure it. Three frameworks are presented here:

1. performance-only measures

2. disconfirmation models

3. importance–performance approaches.

8.4.1 **Performance-only measures**

The simplest approach to measuring service quality is simply to ask customers to rate the performance of a service. In reality, most simple survey forms handed out to customers to provide feedback on service quality ask just a small number of performance-based questions.

Performance-only measures of service quality have their philosophical roots in the quality literature derived from the manufacturing sector. For most manufactured goods, it is possible to define quality in terms of easily measurable criteria, such as the reliability of a car or the quality of gold from which a ring is made. It can be argued by this approach that services are not unique in being shaped in consumers' minds by abstract notions of expectations, when many manufactured goods promote an image and hence an expectation against which performance is based. So, by this argument, if performance-only measures are good for the manufacturing sector, they should also be good for the service sector.

Performance-only measures avoid the need to measure customers' expectations of a service. While the idea of defining a service in terms of its expectations may sound good in principle, actually measuring expectations can be difficult. There are conceptual difficulties in defining just what is meant by expectations, with a number of possible levels of expectation. These conceptual problems are discussed in the following section. There is also the practical difficulty of measuring a customer's expectations. Ideally, expectations should be measured before a service has been consumed. However, in reality, this is often not practical, so researchers are likely to record expectations retrospectively. The danger here is that stated expectations may be influenced by subsequent performance of service delivery, making the retrospective measure of expectations fairly meaningless.

Difficulties with conceptualizing expectations led to the development and application of a more direct form of measurement technique in the form of SERVPERF. This approach requires the customer to rate a provider's performance, typically extending from (1) strongly disagree to (5) strongly agree. The instrument requires the consumer to rate only the performance of a particular service encounter. This eliminates the need to measure expectations on the grounds that customer expectations change when they experience a service, and the inclusion of an expectations measure reduces the content and discriminant validity of the measures (Cronin and Taylor, 1992; McAlexander *et al.*, 1994).

Studies conducted using this performance-based measure found that SERVPERF explained more of the variance in an overall measure of service quality than did performance–expectations models. Cronin and Taylor (1994) acknowledge that it is possible for researchers to infer consumers' disconfirmation through arithmetic means (the P–E gap) but that 'consumer perceptions, not calculations, govern behaviour'.

8.4.2 **Disconfirmation approaches**

By this approach, a service is deemed to be of high quality when consumers' expectations are confirmed by subsequent service delivery. Because of the emphasis on differences between expectations and perceptions, this type of model is often referred to as a **disconfirmation model**. Pre-eminent among these is the work of Berry, Parasuraman and Zeithaml, who have been strong advocates of the need for service organizations to learn more about their customers through a rigorous marketing research-oriented approach which focuses on the expectations and perceptions of customers. They make the point that only customers can judge quality – all other judgements are considered to be essentially irrelevant. They set out to determine what customers expect from services and what the characteristics are that define these services (effectively what is the service in the mind of the customer). Berry, Parasuraman and Zeithaml developed an instrument for measuring customers' perceptions of service quality compared to their expectations. Their findings have evolved from a set of qualitative marketing research procedures culminating in the quantitative technique for measuring service quality which is known as SERVQUAL. The SERVQUAL model has been widely applied.

The SERVQUAL technique can be used by companies to better understand the expectations and perceptions of their customers. It is applicable across a broad range of services industries and can easily be modified to take account of the specific requirements of a company. In effect it provides a skeleton for an investigatory instrument which can be adapted or added to as needed.

SERVQUAL is based upon a generic 22-item questionnaire which is designed to cover five broad dimensions of service quality which the research team consolidated from their original qualitative investigations. The five dimensions covered, with some description of each and the respective numbers of statements associated with them, are as follows:

Dimension	*Statements*
1. tangibles (appearance of physical elements)	1 to 4
2. reliability (dependability, accurate performance)	5 to 9
3. responsiveness (promptness and helpfulness)	10 to 13
4. assurance (competence, courtesy, credibility and security)	14 to 17
5. empathy (easy access, good communications, and customer understanding)	18 to 22

Customers are asked to self-complete the 22 statements relating to their expectations and a perceptions section consisting of a matching set of company-specific statements about service delivery. They are typically asked to score in each instance, on a Likert scale from 1 (strongly agree) to 7 (strongly disagree), whether or not they agree with each statement. In addition, the survey asks for any comments that they wish to make about their experiences of the service, and their overall impression of it. Customers are also asked for supplementary demographic data. The contents of a typical questionnaire are shown in Figure 8.3.

Measures of service quality can be derived quite simply by subtracting expectation scores from perception scores. These scores can be weighted to reflect the relative importance of each aspect of service quality. The outcome from a one-off study is a measure that tells the company whether its customers' expectations are exceeded or not. SERVQUAL results can be used to identify those components or facets of a service for which the company is particularly good or bad. It can be used to monitor service quality over time, to compare performance with that of competitors, to compare performance between different branches within a company, or to measure customer satisfaction with a particular service industry generally.

An organization or industry group can use the information collected in this way to improve its position by acting upon the results and seeking to surpass customers' expectations on a continuous basis. Additionally, the expectations–perceptions results, along with the demographic data, may facilitate effective customer segmentation.

The SERVQUAL methodology highlights the difficulties in ensuring a high quality of service for all customers in all situations. More specifically, it identifies five gaps where there may be a shortfall between expectations and perceptions of actual service delivery.

■ Gap 1: *Gap between consumer expectations and management perception.* Management may think that they know what consumers want and proceed to deliver this, when in fact consumers may expect something quite different.

■ Gap 2: *Gap between management perception and service quality specification.* Management may not set quality specifications or may not set them clearly. Alternatively, management may set clear quality specifications but these may not be achievable.

■ Gap 3: *Gap between service quality specifications and service delivery.* Unforeseen problems or poor management can lead to a service provider failing to meet service quality specifications. This may be due to human error but also mechanical breakdown of facilitating or support goods.

■ Gap 4: *Gap between service delivery and external communications.* There may be dissatisfaction with a service due to the excessively heightened expectations developed through the service provider's communications efforts. Dissatisfaction occurs where actual delivery does not live up to expectations held out in a company's communications.

■ Gap 5: *Gap between perceived service and expected service.* This gap occurs as a result of one or more of the previous gaps. The way in which customers perceive actual service delivery does not match up with their initial expectations.

The five gaps are illustrated in Figure 8.4 where a hypothetical application to a restaurant is shown.

Please complete Part A by indicating your expectations of hotels in general. Then complete Part B indicating your perceptions of this hotel in particular. Please answer on a scale from 1 (Strongly disagree with the statement to 7 (Strongly agree).

PART A

	Strongly disagree ☹	Strongly agree ☺

(1) An excellent hotel will have modern-looking equipment, e.g. dining facility, bar facility, crockery, cutlery, etc.
1 . . . 2 . . . 3 . . . 4 . . . 5 . . . 6 . . . 7

(2) The physical facilities, e.g. buildings, signs, dining room, decor, lighting, carpet etc., at an excellent hotel will be visually appealing
1 . . . 2 . . . 3 . . . 4 . . . 5 . . . 6 . . . 7

(3) Staff at an excellent hotel will appear neat, e.g. uniform, grooming, etc.
1 . . . 2 . . . 3 . . . 4 . . . 5 . . . 6 . . . 7

(4) Materials associated with the service, e.g. pamphlets, statements, table wine, serviettes, will be visually appealing in an excellent hotel
1 . . . 2 . . . 3 . . . 4 . . . 5 . . . 6 . . . 7

(5) When an excellent hotel promises to do something by a certain time, it will do so
1 . . . 2 . . . 3 . . . 4 . . . 5 . . . 6 . . . 7

(6) When patrons have a problem, an excellent hotel will show genuine interest in solving it, e.g. an error in a bill
1 . . . 2 . . . 3 . . . 4 . . . 5 . . . 6 . . . 7

(7) An excellent hotel will perform service right the first time
1 . . . 2 . . . 3 . . . 4 . . . 5 . . . 6 . . . 7

(8) An excellent hotel will provide its services at the time it promises to do so
1 . . . 2 . . . 3 . . . 4 . . . 5 . . . 6 . . . 7

(9) An excellent hotel will insist on error-free service
1 . . . 2 . . . 3 . . . 4 . . . 5 . . . 6 . . . 7

(10) Staff at an excellent hotel will tell patrons exactly when services will be performed
1 . . . 2 . . . 3 . . . 4 . . . 5 . . . 6 . . . 7

(11) Staff at an excellent hotel will give prompt service to patrons
1 . . . 2 . . . 3 . . . 4 . . . 5 . . . 6 . . . 7

(12) Staff at an excellent hotel will always be willing to help patrons
1 . . . 2 . . . 3 . . . 4 . . . 5 . . . 6 . . . 7

(13) Staff at an excellent hotel will never be too busy to respond
1 . . . 2 . . . 3 . . . 4 . . . 5 . . . 6 . . . 7

(14) The behaviour of staff at an excellent hotel will instil confidence in patrons
1 . . . 2 . . . 3 . . . 4 . . . 5 . . . 6 . . . 7

(15) Patrons of an excellent hotel will feel safe in their transactions
1 . . . 2 . . . 3 . . . 4 . . . 5 . . . 6 . . . 7

(16) Staff at an excellent hotel will be consistently courteous with patrons
1 . . . 2 . . . 3 . . . 4 . . . 5 . . . 6 . . . 7

(17) Staff at an excellent hotel will have the knowledge to answer patrons' requests
1 . . . 2 . . . 3 . . . 4 . . . 5 . . . 6 . . . 7

(18) Staff at an excellent hotel will give patrons individualized attention
1 . . . 2 . . . 3 . . . 4 . . . 5 . . . 6 . . . 7

(19) An excellent hotel will have opening hours convenient to all of its patrons
1 . . . 2 . . . 3 . . . 4 . . . 5 . . . 6 . . . 7

(20) An excellent hotel will have staff who give its patrons personal attention
1 . . . 2 . . . 3 . . . 4 . . . 5 . . . 6 . . . 7

(21) An excellent hotel will have the patrons' best interest at heart
1 . . . 2 . . . 3 . . . 4 . . . 5 . . . 6 . . . 7

(22) The staff of an excellent hotel will understand the specific needs of its patrons
1 . . . 2 . . . 3 . . . 4 . . . 5 . . . 6 . . . 7

The **gaps model** is useful as it allows management to make an analytical assessment of the causes of poor service quality. If the first gaps are great, the task of bridging the subsequent gaps becomes greater, and indeed it could be said that in such circum-

271

PART B	Strongly disagree ☹	Strongly agree ☺
(1) The hotel has modern-looking equipment	1 . . . 2 . . . 3 . . . 4 . . . 5 . . . 6 . . . 7	
(2) The physical facilities at the local hotel are visually appealing	1 . . . 2 . . . 3 . . . 4 . . . 5 . . . 6 . . . 7	
(3) Staff at the hotel appear neat	1 . . . 2 . . . 3 . . . 4 . . . 5 . . . 6 . . . 7	
(4) Materials associated with the service are visually appealing	1 . . . 2 . . . 3 . . . 4 . . . 5 . . . 6 . . . 7	
(5) When the hotel promised to do something by a certain time, it did it	1 . . . 2 . . . 3 . . . 4 . . . 5 . . . 6 . . . 7	
(6) When patrons have problems, the hotel shows a genuine interest in solving them	1 . . . 2 . . . 3 . . . 4 . . . 5 . . . 6 . . . 7	
(7) The hotel performs the service rignt the first time	1 . . . 2 . . . 3 . . . 4 . . . 5 . . . 6 . . . 7	
(8) The hotel provides its services at the time it promises to do so	1 . . . 2 . . . 3 . . . 4 . . . 5 . . . 6 . . . 7	
(9) The hotel insist on error-free service	1 . . . 2 . . . 3 . . . 4 . . . 5 . . . 6 . . . 7	
(10) Staff at the hotel were able to tell patrons exactly when services would be performed	1 . . . 2 . . . 3 . . . 4 . . . 5 . . . 6 . . . 7	
(11) Staff at the hotel give prompt service to the patrons	1 . . . 2 . . . 3 . . . 4 . . . 5 . . . 6 . . . 7	
(12) Staff at the hotel are always willing to help patrons	1 . . . 2 . . . 3 . . . 4 . . . 5 . . . 6 . . . 7	
(13) Staff of the hotel are never too busy to respond to patrons	1 . . . 2 . . . 3 . . . 4 . . . 5 . . . 6 . . . 7	
(14) Behaviour of staff at the hotel instils patrons with confidence	1 . . . 2 . . . 3 . . . 4 . . . 5 . . . 6 . . . 7	
(15) Patrons of the hotel feel safe in their transactions	1 . . . 2 . . . 3 . . . 4 . . . 5 . . . 6 . . . 7	
(16) Staff of the hotel are consistently courteous with patrons	1 . . . 2 . . . 3 . . . 4 . . . 5 . . . 6 . . . 7	
(17) Staff of the hotel have the knowledge to answer patrons	1 . . . 2 . . . 3 . . . 4 . . . 5 . . . 6 . . . 7	
(18) The hotel gives patrons individualized attention	1 . . . 2 . . . 3 . . . 4 . . . 5 . . . 6 . . . 7	
(19) The hotel has opening hours convenient to all of its patrons	1 . . . 2 . . . 3 . . . 4 . . . 5 . . . 6 . . . 7	
(20) The hotel has staff who give its patrons personalized attention	1 . . . 2 . . . 3 . . . 4 . . . 5 . . . 6 . . . 7	
(21) The hotel has the patrons' best interest at heart	1 . . . 2 . . . 3 . . . 4 . . . 5 . . . 6 . . . 7	
(22) The staff of the hotel understand the specific needs of its patrons	1 . . . 2 . . . 3 . . . 4 . . . 5 . . . 6 . . . 7	

Figure 8.3 A typical application of the SERVQUAL survey questionnaire, applied here to the hotel sector. (Based on Gabbie and O'Neill, 1997)

stances quality service can only be achieved by good luck rather than good management.

Much attention has been given to the processes by which customers' expectations of service quality are formed. Two main standards of expectations emerge. One standard represents the expectation as a *prediction* of future events (Swan and Trawick, 1981). This is the standard typically used in the satisfaction literature. The other standard is a normative expectation of future events, operationalized as either *desired* or ideal expectations. This is the standard typically used in the service quality literature (Parasuraman *et al.*, 1988).

Zeithaml *et al.* (1993) have proposed that three levels of expectations can be defined against which quality is assessed:

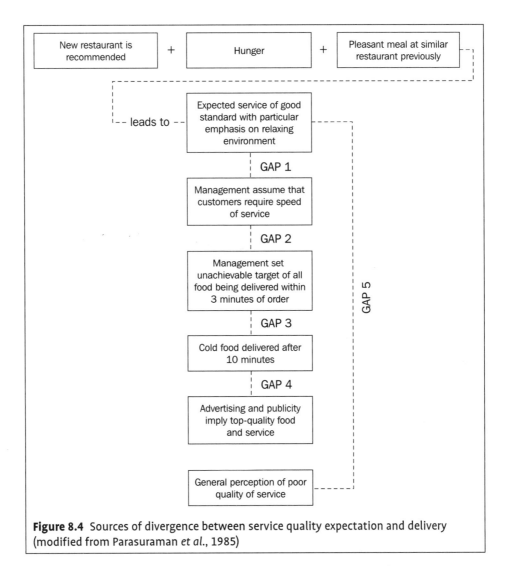

Figure 8.4 Sources of divergence between service quality expectation and delivery (modified from Parasuraman *et al.*, 1985)

1. the *desired* level of service, reflecting what the customer wants

2. the *adequate* service level, defined as the standard that customers are willing to accept

3. the *predicted* service level – that which they believe is most likely to actually occur.

This has led to the idea that *zones of tolerance* may exist in consumers' perceptions of service quality. If perceptions fall below the desired level of service, this may still be acceptable as long as they do not fall below expectations based on an adequate level of service. In other words, rather than a service either meeting or failing a consumer's quality expectations, there is an intermediate zone of tolerance (Figure 8.5).

Disconfirmation models of service quality have been challenged on a number of grounds. One stream of objections holds that absolute measures of attitudes provide

Figure 8.5 Consumers' zones of tolerance for service quality

a more appropriate measure of quality than explanations based on disconfirmation models (Cronin and Taylor, 1994). Researchers have asked whether the calculated difference scores (the difference between expectations and perceptions) are appropriate from a measurement and theoretical perspective. Invariably, customers' expectations are measured after consumption of a service, at the same time as they are asked about their perceptions of a service. Shouldn't expectations be based on a respondent's state of mind before consumption, free of influence from actual consumption? There has been debate about whether it is practical to ask consumers about their expectations of a service immediately before consumption and their perceptions of performance immediately after. It has also been suggested that expectations may not exist or be clear enough in respondents' minds to act as a benchmark against which perceptions are assessed (Iacobucci *et al.*, 1995). Furthermore, expectations are only formed as a result of previous service encounters – that is, perceptions feed directly into expectations (Kahneman and Miller, 1986).

From a measurement perspective, there are three psychometric problems associated with the use of difference scores: reliability, discriminant validity and variance restriction problems. A study by Brown *et al.* (1993) found evidence that these psychometric problems indeed arise with the use of SERVQUAL; they recommend instead use of non-difference score measures which display better discriminant and nomological validity. However, Parasuraman *et al.* respond by arguing that the alleged psychometric deficiencies of the difference-score formulation are less severe than those suggested by critics. Despite their argument that the difference scores offer researchers better diagnostics than separate measurement of perceptions and expectations, from a theoretical perspective, there is little evidence to support the theory of the expectations–performance gap as the basis for measuring service quality (Carman, 1990). Instead, considerable research supports a more straightforward approach of assessing quality on the basis of simple performance-based measures (Bolton and Drew, 1990; Cronin and Taylor, 1994).

It has been claimed that the five dimensions of quality which form the basis of the SERVQUAL scale items are transferable to most services sectors. However, many studies have failed to reproduce the five-factor model.

There have been numerous criticisms of SERVQUAL for the inductive nature of the original research in that it failed to draw on the theory base in the disciplines of psychology, social sciences and economics (Anderson, 1982). Relatively little attention has been devoted to an understanding of how perceptions are formed. It can be argued that disconfirmation models are flawed because *when* a respondent gives a response to his or her perception of service delivery can be just as important as the actual recorded score or the level of expectations against which perceptions are compared. For example, a person may have a very negative attitude towards a haircut immediately after leaving a hairdresser, but that person's perceptions of the haircut may become more favourable over time as he or she gets used to it (O'Neill *et al.*, 1998). It could be argued that in terms of understanding behavioural intention, it is the later measure of perceptions which is most useful to management.

Finally, disconfirmation models do not in themselves indicate the importance to a consumer of individual items of quality, although the SERVQUAL methodology has been adapted to incorporate an additional question asking respondents to rate the importance to them of each item. We will now turn to importance–performance frameworks.

8.4.3 **Importance–performance analysis**

A weakness of disconfirmation approaches to service quality is their failure to explicitly recognize which items are particularly important to consumers. So although an individual item of the SERVQUAL scale may show a high level of dissatisfaction, a manager does not have a clear idea whether this failing represents a particularly important aspect of the service offer. Should the manager concentrate on rectifying an item which is showing a high level of dissatisfaction, but which may be quite unimportant to the consumer, or on rectifying an item that shows only marginal levels of dissatisfaction, but may be absolutely crucial to consumers?

Importance–performance analysis (IPA) is a simple and easy to use approach that compares the performance of elements of a service with the importance of each of these elements to the consumer. The elements which are used to define measurement scales can be derived through exploratory research. In practice, some researchers have used scale items which are very similar to those used in a typical SERVQUAL study. The difference occurs though with the treatment of scores. Instead of calculating a perceptions minus expectations (P–E) score, IPA analysis calculates a performance minus importance (P–I) score. High performance of a relatively important aspect of the service could indicate that management is 'over-delivering' on this aspect of service quality. On the other hand, poor performance of an important item indicates a priority area for management action. The resulting scores for importance and performance can be plotted on a grid (Figure 8.6), with each cell in the grid representing a different course of management action. Particular attention should be given to the extreme observations on the grid since they indicate the greatest disparity between importance and performance.

IPA has been applied within many service sectors, including banking (Joseph *et al.*, 1999), healthcare (Hawes and Rao, 1985), tourism (O'Neill *et al.*, 2002), and education (Wright and O'Neill, 2002; Pike, 2003).

Importance–performance scores are simple to calculate, but their theoretical credibility has been challenged. Bacon (2003) suggested that importance and performance are essentially different constructs and that any measures of difference between them using the same scales 'reflects a "rule of thumb"' guide for action and that attributes that score close to the cross point on the grid may be overlooked or misinterpreted in terms of an appropriate managerial response for action.

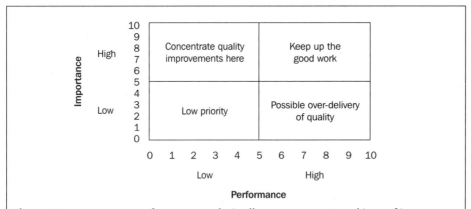

Figure 8.6 Importance–performance analysis allows consumers' rankings of importance and performance of service attributes to be plotted on a grid, from which it is easy to identify management priorities. The top-left-hand quadrant shows priority areas for improvement, while in the bottom-right quadrant, management may be over-delivering and could even save costs by reducing levels of quality.

8.4.4 **Composite models of satisfaction**

A number of attempts have been made to try to measure customer satisfaction at a national level, to provide a baseline when tracking customer satisfaction over time. The large number of currently available approaches for studying customer satisfaction include the Swedish barometer (Fornell, 1992), the Norwegian Customer Satisfaction Barometer (Andreassen and Lindestad, 1998), the American Customer Satisfaction Index (Fornell *et al.*, 1996) and, more recently, the European Customer Satisfaction Index (ECSI) (ECSI Technical Committee, 1998).

The theoretical model for the European Consumer Satisfaction Index (see Figure 8.7) introduces seven interrelated latent variables. The model links image, customer expectations, perceptions of quality and perceived value, to customer satisfaction. The

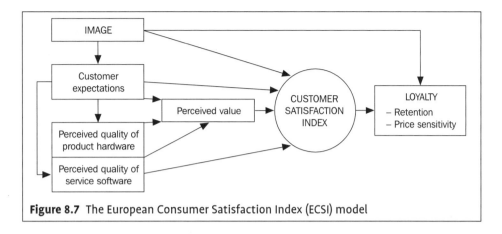

Figure 8.7 The European Consumer Satisfaction Index (ECSI) model

model distinguishes between the tangible and intangible contributors to customer satisfaction by dividing perceived quality into two parts – 'software' and 'hardware'. The 'hardware' component refers to the quality of a product as such, while 'software' relates to associated service like guarantees given, after-sales service provision, conditions of product display and assortment, documentation and descriptions, opening hours, friendliness of the personnel, etc. Only software perceived quality has a direct link with perceived value in the model, and hence the consumer satisfaction index.

The variables on the left-hand side of the model are causative factors which explain customer satisfaction, and those on the right-hand side are indicators of performance. The model shows the main causal relationships, although, in reality, there may exist many more points of dependence between the variables, and also bidirectional interactions (it could also be argued that all causative variables are related to one another). The theoretical ECSI model used is a structural model, employing a probabilistic approach and using simultaneous equation estimation techniques.

The ECSI model is much less detailed and elaborate than many standard company-specific approaches to measuring customer satisfaction. This follows from the fact that it has to be applicable for a number of different industry sectors in parallel. Numerous simplifications and reductions have been introduced in the specification in order to make it as comparable and as useful as possible from industry to industry.

Although composite measures of customer satisfaction such as that represented by ECSI may be too general for many service organizations' internal quality management purposes, these indexes provide an important complement to traditional measures of economic performance, providing useful information not only to the firms themselves, but also to shareholders and investors, government regulators and buyers.

8.5 Setting quality standards

We now move from the conceptualization and measurement of service quality to its management and implementation. A starting point for quality management is to determine the level of quality that a company should provide. A casual observation of most service sectors would indicate a range of quality standards on offer: for example, retailing (compare Marks & Spencer with Matalan); airlines (compare British Airways with Ryanair) and hotels (compare Travelodge with Marriott).

The evidence of a wide range of quality standards occurs despite many services being committed to a 'total quality management' (TQM) approach. In fact, the idea of total quality in the service sector can be quite misleading, for a number of reasons.

- 'Total quality' may be a valid concept in the manufacturing sector where checking and rechecking of components and the finished product can filter out almost all defective products before they reach the customer. How many times have you bought a defective bottle of soft drink or chocolate bar? Even complex manufactured products such as cars can have a TQM approach applied to the many components and sub-assemblies which make up a car, which explains why reliability levels for cars are typically very high. Contrast this situation with that of many services, where the production process is conducted live, much of it in the presence of the customer. The possibilities of filtering out poor performance before the effects reach the consumer are much less. While service companies can aim to improve performance through better training and simplification of service processes, among other things, the pursuit of total quality is much less realistic than is the case with the manufacturing sector.

- Total quality implies that a company has a very deep insight into the mindset of customers. Given that service quality can only be defined in the minds of consumers, the concept of total quality management implies that the target aimed for will vary between customers and may vary with individual customers over the course of time.

It is more realistic to talk about a *return on quality* rather than total quality as an end in itself. It was noted earlier in this chapter that evidence linking high levels of quality with improved profitability is fairly ambiguous. Increased profitability for a company can be achieved by cutting costs or raising revenue, or a combination of the two. In practice, it is difficult for service companies to do both simultaneously. Lower costs invariably (but not always) result in lower quality, and vice versa. It has been noted that during 1999, the low-frills, low-cost airline Ryanair earned over 10 times more than British Airways in total profits and considerably more profit per passenger carried (*The Times*, 1999). Yet this was despite a poorer reliability record, the use of smaller, less convenient airports (e.g. Prestwick instead of Glasgow), providing minimal services (e.g. no in-flight meals and no individual seat allocations) and charging for many ancillary services which are taken for granted with British Airways. A similar picture emerged in the UK retail sector with record performance reported by no-frills operators such as Peacocks and Matalan, while those retailers perceived as having high standards of customer service (e.g. Marks & Spencer and Sainsbury's) suffered falling profits and share prices during the late 1990s.

Are customers prepared to pay for additional quality? The profitable growth of 'budget' airlines suggests that in this sector at least, a large number of customers are prepared to sacrifice quality in return for a lower price. So how far should a company go in improving its levels of quality? The simple answer is, as far as customers are prepared to pay for the enhanced level of quality. To return to the airline example, an operator can invest in additional aircraft to keep in reserve and bring out only when it suffers operating problems (such as bad weather, emergency maintenance, strikes at airports, etc.). This will certainly increase one dimension of quality – reliability – as customers will not have to wait until a defective aircraft is repaired before they can proceed with their journey. However, keeping additional aircraft in reserve can be very expensive, but the improvement in reliability may not be reflected in customers' willingness to pay a higher price which covers the additional costs. Figure 8.8 shows schematically a cut-off point where a service provider should cease investing in service quality improvements.

A precise specification of service standards serves a valuable function in communicating the standard of quality which consumers can expect to receive. It also serves to communicate the standards which are expected of employees. While the general manner in which an organization goes about promoting itself may give a general impression as to what level of quality it seeks to deliver, more specific standards can be stated in a number of ways, which are considered below.

■ At its most basic, an organization can rely on its terms of business as a basis for determining the level of service to be delivered to customers. These generally act to protect customers against excessively poor service rather than being used to proactively promote high standards of excellence. The booking conditions of tour operators, for example, make very few promises about service quality, other than offers of compensation if delays exceed a specified standard or if accommodation arrangements are changed at short notice.

■ A generally worded **customers' charter** goes beyond the minimum levels of business terms by stating in a general manner the standards of performance which the organization aims to achieve in its dealings with customers. In this way, banks publish charters which specify in general terms the manner in which accounts will be conducted and complaints handled. NatWest Bank's Code of Practice for Business Banking, for example, includes general promises to inform customers in writing of any special conditions attached to loans, to discuss the price to be charged for any special services and to investigate any dissatisfaction with service through a formalized complaints procedure.

■ Specific guarantees of service performance are sometimes offered, especially in respect of service outcomes. As an example, parcel delivery companies often guarantee to deliver a parcel within a specified time and agree to pay compensation if they fall below this standard. Many of the public utilities now offer compensation payments if certain specified services are not delivered correctly. For example, Southern Electric aims to restore any loss of power within 24 hours of failure – if it fails in this aim, it pays compensation of £40 plus £20 for each subsequent 12-hour period of power failure. Increasingly, service organizations set their service

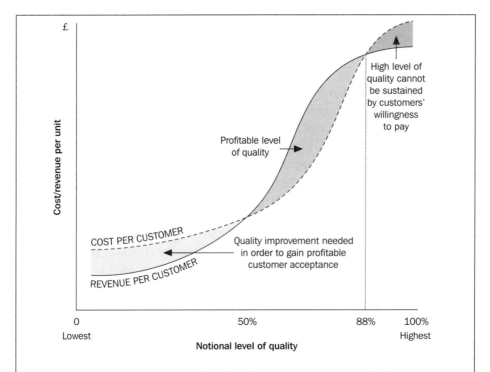

Figure 8.8 What level of service quality should an organization provide for its customers? Too high, and the customers may love the service, but the costs of providing it may lead to a financial loss by the company. Too low, and the company may get insufficient custom at a high enough price to even cover its fixed costs. Management should have a sound understanding of the dynamics of its market, and the willingness of customers to pay extra in return for improved quality levels (or, conversely, the opportunities for cutting quality levels and gaining market share through lower prices). This diagram shows the principles of an ideal level of quality. As a company increases its level of service from a notional '50%' to a notional '100%', its costs per customer climb too, which are indicated by the cost per customer line. But higher levels of quality can be expected to increase the amount that customers are prepared to pay for the service. It can be seen that at above a notional '88% quality', the costs of provision become greater than the price that customers are willing to pay. This is a simplification of reality, and measuring quality for this purpose is likely to be complex and multi-faceted. Costs can also be difficult to measure. However, the diagram illustrates the principle that 'total quality' is not necessarily the most profitable level of quality for a company, and that a sound understanding of costs and markets is needed before determining the ideal level of quality to provide.

guarantees with reference to benchmarks established by best practice companies within their sector, or in a completely different sector. Sometimes, guarantees concentrate on the manner in which a service is produced rather than specifically on final outcomes. In this way, building societies set standards for the time it will take to give a decision on a mortgage application and to subsequently process it. While there can be great benefits from publicizing specific guaranteed performance standards to customers, failure to perform could result in heavy compensation claims, or claims for misleading advertising. Many highly specific targets are therefore restricted to internal use where their function is to motivate and control staff rather than to provide guarantees to potential customers. While the major banks give their branch managers targets for such quality standards as queuing time for counter staff and availability of working ATMs, this does not guarantee a specified level of service to their customers.

■ Many service companies belong to a trade or professional association and incorporate the association's code of conduct into their own service offering. Codes of conduct adopted by members of professional associations as diverse as car repairers, undertakers and solicitors specify minimum standards below which service provision should not fall. The code of conduct provides both a reassurance to potential customers and a statement to employees about the minimum standards expected of them.

■ Of more general applicability is the adoption of ISO quality accreditation. Contrary to popular belief, a company operating to ISO 900 series does not guarantee a high level of quality for its service. Instead, ISO accreditation is granted to organizations that can show that they have in place management systems for ensuring a consistent standard of quality – whether this itself is high or low is largely a subjective judgement. Although this standard was initially adopted by manufacturing industries, it has subsequently found significant use among service companies, including education, leisure centres and building contractors. Increasingly, industrial purchasers of services are seeking the reassurance that their suppliers are ISO registered.

■ In the case of some public-sector services which operate in a monopolistic environment, quality standards are sometimes imposed from outside. In the case of privately owned utilities in the UK, the relevant regulating authority has the power to set specific service targets – for example, the telephone regulatory body, Ofcom, sets limits on what proportion of public telephone kiosks should be out of service at any one time. In the case of UK publicly owned services, the government has issued a series of customer charters setting out the standards of service which users of the service can expect – for example, the period of time which a hospital patient has to wait for an operation. Critics of such charters would argue that they provide little, if any, practical compensation for users of a service who suffer from poor standards of quality. Worse still, they may unrealistically raise users' expectations without providing resources which would allow the organization to meet them.

8.5.1 **Benchmarking studies**

The nature of customers' quality expectations in other similar service industries can be a useful source of information for managers. It is often apparent that customer needs may be similar between different industries, even though the service product on offer is ostensibly quite different. Many common dimensions cut across the boundaries of industries and apply to services in general – for example, courteous and competent staff, a pleasant environment and helpfulness, to name but a few. It can therefore be beneficial to investigate the nature of service provision in closely related service areas, and draw upon the findings of any research that has been made available. In particular, it is worth investigating what is known in those service sectors that have a good track record of analysing and responding to customers' needs and identifying whether this knowledge is applicable to an industry that has only recently adopted a customer-led approach. For example, it is possible to learn a lot about certain aspects of hospital service from what hotel and catering establishments have been researching and practising for some considerable time. Continuing with this theme, many service organizations that have been operating outside the private marketplace for many years can benefit from an understanding of the operations of their counterparts in other countries that have openly marketed their services in a freely competitive market. In this way, managers within the UK National Health Service may learn a lot about customer care by examining health services in the USA.

The term **benchmarking** is frequently used to describe the process by which companies set standards for themselves, based on a study of best practice elsewhere. Best practice could be defined in terms of firms within the same sector or completely different sectors which share similar processes (e.g. benchmarks for waiting time in a bank could be based on benchmarks established within the convenience retail sector).

Benchmarking can be undertaken at a number of levels, based on what is compared and what the comparison is being made against:

- *performance benchmarking* – essentially based on outcome measures (e.g. through-put per hour, profit per customer)

- *process benchmarking* – for example, the efficiency and effectiveness of customer handling procedures

- *strategic benchmarking* – for example, comparing the integrity of a company's strategic plan with best practice in the industry

- *internal benchmarking* – this involves comparing internal processes and structures

- *competitive benchmarking* – this may be with respect to market share, selling price, etc.

- *functional benchmarking* – sometimes the task will be to assess the performance of a company's functions (e.g. advertising or sales) with best practice.

Benchmarking involves a five-step continuous process: plan the study; form the benchmarking team; identify potential benchmarking partners; collect and analyse the information; and adapt and improve. While benchmarking produces a standard against which improvements can be made, these improvements are continuous and benchmarks can go out of date very quickly.

8.6 **Researching service quality**

So far, we have looked in general at conceptual frameworks for understanding service quality. We will now turn our attention to specific research methods that services organizations use to learn more about customers' expectations and perceptions of service quality. A clear, sustained and continuous quality improvement is not possible without some indication of quality performance. To know the real effect of changes over time, managers need measures to compare the quality performance of the service.

Ramaswamy (1996) identified three different sets of measures with which a company must be concerned

1. service performance measures that are primarily internally focused and evaluate the current performance of the service and ensure that it is continuing to reliably meet the design specifications

2. customer measures, which are both internally and externally focused, aimed at assessing the impact of the service performance on customers

3. financial measures, which are indicators of the financial health of the organization.

The correlation between financial and customer measures will determine the revenue-generating potential of the service, while the relationship between service performance measures and customer measures will give some indication as to how the service is performing in customers' eyes. In turn this will have a direct bearing on a company's financial performance and overall market share.

A number of methods for researching customers' expectations and perceptions are available and are examined below. However, as a set of general principles for the effective measurement of service quality, Zeithaml *et al.* stress some requirements for a marketing research programme.

1. Variation. Every research method has its limitations, and in order to overcome this and to achieve a comprehensive insight into a problem, a combination of qualitative and quantitative research techniques should be used.

2. *Ongoing.* The expectations and perceptions of customers are constantly changing, as is the nature of the service offer provided by companies and their competitors. It is therefore important that a service research process is administered on a continuous basis so that any changes can be picked up quickly and acted upon if necessary.

3. *Undertaken with employees.* The closeness of staff to customers within the service sector makes it important that they are asked about problems and possible improvements as well as their personal motivations and requirements.

4. *Shared with employees.* Employees' performance in delivering service quality may be improved if they are made aware of the results of studies of customer expectations, complaint analysis, etc.

8.6.1 **Regular questionnaire surveys**

The incidence of surveys into the level of satisfaction that customers have experienced from service providers is increasing throughout the service sector. The increasing range of competing services available, and customers' growing awareness of the fact that they are in receipt of a service for which they pay a price – whether directly or through taxation – has led them to expect to be consulted and to express an opinion about the level of satisfaction provided. Today, members of the public are in constant receipt of literature from a wide range of service providers asking for comments on the quality of service that they have received. It is probably true to say that most large service providers in both the private and public sectors have jumped on this quality bandwagon, although it is often questionable whether the most appropriate methods are employed to gather the information. Typical applications include filling in a questionnaire on the aeroplane after a holiday, or being asked by the local council to fill in a card headed 'Customer Service Enquiry'. Such surveys usually ask recipients to relate any complaints they may have about the services provided and any comments or suggestions for improving them. The assumption that most people make is that data from such surveys will be used to take corrective action where expectations are not reached. It must however be stated that many of these surveys are of dubious quality and therefore of limited value – many of them smack of a lip-service approach to marketing, research and the issue of quality service.

Questionnaires are often used as a relatively low-cost method of gathering the opinions of a large representative sample of service users. They can range in depth from a small card containing no more than three or four questions and completed by the respondent (see Figure 8.9), through to a multi-page in-depth questionnaire administered by a professional researcher. In addition to the traditional self-completion questionnaire, customer surveys are increasingly carried out by telephone and through the Internet. The latter techniques especially can allow for rapid analysis and dissemination of results.

Although questionnaires may be a relatively low-cost method of gathering information about quality performance, they are subject to a number of limitations. Firstly, a typical questionnaire does not allow for great depth in probing respondents' attitudes towards quality. Most questionnaires tend to focus on the technical aspects of quality rather than the functional aspects. In the case of self-completion questionnaires, it can be difficult to ensure that replies are obtained from a representative sample of service users. There is evidence to suggest, for example, that customers who are particularly satisfied or particularly dissatisfied are more likely to take part in a questionnaire survey than the broad group of customers who would typically be neither satisfied nor dissatisfied.

The timing of the questionnaire can be quite crucial. It was noted above that perceptions of quality could lead to attitude change, which can have an important effect at the time that the next purchase decision is made. Typically, service quality questionnaires are administered immediately after consumption of the service, but there

M

Merton Dene Hotel

PLEASE ☑ TO INDICATE YOUR RATING FOR EACH OF THE FOLLOWING

	Excellent	Good	Poor
Your reception to this hotel	☐	☐	☐
The comfort of your room	☐	☐	☐
The cleanliness of your room	☐	☐	☐
The service in the restaurant	☐	☐	☐
The service provided by our staff	☐	☐	☐
The enjoyment of your breakfast	☐	☐	☐
Value for money	☐	☐	☐

Will you stay at this hotel again? Yes ☐ No ☐

Any general comments which you have time to make will be greatly appreciated.

....

....

....

....

Figure 8.9 Like many services companies, Jurys Inns routinely monitors its customers' level of satisfaction. This simple comment card combines responses which can be measured quantitatively, with an opportunity for customers to express comments in an unstructured manner. Analysis of these responses allows the company to identify differences in performance between its hotels, and to monitor changes in performance over time. Many companies link survey results to bonuses paid to their employees. Like most self-completion surveys, the company must be alert to the representativeness of its respondents, with evidence that very happy and very unhappy customers are more likely to provide comments than customers holding average views. (Reproduced with permission of Jurys Inns)

is evidence that perceived quality scores can change over time (O'Neill and Palmer, 2001). Gestalt analysis, for example, has been used to show how small elements of the service offer which give dissatisfaction can affect perceptions of quality at the time that they occur, but over time fade into the background and do not affect attitude to the service over the long term.

8.6.2 **Qualitative research techniques**

Qualitative techniques are often used by companies to complement their questionnaire-based approaches. The use of qualitative techniques in general has been growing rapidly in recent years, as companies try to gain a much deeper insight into consumers' needs and the nature of individuals' motivators. Qualitative techniques are often used as a precursor to a questionnaire survey. In order to develop meaningful questions in a questionnaire survey, more unstructured qualitative techniques can be useful for generating a list of relevant questions to ask. On other occasions, qualitative research is used to try to interpret the findings of a questionnaire survey, especially where a company has discovered a correlation between a service quality score and some aspects of service delivery, and the company wishes to learn more about the causal relationship.

The focus group is a widely used technique for learning about service quality, although many focus groups would be assembled to discuss a number of aspects of a company's activities or, for example, its image and range of services. Another commonly used technique is a one-to-one unstructured interview with a sample of customers, or selected key customers. In all of these cases, a company cannot hope to gain a representative sample of customer attitudes towards service quality, however it makes up for this through depth of understanding. A key role is played by the individual who leads the research, although many techniques are available to analyse qualitative data in an apparently more objective manner.

8.6.3 Customer panels

These can provide a continuous source of information on customer expectations. Groups of customers, who are generally frequent users, are consulted by a company on a regular basis to study their opinions about the quality of service provided. On other occasions they may be employed to monitor the introduction of a new or revised service – for example, a panel could be brought together by a building society following the experimental introduction of a new branch design format. Research methods used with customer panels can be a combination of qualitative and quantitative research.

The use of continuous panels can offer organizations a means of anticipating problems and may act as an early warning system for emerging issues of importance. Retailers have been involved in the operation of continuous panels to monitor their level of service provision as well as letting panels contribute to new service development research. The validity of this research method is quite dependent on how well the panel represents consumers as a whole. Careful selection should therefore be undertaken to ensure that the panel possesses the same social, economic, demographic, frequency of use, etc., characteristics as the population of customers being analysed. There has been a suggestion that the number of people prepared to become members of panels is not rising as quickly as firms' appetite for information. The result has been the emergence of 'professional' panel members who may not be representative of service users as a whole.

8.6.4 Transaction analysis

An increasingly popular method of evaluative research involves tracking the satisfaction of individuals with particular transactions in which they have recently been involved. This type of research enables management to judge current performance, particularly customers' satisfaction with the contact personnel with whom they have interacted, as well as their overall satisfaction with the service.

The research effort normally involves a mail-out questionnaire survey or a telephone call to individual customers immediately after a transaction has been completed (see Figure 8.10). A wide range of UK service organizations are now using this approach. For example, the Automobile Association (AA) surveys customers who have recently

Figure 8.10 When should you ask customers about their perceptions of service quality? Many service organizations find that the most convenient time to ask customers is immediately after consumption of the service. Details of the service are fresh in customers' memories, and the service provider does not have the trouble and expense of trying to contact customers later by mail or telephone. However, service providers should be interested in the long-term attitude change which results from the perceived quality of the service encounter. It is this longer-term attitude change which is likely to influence whether a customer returns and recommends the service provider to their friends. Sometimes the difference between immediate perceptions of quality and more long-term considered attitudes can be quite great. Hairdressing provides a good example of this. Many people who have been to a hairdresser to have their hair restyled leave the hairdresser with a sense of doubt about their new-look image. At this stage, the hairdresser might score very poorly in any survey of quality. However, given the passage of time, a customer may become used to his or her haircut and, after a few weeks, probably couldn't imagine looking any differently. A few complimentary comments from friends, and the score of the hairdresser after a few weeks will be much higher.

been served by its breakdown service, and many building societies invite customers who have just used their mortgage services to express their views on the service received via a structured questionnaire. An additional benefit of this research is its capability to associate service quality performance with individual contact personnel and link it to reward systems.

8.6.5 **Mystery customers**

The use of 'Mystery customers' is a method of auditing the standard of service provision, particularly the staff involvement in such provision. A major difficulty in ensuring service quality is overcoming the non-conformance of staff with performance guidelines. This so-called service–performance gap is the result of employees being unable and/or unwilling to perform the service at the desired level. An important function of mystery customer surveys is therefore to monitor the extent to which specified quality standards are actually being met by staff.

This method of researching actual service provision involves the use of trained assessors who visit service organizations and report back their observations. Audits tend to be tailored to the specific needs of a company and focus on an issue that it wishes to evaluate. The format of the enquiry is therefore something which is determined jointly by the client and the research organization.

The constructive nature of this research technique has to be stressed, as the mystery customer can quite easily be mistaken by staff for an undercover agent spying on

Can you spot a spy in the pub?

Would you want a 'mystery shopper' trying to measure your performance while you are working? They're not spies but assessors, insists the market research industry. In fact, mystery shoppers are now highly trained, professional assessors. In the early days of mystery shopping, subjective questions were the norm. Today, 80–90% of mystery shopping questionnaires are objective – for example, questions for a mystery shopper survey of a pub include: 'How long was it before I was served? Was I served in turn? Was I offered a clean glass when reordering? Staff working in pubs may still have fun trying to spot the 'mystery customer', and one of the challenges of the industry is to simulate a typical customer. This can be quite a challenge where customers typically use a service in a group, rather than alone, so a mystery shopper acting on their own is likely to stand out.

Rather than being seen as sneaky spying, companies should place a lot of importance in involving staff in the whole measurement process. Not only do staff provide useful insights to the service, if handled correctly they can feel a sense of ownership of the programme. And for those staff who are performing well, there is often a bonus waiting for them at the end of the month.

them on behalf of the management. In particular, if the techniques are applied correctly, they can allow management to know what is really happening at the sharp end of the business. To be effective, mystery shopping surveys need to be undertaken independently, should be objective and must be consistent. The training of assessors is critical to the effective use of this research method and should include, for example, training in observation techniques which allow them to distinguish between a greeting and an acknowledgement.

8.6.6 **Analysis of complaints**

The dissatisfaction of customers is most clearly voiced through the complaints that they make about service provision. For many companies this may be the sole method of keeping in touch with customers. Complaints can be made directly to the provider or perhaps indirectly through an intermediary or a watchdog body. Complaints by customers, referring to instances of what they consider poor-quality service may, if treated constructively, provide a rich source of data on which to base policies for improving service quality. However, customer complaints are at best an inadequate source of information. Most customers do not bother to complain, remain dissatisfied and tell others about their dissatisfaction. Others simply change to another supplier and do not offer potentially valuable information to the service provider about what factors were wrong and caused them to leave.

In truly market-oriented organizations, complaints analysis can form a useful pointer to where the process of service delivery is breaking down. As part of an overall

---

How much is a complaint worth?

How far should a company go in encouraging its customers to complain? Of course, cultures differ greatly in their willingness to complain about bad service. The traditional reserve of the British may seem like a gift to the average duty manager of a restaurant who doesn't have to put up with the rough ride which more demanding Australian or American customers may give. In principle, the idea of collecting feedback from customers is good because of the opportunities which it gives to put things right, both immediately in terms of the complainant's satisfaction, and strategically in terms of designing more effective processes. But could this lead to a culture among some clients of always complaining, just to see what they can get back? Many tour operators can recount stories of customers who routinely submit complaints about trivial matters in an effort to get some compensation which will be put towards the cost of their next holiday. How does a company strike a balance between listening to customer complaints and keeping its costs of compensation down, especially when it is positioning itself as a low-cost supplier and operating in an environment where things are quite likely to go wrong?

programme for keeping in touch with customers, the analysis of complaints can have an important role to play. The continuous tracking of complaints is a relatively inexpensive source of data which enables a company to review the major concerns of customers on an ongoing basis and hopefully rectify any evident problems. In addition, the receipt of complaints by the firm enables staff to enter into direct contact with customers and provides an opportunity to interact with them over their matters of concern. As well as eliciting customers' views on these issues in particular, complainants can also contribute views about customer service in general. Many companies have gone to great lengths to make it easy for customers to complain, for example by creating freefone telephone lines and making comment cards readily available.

8.6.7 Employee research

Research undertaken among employees can enable their views about the way that services are provided, and their perceptions of how they are received by customers, to be taken into account. Data gathered from staff-training seminars and development exercises, feedback from quality circles, job appraisal and performance evaluation reports, etc., can all provide valuable information for planning quality service provision. One way in which formal feedback from staff can be built into a systematic research programme is the operation of a staff suggestion scheme. The proposals which staff may make about how services could be provided more efficiently and/or effectively certainly can have an important role to play in improving service quality.

Research into employees' needs can also allow identification of policies which improve their motivation to deliver a high quality of service. Many of the techniques employed to elicit the views of employees as internal customers are in principle the same as those used in studies of external customers. Interviews and focus groups may be used in the collection of qualitative data on employee needs, wants, motivations and attitudes towards working conditions, benefits and policies. This can be followed up with appropriate quantitative analysis, such as the SERVQUAL methodology, which it is suggested can equally be applied to internal employee studies.

In Chapter 12 the issue of obtaining the involvement and participation of the workforce is considered in some detail. In this respect, involving employees in the research process and its findings, for example by using them to gather data, showing them videotapes of group discussions and interviews with customers, and circulating them with the findings of research reports, can do a lot for improving their understanding of service quality issues throughout their organization. In high-contact, people-intensive service sectors, the importance of employees as sources of information about customers' perceptions of service quality, cannot be over-emphasized. There are many barriers to the flow of information from employees to managers, especially in organizations where there is no culture of listening to staff. Where there are clearly identified means of listening, and for acting on the results, a shared commitment to improving quality can greatly improve customers' perceptions.

8.6.8 **Intermediary research**

It has already been noted that services intermediaries often perform a valuable function in the process of service delivery, performing their role in quite a different manner to goods intermediaries. Research into intermediaries focuses on two principal concerns.

1. Where intermediaries form an important part of service delivery processes, the quality perceived by customers is to a large extent determined by the performance of intermediaries. In this way, the perceived quality of an airline may be tarnished if its ticket agents are perceived as being slow or unhelpful to customers. Research through such techniques as mystery customer surveys can be used to monitor the standard of quality delivered by intermediaries.

2. Intermediaries as co-producers of a service are further down the channel of distribution and hence closer to customers. They are therefore in a position to provide valuable feedback to the service principal about consumers' expectations and perceptions. As well as conducting structured research investigations of intermediaries, many **service principals** find it possible to learn more about the needs and expectations of their final customers during the process of providing intermediary support services such as training.

8.6.9 **Management by walking about**

All of the techniques described above are essentially involved in providing senior management with insights into service quality as it is perceived by customers at the point of delivery. A small service provider, such as a self-employed decorator or builder, is in a good position to understand customers' perceptions of quality, from the comments which they receive back directly from customers, and from customer referrals and repeat business. In the large multi-outlet corporation, this opportunity for customer feedback is not available to key corporate decision-makers on a regular basis. Many large organizations have therefore developed programmes for sending their senior staff back to the front line in order that they can understand at first hand the expectations of customers and the delivery performance of the company.

Management by walking about (MBWA) has become a popular way in which senior executives try to gain knowledge about aspects of their operations that is not immediately apparent from structured reporting systems. Archie Norman, when head of the retailer Asda, is reported to have introduced a number of innovations learnt during his regular visits to the company's shop floors. Some companies have adopted a formal system of role exchanges where senior executives spend a period at the sharp end of the business. Even the vice chancellors of some universities have taken the bold step of trying to live the student life for a day or a week, experiencing classrooms and lectures at first hand. It was hoped that this would give vice chancellors a better understanding of the day-to-day issues which are of greatest concern to students. Although many service organizations have developed similar programmes for their senior management, others have been critical of the idea. To some, management by walking about is no more than a gimmick, while others adopt the arguments of the scientific management approach by claiming that the time of a highly paid executive is spent more cost-effectively in the boardroom rather than doing relatively unskilled work on the shop floor.

8.7 Managing the marketing mix for quality

Service quality management is the process of attempting to ensure that the gap between consumer expectations and the perceived service delivery is as small as possible. There are a number of important dimensions to this task.

Firstly, the marketing mix formulation and its communication to potential customers must be as realistic as possible. Exaggerated claims merely lead to high expectations which an organization may not be able to deliver and thus the service is likely to be perceived as being of a poor quality.

Secondly, non-marketer dominated factors such as word-of-mouth information, traditions, etc., also need to be considered as, once again, their presence may have the effect of raising expectations.

Finally, service companies must recognize that the relationship between customers' perceptions and expectations is dynamic. Merely maintaining customers' level of perceived quality is insufficient if their expectations have been raised over time. Marketing mix management is therefore concerned with closing the quality gap over time, either by improving the service offer, or restraining customers' expectations (see Figure 8.11).

Quality affects all aspects of the marketing mix – decisions about service specification cannot be taken in isolation from decisions concerning other elements of the mix. All can affect the level of customer expectations and the perceived standard of service delivery.

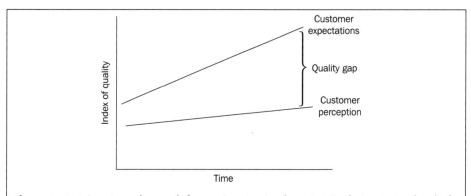

Figure 8.11 It is not good enough for services to simply maintain their existing level of quality, because consumers' expectations are likely to have moved on. Even a company which strives to improve its performance may find its quality ratings falling if its customers' expectations have moved ahead faster than its improvement in performance.

8.7.1 Promotion decisions

Promotion decisions have the effect of developing consumers' expectations of service quality. Where marketer-dominated sources of promotion are the main basis for evaluating and selecting competing services, the message as well as the medium of communication can contribute in a significant way towards customers' quality expectations. Invariably, promotion sets expectations which organizations struggle to meet.

On some occasions however, the image created by promotion may actually add to the perceived quality of the service. This is quite common for goods of conspicuous consumption, where the intangible image added to products such as beer can actually lead to consumers believing that the beer is of higher quality than another beer of identical technical quality, which has been promoted in a different way. The possibility for achieving this with services is generally less, on account of the greater involvement of customers in the production/consumption process and the many opportunities which occur for judging quality. It is, however, possible in the case of some publicly consumed services, where high-profile advertising may actually add to the perceived quality of the service. In this way, the promotion of an exclusive gym may add to customers' feeling that they have an exclusive and prestigious facility. Without the advertising, the prestigious value of the gym would not be recognized by others.

8.7.2 Price decisions

Price decisions affect both customers' expectations and perceptions of service quality, as well as the service organization's ability to produce quality services. In cases where all other factors are equal, price can be used by potential customers as a basis for judging service quality. If two outwardly similar restaurants charge different prices for a similar meal, the presumption may be made that the higher-priced restaurant must offer a higher standard of service, which the customer will subsequently expect to be delivered. It will be against this benchmark that service delivery will be assessed.

The price charged can influence the level of quality which a service organization can build into its offering. The concept of price positioning was raised in Chapter 7, where it was noted that while any position along a line from high price/high quality to low price/low quality may be feasible, high price/low quality and low price/high quality positions are not generally sustainable over the long term. As an example, the low prices which many UK tour operators have offered relative to the levels charged in many overseas markets have resulted in insufficient margins to provide a high quality of service. Delays and inconvenience due to over-scheduled aircraft or overbooked flights have been among the consequences.

8.7.3 Accessibility decisions

Place, or accessibility, decisions can affect customers' expectations of quality as well as actual performance. A poor-quality service sold through a high-quality agent may give heightened expectations of quality. Poor delivery may subsequently harm the image of the agent itself, which partly explains why many travel agents are reluctant to continue to act as intermediaries for tour operators with poor service quality records. The manner in which an intermediary initiates, processes and follows up the service delivery process can often affect perceived quality received by the customer – for example, an agent who incorrectly fills out the departure time for a coach ticket harms the quality of the service which the customer receives. For these reasons, an important element of quality management involves the recruitment and monitoring of a network of intermediaries who are able to share the service principal's commitment to quality standards.

8.7.4 Personnel

Personnel, especially front-line contact personnel, are important elements of consumers' perceptions of functional quality, and therefore the nature of the buyer–seller interaction becomes crucial in the management of service quality. Recruitment, training, motivation and control of personnel are therefore important elements of the marketing mix which impact on quality standards. Front-line employees have the best possible vantage point for observing quality standards and are best placed to identify any impediments. Whether these contact personnel have the ability to articulate these failings can be another matter.

8.8 Organizing and implementing service quality

Service quality does not come about by chance – organizations need to develop strategies for ensuring that they deliver consistent and high-quality services. A number of people have sought to identify the organizational factors which are most commonly associated with successful quality management. Kotler (1991), as a result of research involving successful service firms in the USA, proposed the following requirements.

1. A strategic concept which is customer focused.

2. A history of top-management commitment to quality, i.e. seeing quality indicators as being just as important as financial indicators.

3. The setting of high standards and communicating these expected standards to employees.

4. Systems for monitoring performance. Top service firms regularly evaluate their own and their competitors' performance.

5. Systems for satisfying complaining customers. It is important to respond quickly and appropriately to customers' complaints.

6. Satisfying employees as well as customers. Successful organizations understand the importance of contact personnel and see an important role for 'internal marketing', i.e. 'applying the philosophies and practices of marketing to people who serve

the external customers so that (1) the best possible people can be employed and retained and (2) they will do the best possible work' (Berry, 1980). The subject of 'internal marketing' is discussed in more detail in Chapter 12.

Service personnel have emerged as a key element in the process of quality management. Maintaining a consistent standard of quality in labour-based services becomes very difficult on account of the inherent variability of personnel, as compared to machines. Furthermore, it has already been noted that the inseparability of most services does not generally allow an organization to undertake quality control checks between the points of production and consumption. Many service organizations link employees' salaries to customer satisfaction scores achieved by the team that they work in – for example, it is reported that at the fast-food chain KFC about 35% of a manager's annual bonus is tied to the customer satisfaction scores achieved. We will return to the subject of employee rewards linked to service quality in Chapter 12.

Responsibility for developing a culture of quality rests with senior management. In addition to introducing reward systems linked to quality performance, successful service organizations have introduced a participative culture in which knowledge is shared and a commitment made to continually improve quality performance. One widely used approach is the **quality circle** (QC). QCs consist of small groups of employees who meet together with a supervisor or group leader to discuss their work in terms of production and delivery standards. QCs are especially suited to high-contact services where there is considerable interaction between employees and consumers. Front-line service staff who are in a position to identify quality shortcomings as they impact on customers are brought together with operational staff who may not interact directly with customers but can significantly affect service quality. By sitting down and talking together, employees have an opportunity to jointly recognize and suggest solutions to problems. In this way, a QC run by a car repair garage would bring together reception staff who interact with the public and mechanics who produce the **substantive service**. By analysing a quality problem identified by the receptionists (e.g. delays in collecting completed jobs), the mechanics might be able to suggest solutions (e.g. rescheduling some work procedures).

To be successful, the QC leader has to be willing to listen to and act upon issues raised by QC members. This is essential if the QC is to be sustained. Circle members must feel that their participation is real and effective, thus the communication process within the QC must be two way. Consent can be real or perfunctory. In the latter case, if the QC appears to become only a routinized listening session, circle members may consider it to be just another form of managerial control. While circle members might consent to such control, their active participation in processes to improve service quality may be absent.

QC members need speedy and real feedback on ideas they might suggest to solve operational problems. Where a QC has successfully identified reasons why marketing objectives are not being attained, its suggestions should be commented on in a constructive manner.

Case study

To guarantee or not to guarantee?

By Rod McColl, Groupe ESC Rennes, France

Pierre Legrand, marketing director of a four-star hotel chain operating in France, was considering whether or not to recommend the introduction of a service guarantee for his chain. He had just returned, excited, from an international management conference where many examples of successfully introduced service guarantees were outlined. Although the concept of product guarantees dates back to the 1850s, an interesting trend was emerging where service companies were also introducing guarantees. Examples were presented across many service sectors, such as retailing, real estate, financial services, insurance, transport, fast food, video rental and leisure industries. If service guarantees could work for these companies, why shouldn't they work in Legrand's hotel chain?

Legrand was already familiar with examples of the two main types of service guarantees: *conditional (or specific) guarantees* and *unconditional guarantees*. Within the hotel sector, Ibis already offered a conditional guarantee in its promise that 'any problems caused by the hotel will be rectified within 15 minutes'. A *conditional guarantee* spells out certain elements of the service offering which an organization chooses to stand behind. Radisson Hotels, on the other hand, offered an *unconditional guarantee*, by offering a '100% satisfaction guarantee' across its hotels worldwide. Such unconditional guarantees are generally simple to understand and usually have no hidden clauses or conditions.

The table overleaf shows a selection of service guarantees that were presented at the conference.

From the examples presented, it appeared that service guarantees were implemented for three main reasons: as a *marketing tool*; as a *quality tool*; or as *a customer service device*. As a *marketing tool*, one presenter from a real estate company said that their service guarantee differentiated them from the competition. The firm promised that 'the client will pay no fees unless the property is sold'. This was an important factor for clients used to paying substantial advertising fees even if their property was not sold at auction. To marketers, the service guarantee can build trial and help to reduce the perceived risk, particularly when purchasing a highly intangible service. It also potentially generates positive word of mouth from satisfied customers by reducing 'referral fear'.

The most comprehensive case of a company using the service guarantee as a *quality tool* came from AAMI, a medium-sized Australian insurance company. Its guarantee was introduced as a strategic tool to drive its internal quality programme and to give an operational focus to the way in which insurance claims were dealt with. The company sought to ensure that its service standards met customers' expectations.

AAMI executives said that the guarantee process helped the company's quality initiatives in a number of ways.

Overview of a range of service guarantees

Case/industry	Guarantee type	Conditions	Invoking authority	Compensation
Banking – ANZ Bank	Conditional	Five minutes in a queue or $5 back	Customer and/or company	Monetary $5
Communications – Telstar	Conditional	$25 of rental reduction per month for each day phone is out of order	Customer and/or company	Monetary $25
Video rental – Home Video	Conditional	If you don't like the movie you can return the video at no charge	Customer	Monetary (refund)
Postal services – Australia Post	Conditional	Express Post Pack – if the package does not reach destination by next day, you receive a free bag	Customer	Monetary (replacement)
Insurance – AAMI	Conditional/ service charter	Service charter includes 18 service promises	Customer and/or company	Monetary $25
Real Estate – Hayden Real Estate	Conditional	No fees unless the property is sold	Customer and/or company	Monetary (no charge)
Hotel – Radisson Hotels	Unconditional	100% satisfaction or money refunded	Customer	Monetary (refund)
Plumbing – ABC Plumbing	Conditional	On-time arrival for all appointments	Customer	Monetary (refund)

- It defined and focused on customers' most important needs and concentrated resources on those needs. In doing so, it created a sense of urgency about service priorities.

- It helped to understand the service-delivery process, including the controllable and uncontrollable variables and possible weaknesses or failure points such as human resources or outside supplier quality.

- It helped to establish customer-satisfaction measures as key performance indicators.

- It allowed errors to be tracked better rather than relying on customer complaints.

- The process established a feedback loop for continual improvement.

AAMI claimed that its guarantee gave a 'fresh focus' as 'previous attempts to improve customer service had been quite disparate'. Despite the fact that the Australian general insurance industry Code of Practice required a minimum standard of performance, AAMI launched its more demanding guarantee requirements to pre-empt and exceed any efforts by competitors to move beyond the minimum requirements of the Code of Practice. As part of its continuous improvement process, additional service promises are generated from customer complaints, market research and staff research. A guarantee committee evaluates the potential for including new promises in the guarantee. For example, research identified that customers making insurance claims were unhappy about the delay between the agreement of a settlement and actually receiving the cheque. Customers expected a delay of no more than five working days but the average for the company was more than 15 days. The company's operations were modified to deliver against the customer's expectation and so this promise was added to the guarantee.

Other companies were using service guarantees not as a marketing or quality tool, but as a *customer service device* to encourage dissatisfied customers to complain. Complaints were then tracked as a monitor of the service level.

All company executives agreed that an effective service guarantee should be easy to understand, well communicated, meaningful to the customer, easy for the customer to invoke and easy for a customer to receive a payout. Guarantee design issues were therefore very important and went beyond just the type of guarantee and stating any conditions. Legrand felt that he would need to consider the issues of compensation and invoking authority, making the guarantee process more complex than he first realized.

Most of the conference presenters felt that it was important to enhance the credibility of the service guarantee through the promise of compensation. In the case of AAMI, a penalty was established at a level where it could hurt the company and the effort of complaining for the customer was warranted. According to AAMI, '$25 isn't very much if you have a major disagreement with the company, but for something minor like not having a decision-maker on hand at the time of your call, it is quite high'. AAMI's service guarantee (described by the company as a charter) outlined 18 specific service standards that customers can expect from the company. Any breaches of the guaranteed conditions are independently audited by a national accounting and audit firm. AAMI's performance against each service promise is then publicly available in an annual report.

In another case, Australia Post offered a postal pack that is guaranteed to arrive by 10.00 am the next day. It promised to supply a free replacement courier bag as compensation in the event of the original parcel not arriving by the specified time. The company claimed that it meets its published deadlines 99 times out of 100, as audited by an independent accounting firm. This translated to around 30 000 parcels per year that failed to meet the promised delivery times. A company representative noted 'even if we had to compensate every one of those 30 000 customers with a replacement courier bag, it is such a small cost compared with the benefits of customer satisfaction'.

Another key consideration in the design of a service guarantee is deciding who has the authority or responsibility for invoking the service guarantee should the need arise: the customer, the company, or either party. By virtue of its design, the unconditional guarantee implies that authority and responsibility for invoking the guarantee rests with the customer. This was illustrated by the Radisson Hotels representative's response that 'the customer is the ultimate judge of quality under our 100% satisfaction guarantee'.

Australia Post required a disgruntled customer to contact his or her local post office or to call the customer service department and quote their parcel's barcode number in order to invoke the guarantee. At AAMI between 70 and 80% of the penalties paid under its guarantee were initiated by employees rather than customers.

Presenters generally agreed that any service guarantee that was entirely dependent upon the customer initiating a claim was less powerful than one that could be initiated by either party or by the service company only. However, for the company-invoked guarantee, respondents were concerned that employees might be under pressure not to invoke the guarantee if it reflected poorly on them personally or on their department. For example, if the housekeeping department of a hotel was more frequently cited for causing guests to activate the guarantee, housekeeping staff may become discouraged from initiating further payouts. The company-invoked guarantee 'may, on the other hand, act as a pleasant surprise to a guest in the service recovery process, particularly if the guest had been unaware of the existence of the service guarantee'.

At Australia Post, experience showed that some customers would demand compensation for late deliveries beyond a replacement courier bag, which was the offer stated in the service guarantee. This was the case for misplacing important documents such as job applications that did not arrive at the destination on time. The response of Australia Post has been to 'judge each claim individually on its merit'. In one instance, when football final tickets went astray, the company arranged for replacement tickets.

Examples of poor guarantee experiences were also raised at the conference. For example, some years ago Lufthansa Airlines guaranteed a number of conditions to passengers including that they would receive a seat in the class in which they booked and that their luggage would arrive with them at the destination. These promises were considered so fundamental to passengers that they weakened the impact of the guarantee and raised doubts in their minds that these promises may not be fulfilled. Another airline in the USA suffered from implementing a 100% satisfaction guarantee as customers claimed for all sorts of minor disputes, such as the ice-cream served during the in-flight meal was too soft.

ANZ Bank subsequently discontinued its service guarantee of 'more than 5 minutes in a queue or receive $5' claiming it had enabled the bank to demonstrate successfully its commitment to better customer service. Some observers argued that the service guarantee was discontinued because it conflicted with the bank's policy of discouraging branch banking in favour of Internet, telephone and automatic teller machine banking. A guarantee of not spending more than five minutes in a queue may have actually encouraged customers to visit the branches.

Legrand was now about to provide a recommended strategy to his managing director and was again reviewing the notes he made during the conference. He seemed to have more questions than answers on the issue. He could see the possible benefits of providing a written guarantee of service but there were also potential risks. What type of guarantee would work best? Do the cultural differences of a nation impact on the effectiveness of the guarantee? For example, perhaps his mainly French clients are less demanding than British customers. It was clear that the issue of whether or not to introduce a service guarantee had profound implications for his company, and the decision was not an easy one.

Case study review questions

1. Address the questions raised by Legrand in the last paragraph.

2. What would you recommend if you were in Legrand's position?

Chapter summary and links to other chapters

Quality is a complex concept when applied to services, and this chapter has reviewed some of the difficulties in seeking to measure a concept which can only be defined in consumers' minds. Much of what passes for service quality measurement is ad hoc and misleading. However, there is disagreement over more comprehensive approaches to service quality measurement and the role of expectations in influencing quality evaluations. Quality measurement alone is of little value if management does nothing to set standards for quality and implement these standards successfully. This chapter has reviewed issues involved in the management of quality to which we will return in **Chapter 12** in the context of human resource management.

A large part of this chapter's discussion on quality can be related back to the chapter discussing service encounters – blueprinting can be a valuable tool for designing services processes that consistently meet customers' expectations (**Chapter 3**). Quality delivery of service is a prerequisite to the development of stable long-term buyer–seller relationships (**Chapter 5**) and is an issue which should be shared between a company and its intermediaries (**Chapter 9**) to create quality through a value chain. The need for a constant flow of information to monitor quality standards was underlined in **Chapter 6**.

Chapter review questions

1. Discuss the reasons why quality has become an increasingly important issue in services marketing.

2. In what ways can an airline attempt to measure the quality of its services?

3. Using a public-sector organization of your choice, give examples of the methods by which the organization can seek to manage quality.

4. Giving examples, distinguish between the concepts of 'functional' and 'technical' quality.

5. Critically assess the usefulness of the SERVQUAL technique for measuring quality in an industry of your choice.

6. In what ways can the personnel input to services be managed in order to achieve more consistent quality standards?

Activity

Gather together a sample of questionnaires from service companies, which are designed to give the company an indication of its service quality performance. Then critically assess the contribution that you think each of the questionnaires will make in giving the company a good indication of its performance. What, if any, changes would you recommend to the questionnaire? What additional sources of information would you recommend in order to better inform the company's service quality management?

Key terms

Benchmarking Setting performance standards by reference to best practice elsewhere.

Customers' charter A statement by a service organization to its customers of the standards of service it pledges to achieve.

Customers' expectations The standard of service against which actual service delivery is assessed.

Disconfirmation model Customers prior expectations of a service are not confirmed by subsequent delivery of the service.

Functional quality Customers' subjective judgements of the quality of service delivery.

Gaps model An analysis of the causes of differences between what customers expect and what they get.

Management by walking about (MBWA) A process by which key decision-makers in an organization keep in touch with issues at the point of service production and delivery.

Quality circles Groups of employees formed to discuss methods of better meeting customers' expectations of quality.

Service principals A relational term describing an organization which produces a service, but which makes some or all of the benefits available through intermediaries.

Service–profit chain The linkage between service production processes, value creation in the eyes of customers and, ultimately, the level of profitability achieved by an organization.

Substantive service The essential function of a service.

Technical quality Objective measures of quality; not necessarily the measures that consumers consider to be important.

Selected further reading

The following offer an introduction to the overlapping and related concepts of quality, satisfaction and value.
Oliver, R. (1997) *Satisfaction: A Behavioral Perspective of the Consumer*, McGraw-Hill, New York.
Bolton, R. and Drew, J. (1991) 'A multistage model of customers' assessments of service quality and value', *Journal of Consumer Research*, 17 (March), 375–84.
Zeithaml, V.A., Berry, L.L. and Parasuraman, A. (1996) 'The behavioral consequences of service quality', *Journal of Marketing*, 60, 31–46.
Iacobucci, D., Ostrom, A. and Grayson, K. (1995) 'Distinguishing service quality and customer satisfaction: The voice of the consumer', *Journal of Consumer Psychology*, 4 (3), 277–303.
Grönroos, C. (2001) 'Guru's view: The perceived service quality concept – a mistake?', *Managing Service Quality*, 11 (3), 150–2.

The effects of services' intangibility on consumers' expectations are explored in the following.
Boulding, W., Kalra A., Staelin, R. and Zeithaml, V.A. (1993) 'A dynamic process model of service quality: From expectations to behavioural intentions', *Journal of Marketing Research*, 30 (1), 7–27.
Bebko, C. (2000) 'Service intangibility and its impact on consumer expectations of service quality', *Journal of Services Marketing*, 14, 9–24.

The pre-eminent disconfirmation model of service quality – SERVQUAL – is described in the following widely cited paper.
Parasuraman, A., Zeithaml, V. and Berry, L. (1988) 'SERVQUAL: A multiple-item scale for measuring consumer perceptions of service quality', *Journal of Retailing*, 64 (1), 12–40.

The following paper provides an overview of importance–performance analysis.
Bacon, D.R. (2003) 'A comparison of approaches to importance–performance analysis', *International Journal of Market Research*, 45 (1), 55–71.

The link between service quality, customer loyalty and profitability is discussed in the following papers.
Bates, K., Bates, H. and Johnston, R. (2003) 'Linking service to profit: The business case for service excellence', *International Journal of Service Industry Management*, 14 (2), 173–83.
Vilares, M.J. and Coelho, P.S. (2003) 'The employee–customer satisfaction chain in the ECSI model', *European Journal of Marketing*, 37 (11), 1703–22.
Paraskevas, A. (2001) 'Exploring hotel internal service chains: A theoretical approach', *International Journal of Contemporary Hospitality Management*, 13 (5), 251–8.
Bloemer, J., de Ruyter, K. and Wetzels, M. (1999) 'Linking perceived service quality and service loyalty: A multi-dimensional perspective', *European Journal of Marketing*, 33, 1082–106.

Discussion of service quality through electronic channels is brought up to date in the following article.
Zeithaml, V.A., Parasuraman, A. and Malhotra, A. (2002) 'Service quality delivery through web sites: A critical review of extant knowledge', *Academy of Marketing Science Journal*, 30 (4), 362–74.

References

Anderson, E.W. and Fornell, C. (1994) 'A customer satisfaction research prospectus', in R.T. Rust and R.L. Oliver (eds), *Service Quality: New Directions in Theory and Practice*, Sage Publications, Thousand Oaks, CA, 241–68.
Anderson, E.W., Fornell, C. and Lehmann, D.R. (1994) 'Customer satisfaction, market share and profitability', *Journal of Marketing*, 58 (3), 53–66.
Anderson, P. (1982) 'Marketing, strategic planning and theory', *Journal of Marketing*, (Spring), 15–26.
Andreassen, T.W. and Lindestad, B. (1998) 'The effects of corporate image in the formation of customer loyalty', *Journal of Service Research*, 1 (1), 82–92.
Bacon, D.R. (2003). 'A comparison of approaches to importance–performance analysis', *International Journal of Market Research*, 45 (1), 55–71.
Bates, K., Bates, H. and Johnston, R. (2003) 'Linking service to profit: The business case for service excellence', *International Journal of Service Industry Management*, 14 (2), 173–83.
Bebko, C.P. (2000) 'Service intangibility and its impact on consumer expectations of service quality', *Journal of Services Marketing*, 14 (1), 10–26.
Berry, L.L. (1980) 'Services marketing is different', *Business*, 30 (3), 24–9.
Bitner, M. (1990) 'Evaluating service encounters: The effects of physical surroundings and employee responses', *Journal of Marketing*, 51 (April), 69–82.
Bolton, R. and Drew, J. (1991) 'A multistage model of customers' assessments of service quality and value', *Journal of Consumer Research*, 17 (March), 375–84.
Bolton, R.N. and Lemon, K.N. (1999) 'A dynamic model of customers' usage of services: Usage as an antecedent and consequence of satisfaction', *Journal of Marketing Research*, 36 (2), 171–86.
Brady, M.K. and Cronin, J.J. (2001) 'Some new thoughts on conceptualizing perceived service quality: a hierarchical approach', *Journal of Marketing*, 65, 34–49.
Brown, T.J., Churchill, G.A. and Peter, J.P. (1993) 'Improving the measurement of service quality', *Journal of Retailing*, 69 (1), 127–39.

Carman, J.M. (1990) 'Consumer perceptions of service quality: An assessment of the SERVQUAL dimensions', *Journal of Retailing*, 66 (1), 33–55.

Cronin, J.J. (2003) 'Looking back to see forward in services marketing: Some ideas to consider', *Managing Service Quality*, 13 (5), 332–7.

Cronin, J.J. and Taylor, S.A. (1992) 'Measuring service quality: A re-examination and extension', *Journal of Marketing*, 56 (July), 55–68.

Cronin, J.J. and Taylor, S.A. (1994) 'SERVPERF versus SERVQUAL: Reconciling performance-based and perceptions-minus-expectations measurement of service quality', *Journal of Marketing*, 58 (1), 125–31.

Crosby, P.B. (1984) *Quality Without Tears*, New American Library, New York.

Dick, A.S. and Basu, K. (1994) 'Customer loyalty: Toward an integrated conceptual framework', *Journal of the Academy of Marketing Science*, 22 (2), 99–113.

ECSI Technical Committee (1998) *European Customer Satisfaction Index Foundation and Structure for Harmonized National Pilot Projects*, ECSI.

Feinberg, R.A., Kadam, R., Hokama, L. and Kim, I. (2002) 'The state of electronic customer relationship management in retailing', *International Journal of Retail and Distribution Management*, 30 (10), 470–81.

Fornell, C. (1992) 'A national customer satisfaction barometer: The Swedish experience', *Journal of Marketing*, 55 (January), 6–21.

Fornell, C., Johnson, M.D., Anderson, E.W., Cha, J. and Bryant, B.E. (1996) 'The American Customer Satisfaction Index: Nature, purpose, and findings', *Journal of Marketing*, 60 (4), 7–18.

Galloway, L. (1999) 'Hysteresis: A model of consumer behaviour?', *Managing Service Quality*, 9 (5), 360–70.

Getty, J.M. and Thompson, K.N. (1994) 'The relationship between quality, satisfaction and recommending behaviour in lodging decisions', *Journal of Hospitality and Leisure Marketing*, 2 (3), 3–22.

Grant, L. (1998) 'Your customers are telling the truth', *Fortune*, 16 February, 164–6.

Grönroos, C. (1984) 'A service quality model and its marketing implications', *European Journal of Marketing*, 18 (4), 36–43.

Gwynne, A., Ennew, C. and Devlin, J. (1999) 'Service quality and customer satisfaction: A longitudinal analysis', *Proceedings of the 28th European Marketing Academy Conference*, Humboldt University, Berlin, 25.

Hawes, J.M. and Rao, C.P. (1985) 'Using importance–performance analysis to develop health care marketing strategies', *Journal of Health Care Marketing*, 5 (Autumn), 19–25.

Heskett, J.L., Sasser, W.E. and Schlesinger, L.A. (1997) *The Service Profit Chain*, The Free Press, New York.

Iacobucci, D., Ostrom, A. and Grayson, K. (1995) 'Distinguishing service quality and customer satisfaction: The voice of the consumer', *Journal of Consumer Psychology*, 4 (3), 277–303.

Johnston, R. (2001) 'Linking complaint management to profit', *International Journal of Service Industry Management*, 12 (1), 60–9.

Joseph, M., McClure, C. and Joseph, B. (1999) 'Service quality in the banking sector: The impact of technology on service delivery', *International Journal of Bank Marketing*, 17 (4), 182–91.

Juran, J.M. (1982) *Upper Management and Quality*, Juran Institute, New York.

Kahneman, D. and Miller, D.T. (1986) 'Norm theory: Comparing reality to its alternatives', *Psychological Review*, 93, 136–53.

Kotler, P. (1991) *Marketing Management: Analysis, Planning, Implementation and Control*, Prentice Hall.

McAlexander, J.H., Kaldenberg, D.O. and Koenig, H. (1994) 'Service quality measurement', *Journal of Health Care Marketing*, 14 (3; Fall), 34–9.

Mels, G., Boshoff, C. and Deon, N. (1997) 'The dimensions of service quality: the original European perspective revisited', *The Service Industries Journal*, 17 (January), 173–89.

Muhanna, W.A. and Wolf, J.R. (2002) 'The impact of e-commerce on the real estate industry: Baen and Guttery revisited', *Journal of Real Estate Portfolio Management*, 8 (2), 141–53.

Newberry, C.R.F., Klemz, B.R. and Boshoff, C. (2003) 'Managerial implications of predicting purchase behavior from purchase intentions: A retail patronage case study', *Journal of Services Marketing*, 17 (6), 609–20.

Oliver, R. (1997) *Satisfaction: A Behavioral Perspective of the Consumer*, McGraw-Hill, New York.

O'Neill, M. and Palmer, A. (2001) 'Survey timing and consumer perceptions of service quality: An overview of empirical evidence', *Managing Service Quality*, 11 (3), 182–90

O'Neill, M., Palmer, A. and Beggs, R. (1998) 'The effects of survey timing on perceptions of service quality', *Managing Service Quality*, 8 (2), 126–32.

O'Neill, M., Palmer, A. and Charters, S. (2002) 'Wine production as a service experience – the effects of service quality on wine sales', *Journal of Services Marketing*, 6 (4), 342–60.

Paraskevas, A. (2001) 'Exploring hotel internal service chains: a theoretical approach', *International Journal of Contemporary Hospitality Management*, 13 (5), 251–8.

Parasuraman, A., Zeithaml, V.A. and Berry, L. (1985) A conceptual model of service quality and its implications for future research', *Journal of Marketing*, 49 (Fall), 41–50.

Parasuraman, A., Zeithaml, V.A. and Berry, L.L. (1988) 'SERVQUAL: A multiple-item scale for measuring consumer perceptions of service quality', *Journal of Retailing*, 64 (Spring), 12–40.

Passikoff, R. (1997) 'The limits of customer satisfaction', *Brandweek*, 38 (9), 17.

Pike, S. (2003) "Hot chicks", "better parties" or academic stuff – Perceptions of a regional university campus using repertory grid analysis and importance–performance analysis', *Proceedings of the Australia and New Zealand Marketing Academy Conference (ANZMAC)*, Adelaide, 1–3 December, 1288–95.

Ramaswamy, R. (1996) *Design and Management of Service Processes: Keeping Customers for Life*, Addison-Wesley Publishing Co., Reading, MA.

Swan, J.E. and Comb, L.J. (1976) 'Product performance and consumer satisfaction: A new concept', *Journal of Marketing*, 40 (April), 25–33.

Swan, J.E. and Trawick, I.F. (1981) 'Disconfirmation of expectations and satisfaction with a retail service', *Journal of Retailing*, 57 (Fall), 49–67.

Thornton, J. and Marche, S. (2003) 'Sorting through the dot bomb rubble: How did the high-profile e-tailers fail?' *International Journal of Information Management*, 23, 121–38.

Times, The (1999) 'Ryanair shareholders reduce their stakes through public offerings', 29 May, 26.

Wright, C. and O'Neill, M. (2002) 'Service quality evaluation in the higher education sector: An empirical investigation of students' perceptions', *Higher Education Research & Development*, 21 (1).

Zeithaml, V.A., Berry, L.L. and Parasuraman, A. (1993) 'The nature and determinants of customer expectations of service', *Journal of the Academy of Marketing Science*, 21 (1), 1–12.

Zeithaml, V.A., Berry, L.L. and Parasuraman, A. (1996) 'The behavioral consequences of service quality', *Journal of Marketing*, 60, 31–46.

Zeithaml, V., Parasuraman, A. and Berry, L. (1990) *Delivering Service Quality: Balancing Customer Perceptions and Expectations*, The Free Press, New York.

Zeithaml, V.A., Parasuraman, A. and Malhotra, A. (2002) 'Service quality delivery through web sites: A critical review of extant knowledge', *Academy of Marketing Science Journal*, 30 (4), 362–74.

Making services accessible to consumers

Learning objectives

This chapter will explain:

- the effects of inseparability on decisions about service production/consumption location

- accessibility as a feature to be designed into service production decisions

- models to assist service location decisions

- the role of service intermediaries as co-producers of a service

- methods used to select, motivate and monitor service intermediaries

- types of service intermediary, including agents and franchisees.

9.1 **Introduction**

Consider the following successful service innovations:

- First Direct telephone banking from home
- McDonald's out-of-town 'drive thru' restaurants
- Domino's Pizzas home delivery service.

In each case, success has been based on making an existing service more readily accessible to customers. So the bank customers no longer need to visit their local branch to carry out many types of transactions; people looking for a Big Mac need no longer leave their car; and pizza eaters need not even leave their home.

Actually achieving these high levels of accessibility calls for a strategy which is capable of achieving desired levels within a specified time period. For the pizza company to be able to put a pizza in anyone's home requires an effort which is probably not achievable by the company acting alone. It may therefore seek a variety of arrangements, such as franchising, with local companies who are able to implement its strategy better than it could itself.

The inseparability of services makes the task of passing on service benefits much more complex than is the case with manufactured goods. Inseparability implies that services are consumed at the point of production – in other words, a service cannot be produced by one person in one place and handled by other people to make it available to customers in other places. A service cannot therefore be produced where costs are lowest and sold where demand is greatest – customer accessibility must be designed into the service production system.

In this chapter, strategies to make services accessible to customers will be analysed by focusing on four important, but related issues.

1. Where and when is the service to be made available to the consumer?

2. What is the role of intermediaries in the process of service delivery?

3. How are intermediaries selected, motivated and monitored?

4. How are tangible goods, which form a part of many service offers, to be made available to final consumers?

9.2 **Service location decisions**

In this section, choices facing service providers about the place and time at which a service is to be provided are considered. Firstly, it should be repeated that because consumers of services are usually involved as **co-producers** of the service, the time and place at which they are expected to take part in this process becomes an important criterion for evaluation. Production location decisions therefore cannot be taken in isolation from an analysis of customers' needs. While service organizations often have a desire to centralize production in order to achieve economies of scale, consumers usually seek local access to services, often at a time which may not be economic for the producer to cater for. Service location decisions therefore involve a trade-off between the needs of the producer and the needs of the consumer. This is in contrast to goods manufacturers who can manufacture goods in one location where production is most economic then ship the goods to where they are most needed.

For some services, production is very inflexible with respect to location, resulting in relatively production-led location decisions. In other cases, production techniques may by their nature allow much greater flexibility, but location decisions are constrained by the inflexibility of consumers to travel to a service outlet, either because of their physical inability or merely their unwillingness. In the case of some intangible, low-contact services, it is possible to separate production from consumption, using some of the methods described later in this chapter. In such cases, services can be produced in the most economic location and made available wherever customers are located.

9.2.1 Flexibility in production

The extreme case of inflexibility in production is provided by services where the whole purpose of the service is to be at one unique location – for example, tourism-related services based on a unique historic site by their very nature cannot be moved. A further group of services are locationally inflexible because they can only sensibly be produced in large-scale centralized production facilities. This can be the case where the necessary supporting equipment is expensive and offers opportunities for significant economies of scale. Where this equipment is also highly immobile, customers must come to a limited number of central service points to receive service. This is true with much of the specialized and expensive equipment needed for complex medical care, such as trauma care which tends to be provided at a small number of central locations. In cases where the equipment offers less scope for economies of scale and is more easily transported, service production can be distributed more widely. This explains why breast-screening services are frequently taken to users, while users must travel to trauma centres.

Some service organizations operate a 'hub and spoke' system where the benefits of large-scale, centralized production of specialized services are combined with locally accessible outlets. In the banking sector, specialized business and investment services can often only be competitive if they are produced in units which have a high enough critical mass to support the payment of experts in that field of activity. The major British banks have accordingly developed specialized business advisory centres located in a few key locations. Their services are subsequently made available through local branches by a combination of telephone, mail, computer link or a personal visit from the centrally based expert. Similarly, much of the processing work involved in producing a service can be transferred to an efficient regional centre, leaving local outlets to act as an interface with customers. In this way, many banks and building societies have transferred mortgage processing from high-street branches, leaving the latter to act as little more than sales outlets. The principal components of a 'hub and spoke' system are illustrated in Figure 9.1.

As well as internal economies of scale, external economies of scale are sometimes an important influence on a firm's location decisions. The first kind of external economies occur where a location close to other service producers reduces a firm's input costs. For this reason, many diverse financial services companies have congregated in the city of London. A ship-broking agency may find significant benefits from being located within walking distance of Lloyds insurance market and banks for sources of finance. Similarly, clusters of advertising agencies, graphic designers, typographers and typesetters can be found to maximize benefits from internal trading, to the benefit of suppliers and customers alike. However, the importance of such external economies of scale to location decisions is declining due to technological developments which allow production to be separated from consumption. In both of the above examples, service benefits can now be delivered electronically, reducing the need for direct interaction, although the importance of social contact between companies remains.

A second source of external economies of scale can result from locating in a recognized local marketplace, as occurs where jewellers or estate agents locate in one

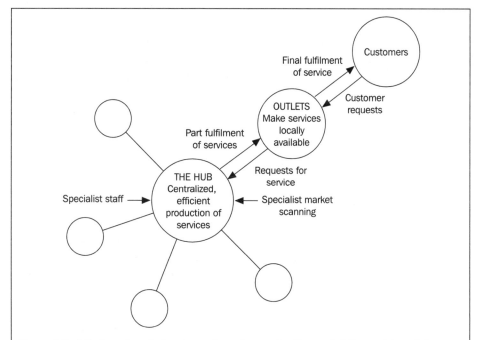

Figure 9.1 A 'hub and spoke' system of service production and delivery. A lot of the processing of services can often be undertaken in a central processing facility, and then made available locally to customers through branch networks. For highly intangible services, many customers have opted to deal directly with the central processing centre by telephone, Internet or mail, rather than accessing the service through the branch network.

neighbourhood of a town. Because the existence of the marketplace is widely recognized, any firm locating within it will need to spend less on promotion to attract potential customers to its location.

Production considerations are likely to be a less important influence on location decisions where economies of scale are insignificant. In a market environment, competitive advantage will be gained by maximizing availability though more widespread distribution outlets, rather than cost saving through centralization. To illustrate this, hairdressing offers fairly limited scope for economies of scale, and competitive advantage is gained by providing small outlets which are easily accessible to customers.

Finally, the competitiveness of the market environment can affect the locational flexibility of service producers. A service producer which is able to be flexible in its location decisions may nevertheless be unwilling to be flexible if its customers have little choice of supplier. For this reason, many government-provided services (e.g. Inland Revenue offices) are provided through centralized administrative offices which may be inconveniently located for most users.

9.2.2 **Flexibility in consumption**

Decisions on service location are also influenced by the extent to which consumers are willing or able to be flexible in where they consume a service. Inflexibility on the part of consumers can arise for a number of reasons.

- Where a service is to be performed on a customer's possessions, those possessions may themselves be immovable, requiring the supplier to come to the customer (e.g. building repairs).

- Sometimes, the customer may also be physically immobile (e.g. physically disabled users of healthcare services).

- For impulse purchases, or services where there are many competitive alternatives, customers are unlikely to be willing to travel far to seek out a service.

- For specialist services, customers may show more willingness to be flexible in where they are prepared to receive the service, compared to routine purchases for which they would be unwilling to travel.

In reality, most consumers' decisions involve a trade-off between the price of a service, the quality of delivery at a particular location, the amount of choice available and the cost to the consumer in terms of the time and money involved in gaining access to a service. For the buyer of a few odd items of groceries, price and choice are likely to be relatively unimportant compared to ease of access – hence the continued existence of many small corner shops. For a consumer seeking to purchase the week's groceries, price and selection may become much more important relative to ease of access. For more specialized services, such as cosmetic surgery, consumers may be willing to travel longer distances to a service provider which offers competitive prices and/or a wide selection of treatments.

It follows therefore that access strategies should be based on an identification of market segments made up of users with similar accessibility needs. Access strategies can then be developed which meet the needs of each segment.

- Age frequently defines segments in terms of the level of access sought. For many elderly users of personal care services, there is sometimes an unwillingness or inability to leave the home, making home availability of a service a sought attribute. For other groups, such as older teenagers, the very act of getting away from home to receive a service may be attractive. This could explain continuing interest in going out to see a film at a cinema in the face of the competing alternatives provided by local video rental shops and satellite television services.

- Segmentation on the basis of an individual's economic status can be seen in the willingness of more affluent segments to pay premium prices in order to consume a service at a point and time which is convenient to themselves rather than the service provider. Evidence of this is provided by home delivery food services which target groups with higher disposable incomes.

- Psychographic segmentation can be seen in the way groups of people seek out services which satisfy their lifestyle needs. As an example, some segments of the population are prepared to travel long distances to a restaurant whose design and ambience appeals to them.

- The cultural background of some individuals can predispose them to seek a particular kind of accessibility. This can be seen in the reluctance of some groups to become involved in service delivery methods which remove regular personal contact with the service provider. Insurance companies that collect premiums from the homes of customers may give reassurance to some segments who have been brought up to distrust impersonal organizations, whereas telephone banking or annual payment by post may satisfy the needs of other segments.

- Access strategies can be based on the type of benefit which users seek from a service. As an example, customers are often prepared to travel a considerable distance to a restaurant for a celebration meal, but would expect it to be easily accessible for a lunchtime snack.

- High-frequency users of a service may place a higher premium on easy accessibility than casual users.

- In the case of business-to-business services, the level of access to a service can directly affect the customer's operating costs. A computer repair company which makes its services available at buyers' offices avoids the costs which the latter would incur if it had to perform part of the service – delivery and collection – itself.

For some services, the location of the service delivery point is the most important means of attracting new business. This can be true for low-value services for which consumers show little willingness to pre-plan their purchase or to go out of their way to find. Location is also very important in the case of impulse purchases. Petrol filling stations, tea shops in tourist areas and guest houses are typically chosen as a result of a customer encountering the service outlet with no prior planning. It is unlikely for instance that many motorists would follow media advertisements and seek out a petrol station which is located in a back street – a visible location is a vital factor influencing consumers' choice.

The perishability of service offers results in their time accessibility being important as well as their spatial location. Again, customers can be segmented according to their flexibility with respect to the time at which they are prepared to consume a service. At one extreme, some segments for some services may be prepared to wait until a specified time to receive the service – as an example, ardent fans of a pop group would probably buy a ticket for a concert regardless of the time and date that it takes place. In other cases, no purchase would be made if a service is not instantly available – for example, a taxi operator that makes its service available only at specified times will probably lose all custom outside these times to other operators.

Service accessibility by time can be used to give an organization competitive advantage in much the same way as spatial accessibility. When building societies started offering banking services from the mid-1980s, their longer opening hours gave them a competitive advantage over banks and attracted many disloyal bank customers who found banking hours of 9.30 am to 3.30 pm too restrictive. Having lost significant elements of their core business to building societies, banks were forced to respond by opening certain branches on Saturdays and extending their opening hours in the afternoon.

9.2.3 A typology of service location influences

An attempt to develop a typology of service location decisions is shown in Figure 9.2 where inseparable services are classified in a matrix according to their degree of flexibility in production and consumption.

Services in the upper-left quadrant often have little locational flexibility because they are associated with a unique site, for example outstanding scenery or a historical

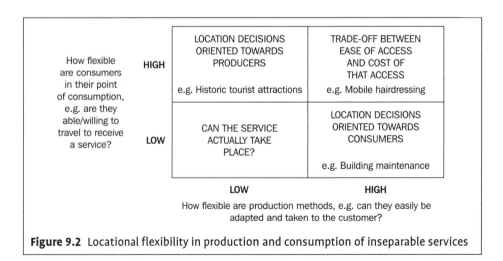

Figure 9.2 Locational flexibility in production and consumption of inseparable services

association. Nevertheless, attempts have sometimes been made to replicate the original site at a point which is closer to consumers – for example, the creation of Disneyworld Paris was an attempt to bring the unique features of the American Disneyland to a European audience.

Services in the bottom-right quadrant may have little locational flexibility because consumers are unable to move themselves or their possessions. In the case of some fixed assets such as buildings, this inflexibility may be absolute and the service provider must come to the consumer. However, consumers may merely be unwilling to be flexible or it may be part of their expectations that a service should come to them.

It is in the upper-right quadrant where trade-offs between convenience for the consumer and for the producer are greatest. Here, markets can often be segmented by accessibility preferences and producers adapt their production methods to the price/convenience preferences of each segment. The retailing sector shows a wide variation from large hypermarkets, which are efficient for the producer but relatively inaccessible to most consumers, through to corner shops which are more accessible but less efficient. Many consumers are prepared to pay a premium for ease of access, even to have goods delivered to their door.

Where both producer and consumer are inflexible, it may be difficult for any service to take place at all, and where it does it may be under distress conditions (e.g. hospital emergency admissions). With developments in technology, it is sometimes possible to increase the production flexibility (e.g. through mobile operating theatres and tele-medicine).

We will consider later in this chapter the case of services whose production can be separated from their consumption, for example through the use of the Internet (see Figure 9.3).

9.2.4 **Service location models**

Before a network of service outlets can be designed, an organization must clearly define its accessibility objectives. In particular, it must have a clear idea of the volume of business, market share and customer segments that it seeks to attract. Accessibility objectives derive from the positioning strategy for a service. A high level of accessibility may only be compatible with business objectives if it is also associated with a premium price position. A high level of accessibility may also reduce and change the role played by promotion within the marketing mix. By contrast, a strategy which involves a low level of accessibility may need to rely heavily on promotion to make potential customers aware of the location of service outlets.

Examples of accessibility objectives include:

- providing a hotel location in all towns with a population of 200 000 or more

- developing supermarket sites which are within 10 minutes' driving time of at least 50 000 people

- locating retail sites where pedestrian or vehicular traffic exceeds a specified threshold.

Figure 9.3 For a number of decades, the tendency in European grocery retailing was for customers to have to put more effort into getting access to a retail outlet, as retailers abandoned home delivery services and concentrated on large hypermarkets at the expense of local neighbourhood stores. Customers were going to the service, rather than the service coming to them. More recently, a number of retailers have sought to bring their services closer to customers, with the development of online shopping and home delivery. The development of the Internet has resulted in home delivery of groceries being a growth area for many supermarket operators, fuelled by rising real household incomes and increasingly busy lifestyles. However, although the cost of using the Internet has fallen, the cost of delivering goods and services to the home has tended to increase, in line with rising wage costs and employment legislation. While home delivery may be an attractive option for some segments, other consumers prefer to make a trade-off by going to the service provider where they can often obtain lower overall prices, wider choice and immediate availability. (Reproduced with permission of Sainsbury's Supermarkets Ltd)

Service location decisions are used at both a macro and a micro level. At the macro level, organizations seek the most profitable areas or regions in which to make their service available, given the strength of demand, the level of competition and the costs of setting up in an area. Micro-level decisions refer to the choice of specific sites.

Macro analysis begins with a clear statement of the profile of customers that an organization is targeting. Areas are then sought that have a geodemographic profile closely matching that of the target market. At its simplest, indicators can be used to identify potentially attractive locations. As a simple example, a financial service company seeking to set up a national chain of outlets offering home equity loans to elderly people may select the most promising areas on the basis of three pieces of information: the average value of houses in an area (available from the Chartered Institute of Surveyor's regular monitoring report); the percentage of the population who are elderly (available from the Census of Population); and the percentage of the population who are owner-occupiers (available from Regional Trends). The attractiveness of a market could be indicated by a weighted index of these factors and subjected to a more detailed analysis of competitor activity in each area. A number of more specialized segmentation methods have been developed which allow organizations to evaluate the profile of an area. An example is MOSAIC, developed by Experian Ltd, which is based on an analysis of postcodes.

Methods used by an organization to select service outlet locations tend to become more complex as the organization grows. In the early stages of growth, simple rule-of-thumb methods may be acceptable. With further growth, simple indexes and ratios are commonly used. With more service outlets established, an organization can begin to gather sufficient data to analyse the performance of its existing outlets, and from this to develop models which can be used to predict the likely performance of proposed new locations. Regression techniques are used to identify relationships between variables and the level of significance of each variable in explaining the performance of a location. The development of regression models requires considerable initial investment in creating an information base and calibrating the model, but once calibrated they can help to reduce the risk inherent in new service location decisions. It should be noted, however, that models cannot be extrapolated to cover types of decisions which were not envisaged in the model as originally calibrated – for example, a model calibrated for UK site location decisions may be inappropriate for making site location decisions in France.

A number of additional problems in the application of regression-modelling techniques can be noted. Because such techniques require large amounts of data for

Where are the supermarket customers?

The level of risk associated with opening a new supermarket in a fiercely competitive environment can be considerable, yet large retailers claim that they can predict the turnover of a new store opening to within a few percentage points. While a small general retailer may be able to rent shop space on low-risk short-term leases, modern supermarkets require considerable investment in purpose-built facilities which meet customers' ever-increasing needs and expectations. A study by Jones and Mock of a small American supermarket chain illustrates the value of regression-modelling techniques. The supermarket chain being studied had previously relied on rule-of-thumb methods for store location, but as the size of its new stores increased, so too did the level of risk. As its business grew, it was also able to gather more data to understand the factors that are associated with the success of a particular store.

The regression modelling started by grouping sites according to similarities in their environments. On the basis of socio-economic data, five distinctive environments were identified – city centre, suburbs, old-established shopping streets, the urban fringe and non-metropolitan locations. To find out which of the many variables available were the most relevant for each retailing environment, a series of cross-tabulations between individual key variables was carried out. The relevant variables were then put into a series of stepwise regression models, one for each environment, allowing the identification of the variables which were most effective in explaining sales performance. In the case of suburban stores, variation in store sales was best explained by three measures – the percentage of the neighbourhood which had recently been developed, accessibility of the site by car and the number of competitors located within three blocks. Each increase of 1% in the share of new houses resulted in an additional weekly sales turnover of $120, whereas each nearby competitor reduced sales by $656.

Such models tend to give good results when the business environment is stable. But how useful are they when it is possible for operators to set up rival facilities quickly, changing the assumptions on which the model is based? After all, if one supermarket is running such a model, its competitors are probably doing the same and coming up with similar results. Should they be concentrating on flexibility so that the start-up and close-down costs are reduced?

calibration, they are only really suited to high-volume services. It can also be difficult to identify the key variables that cause variation in sales turnover, or to exclude interaction among the variables. Simple linear regression models may not be adequate to explain complex non-linear relationships (for example, one or two nearby competitors for a restaurant may detract from sales at a prospective site; however, a large number of competitors may actually increase sales, if the clustering of restaurants creates a hot spot which attracts diners looking for a choice of restaurants). Finally, regression is essentially an incremental planning technique which is less appropriate for designing networks of service outlets, such as may occur following the merger of two service organizations resulting in a need to rationalize outlets. For the latter, an alternative approach is to use a spatial location model.

Spatial location models measure the geographical dispersion of demand and seek to allocate this demand to service outlets on the basis that the probability of a consumer using a particular outlet will be:

- positively related to the attractiveness of that outlet, and

- negatively related to its distance from the points where demand is located.

These principles are developed in the following model (Huff, 1966), which has frequently been used as a basis for retail location models, but also has applications in locating leisure facilities and health services, etc.

$$P_{ij} = \frac{\dfrac{A_j^a}{d_{ij}^b}}{\displaystyle\sum_{n=1}^{i} \dfrac{A_j^a}{d_{ij}^b}}$$

where P_{ij} = the probability of a trip from origin i to destination j

A_j = the attractiveness of destination j

d_{ij} = the distance between origin i and destination j

a and b = parameters to be empirically determined

The intuitive appeal and simplicity of such a model can hide a number of conceptual and practical problems in their application and this has triggered considerable research in an attempt to operationalize the basic model. The concept of attractiveness can be difficult to measure. Fishbein (1967) has pointed out that although an individual may have a belief that a location is attractive, this attractiveness may not be of importance to that particular individual, and may consequently not affect his or her behaviour. Distance itself can be difficult to measure and can be measured objectively (e.g. mileage or average travelling times), or subjectively according to users' perceptions of distance. As an example of research into the distance components of such models, Mayo and Jarvis (1981) showed that subjectively perceived distances increase proportionately less than the objective measured distance.

Spatial location-allocation models are powerful tools which emphasize long-term marketing strategies rather than short-term decisions about opening or closing a specific location. They can be used to evaluate all possible combinations of location possibilities in relation to the geographical pattern of demand. The criteria for selecting the most efficient network of outlets usually involves balancing the need to maximize its attractiveness to customers against the service provider's need to minimize the cost of operating the network. Sophisticated computer models allow assumptions about consumer behaviour to be varied – for example, the maximum distance which people are prepared to walk to an outlet. Such models are expensive to develop in view of the data requirements and the need to use specialized staff to develop them. Where the risks associated with a bad location decision are low, it may be more cost-effective to use rule-of-thumb methods than to commission such a model. In the UK, the high cost of acquiring and refurbishing property in the mid-1980s led to spatial location models becoming very popular as risk reducers. However, the fall in property-related costs – and associated risk levels – which occurred in the 1990s saw many companies (such as Sketchley's Dry Cleaners) dropping their use and reverting to more cost-effective rule-of-thumb methods or regression models. Spatial allocation models do, however, continue to be used extensively in both the private and public sectors (e.g. in planning a network of clinics which minimizes patients' travel distances).

9.2.5 The Internet as a means of reducing locational dependency

The traditional idea that service production and consumption are inseparable would appear at first sight to pose problems in achieving both maximum productive efficiency and maximum accessibility to a service. One method of resolving this apparent problem is to try to make production and consumption separable – that is, to design a service which can be produced where it is most efficient and consumed where it is most needed.

Telecommunications can be used to allow the substantive element of a service to be produced at a central processing unit and made available at any point of consumers' choice. Information databases used by businesses and pre-recorded telephone information used by personal consumers are typical of the type of service where this separation has been possible. Banks have recognized the distribution implications of improved telephone and Internet technology and most of the large banks in the UK have developed telephone-based banking services. These allow customers to receive statements and to transfer funds from one account to another, or to pay bills to outside organizations, direct from the customers' home or office. The bank may actually answer the telephone call in a relatively low-cost country, such as India, which is distant from the customer. Internet banking and TV banking have extended the possibilities for spatial separation of customer and provider. The locational implications of such delivery systems are quite significant. Banks have been steadily reducing their costly branch networks and seeking to channel more of their business through electronic media. As well as cutting costs through the use of an efficient centralized administration centre, Internet banking makes the banks' services available to customers at any location and at any time of day. Nevertheless, problems remain with excessive reliance on the Internet, as many services usually involve a tangible benefit which must be transferred from producer to consumer at some point. Bank customers usually require cash, necessitating physical locations to supplement the Internet-based service delivery.

In the early stages of Internet development, the technology has been used to provide a modest incremental improvement on what was previously possible using voice telephone or postal services. With increasing sophistication, possibilities arise for the Internet to provide additional benefits which are not possible using more traditional distribution methods. Personalization of websites can facilitate reordering of routinely purchased services (e.g. an airline site which opens with previously recorded preferences). Many websites are now linked with other complementary value-adding services (e.g. a travel informediary's (see p. 326) website, which has links to national and regional tourist board websites).

How much will it cost to get access to the cash?

Banks have been at the forefront of efforts to tackle the problems of service inseparability. The big four UK banks run large and expensive branch networks and have faced increased competition from new low-cost telephone and postal banking services. Many non-bank competitors have appeared, especially supermarkets who have developed banking to complement their customer relationship building activities. A study by Ernst & Young in 1997 indicated some of the reasons why banks were keen to reduce their dependence on a large branch network. The study found that each transaction in a bank branch cost an average of 64p. By contrast, the average cost of transactions by telephone was 32p; 27p through an ATM and just 0.5p through the banks' Internet services. But how do banks exploit the opportunities made available by new means of separating production and consumption? Closing local branches is never popular with customers and may lead to the defection of profitable ones to competitors. Some banks have tried differential pricing by charging a fee for users of counter facilities. When Abbey National began charging its Instant Access account customers £1 each time they cashed a cheque within a branch, there was understandable bad publicity. The company was clearly trying to encourage its customers to use its ATMs and telephone banking facility. But how large and fast growing is the market segment which is prepared to sacrifice personal face-to-face contact for a cheaper and more efficient machine-based method of distribution?

9.3 The role of intermediaries in distributing services

Having now discussed issues of *where* services should be made available to consumers, this chapter now considers *how* they should be made available. More specifically, *who* should be involved in the process of delivering the benefit of a service to consumers? Should a company seek to perform the whole service process itself? If not, who should it involve, and at what stages of the production process?

In the context of goods marketing, the concept of an **intermediary** can be understood as being a person who handles goods as they pass from the organization that manufactured them to the individual or business which finally consumes them. The intermediary may physically handle the goods, splitting them into progressively smaller volumes as they pass through channels of distribution, or it may simply buy and sell the rights to goods in the role of a commodity dealer.

Any discussion of service intermediaries immediately raises a number of conceptual issues:

- services cannot be owned, therefore it is difficult to talk about service ownership being transferred through channels of distribution

- pure services are intangible and perishable, therefore stocks cannot exist

- the inseparability of most services should logically require an intermediary to become a co-producer of a service.

A distinction should be made between intermediaries as co-producers and their role as mere sales agents. While the former is an active part of the production process, the latter doesn't actually deliver a service itself, only the right to a service. As an example, a shop selling postage stamps is not significantly involved as a co-producer of postal services. It can be difficult to distinguish between these two situations – a theatre ticket agency, in addition to merely selling the right to a service may provide a valuable service for consumers in procuring specific seats.

Service intermediaries perform a number of important functions on behalf of service organizations (the latter are often referred to as 'service principals'). The role expectations of intermediaries vary according to the nature of the service in question and some of the most important are described below.

- As a co-producer of a service, an intermediary assists in making a service available locally to consumers at a place and time that is convenient to consumers. An estate agent providing a cheque cashing facility for a building society is assisting in the process of producing and making financial services available to consumers. In other cases, an intermediary may become the dominant partner involved in co-production. A national key-cutting or shoe-heeling service may put almost the entire service production process in the hands of intermediaries, leaving the principal to provide administrative and advertising support and to monitor standards.

- Intermediaries usually provide sales support at the point of sale. For some customers of personal services, a two-way personal dialogue with a local intermediary may be more effective at securing a sale than advertising messages derived centrally from a service principal.

- Consumers may prefer to buy services from an intermediary who offers a wide choice, including the services offered by competing service principals. A holiday tour company seeking to sell its holidays direct to the public might encounter resistance from segments of the population who prefer to have choices from many companies presented to them at one location.

- Consumers may enjoy trusting relationships with intermediaries and prefer to choose between competing alternatives on the basis of the intermediaries' advice. In the financial services sector, intermediaries develop trust with their clients in guiding them through often complex choices. To be successful with such segments of buyers, a financial services company must establish its credentials with the intermediary if its products are to enter the final consumer's shortlisted choice set.

- An intermediary as co-producer of a service often shares some of the risk of providing a service. This can come about where a service principal requires intermediaries to contribute some of their own capital to the cost of acquiring equipment, and both share any subsequent operating profit or loss.

- The use of independent intermediaries can free up capital which a service principal can reinvest in its core service production facilities. An airline which closes its own ticket shops and directs potential customers to travel agents is able to reinvest the proceeds in updating its aircraft or reservation systems which may give it greater competitive advantage than having its own ticket outlets.

■ Once the initial service act is completed, there may be a requirement for 'after-sales' services to be provided. Intermediaries can make this support more accessible to the consumer and assist the service principal as co-producer of the after-sales support. Insurance is a good example where many segments of the insurance buying public feel happier with easy local access to a local agent who can give advice about making a claim. The agent in turn simplifies the task of the insurance company by handling much of the paperwork involved in making a claim, thereby reducing the latter's workload.

9.3.1 **Push and pull relationships with intermediaries**

'Push' and 'pull' channels of distribution are familiar concepts in the marketing of goods, but they also have application within the service sector. A traditional 'push' **channel of distribution** involves a service principal aggressively promoting its service to intermediaries by means of personal selling, trade advertising and the use of trade incentives. The intermediary in turn aggressively sells the service to final consumers, often having to strike a balance between maximizing the customer's benefit and maximizing the incentives offered to the intermediary by the service principal. This approach sees the service as essentially a commodity – the consumer starts with no preference of service principal and seeks the best value available from an intermediary. A push channel is typical of the way in which basic motor insurance is made available to customers. For many buyers, insurance is a 'distress' purchase where the only perceived difference between policies is the price. Many people rely on their intermediary to suggest the lowest-cost insurance available to them. Intermediaries will be most aggressive in the sale of policies which meet buyers' criteria and on which they receive the most attractive commission payments.

For service principals, push strategies can be quite risky, as any product differentiation policy can only be effective if the intermediary effectively communicates the unique benefits to potential customers, rather than relying on price alone as the point of differentiation. To try to reduce this risk, service principals can aim messages directly at consumers, seeking to establish at an early stage in the buying process the values which their brand stands for. Having developed an attitude towards a brand, consumers are more likely to specifically ask for that brand from an intermediary or to express a preference for it when offered a choice by the intermediary. For a 'pull' strategy, the intermediary's role is reduced to one of dispensing pre-sold branded services. The UK pensions industry has seen considerable activity by companies such as Prudential, Legal & General and Standard Life, seeking to build up favourable images of their services so that potential customers enter discussions with intermediaries with a favourable predisposition towards the insurance company. Buyers may know very little about the merits of one pension policy over another, but they approach an intermediary with attitudes about their preferred principal. Push and pull strategies are compared in Figure 9.4.

It can sometimes be difficult to distinguish between pure push and pull strategies. A company may act as an intermediary for some services, but as a service principal

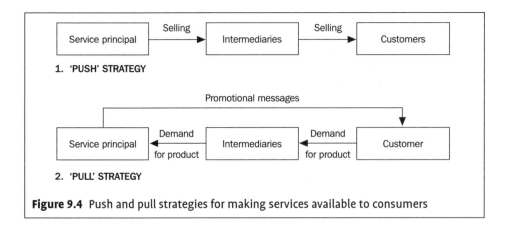

Figure 9.4 Push and pull strategies for making services available to consumers

for other similar services. As well as selling a service for a principal as an intermediary, the latter could buy in rights to services as though the principal was in fact a subcontractor. In this way, small local travel agents sometimes put together package holidays aimed at segments of their own market. An agent which acts as intermediary for the sale of other tour operators' coach holidays may buy in hotel, coach and sightseeing services direct from the principals and sell the entire tour under its own brand name. The travel agent effectively becomes a principal. While there is potential benefit from being able to earn both the retail agent's and the tour operator's profit margin, this strategy poses potential risk for the intermediary, who must cover all the fixed costs of the principal, rather than just earning a commission on every service sold.

9.3.2 Service characteristics as an influence on the role of intermediaries

Services are not homogeneous and this is reflected in the role played by intermediaries. While some services can be handled by a large number of intermediaries, others cannot easily be handled by intermediaries at all. The characteristics of services and of customers' expectations need to be considered before a strategy for intermediaries is developed.

- Some services experience highly variable outcomes, making efforts at controlling quality through intermediaries very difficult to achieve. This is particularly true of personal services such as hairdressing which are most commonly provided by small businesses direct to final consumers without the use of intermediaries.

- Some services may be highly specialized and likely to be neglected by intermediaries with inadequate training or knowledge. A service principal may gain no competitive advantage if intermediaries are incapable of giving appropriate sales and co-production support. Where a service is complex, the service principal must pay careful attention to the selection of intermediaries or, alternatively, deal directly with consumers. Within the package holiday industry, trekking and activity holidays are quite specialized services which most travel agents have inadequate knowledge to handle effectively. Some operators of these holidays have chosen to operate through specialized intermediaries such as specialist outdoor pursuit agencies, while many more prefer to deal directly with their target markets.

- Margins available on a service may be insufficient to support many intermediaries, if any at all. Domestic and industrial cleaning services often operate on very low margins, resulting in most services being provided direct to consumers.

- Legislation or voluntary codes of conduct may limit the choice of intermediary available to a service principal, or make it impossible to act through them at all. In the UK, the Financial Services Act 1986 is a good example of legislation which directly constrains the distribution opportunities available for certain services. The Act requires that specified financial services may only be handled by authorized intermediaries. Also, voluntary codes provide an additional constraint for some services. An example is that operated by the Association of British Travel Agents (ABTA) governing the manner in which package holidays can be sold. ABTA does not generally allow its retail agent members to sell any overseas holidays run by tour operators who are not themselves members of the association.

9.4 **Direct sale**

Should a service principal involve intermediaries at all? Direct sale is a particularly attractive option for service providers where the service offer is complex and variable and where legal constraints make the involvement of intermediaries difficult. With increasing use of centralized electronic databases and the Internet, direct sale is becoming more important for many organizations. The attractions of direct sale are numerous.

- The service provider is in regular direct contact with consumers of its service, making faster feedback of customer comments a possibility. This can facilitate the process of improving existing services or developing new ones.

- It can be easier for service principals to develop relationships with customers if they are in regular contact. Databases can be built up to provide a profile of individual customers, allowing for more effective targeting of new service offers.

- Intermediaries may jealously guard their customers from the service principal, in the fear that any initial contact between the service principal and consumer could result in the role of the intermediary being diminished. Having spent time and effort attracting their customer, they do not wish to see the service principal picking up the long-term benefits of repeat business without the revenue-earning involvement of the intermediary. The service principal therefore loses a lot of valuable feedback. In the travel industry, agents have deliberately not passed on the addresses of customers to the tour operating company with whom they are booked, disclosing only a telephone number for emergency use.

- In the public sector, political considerations or fears over confidentiality may prevent services being provided by private-sector intermediaries. Definitions of what is politically acceptable change over time. In the UK many have considered that school catering and leisure centre services are vital public services which could only be supplied directly by public-sector bodies. It is now widely accepted that these can be provided through service intermediaries of one form or another, although debate continues about whether more contentious services such as prisons and security services should be provided through private-sector intermediaries. From the opposite approach, the use of public-sector organizations as intermediaries has increasingly been accepted. As an example, hospitals are being used to make a widening range of private-sector health-related services available, including financial and legal services.

- The service principal can retain for itself the profit margin which would have been paid to an intermediary. This could be beneficial where its own distribution costs are lower than the commission that it would have paid to an intermediary.

Quite often, service principals choose to make their services available both directly and through intermediaries. This can be an attractive option as it allows the principal to target segments which may have very different buying behaviour. As an example, one segment of the holiday buying public may seek the reassurance provided by being able to walk into and talk to a travel agent, while another segment might be more confident, price sensitive and short of time, for whom direct booking with a tour operator by telephone or Internet is attractive. Against the advantages of segmenting the market in this way can come significant problems. Intermediaries can become demotivated if they see a principal for whom they are working as agent selling the same services direct to the public. To make matters worse, direct sale promotional material often emphasizes the benefits of not using an intermediary, typically lower prices and faster service. One solution is to split an organization into two distinct operating units with their own brand identity, one to operate through intermediaries and the other to sell direct to the final consumer. This was the solution adopted by the Thomson holiday group, which in addition to selling holidays through travel agents under the Thomson brand name (among others) also sells basically similar holidays direct to the public under the Portland brand name.

9.4.1 The internet and 'disintermediation'

With the early development of the Internet, it was widely predicted that service principals would be able to dispense with intermediaries and distribute their services directly to each customer (see Figure 9.5). The growth of direct selling intermediaries such as Direct Line Insurance appeared to confirm the ability to cut out intermediaries, who were often portrayed as parasitic and delaying middlemen. The inelegant

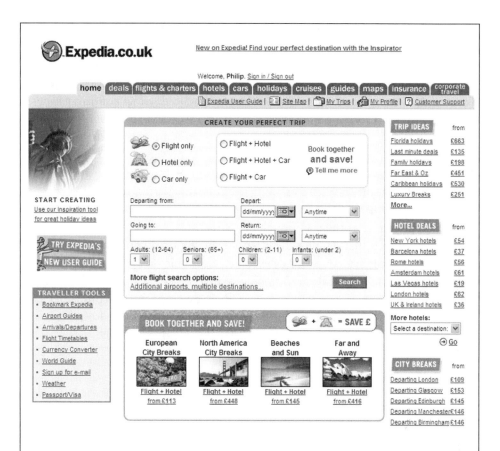

Figure 9.5 Many people thought that the Internet would fundamentally change the pattern of distribution for services, by allowing service principals to distribute their services efficiently and effectively without the use of intermediaries. In the travel sector, budget airlines have been notable for the way in which they have managed to use their websites to cut out intermediaries and thereby pass on cost savings to customers (easyJet, for example, claims that over three-quarters of its customers book through its website). However, customers looking for choice in one location may prefer to use the website of one of the many web-based travel intermediaries that have emerged. Expedia.co.uk is one of the UK's largest web-based travel intermediaries and is particularly valuable to consumers where guidance is needed on the options available. easyJet's services comprise relatively simple point-to-point journeys within Europe, and the company has undertaken extensive promotion to create awareness of its site. For more complex travel needs, such as a journey from London to Australia involving a break of journey, a prospective buyer may not be aware of the full range of airlines that are available to complete the journey. By reducing search costs, an intermediary such as Expedia adds value for consumers, in much the same way as traditional high-street travel agents. © 2004 Expedia, Inc. All rights reserved. Expedia, and Expedia.com, are either registered trademarks or trademarks of Expedia, Inc. in the United States and/or other countries. Other company and product names mentioned herein may be trademarks of their respective owners. (Reproduced with permission of Expedia.co.uk)

term **disintermediation** has been used to describe the process of removing inter-mediaries from a distribution channel and developing direct communications.

The Internet does not change the basic principles of the role of intermediaries who exist to simplify buyers' choice processes. When several companies seek to develop direct relationships with their customers, buyers are faced with a confusing array of messages. Faced with dozens of insurance companies seeking to sell insurance directly, consumers are likely to simplify their choice process by using an intermediary who can carry out some of the buyer's search activity on their behalf. The result has therefore been the emergence of a new generation of Internet intermediaries, or **informediaries**. In the travel sector, numerous informediaries, such as Expedia and Travelocity, have emerged to simplify consumers' buying process, fulfilling very much the same type of role as the traditional high-street travel agent. Many service principals have realized that gaining the attention of the final consumer is becoming increasingly difficult in a congested cyberspace. 'Electronic shelf space' may be almost infinite, but service principals need to be sure that target customers will come past their site. So instead of heavily promoting their own site, many companies have resorted to using informediaries. Disintermediation has turned into **reinter-mediation** and the basic principles of channel design are little changed.

9.5 Selection of intermediaries

Service principals often decide that the most efficient and effective means of deliver-ing their service is in collaboration with intermediaries of various types. Service intermediaries take many forms in terms of their size, structure, legal status and rela-tionship to the service principal. Because of this diversity, attempts at classification can become confused by the level of overlap present. In this section, attention is focused on the characteristics of four types of intermediary: agents, retailers, whole-salers and franchisees.

9.5.1 Service agents

A **service agent** is someone who acts on behalf of a principal and has the authority to create a legal relationship between the customer and service principal as if it was made directly between the two. Principals are vicariously liable for the actions of their agents. Agents are usually rewarded for their actions by being able to deduct a com-mission before payment is passed on to their principal, although in many cases, agents may be paid a fixed fee for the work actually done – for example, in preparing a new market prior to the launch of a new service.

For service principals, the use of agents offers many advantages.

- Capital requirements for creating a chain of distribution outlets are minimized.

- Consumers may expect choice at the point of service purchase and it is usually easier for an independent agent to do this rather than for the service principal to set up distribution outlets which sell competing products. (In the case of many financial services, the UK Financial Services Act 1986 makes it difficult for service principals to both sell their own products and those of competitors – for example, banks and building societies must choose between becoming a 'tied' agent of one service principal and offering a genuine choice to customers.)

■ Where a service principal is entering a new market, it may lack the knowledge which allows it to understand buyer behaviour and the nature of competition in that market. Some overseas financial institutions with a poor understanding of the UK mortgage market chose to make mortgage services available by means of independent mortgage brokers and, in some cases, established UK building societies.

■ In the case of overseas markets, it may be illegal for a service principal to deal directly with the public, a problem which can be remedied by acting through a local licensed agent.

■ In some cases, special skills are required by a service principal which would be very costly to develop in-house. A shipping company may not have the need for a full-time employee to negotiate sale of its capacity in the open charter market, and it may therefore be more sensible to employ an agent to do this on its behalf as and when required, either on a commission or fixed-charge basis.

9.5.2 **Retail outlets**

The notion of a retailer in the service sector poses conceptual problems, for it has already been established that a retailer cannot carry a stock of services, one of the important functions of a retailer of goods. The distinction between a retailer and an agent or franchisee (see below) can be a fine one. In general, a retailer operates in a manner which does not create legal relations between the service principal and the final customer – the customer's relationship is only with the retailer.

Many services which pass through retailers have a significant goods element. As an example, many film-processing companies sell their services through retail chemists under the brand name of the chemist. The latter takes a profit margin while allowing the film-processing company to make its service available locally. Many services, such as key-cutting and fast-food catering are often retailed in the form of a franchise agreement, which is discussed below.

Sometimes, service retailers undertake another of the traditional goods retailer's functions in taking risk. A retailer can buy the right to a block of service transactions and if these rights are not sold by the time the service is performed, the value of these rights disappears. This can happen where a theatre ticket agent buys a block of tickets on a no-return basis from an event organizer.

9.5.3 **Service wholesalers**

Similar conceptual problems apply to the role of the wholesaler. For services, the term is most sensibly understood where an intermediary buys the right to a large volume of service transactions and then proceeds to break these down into smaller units of rights to a service for handling by retailers or other intermediaries. Hotel-booking agencies who buy large blocks of hotel accommodation earn their margin by buying in volume at low prices and adding a mark-up as a block booking is broken down into smaller units for sale to retailers or agents. As with retailers, it can be difficult to distinguish a wholesaler from an agent. A hotel wholesaler may have some rights to return unsold accommodation to the hotels concerned and may include in their dealings with customers a statement that the transaction is to be governed by conditions specified by the service principal.

9.6 Franchised service distribution

The term **franchising** refers to a relationship where one party – the franchisor – provides the development work on a service format and monitors standards of delivery, while coming to an arrangement with a second party – the franchisee – who is licensed to deliver the service, taking some share of the financial risk and reward in return. Vertical franchising occurs where a manufacturer allows a franchisee an exclusive right to sell its goods within a specified area. The more recent business-format franchising occurs where an organization allows others to copy the format of its own operations.

The International Franchise Association has defined a franchise operation as:

. . . a contractual relationship between the franchisor and franchisee in which the franchisor offers or is obliged to maintain a continuing interest in the business of the franchisee in such areas as know-how and training; wherein the franchise operates under a common trade name, format or procedure owned by or controlled by the franchisor, and in which the franchisee has made or will make a substantial capital investment in his business from his own resources.

The service sector has seen considerable recent growth in franchising. According to the annual NatWest/British Franchise Association annual survey, the total number of franchise systems in the UK in 2004 was 695. These were linked to a total of 33 800 franchisees, with an annual turnover of £9.65 billion and employed 330 000 people. A total of 95% of franchisees were profitable (British Franchise Association, 2004). Franchising offers particular opportunities for service industries which are people intensive, by combining the motivation of self-employed franchisees with the quality control and brand values of the franchisor.

Franchise agreements cover a diverse range of services, from car hire to fast food, kitchen design services, veterinary services and hotels. Of the top 10 UK business franchise operations (in terms of turnover), all are involved in essentially service-based activities, ranging from fast food to car hire and car servicing. Although most franchisees are self-employed individuals or small companies, they can also be very large organizations. To illustrate this, it is quite common to find corporate franchisees who operate a large number of hotels for a franchisor, making the franchisee a very large organization. Franchising also has applications within the public sector (see below).

Once franchising has taken hold within an organization, it tends to expand rather than contract. If a franchisor has built up a successful brand format, coupled with successful management, it can usually achieve greater returns on its capital by selling the right to use its name rather than operating its own outlets. The British School of Motoring (BSM), for example, has steadily increased the proportion of its outlets that are franchised from 24% in 1980 to over 80% in 2002. Other examples of strongly managed brands which have followed this route include Kallkwik (Figure 9.6), McDonald's restaurants and Swinton Insurance.

Figure 9.6 Franchising has firmly taken root in the market for fast printing services, with names such as Kallkwik, Kwik-Print and Kinko's being familiar, well-developed franchise systems. The development of low-cost offset litho and photocopying machines lowered the entry barriers to printing, which had previously been confined to craft-trained individuals. Kallkwik is typical in selling a franchise to people who can demonstrate commitment to high standards and profitable growth. For small investors looking for a business of their own, a Kallkwik franchise offers the security of a brand name that customers have come to trust. Like most fast-printing companies, Kallkwik's franchisees offer essentially simple, straightforward printing services that can easily be described in a business blueprint. More complex and variable printing services, such as carton printing, tickets and high-volume magazine printing, are less likely to be franchised out. (Reproduced with permission of Kallkwik)

There is a limit to which operations can be franchised and most franchisors choose not to franchise their operations entirely. There are two important reasons for this. Firstly, new product development is usually easier to carry out in-house rather than at a distance through a franchise. In this way it avoids alienating franchisees should experimental new services fail. Secondly, some operations may be too specialized to expect a franchisee to have the standard of training to ensure a consistent standard of delivery, and the franchisor may choose to retain responsibility for providing these.

Maintaining and motivating franchisees is a constant challenge for franchisors. Franchisees can become only too aware of the payments which the franchisor takes from them on an ongoing basis in return for dubious support. In the USA, some franchisee associations have brought legal actions against their franchisor for granting excessive numbers of franchises which have adversely affected existing franchisees. In such situations, many franchisees may be tempted not to renew their franchise at the end of their agreement and to either go it alone or sign up with another franchise operation. Where brands are strong, the former route can be very risky – for example, Prontaprint retail franchisees who have used their premises to provide their own competing service format have lost customers when the franchisor creates a new outlet in the locality. Payment of franchise fees represents good value to a franchisee for as long as it receives good back up from the franchisor and a steady supply of customers who are attracted by the reputation of the franchise brand.

9.6.1 The nature of a franchise agreement

A franchise agreement sets out the rights and obligations of the franchisor and franchisee and typically includes the following main clauses.

- The nature of the service which is to be supplied by the franchisee is specified. This can refer to particular categories of service which are to be offered – for example, a car repair franchise would probably indicate which specific service operations (such as brake replacement, engine tuning, etc.) are covered by the franchise agreement.

- The territory in which the franchisee is given the right to offer a service is usually specified. The premium which a franchisee is prepared to pay for a franchise usually reflects the exclusivity of its territory.

- The length of a franchise agreement is specified – most franchises run for a period of 5 to 10 years with an option to renew at the end of the period.

- The franchisee usually agrees to buy the franchise for an initial fee and agrees the basis on which future payments are to be made to the franchisor. The level of the initial fee reflects the strength of an established brand – a high initial fee for a strong established brand can be much less risky for a franchisee than a low price for a relatively new franchise. Payment of ongoing fees to the franchisor is usually calculated as a percentage of turnover. The agreement also usually requires the franchisee to buy certain supplies from the franchisor. Agreements vary widely – for example, BSM makes no initial charge to franchisees, but subsequently charges a fixed weekly fee which includes much of the equipment the franchisee uses.

- The franchisee agrees to follow instructions from the franchisor concerning the manner of service delivery. Franchisees are typically required to charge according to an agreed scale of prices, maintain standards of reliability, availability and performance in the delivery of the service and to ensure that any advertising follows the franchisor's guidelines.

- The franchisee usually agrees not to act as an intermediary for any other service principal, insisting that their franchised outlets show the same loyalty to the organization as if they were actually owned by the organization. Thus the operator of a Pizza Express franchise cannot use a franchised outlet to sell the services or goods of a competing organization such as Burger King. Franchising implies a degree of control which the franchisor has over the franchisee, unlike a retail agent who usually has considerable discretion over the manner in which they conduct their business. For the franchisor, considerable harm could result from its promotion being used to draw potential customers into the franchisee's outlets, only for them to be cross-sold a service over which the franchisor has no control nor is likely to receive any financial benefit. However, in many cases, service franchises are sold on the understanding that they will form just one small part of the franchisee's operations – for example, a franchise to operate a courier service's collection point may be compatible with the business of a service station or newsagent franchisee.

- The franchisor agrees to provide promotional support for the franchisee. The aim of such support is to establish the values of the franchisor's brand in the minds of potential customers, thereby reducing the promotion which the franchisee is required to undertake. The franchise agreement usually requires certain promotional activity of the franchisee to be approved by the franchisor.

- The franchisor usually agrees to provide some level of administrative and technical support for the franchisee. This can include the provision of equipment (e.g. printing machines for a fast-print franchise) and administrative support such as accounting.

- Franchise agreements usually give either party the right to terminate the franchise and for the franchisee to sell the franchise. The right to terminate can act as a control mechanism should either party fail to perform in accordance with the conditions of the franchise. A successful franchisee would want a clause in an agreement allowing him or her to sell the goodwill of a franchise which they have developed over time.

9.6.2 **Public-sector franchising**

Public services are increasingly being delivered by franchise agreements in order to capitalize on the motivation of smaller-scale franchisees which was described above. Franchising can take a number of forms, as outlined below.

- The right to operate a vital public service can be sold to a franchisee who in turn has the right to charge users of the facility. The franchisee will normally be required to maintain the facility to a required standard and to obtain government approval of prices to be charged. In the UK, the government has offered private organizations franchisees to operate vital road links, including the Dartford river crossing and Severn Bridge. In the case of the latter, an Anglo-French consortium acquired the right to collect tolls from users of the bridge, and in return paid to develop a second river crossing and agreed to carry out routine maintenance work.

- Government can sell the exclusive right for private organizations to operate a private service which is of public importance. Private-sector radio and television broadcasting is operated on a franchise basis where the government invites bids from private companies for exclusive rights to broadcast in specified areas and/or at specified times.

- Where a socially necessary but economically unviable service is provided in a market-mediated environment, government can subsidize provision of the service by means of a franchise. In the UK, rail passenger services are provided by private train operators who have a franchise to operate a route, typically for about seven years. As most rail services are loss-making, this has entailed government paying franchisees to operate a service, with franchisees being selected on the basis of, among other things, the amount of subsidy they would need to operate a service. Successful bidders keep the revenue which they generate from passengers, subject to meeting the minimum requirements of the rail regulator in terms of timetables, reliability, fares, etc.

- Even though a public service is not market mediated at the point of delivery, production methods may nevertheless be market mediated and part of the production function provided through a franchise agreement. Such an arrangement can have benefits for customers where the franchisee is rewarded partly on the basis of feedback from users. A recent application of this type of franchise can be found in the field of higher education where many universities have franchised their courses to colleges of further education.

- In the UK, possibly the longest-established public-sector franchise is seen in the Post Office. In addition to government owned 'Crown' post offices, 'sub' post offices have traditionally been operated on a franchise basis in smaller towns and in villages. Franchises have been taken up by a variety of small shops and newsagents, and generally offer a more limited range of postal services compared to Crown offices.

University degrees made accessible through franchises

The past 20 years have seen many major changes in the way higher education is managed in the United Kingdom, with marketing playing a much greater role. Underlying this has been a growth in numbers entering higher education, rising from under 10% in the 1980s to nearly 40% of all 18 year olds in a few decades. Making additional capacity available to the enlarged number of students has been a challenge for universities, whose facilities have become increasingly stretched. One solution adopted by many universities has been franchising, using principles borrowed from the private business sector.

Franchising offered benefits to universities and to franchisee colleges of further education who would deliver part of the university's programmes. For universities, local accessibility to courses and expansion in numbers was allowed using the staff and facilities of another organization. It could allow the university to concentrate on higher-level teaching and research, while colleges undertook foundation courses. For colleges, a franchise would allow a broader portfolio of courses to be marketed, which was especially important, given the rising levels of competition from schools for its traditional students.

Both the university and the local college become involved in the marketing of franchised courses. The franchisee college can appeal to its local population on the basis of being a caring local community facility, while the university can add to this at both a local and national level. If the reputation of the university is itself weak, the task of recruiting students for franchised colleges will be more difficult.

At the heart of an educational franchise is the requirement to maintain consistent standards so that a student studying at a franchised college receives substantially the same education as one studying at the franchising university. Vetting of colleges at the outset is crucial to ensure that they have the staff, accommodation and technical resources capable of delivering the specified course. Once a scheme is running, close monitoring is required from the university on such matters as assessment standards and the quality of teaching materials delivered.

Quality control of franchise colleges has been highlighted in numerous reports by the government's Quality Assurance Agency (QAA). These have often pointed to a failure of quality control from the beginning of many franchise operations – for example, through poor specification of requirements at the outset and through some of the essential quality requirements not having been met. Subsequent reports have shown the difficulties which some universities have got into, especially when franchising their courses to overseas colleges where quality control is much more difficult.

What is the future of higher education franchising? If the experience of most other service sectors is anything to go by, it will continue to have a role. A franchise relationship between university and college will last for as long as it is in both organizations' interests for it to do so.

A college could in some cases run a course on its own without reference to a university, but against the saving in franchise fees must be set the greater cost and difficulty of recruiting students who may be unaware of the existence or the standards of the college. Students may perceive a franchised course which is validated by a university as being much more valuable than one validated by a local college in its own name. But given that quality control is crucial to maintaining the good brand image of the franchising university, will many come to think that maintaining such controls over culturally different and geographically dispersed colleges is too much effort? Could they overcome their capacity problems or exploit the new accessibility possibilities opened up by the Internet?

9.7 Accessibility through co-production

Some service organizations choose to make their services available to consumers in combination with other goods and services, with the collaboration of another producer. The outputs of the two organizations can be quite diverse – for example, a finance company could offer loan facilities in conjunction with customers buying audio equipment. Other examples include a combined train fare and museum admission ticket and a combined hotel and travel offer.

On other occasions, a service can be made available in combination with similar services provided by potential competitors. The basis for doing this is that the combined value of the enlarged service offer will generate more business and ultimately be of benefit to all service providers involved. In this way, many regional travel tickets allow passengers to travel on the trains and buses of potentially competing operators, thereby making public transport as a whole a relatively attractive option. Similarly, banks benefit by sharing cash dispenser networks – those sharing gain a competitive advantage over a bank which chooses to go it alone with its own dedicated but smaller network. In Britain, as in most western countries, legislation exists to restrict such collaborative activities where they are deemed to be anti-competitive and therefore against the public interest. Banks, for example, were accused of collusion in 2000 when they collectively agreed a scale of charges for using each other's ATMs, and which was deemed by many to be far in excess of the banks' actual costs.

9.8 Making the tangible components of the service offer available to consumers

For some services, tangible goods are a vital element of the overall service offer and a strategy is needed for making them available to consumers. Managing the availability of tangibles assumes importance for a number of reasons:

- Tangibles may be vital in giving pre-sales evidence of a service offer in the form of printed brochures, order forms, etc. An indication of the logistical problems in making brochures available to potential customers is provided by the task facing Thomson Holidays. If the company was to distribute 50 copies of its main summer holiday brochure to each of over 7000 travel agents in Britain, it would need to move over 350 000 brochures. The fact that Thomson produces multiple brochures aimed at different segments of the holiday market makes the logistical task even greater.

- Tangibles often form an important component of a service offer, and failure to deliver tangibles reduces the quality of a service or makes it impossible to perform at all. This is true of fast-food restaurant chains for whom perishable raw materials have to be moved regularly and rapidly.

- Sometimes the fundamental purpose of a service process is to make goods available. Retailers and equipment rental companies provide a service, but without a strategy to move the associated goods effectively, their service becomes of little value.

- The freight transport service sector exists solely to move goods.

Where tangibles form an important part of a service offer, their efficient and effective distribution can give an organization a competitive advantage. An inefficient and unreliable distribution system can negate a restaurant chain's efforts at improving service quality if it is unable to deliver advertised meal offers. There are many texts covering the subject of physical distribution management in detail (see the 'Selected further reading' section at the end of this chapter). Here, a brief overview of the key elements of a physical distribution system is offered.

9.8.1 **Physical distribution management**

The design of a physical distribution system begins by setting objectives. Ideally, a system should make the right goods available in the right places at the right time. Against this must be balanced the need to minimize the cost of distribution, so objectives are stated in a form which involves a trade-off – for example, a holiday tour operator might realistically aim to deliver 80% of brochure requests to travel agents within three working days at the minimum possible cost. Distribution objectives in turn are based on an assessment of customers' needs. While a fast-food restaurant chain might be happy to live with a three-day delivery objective for orders for packaging materials, 24-hour delivery may be required for perishable foods. The importance of rapid and reliable delivery of fresh food would be reflected in a greater willingness to pay premium prices for a service which is capable of meeting objectives – failure to deliver could have a serious effect on sales and reputation.

Physical distribution systems can be seen as comprising six basic elements which can be manipulated to design an optimum system. These are shown in Figure 9.7, and the management decisions which need to be made in respect of each of these are considered briefly below.

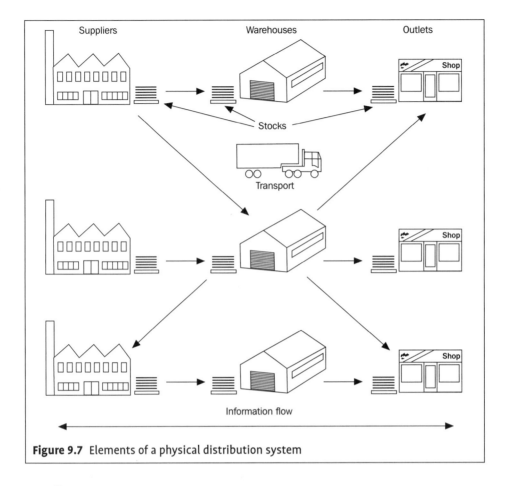

Figure 9.7 Elements of a physical distribution system

Suppliers

A marketing-oriented service organization must balance the need to have supply sources close to customers against economies of scale which may be obtained from having one central point of supply. Where markets are turbulent, the distribution system may favour suppliers who are closest to the customer rather than necessarily the cheapest sources of production. During a period of market turbulence, a domestic tour operator may source brochures at home rather than wait for them to be delivered from a possibly cheaper source overseas.

Outlets

These can range from the individual household through to the largest hypermarket. If the unique offer of a service is home delivery, strategy must identify the most efficient and effective means of moving associated tangibles to customers' homes.

Stocks

These need to be held in order to provide rapid availability of goods and to provide contingencies against disruptions in production. Stocks also occur because of the need to achieve economies of scale in production, resulting in initially large stock-holdings which are gradually reduced until the next production run. Seasonal patterns of production and consumption may also contribute towards fluctuating stock levels. The need to make stock readily available has to be offset against the need to minimize the cost of stockholding which can result from capital charges, storage charges and the risk of obsolescence.

Warehouses

These are incorporated into a system to provide a break of bulk point, and to hold stocks. A company must decide on the number and nature of the warehouses which are incorporated into its system, in particular the balance between the need for local and accessible warehouses against the need for efficiency savings which favour large warehouses. Automation of warehouses with the development of computerized picking systems is increasingly favouring larger warehouses – a typical national supermarket in the UK would now include just half a dozen strategically located warehouses in its distribution system to serve a national chain of outlets.

Transport

This moves stocks from manufacturers to retail outlets and sometimes – as in the case of mail order or home delivery of milk – to final consumers. Transport is becoming an increasingly important element of distribution systems, with goods tending to travel for longer average distances between larger, centralized warehouses within the system. Road haulage has become the dominant form of goods transport within Britain.

Information flow

The need to respond to customers' requirements rapidly, while at the same time keeping down stock-holding levels, demands a rapid flow of information. The development of 'just-in-time' (JIT) systems has only been possible with the improvement of data-processing techniques. The introduction of barcodes has achieved notable results in this respect. A supermarket can now know minute by minute the state of stocks for all of its products and can order replacement stocks – by an electronic data link – for delivery from a regional distribution centre the following day. The regional distribution centres can similarly rapidly reorder stocks from their suppliers. The development of just-in-time systems has not only allowed a more reliable level of availability of goods to the final consumer, but it has also allowed retailers to reduce warehouse space provided within shops. Because it is no longer necessary to hold large stocks locally, warehouse space can be turned over to more valuable sales floor space.

Case study

Domino's cooks up millionaire franchisees

Domino's Pizza is now recognized as the world's leading pizza delivery company. Its expertise and passion for delivering hot and fresh pizza is reflected in its mission statement which talks about employing exceptional people on a mission to be the best pizza delivery company in the world. Founded in 1960, Domino's makes and delivers nearly 6 million pizzas a week in more than 60 countries around the world. It has more than 7000 stores with worldwide sales in 2001 of more than $3.78 billion. From humble beginnings in 1960, franchising has been a key element of the company's mission to bring pizza to the world. In 2001, 85% of its outlets were owned by franchisees.

The UK was an early target for Domino's expansion, and it established a subsidiary company, Domino's Pizza Group Limited, which holds the exclusive master franchise to own, operate and franchise Domino's Pizza stores in the UK and Ireland.

Fast food may be looked down on by many as not being a 'proper' career, but Domino's has used the energy of talented and hard-working individuals to deliver good financial rewards to its franchisees and quality pizzas to its customers. In 2004, Domino's reported that 10 of its 100-plus UK and Ireland franchisees owned businesses which were worth more than £1 million each. These figures are based on a standard calculation of twice annual turnover. With an average start-up cost of £183 000 this is a significant return on franchisees' initial investment. Only two years previously one in ten of Domino's stores had a turnover of £10 000 a week, by 2004 this figure was one in three. In 2002, Domino's franchisees earned around £120 000 a year on average (although some considerably more) which was more than three times the average income of a typical business manager (£38 107). Furthermore, no Domino's franchise failed during the year, compared with over 22 000 business failures elsewhere in the UK economy.

Domino's research into the skills set and characteristics of the most successful franchisees both in the UK and internationally has uncovered that the majority of franchisees believe the traditional corporate management career path failed to offer either the scope to succeed or the financial rewards within the time scale they want.

Typical of the hard-working individuals attracted to a Domino's franchise was James Swift. As a 16-year-old delivery driver for Domino's Pizza, Swift spotted the potential to run his own business at an early age. He soon secured a position as the manager of Domino's branch in Swindon and learned everything there was to know about running a store. This operational experience was critical for learning everything from how to make a pizza to how to manage a big team. It was about three years later that he got the chance to buy a share in the franchise. By the age of 24, he had become co-franchisee of three Domino's outlets in Swindon, Newbury and Bath. He put his success down to sheer hard work and determination, with the backing of a renowned brand and the commitment that only an owner of a business can give.

Maybe one day, James Swift will match the success of Richard P. Mueller, Jr,

Domino's Pizza's most successful global franchisee. Mueller joined Domino's in 1967 as a delivery driver and became a franchisee in 1970. By 2003 he owned 158 stores in the USA and employed over 3000 team members. His company sold over 10 million pizzas a year, as many as the entire UK Domino's business. That equated to 5 million pounds of dough, 5 million pounds of cheese and enough pizza sauce to fill a large swimming pool. In the process of growing his business, Mueller had become a millionaire.

Given the stressful, tedious conditions of most fast-food operations, it is vital that staff are motivated to succeed. While many part-time staff, such as students and parents of young school children, are happy to do just a few hours of work in return for a bit of extra cash, the business needs to be able to accommodate the ambitions of people who could make good leaders of people. A bureaucratic 'jobsworth' culture will not allow a pizza company to compete effectively with more agile and committed competitors. The success of Domino's illustrates the value of having committed franchisees who benefit directly from having rising numbers of satisfied customers.

However, although franchising is the dominant form of distribution for Domino's, the company retains a proportion of directly managed outlets. As well as providing an internal benchmark against which franchisees can be judged, these outlets are useful for developing new service ideas which may be too risky for individual franchisees to undertake on their own. One outcome of this process has been the development of a bluetooth and GPS enabled system which can pinpoint a pizza delivery person's exact location via satellite. Information can then be transmitted to the delivery person's bluetooth headset, providing guidance on the best route to take to the next customer via the GPRS (general packet radio service) system based at the store. Would such developments be possible without the support of a strong centrally managed franchise?

Source: based on material provided by Domino's (www.dominos.com) and the British Franchise Association (www.british-franchise.org) websites.

Case study review questions

1. Discuss the relative merits of franchising and direct management for fast-food outlets.

2. What problems does a franchise such as Domino's face in trying to reconcile the individualism of entrepreneurial franchisees with the need for brand consistency?

3. Why do you think that 15% of Domino's outlets are managed directly by the company, rather than by franchisees?

Chapter summary and links to other chapters

Making services accessible to consumers involves some different principles compared to goods, largely arising out of the inseparability and intangibility of services. In particular, intermediaries become co-producers of a service. Services vary in the extent to which producers and consumers are able or willing to travel to each other in order for an inseparable service to be performed. Service firms in many sectors have sought to reduce the effects of inseparability through mail, telephone and Internet access systems.

Intermediaries are often the main contact a customer has with an organization, therefore they can be critical to successful service encounters (**Chapter 3**) and contribute to the overall quality of a service (**Chapter 8**). Increasingly, intermediaries are being used to promote service firms' relationship marketing strategies, although problems still remain where intermediaries are suspicious of service principals who they fear are trying to reduce or eliminate their role (**Chapter 5**). The level of accessibility to a service is often reflected in the price charged for a service at a particular time and location (**Chapter 10**). When firms seek to expand overseas, new problems in developing accessibility are raised, and these are discussed in **Chapter 14**.

Chapter review questions

1. What are the most important factors influencing the location decision for a proposed new gymnasium?

2. Of what value are modelling techniques in deciding on retail store location?

3. In what ways does a travel agent assist tour operators in the process of making holidays available to its customers?

4. In what situations is a service principal likely to prefer dealing directly with its customers, rather than through intermediaries?

5. Using examples, contrast the role of 'push' and 'pull' methods of making services available within the service sector.

6. Analyse the potential problems and opportunities for a dry cleaning company seeking to expand through franchising.

Activity

Take a close look at fast-food outlets in your area. Can you tell which are run by franchisees and which are run directly by a brand owner? What, if any, differences in service provision are evident between the two types of service outlet?

Key terms

Channel of distribution The people and organization involved in getting a service to the final consumer.

Co-producers More than one individual or organization is involved in producing a service.

Disintermediation Simplifying a channel of distribution by reducing the role of intermediaries.

Franchising An agreement where a franchisor develops a good service format and marketing strategy, and sells the rights for other individuals or organizations ('franchisees') to use that format.

Informediaries Intermediaries whose main resource is information, collected and distributed using information technology.

Intermediary An individual or organization involved in transferring service benefits from the producer to the final consumer. For services, this usually requires the intermediary to become a co-producer of the service.

Reintermediation Increasing the role played by intermediaries in a channel of distribution.

Service agents Intermediaries who assist a service principal in making service benefits available to consumers. An agent is usually a co-producer of a service and acts on behalf of the service principal, with whom customers enter into legal relations.

Selected further reading

For a general discussion of the principles of distribution and the use of intermediaries, the following texts are useful.
Frazier, G.L. (1999) 'Organizing and managing channels of distribution', *Journal of the Academy of Marketing Science*, 27 (2; Spring), 226–40.

Löning, H. and Besson, M. (2002) 'Can distribution channels explain differences in marketing and sales performance measurement systems?' *European Management Journal*, 20 (6; December), 597–609.

Much of the literature on relationship marketing is relevant to the analysis of relationships between service principals and their intermediaries. The following are useful.
Gummesson, E. (2001) *Total Relationship Marketing*, Butterworth-Heinemann, London.
Varey, R.J. (2002) *Relationship Marketing: Dialogue and Networks in the E-commerce Era*, Wiley, Chichester.
Christopher, M., Payne, A. and Ballantyne, D. (2001) *Relationship Marketing: Creating Stakeholder Value*, Heinemann, London.
Sheth, J.N. and Parvatiyar, A. (2000) *Handbook of Relationship Marketing*, Sage, USA.

The effects of the Internet on service distribution channels is discussed in the following.
Porter, M.E. (2001) 'Strategy and the Internet', *Harvard Business Review*, March–April, 63–78.
Law, R., Leung, K. and Wong, R. (2004) 'The impact of the Internet on travel agencies', *International Journal of Contemporary Hospitality Management*, 16 (2), 100–7.
Joseph, M. and Stone, G. (2003), 'An empirical evaluation of US bank customer perceptions of the impact of technology on service delivery in the banking sector', *International Journal of Retail and Distribution Management*, 31 (4), 190–202.
Pitt, L., Berthon, P. and Berthon, J.P. (1999) 'Changing channels: The impact of the Internet on distribution strategy', *Business Horizon*, 42 (2; March–April), 19–28.

This chapter has considered only briefly the principles of physical distribution management as they affect the tangible elements of a service offer. The following references offer further discussion of the principles.
Christopher, M. and Peck, H. (2003) *Marketing Logistics and Customer Services*, Butterworth-Heinemann.
Fawcett, S.E. and Magnan, G.M. (2002) 'The rhetoric and reality of supply chain integration', *International Journal of Physical Distribution and Logistics Management*, 32 (5), 339–61.

References

British Franchising Association (2004) *The NatWest/British Franchising Association Annual Survey of Franchising*, BFA, Henley-on-Thames.
Fishbein, M. (1967) *Readings in Attitude Theory and Measurement*, John Wiley & Sons, New York.
Huff, D.L. (1966) 'A programmed solution for approximating an optimal retail location', *Land Economics*, 42, 293–303.
Mayo, E.J. and Jarvis, L.P. (1981) *The Psychology of Leisure Travel*, CBI Publishing Co., Boston, Mass.

The pricing of services

Learning objectives

This chapter will explain:

- the effects of inseparability on service firms' ability to offer finely segmented prices

- factors influencing an organization's price decisions, including organizational objectives, cost levels, strength of demand and level of competition

- the role of external government regulation on service pricing

- pricing strategy and tactics used by service firms

- price bundling of complex, interdependent service offers

- pricing constraints and opportunities for public-sector services.

10.1 **Introduction**

Within the service sector, the term 'price' often passes under a number of names, sometimes reflecting the nature of the relationship between customer and provider in which exchange takes place. Professional service companies therefore talk about fees, while other organizations use terms such as fares, tolls, rates, charges and subscriptions. The art of successful pricing is to establish a price level which is sufficiently low that an exchange represents good value to buyers, yet is high enough to allow a service provider to achieve its financial objectives.

The importance of pricing to the development of marketing strategy is reflected in the diverse range of strategic uses to which it is put.

- At the beginning of the life of a new service, pricing is often used to gain entry to a new market. As an example, a firm of estate agents seeking to extend its operations to a new region may offer initially very low commission rates in order to build volume in a new market.

- Price is used as a means of maintaining the market share of a service during its life and is used tactically to defend its position against competitors.

- Ultimately, for organizations working to profit objectives, prices must be set at a level which allows them to meet their financial objectives.

Services are more likely than goods to be made available to consumers by methods where price is not the focal point of the exchange. Many public-sector services are provided to the end consumer at either no charge or at a charge that bears little relation to the value of a service to the consumer or producer. Public services such as museums and schools which have sought to adopt marketing principles often do not have any control over the price element of the marketing mix. The reward for attracting more visitors to a museum or pupils to a school may be additional centrally derived grants, rather than income received directly from the users of the service.

10.2 **Organizational influences on pricing decisions**

Organizations show a wide variation in the objectives which they seek to achieve. An analysis of corporate objectives is a useful starting point for understanding the factors that underlie price decisions. Some commonly found organizational objectives and their implications for price decisions are analysed below.

- *Profit maximization.* It is often assumed that all private-sector organizations exist primarily to maximize their profits and that this will therefore influence their pricing policies. In fact, the notion of profit maximization needs to be qualified with a time dimension, for marketing strategies which maximize profits over the short run may be detrimental to achieving long-term profits. An organization charging high prices in a new market may make that market seem very attractive to new entrants, thereby having the effect of increasing the level of competition in subsequent years, and so reducing long-term profitability. Also, the time frame over which profitability is sought can affect pricing decisions. If an innovative service is given an objective to break even after just one year, prices may be set at a low level in order to capture a large share of the market as quickly as possible, whereas a longer-term profit objective may have allowed the organization to tap relatively small but high-value segments of its markets in the first year and save the exploitation of lower-value segments until subsequent years. The notion of profit maximization has a further weakness in the service sector where it can be difficult to establish clear relationships between costs, revenue and profits (see below).

- *Market share maximization.* It has frequently been argued (e.g. Cyert and March, 1963) that it is unrealistic to expect the managers of a business to put all of their efforts into maximizing profits. To begin with, there can be practical difficulties in establishing relationships between marketing strategy decisions and the resulting change in profitability. Secondly, management often does not directly receive any reward for increasing its organization's profits – its main concern is to achieve a satisfactory level of profits rather than the maximum possible. Managers may be more likely to benefit from decisions which increase the market share of their organization (e.g. through improved career opportunities and job security). An objective to maximize market share may be very important to service industries where it is necessary to achieve a critical mass in order to achieve economies of scale, and therefore a competitive advantage. The price competition which accompanied the emerging market for Internet Service Providers in the late 1990s was based on the desire of the main competitors to achieve a critical size which made them consumers' first choice for Internet-related activities.

- *Survival.* Sometimes, the idea of maximizing profits or market share is a luxury to a service provider whose main objective is simply to survive and to avoid the possibility of going into receivership. Most businesses fail when they run out of cash flow at a critical moment when debts become due for payment. In these circumstances, prices may be set at a very low level simply to get sufficient cash into the organization to tide it over its short-term problems. During the Iraq War in 2003, **demand** for air travel fell significantly, putting severe pressure on the resources of many airlines, which suffered further from the increase in aviation fuel prices. In a bid to stay afloat, many airlines were forced to lower fares dramatically simply in order to keep cash flowing into the business over what they thought would be the last hurdle before regaining a long-term growth path.

- *Social considerations.* Profit-related objectives have little meaning to many public-sector services. At one extreme, the price of many public services represents a tax levied by government based on wider considerations of the ability of users to pay for the service and the public benefits of providing that service (e.g. fixed charges for National Health Service dental work in the UK with exemptions for disadvantaged groups). Where public services are provided in a more market-mediated environment, pricing decisions may nevertheless be influenced by wider social considerations (e.g. non-vocational educational classes run by local authorities may charge a nominal fee for an adult literacy class, but a much higher fee for a golf tuition class). Although social objectives are normally associated with public-sector services, they can sometimes be found within the private sector. Services provided by employers for their staff are often provided at a price which does not reflect their true value, but instead contribute towards staff members' total benefit package – examples include staff restaurants and sports clubs which are often priced at much lower levels than their normal market value.

In practice, organizations work to a number of objectives simultaneously – for example, a market share objective over the short term may be seen as a means towards achieving a long-term profit maximizing objective.

10.3 Factors influencing pricing decisions

An organization's objectives determine the desired results of pricing policies. Strategies are the means by which these objectives are achieved. Before discussing pricing strategy, it is useful to lay the groundwork by analysing the underlying factors that influence price decisions. Four important bases for price determination can be identified:

1. what it costs to produce a service

2. the amount that consumers are prepared to pay for it

3. the price that competitors are charging

4. the constraints on pricing that are imposed by regulatory bodies.

The cost of producing a service represents the minimum price that a commercial organization would be prepared to accept over the long term for providing the service. The maximum price achievable is that which customers are prepared to pay for the service. This will itself be influenced by the level of competition available to customers to satisfy their needs elsewhere. Government regulation may intervene to prevent organizations charging the maximum price that consumers would theoretically be prepared to pay. These principles are illustrated in Figure 10.1.

10.4 Costs as a basis for pricing

Many empirical studies have shown the importance of costs as a basis for determining prices within the service sector. For example, Zeithaml *et al.* (1985), in their study of service firms in the USA, found that it was the dominant basis for price determination.

At its most simple, a **cost-plus pricing** system works by using historical cost information to calculate a unit cost for each type of input used in a service production process. Subsequent price decisions for specific service outcomes are based on the

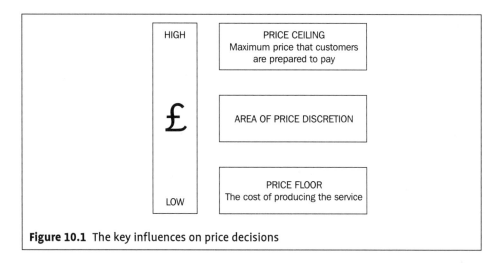

Figure 10.1 The key influences on price decisions

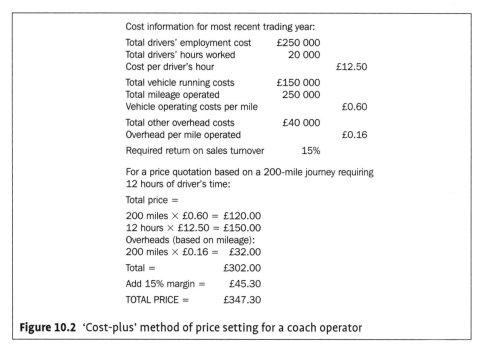

Figure 10.2 'Cost-plus' method of price setting for a coach operator

number of units of inputs used, multiplied by the cost per unit, plus a profit margin. This method of setting prices is widely used in service industries as diverse as catering, building, accountancy and vehicle servicing. An example of how a coach hire operator might calculate its prices on this basis is shown in Figure 10.2.

There are many reasons why 'cost-plus'-type pricing methods are so widely used in the service sector.

■ Prices are easy to calculate and allow the delegation of price decisions for services which have to be tailored to the individual needs of customers. For example, every building job, vehicle repair or landscape gardening job is likely to be unique and a price for each job can be calculated by junior staff using standard unit costs for the inputs required to complete the job and a predetermined profit margin.

■ Where an agreement is made to provide a service, but the precise nature of the service which will actually be provided is unknown at the outset, a contract may stipulate that the final price will be based in some way on costs incurred. A garage agreeing to repair a car with an unidentified engine noise brought in by a customer could not realistically give a price quotation before undertaking the job and examining the nature of the problem. In these circumstances, the customer may agree to pay an agreed amount per hour for labour, plus the cost of any parts which the garage buys in.

■ Trade and professional associations often include codes of conduct that allow a service provider only to increase prices beyond those originally agreed in an estimate on the basis of the actual costs incurred. Solicitors and accountants, for example, who need to commit more resources to complete a job than was originally allowed for in their price estimate are bound by their professional bodies to pass on only their reasonable additional costs.

Against these attractions, pricing services on the basis of historic costs presents a number of problems.

■ In itself, cost-based pricing does not take account of the competition which a particular service faces at any given time, nor of the fact that some customers may value the same service more highly than others.

■ Calculating the costs of a service can in fact be very difficult, and often more difficult than in the case of goods. One reason for this is the structure of costs facing many services businesses (discussed below).

■ While it may be possible to determine costs for previous accounting periods, it can be difficult to predict what these costs will be in the future. This is a particular problem for services which are contracted to be provided at some time in the future. Unlike goods, it is not possible to produce the service at known cost levels in the current period and to store it for consumption in some future period. Historical cost information is often adjusted by an inflation factor where service delivery is to be made some time in the future, but it can be difficult to decide what is the most appropriate inflation factor to use for a specific input. Where input costs are highly volatile (e.g. aviation fuel), one solution is for a service producer to pass on part of the risk of unpredictable inflation to customers. Charter airlines frequently do this by requiring customers to pay for any increase in fuel costs beyond a specified amount.

10.4.1 Cost structures

The costs of producing a service can be divided into those that are variable and those that are fixed. Variable costs increase as service production increases, whereas **fixed**

costs remain unchanged if an additional unit of service is produced. Fixed costs therefore cannot be attributed to any particular unit of output. In between these two extremes of costs are semi-fixed costs which remain constant until a certain level of output is reached, when expenditure on additional units of productive capacity is needed. The particular problem of many services industries is that fixed costs represent a very high proportion of total costs, resulting in great difficulty in calculating the cost of any particular unit of service.

The importance of fixed costs for a number of services industries is illustrated in Figure 10.3, where variable costs are defined as any cost which varies directly as a result of one extra customer consuming a service for which there is currently spare capacity. Thus one more passenger on a domestic flight from London to Aberdeen will probably only result in nominal additional variable costs of an additional in-flight meal and airport departure and security charges which have to be paid for each passenger. The cost of cabin crews and aircraft depreciation would not change, nor would those more remote fixed costs such as head office administration and promotion.

It can be argued that, over the long term, all costs borne by a business are variable. In the case of the airline, if the unit of analysis is a particular flight rather than one individual passenger, the proportion of costs which are variable increases. So, if the airline withdrew just one return journey between the two points, it would save fuel costs, making fuel a variable cost. It would probably also save some staff costs, but may still have to incur aircraft depreciation costs and the more remote head office administration costs. If the whole route was closed, even more costs would become variable – staff employed at the terminal could be cut, as could the flight crews. It may be possible for the airline to avoid some of its aircraft depreciation costs by reducing the size of its fleet. Even promotional costs would become variable as part of the airline's advertising may no longer need to be incurred if the service was closed completely.

Service	Fixed costs	Variable
Restaurant	Building maintenance Rent and rates Waiters and cooks	Food
Bank mortgage	Staff time Building maintenance Corporate advertising	Sales commission Paper and postage
Domestic air journey	Aircraft maintenance and depreciation Head office administrative costs	Airport departure tax In-flight meal
Hairdresser	Building maintenance Rent and rates	Shampoos used

Figure 10.3 Examples of fixed and variable costs in selected service industries

High levels of fixed costs are associated with high levels of interdependency between the services which make use of the fixed-cost elements. To illustrate this, the cost of maintaining a retail bank branch network is fixed over the short to medium term, yet the network provides facilities for a wide range of different service activities – current accounts, mortgages, business loans and foreign currency business, to name but a few. Staff may be involved in handling each of these activities in the course of a working day and it is likely that no special space is reserved exclusively for each activity. For many of these activities, the short-term direct costs are quite negligible – for example, the direct cost of one order to change Sterling into dollars is little more than the cost of a receipt slip. But users of this service would be expected to contribute towards the overhead costs of staff and space. There is frequently no obvious method by which these fixed costs can be attributed to specific units of output, nor even to particular types of service. The fixed costs for money exchange could, for example, be allocated on the basis of the proportion of floor space occupied, proportion of staff time used, proportion of total turnover, or some combination of these bases. Allocation bases are often the result of judgement and political in-fighting. They can change as a result of argument between cost centre managers who invariably feel that their product is contributing excessively to fixed costs and may put forward an argument why their pricing base is putting them at a disadvantage in the marketplace against competitors who have a simpler cost structure. In the end, cost allocation is a combination of scientific analysis and bargaining.

10.4.2 Marginal cost pricing

A special kind of cost-based pricing occurs where firms choose to ignore their fixed costs. The price which any individual customer is charged is based not on the total unit cost of producing it, but only the additional costs which will result directly from servicing that additional customer. It is used where the bulk of a company's output has been sold at a full price which recovers its fixed costs, but in order to fill remaining capacity, the company brings its prices down to a level which at least covers its variable or avoidable costs. Marginal cost pricing is widely used in service industries with low, short-term supply elasticity and high fixed costs. It is common in the airline industry where the perishability of a seat renders it unsaleable after departure. Rather than receive no revenue for an empty seat, an airline may prefer to get some income from a passenger, so long as the transaction provides a contribution by more than covering the cost of additional food and departure taxes. The Internet has seen the emergence of a number of companies which specialize in selling surplus capacity at low rates (Figure 10.4).

Against the attraction of filling spare capacity and getting a contribution towards fixed costs where otherwise there would have been none, marginal cost pricing does have its problems. The biggest danger of pricing on this basis is that it can be taken too far, allowing too high a proportion of customers to be carried at **marginal cost**, with insufficient customers charged at full price to cover the fixed costs. Many airlines

Figure 10.4 'Late deals' have for a long time been a feature of the package holiday industry, as tour operators and airlines use marginal cost pricing to sell spare capacity. The companies realize that if a holiday is not sold by the time of departure, the opportunity to sell it will be lost for ever. Some revenue is better than no revenue, as long as it covers the company's variable costs and makes a contribution to fixed costs. Many holiday buyers deliberately leave booking their holiday until late in the day, hopeful that they may pick up a bargain late-availability deal. The online travel intermediary lastminute.com has successfully made use of marginal cost pricing by bringing together companies who have spare capacity, with buyers who are looking for a bargain. (Reproduced with permission of lastminute.com)

and holiday tour operators have fallen into the trap of selling holidays on this basis, only to find that their fixed costs have not been fully covered. Another problem is that it may devalue customers' perception of a service. If a service promoted for its prestige value can be sold for a fraction of its original price, this may leave potential customers wondering just what the true value of the service is. It may also cause resentment from customers who had committed themselves to a service well in advance, only to find that their fellow consumers obtained a lower price by booking later (and thereby also making marketing planning much more difficult for many service operators). Companies can try to overcome problems of marginal cost pricing by differentiating the marginally costed product from that which is purchased at full price. Holiday tour operators, for example, reduce the price of last-minute standby holidays but offer no guarantee of the precise accommodation to be used – or even the precise resort, unlike the full-price holiday, where this is clearly specified.

10.5 **Demand-based pricing**

The upper limit to the price of a service is determined by what customers are prepared to pay. In fact, different customers often put differing ceilings on the price which they are prepared to pay for a service. Successful demand-based pricing, therefore, segments markets to achieve the maximum price from each segment. Price discrimination, as it is often called, can be carried out on the basis of:

- discrimination between different groups of users
- discrimination between different points of use
- discrimination between different types of use.

10.5.1 **Price discrimination between different groups of users**

Effective price discrimination requires groups of consumers to be segmented in such a way that maximum value is obtained from each segment. Sometimes this can be achieved by simply offering the same service to each segment, but charging a different price. In this way, a hairdresser can offer students or senior citizens a haircut which is identical to the service offered to all other customer groups in all respects except price. The rationale could be that these segments are more price sensitive than other segments, and therefore additional profitable business can only be gained by sacrificing some element of margin. By performing more haircuts, even at a lower price, a hairdresser may end up having increased total revenue from this segment, while still preserving the higher prices charged to other segments.

On other occasions, the service offering is slightly differentiated and targeted to segments who are prepared to pay a price which reflects its differential advantages. This is particularly important where it is impossible or undesirable to restrict availability of a lower price to certain predefined groups. Thus airlines operating between London and New York offer a variety of fare and service combinations to suit the needs of a number of segments. One segment requires to travel at short notice and is typically travelling on business. For the employer, the cost of not being able to travel at short notice may be high, so this group is prepared to pay a relatively high price in return for ready availability. A sub-segment of this market may wish to arrive refreshed ready for a day's work and be prepared to pay more for the differentiated business or first-class accommodation. For non-business travellers, one segment may be happy to accept a lower price in return for committing themselves to a particular flight several weeks before departure (Figure 10.5).

Another segment with less income to spend on travel may be prepared to take the risk of obtaining a last-minute standby flight in return for a lower-priced ticket still.

The intangible and inseparable nature of services make the possibilities for price discrimination between different groups of users much greater than is usually the case with manufactured goods. Goods can easily be purchased by one person, stored and sold to another person. If price segmentation allowed one group to buy bread at a discounted price, it would be possible for this group to buy bread and sell it on to people in higher priced segments, thereby reducing the effectiveness of the segmentation exercise. Because services are produced at the point of consumption, it is possible to control the availability of services to different segments. Therefore a hairdresser which offers a discounted price for a student segment is able to ensure that only students are charged the lower price, for example by requiring to see a Students Union identity card. A student cannot go into the hairdressers to buy a haircut and sell it on to a higher price segment.

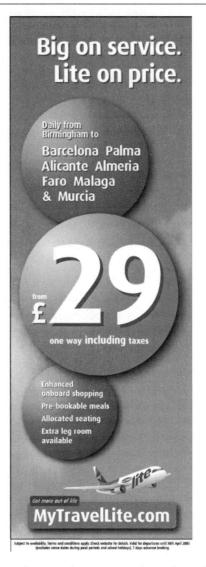

Figure 10.5 Budget airlines discovered a segment of travellers who were highly responsive to lower air fares. These airlines have simplified their operations, for example by using cheaper but less accessible airports, cutting out free in-flight catering and not paying travel agents' commission. The result has been a lower cost structure which has been passed on in lower prices, with the price of a return fare from London to Glasgow falling in some cases to less than the price of a pair of jeans. Low prices have tempted many customers to fly with 'budget' airlines. Some of these customers would have transferred from other full-service airlines, on the basis that a low price is a fair trade-off for the loss of some of the additional facilities offered by full-service airlines. For some people, low prices by air meant that they switched from competing rail and road services, while for others, new possibilities for taking short holidays or visiting friends were opened up which had previously not been affordable. (Reproduced with permission of MyTravelLite)

> ## Price discrimination by supermarket backfires
>
> Many service-sector companies have offered reduced prices for segments of senior citizens, calculating that these segments are more price sensitive than others and could usefully fill spare capacity at a profit, even at the lower prices charged. Services marketers are more fortunate than marketers of goods, where price discrimination can backfire. With services, a supplier can insist that only the senior citizen receives the benefit of the service that has been paid for (for example, by insisting on seeing proof of age during a train journey). But goods can be bought by a low-price segment and sold on to a relatively high-price one. The pitfalls of this approach to market segmentation were learnt by a German grocery retailer which offered 20% off the price of all purchases made by senior citizens at selected times of the week. Entrepreneurial senior citizens were then seen lining up outside the supermarket offering to do other customers' shopping for them. The 20% price saving was split between the senior citizen and the person needing the goods, saving effort for the latter and making additional income for the former, but making a mockery of the retailer's attempts at price discrimination. Had it been haircuts which were being offered at 20% discount to senior citizens, it would have been impossible for these to be sold on to other market segments.

10.5.2 Price discrimination between different points of consumption

Service organizations frequently charge different prices at different service locations. The inseparability of service production and consumption results in service organizations being able to define their price segments both on the basis of the point of consumption and the point of production. An example of this is found in chains of retail stores, which, in addition to using price to target particular groups of customers, also often charge different prices at different stores. For example, Marks & Spencer charges higher prices for some of its products in its central London stores than in its stores in the provinces. For its overseas branches, it is faced with very different markets again, requiring separate price lists. Some retailers with a combination of large superstores and small convenience stores can justify charging higher prices in their convenience stores. A town centre branch of Tesco Metro is likely to attract people calling in for a few items for which they would be less prepared to shop around than if they were doing a week's shopping.

Some production locations offer unique advantages to consumers. Unlike goods, the service offering cannot be transferred from where it is cheapest to produce to where it is most valued, hence service providers can charge higher prices at premium sites. Hotels fall into this category with high premiums charged by chains for those hotels located in 'honeypot' areas. A hotel room in the centre of Stratford-upon-Avon offers much greater benefit to consumers who wish to visit the theatre without a long drive back to their accommodation. Hotel prices for comparable standards of hotel therefore fall as distance from the town increases.

Travel services present an interesting example of price discrimination by location, as operators frequently charge different prices at each end of a route. The New York to London air travel market is quite different from the London to New York market. The state of the respective local economies, levels of competition and customers' buying behaviour differs between the two markets, resulting in different pricing policies in each. Because of the personal nature of an airline ticket and the fact that discounted return tickets specify the outward and return dates of travel, airlines are able to avoid tickets being purchased in the low-priced area and used by passengers originating from the higher-priced area.

Within Britain, price discrimination by location is frequently used by train operators for journeys to and from London. Fares from provincial towns to London are frequently priced at a lower rate than equivalent fares from London, reflecting – among other things – the greater competitive advantage which train operators have in the London-based market.

10.5.3 Price discrimination by time of production

Goods produced in one period can usually be stored and consumed in subsequent periods. Charging different prices in each period could result in customers buying goods for storage when prices are low, and running down their stockpiles when prices are high. Because services are instantly perishable, much greater price discrimination by time is possible.

Services often face uneven demand which follows a daily, weekly, annual, seasonal, cyclical or random pattern. At the height of each peak, pricing is usually a reflection of:

- the greater willingness of customers to pay higher prices when demand is strong, and

- the greater cost which often results from service operators trying to cater for short peaks in demand.

The greater strength of demand which occurs at some points in a daily cycle can occur for a number of reasons. In the case of rail services into the major conurbations, workers must generally arrive at work at a specified time and may have few realistic alternative means of getting to work. A railway operator can therefore sustain a higher level of fares during the daily commuter peak period. Similarly, the higher rate charged for telephone calls during the daytime is a reflection of the greater strength of demand from the business sector during the daytime (see Figure 10.6). As well as price discrimination between different periods of the day, it can also occur between different periods of the week (e.g. higher fares for using many train services

University Sport Club Annual Membership

Full-time student	£6.00
Full-time student and family	£19.00
Part-time student	£17.00
Part-time student and family	£34.00
Staff (individual)	£17.00
Staff and family	£34.00
Graduate (individual)	£25.00
Graduate and family	£50.00
Associate (individual)	£40.00
Associate and family	£80.00
Senior citizen	£30.00
Student (non-university)	£17.00
Associate college	£12.00

Figure 10.6 Although the costs of serving different groups of individuals may not vary much, this university sports centre practises price discrimination by charging different prices for different groups of users. Sometimes, lower prices are offered to fill capacity at quiet times when the marginal cost of providing facilities is particularly low (for example, many sports centres have low-priced membership schemes which are only available for use during off-peak periods). However, in the absence of clear product differentiation, the reputation of a service provider may be harmed by a feeling of unfairness on the part of those groups who fail to qualify for a lower price.

on a Friday evening), or between different seasons of the year (holiday charter flights over public holiday periods).

Price discrimination by time can be effective in inducing new business at what would otherwise be a quiet period. Hotels in holiday resorts frequently lower their prices in the off-peak season to try to tempt additional custom. Many of the public utilities lower their charges during off-peak periods in a bid to stimulate demand. Lower electricity tariffs are available during the night in order to appeal to a price-sensitive market which is able and willing to programme washing machines to operate at night time.

Cookies allow price discrimination at Amazon

The Internet and electronic databases have opened up vast new possibilities for companies to practise price discrimination between different groups of customers. Airlines and hotels have for some time practised revenue management techniques, designed to get the highest price possible for each unit of output. We are now all familiar with the idea that the price of a ticket for a plane journey on a specific route on a specific date at a specific time may vary – you may see it on an airline's website at one price today, but by tomorrow it may have gone up or down.

There are dangers in practising price discrimination too avidly, as the online retailer Amazon.com found to its cost. In September 2002, the company attempted to implement a differential pricing structure by tracking customers' online purchasing behaviour, in order to charge loyal customers higher prices for its DVDs. Consumers were quick to discover the price differences and complaints followed. Amazon customers on DVDTalk.com, an online forum, reported that certain DVDs had three different prices, depending on the so-called **cookie** a customer received from Amazon. **Cookies** are small files that websites transfer to customers' hard drives through the browsers they use. These files allow sites to recognize customers and track their purchase patterns. Depending on previous purchases, a DVD such as *Men in Black* could cost $33.97, $25.97 or $27.97. The list price was $39.95. One customer is reported to have ordered the DVD of *Julie Taymour's Titus*, paying $24.49. The next week he went back to Amazon and saw the price had jumped to $26.24. As an experiment, he stripped his computer of the electronic tags that identified him to Amazon as a regular visitor and the price fell to $22.74. One angry message posted on DVDTalk.com stated, 'Amazon apparently offers good discounts to new users, then once they get the person hooked and coming back to their site again and again, they play with the prices to make more money' (cited in Bicknell, 2000). Loyal, repeat customers were particularly incensed.

Amazon.com quickly issued reports claiming that it had been presenting different prices to different customers but denied that it had done so on the basis of any past purchasing behaviour at Amazon. A spokesman stated that the company had just been carrying out a simple price test and was not discriminating against loyal customers. However, the company later admitted that it had been carrying out **discriminatory pricing**, justifying its use by the fact that the practice was commonplace among both Internet and bricks-and-mortar companies. Faced with vociferous criticism from its loyal customers, the company quickly ended its use of cookies to discriminate between customers and refunded the difference to customers who had paid the higher prices. Amazon.com may have had to retreat on this occasion, but the case emphasizes that traditional methods used to calculate prices are sledgehammers compared with the Internet's sharp scalpel. The web provides a continuous feedback loop in that the more a customer buys from a website, the more the site knows about him or her and the weaker is his bargaining position. As one commentator put it, 'It's as if the corner drugstore could see you coming down the sidewalk, clutching your fevered brow, and then doubled the price of aspirin.' Is the use of cookies to determine prices charged to individuals an ethical practice?

Source: based on Streitfeld, 2002.

In most cases of price discrimination by time, there is also some relationship to production costs. An argument of telephone operators and electricity generators is that the marginal cost of producing additional output during off-peak periods is relatively low – as long as peak demand has covered the fixed costs of providing equipment, off-peak output can be supplied on a marginal cost basis (see above).

10.5.4 Auctions and one-to-one pricing

Price discrimination between groups of buyers may sound fine in theory, but there can be problems in actually implementing it. First, it can be very difficult to identify homogeneous segments in terms of individuals' responsiveness to price changes. Secondly, it can be very difficult to predict just what level of price will be acceptable to that group, and a lot of trial and error may be necessary to establish the most appropriate price. One alternative adopted by some companies is to leave price determination to a process of individual negotiation between buyer and seller. For high-value commercial goods and services, individual negotiation of prices has always been quite commonplace. But in the case of mass-market services, the existence of a published price list has simplified the process of exchange for buyer and seller, who do not need to spend time negotiating a price on each occasion that a relatively low-value service is sought. It has been quite rare for relatively low-value consumer sales to be individually negotiated. However, auctions provide an opportunity for a seller to get the highest price possible for a individual consumer product. The emergence of Internet-based auction sites has offered new opportunities for service providers to set their prices on the basis of what the highest bidder is prepare to pay.

Auction sites such as eBay.com and QXL.com essentially put the onus of pricing on the buyer by allowing customers to disclose the price at which they would be prepared to purchase. Faced with surplus aircraft seats, hotel rooms or theatre seats, service providers can make them available on a website and sell them to bidders who bid the highest amount, so long as this is above a minimum reserve price. If the system is working effectively, the services provider can be reasonably sure that it has secured the maximum achievable price for the services on offer.

While auctioning of services to the highest bidder has numerous attractions, there are also problems. An auction may be good in the short-term for clearing spare capacity, but in itself does nothing to develop strong brand values. In fact, auctions may treat a service like a commodity in which the only distinguishing feature is price. Auctions can be difficult to administer, even with the use of the Internet. It can be difficult to control auction sites to ensure that bidders actually pay for the service that they successfully bid for and that suppliers deliver their promises. Many consumers would prefer the certainty of fixed prices rather than taking a chance with an auction where neither the availability of a specific service nor its price can be guaranteed.

As well as consumer sales, Internet auctions have found a valuable role for business-to-business procurement (Timmins, 2003). A company can put out a tender and invite suppliers to bid, following which it would choose the lowest price bidder.

Haggling by computer?

What is there in common between the haggling over prices which takes place in many eastern markets, and modern direct marketing? At first sight the two would appear to be worlds apart, but in fact they can both be processes by which the seller seeks to establish the maximum amount that a buyer is prepared to pay. In the eastern bazaar, the seller will learn that some buyers are more price sensitive than others, resulting in each transaction being uniquely priced. This is exactly what modern direct-marketing firms often seek to achieve, except that they are likely to have a mass of information on each potential customer to initiate a price or a level of purchase incentive. And if this price is too high, the company might try again with a lower price or better incentive, knowing what the likely reaction of a particular market segment will be to the lower price. Credit card companies, mortgage lenders and banks have used such techniques and are becoming increasingly sophisticated in their use. Can a centralized database do a better job than one-to-one haggling in a marketplace?

10.5.5 **Customer lifetime pricing**

It will be recalled from Chapter 5 that the development of ongoing buyer–seller relationships is becoming a much more important part of business strategy. Rather than seeing each transaction in isolation, companies are trying to view each transaction with a customer in the context of those that have gone before, and those that they hope will occur in the future. Information technology is increasingly allowing companies to track individual customers and charge a price which is appropriate to their position in the relationship life cycle, creating what, in effect, is **customer lifetime pricing**.

A very low price may be needed to tempt a customer to try a supplier in the first place (for example, satellite television companies and Internet service providers often offer free or reduced-price trials of their services). With repeated transactions, a company can build up a picture of a customer's price sensitivity with regard to different types of services. As the relationship develops, the nature of the service may become tailored to the precise needs of the customer, such that the customer will be happy to pay a higher price in return for the benefit received. To switch to a lower-cost provider would involve the psychological cost of searching and explaining their needs to a new supplier and possibly having to understand a new service production system. A customer who has found a reliable car repair garage may come to be happy paying a little bit over the odds if they can trust the garage to understand their needs and to satisfy them effectively.

Sometimes, there may be financial as well as psychological switching costs when a relationship develops into some form of structural tie between buyer and seller.

Customers frequently sign service supply agreements which bind them to a supplier for a specified period of time (e.g. a 12-month contract for a mobile phone). At other times the structural bonds may be more subtle, as when a commercial customer has invested heavily in a computer software system and switching to another company for service support or upgrades may be very expensive.

Sometimes, inertia sets in and a supplier may try to raise its prices in the expectation that a buyer could not be bothered to shop around. Many private customers of telephone companies do not switch to cheaper alternatives because the psychological cost of doing so is seen as too great in relation to the likely financial benefits.

10.6 **Competitor-based pricing**

There are very few situations where an organization can set its prices without taking account of the activities of its competitors. The competition against whom prices need to be compared must be considered carefully, for competition can be defined in terms of the similarity of the service offered, or merely the similarity of the underlying needs which a product satisfies. For example, a chain of video rental shops can see its competition purely in terms of other rental chains, or wider to include cinema and satellite television services, or wider still to include any form of entertainment.

Having established what market it is in and who the competition is, an organization must establish what price position it seeks to adopt relative to its competitors (see Chapter 7). This position will reflect the service's wider marketing mix strategy, so if the company has invested in providing a relatively high-quality service whose benefits have been promoted effectively to target users, it can justifiably pitch its price at a higher level than its competitors.

For services targeting similar sub-segments of a market, the pricing decisions of competitors can have a direct bearing on an organization's own pricing decisions. Price in these circumstances can be used as a tactical weapon to gain short-term competitive advantage over rivals. However, in a market where competitors have broadly similar cost structures, price-cutting can be destabilizing and result in costly price wars with no sustainable increase in sales or profitability. An example of price being used to gain short-term competitive advantage is provided by the decision of Midland Bank (now HSBC) to offer free banking for customers who kept their accounts in credit. While the Midland's market share increased in the short term, it was neutralized during the following year when competing banks offered free banking to match that originally offered by Midland. The market eventually stabilized with all of the main competitors offering free banking and all had lost revenue as a result of the continuance of free banking.

10.6.1 **Going rate pricing**

In some services markets which are characterized by a fairly homogeneous service offering, demand is so sensitive to price that a firm would risk losing most of its business if it charged just a small amount more than its competitors. On the other hand, charging any lower would result in immediate retaliation from competitors.

Where cost levels are difficult to establish, charging a **going rate price** can avoid the problems of trying to calculate costs. As an example, it may be very difficult to calculate the cost of renting out a video film, as the figure will be very dependent upon assumptions made about the number of uses over which the initial purchase cost can be spread. It is much easier to take price decisions on the basis of the going rate among nearby competitors (Figure 10.7).

Many service providers face 'price points' around which customers expect to pay for a service. The UK market for Internet Service Providers (ISPs), for example, has developed a number of price points, and customer evaluation processes may begin with the question 'How much do I want to spend?'; comparison is then based on what level of service (e.g. peak/off-peak availability, free telephone calls, helpline

Figure 10.7 An example of going rate pricing is often found in areas where a number of restaurants cluster closely together, all offering a basically similar service at a similar price. For the price-sensitive diner, the 'dish of the day' may be set at the going rate, while more specialized dishes for which there is less direct competition are priced at a premium rate. Where a 'going rate' is clearly recognized by consumers, the task of the service provider may be to design a service around the price point. Just what menu can the restaurant include in a going rate price of £6, and still make a profit? If it is forced to offer a low 'going rate' price to tempt customers in, can it increase its margin by selling additional items (e.g. drinks), which are not included in the going rate price?

availability, etc.) that they can obtain within this price. The service provider's task then becomes one of designing a profitable service around the price point, rather than designing the service and then fixing a price.

10.6.2 Sealed bid pricing

Many industrial services are provided by means of a sealed bid tendering process where interested parties are invited to submit a bid for supplying services on the basis of a predetermined specification. In the case of some government contracts, the organization inviting tenders may be legally obliged to accept the lowest priced tender, unless exceptional circumstances can be proved. Price therefore becomes a crucial concern for bidders, regardless of their efforts to build up long-term brand values which in other markets might have allowed them to charge a premium price. The first task of a bidding company is to establish a minimum bid price based on its costs and required rate of return, below which it would not be prepared to bid. The more difficult task is to try to put a maximum figure on what it can bid. This will be formed on expectations of what its competitors will bid, based on an analysis of their strengths and weaknesses.

In Britain, the Local Government Acts of 1980 and 1988, and the Housing and Local Government Act 1989 required a comprehensive list of local authority services to be opened up to competitive tendering. The desire of many organizations to gain market share by underbidding resulted in many financial failures part way through the operation of a contract. Although compulsory competitive tendering has been replaced by a more general requirement of local authorities to obtain 'best value', tendering remains important for many high-value government service contracts.

10.7 Distortions to market-led pricing decisions

Services are more likely than goods to be supplied in non-competitive environments. As an example, the high fixed costs associated with many public utility services means that it is unrealistic to expect two companies to compete (can you imagine two competing sets of water supply pipes running down each road?). More importantly, much investment in services infrastructure is fixed and cannot be moved to where market opportunities are greatest. While a car manufacturer can quite easily redirect its new cars for sale from a declining market to an expanding one, a railway operator cannot easily transfer its track and stations from one area to another. The immobility of many services can encourage the development of local monopoly power. The nature and consequences of such market distortions, and government responses, are discussed below.

In most western countries there is a presumption that competition is necessary as a means of minimizing prices charged to consumers. However, while price competition may appear to act in the short-term interests of consumers, this normally restrains the combined profits of competitors. It is common, therefore, for competing organizations to seek to come to some sort of agreement (formal or informal) among themselves about prices to be charged, in order to avoid costly price competition.

Anti-competitive pricing occurs not just at a national level between large organizations, but also locally for services where the possibility of newcomers entering a market is limited by technical, economic or institutional barriers. Many local service providers have understandings – if not outright agreements – which have the effect of limiting price competition. In this way, local estate agents and building contractors have sometimes been accused of covert collusion to not engage in price competition, although obtaining evidence of such collusion can be very difficult.

To counter market imperfections, most western governments have actively sought to eliminate anti-competitive pricing practices. Government regulation of prices charged by private-sector service providers can be divided into two broad categories:

1. direct government controls to regulate monopoly power

2. government controls on price representations.

10.7.1 **Direct government controls to regulate monopoly power**

The Competition Act 1998 reformed and strengthened UK competition law by prohibiting anti-competitive behaviour. The act introduced two basic prohibitions: a prohibition of anti-competitive agreements, based closely on Article 85 of the EC Treaty; and a prohibition of abuse of a dominant position in a market, based closely on Article 86 of the EC Treaty. The act prohibits agreements which have the aim or effect of preventing, restricting or distorting price competition. Since anti-competitive behaviour between companies may occur without a clearly delineated agreement, the prohibition covers not only agreements by associations of companies, but also covert practices. The Enterprise Act 2002 strengthened the Competition Act by including provision for a new Competition Appeal Tribunal (CAT) and its supporting body the Competition Service. The act introduced criminal sanctions with a maximum penalty of five years in prison for companies that operate agreements to fix prices, share markets, limit production and rig bids. The voice of consumers was strengthened with designated consumer bodies able to make 'super-complaints' to the Office of Fair Trading.

The Competition Commission has the power to investigate alleged anti-competitive pricing practices referred to it by a number of designated bodies, including the Secretary of State for Trade and Industry, the Office of Fair Trading and industry regulatory bodies. The following are examples of previous investigations by the Commission.

■ In a 2003 report, the Competition Commission concluded that a monopoly situation existed for the supply of extended warranties for electrical goods. This had resulted in a lack of choice, excessive prices, insufficient information and lack of competition at the point of sale, leaving customers unduly pressurized to agree to disadvantageous terms. The Commission estimated that the top five providers of extended warranties – Dixons Group, Comet, Powerhouse, Littlewoods and Argos – had collectively made between £116 and £152 million more profit each year than they would have done had they been operating in a competitive market environment. The Commission accordingly recommended a series of actions to overcome this market imperfection, including making prices clearer at the outset, providing written quotations and allowing cancellation within 30 days.

■ A report in March 2000 accused the main UK banks of colluding through their shared 'Link' cash dispenser network to set fees for withdrawing cash at an unreasonably high level which bore no relation to actual costs incurred.

■ The Competition Commission doesn't just involve itself with national organizations – it also investigates local abuse of monopoly power. Since the deregulation of the UK bus industry, the Commission has investigated several alleged anti-competitive practices by bus companies. For example, during an investigation of bus services in Darlington, the Commission found a scale monopoly that acted in favour of the Stagecoach and Go-Ahead Northern bus companies. It found that Stagecoach recruited most of the drivers of the ailing Darlington Transport Company, registered services on all its routes and then ran free services, causing the sale of the municipal bus company to fall through and the company to collapse. The Director General of Fair Trading sought undertakings from Stagecoach and Go-Ahead Northern that they would maintain fares and service frequencies for three years after a competitor withdrew from a route, if their lower fares or increased frequencies had been responsible for the competitor withdrawing. The Commission eventually recommended a 12-month fares and frequencies freeze, despite protests by both companies that their behaviour had been in the public interest, pointing to their investment in new vehicles and staff training.

During the 1980 and 1990s, the privatization of many UK public-sector utilities resulted in the creation of new private-sector monopolies. To protect the users of these services from exploitation, the government's response has been two-fold. Firstly, it has sought to increase competition, in the hope that this in itself will be instrumental in moderating price increases. In this way, the electricity generating industry was divided into a number of competing private suppliers (National Power, Powergen, Nuclear Electric, Scottish Power and Scottish Hydro), while conditions were made easier for new generators to enter the market. In some cases, measures to increase competition have had only limited effect, as in the very limited competition faced by the privatized water supply companies. Even within the apparently more competitive telecommunications sector, the regulator has frequently intervened with instructions to operators to reduce specific categories of prices. In 2003, Oftel published the result of an investigation by the Competition Commission into the 'termination charges' levied by mobile phone operators for calls coming in from other networks. The regulator found evidence of overcharging and ordered termination costs to be cut (White, 2003).

Prices may still fly high with deregulated markets

Americans are devoted to the idea that air travel is cheap following deregulation back in the 1970s. But are low prices in fact a myth? Is it enough to simply deregulate a market in order to ensure price competition?

The theory of airline deregulation in the USA was irresistible. Any airline would be allowed to operate on any route, setting its fares as it liked. New airlines soon appeared and initially held down fares through competitive pressures. However, the major carriers have since acquired such a dominant position that US air fares rose on average 20% during 1997 and have risen faster than the general rate of inflation since. What went wrong?

The established airlines have managed to control 'slots' at the principal hub airports, making it difficult for new entrants to obtain slots. Many of the larger airlines have resorted to predatory pricing to keep away newcomers. This involves offering low fares on routes and at times that are competitive with other airlines, but charging higher fares where it has an effective monopoly. Some have argued that airport operators didn't want to rock the boat and were quite happy to put the interests of established carriers first, because these tended to pay higher landing fees than the low-cost 'budget' airlines. The lesson from US airline deregulation is that price competition may be expected in theory, but there are many reasons why it doesn't happen in practice.

For many of the newly privatized monopolies, effective competition proved to be an unrealistic possibility. The result has been the creation of a series of regulatory bodies which can determine the level and structure of charges made by these utilities. Thus British Telecom, British Gas and the regional water companies are controlled by Ofcom, Ofgem and Ofwat respectively. In the case of British Gas, Ofgem regulations allow the company to increase gas supply charges in line with changes in energy prices, but the price charged for ancillary services such as standing charges and repairs can only rise by the rate of inflation, less 2%. The regulatory bodies have power to prohibit any practices which allow the companies to exploit their monopoly position. In one case, Oftel (a predecessor of Ofcom), investigated complaints from rival telephone companies that BT had abused its dominant market position by offering low prices on combined telephone/satellite television packages with BSkyB. Oftel upheld cable television companies' claims that the bulk of BT customers were cross-subsidizing those BT customers who were most vulnerable to competition from cable operators.

10.7.2 Government controls on price representations

In addition to controlling or influencing the actual level of prices, government regulations often specify the manner in which price information is communicated to potential customers. This is particularly important for services which are mentally intangible and for which many customers would be ill-equipped to make valid comparisons between competing suppliers. In the UK, the Competition Act 1998 requires that all prices shown should conform to a code of practice on pricing. Misleading price representations which relegate details of supplementary charges to small print or give attractive low lead-in prices for services which are not in fact available are made illegal by this act. There are other regulations which affect specific industries. The Consumer Credit Act 1974 requires that the charge made for credit must include a statement of the annual percentage rate (APR) of interest. Also, within the financial services sector, the Financial Services Act 1986 has resulted in quite specific requirements in the manner which charges for certain insurance-related services are presented to potential customers.

10.8 Pricing strategy

The fundamental economic, organizational and legal factors which underpin pricing decisions have now been described. This section moves on to analyse how organizations give strategic direction to pricing policy in order that organizational objectives can be met. The challenge here is to make pricing work as an effective element of the marketing mix, combining with the other mix elements to give a service provider a profitable market position. An effective strategy must identify how the role of price is to function as a service goes through different stages in its life from the launch stage through growth to maturity.

This analysis of pricing strategy will consider firstly the development of a strategy for a new service launch and, secondly, price adjustments to established services. In practice, of course, it is often not easy to distinguish between the two situations, as where an existing service is modified or relaunched.

10.9 New service pricing strategy

In developing a price strategy for a new service, two key issues need to be addressed.

1. What price position is sought for the service?

2. How novel is the service offering?

We saw in Chapter 7 that the choice of price position cannot be separated from other elements of the marketing mix. For many consumer services, the price element can reinforce a quality position. This is especially important where consumers have difficulty in distinguishing between competing services before consumption, and the price charged is one of the few – or only – indicators of likely service quality. Private consumers choosing a painter or decorator with no knowledge of their previous work record may be cautious about accepting the cheapest quotation on the basis that it may reflect an inexperienced decorator with a poor quality record.

The novelty of a new service offer can be analysed in terms of whether it is completely new to the market, or merely new to the company providing it, but already available from other sources. In the case of completely new innovative services, the company will have some degree of monopoly power in its early years. On the other hand, the launch of a 'me-too' service to compete with established services is likely to face heavy price competition from its launch stage. The distinction between innovative services and copycat services is the basis of two distinct pricing strategies – 'price skimming' and 'saturation pricing' – which are now examined in more detail.

10.9.1 **Price-skimming strategy**

Most completely new product launches are aimed initially at the segment of buyers who can be labelled 'innovators'. These are buyers who have the resources and inclination to be the trend-setters in purchasing new goods and services. This group includes the first people to buy innovative services such as mobile photo messaging. Following these will be a group of early adopters, followed by a larger group often described as the 'early majority'. The subsequent 'late majority' group may only take up the new service once the market itself has reached maturity. Laggards are the last group to adopt a new service and do so only when the product has become a social norm and/or its price has fallen sufficiently (diffusion models are described in the following chapter).

Price-skimming strategies seek to gain the highest possible price from the early adopters. When sales to this segment appear to be approaching saturation level, the price level is lowered in order to appeal to the early adopter segment which has a lower price threshold at which it is prepared to purchase the service. This process is repeated for the following adoption categories.

The art of effective pricing of innovative services is to identify who the early adopters are, how much they are prepared to pay and how long this price can be sustained before competitors come on the scene with imitation services at a lower price. A price-skimming strategy works by gradually lowering prices to gain access to new segments and to protect market share against new market entrants. Pricing strategy is therefore closely related to the concept of the product life cycle and a typical price-skimming strategy showing price levels through time is shown in Figure 10.8(a), see page 369.

While the above analysis may be true of services bought by private consumers, is the same effect likely to be true for services bought by businesses? A business buyer is less likely to want to be a trend-setter for its own sake, although individuals within an organization may gain status by being the first to have an innovative service. Sometimes, using a new service ahead of competitors can give a forward-thinking firm a price advantage over its competitors (e.g. the first courier delivery companies to equip their fleets of vehicles with geographical positioning systems gained cost advantages over their competitors and were able to offer a better service to customers).

For many innovative services, the trend of falling prices may be further enhanced by falling costs. Lower costs can occur due to economies of scale (e.g. the cost per

> ### How many pints of beer is a phone call worth?
>
> To what extent do buyers of services shop around and compare prices when choosing between competing services? Do they even have any idea of a baseline price for a category of service? The BT Business Price Perception Survey suggests that even business buyers – who are sometimes thought to act with greater economic rationality than private buyers – are often wide of the mark when it comes to understanding services prices. In its 1997 survey, it found knowledge of telephone prices to be particularly bad, probably reflecting the plethora of price plans which have emerged in recent years. Respondents gave the average price of a five-minute peak national call as £2.15, whereas in fact it was only 44p. Another service sector with confusing price structures is railways. Here, respondents estimated the price of a second-class return ticket from London to Edinburgh at £54, compared to the actual price of £64. By contrast to the wide variations in service price estimates, respondents were quite accurate in their assessment of the price of a pint of beer. The average estimate of £1.73 for a pint of lager was just 2p off the true average. What does this say about service companies' pricing policies? Has the process of price discrimination been taken so far that it leaves buyers confused? Is there sometimes a case for adopting an 'everyday low price' approach by offering a limited number of prices for a given service, something which has been adopted by many of the new low-cost, no-frills airlines?

customer of providing the technical support for a home shopping service declines as fixed costs are spread over more volume of throughput) and also to the experience effect. The latter refers to the process by which costs fall as experience in production is gained. It is of particular strategic significance to service industries, since by pursuing a strategy to gain experience faster than its competitors, an organization lowers its cost base and has greater scope for adopting an aggressive pricing strategy. The combined effects of these two factors can be seen in the UK mobile phone market, where high initial prices have been brought down by the ability of network operators to spread their capital costs over increasing numbers of users. Also, operators have learnt from experience how a given level of service can be provided more efficiently, for example through adjusting transmitter locations.

10.9.2 Saturation-pricing strategy

Many 'new' services are launched as copies of existing competitors' services. In the absence of unique features, a low initial price can be used to encourage people who show little brand loyalty to switch service suppliers. Once an initial trial has been made, a service provider would seek to develop increased loyalty from its customers, as a result of which they may be prepared to pay progressively higher prices. A saturation pricing strategy is shown diagrammatically in Figure 10.8(b).

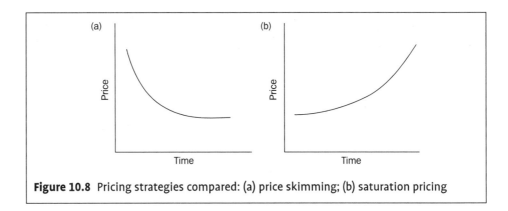

Figure 10.8 Pricing strategies compared: (a) price skimming; (b) saturation pricing

The success of a saturation-pricing strategy is dependent upon a sound under-standing of the buying behaviour of the target market; in particular, the following aspects.

- *The level of knowledge which consumers have about prices.* For some services, such as the rate of interest charged on credit cards, consumers typically have little idea of the charge which they are currently paying, or indeed of the 'going rate' for such charges. There is now considerable research showing the effects of consumers' knowledge of prices on their buying behaviour (e.g. Dickson and Sawyer, 1990; Wakefield and Inman, 1993). Any attempt to attract new customers on the basis of a differential price advantage may prove unsuccessful if knowledge of prices is low. Other incentives (e.g. free gifts or money-off vouchers) may be more effective at inducing new business. Sometimes, companies offering a diverse range of services may offer low prices on services where price comparisons are commonly made, but charge higher prices on other related services where consumer knowledge is lower. Customers of solicitors may shop around for a standard service such as house conveyancing, but may be more reluctant to do so when faced with a non-routine purchase such as civil litigation.

- *The extent to which the service supplier can increase prices on the basis of perceived added value of the service offering.* The purpose of a low initial price is to encourage new users of a service to try it and return later, paying progressively higher prices. If the new competitor's service is perceived to offer no better value than is offered by the existing supplier, the disloyalty which caused the initial switching could result in a switching back at a later date in response to a competitor's tactical pricing. Worse still, a new service could be launched and experience teething troubles in its early days, doing nothing to generate a perception of added value.

- *The extent to which the service supplier can turn a casually gained relationship into a long-term committed relationship.* Incentives are frequently offered to lessen the attractiveness of switching away from the service provider. These can take the form of a subscription rate for regular purchase of a service, or offering an ever-increasing range of services which together raise the cost to the consumer of transferring his or her business elsewhere. Banks may offer easy transfers between various savings and investment accounts and, in doing so, aim to reduce the attractiveness of moving one element of the customer's business elsewhere. A loyalty programme can have the effect of tying a customer to a seller.

Price alone won't sell burgers

How easily swayed are consumers of fast food by a price cut? The market for fast food in the USA and western Europe has become increasingly saturated, leading McDonald's, the market leader, to reverse its expansionary policies with a worldwide programme of branch closures in 2002. In that year, it announced the first annual loss in its history. The woes of the burger market came despite vigorous price competition by the company. One campaign in the USA during 1997 cost $200 million in promotion and involved reducing the cost of a Big Mac from $1.90 to 55 cents. But price alone seemed to have little effect in the continuing war against arch-rival Burger King. The heart of the problem seemed to be that baby-boomers had got older and cared more about taste and healthy eating. Yet armies of fast-food critics argued that McDonald's had failed to improve the taste and range of its meals in the 1990s as much as its rivals, to the point where even price-cutting would not prevent customers wandering down the road to the second-rated Burger King or third-place Wendys. A Big Mac, it seemed, had become substitutable with an ever-widening range of fast food, and it was no longer able to command a price premium.

Lowballing among solicitors

Solicitors in the UK have traditionally enjoyed a high professional status in which high charges and slow service almost became an expectation. But a series of measures at deregulation (for example, the authorization of licensed conveyancers to share the solicitors' previous monopoly on house conveyancing) has led to much greater price awareness among buyers. This has been particularly true in the case of legal services provided to businesses, where many companies now routinely shop around for the lowest priced solicitors. The old loyalty of client to lawyer has waned as clients are seduced by the lure of low fees elsewhere. But are legal services a commodity which buyers can shop around for as and when they are required? Lawyers argue that the practice of 'lowballing' (offering very low fees to attract business) can create problems for the client as well as for the lawyer. Clients may believe that by holding down fees on professionals who are guaranteed to provide a competent service, they have nothing to lose by going for the cheapest possible deal. But are those practices which are willing to provide services at rock bottom prices likely to try to achieve a profit by cutting corners? Rather than offering low fees, is there a significant segment of business clients who would prefer value to be added to a business relationship, for example by organizing seminars on subjects of topical legal interest?

In some cases, a high initial uptake of a new service may itself add value to the service offering. This can be true where co-production of benefits among consumers is important. A telecommunications operator offering data exchange facilities will be able to offer a more valuable service if large numbers of users are contracted to its system, offering more communications possibilities for potential new users. In the same way, airport landing slots become increasingly valuable to an airline as an airport becomes progressively busier, as each airline is able to offer a more comprehensive and valuable set of potential connections to customers. In both cases, a low initial price may be critical to gain entry to a market, while raising prices is consistent with increasing value to the users of the service.

10.9.3 Evaluating strategic pricing options

In practice, pricing strategies often contain elements of skimming and saturation strategies. The fact that most new services are in fact adaptations and are easy to copy often prevents a straightforward choice of strategy. Even when a price strategy has been adopted and implemented, it may run off target for a number of reasons.

■ Poor market research may have misjudged potential customers' willingness to pay for a new service. As an example, National Westminster Bank sought to charge personal customers £30 for using its then innovative Internet-based banking service, 'NatWest Online'. Take-up was reported to be less than expected, with the result that the charge was abolished soon after launch. A service provider may have misjudged the effect of price competition from other services, which, although different in form, satisfied the same basic needs.

■ Competitors may emerge sooner or later than expected. The fact that new services can often be copied easily and quickly can result in a curtailment of the period during which an organization can expect to achieve relatively high prices. As an example, an optician opening the first eye care centre in an expanding market town may expect to enjoy a few years of higher price levels before competitors drive down price levels, only to find that another optician had a similar idea and opens a second eye care centre shortly afterwards.

■ The effects of government regulation may be to extend or shorten the period during which a company has a protected market for its new service. The announcement by the British government in 1991 that it was to license a number of new cellular telephone networks had the effect of bringing forward the time when the existing operators had to face fiercer price competition.

10.9.4 **Price leader or follower?**

Many services markets are characterized by a small number of dominant suppliers and a large number of smaller ones. Perfect competition and pure monopoly are two extremes which rarely occur in practice. In markets which show some signs of interdependency among suppliers, firms can often be described as price-makers or price-followers. Price-makers tend to be those who as a result of their size and power within a market are able to determine the levels and patterns of prices which other suppliers then follow. Within the UK insurance industry, the largest firms in the market often lead changes in rate structures. Price-takers, on the other hand, tend to have a relatively low size and market share, and may lack product differentiation, resources or management drive to adopt a proactive pricing strategy. Smaller estate agents in a local area may find it convenient to simply respond to pricing policies adopted by the dominant firms – to take a proactive role themselves may bring about a reaction from the dominant firms which they would be unable to defend on account of their size and standing in the market.

10.10 **Service portfolio pricing**

Multi-output service providers usually set the price of a new service in relation to the prices charged for other services within their portfolio. A number of product relationships within a product portfolio can be identified for pricing purposes:

- optional additional services
- captive services
- competing services.

Optional additional services

These are the service that a consumer chooses whether or not to add to the core service purchase, often at the time that the core service is purchased. As a matter of strategy, an organization could seek to charge a low lead-in price for its core service, but to recoup a higher margin from the additional optional services. Simply breaking a service into core and optional components may allow for the presentation of lower price indicators, which through a process of rationalization may be more acceptable to buyers. Research may show that the price of the core service is in fact the only factor which buyers take into account when choosing between alternative services. In this way, many travel agents and tour operators cut their margins on the core holiday which they sell, but make up some of their margin by charging higher mark-ups for optional extras such as travel insurance policies and car hire.

Captive services

These occur where the core service has been purchased and the provision of additional services can only be provided by the original provider of the core service.

Where these are not specified at the outset of purchasing the core service, or are left to the discretion of the service provider, the latter is in a strong position to charge a high price. Against this, the company must consider the effect which the perception of high exploitative prices charged for these captive services will have on customer loyalty when a service contract comes due for renewal. An example of captive service pricing is provided by many car insurance companies who, after selling the core insurance policy, can treat the sale of a 'green card' (which extends cover beyond the geographical limits defined in the policy) as a captive sale.

Competing services

These, within a company's portfolio, occur where a new service targets a segment of the population which overlaps the segments served by other products within the portfolio. By a process of 'cannibalization', a service provider could find that it is competing with itself. In this way, an airline offering a low-priced direct service from Glasgow to Frankfurt may find that the low price – in addition to generating completely new business – has an important side-effect in abstracting traffic from its connecting services from Glasgow to London and from London to Frankfurt.

10.10.1 **Price bundling**

Price bundling is the practice of marketing two or more services in a single package for a single price. Bundling is particularly important for services on account of two common characteristics of services. Firstly, the high ratio of fixed to variable costs which characterizes many service organizations makes the allocation of costs between different services difficult and sometimes arbitrary. Secondly, there is often a high level of interdependency between different types of service output from an organization. In this way, the provision of an ATM card and cheque guarantee card becomes an interdependent part of the current bank account offering which most UK banks do not charge for separately. For some services, the administrative cost of charging for individual elements of a service offer may cost as much as the provision of the service itself. (For example, Internet Service Providers realized from an early stage that it would not be practical to charge for each individual e-mail message that is sent, because the amount of information that would have to be transmitted to create a bill may be more than the amount of information transmitted by the e-mail message itself.)

Price bundling of diverse services from an organization's service portfolio is frequently used as a means of building relationships with customers. In this way, a mortgage could be bundled with a household contents insurance policy or a legal protection policy. Where the bundle of service represents ease of administration to the consumer, the service organization may be able to achieve a price for the bundle which is greater than the combined price of the bundle's components.

'Pure' bundling occurs where services are only available in a bundled form (e.g. where a tour operator includes insurance in all of its package holidays), whereas 'mixed' bundling allows customers to choose which specific elements of the service offering they wish to purchase. In his study of price bundling, Guiltinan (1987) showed that as service firms expand their range of service outputs, simple cost-based or price-follower strategies become too simplistic for two reasons. Firstly, as the number of services offered increases, the opportunities for differentiation and bundling are enhanced. Secondly, the high ratio of fixed to variable costs typical of many services industries makes cost-based pricing increasingly arbitrary as fixed cost allocations change with the expansion of the service range. Bundling reduces the need to allocate fixed costs to individual services.

A service provider may feel compelled to bundle services in a way which is in accordance with consumers' expectations, leading to the development of a dominant pricing model. Sometimes, this standard pricing model is challenged by a new entrant, with the result that consumers' expectations are changed. The effect of dominant pricing models can be seen in the development of Internet Service Providers (ISPs) in the UK. Until 1998, the dominant pricing model for ISPs serving the private consumer market was a monthly fee giving entitlement to a specified number of hours online. In 1998, Freeserve challenged this pricing model by making its service free to consumers, but made up the income loss by selling advertising banner space and recouping a percentage of the amount consumers paid in telephone calls. Shortly afterwards, the majority of ISPs were forced to respond by copying Freeserve's pricing model.

Although price bundling may appear attractive to many service organizations, there are dangers that they may fall foul of competition legislation. In the UK, the Office of Fair Trading has investigated the anti-competitive effects of mortgage lenders bundling household insurance with their core offer and of travel agents bundling insurance with package holidays. In both cases, firms were held to be abusing their position to sell these additional services.

10.11 Tactical pricing

In practice, manoeuvrability around the central pricing strategy will be needed to allow detailed local application of the overall strategy. This is the role of tactical pricing. The distinction between strategic and tactical pricing can sometimes be difficult to draw. In highly competitive, undifferentiated services markets, the development of tactical plans can be all important and assume much greater importance than for a service where an organization has more opportunity for developing a distinctive strategic price position. Some of the tactical uses of pricing are analysed below.

- Tactical pricing can provide short-term competitive advantage. Periodic price reductions can be a means of inducing potential customers to try a service, whether it is new or established. The price cut can be a general across-the-board reduction, or it could be targeted (e.g. by the use of vouchers). The extent of the uptake will be dependent on the importance of price comparisons, the extent to which consumers of that type of service typically make casual purchases and are not tied to a relationship with another supplier (e.g. lower single bus fares may result in little additional demand if a large proportion of travellers are tied to a season ticket with another operator) and consumers' perceptions of the price offer. Economic rationality may expect that sales of a service will increase as its price is reduced. However, the price reduction may reduce the perceived value of a service, leading to a feeling that its quality has been eroded. Subsequent price increases may lead to the feeling that the service is over-priced if it could be offered previously at a lower price. There may also be significant price points at which a service is perceived as being of good value. A trans-Atlantic air ticket priced at £199 may be perceived as offering much better value than a ticket priced at £200.

Even if economic rationality is assumed on the part of consumers, it can be difficult to predict the effects of a price change. Comparison with previous occasions when price was adjusted assumes that all other factors are the same, whereas in reality, many factors, such as the availability of competitors' services and general macro- environmental considerations require some judgement to be made about how a similar price change might perform this time around.

- Tactical pricing can be used to remove unplanned excess supply. The strategic price position sought by an organization may be incapable of achievement on account of excess supply, both within the organization and within the market generally. A temporary price cut can be used to bring demand and supply back into balance. Pricing can also be used to capitalize on excess demand relative to supply. In addition to removing discounts and increasing prices, firms can remove low-margin elements from their service portfolio in order to maximize their returns from high-margin lines.

- Short-term tactical pricing can be used to protect markets against new entrants. Where a new entrant threatens the existing market of an established supplier, the latter may react with short-term price reductions where price comparisons are commonly made. If the new entrant is a small opportunist company seeking to make inroads into the larger dominant firm's market, a low price may force the new company to respond with low prices, putting strain on its initial cash flow and possibly resulting in its withdrawal from the market, if not ceasing to trade completely. Many established operators of a bus route have responded to new market entrants by lowering their prices or even running free buses, in the hope that they might drive the new competitor out of the market. However, such pricing may be deemed anti-competitive by regulatory agencies.

- Differential pricing with respect to time which may have been part of the strategic pricing plan can be implemented by a number of tactical programmes. Off-peak discounts are frequently used in industries such as rail travel, telecommunications and hotels. The converse of peak surcharges can also be employed, for example the supplementary charge levied by train operators for travel on certain West Country holiday trains during the busiest summer weekends. Other options include offering added-value price bundles at certain periods (e.g. shopping vouchers for off-peak cross-Channel car ferry passengers) and subtly altering a service offering and making it available only at certain times (e.g. a restaurant may slightly differentiate lunch from dinner and charge more for the latter on account of the willingness of customers to pay more for an evening social meal).

- Similarly, differential pricing with respect to place must be translated from a strategic plan to a tactical programme. Implementing differential pricing by area is relatively easy for services on account of the difficulty in transferring service consumption. Hotels and shops – among others – often use different price lists for different locations, depending upon the local competitive position and such lists are often adjusted at short notice to respond to local competitive pressure. Sometimes a common base price is offered at all of an organization's service outlets, and tactical objectives are achieved by means of discounts which are only available at certain locations. Reduced-price vouchers offered by a national hotel chain may have their validity restricted to those locations where demand is relatively weak. In some cases, companies advertise a number of core services nationally at a fixed rate, while related services are priced according to local market conditions.

- For differential pricing between different consumer segments, the problem of turning a strategy into a tactical programme hinges on the ease with which segments can be isolated and charged different prices. Because services are consumed at the point of production, it is often easy to confine price differences within small segments of a market. In this way, cinemas are able to ensure that only students are able to use reduced-price student tickets by asking for identification as the service process is being undertaken. Sometimes the implementation of a highly segmented pricing programme can cause problems for service providers where compromise needs to be made between the desire for small, homogeneous segments and the need for segments which are of a worthwhile size to service. As an example, UK train operators place all elderly people in one segment which is offered a low-price Senior Citizen Railcard. However, the simplicity of this large homogeneous segment is offset by the fact that many people in it are well off and less price sensitive, and may even be travelling on business. There is also the problem with this form of price segmentation that goodwill can be harmed where arguments develop over a customer's eligibility for a particular price offer (see Figure 10.9).

- Tactical pricing programmes are used to motivate intermediaries. Where a service is provided through an intermediary, the difference between the price that a customer pays and the amount that the service principal receives represents the intermediary's margin. In some cases, the price sensitivity of the final consumer is low, but awareness of margins by the intermediary high, requiring tactical pricing to be directed at maintaining intermediaries' margins relative to those offered by competitors. An example is provided by holiday insurance offered by travel agents – customers do not typically shop around for this ancillary item of a package

Julia's Salon

PRICE LIST

Cut	Ladies	£25
	Gentlemen	£17
Cut and blow dry	Ladies	£32
	Gentlemen	£25
Permanent waving	from	£42
Colouring		by quotation
Highlights		by quotation

SPECIAL RATES

Senior citizens	10% off all prices Monday–Thursday only
Students	20% off on Wednesday afternoon
Children	25% off all prices

Figure 10.9 It is not just large service organizations that practise price discrimination. Many smaller businesses, such as this hairdressing salon, charge different prices for different groups, typically offering discounts for students and senior citizens. Price discrimination would work for a haircut (unlike most goods), because one person cannot buy a cheap haircut and sell it on to another person who is not eligible for a lower price. However, even small businesses must ensure that discriminatory pricing does not create feelings of resentment from those who pay a higher price for an essentially similar service.

holiday, but travel agents themselves decide which policy to recommend to their clients largely on the basis of the commission level they can earn. Price charged to the final consumer can also affect an intermediary's motivation to sell a principal's service – if the agent perceives the selling price to be too high, they may give up trying to promote it in favour of a more realistic and attractive competitor. On the other hand, if the price is too low, intermediaries working on a percentage commission basis may consider that the reward for them is not worth their effort.

10.12 Pricing strategies for public-sector services

It was noted at the beginning of this chapter that price is often a very constrained element of the marketing mix for public services where there is much less freedom to implement the strategies and tactics of pricing described above. At one extreme, some publicly provided services can operate in a market-mediated environment where pricing policies do not differ significantly from the private sector – indeed, legislation frequently requires such services to act as though they were a private-sector operator. Local authority operated bus services are such an example. At the other extreme, some public services can only sensibly be distributed by centrally planned methods where price loses its role as a means of exchange of value.

The pricing of services which, by their very nature require a high degree of central planning, but which are expected to exhibit some degree of marketing orientation, presents particular challenges for marketers. It may be difficult or undesirable to implement a straightforward price–value relationship with individual service users for a number of reasons.

■ External benefits may be generated by a service which are difficult or impossible for the service provider to appropriate from individual users. For example, road users within the UK have not generally been charged directly for the benefits which they receive from the road system. This reflects the technical difficulties in appropriating charges from users and the political problem that access to road space is deemed to be a 'birthright' which should not be restricted by direct charging. Nevertheless, the London 'Congestion Charge' (Figure 10.10) shows how change in the technical and political environment has allowed governments to charge more directly for road space used.

Figure 10.10 With the exception of toll bridges and some toll motorways, roads have been provided throughout Europe without a specific charge being made to users. Instead, road users have paid through general taxation and specific taxes on motor-related expenditure (e.g. an annual licence fee and tax on petrol). For a long time, this system was seen as the fairest and – just as importantly – the most practical way of paying for roads. More recently, improvements in technology and worsening problems of congestion have led to a search for alternative forms of road pricing. The Congestion Charge was introduced in London in 2003, requiring drivers in a specified area to pay a fee of £5 per day to use their car there. The results provide evidence that pricing a public service can change consumers' behaviour, with traffic volumes reported to have fallen by 16% in the months following the introduction of the charge. Further UK towns are now studying the feasibility of road pricing in their areas.

- The benefits to society at large may be as significant as the benefits received by the individual who is the immediate recipient of a public service. An early argument for the free provision of doctors' services was that society as a whole benefited from an individual being cured of a disease, and therefore not spreading it to other members of the community. Similarly, education and training courses may be provided at below cost in order to add to the level of skills available within an economy generally.

- Pricing can be actively used as a means of social policy. Subsidized prices are often used to favour particular groups, for example prescription charges are related to consumers' ability to pay, with exemption for the very ill and unemployed, among others. Communication programmes are often used by public services to make the public aware of the preferential prices to which they may be eligible. Sometimes, the interests of marketing orientation and social policy can overlap. For example, reduced admission prices to museums for the unemployed may at the same time both help a disadvantaged group within society, while generating additional overall revenue through segmenting the market in terms of ability to pay.

Problems can occur in public services which have been given a largely financial, market-oriented brief, but in which social policy objectives are superimposed, possibly in conflict. Museums, leisure centres and car park charges have frequently been at the centre of debate about the relative importance of economic and social objectives. One solution which has sometimes been adopted is to split a service into two distinct components, one part being an essentially public service which is provided for the benefit of society at large, and the other part comprising those elements which are indistinguishable from commercially provided services. In this way, museums have often retained free entry or nominally priced admission charges for the serious, scholarly elements of their exhibits, while offering special exhibitions which match the private sector in the standard of production and the prices charged.

10.13 **Internal market pricing**

The development of matrix-type organizations (discussed further in Chapter 12) can result in significant internal trading of services occurring within an organization. Services that are commonly traded internally include photocopying, cleaning, transport and catering. Very often, the price at which services are traded between a department which uses a resource and a department which produces that resource does not reflect a competitive market price – indeed, a market as such may not exist. Setting transfer prices can raise a number of issues for an organization, even where external market prices can readily be ascertained. Allowing users of resources to purchase their services from the cheapest source – internal or external – could result in the in-house supplier losing volume to the point where it ceases to be viable. This could result in the loss of an internal facility to perform specialized jobs which cannot easily be handled by outside contractors. By allowing part of its requirements to be bought in from outside, an organization may increase the loss incurred by its internal supplier, while adding to the profits of outside companies. The internal pricing of services therefore needs to reconcile the possibly conflicting requirements of the in-house production unit to make profits and maintain some capacity, against the resource users' requirements to minimize their total expenditure.

A number of possible solutions to the problem of internal pricing can be identified.

- If an external market exists, a 'shadow' price can be imputed to the transfer, reflecting what the transaction would have cost had it been bought in from outside.

- Where no external market exists, bargaining between divisional managers can take place, although the final outcome may be a reflection of the relative bargaining strength of each manager.

- Corporate management could instruct all divisions to trade on an agreed full cost-pricing basis.

- A system of dual pricing can be adopted where selling divisions receive a market price (where this can be identified) while the buying division pays the full cost of production. Any difference is transferred to corporate accounts.

- A proportion of the internal service producer's fixed costs can be spread over all resource users as a standing charge, regardless of whether they actually use the services of the unit. This would enable the internal supplier to compete on price relatively easily, while still allowing resource users for whom a higher standard of service is worth paying a premium to buy in their requirements from outside.

Public services which are provided free of charge to users are nevertheless often traded within the public sector on the basis of price. During the 1990s, the UK National Health Service moved from being a centrally planned organization to one which was based on negotiated contracts between hospitals that provide care services and the health authorities and fund-holding general practitioners who buy services on behalf of their patients. The fund-holding health authorities and GPs clearly wanted their funds to buy the best available care for their patients at the lowest possible price. The early days of internal trade within the National Health Service saw many of the pricing problems commonly associated with internal trading. The wide discrepancies in prices quoted by different hospitals for the same operation reflected a lack of costing information on which prices were based and the high level of overhead costs associated with many medical facilities. The prospect emerged of whole hospitals suddenly being closed because of their lack of price competitiveness, undoing the benefits of centralized planning which had sought to balance supply and demand for specialized facilities at a regional level. The problems of effectively managing an internal price-led market for health services subsequently resulted in greater resort to centralized planning and resource allocation through Primary Care Groups.

Case study

Manchester to London for £19 – or £286?

Visitors to Britain are often confused by the seemingly endless range of ticket prices for a journey between two points. French rail users, for example, are accustomed to no more than five or six possible prices for a journey. Compare this with a train journey from Manchester to London, where in 2004 the ticket booking website www.thetrainline.com indicated no fewer than 23 different fares.

Some British train fares – mainly standard single and return fares – are regulated by the Office of Rail Regulation (Ofrail), but privatized rail operators are generally free to set their own prices for promotional fares. A number of market segments have been identified and a distinctive marketing mix has been developed for each. The business traveller typically has a need for the flexibility of travelling at any time of the day and because an employer is often picking up the bill, this segment tends to be relatively insensitive to the price charged. Some segments of the business market demand higher standards of quality and are prepared to pay a price of £286.80 for a 'Virgin Business First' executive package from Manchester to London. This includes 'first class' accommodation and additional services such as meals and car parking. Leisure segments are on the whole more price sensitive and prepared to accept a lower level of flexibility. Those who are able to book their ticket one week in advance can pay just £19 for a return ticket from Manchester to London.

A keen eye is kept on the competition in determining prices. Students are more likely than business travellers to accept the coach as an alternative and therefore the Manchester to London student Saver rail fare of £32 is pitched against the equivalent student coach fare of £20, the higher rail fare being justified on the basis of a superior service offering. For the business traveller, the comparison is with the cost of running a car, parking in London and, more importantly, the cost of an employed person's time. Against these costs, the executive fare of £286.60 may be perceived as being good value. For the family market, the family car presents the most serious competition, so a family discount railcard allows the family as a unit to travel for the price of little more than two adults. Airlines have become important competitors on longer routes such as London–Glasgow and London–Edinburgh, where off-peak book-ahead fares with easyJet and Ryanair are often cheaper than the train.

The underlying cost of a train journey is difficult to determine as a basis for pricing. Fixed costs have to be paid by train-operating companies to Network Rail for the use of the track and terminals. In addition, trains and staff represent a fixed cost, although many companies have sought to make these more flexible. Companies recognize that trains operating in the morning and afternoon peak periods cost more to operate, as fixed costs of vehicles used solely for the peak period cannot be spread over other off-peak periods. The underlying costs of running commuter trains have been cited publicly by train-operating companies as the reason for increasing season ticket prices by greater than the rate of inflation during recent years, although the fact that commuters often have no realistic alternative means of transport may have also been an important consideration in raising prices.

The political environment has had an important effect on rail-pricing policies. Before the 1960s, railways were seen as essentially a public service and fares were charged on a seemingly equitable basis that was related to operating costs. Fares were charged strictly on a cost per mile basis, with a distinction between first and second class, and a system of cheap day returns which existed largely through tradition. From the 1960s, British Rail moved away from social objectives with the introduction of business objectives. With this came recognition that pricing must be used to maximize revenue rather than to provide social equality. However, government intervention occasionally came into conflict with British Rail's business objectives – for example, it was instructed to curtail fare increases during the 1980s as part of the government's anti-inflation policy and again in the autumn of 1991 it was instructed to reduce some proposed Inter City fare increases on account of the poor quality of service on some routes.

The privatization of British Railways in the mid-1990s led to further developments in pricing. Recognizing the importance of maintaining an integrated passenger network, the government appointed a regulator of rail services with powers to specify fares charged for a range of types of tickets and to ensure that through tickets are still available for journeys that involve more than one rail company. However, the newly privatized companies exploited opportunities to offer new types of tickets targeted at different segments of the population. Virgin Railways used the experience of its airline to promote book-ahead tickets through its website (www.virgintrains.co.uk) which offers bargain prices to fill off-peak capacity. At the same time, signs of genuine price competition between rival rail operators began to appear. Segments of the London–Scotland market were contested by Great North Eastern Railways and Virgin, while Chiltern Railways sought to appeal to the price sensitivity of travellers from Birmingham to London.

Privatization had resulted in a huge range of new marketing initiatives, and a seemingly bewildering array of special ticket prices has appeared from each of the rail franchise operators. With titles such as 'Virgin Value 7' and 'Network Stayaway', the public had become confused by the choices available. As a result, the Train Operators' Association, which represents the franchise operators, agreed to co-operate in offering just six 'families' of ticket types, based on the validity of the ticket.

Case study review questions

1. Should governments intervene to regulate rail fares?

2. Evaluate the financial benefits to rail operators of offering reduced fares to students.

3. Are train fares too expensive?

Chapter summary and links to other chapters

The prices charged by an organization are the result of a range of factors, including the organization's objectives, the nature of the service and the competitiveness of the market in which it operates. Very big differences frequently exist in the price charged for two identical services. This reflects the ability of many service firms to practise price discrimination between different groups of customers and a high level of fixed costs which allows services to be charged at low marginal costs. The perishability of services further encourages wide variation in prices charged for a service.

Pricing is a crucial tool in the management of peaks and troughs in demand (**Chapter 13**). In many cases, a service offered at one time is totally different to that offered at another (**Chapter 2**). A high-priced ticket for a commuter train may be no substitute for a lower priced ticket which is only available on off-peak trains. In circumstances where it is difficult to evaluate a service prior to consumption, customers use price as an indicator of the expected quality of a service (**Chapters 8**). Pricing is also an important part of many service organizations' relationship marketing strategies (**Chapter 5**). On the one hand, price discounts are often given to reward loyalty, but, on the other hand, firms would expect loyal customers to be less price sensitive. Finally, price is one aspect of the positioning of an organization and its service offers, and the price position adopted must be consistent with positions adopted with respect to quality, accessibility and promotion (**Chapters 8, 9 and 11**).

Chapter review questions

1. What is the relationship between product life cycle theory and pricing strategy?

2. Give examples to illustrate situations where price competitiveness may be largely absent in services markets.

3. Analyse the product mix of a diverse service organization and identify the pricing strategies used to increase total revenue.

4. Using examples, compare the advantages and disadvantages of cost-plus and marginal cost pricing.

5. Using a service company of your choice, analyse how price discrimination is practised between different groups of customers.

6. Examine the role that is likely to be played by pricing for a local authority owned leisure centre.

Activity

Gather together price lists from a selection of any of the following services organizations in your area: sports centres; cinemas/theatres; restaurants. Analyse their pricing and the extent to which cost-based, customer-based and competitor-based pricing is being applied.

Key terms

Cookie A small programme embedded in a computer which collects information that can be forwarded and interrogated by a remote computer.

Cost-plus pricing A pricing method in which a percentage mark-up is added to the costs of producing a product.

Customer lifetime pricing An approach to pricing which is based on developing a profitable long-term relationship with customers.

Demand The willingness and ability of buyers to buy a particular product at a particular time at a given price.

Discriminatory pricing Selling a product at two or more prices, where the difference in prices is not based on differences in costs.

Fixed costs Costs that do not increase as total output increases.

Going rate price A uniform price charged within a market for an essentially similar product.

Marginal cost The addition to total cost resulting from the production of one additional unit of output.

Price bundling Charging a combined price for a number of service elements, rather than setting prices for each individual element.

Selected further reading

For a general overview of the principles of effective pricing, the following are useful.
Nagle, T. and Holden, R. (2001) *The Strategy and Tactics of Pricing*, Prentice Hall, New Jersey.
Gourville, J. and Soman, D. (2002) 'Pricing and the psychology of consumption', *Harvard Business Review*, 80 (9), 90–6.
Trout, J. and Rivkin, S. (1998) 'Prices: Simple guidelines to get them right', *Journal of Business Strategy*, 19 (6), 13–17.

The intangible nature of services and the problems which this can give rise to in consumers' pre-purchase evaluation are discussed in the following.
Docters, R., Reopel, M., Sun, J.-M. and Tanny, S. (2004) 'Capturing the unique value of services: Why pricing of services is different', *Journal of Business Strategy*, 25 (2), 23–8.

Berry, L.L. and Yadav, M.S. (1996) 'Capture and communicate value in the pricing of services', *Sloan Management Review*, Summer, 41–51.

Yelkur, R. and Herbig, P. (1997) 'Differential pricing for services', *Marketing Intelligence and Planning*, 15 (4–5), 190–5.

The following papers discuss how multi-product service firms can effectively price combinations of different services rather than selling individual services in isolation.

Naylor, G. and Frank, K.E. (2001) 'The effect of price bundling on consumer perceptions of value', *Journal of Services Marketing*, 15 (4), 270–81.

Guiltinan, J.P. (1987) 'The price bundling of services: A normative framework', *Journal of Marketing*, 51 (April), 74–85.

The impact of the Internet on pricing is discussed in the following.

Carr, N.G. (1999) 'Redesigning business', *Harvard Business Review*, 177 (6), 19.

Yelkur, R. and DaCosta, M.M.N. (2001) 'Differential pricing and segmentation on the Internet: The case of hotels', *Management Decision*, 39 (4), 252–62.

References

Bicknell, C. (2000), 'The Amazon story', *Wired News*, 21 July.

Cyert, R.M. and March, J.G. (1963) *A Behavioural Theory of the Firm*, Prentice-Hall, Englewood Cliffs, NJ.

Dickson, P.R. and Sawyer, A.G. (1990) 'The price knowledge and search of supermarket shoppers', *Journal of Marketing*, 54 (July), 42–53.

Guiltinan, J.P. (1987) 'The price bundling of services: A normative framework', *Journal of Marketing*, 51 (April), 74–85.

Streitfeld, D. (2002) 'Ads on web don't click', *Washington Post*, 29 October, 1.

Timmins, N. (2003) 'A bid to save money for the government: Online auctions', *Financial Times*, 29 January, 12.

Wakefield, K.L. and Inman, J.J. (1993) 'Who are the price vigilantes? An investigation of differentiating characteristics influencing price information processing', *Journal of Retailing*, 69, 216–33.

White, D. (2003) 'Mobile pricing riles operators', *Daily Telegraph*, 18 January.

Zeithaml, V.A., Parasuraman, A. and Berry, L.L. (1985) 'Problems and strategies in services marketing', *Journal of Marketing*, 49 (Spring), 33–46.

Promoting services

Learning objectives

This chapter will explain:

- the effects of service intangibility on buyers' perception of riskiness, and the role of promotion to address this perceived risk

- the communication process and its role in reducing perceived risk

- the extended promotional mix for services

- front-line employees' promotional roles

- the importance of word-of-mouth recommendation for services.

11.1 Introduction

Well-developed marketing strategies and tactics should have the effect of reducing reliance on promotion as a means of achieving customer take-up of a service. A well-formulated service offer, distributed through appropriate channels at a price which represents good value to potential customers, places less emphasis on the promotion element of the marketing mix. Nevertheless, few services – especially those provided in competitive markets – can dispense with promotion completely. The purpose of this chapter is to examine the nature of the strategic and tactical decisions which service organizations must take in formulating this element of the marketing mix.

This chapter considers some of the basic principles of promotion decisions, but places particular emphasis on the distinctive needs of services promotion. These distinctive needs derive from the distinguishing characteristics of services, in particular:

■ the intangible nature of the service offer often results in consumers perceiving a high level of risk in the buying process, which promotion must seek to overcome

■ promotion of a service offer cannot generally be isolated from promotion of the service provider

■ visible production processes, especially service personnel, become an important element of the promotion effort

■ the intangible nature of services and the heightened possibilities for fraud result in their promotion being generally more constrained by legal and voluntary controls than is the case with goods.

The promotion function of any service organization involves the transmission of messages to present, past and potential customers. At the very least, potential customers need to be made aware of the existence of a service. Eventually, in some way, they should be influenced towards purchase and subsequent repurchase.

It should not be forgotten that the promotion industry is a major service sector in its own right. Public relations agencies, direct mail operators and advertising agencies not only provide vital inputs to other firms' marketing efforts, but they themselves have to develop promotional plans for their own business.

11.2 The communication process

Promotion involves an ongoing process of communication between an organization and its target markets. The process is defined by the answers to the following questions.

■ WHO is saying the message?

■ TO WHOM is the message addressed?

■ HOW is the message communicated?

■ To what EFFECT was the communication made?

387

The elements of this process are illustrated in Figure 11.1 and are described in more detail below.

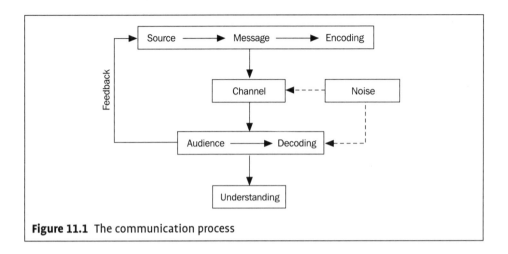

Figure 11.1 The communication process

11.2.1 **To whom is the message addressed**

The most important element of the communication process is the audience at which communication is aimed. The audience of a message determines what is to be said, when it is to be said, where it is to be said and who is to say it. The target audience of a communication must be clearly defined and this can be done in a number of ways.

- The most traditional method of defining audiences is in terms of social, economic, demographic and geographical characteristics. In this way, audiences are defined using parameters such as age, sex, social class, area of residence, etc.

- Audiences can be defined in terms of the level of involvement of potential recipients of the communication – for example, a distinction can be made between those people who are merely *aware* of the existence of a service, those who are *interested* in possibly purchasing the service and those who *wish to purchase* the service.

- An audience can be defined on the basis of target customers' usage frequency (e.g. regular users of an airline are likely to respond to communications in a different way compared to occasional users).

- Similarly, audiences can differ in the benefits which they seek from a category of service. Train operators aim different messages at leisure users who may seek benefits in terms of social togetherness, compared to business users for whom the benefits of speed and reliability are of greatest importance.

- In the case of services supplied to corporate buyers, audiences can be defined in terms of the type and size of business and their geographical location. More importantly, the key decision-makers and influencers must be identified and used in defining the audience (e.g. for many corporate travel services, secretaries can be important in choosing between competing services rather than the actual service user, and should therefore be included in a definition of the target audience).

Having defined its target audience, the communicator must then research a number of its important characteristics. For services, one vital aspect to explore is the audience's image of the organization and its services, and the degree of image consistency among the audience. An image tends to persist over time with people continuing to see what they expect to see rather than what actually exists. The image of a service firm and its service offers can be significantly influenced by how they are delivered and therefore contact personnel play a vital role in the development of this image.

Of course, some elements of an organization's image can be derived through channels other than the formal communication process. There is a lot of evidence, for example, that when differentiating between professional service providers, customers prefer to be guided by information from friends and other personal contacts rather than the usual promotion mix (e.g. Walker, 2001; Susskind, 2002).

A second important characteristic of the audience justifying research is its degree of perceived risk when considering the purchase of a new service. For purchases which are perceived as being highly risky, customers are likely to use more credible sources of information (e.g. word-of-mouth recommendation) and engage in a prolonged search through information sources. People differ markedly in their readiness to try new products and a number of attempts have been made to classify the population in terms of their level of risk-taking. Rogers (1962) defined a person's 'innovativeness' as the 'degree to which an individual is relatively earlier in adopting new ideas than the other members of his social system'. In each product area, there are likely to be 'consumption pioneers' and early adopters, while other individuals only adopt new products much later. This has led to a classification of markets into the following adopter categories:

- innovators

- early adopters

- early majority

- late majority

- laggards.

The **adoption process** is represented as a normal distribution when plotted over time. After a slow start, an increasing number of people adopt the innovation. The number then reaches a peak before diminishing as fewer non-adopters remain. A typical adoption distribution pattern is illustrated in Figure 11.2. Innovators are venturesome in that they try new ideas at some risk. Early adopters are opinion leaders in their community (see below) and adopt new products early but carefully. The early majority adopt new ideas before the average person, taking their lead from opinion leaders. The late majority are sceptical, tending to adopt an innovation only after the majority of people have tried it. Finally, laggards are tradition bound, being

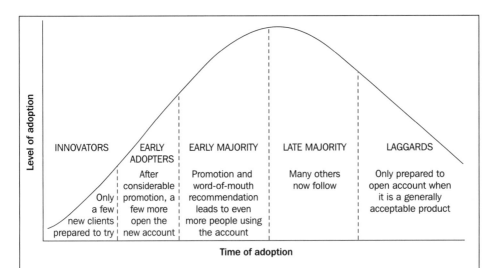

Figure 11.2 A typical buyer adoption pattern for a new type of bank account. This distribution is most likely to apply where the service is highly innovative and consumers are faced with a high level of perceived risk when deciding whether to adopt it. It is less useful for understanding adoption processes for 'copycat' banking services (this pattern may apply to take-up of a new type of UK savings account which offers added-value features, such as advice on equity investments, but not to another basic cheque account).

suspicious of changes. They only adopt a new service when it has become sufficiently widespread that it has now taken on a measure of tradition in itself.

Although adoption processes for goods and services are in principle similar, differences can result from services being perceived as riskier than goods, especially where they entail a high level of involvement by the consumer. Evaluation of quality and value before purchase is difficult, and effective promotion of services must therefore start by understanding the state of mind of potential customers and the information they seek in order to reduce their exposure to risk.

11.2.2 **Audience response**

Having identified the target audience and its characteristics, the communicator must consider the type of response required from it. The required response will have an influence on the source, message and channel of communication.

In most cases, customers are seen as going through a series of stages before finally deciding to purchase a service. It is therefore critical to know these buyer-readiness stages and to assess where the target is at any given time. The communicator will be seeking any one or more of three audience responses to the communication:

1. cognitive responses – the message should be considered and understood

2. affective responses – the message should lead to some change in attitude

3. behavioural responses – finally, the message should achieve some change in behaviour (e.g. a purchase decision).

Many models have been developed to show how marketing communication has the effect of 'pushing' recipients of messages through a number of sequential stages, finally resulting in a purchase decision. The stages defined in three widely used models of communication – **AIDA**, the Hierarchy of Effects, and Innovation–Adoption – are shown in Figure 11.3.

Domain	AIDA model	Hierarchy of Effects model (Lavidge and Steiner, 1961)	Innovation–Adoption model (Rogers, 1962)
Cognitive	Awareness	Awareness	Awareness
		Knowledge	
Affective	Interest	Liking	Interest
	Desire	Preference	Evaluation
Behavioural	Action	Conviction	Trial
		Purchase	Adoption

Figure 11.3 Models of buyer states. The communication process often has to take prospects from the stages of being unaware of the existence of a service, to awareness, liking and eventual purchase. In addition, prospects who have actually become customers must have their positive attitude towards the service reinforced, so that they repurchase and recommend the service to friends.

Communication models portray a simple and steady movement through the various stages, although this should not be seen as ending when a sale is completed. It was noted in Chapter 5 that service organizations increasingly seek to build relationships with their customers, so the behavioural change (the sale) should be seen as the starting point for making customers aware of other offers available from the organization and for securing repeat business. Smooth progress through these stages is impeded by the presence of a number of 'noise' factors, which are discussed below. The probabilities of success in each stage cumulatively decline due to noise and therefore the probability of the final stage achieving an actual purchase is very low.

11.2.3 **Communication source**

The source of a message – as distinct from the message itself – can influence the effectiveness of any communication. Aaker and Myers (1982) identified a few major features of sources that influence communication effectiveness.

■ If a source is perceived as having power, then the audience response is likely to be compliance.

■ If a source is liked, then identification by the audience is a likely response. Important factors here include past experience and reputation of the service organization, in addition to the personality of the actual source of the communication. A salesperson, any contact personnel, a TV/radio personality, etc., are all very important in creating liking.

- If a source is perceived as credible then the message is more likely to be internalized by the audience. Credibility can be developed by establishing a source as important, high in status, power and prestige, or by emphasizing reliability and openness.

- For many low-risk, low-involvement services, endorsement by an individual's peer group can be important. 'If people like me are happy using this service, then I will be happy as well' is a typical rationalization. A company may build on this by using an ordinary person as the message source. During 2003, the grocery retailer Tesco used a seemingly ordinary (although slightly eccentric) pensioner to promote its low prices, and many similar pensioners doubtless empathized with what she was saying.

- Celebrities are often used to endorse a service or an organization. We have a tendency to impute to the endorsed product the qualities that we have come to like about our favourite celebrity characters. There have been numerous studies of the effects of celebrity endorsement (e.g. Chung-kue and McDonald, 2002). To be effective, the celebrity must be chosen carefully to match the aspirations of a product's target market (for example, the TV chef Jamie Oliver has developed a loyal following among aspirational cooks which has been exploited by the grocery retailer Sainsbury's, which employed the chef to front its advertising campaign demonstrating meals made with Sainsbury's groceries).

Closely related to the notion of credibility is the 'halo effect'. Coulson-Thomas (1985) defined this as the 'tendency to impute to individuals and things, the qualities of other individuals and things with which they are associated'. The closer the perceived link between 'personality' and service, the stronger the halo effect. However there is also a phenomenon known as the 'sleeper effect' in which the credibility of a source – and hence message retention – is built up over a period of time. The implication of this is that company and product reputation need regular reinforcement, both from formal **advertising** and from satisfying contacts between customers and front-line employees.

11.2.4 **The message**

A message must be able to move an individual along a path from awareness through to eventual purchase. In order for a message to be received and understood, it must gain attention, use a common language, arouse needs and suggest how these needs may be met. All of this should take place within the acceptable standards of the target audience. However, the service itself, the channel and the source of the communication also convey a message and therefore it is important that these do not conflict.

Three aspects of a communication message can be identified: content, structure and format. It is the content which is likely to arouse attention, and change attitude and intention. The appeal or theme of the message is therefore important. The formulation of the message must include some kind of benefit, motivator, identification or reason why the audience should think or do something. Appeals can be rational, emotional or moral.

Messages can be classified into a number of types, according to the dominant theme of the message. The following are common focal points for messages.

- The nature and characteristics of the organization and the service on offer – for example, television advertisements for the airline Cathay Pacific emphasize the high quality of its in-flight service.

- Advantages over the competition – for example, promotion by the airline Ryanair has emphasized the low cost of its fares compared to those of its competitors.

- Adaptability to meet buyers' needs – many insurance companies stress the extent to which their policies have been designed with the needs of particular age segments of the population in mind.

- Experience of others – in this way, testimonials of previous satisfied customers are used to demonstrate the benefits resulting from use and the dependability of the service provider – for example, the Prudential Assurance company has used the opinions of ordinary investors to extol the virtues of a Prudential pension plan.

Recipients of a message must see it as applying specifically to themselves and they must see some reason for being interested in it. The message must be structured according to the job it has to do (Figure 11.4). The points to be included in the message must be ordered (strongest arguments first or last) and consideration given to whether one-sided or two-sided messages should be used. The actual format of the message will be very much determined by the medium used, e.g. the type of print if published material, the type of voice if broadcast media, etc.

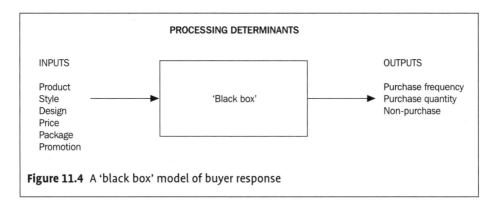

Figure 11.4 A 'black box' model of buyer response

Guerrilla tactics

In the world of military warfare, the most dangerous enemy is the surprise attacker whose behaviour is unpredictable and who can have an impact disproportionate to his or her efforts. So too with promotion by commercial organizations. When advertising begins to blend in with the wallpaper, it can take guerrilla tactics to grab buyers' attention.

The term 'guerrilla marketing' is not new and can be traced back to the mid-1980s. Jay Conrad Levinson describes the concept as being all about achieving conventional goals, such as increased profits, with unconventional methods, such as investing energy instead of money (Levinson, 2003). Just as guerrilla warfare tactics can serve the interests of small dissident groups, guerrilla marketing is particularly suitable for smaller services businesses. Nightclubs, bars and online information services have been frequent users of guerrilla tactics. Inevitably, many of the practices of guerrilla marketing can be questioned on ethical grounds.

One of the principles of guerrilla marketing is to get a message through to the target audience when the audience would least be expecting a selling message. Instead of perceptually filtering out what might be seen as a sales message, the target may be more amenable to persuasion.

When guerrilla tactics get hooked up to the Internet, the results can be even more questionable. FriendGreetings.com built up a mailing list of e-mail addresses and thousands of people followed its link to a greeting card which the company claimed was waiting for the recipient. Users were then invited to install an ActiveX control in order to view their e-card. Two lengthy end-user licence agreements were displayed stating that by running the application the user is giving permission for a similar e-mail to be sent to all addresses found in the user's Outlook address book. Of course, most users would not bother to read the licence agreement and therefore allowed numerous unwanted e-mails to be sent from their e-mail address. Such a 'worm', which creates a flood of unwanted e-mails, can be just as much a nuisance as a virus. Guerrilla tactics had achieved their aim of attracting attention. As the message took the form of an e-card sent by somebody that the user knew, they did not suspect that clicking on the link would result in anything untoward occurring.

Are the practices of companies such as FriendGreetings.com ethical? Would such practices be self-defeating because the company would simply acquire a bad reputation for itself? Is it right that 999 people could be inconvenienced so that the company can get profitable business from just 1 person out of each 1000 that it targets? Is it possible to stop practices of this type? After all, users had technically given permission for a worm to get into their computer, even if the request was deviously hidden in a lengthy licence agreement?

11.2.5 **Noise**

The creator of a message needs to encode it into some acceptable form for an audience to decode and comprehend. Unfortunately, there is likely to be interference between the stages of encoding and decoding, and although it is difficult to totally eliminate such interference in the communication process, an understanding of the various elements of this 'noise' should help to minimize its effects. The potential for 'noise' to hinder the effective communication is usually greater for services than for manufactured goods. Because of the intangible nature of services, expectations of service delivery must be created in people's minds without the help of tangible evidence which can be used to describe manufactured goods.

The nature of 'noise' factors can be examined in terms of a simple 'black box' model of buyer response (Figure 11.4). A communication of some sort (originating either from within a company or extraneously) is seen as a stimulus to some form of customer response. Response can be expressed in terms such as quantity purchased, frequency of purchase or even non-purchase. The final response, however, is not a straightforward response to the initial stimulus. The initial stimulus is distorted within the 'black box' process, resulting in different individuals responding in different ways to a similar stimulus. The variables at work within the black box are the noise factors and can be divided into two major types.

1. *Factors that relate to the individual, i.e. psychological factors.* Both positive and negative previous experiences predispose an individual to decode messages in a particular way. Also, the personality of specific members of an audience can significantly influence interpretation of a message – for example, an extrovert may interpret a message differently to an introvert. Similarly, an individual's motives can influence how a message is decoded. An individual who has just come home from work hungry and is about to eat dinner is unlikely to be amenable to information communicated by a life assurance salesperson which may satisfy some higher-order need for family security.

2. *Factors that relate to other groups of people, i.e. sociological factors.* Important sociological influences on behaviour include culture and social class. Individual members of different cultures and classes are likely to interpret messages in different ways. In this way, communications offering credit facilities may be interpreted with suspicion within certain social groups who have been conditioned to live within their means, whereas members of other social groups may welcome the opportunities represented by the message.

11.3 **Developing the promotional mix**

Having considered 'who says what to whom and with what effect', the next area of concern is 'how?' Developing the promotional mix entails selecting and blending different channels of communication in order to achieve the promotional objectives of the marketing mix. Specifying the objectives of a communication is important if appropriate messages are to be targeted accurately through the most appropriate channels in the most cost-effective manner possible. Typical promotional objectives might be:

- to develop an awareness of, and an interest in, the service organization and its services or products.

- to communicate the benefits of purchasing a service

- to influence eventual purchase of the service

- to build a positive image of the service firm

- to differentiate the service from its competitors

- to remind people of the existence of a service and/or the service firm.

Ideally, these objectives should be quantified as far as possible, thus promotional objectives for a new type of motor insurance policy may begin with an objective to achieve awareness of the brand name by 30% of the 25–55-year-old insurance-buying public in the UK within one year of launch.

The promotion mix refers to the combination of channels which an organization uses to communicate with its target markets. Communication is received by audiences from two principal sources – sources within an organization and external sources. The latter includes word-of-mouth recommendation from friends, editorials in the press, etc., which it has already been noted may have high credibility in the service evaluation process. Sources originating within an organization can be divided into those originating from the traditional marketing function (which can be divided into personal two-way channels such as personal selling and impersonal one-way channels such as advertising), and those originating from front-line production resources. Because services normally involve consumers in the production process, the promotion mix has to be considered more broadly than is the case with manufactured goods. Front-line operations staff and service outlets become valuable channels of communication. The elements of the services promotion mix are illustrated in Figure 11.5.

The choice of a particular combination of communication channels will depend primarily on the characteristics of the target audience, especially its habits in terms of exposure to messages. Other important considerations include the present and potential market size for the service (advertising on television may not be appropriate for a service that has a local niche market, for example), the nature of the service itself (the more personal the service, the more effective the two-way communication channel) and of course the costs of the various channels.

A very important consideration is the stage that a service has reached in its life cycle (see Chapter 7). Advertising and public relations are more likely to form important channels of communication during the introductory stage of the life cycle where the major objective is often to increase overall audience awareness. Sales promotion can be used to stimulate trial and, in some instances, personal selling can be used to

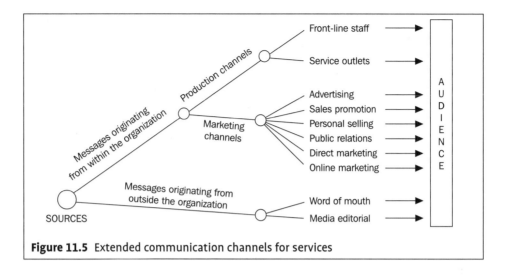

Figure 11.5 Extended communication channels for services

acquire distribution coverage. During a service's growth stage, the use of all communication channels can generally be reduced as demand during this phase tends to produce its own momentum through word-of-mouth communications. However, as the service develops into its maturity stage, there may be a call for an increase in advertising and sales promotion activity. Finally, when the service is seen as going into decline, advertising and public relations are often reduced, although sales promotion can still be quite usefully applied. Sometimes, services in decline are allowed to die quietly with very little promotion. In the case of many long-life financial services which a company would like to delete but cannot for contractual reasons, the service may be kept going with no promotional support at all.

In the following sections, each of the elements of the promotion mix through which communications can be directed is discussed. Before the traditional elements of advertising, sales promotion, personal selling and public relations are considered, attention is given to the role of production process inputs to the promotion mix of service firms.

11.4 The producer–customer interface of the services promotion mix

Inseparability results in consumers being involved in a series of encounters with service producers. During each of these encounters, a service organization has an opportunity to communicate with its customers. Without any effort on the part of an organization, customers will pick up messages, whether they are good or bad. With more planning, an organization can ensure that every encounter is turned into an opportunity to convey positive messages that encourage repeat business from customers and encourage them to pass on the message to others. Two important sources of non-marketer-derived messages can be identified within the extended promotion mix of services – front-line employees and the physical environment of the service encounter.

11.4.1 The promotional role of employees

The important role played by front-line operational personnel as 'part-time marketers' has been stressed on many previous occasions in this book. It has also been noted that the activities of such staff can be important in creating an image of an organization which can live on to influence target customers' perceptions of an organization.

Staff who have front-line encounters with customers should be trained to treat these encounters as promotional opportunities. Without appropriate training and explanation of expectations, a call for such employees to promote their service more effectively can be little more than rhetoric. Training might seek to develop a number of skills in front-line staff, as described below.

- An ability to spot cross-selling possibilities can call for empathy on the part of front-line staff. A bank clerk who sees a customer repeatedly using a service that is not adequately fulfilling his or her needs could be trained to try to sell another service which better meets the customer's needs. Training should make such employees aware of the services available and give them skills in approaching customers effectively and referring them on to appropriate personnel.

- Many operational staff have quite clearly defined sales responsibilities – for example, restaurant waiters may be expected to encourage customers to spend more on their visit to the restaurant.

- The general manner of staff members' interaction with customers is important in encouraging customers to return and to tell their friends about their good experience. Again, training should emphasize those behaviours that have a positive effect on customers' evaluation of their encounter.

- Staff can directly influence future purchases by encouraging customers to book a repeat service or by giving them literature to pass on to friends.

It can be difficult to draw a distinction between production staff and marketing staff in terms of their contribution towards the promotion of an organization. Organizational boundaries should not prevent operational staff being considered an important element of promotion mix planning.

11.4.2 The promotional role of service outlets

From the outside, service outlets can be seen as billboards capable of conveying messages about the services which take place within them. They are therefore powerful tools in appealing both to customers and non-customers (Figure 11.6). The general appearance of an outlet can promote the image of a service organization. A brightly coloured and clean exterior can transmit a message that the organization is fast, efficient and well run. Outlets can be used to display advertising posters, which in heavily trafficked locations can result in valuable exposure. Many retailers with town-centre locations consider that these opportunities are so great that they do not need to undertake more conventional promotion. Among the large UK retailers, Marks & Spencer until the 1980s paid for very little promotional activity, arguing that over half the population passed one of its stores during any week, thereby exposing them to powerful 'free' messages. Although the company's promotional mix now includes more purchased advertising, store locations are still considered to be valuable promotional media.

Service outlets can also provide valuable opportunities to show service production processes to potential customers, something which is much more difficult to achieve

Figure 11.6 The idea that buildings should form an important part of a service organization's promotion mix is not new. Today, a grand reception area and an imposing atrium in an accountant's headquarters may send out a message that the firm of accountants is a substantial one and has the resources to be a reliable long-term service provider. A century ago, before the age of modern regulation, banks needed to earn the trust of their customers. With lots of small, regional banks competing for business, and frequent bankruptcies robbing investors of their savings, how could anyone be sure that the bank where they invested their savings was not going to disappear with their savings? One solution adopted by many banks was to construct substantial buildings, often designed to look like cathedrals. This bank may now stand out as a listed building, but when it was built the design served to send out a message to customers that the bank would be around for as long as the cathedrals which the building emulated.

through conventional media. A fast printing shop displaying sophisticated printing equipment and a tyre retailer's large stocks and tidy appearance all help to promote an organization's processes as much as its outcomes.

11.5 Advertising and the media

Advertising is mass, paid communication which is used to transmit information, develop attitudes and induce some form of response on the part of the audience. It seeks to bring about a response by providing information to potential customers, by trying to modify their desires and by supplying reasons why they should prefer that particular company's services.

Advertising objectives should be clearly specified in terms of target audiences and desired effects. However, in monitoring the performance of advertising, it can be extremely difficult to prove that this alone is responsible for a sales increase. Sales, after all, can be the result of many intervening variables, some of which are internal to the organization (e.g. public relations activity, pricing policy), while others are external (e.g. the state of the national economy). It is therefore too simplistic to set advertising objectives simply in terms of increasing sales by a specified amount. Given the existence of diverse adopter categories and the many stages in the communication process which were described earlier, more appropriate objectives can often be specified in terms of levels of awareness or comprehension.

11.5.1 Media characteristics

The choice of media is influenced by the characteristics of each medium and its ability to achieve the specified promotional objectives. The following are some of the most common types of media and their characteristics.

Newspapers

Daily newspapers tend to have a high degree of reader loyalty, reflecting the fact that each national title is targeted to specific segments of the population. This loyalty can lead to the printed message being perceived by readers as having a high level of credibility. Newspapers can be used for creating general awareness of a product or a brand as well as providing detailed product information. In this way, banks use newspapers both for adverts designed to create brand awareness and liking for the organization, as well as adverts for giving specific details of savings accounts. The latter may include an invitation to action in the form of a freepost account opening coupon.

Magazines/journals

Within the UK, there is a wide range of magazine and journal titles available to advertisers. While some high-circulation magazines appeal to broad groups of people (e.g. *Radio Times*), most titles are specialized in terms of their content and targeting. In this way, *Which Mortgage?* can prove to be a highly specific medium for building societies to promote mortgages. Specialist trade titles allow messages to be aimed at service intermediaries – for example, a tour operator seeking to promote a holiday offer may first gain the confidence and support of travel agents through such magazines as the *Travel Trade Gazette*. Although advertising in magazines may at first seem relatively expensive compared to newspapers, they represent good value to advertisers in terms of their high number of readers per copy and highly segmented audiences.

Outdoor advertising

This is useful for reminder copy and can support other media activities. The effect of a television advertisement can be prolonged if recipients are exposed to a reminder poster on their way to work the following day. If strategically placed, the posters can appeal to segmented audiences – e.g. London Underground sites in the City of London are seen by large numbers of affluent business people. The sides of buses are often used to support new service facilities (e.g. new store openings) and have the ability to spread their message as the bus travels along local routes. Posters can generally only be used to convey a simple communication rather than complex details.

Television

This is an expensive, but very powerful medium. Although it tends to be used mainly for the long-term task of creating brand awareness, it can also be used to create a rapid sales response. The very fact that a message has been seen on television can give credibility to the message source and many smaller service companies add the phrase 'as seen on TV' to give additional credibility to their other media communications. The power of the television medium is enhanced by its ability to appeal to both the senses of sight and sound, and to use movement and colour to develop a sales message.

A major limitation of television advertising is its cost – for most local service providers, television advertising rates start at too high a level to be considered. Also, the question must be asked, how many people within the target audience are actually receptive to television advertising. Is the target viewer actually in the room when an advertisement is being broadcast? If the viewer is present, is he or she receptive to the message? Against this, television advertising has become an increasingly flexible medium, with cable channels offering geographical and lifestyle targeting of audiences. Digital television is also able to offer an immediate response function, so a pizza delivery company can use television not only for creating brand awareness, but also for immediate need fulfilment.

The Internet

Most large service organizations now have their own websites which are used to disseminate messages to customers and potential customers. In addition to listing their sites with search engines, companies often buy advertising space on other websites, with hotlinks provided to their own site. The Internet is good at assessing the number of visitors to a site and advertisers can learn how visitors move around a site as they seek out information. The greatest power of the Internet is that it can become a medium for personalized messages, thereby not strictly falling within the definition of advertising given earlier. For this reason, further consideration of the Internet as part of an organization's promotion mix will be given in the later section on direct marketing.

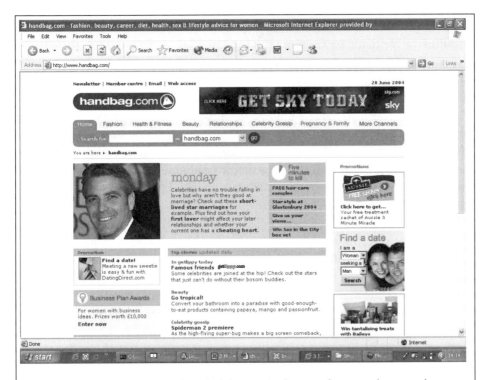

Figure 11.7 Service companies have led the way in the use of Internet banner ads. handbag.com is a service provider in its own right and offers its business customers opportunities to target buyers with quite specific messages. Through the use of cookies, handbag.com can learn about visitors to its site and ensure that the adverts which appear on its pages are the ones to which a visitor will be most receptive. If a visitor has previously been surfing through travel-related websites, this may be a sign that the visitor is in the market for travel services. This ability to try to understand the visitor's needs and preferences has led to banner adverts becoming popular with entertainment, travel and personal finance service suppliers, among others. Internet banner ads have a lot of additional advantages compared to a newspaper or TV advert. Hotlinks can take a viewer directly to further information, something that is not possible with most forms of advertising. So a banner ad for a bank may provide a link to the bank's website where the cost of a loan tailored to the needs of an individual customer can be calculated. An Internet advertiser has much more information about visitors to a site than would be available to a newspaper or television advertiser. By using cookies, Internet advertisers can even change the message that a person sees depending on the sites that they have visited previously. (Reproduced with permission of handbag.com)

Cinema

Because of the captive nature of cinema audiences, this medium can potentially have a major impact. It is frequently used to promote local services such as taxi operators and food outlets whose target market broadly corresponds to the audience of most cinemas. However, without repetition, cinema advertisements have little lasting effect, but do tend to be useful for supporting press and television advertising.

Commercial radio

Radio advertising has often be seen as the poor relation of television advertising, appealing only to the sense of sound. The threshold cost of radio advertising is much lower than for television, reflecting much more local segmentation of radio audiences and the lower production costs of radio adverts. A major advantage over other media is that the audience can be involved in other activities – particularly driving – while being exposed to an advertisement. Although there are often doubts about the extent to which an audience actually receives and understands a message, it forms a useful reminder medium when used in conjunction with other media.

11.5.2 Media selection criteria

In addition to the characteristics of the media themselves, a number of other important factors must be taken into account in selecting the media mix for a particular advertising campaign. These factors are:

- the characteristics of the target audience
- the level of exposure of the target audience to the communication
- the impact which advertising will have on the target audience
- the extent to which the effects of a particular advertising message 'wear out' over time
- the cost of advertising through a particular medium.

Target audience

The media habits of the target audience must be fully understood. If a firm's target market is not in the habit of being exposed to a particular medium, much of the value of advertising through that medium will be wasted. As an example, attempts to promote premium credit cards to high-income segments by means of television commercials may lose much of their value because research suggests that the higher socio-economic groups tend to spend a greater proportion of their viewing time watching BBC rather than commercial channels. On the other hand, they are heavy readers of Sunday newspaper magazine supplements.

Information about target audiences' media habits is obtained from a number of sources. Newspaper readership information is collated by the National Readership Survey. For each newspaper, this shows reading frequency and average issue readership (as distinct from circulation) broken down into age, class, sex, ownership of consumer durables, etc. Television viewing information is collected by the Broadcasters' Audience Research Board (BARB). This indicates the number of people watching particular channels at particular times by reference to two types of television ratings (TVRs) – one for the number of households watching a programme/advertising slot and one for the number of people watching.

Advertising exposure

The number of advertising exposures of a particular communication is determined by two factors: cover/reach and frequency. 'Cover', or 'reach', is the percentage of a particular target audience reached by a medium or a whole campaign, while 'frequency' is the number of times a particular target audience has an 'opportunity to see/hear' (OTS/OTH) an advertising message. The combination of these two factors results in an index of advertising exposure which is usually stated in terms of 'gross rating points' (GRPs). For example, if an objective is to reach 50% of the target audience three times a year, this would be stated as a GRP of 150 (i.e. 50 x 3). Within a given budget, there has to be a trade-off between coverage/reach and frequency.

Advertising impact

Impact is usually more closely related to the message than the media. If, however, the medium is the message, then advertising impact should be an important criterion for media selection. Different media vehicles can produce different levels of awareness and comprehension of an identical message. In this way, the image of Ronald McDonald presented via television is very much more powerful compared to that presented via radio.

Wearout

The concept of advertising exposure assumes that all advertising insertions have equal value. However, the effect of additional insertions may in fact decline, resulting in diminishing returns for each unit of expenditure. There is usually a 'threshold' level of advertising beneath which little audience response occurs. Once over this threshold, audience response tends to increase quite rapidly through a 'generation' phase until eventually a saturation point is reached. Any further advertising may lead to a negative or declining response, i.e. 'wearout'.

Cost

The cost of using different media varies markedly, and while a medium which at first sight appears to be expensive may in fact be good value in terms of achieving promotional objectives, a sound basis for measuring cost is needed. There are generally two related cost criteria.

1. *Cost per gross rating point.* This is usually used for broadcast media and is the cost of a set of commercials divided by the gross rating points.

2. *Cost per thousand.* The **cost per 1000** is used for print media to calculate the cost of getting the message seen by 1000 members of the target market.

These measures can be used to make cost comparisons between different media vehicles. However, a true comparison needs to take into consideration the different degrees of effectiveness each medium has. In other words, the strength of the media vehicle needs to be considered, as does the location, duration, timing and – where relevant – size of the advertisement plus a variety of more complex factors. These are all combined to form 'media weights' which are used in comparing the effectiveness of different media. Cost-effectiveness, therefore, is calculated using the following formula:

$$\text{Cost-effectiveness} = \frac{\text{Readers/viewers in target} \times \text{Media weight}}{\text{Cost}}$$

11.5.3 Determining the advertising budget

Advertising expenditure could become a drain on an organization's resources if no conscious attempt is made to determine an appropriate budget and to ensure that expenditure is kept within the budget. A number of methods are commonly used to determine an advertising budget.

- *What can be afforded.* This is largely a subjective assessment and pays little attention to the long-term promotional needs of a service. It regards advertising as a luxury which can be afforded in good times, to be cut back during lean times. In reality, this approach is used by many smaller service companies for whom advertising spending is seen as the first and easy short-term target for reducing expenditure in bad times.

- *Percentage of sales.* By this method, advertising expenditure rises or falls to reflect changes in sales. In fact, sales are likely to be influenced by advertising rather than vice versa, and this method is likely to accentuate any given situation. If sales are declining during a recession, more advertising may be required to induce sales, but this method of determining the budget implies a cut in advertising expenditure.

- *Comparative parity.* Advertising expenditure is determined by the amount spent by competitors. Many market sectors see periodic outbursts of promotional expenditure, often accompanying a change in some other element of firms' marketing mix. During 2004, an increase in promotional expenditure by the Channel Tunnel operator, aimed at increasing its market share of the UK–France travel market, triggered an increase in advertising by ferry companies operating on the route. However, merely increasing advertising expenditure may hide the fact that it is the other elements of the marketing mix which need adjusting in order to gain a competitive market position in relation to competitors.

- *Residual.* This is the least satisfactory approach and merely assigns to the advertising budget what is left after all other costs have been covered. It may bear no relationship whatever to promotional objectives.

- *Objective and task*. This approach starts by defining clearly promotional objectives. Tasks are then set which relate to specific targets. In this way, advertising is seen as a necessary – even though possibly risky – investment in a brand, ranking in importance with other more obvious costs such as production and salary costs. This is the most rational approach to setting a promotional budget.

11.5.4 Developing the advertising campaign

An advertising campaign brings together a wide range of media-related activities so that instead of being a discrete series of activities, they can act in a planned and co-ordinated way to achieve promotional objectives. The first stage of campaign planning is to have a clear understanding of promotional objectives (see above). Once these have been clarified, a message can be developed that is most likely to achieve these objectives. The next step is the production of the media plan. Having defined the target audience in terms of its size, location and media exposure, media must be selected which achieve desired levels of exposure/repetition with the target audience. A media plan must be formulated that specifies:

- the allocation of expenditure between the different media

- the selection of specific media components – for example, in the case of print media, decisions need to be made regarding the type (tabloid versus broadsheet), size of advertisement, whether use of a Sunday supplement is to be made and whether there is to be national or local coverage

- the frequency of insertion

- the cost of reaching a particular target group for each of the media vehicles specified in the plan.

Finally, the advertising campaign must be co-ordinated with the overall promotional plan – for example, by ensuring that sales promotion activities reinforce advertising messages.

While the principles of planning a campaign for a service organization are in principle the same as would be followed by a manufacturing company, the intangible, inseparable and variable nature of services does need to be borne in mind when planning a campaign. Advertising alone is unlikely to be successful in helping customers make services purchase decisions, but their effectiveness can be increased by following a few guidelines. The following have been proposed by George and Berry (1980).

- *Use clear and unambiguous messages*. The very intangibility of services can make it very difficult to communicate information defining the service offer. This is particularly true in the case of highly complex services. Here, advertising copy should emphasize the benefits of a service and how these match the benefits sought, i.e. a customer orientation rather than a product/service orientation.

- *Build on word-of-mouth communication*. An important influence on buyers' decision-making is recommendation from others, therefore advertising should be used to enhance this. For example, advertising can be used to persuade satisfied customers to let others know of their satisfaction. Organizations can develop material that customers can pass on to non-customers or persuade non-customers to talk to present customers. Finally, advertising campaigns can be aimed at opinion leaders who will then 'trickle down' information.

- *Provide tangible cues.* Organizations selling manufactured goods tend to differentiate their products from their competitors' by emphasizing intangible features such as after-sales service, guarantees, etc. Service marketers, however, tend to differentiate their services by emphasizing tangible cues or 'physical evidence'. The use of well-known personalities and objects can act as surrogates for the intangible features of a service. The use of consistent logos, catchphrases, symbols and themes can help to overcome the transitory nature of intangibility and encourage a durable company identity in the customer's mind.

- *Promise what can be delivered.* The intangible nature of services results in customers holding abstract expectations about the standard of service delivery. You will recall from Chapter 8 that customers are likely to judge a service to be of poor quality where perceived delivery does not live up to these abstract expectations. Advertising should not therefore over-promise.

- *Aim advertising at employees too.* Most services are labour intensive and advertisers need to be concerned with both the encouragement of employees to perform as well the encouragement of customers to buy (see the vignette below). Advertisements that emphasize personal service can motivate contact personnel to perform their duties more effectively as well as influencing consumer choice.

- *Remove post-purchase anxiety.* Consumption of a service usually involves a high degree of customer involvement and therefore there is a greater likelihood of post-purchase dissonance occurring than is the case with most goods purchases. There is little tangible evidence to use in the post-purchase evaluation process and therefore advertising should be used to reinforce positive post-purchase feelings.

Selling an organization to its employees

Although the primary target audience of an advertisement may be customers, its effects on employees should not be forgotten. This is especially true of labour-intensive services industries where an advert can provide encouragement for front-line employees to perform their jobs with pride, as well as encouraging customers to buy. If cabin crew of British Airways see the airline's advertisements casting them in the role of helpful and friendly problem-solvers, they should be able to identify with this role and carry it out effectively and with pride.

Employees can become highly involved in the adverts where they are used in place of professional actors. The DIY retailer B&Q has for a long time used its own employees from different branches to promote its store offers, providing a sense of realistic credibility to customers and involvement from employees.

Employees who have heard rumours about poor financial prospects for a company amid talk of falling sales may have some of their confidence restored by the sight of advertisements to drum up new business.

At times, however, advertisements can only serve to demotivate staff. Advertising claims may be made which front-line staff are simply incapable of delivering, perhaps due to inadequate training or insufficient resources to keep promises made in an advert. If employees don't believe the claims of an advert, why should customers? On occasions, adverts can actually annoy staff by casting them in a demeaning role, something which the retailer Sainsbury's learnt to its cost following a series of adverts in its 'Value to shout about' campaign. These used the actor John Cleese to promote the grocery retailer's low prices, but in doing so the scenes belittled staff and their knowledge of the new low prices. After representations from staff – and some suggestion that the campaign wasn't working with customers – the adverts were pulled.

University of fun?

How do you strike a balance between an advertising campaign being eye-catching and accessible on the one hand, while preserving the core values of the product on the other? Retailers, banks and insurance companies have all encountered problems when their traditional mature audiences have been alienated by advertising which was aimed at increasing the number of younger customers. Wacky advertising may attract attention, but what does it say about the nature of the product on offer? Liverpool-based John Moores University used an unconventional approach to advertising its courses in 1999. Its prospectus paid relatively little attention to the details of the courses on offer, but gave great emphasis to the pubs and clubs in town. It may well be that this was based on a sound analysis of the factors that influence students' choice of university. Most prospective students have only a limited ability to distinguish between the academic credentials of competing courses, whereas nightlife is an easier point of reference. But the media picked up the story, claiming that this was further evidence of 'dumbing down' in education generally, and at John Moores University in particular. Even existing students claimed that the value of their degrees would be demeaned by advertising which made their institution appear to the outside world like a 'good time university'. But if the university went back to stuffy advertising and prospectuses, would it lose a point of difference with its nearby competitors? Would the target audience stop to read its messages?

11.6 **Sales promotion**

Sales promotion involves those activities, other than advertising, personal selling and **public relations**, that stimulate customer purchase and the effectiveness of intermediaries. Although it can be used to create awareness, sales promotion is usually used for the later stages of the buying process, that is, to create interest, desire and – in particular – to bring about action. Sales promotion can quite successfully complement other tools within the promotion mix, for example by reinforcing a particular image or identity developed through advertising.

Over the last few years there has been a rapid increase in the use of sales promotion, for a number of reasons.

- Internally, there has been a greater acceptance of the use of sales promotion by top management and more people are now qualified to use it. In addition, there is greater pressure today to obtain a quick sales response, something which sales promotion is good at achieving.

- There has been a general proliferation of brands with increased competitive pressure. As a result of this and the changing economic environment, consumers are more 'deal oriented' and this has led to pressure from intermediaries for better incentives from manufacturers and service principals.

- It has been argued by many that advertising efficiency is declining due to increasing costs and media clutter.

- New technology in targeting has resulted in an increase in the efficiency and effectiveness of sales promotion.

The public and professional service sectors have also accepted the role of sales promotion in many areas – for example, leisure centres and opticians respectively. As a promotional tool, sales promotion is likely to continue to grow in the future.

11.6.1 **Sales promotion planning**

Sales promotion contributes in a number of ways to achieving overall promotional objectives. While it can be used merely to gain attention for a service, it is more likely to be used as an incentive incorporating an offer which represents value to the target audience. It can also act as an invitation to engage in a transaction now rather than later. Sales promotion usually attracts brand-switchers but is unlikely to turn them into loyal brand users without the use of other elements of the promotion mix. In fact, it is usually considered that sales promotion is used to break down brand loyalty, whereas advertising is used to build it up. Sales promotion can gain new users or encourage more frequent purchase but it cannot compensate for inadequate advertising, poor delivery or poor quality.

It has been suggested that the role of sales promotion for services is much more limited than is the case with goods. The fact that services cannot be stored may appear to limit the ability of a service firm to offload unused services at a cheap

---

Is there such a thing as a free gift?

In many markets where services are perceived by buyers as being basically similar, it may be necessary to offer an incentive in order to initiate a dialogue. Eager to enter buyers' choice set, many insurance companies provide a token gift in order to generate an initial response. Many offer further incentives that are given following a completed purchase. Sales promotion activities of this type may be particularly important where consumers' ability to differentiate between competing products is low and an incentive offers a tangible basis for differentiation. Some more discerning customers who have greater product knowledge may appreciate that there is 'no such thing as a free gift' and may consider that if the insurance policy is good in its own right, it should not need an incentive to encourage purchase.

---

price, something which is commonly undertaken by goods manufacturers using sales promotion. On the other hand, off-peak sales promotional activity can help to alleviate such a problem in the future. There is also a view that some promotional tools – such as the use of free samples – cannot be used for services as the sample would have to involve the whole service. However, a free first consultation by a solicitor, for example, could be thought of as an equivalent form of sales promotion.

As in the case of advertising, effective sales promotion involves an ongoing process with a number of distinct stages.

- Establishment of objectives, which could include the encouragement of increased usage or the building of trial among non-users or other brand users.

- Selection of promotional tools, which can include free samples/visits/consultations (which can be an important means of demonstrating an intangible service process); money-off price incentives (although these tend to be expensive to the service provider, as the incentive is given to customers regardless of its motivational effect on an individual customer); coupons/vouchers (which can offer targeted invitations to try a new service or to reward customer loyalty); gift offers (which can help to give tangible cues to the service company's offering as well as offering an incentive for immediate purchase); and competitions (which can add to the perceived value of a service).

- Planning the sales promotion programme – especially the timing and size of incentive to be offered.

- Pre-testing, in order to ensure that potentially expensive problems are discovered before the full launch of a promotion (e.g. false assumptions of redemption rates for an incentive may lead to the budget being exceeded, as happened in an offer by Hoover of free air tickets in return for purchases of electrical equipment where the company seriously under-estimated the subsequent take-up rate of the incentive by customers).

Figure 11.8 Coupons have been a valuable tool of service marketers, and given out to target customers to encourage trial of a new or existing service. Because of the inseparable nature of services, service markets have been able to ensure that only the target benefits from the incentive offered by a coupon (for example, a coupon offering students concessionary prices at a concert may require customers taking up the offer to present some proof that they are students). By restricting the distribution of coupons to those in whom it is most interested, a company avoids giving a price reduction to everyone, including those who are loyal and probably find its prices good value. More recently, the Internet has allowed electronic coupons to be distributed more efficiently and effectively. By studying site visitors' previous behaviour, unique coupons can be generated. These can either be used online, printed for use elsewhere, or sent as an SMS message to a mobile device. The online retailer Amazon.com has made extensive use of coupons to promote sales, such as this one, which is configured according to the information that the company has available about specific targets. Combined with a carefully planned Internet-based promotion programme and an active affiliates programme, Amazon has become the leading online book retailer in the UK. (Reproduced with permission of Amazon.co.uk)

- Implementation must specify the 'lead time' (the time necessary to bring the programme up to the point where the incentive is to be made available to the public) and the 'sell in time' (the period of time from the date of release to when approximately 90–95% of incentive material has been received by potential customers).

- Evaluation: with the use of customer databases, methods of evaluation are improving. However, it can be extremely difficult to separate out the effects of sales promotion activity from other promotional activity – or indeed from other marketing mix and extraneous factors.

411

Sales promotion activity can be aimed at intermediaries as well as the final consumers of a service. Sales promotion activity aimed at intermediaries includes: short-term increases in sales commission; competitions and gifts (useful motivators where individual sales personnel benefit directly from the incentive); point-of-sale material (e.g. tour operators who arrange a film evening for its travel agencies' clients); and co-operative advertising, where a service principal agrees to subscribe to local advertising by an intermediary, often in conjunction with a significant event, e.g. the opening of a new outlet by the intermediary. Sometimes, a service principal targets sales promotions at individual employees of its intermediaries (e.g. tour operators have given free holiday vouchers to travel agency clerks who sell a certain quota of the tour operator's holidays). This can raise ethical issues about whether employees should accept incentives when their first duty is to their employer who in turn seeks to develop the best long-term relationship with its customers.

11.7 **Personal selling**

Personal selling is a powerful two-way form of communication. It allows an interactive relationship to be developed between buyer and seller in which the latter can modify the information presented in response to the needs of the audience. Personal selling allows for the cultivation of a friendship between buyer and seller, which can be an important element of a relationship marketing strategy. It can also be powerful in creating a feeling of obligation by the customer to the salesperson, thereby helping to bring about a desired response.

Although the principles of personnel selling are basically the same for goods and services industries, services sales personnel are more likely to combine their sales duties with other operational duties, for example in the way that a travel agent – as well as being an expert on travel reservation systems – is expected to perform a selling role.

11.7.1 **The salesperson's activities**

The actual selling act is only a small part of the overall salesperson's role. In addition to their specific selling role, two further principle roles can be identified – servicing and intelligence.

The servicing element can be an important contributor to the development of long-term customer relationships where the service in question is perceived as being highly risky. Such relationships need to be regularly attended to, even if there is no short-term prospect of a sale. In a study of the life assurance sector, George and Myers (1981) found that customers viewed their purchases as being highly risky and therefore unpleasant. As a consequence, they attached particular importance to the level of support they received from a salesperson in particular and their organization in general. There have now been many studies to identify the factors that contribute towards relationship satisfaction between buyer and seller (e.g. Crosby *et al.*, 1987).

As well as being the mouthpiece of an organization, sales personnel can also be its ears. They can be extremely useful in marketing research, for example by reporting on customers' comments, or providing information about competitors' activity. Organizations should develop systems for capturing information collected by sales personnel.

In respect of their selling role, a number of types of selling situation can be identified:

- trade selling, where their role is to facilitate sales through intermediaries

- technical selling, which involves giving advice and technical assistance to customers; this type of salesperson becomes a consultant and assumes importance in many types of business-to-business service sales – e.g. business travel agencies

- missionary selling, where the salesperson is not expected to take orders but to 'prepare the ground' by building goodwill

- New business selling, which involves the acquisition of new accounts and may sometimes involve 'cold calling'.

The task of selling can be broken down into sequential stages, as follows.

- *Prospecting* (i.e. finding new customers). Sales leads can be developed in a number of ways – for example, records of past customers, past enquiries and referrals from existing customers and suppliers.

- *Preparation and planning.* A salesperson should attempt to gain as much information as possible about a prospect before actual contact takes place, for example in regard to their previous buying behaviour or aspirations.

- *The sales presentation.* The salesperson should be recognized as a surrogate for the service – for low-contact services such as life insurance, the salesperson may be perceived as *being* the service. Appearance and demeanour are therefore very important in creating the right impression of the service offer. The sales presentation should help to tangibilize an intangible service. Samples of supporting goods, brochures or audio-visual aids can often give a better and more credible description of a service process than a salesperson alone. The salesperson should show a deep knowledge of their particular area, therefore the training of sales personnel in technical as well as sales skills is important. The sales presentation shouldn't offer what cannot be delivered – this applies to both goods and services but is particularly important where abstract expectations of service quality are not matched by actual performance. Customers should be given early opportunities to assess service quality, either by producing evidence of previous outcomes (e.g. previous performance of an investment fund) or by sampling the service process.

- *Handling objections.* Objections to the sales presentation can be rational (for example, objections to the price or the service itself) or irrational (e.g. objections based on resistance to change, apathy, prejudice, etc.), and need to be acknowledged, isolated and discussed.

- *Closing the sale.* This is a difficult stage in that knowing how and when to close is a skill in itself.

- *Follow-up.* This stage is often neglected but is essential to ensure customer satisfaction and repeat business. A letter of thanks or a phone call can help to reduce post-purchase dissonance, which is especially valuable for services where benefits are to be delivered in the distant future.

11.8 Direct marketing

Direct marketing has been defined by the UK Direct Marketing Association as 'an interactive system of marketing which uses one or more media in acquiring a measurable response at a given location'. Its aim is to create and exploit a direct relationship between service producers and their customers. In recent years there has been a dramatic increase in the use of direct marketing for promoting services, largely due to the development of new technology which enables organizations to accurately target their messages. In the UK, total direct marketing expenditure grew by 80% in the period 1996 to 2001, rising from £6.1 billion to £11.14 billion (Direct Marketing Association UK, 2002), with a large share of this accounted for by the financial services sector, particularly pensions and insurance companies. Travel companies, retailers and hotels have been more recent adopters of direct marketing methods on a large scale. While direct marketing may include personal selling, it is the other elements of direct marketing which are of interest here, including **telemarketing**, direct mail and directories.

The key elements of a direct marketing system are:

- an accurate record of the names of existing customers, ex-customers and prospective customers classified into different groups

- a system for recording the results of communications with targets; from this, the effectiveness of particular messages, and the responsiveness of different target groups, can be assessed

- a means of measuring and recording actual purchase behaviour

- a system to follow up with continuing communication where appropriate.

Direct marketing is closely linked to firms' efforts to build long-term relationships with their customers (Chapter 5), and the importance of accurate and up-to-date information about customers was stressed in Chapter 6. Direct marketing allows a company to assess its customers' and potential customers' level of profitability, and to deliver services and messages which are very closely related to their unique needs.

The three most common media used by service organizations are telemarketing, direct mail and electronic media. We will return to electronic media in Section 11.11.

Over-enthusiastic selling of pensions

Can a salesperson be too successful? Many sales personnel have responded to bonus or other incentives offered by their employers to vigorously achieve sales which looked good at the time, but later came back to haunt the company. One of the key characteristics of a good salesperson is his or her ability to listen and to gain a good understanding of a buyer's needs. But what happens when the customer doesn't really have a very good understanding of his or her own needs? Furthermore, what happens when you couple this with a salesperson who would rather earn his or her sales commission as easily as possible rather than probing the true needs of the customer? The result has been a series of mis-selling scandals that have tarnished the reputation of a number of business sectors, especially financial services.

The term 'caveat emptor' ('let the buyer beware') has been used to excuse the situation where a salesperson sold an individual an item that was not at all suited to the person's needs. It was assumed to be the buyer's fault for buying wrongly, rather the seller's fault for selling wrongly. The balance is now tilting in the consumer's favour as society's expectations of sellers rise. This has been demonstrated through the mis-selling of a range of financial services during the 1980s and 1990s. Perhaps the most serious occurred where sales personnel employed by the big UK pensions companies persuaded employees to cash in the pension scheme they had with their employer and take out a new scheme with their company. By 2003 the value of personal pensions had fallen sharply following a fall in stock market prices. Why did so many people give up a good employer's pension scheme for a much more dubious personal pension scheme? Many may have been tempted by a one-off payment from the government and the salesperson may have been tempted to sell personal pensions aggressively by a hefty commission payment on the sale. The customers may have thought that they were buying into a good deal, but most buyers were not able to understand the complexities of a pension scheme. In most cases the customers were badly advised and found that the pension they had bought into was worth much less than the employer's pension they had given up. This over-enthusiastic selling resulted in the big pensions companies being reprimanded by their industry watchdog and forced to pay millions of pounds in fines and compensation to customers. They were forced to rethink the way they managed their sales personnel, but much of the change simply involved going back to traditional best practice for the salesforce – listening to the customers and understanding what they really need; training the salesforce with greater product knowledge; and structuring their rewards to recognize a balance between the need for short-term incentives and long-term relationships.

11.8.1 **Telemarketing**

Telemarketing involves two-way communication by telephone – 'outbound' tele-marketing occurs where suppliers take the initiative and 'inbound' where customers act in response to another stimulus, such as a newspaper advertisement. There has been a rapid increase in inbound telemarketing using toll-free 0800 numbers, particularly by the financial services sector. Companies need to be able to handle surges in incoming calls, otherwise the cost of generating leads is wasted and prospective customers who cannot get through may get such a bad impression of the company that they do not bother calling back. Research by Mintel into 2000 users of call centres found that by far the biggest complaint when telephoning a call centre was the time spent waiting on hold, with some 60% complaining about this. Those aged between 25 and 34 were the least tolerant towards call centres, with around 35% abandoning calls. Just 5% of consumers had never experienced a problem with a call centre (Mintel, 2002).

Inbound telemarketing is very powerful when combined with other media and an incentive for customers to act promptly. Outbound telemarketing has sometimes been used as an alternative to personal selling, especially where some customers are seen as potentially less profitable than others and telemarketing is used for these instead of more expensive face-to-face personal selling.

The effectiveness of telemarketing can be assessed in a number of ways. One possibility is to measure the cost per telephone call and, from this, the cost per successful call. Alternatively effectiveness can be measured in terms of the cost per telephone hour which includes the costs incurred in managing the system. A more useful approach is to assess effectiveness in terms of benefits as well as costs. The simplest measure of benefit is the number and quality of enquiries received. Furthermore, by asking questions of enquirers, the source of particularly effective supporting advertisements can be identified. It can often be possible to measure the cost-effectiveness of telemarketing in terms of the value of sales generated, especially where there is little extraneous media advertising which could itself have explained sales success.

11.8.2 **Direct mail**

Direct mail describes the way in which an organization distributes printed material aimed at specifically targeted potential customers with a view to carrying on direct interchange between the two parties. Its use is becoming increasingly popular among services industries and a number of important advantages which it has over the other promotional tools can be identified.

- It can be used very selectively to target quite specific groups of potential private or business customers.

- The sales message can be personalized to the needs of individual recipients.

- Direct mail offers a very versatile and creative medium and is flexible in the range of materials that can be used.

- It can be timed effectively to fit in with the overall marketing strategy and is quick to implement and to produce results.

- Direct mail can include tangible evidence of a highly intangible service offer (e.g. pictures of hotels).

Direct Mail can be employed to achieve a number of promotional objectives, including the generation of enquiries, keeping prospects interested, keeping customers informed of new developments and improving the effectiveness of the salesperson (i.e. it can be used as a 'door opener').

Compared to advertising, the direct mail message can be more detailed. Much more space is available on a direct mailshot and this allows long and complex messages to be presented – a point which partly explains the popularity of direct mail with financial services companies, whose sales messages are typically very complex. Leaflets, inserts, pop-ups, etc., can also be included in the mailshot. The response medium serves a variety of purposes. It can be used to obtain expressions of interest, to obtain sales orders and to measure the effect of the promotion. It is therefore extremely important to know who has responded and what the response actually is.

With the use of reply-paid envelopes and freefone numbers, response from recipients of direct mail is facilitated. The results of individual targeted mailshots can be assessed quite easily and, through further refinement of customer profiling and targeting, the cost of contact per person can be reduced to a low level. It is also important to consider non-respondents and why they did not respond.

11.9 **Public relations**

Public relations is an indirect promotional tool whose role is to establish and enhance a positive image of an organization and its services among its various publics. It is defined by the Institute of Public Relations as 'the deliberate, planned and sustained effort to establish and maintain mutual understanding between an organization and its publics'. It seeks to persuade people that a company is an attractive organization with which to relate or do business, which is important for the service sector as it has already been noted that services are evaluated very subjectively and often rely on word-of-mouth recommendation. Public relations facilitates this process of subjective evaluation and recommendation.

Because public relations is involved with more than just customer relationships, it is often handled at a corporate level rather than at the functional level of marketing management. As an element within the promotion mix, public relations presents a number of valuable opportunities as well as problems. Some of its more important characteristics are described below.

- *Low cost.* The major advantage of public relations is that it tends to be much cheaper in terms of cost per person reached than any other type of promotion. Apart from nominal production costs, much public relations activity can be carried out at almost no cost, in marked contrast to the high cost of buying space or time in the main media.

- *Audience specificity.* Public relations can be targeted to a small specialized audience if the right media vehicle is used.

- *Believability.* Much public relations communication is seen as credible because it comes from an apparently impartial and non-commercial source. Where information is presented as news, readers or viewers may be less critical of a message than if it was presented as a biased advertisement.

- *Difficult to control.* A company can exercise little direct control over how its public relations activity is subsequently handled and interpreted. If successful, a press release may be printed in full, although there can be no control over where or when it is printed. At worst, a press release can be misinterpreted and the result could be very unfavourable news coverage.

- *Competition for attention.* The fact that many organizations compete for a finite amount of attention puts pressure on the public relations effort to be better than that of competitors.

11.9.1 **The publics of public relations**

Public relations can be distinguished from customer relations because its concerns go beyond the creation of mutually beneficial relationships with actual or potential customers. The following additional audiences for public relations can be identified.

- *Intermediaries.* These may share many of the same concerns as customers and need reassurance about the company's capabilities as a service principal. Service organizations can usually develop this reassurance through the use of company newsletters, trade journal articles, etc.

- *Suppliers.* These may need assurances that the company is a credible one to deal with and that contractual obligations will be met. Highlighting favourable annual reports and drawing attention to major new developments can help to raise the profile and credibility of a company in the eyes of its suppliers.

- *Employees.* Here, public relations overlaps with the efforts of internal marketing (see Chapter 12) and assumes great importance within the service sector where personnel become part of the service offer, and it is important to develop participation and motivation among employees. In addressing its internal audiences, public relations uses such tools as in-house publications, newsletters and employee recognition activities.

- *Financial community.* This includes financial institutions that have supported, are currently supporting or who may support the organization in the future. Shareholders – both private and institutional – form an important element of this community and must be reassured that the organization is going to achieve its stated objectives.

- *Government*. In many cases, the actions of government can significantly affect the fortunes of an organization and therefore relationships with government departments – at local, national and supranational level – need to be carefully developed. This can include lobbying of Members of Parliament, communicating the organization's views to government enquiries and civil servants, and creating a favourable image for itself by sponsoring public events.

- *Local communities*. It is sometimes important for an organization to be seen as a 'good neighbour' in the local community. Therefore, the organization can enhance its image through the use of charitable contributions, **sponsorship** of local events, being seen to support the local environment, etc.

11.9.2 **The tools of public relations**

A wide range of public relations tools are available and the suitability of each is dependent upon the promotional objectives at which they are directed. In general, the tools of public relations are best suited to creating awareness of an organization or liking for its services, and tend to be less effective in directly bringing about action in the form of purchase decisions. While there can be argument as to just what constitutes public relations activity, some of the important elements which are used within the promotion mix are described below.

- *Press releases*. This refers to activities undertaken by firms to obtain editorial space in the media which are likely to be seen or heard by the company's target customers. The aim of the press release is more likely to be promoting the image of an organization rather than achieving an immediate sale. Because of their important contribution towards the promotion mix, press relations are considered in more detail below.

- *Lobbying*. Professional lobbyists are often employed in an effort to inform and hence influence key decision-makers who may be critical in allowing for elements of a marketing plan to be implemented. Lobbying can take place at a local level (e.g. a bus company seeking to convince a local authority of the harm which would result to the public in general if streets in a town centre were closed to buses); at a national level (e.g. lobbying by British Telecom to reduce the regulatory constraints on its pricing); and at a supranational level (e.g. lobbying by airlines to the European Commission which took place at the time that the Commission was deciding whether to allow a proposed merger between British Airways and American Airlines to proceed).

- *Education and training*. In an effort to develop a better understanding – and hence liking – of an organization and its services, many service organizations aim education and training programmes at important target groups. In this way, banks frequently supply schools and colleges with educational material which will pre-dispose recipients of the material to their brand when they come to open a bank account. Open days are another common method of educating the public by showing them the complex 'behind the scenes' production processes involved, a tactic commonly employed by theatres.

- *Exhibitions*. Most companies attend exhibitions not with the intention of making an immediate sale, but to create an awareness of their organization which will result in a sale over the longer term. Exhibitions offer the chance for potential cus-tomers to talk face to face with representatives of the organization and the physical layout of the exhibition stand can give valuable tangible evidence about the nature of the service on offer. Exhibitions are used for both consumer services and busi-ness-to-business services. As an example of the latter, the annual World Travel Market in London offers the chance for a wide range of tourism-related service industries to meet quite narrowly targeted customers and to display tangible cues to their service offering (e.g. brochures and staff).

- *In-house journals*. Many service organizations have developed their own magazines which are given to customers or potential customers. By adopting a news-based magazine format, the message becomes more credible than if it was presented as a pure advertisement. Often, outside advertisers contribute revenue which can make such journals self-financing – this commonly happens with in-house magazines published by banks. Travel operators often publish magazines which are read by a captive travelling public.

- *Special events*. In order to attract media attention, organizations sometimes arrange an event which is in itself newsworthy and will create awareness of the organization. One example was the world's first non-stop passenger plane flight between Britain and Australia, made by a Qantas aircraft. Although Qantas had adapted the aircraft and the journey could not be made under normal operating conditions, the fact that it was a 'first' made it newsworthy and created significant awareness of Qantas. Of course, if badly managed, a special event can turn into a public relations disaster.

- *Sponsorship*. There is argument about whether this strictly forms part of the public relations portfolio of tools. It is, however, increasingly being used by services com-panies and is described in more detail below.

11.9.3 **Press relations**

Service organizations realize that an important way of promoting a favourable corporate image is through effective relationships with the main media. They aim to create over the longer term a feeling of mutual understanding between the organization and the media, which is achieved by means of the following.

- *Press releases*. There are the most frequent form of press relations activity and is commonly used to announce new service launches, new appointments or significant achievements. Press releases have the advantage of being a relatively inexpensive promotional tool which can reach large audiences with a high degree of credibility. Against this, a major disadvantage is the lack of control which the generator of a press release has over how it is subsequently handled, in terms of appearance, timing and content (it is likely to be edited). Because of the competition from other organizations for press coverage, there can be no guarantee that any particular item will actually be used.

- *Press conferences.* These are used where a major event is to be announced and an opportunity for a two-way dialogue between the organization and the media is considered desirable.

- *Availability of specialist commentators.* Faced with a news story on which the media wishes to report, a newspaper or radio station may seek specialists within an industrial sector who are knowledgeable on the issues involved. For example, a local tour operator may be asked by a local newspaper to comment upon

---

PR on the line

Service companies have begun to appreciate the PR value of the Internet as a convenient way to disseminate information quickly and widely. But against this is the realization that corporate reputations can be savaged as disgruntled customers and shareholders swap comments on the World Wide Web. Thorns in the side of PR people include the McSpotlight site (www.mcspotlight.org), which carries information critical of McDonald's restaurants, and the Lostminute.com site for disgruntled investors in Lastminute.com. Such sites can be created without the companies' knowledge, if they are not monitoring, and contributing to, the forums and chat rooms. They can end up disseminating a damaging mix of rumour and untruths.

PR agencies that have the technical expertise have set up monitoring services. The UK's third largest PR consultancy, Edelman, monitors the Internet, checking on 33 000 user groups and bulletin boards, and regularly prepares web pages for its clients in anticipation of crises. These are then 'hidden' on the website, ready to be activated if needed.

PR professionals have had to face up to the new realities of the Internet. Response times need to be immediate, with no specific deadlines that are typical of conventional published media. But quite apart from the battle of technology are the fundamental questions: Why did a company allow itself to get into the position of exposing itself to criticism? Could this not have been foreseen? If there is little for people to campaign about, the dissident websites would probably lose much of their support.

the consequences of a hurricane in an overseas resort. This helps both the reporter and the service organization in question, whose representative is fielded as an expert.

11.9.4 Crisis management

An important element of public relations is avoiding negative publicity. Because services can be highly variable, there is always the possibility that the media will pick up on one bad incident and leave its audience thinking that this is the norm for that services provider. This is particularly a problem for highly visible public or quasi-public services for which readers enjoy reading bad news stories to confirm their own prejudices. External events may also lead to bad publicity, or the negative actions of similar service organizations may lead to a generally poor reputation of the sector as a whole. In all situations, an organization needs to establish contingency plans to minimize any surprise and confusion resulting from the publicity. Bad publicity is more likely to be managed effectively if an organization has invested time and effort in developing mutually supportive good relations with the media.

Service organizations, by the very nature of their operating environment, face unpredictable major crises, such as a train crash or a fire at a nightclub. At such times, the provision of timely, appropriate and honest information can help to preserve a company's image as a caring and honest organization. Service organizations therefore often prepare and practise plans to be implemented when a disaster occurs. Following a serious train crash outside London's Paddington Station in 1999, the quality of communication was one bright spot in an otherwise devastating incident and showed evidence of previous rehearsal. Where a company appears to be caught on the hop and is perceived to be making things up as it goes along, the effects can cause a crisis to be remembered for even longer. The handling of a crash by a TWA aircraft on its way from New York to Paris in 1998 is cited as an example of bad crisis management.

11.10 Sponsorship

One way that service organizations can try to 'tangibilize' their services is to attempt to get customers to link the image of the organization or of specific services with a more tangible event or activity. While publicity can perform this function successfully, sponsorship can also have long-term value.

Sponsorship involves investment in events or causes in order that an organization can achieve objectives such as increased awareness levels, enhanced reputation, etc. Sponsorship activities include such examples as a bank sponsoring cricket matches (e.g. the NatWest Trophy) and the sponsorship of specific television programmes (such as Powergen's sponsoring of weather forecasts on ITV).

Sponsorship is attractive to service companies as it allows the relatively known characteristics of an event or activity being sponsored to help enhance the image of

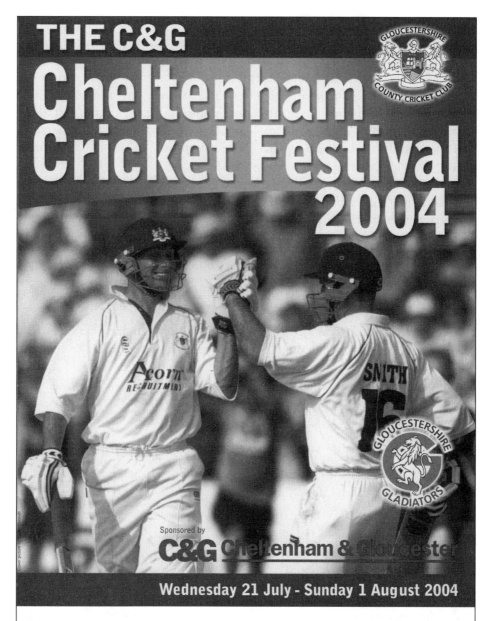

Figure 11.9 Service organizations have a long tradition of sponsoring sporting events, in an effort to link the intangible and possibly unknown nature of their service with the tangible and known nature of a major sports event. Cheltenham & Gloucester – the third largest provider of household mortgages in the UK – uses sponsorship, among other things, to differentiate itself from dozens of other banks and building societies with which it competes. By sponsoring a public activity, the brand name is exposed to potential buyers, especially, in this case, cricket fans, for whom C&G may be high on the list of brands that are spontaneously recalled. The company's financial services products are also likely to be attributed with some of the characteristics of cricket – traditional, very English, reliable, etc. (Reproduced with permission of Cheltenham & Gloucester)

an organization's own inherently intangible services (Figure 11.9). As an example, an insurance company wishing to associate itself with high quality may seek to sponsor the activities of a leading arts organization noted for the quality of its productions. A further advantage of sponsorship is that it allows a company to avoid the general media clutter usually associated with advertising. Furthermore, audiences can be segmented and a sponsorship vehicle chosen whose audience matches that of the sponsoring company, in terms of socio-economic, demographic and geographic characteristics. In this way, a regional insurance broker might sponsor a local theatrical group operating solely in its own business area.

It is difficult to evaluate sponsorship activities because of the problem of isolating the effects of sponsorship from other elements of the promotion mix. Direct measurement is only likely to be possible if sponsorship is the predominant tool. Sponsorship should therefore be seen as a tool that complements other elements of the promotion mix.

11.11 Online marketing

The Internet has emerged as a versatile element of the **communication mix** which often combines a promotional function with a distribution function. In the early days of online marketing, there were many claims that the Internet would come to dominate companies' promotion mix. Of course, many people's early hopes for the Internet have since been moderated and it may be more realistic to regard online marketing not as a standalone activity, but as just one component of a company's integrated marketing communications.

We have already mentioned some of the advantages of online marketing in our previous discussion of the elements of the promotion mix and noted the overlap between promotion mix elements.

- Our definition of advertising includes web pages which broadcast to large numbers of people but are not interactive.

- Personal selling is increasingly relying on online communication to support the efforts of sales personnel.

- Public relations professionals have understood the impact of chat rooms and dissident websites on a company's reputation and have developed web-based tools of their own.

- Online media have become an integral element of direct marketing by opening up an additional channel through which a company can enter an interactive dialogue (**e-business**) with its customers.

11.11.1 Objectives and development of online media

Communication using online media involves a number of stages of development. At the most basic level, a company's website can simply give additional information about its services, for example many hotels have websites which give information about their location and the facilities available. At this stage of development, the Internet is being used simply as an online form of the traditional printed brochure. Although a static, one-to-all website may now seem quite unadventurous, we should nevertheless recognize the advantages that web pages have over traditional printed brochures.

- They are much less expensive to produce.

- They can be updated very rapidly (e.g. in response to a price change) without the need to destroy existing stocks of brochures.

- Information can be provided immediately to prospective customers anywhere in the world, without the need to wait for a postal delivery.

- Comprehensive information can be provided within the site – more than could realistically be provided within the confines of a printed brochure.

- Links can be provided to other related information (for example, a hotel can include a link to local tourist attractions).

The second stage of online development allows some degree of interactive dialogue between a company and visitors to its website. At its simplest, this can take the form of a facility for visitors to enter a dialogue with the company by e-mail, perhaps to find out further information. Interactivity could be added by creating a script which allows the visitor to ask simple questions and for the site to generate answers which are of direct relevance to the customer. This could take the form of a simple ready-reckoner type of calculator to allow the user to calculate the monthly repayments on a mortgage, in which they are invited to enter various loan amounts and repayment periods. More complex interactivity can be developed by linking the customer's request to a database of information. This is used by railway operators (e.g. www.nationalrail.co.uk) to provide precise information on possible rail journeys in response to a customer's request for information on train times between two specified points at a specified time. Many online service providers use targeted e-mail services to encourage customers to visit their sites. The travel and leisure company Lastminute.com, for example, claims to send more than 2 million e-mails to customers every week. The content of these e-mails is tailored to fit the recipient's age, lifestyle and other factors (Kirchgaessner, 2003).

The third stage of online development is to allow immediate fulfilment of a request, such as confirmation of a hotel booking or reservation of a plane ticket. By linking a customer's online request to a real-time database of availability, the company is able to immediately communicate a specific price/product offer. Many airline and hotel companies have used the principles of yield management to continually change their price and product offer to reflect the changing balance between supply and demand, so the message that it sends to a site visitor may be quite different to one that it sent even just half an hour ago.

The Internet is used extensively for comparison shopping and a lot of research has gone into understanding which sites produce the best results in terms of moving an individual through the stages of purchase. A regularly updated site which contains information of direct relevance to a user and which is fast to download has become a minimum requirement for most users of the medium.

Online communication is particularly attractive for services, such as travel and financial services, where the cost of delivering tangible elements is not a major constraint. It has been predicted that, by 2010, the majority of package holidays will be bought through the Internet and high-street travel agencies will serve only a small niche market. According to Forrester Research (in Flood, 2001), Internet airline ticket sales topped $7 billion in 2000 and US online hotel bookings were over $2 billion. Although research estimates and forecast sales vary widely, most surveys agree that travel is the largest e-commerce sector by value.

In most western countries, the majority of the population now has access to the Internet, either at home, work or their place of study. The Internet is now firmly established as a communication medium in most organizations, and in a growing proportion of households use of the Internet is becoming as commonplace as switching on the television. An important consideration for marketers is that those households who have innovated with Internet access tend to be the high-income households and opinion leaders which many companies are particularly keen to target (Kwak *et al.*, 2002). The development of high-capacity fibre-optic lines will

---

Short message – quick results?

Companies have taken on board the basic functions of SMS text messaging to target customers and potential customers. During 2003 the Hilton Hotel Group used SMS messaging to communicate details of promotional offers to members of its database. Using SMS allowed the hotel to get the messages out instantly and at the most appropriate time of day, and achieved a claimed 10–25% uptake of offers. SMS text messages can only allow a very short message to be communicated and, to be effective, need to be linked to other methods of demographic data collection and profiling. Early experience of mobile internet facilities through wireless application protocol (WAP) technology was disappointing, but the development of 'third generation' mobile telephony offers new opportunities for interactive dialogue at any location. By linking wireless access to global positioning systems (GPSs), individuals can be targeted with information which is relevant to their immediate needs. Examples include restaurants seeking to fill spare capacity by sending messages to mobile phone users who have previously registered an interest in receiving alerts and who are in the area at a time when the restaurant has spare capacity.

increase the amount of data which can be transmitted through the Internet, thereby reducing the problems of slow speed which have inhibited e-commerce.

11.11.2 **Limitations of online media**

Online media have developed rapidly over the last decade and provided benefits to buyers and sellers which would previously have been almost unimaginable. Rapid growth inevitably brings developmental problems and some of the limitations of online media are summarized below.

- Systems often require high capital outlay, and there may be a slow return on investment. Compatibility within the technological architecture can be a limitation with new technologies continually requiring additional investment from companies. In the early days of the 'dotcom' boom, investors were eager to invest in new technology, often unwisely as it turned out. Given a previous history of failed web initiatives, raising capital for next generation technology can be a challenge.

- As use of the Internet as a communication medium has increased, it has become increasingly cluttered. This effect has been seen during the development of all media, and companies using the Internet have faced increasing challenges in drawing people to their websites. Getting a high ranking in search engines has become a critical skill and specialist companies are often employed to raise a client's rankings. From being a very cheap source of messages, companies are having to spend increasing amounts of money promoting their web presence, both online and offline. A new generation of 'informediaries' has appeared to simplify communication between online buyers and sellers. Buying access to target customers on the Internet has become an important activity, with portals such as Yahoo! charging for the use of **banner advertisements** on their popular websites. A number of companies, such as Doubleclick.com, exist to collect information about individuals' usage patterns with a view to improving the targeting of advertisements through paid-for websites.

- Many companies have been keen to move communication with customers to the Internet and away from other more expensive media. Research undertaken by Oxford Associates in a number of US-based industries suggested that most companies achieved a 20–40% reduction in transaction costs when selling through distributors and partners, 40–45% when selling through call centres, and over 50% when selling over the Internet. However, they warned against following a cost reduction strategy that does not take account of buyer behaviour. A company could too easily lose key customers as it cuts back its salesforce and call centres, hoping that buyers will migrate to the internet. There have been many cases of online systems that have faced lengthy teething problems, costing a lot in lost customer goodwill.

Switch in Amazon promotion strategy

One of the early paradoxes of the 'new media' of the late 1990s was their reliance on 'old' media. To those who had advocated a revolution in media channels, it would seem odd that some of the biggest newspaper and television advertisers in 1999 were Internet-related service companies, with companies such as Lastminute.com, Freeserve and Yahoo! spending huge amounts to promote their Internet-based services.

In among the big spenders was Amazon.com, which had soaked up billions of dollars of its investors' capital in developing a high-profile brand, backed up by high levels of service. Until 2002, Amazon had used its TV advertising for both brand-building and driving immediate sales. The company's TV ad campaign – which in 2001 cost an estimated $50 million – focused on the advantages of shopping online versus going to a shopping mall. The company had not promoted its new product categories, or 'stores', via TV ads. Instead, the company had an impressive web presence which promoted the company and its products.

In 2002 Amazon decided to stop all TV advertising. Was this just another wild idea by a company whose chairman, Jeff Bezos, had ruffled the feathers of many investors through his seemingly wacky ideas? Or was the decision simply a reflection of the fact that the promotional objectives of Amazon had changed, and therefore called for new communication tools?

The company had carried out extensive research into what was now a substantial customer base. Simply encouraging existing customers to buy more (for example, through new product ranges) was one way of securing additional sales. But its research also showed that shipping costs were a major point of contention with existing and would-be customers. With local high-street bookstores offering attractive prices and long opening hours, plus free ordering and collection services, people often felt miffed about having to pay a $3 shipping charge for an item that only cost $25. Although the company felt that the creative message of its TV adverts was working, it thought that free shipping and lower prices would bring an even greater return on its investment.

The company switched its advertising budget to fund a sales promotion of free shipping costs for purchases over $25. During 2001, Amazon reported in its financial results a $41 million loss on its shipping costs. After an initial trial, the free-shipping promotion was extended in 2003 to the British market for purchases over £39.

Amazon had another promotional tool up its sleeve which it planned to use fully – its network of associates who place a banner ad on their websites and take a small percentage of sales revenue when a visitor to their website clicks through to Amazon and makes a purchase. The company had also been a big spender on banner adverts on other companies' sites, and strengthened this form of promotion, helped by a slump in charges for banner ads as other dotcom advertisers were removed from the market through bankruptcy.

Stopping all television advertising is an unusual move for a major brand such as Amazon. Its brand had been successfully built, to the extent that it scored highly in unprompted recall of booksellers' names. But could it have built the brand entirely online without television and newspaper support? Would the brand need refreshing with further TV advertising to protect it against new 'clicks and mortar' bookstores?

Source: based on Kawamoto, D., 'Amazon has turned off its television ads', CNET News.com, 10 February 2003.

11.12 **Word-of-mouth**

Of course, an organization's image can be derived through channels other than the formal communication process. There is a lot of evidence, for example, that when differentiating between professional and personal service providers, customers prefer to be guided by information from friends and other personal contacts rather than the usual promotion mix (e.g. Walker, 2001; Susskind, 2002). Of course, positive word-of-mouth recommendation is generally dependent on customers having good experiences with an organization, and studies have shown how unexpectedly high standards of service from a company can promote recommendation (Derbaix and Vanhamme, 2003). On the other hand, a bad experience can rapidly be spread as negative word-of-mouth discouragement (Laczniak *et al.*, 2001). An important communication objective is therefore often to leverage this 'free' form of positive promotion and to limit the damage caused by negative word-of-mouth by encouraging dissatisfied customers to resolve their problems before they tell others. In addition to providing a good service that people would want to recommend to their friends, firms facilitate word-of-mouth recommendation through such means as customer referral cards.

Word-of-mouth recommendation has been further facilitated by the Internet. As well as telling their friends, messages left with bulletin boards and chat rooms can spread a message very rapidly. Many companies have embraced the Internet to develop 'viral' marketing, in which a message can rapidly be spread from one person who informs a handful of friends, who each in turn inform a handful of their friends (Gelb and Sundaram, 2002; Welker, 2002).

For many people, buying a mobile phone is very daunting, with countless permutations of networks, tariffs and handsets, communicated through a barrage of advertising messages. Carphone Warehouse has recognized the importance of word-of-mouth recommendation in simplifying buyers' decision processes, and offers existing customers an incentive to pass on their recommendation to friends.

Case study

Co-op Bank smiles with ethical promotion

The banking sector has been dominated by the 'big four' banks, yet despite their domination, smaller challengers manage to achieve success in niche markets. One of these is the Co-operative Bank, a minnow compared to rivals such as Barclays, Lloyds TSB, HSBC and Royal Bank of Scotland. The use of a distinct promotional positioning has been the key to the Co-operative Bank's survival and expansion in a competitive and consolidating marketplace.

The Co-operative Bank was originally founded in 1872 by the Co-operative Wholesale and Retail Societies, who had a vision of providing all the goods and services that an individual would need from cradle to grave, free from capitalist profiteering. By the mid-1980s the bank had enjoyed a period of steady growth when its branch size passed 100, helped by several innovative new services such as free in-credit banking, extended opening hours and interest-bearing cheque accounts. However the bank found its market position steadily being eroded by increased competition from the major clearing banks and particularly the larger building societies. Following deregulation of the UK banking sector in the 1980s, these had been able to enter the personal banking sector and many had established their own personal cheque accounts. Partly as a result of this new competition, the Co-operative Bank saw its market share fall from 2.7% in 1986 to 2% by 1991.

Alongside this trend the bank faced a changing customer profile. Traditionally the bank had attracted a high proportion of its customers from the more affluent ABC_1 social groups. By 1992 an increasing number of new accounts were being attracted from the C_2DE social groups, while at the same time the bank was losing its core ABC_1 accounts. This trend was diluting its position as a more upmarket bank and reducing its potential to cross-sell more profitable financial products such as insurance and personal loans.

The bank's research showed that outside of its customer base, it lacked a clear image, being seen mainly as rather staid, old-fashioned and with left-wing political affinities. Many people linked the image of the bank with the Co-op shops, which in the 1980s were often looking tired alongside their more dynamic competitors. Furthermore, spontaneous recall of the Co-operative Bank name had steadily fallen despite extensive advertising of its innovative new products.

The bank realized that immediate action was necessary to rebuild its image and stem the loss of its ABC_1 accounts. The size of the bank and its profitability meant that the advertising budget had to be modest and therefore a focused campaign with maximum effectiveness was crucial.

BDDH was appointed as advertising agency to devise a promotional campaign. The agency carried out an audit of the Co-operative Bank to identify any distinctive competencies that it could build a campaign upon. It soon found that the bank's heritage offered a unique positioning opportunity against other mainstream banks. This derived in particular from its sourcing and distribution of funds which had been governed by an unwritten ethical code, with the effect that the bank never lent money to environmentally or politically unsound organizations. BDDH set out to transform the results of its audit into a relevant and motivating proposition that would appeal beyond the bank's current customer base. A key strategic decision was made to target promotional activity at the growing number of 'ethical consumers' who, importantly, were found to have a more upmarket ABC_1 profile.

The 'ethical bank' formed the foundation upon which BDDH built its campaign. Initially this was tested on the bank's existing customers, where it gained a high level of approval. The bank recognized that advertising claims must be met by actual practice and incorporated its ethical stance into its customer charter. The bank was well aware that the media enjoys making trouble for companies that claim to be ethical but in fact are caught out undertaking unethical practices. Advertising was initially used to raise awareness of the bank's positioning. The creative work was deliberately provocative and motivating, while at the same time maintaining the bank's credentials as a high-street lender. The creative images used were often simple and stark.

The key objectives of the campaign were:

1. build customer loyalty and so stem the outflow of ABC_1's.

2. expand the customer base, targeting ABCs.

3. expand the corporate customer base.

National press and regional television in the banks 'northern heartland' were the primary media used in the initial stages of the campaign. Cinema advertising was used as the campaign progressed.

The marketing objectives were exceeded as a result of the promotional campaign. The bank established a strong and differentiated brand platform which it subsequently used to launch new services, including its 'Smile' Internet-banking operation (www.smile.co.uk). The campaign was carefully targeted, with the aim of achieving maximum impact which enabled the message to be delivered cost-effectively. The case clearly demonstrates how effective promotional activity, linked closely to business and marketing objectives and strategy, can provide a long-term sustainable competitive position in the marketplace.

In 2004, the bank reported its tenth year of increased profits, up in 2003 to £130m. Although the bank's margins had been falling, it remained prudent in its lending, with a mortgage loan-to-value ratio of 50% – considered good for the industry, and further evidence that the bank was not reliant on poorer socio-economic groups who tend to borrow a higher proportion of a property's value. Of course, the bank's rising profitability could not be entirely attributed to its campaign, but the bank's successful promotional positioning can be put down to a clear understanding of its customer base and its own unique competencies.

Case study review questions

1. Identify a programme of research that might indicate whether the Co-operative Bank's ethical promotional positioning has been effective.

2. How sustainable is an ethical positioning by a bank? To what extent have the Co-operative Bank's rivals sought to establish their ethical credentials? What barriers prevent an even wider uptake of an ethical position?

3. What – if any – new challenges or threats arise for the Co-operative Bank's ethical promotion as a result of greater use of online banking services?

Chapter summary and links to other chapters

This chapter has explored the role of promotion in the marketing planning of services. While many of the principles of communication for services are similar to those for goods, the promotion of services poses additional problems and opportunities. Perceived risk, caused by intangibility, must be addressed by promotion, and techniques for seeking to achieve this have been discussed. The presence of consumers in the production process for services opens possibilities for promotion which are not generally available to the goods manufacturer.

Promotion has a vital role in guiding buyers through the purchase decision process (**Chapter 4**). With the development of relationship marketing strategies (**Chapter 5**), the promotional emphasis in many companies has moved from recruitment of new customers to retention of existing ones. With the development of direct marketing, promotion and accessibility strategies are becoming increasingly closely connected (**Chapter 9**). Finally, promotion strategy contributes towards the positioning strategy of a service (**Chapter 7**) and implementation requires adequate information for planning and monitoring purposes (**Chapter 6**).

Chapter review questions

1. To what extent does the intangibility of a service influence the promotional methods used by a service organization?

2. Why do you think that certain professional services still consider sales promotion to be unethical?

3. What is the link between 'internal marketing' and the promotion of services?

4. To what extent can the application of direct marketing be effective in the promotion of a university?

5. Public relations may be a more effective promotional tool for services than other communication methods. Why do you think this may be the case?

6. Identify the problems likely to be faced by an airline in evaluating the effectiveness of its promotion for a newly introduced service.

Activity

Gather together advertising messages from banks promoting their current accounts. To what extent are the banks advertising claims consistent with your experience of banks' service delivery? Who are the advertisements aimed at? To what extent are they aimed at the banks' own employees?

Key terms

Adoption process Rate at which individuals start buying a product.

Advertising The process by which an advertiser communicates with target audiences through paid-for messages.

AIDA (Attention, Interest, Desire, Action) A mnemonic used to describe the process of communicating a series of messages.

Banner advertisements Paid-for advertisements on other companies' websites.

Communication mix The various media and messages which are used to communicate with the target audience.

Cost per 1000 Used in advertising as a measure of cost per 1000 people viewing or reading an advertisement.

Direct marketing Direct communication between a seller and individual customers using a method of promotion other than face-to-face selling.

E-business The ability to integrate local and wide area networks through the use of Internet protocols to effectively remove the barriers between businesses, their customers and their suppliers.

Guerrilla marketing The use of unconventional promotional tactics which are unexpected by the target audience.

Public relations The deliberate, planned and sustained effort to establish and maintain mutual understanding between an organization and its publics.

> **Sales promotion** Techniques and incentives used to increase short-term sales.
>
> **Sponsorship** Payment by a company to be associated with a particular event or activity.
>
> **Telemarketing** Sales activity which focuses on the use of the telephone to enter into a two-way dialogue with present and potential customers.

Selected further reading

For a fuller discussion of the general principles of promotion, the following texts cover the main elements of the promotion mix.

Smith, P. (2001) *Marketing Communications: An Integrated Approach*, Kogan Page, London.

Fill, C. (2001) *Marketing Communications: Contexts, Strategies, and Applications*, FT Prentice Hall, London.

Picton, D. and Broderick, A. (eds) (2000) *Integrated Marketing Communications*, FT Prentice Hall, London.

Jefkins, F. and Yadin, D. (2000) *Advertising*, 4th edn, FT Prentice Hall, London.

Cheverton, P. (2001) *Key Account Management*, Kogan Page, London.

Cummins, J. and Mullin, R. (2002) *Sales Promotion: How to Create, Implement and Integrate Campaigns That Really Work*, Kogan Page, London.

Oliver, S. (2001) *Public Relations Strategy: A Guide to Corporate Communications Management*, Kogan Page, London.

Tapp, A. (2001) *Principles of Direct and Database Marketing*, 2nd edn, FT Prentice Hall, London.

Chaffey, D. and Smith, P.R. (2001) *E-marketing Excellence*, Butterworth-Heinemann.

During the early days of the services marketing literature, a number of articles sought to define the ways in which the promotion of services differed from that of goods. Some early articles, and more recent discussion, can be found in the following.

Firestone, S.H. (1983) 'Why advertising a service is different', in L.L. Berry, G.L. Shostack and G.D. Upah (eds), *Emerging Perspectives in Services Marketing*, American Marketing Association.

George, W.R. and Berry, L.L. (1980) 'Guidelines for the advertising of services', *Business Horizons*, 24 (July/August), 43–9.

George, W.R., Kelly, J.P and Marshall, C.E. (1983) 'Personal selling of services', in L.L. Berry, G.L. Shostack and G.D. Upah (eds), *Emerging Perspectives in Services Marketing*, American Marketing Association.

Mortimer, K. (2000) 'Are services advertised differently? An analysis of the relationship between product and service types and their information content', *Journal of Marketing Communications*, 6, 121–34.

Zinkhan, G.M. (2002) 'Promoting services via the Internet: New opportunities and challenges', *Journal of Services Marketing*, 16 (5), 412–23.

References

Aaker, D.A. and Myers, J.G. (1982) *Advertising Management*, Prentice Hall.

Chung-kue Hsu and McDonald, D. (2002) 'An examination on multiple celebrity endorsers in advertising', *Journal of Product and Brand Management*, 11 (1), 19–29.

Coulson-Thomas, C.T. (1985) *Marketing Communications*, Heinemann.

Crosby, L.A., Evans, K.R. and Cowles, D. (1990) 'Relationship quality in services selling: An interpersonal influence perspective', *Journal of Marketing*, 54 (July), 68–81.

Derbaix, C. and Vanhamme, J. (2003) 'Inducing word-of-mouth by eliciting surprise – A pilot investigation', *Journal of Economic Psychology*, 24 (1), 99–116.

Direct Marketing Association (2002) *Census of the UK Direct Marketing Industry*, Direct Marketing Association, London.

Flood, G. (2001) 'Online travel businesses fly high on the net', *Computing (UK)*, 8 March, 48–9.

Gelb, B.D. and Sundaram, S. (2002) 'Adapting to "word of mouse"', *Business Horizons*, 45 (4), 21–5.

George, W.R. and Berry, L.L. (1980) 'Guidelines for the advertising of services', *Business Horizons*, 24 (July/August), 43–9.

George, W.R. and Myers, T.A. (1981) 'Life underwriters' perceptions of differences in selling goods and services', *CLU Journal*, April.

Kirchgaessner, S. (2003) 'Need inflatable sheep, fast? Lastminute.com: Speed and reliability are essential ingredients for online success', *The Financial Times*, 5 February, 4.

Kwak, H., Fox, R.J. and Zinkhan, G.M. (2002) 'What products can be successfully promoted and sold via the Internet?', *Journal of Advertising Research*, 42 (1), 23–38.

Laczniak, R.N., DeCarlo, T.E. and Ramaswami, S.N. (2001) 'Consumers' responses to negative word-of-mouth communication: An attribution theory perspective', *Journal of Consumer Psychology*, 11 (1), 57–73.

Levinson, J.C. (2003) *Guerrilla Marketing for the 21st Century*, Houghton Mifflin.

Mintel (2002) *Optimising the power of call centres*, Mintel, London.

Rogers, E.M. (1962) *Diffusion of Innovation*, Free Press, New York.

Susskind, A.M. (2002) 'I told you so! Restaurant customers' word-of-mouth communication patterns', *Cornell Hotel & Restaurant Administration Quarterly*, 43 (2), 75–85.

Walker, L.J.H. (2001) 'The measurement of word-of-mouth communication and an investigation of service quality and customer commitment as potential antecedents', *Journal of Service Research*, 4 (1), 60–75.

Welker, C.B. (2002) 'The paradigm of viral communication', *Information Services and Use*, 22 (1), 3–8.

The marketing impacts of services employees

Learning objectives

This chapter will explain:

- the interrelationship of marketing, human resource management and operations management

- the contribution of employee performance to customer satisfaction and subsequently to an organization's profitability

- internal marketing as an integration of marketing and human resource management practices

- key issues involved in the recruitment, motivation, training and control of staff employed in the service sector, especially those involved in front-line service encounters

- organizational structures and processes for effective services marketing

- methods to reduce a service organization's dependency on human resources.

12.1 **Introduction**

Consider a weekend leisure break in a hotel and the things which, typically, are most likely to go wrong:

- the checking-in procedure is slow and unfriendly

- facilities in the room are not as promised and the hotel is slow to put things right

- the promised wake-up call doesn't materialize

- the bill is wrongly made up and it takes a lot of effort by the customer to put it right.

All of these instances illustrate the importance of employee management as a means of meeting customers' quality expectations. Appropriate actions by front-line employees, and effective management of these employees could have avoided many of these problems. Of course, employees can also be responsible for particularly good service encounters, such as the hotel receptionist who spends considerable time in trying to find a Japanese-speaking babysitter for guests who request one.

The importance of people as a component of the service offering has been stressed on many occasions in previous chapters of this book. Most service production processes require the service organization's own personnel to provide significant inputs to the service production process, both at the front-line point of delivery and in those parts of the production process which are relatively removed from the final consumer. In the case of many one-to-one personal services, the service provider's own personnel constitute by far the most important element of the total service offering. The focus of this chapter is on personnel employed by the service organization. The management of this input, in terms of recruiting the best personnel, and training, motivating, rewarding and controlling them becomes crucial in influencing the perceived quality of service.

Services management has often been described as the bringing together of the principles of marketing, operations management and human resource management, in which it can sometimes be difficult – and undesirable – to draw distinctions between the three approaches (Figure 12.1). In this way, methods to improve the service provided by staff of a fast-food restaurant can be seen as a marketing problem (e.g. the need to analyse and respond to customer needs for such items as speed, variety and cleanliness), or an operations management problem (scheduling work in a manner which reduces bottlenecks and allows a flexible response to patterns of demand), or a human resource management problem (selecting and motivating staff in a way that maximizes their ability to deliver a specified standard of service).

It can be almost a cliché to say that for some businesses, the employees *are* the business – if they are taken away, the organization is left with very few assets with which it can seek to gain competitive advantage in meeting customers' needs. Numerous studies have demonstrated the effects of employees' customer orientation on service performance (e.g. Donavan *et al.*, 2004). While for some organizations the management

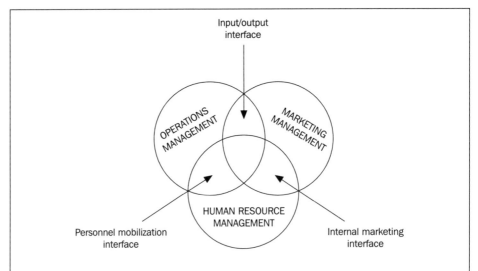

Figure 12.1 The interfaces between marketing management, operations management and human resource management

of personnel can be seen as just one other asset to be managed, for others human resource management is so central to the activities of the organization that it cannot be seen as a separate activity. Some indication of the importance attached to human resource management (HRM) within any organization can be gained by examining two aspects of personnel:

1. the proportion of total costs which are represented by employee costs

2. the importance of customer–employee encounters within the service offer.

In Figure 12.2 these two dimensions are shown in a matrix form with examples. For HRM, the most critical group of services is found where employees account for a high proportion of total costs and form an important part of the service offering perceived by the consumer. Many personal services such as hairdressing fall into this category. In other cases, employee costs may be a small proportion of total costs, but can represent key individuals who can significantly affect consumers' perceptions of a service. In this way, personnel costs are typically a relatively small proportion of the operating costs of a telephone service, yet the performance of key front-line staff such as telephone operators or service engineers can significantly affect judgements of quality.

The human input to services can by its nature be highly variable, resulting in variability in perceived quality. For this reason, many service organizations have sought to replace personnel with equipment-based inputs, often resulting in fewer, but more highly trained personnel being required.

The importance attached to HRM is also a reflection of the competitiveness of the environment in which an organization operates. At one extreme, the highly competitive environment which faces most west European fast-food restaurants requires

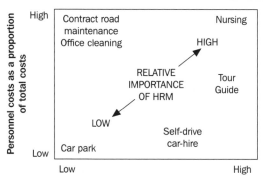

Figure 12.2 The importance of personnel within the service offer. The challenge of internal marketing is particularly great where employees account for a high proportion of an organization's total costs, and where employees have a high level of interaction with customers.

organizations to ensure that their staff meet customers' needs for speed, friendliness and accuracy more effectively than their competitors. On the other hand, organizations with relatively protected markets (for example, many public-sector services) can afford to be less customer-led in the manner in which their human resources are managed.

The world's favourite airline crews?

Established airlines have faced increasing competition as a result of deregulation and the emergence of budget, 'no-frills' airlines such as easyJet and Ryanair. While these new airlines have been particularly successful in attracting price-sensitive travellers, a large part of the market still prefers to travel with a 'full service' airline and is prepared to pay more than the rock-bottom prices sometimes advertised by budget airlines. British Airways promotes the fact that it has achieved high customer satisfaction ratings through the actions of its employees. Its reputation for good staff is based not just on smiling at customers, but being able to empathize with customers and to solve their problems. Operating aircraft is subject to all sorts of uncertainties, such as aircraft failure, bad weather and overbooking, all of which can have an immediate and profound impact on customers. An important role of employees is to ameliorate the effects of such uncertainties and to use initiative to solve customers' problems.

12.2 Internal marketing

The term '**internal marketing**' has come to be widely used to describe the practice of turning many of the established techniques of marketing inwardly by focusing on employees. Of course, services marketers have a lot to learn from human resource management (HRM). The role of marketing is to achieve organizational goals by satisfying customers' needs. HRM is concerned with achieving organizational goals. It therefore follows that HRM must itself be concerned with satisfying the needs of external customers. HRM can be contrasted with the more traditional personnel management which is often seen as being isolated and separate from the business aims of firms. Personnel management has frequently been oriented towards control and administrative activities rather than the alignment of human resources towards achieving strategic organizational goals. In doing so, personnel management has often become too concerned at achieving its own set of sub-goals which are not necessarily related to the marketing needs of an organization. In this way, the maintenance of a uniform pay structure may have been seen as a desirable objective in its own right by personnel managers despite the fact that the marketing needs of an organization may require more flexibility in the manner in which staff are paid.

The term 'internal marketing' came to prominence during the 1980s and an early definition of internal marketing provided by Berry (1980) was:

… the means of applying the philosophy and practices of marketing to people who serve the external customers so that (i) the best possible people can be employed and retained and (ii) they will do the best possible work.

It may be easy to say that there should be no barriers between the marketing and HRM functions of an organization, but in practice, jealousies and conflict can arise. In most organizations, HRM has its own hierarchical structure which is distinct from marketing. Even as an academic discipline, the two are usually taught as distinct subjects. This has led many people to criticize marketers' approach to internal marketing as being superficial and not being informed by the large body of knowledge on HRM which has gone before it.

In an attempt to clarify the concept of internal marketing, Varey and Lewis (1999) have conceptualized a number of its dimensions.

- *Internal marketing as a metaphor.* Organization jobs and employment conditions are 'products' to be marketed and managers should think like a marketer when dealing with people. However, it is the employer who is both buyer and consumer in the employment relationship, rather than the employee.

- *Internal marketing as a philosophy.* Managers may hold a conviction that HRM requires 'marketing-like' activities. However this does not address employees' divergent needs and interests which may themselves be quite different from those of the organization. This is especially the case if the 'marketing' activities are actually promotional advertising and selling of management requirements. Employees may merely be seen as the manipulable subject of managerial programmes.

- *Internal marketing as a set of techniques.* HRM may adopt market research, segmentation and promotional techniques in order to inform and persuade employees. But internal marketing as the manipulation of the '4Ps' imposes management's point of view on employees and cannot be said to be employee (customer) centred.

Therefore, it is employees who must change their needs or must understand the position of the employer as they respond to the market.

■ *Internal marketing as an approach.* There is an explicit symbolic dimension to HRM practices, such as employee involvement and participation, and statements about the role of employees within the organization. These are used to bring about indirect control of employees. Nevertheless, the symbolism of internal marketing may reveal many contradictions. For example, individualism contradicts team-working, and the service culture as defined by management may contradict attitudes towards employee flexibility and responsibility. The complexities of managing people and their actions and knowledge may be reduced to mere 'techniques' of symbolic communication.

Much debate surrounds just how internal marketing fits within traditional HRM structures and processes. Hales (1994), for example, is critical of the 'managerialist' perspective on internal marketing and of the literature on internal marketing as an approach to HRM. Viewed as an activity in isolation, internal marketing is unlikely to succeed. For that to happen, the full support of top management is required.

12.2.1 Employees as internal customers

Every organization can be considered to be a marketplace consisting of a diverse group of employees who engage in exchanges between each other (Foreman and Money, 1995). In order to have their needs met, employees are often dependent upon internal services provided by other departments or individuals within their organization. As in the case of external customers, these internal customers engage in numerous service encounters to satisfy the many needs they bring to the encounter. These internal encounters include relationships between customer-contact staff and the backroom staff, managers and the customer-contact staff, managers and the backroom staff, and, for large organizations, between the head office and each branch. In the most general sense, employees have been seen by some as 'consumers' of services provided by their employer, such as a pleasant working environment, provision of a pension scheme and good facilities for performing their tasks.

Increasingly, organizations are requiring internal service departments, such as information technology, human resources, accounting and media services, to be more accountable. In a growing number of instances, organizations have outsourced the services traditionally provided by such internal departments, resulting in extended 'network' or 'virtual' organizations. This has resulted in employees effectively trading services with other employees within their organization.

This view of different internal suppliers and customers, some which deal directly within the service delivery process and some which provide support services to the service delivery process, appears to be closely related to the concept of the value chain (Porter, 1980). A modified value chain in terms of internal suppliers is shown in Figure 12.3.

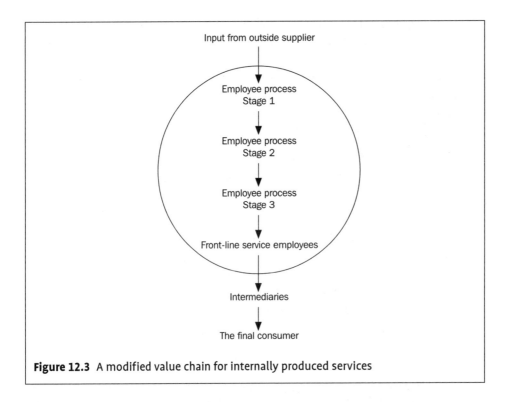

Figure 12.3 A modified value chain for internally produced services

This idea of a value chain and internal trading of services is closely related to the idea developed in the total quality management literature of 'next operation as a customer' (NOAC; Denton, 1990). NOAC is based on the idea that each group within an organization should treat the recipients of their output as an internal customer and strive to provide high-quality outputs for them (e.g. Lukas and Maignan, 1996). Through this approach, quality will be built into the service delivered to the final customer.

Attempts have been made to apply external service quality dimensions to the measurement of internal service quality between employees (e.g. Varey, 1995; Reynoso and Moores, 1997). This has been justified on the basis that the interaction between the company and the customer is simply one link in a large network of relationships, many of which occur within the boundaries of the company. The implication is that the principles and techniques for the creation and measurement of service quality can be transferred to the internal environment.

There are, however, problems in drawing analogies between internal and external markets for services. External customers can usually take their business elsewhere if they are not satisfied with the service provided, while internal customers may be required to use a designated service unit within their organization. Consequently, the internal customer is frequently a *captive* customer (Albrecht, 1990). Employees as customers may be tied to employment contracts with little short-term prospect of 'buying' employment elsewhere.

Many studies of internal marketing which focus on internal customers and suppliers have not differentiated between the different types of internal customers which may exist within the firm and their differing internal service expectations. This would appear to be no more marketing oriented than a marketing plan which treats all external customers as homogeneous. There is a need to explore the service expectations of different internal customer segments within the internal market and to identify any differences between these segments. This knowledge can then be applied to the internal marketing programme to maximize its effectiveness.

There is a widely held view that if employees are not happy with their jobs, external customers will never be uppermost in their minds. Researchers have tended to agree that satisfied internal customers are a critical prerequisite to the satisfaction of external customers. From an internal marketing perspective, there is an argument that by satisfying the needs of their internal customers, firms enhance their ability to satisfy the needs of their external customers. Nevertheless, it has also been recognized that service encounters are a three-way fight between the firm, the contact personnel and the customer. The service encounter is thus a 'compromise between partially conflicting parties' (Bateson, 1989). To give an example, it may sound like a good idea to give employees longer rest breaks because this satisfies their needs as internal 'customers'. But longer rest breaks may result in greater waiting time for external customers as

Customers before employees?

Many companies have developed a philosophy of putting their employees first. This at first might sound contradictory to the marketing philosophy which puts customers at the centre of a firm's thinking, but there are many examples of companies who have made this proud claim and achieved credible results. The American South Western Airlines has frequently been cited as an advocate of this approach, and has expanded rapidly and profitably. The airline has argued that employees are a major part of its service offer and that if they are not happy, it is unlikely that the airline's customers will be happy. Being a relatively new airline with no history of poor industrial relations undoubtedly helps employees to identify with the company's mission. Having staff incentive schemes which encourage employees to perform at their best in a highly competitive market also helps. But can this approach work in all situations? If employees do not share a company's mission, management's attempts to put employees first may not be reciprocated in the form of employees' enthusiastic contribution to the business. And if there is very little external competition to spur them on, captive customers may come second best by a long way.

In reality, it is difficult to talk about employees coming first if, by implication, customers come second. They should both be seen as part of a virtuous circle in which attention given to one reinforces attention given to the other.

fewer staff are now available to serve them. A fine balance has to be drawn and there is no conclusive proof that in all situations happier employees necessarily result in happier external customers and a more profitable service operation (see Silvestro, 2002).

12.3 Controlling and empowering staff

It follows from the previous discussion that there are two basic approaches to managing people. On the one hand, staff can be supervised closely and corrective action taken where they fail to perform to standard. On the other hand, staff can be made responsible for controlling their own actions. The latter is often referred to as 'empowering' employees. The problem of control is particularly great with service industries as it is usually not possible to remove the results of poor personnel performance before their effects are felt by customers. While the effects of a poorly performing car worker can be concealed from customers by checking his or her tangible output, the inseparability of the service production/consumption process makes quality control difficult to achieve. There is an argument that because many services are carried out on a one-to-one basis with little possibility of management intervention, day-to-day control by management is impossible. Nevertheless, many companies which use industrialized service processes rely on control powers with varying degrees of formality.

Should employees of service organizations be closely controlled, or should they be empowered to act in the best way they see fit? It was noted in Chapter 3 that **empowerment** may be crucial for turning service failures into effective recovery, and for closely tailoring a service to individual customers' needs. The degree of empowerment given to employees, or the control exercised over them depends on the format of a service delivery system. For low-contact, standardized services, employees can be controlled by mechanistic means such as rules and regulations. For high-contact, highly divergent services, high levels of empowerment may be more appropriate.

One of the underlying assumptions of those advocating empowerment is that employees' values will be in line with those of the organization. Organizations must be prepared to allow employees the freedom to act and to make decisions based on their own judgement. For example, if a service employee is empowered, then that employee must be able to decide how best to deal with the needs of customers, and should be accountable and responsible to deal with problems of customer complaints and operational difficulties caused.

Empowerment essentially involves giving employees discretion over the way they carry out their tasks. Kelley (1993) distinguished between three types of employee discretion: routine, creative and deviant.

- *Routine discretion* occurs where employees are allowed to select an alternative from a prescribed list of possible actions in order to do their job (e.g. a service engineer having a choice of three sub-systems to install in order to rectify a specified problem).

- *Creative discretion* is exercised where employees are required to develop alternative methods of performing a task (e.g. an interior design consultant may have complete freedom to choose their own designs).

- *Deviant discretion* is negatively regarded by the employer as it involves behaviours that are not part of the employees' formal job descriptions and which are outside their areas of authority.

Berry (1995, p. 208) noted that empowerment is essentially a state of mind. An employee with an empowered state of mind should experience feelings of: (1) control over how his or her job is performed; (2) awareness of the context in which the job is performed; (3) accountability for his or her work output; (4) shared responsibility for unit and organizational performance; and (5) equity in the rewards based on individual and collective performance. Discussion of empowerment frequently stresses the need to share information, so that employees understand the context in which they work.

Empowered employees need to be rewarded in a timely fashion and their initiatives, triumphs and achievements acknowledged. Empowerment also implies a culture which encourages employees to experiment with new ideas and can tolerate them making mistakes and learning from them. Such a culture would be more in line with the image of the 'Learning Organization' (Garvin, 1993).

The reasons for empowering employees can be divided into the mutually supportive dimensions of those that improve the motivation and productivity of employees and those that improve service delivery for consumers.

On the motivational side, empowerment of front-line service employees can lead to both attitudinal and behavioural changes in employees. Attitudinal changes resulting from empowerment include increased job satisfaction and reduced role stress. A consequence of increased job satisfaction is greater enthusiasm for their job which can be reflected in better interaction with customers.

Behaviourally, empowerment can lead to a quicker response by employees to the needs of customers, as less time is wasted in referring customers' requests to line managers. In situations where customer needs are highly variable, empowerment can be crucial in allowing employees to customize service delivery. In the event of a service failure, empowerment can facilitate a rapid recovery (Hart *et al.*, 1990). If service failures are not rectified quickly and satisfactorily, customers may lose trust and confidence in a service provider.

Advocates of tighter control mechanisms point to the disadvantages of empowerment. One of the consequences of empowerment is that it increases the scope of employees' jobs, requiring employees to be properly trained to cope with the wider range of tasks which they are expected to undertake. It also impacts on recruitment as it is necessary to ensure that employees recruited have the requisite attitudinal characteristics and skills to cope with empowerment. Hartline and Ferrell (1996) found that while empowered employees gained confidence in their abilities, they also experienced increased frustration and ambiguity through role conflict. Additionally, because empowered workers are expected to have a broader range of skills and to perform a greater number of tasks, they are likely to be more expensive to employ because of their ability to command higher rates of pay.

Far from improving the efficiency of service delivery processes, empowerment can actually slow them down. An employee who is empowered to customize each service to individuals' specific requirements will be less efficient than one who is quite strictly controlled as to how much customization is to be carried out. Of course, it is another matter whether the empowered employee is more effective at satisfying customers' needs, but if the service blueprint is based on a no-frills, low-cost proposition, excessive empowerment and customization by employees may not be viable for a company. The company could in the short term cause delays to waiting customers who seek a standard service, and in the long term find itself delivering excessive value to customers. Customization of service could also be perceived by some customers as unfair in situations where employees are observed to be favouring some customers rather than others. It has been pointed out by Martin (1996) that employees may, consciously or unconsciously, discriminate to give better service to friends or people who are similar to themselves in terms of age, gender or ethnicity.

Finally, empowering employees can cost actual money in the short term, which has to be balanced against possible revenue gains in the long term. Faced with a service failure, an empowered employee may over-compensate customers, not only incurring immediate costs for the company, but raising expectations for compensation next time a service failure occurs.

Even with highly empowered employees, some residual forms of control are necessary. Control systems are closely related to reward systems in that pay can be used to control performance – e.g. bonuses forfeited in the event of performance falling below a specified standard. In addition, warnings or ultimate dismissal form part of a control system. In an ideal service organization which has a well-developed HRM policy, employees' involvement in their work should lead to considerable self-control or informal control from their peer group. Where such policies are less well developed, three principal types of control are used – simple, technical and bureaucratic.

■ *Simple controls* are typified by direct personal supervision of personnel – for example, a head waiter can maintain a constant watch over junior waiters and directly influence performance when this deviates from standard.

■ *Technical controls* can be built into the service production process in order to monitor individuals' performance – for example, a supermarket checkout can measure the speed of individual operators and control action (e.g. training or redeployment) taken in respect of those shown to be falling below standard.

■ *Bureaucratic controls* require employees to document their performance – for example, the completion of work sheets by a service engineer of visits made and jobs completed. Control action can be initiated in respect of employees who, on paper, appear to be under-performing.

In addition to these internal controls, the relationship which many front-line service personnel develop with their customers allows customers to exercise a degree of informal control. College lecturers teaching to a class would in most cases wish to avoid the hostility from their class which might result from consistently delivering a poor standard of performance – in other words, the class can exercise a type of informal control.

So in what situations should a service provider decide to empower its employees, rather than to tightly control them? A number of authors have suggested a contingency approach to empowerment. Ahmed and Rafiq (2003) have built on the work of Bowen and Lawler (1992) to develop a model of five factors which influence whether a control or empowerment approach is most appropriate, namely: business strategy, tie to the customer, technology, business environment, and types of employees.

1. *Business strategy.* Firms undertaking a differentiation business strategy, or a strategy that involves high degrees of **customization** and personalization of services should empower their employees. However, firms pursuing a low-cost high-volume strategy should use a production-line approach to controlling employees.

2. *Tie to the customer.* Where service delivery involves managing long-term relationships with customers rather than just performing a simple one-off transaction, empowerment is vital. Employees should be able to identify and respond flexibly to customers' changing needs over time, something which may be inhibited by a tightly scripted control approach.

3. *Technology.* If the technology involved in service delivery simplifies and industrializes the tasks of employees, a production line approach is more appropriate than empowerment. However, where the technology is non-routine or complex, empowerment is more appropriate.

4. *Business environment.* Some environments are more variable than others, for example the operating environment of an airline is more variable than that of a fast-food restaurant. A company may make its environment more complex – for example, an airline may offer to cater for special meal and accessibility requirements, or such complexity may be forced on it by generally held expectations within the market. A production line approach is more appropriate where customer requirements are simpler and more predictable.

5. *Types of employees.* Bowen and Lawler (1992) recognized that empowerment and control approaches require different types of employees. Employees most likely to be empowered effectively are those who have high growth needs and who need to have their abilities tested at work. Where empowerment requires teamwork, employees should have strong social and affiliative needs and good interpersonal and group skills. Empowerment requires 'Theory Y'-type managers who allow employees to work independently to the benefit of the organization and its customers. The control approach requires 'Theory X'-type managers who believe in close supervision of employees (McGregor, 1960).

12.4 Creating involvement by employees

Strategies to empower employees to make for more effective service encounters are less likely to be successful if employees do not feel involved in their jobs. Motivation, consent, participation and communication form essential focal points for an organization's HRM strategy to bring about a sense of involvement which underlies empowerment. HRM stresses the individual employee and their importance to the organization and this importance cannot be made real if employees do not feel motivated to share organizational goals. Research has shown that service employee perceptions of how they are treated by their organization, are associated with more effective service delivery and enhanced customer perceptions of service quality (Bienstock *et al.*, 2003).

Motivation concerns the choices which employees make between alternative forms of behaviour in order that they, as employees, attain their own personal goals. The task of management is to equate the individual's personal goals with those of the organization – that is, getting employees morally involved with the service which they help to produce. This in turn requires employees to consent to the management of their work activity. Where this consent is obtained, employees can be motivated by some form of participation in the organization. Such participation gives the employees a small stake in the organization, be it financial or in the form of discretionary control over the performance of their work function.

12.4.1 Consent

The term 'consent' covers a variety of management-led initiatives and strategies which seek to give management authority without actively emphasizing its coercive power. For many services provided on a one-to-one basis, direct monitoring and supervision of employees by management may be impossible to achieve anyway. Active consent is therefore of great use to the management of service organizations.

In the UK during the 20th century there were various forms of employee participation and involvement designed to aid management in the generation of consent. Such initiatives have included scientific management, paternalism and the human relations approach. Each initiative has its own prescription for the generation of consent.

Scientific management approaches seek co-operation between employer and employee in terms of the division of labour, whereby individual employees work in pre-defined ways as directed by management. Advocates of scientific management saw mutual benefits for the employee and employer. For employees, specializing in one work activity would give the opportunity to earn more, especially through piece rate pay systems, while management would benefit through greater work control and higher productivity. What Taylor, the leading advocate of scientific management, did not expect was the hostility of employees to what is often described as the process of deskilling. Within the service sector, many attempts have been made to deskill jobs in accordance with the scientific management prescription. However, it is necessary to balance the benefits of specialization and improved efficiency against employees' sense of alienation from their job which occurs where they are involved in only a very small part of a service delivery process. In this way, scientific management might suggest that a visitor attraction employ guides who each conduct tours of just a part of the attraction, before handing over to another guide who specializes in another area. However, a much greater sense of involvement from employees may occur if guides are trained to be able to deliver a complete guided tour of the attraction themselves from beginning to end, although this might call for additional training.

Paternalism is often associated with Quaker employers such as Cadbury or Rowntree, who attempted to show that they were interested in their workforce at home as well as at work. Within the service sector, many retail employers, such as Marks & Spencer, have taken a paternalistic attitude towards their employees by providing such benefits as on-site services or temporary accommodation for their employees. This and other benefits, such as subsidized social clubs, are often designed to encourage employee identification with the company, and therefore loyalty, which legitimizes managerial authority and hence consent to it.

In contrast to the economically based consent strategies of scientific management, the *human relations* approach looks at a person as a social animal. Elton Mayo, in his study of General Electric in the United States, argued that productivity was unrelated to work organization and economic rewards as suggested by scientific management. Mayo emphasized the importance of atmosphere and social attitudes, group feelings and the sense of identification which employees had. He suggested that the separation of employees, which scientific management had created prevented them from experiencing a sense of identification and involvement which is essential for all humans. Hence one solution was to design group structures into production processes. Such processes were thought to assist in the generation of employees' loyalty to their organization via the work group. Mayo's work is similar in focus to that of Frederick Herzberg and Abraham Maslow (Buchanan and Huczynski, 2001). Maslow suggested that humans have psychological as well as economic needs. To Herzberg, humans have lower- and higher-order needs. The former are the basic economic needs of food and shelter whereas the latter are more psychologically based in terms of recognition and contribution to the group and organization.

All of the management initiatives and strategies described in this section are in part efforts to generate employee consent to management authority without management exercising its authority via coercion.

12.4.2 **Moral involvement**

Moral involvement refers to some mechanism whereby employees can identify with the corporate goals of their employer and relay their feelings about these goals back to management. Essentially, employees need some institutional process through which, directly or indirectly, they can voice their concerns over decisions which affect them.

Mechanisms to develop moral involvement are closely related to policies which generate consent. Mechanisms can operate collectively, as with collective bargaining or professional recognition via professional associations. Management can generate moral involvement through joint consultation with employees on decisions made by management. Alternatively they can be individual through quality circles, team briefings (discussed later in this chapter), appraisals or the 'open door' policies encouraged by the human relations approach. HRM highlights the importance of the individual worker to the success of the organization and therefore stresses individual training and development.

12.4.3 **Motivation**

Motivation concerns goals and rewards. Maslow (1943) argued that motivation is based on individuals' desire to satisfy various levels of need. These levels range from the need to realize potential and self-development down to the satisfaction of basic needs such as hunger and thirst. Rewards for reaching goals can be tangible (for example, money) or intangible (for example, commendations or awards which add to status or self-esteem). An organization has to bring about a congruence between its own goals and those of its employees. This is the basis for designing an appropriate motivation package. Within the UK tourist attractions sector, a comparison can be made between many commercial operations (e.g. Alton Towers and Warwick Castle) where financial incentives are an important motivator, and the National Trust, which attracts many unpaid volunteers, motivated by a desire to share in the preservation of historic buildings. Employees' attitudes and opinions about their colleagues and the work environment may make all the difference between workers merely doing a good job and delivering exceptional service (Arnett *et al.*, 2002).

12.4.4 **Participation**

An employee's participation in an organization may be limited to purely economic matters – payment is received in return for work performed. Alternatively, participation may manifest itself through more qualitative measures such as employee involvement in decision-making through quality circles or team briefings (discussed later in this chapter). The process of moral involvement can take the form of a devolution of some areas of traditional personnel activity to line management in order that the employees actually doing the work and those responsible for managing particular sections feel that they are somehow involved in it together. This can apply, for example, to selecting, recruiting and appraising employees within a work group.

12.4.5 **Communication**

To many people, internal marketing is essentially about improving communication between a company and its employees. Unfortunately, many service organizations consider effective communication to be based on a one-way channel of information from managers to employees through such media as staff newsletters. This is no more a definition of internal marketing than advertising is a definition of marketing. As in the case of marketing to external customers, communication to employees needs to be based on a sound understanding of the needs of individual segments within the workforce. There should also be some facility for feedback from employees.

Communication as an element of internal marketing is most notable when it is absent. Rumours about revised working arrangements, reductions in the workforce and changes to the terms of employment often circulate around companies, breeding a feeling of distrust by employees in their management. Some managers may take a conscious decision to give employees as little information as possible, perhaps on the basis that knowledge is power. There are sometimes strategic reasons for not disseminating information to employees (for example, business strategy may be a closely guarded secret in order to keep competitors guessing). However, in too many service organizations information is unnecessarily withheld from employees, creating a feeling of an underclass in terms of access to information. Such practices do not help to generate consent and moral involvement by employees.

In good practice organizations, information can be communicated through a number of channels. The staff newsletter is a well-tried medium, but in many instances is seen as being too little too late, and with inadequate discussion of the issues involved. Many organizations use team briefings (see below) to cascade information down through an organization and to communicate back upwards again. Company intranets and e-mail have developed new opportunities for communicating information to a company's employees, allowing much greater personalization to the specific needs of individual employees, and also facilitating feedback. External advertising should regard the internal labour force as a secondary target market. The appearance of advertisements on television can have the effect of inspiring the confidence of employees in their management and pride in their company.

12.4.6 Strategies to increase employees' involvement

The methods which an organization uses to encourage involvement among its employees are likely to be influenced by the type of person it employs and the extent to which their jobs present opportunities to exercise autonomy (that is, the extent to which employees are able to control their own work processes) and discretion (the degree of independent thinking they can exercise in performing their work).

This section considers various strategies to increase employees' involvement and comments on their suitability for service organizations. In practice, organizations are more likely to be concerned with securing greater employee involvement by making individual employee objectives more congruent to those of the whole organization rather than through what could be described as collective participation. This type of involvement may be available to all employees but the extent to which their participation is real and effective may well depend on where they are positioned in the employment hierarchy – that is, whether they are within the core or the peripheral groups of workers. Increased participation is brought about by a combination of consultation and communication methods, and team briefings.

- 'Open door' policies encourage employees to air their grievances and to make suggestions directly to their superiors. The aim of this approach is to make management accessible and 'employee friendly'. To be effective, the human relations approach would require employees to feel that they do in fact have a real say in managerial matters. As a consequence, management must appear to be open and interested in employee relations. It is likely that this approach to managerial style and strategy will emphasize open management through some of the methods described below.

- Team briefings are a system of communication within the organization where a leader of a group provides group members (up to about 20) with management-derived information. The rationale behind briefing is to encourage commitment to and identification with the organization. Team briefings are particularly useful in times of organizational change, although they can be held regularly to cover such items as competitive progress, changes in policy and points of future action. Ideally, they should result in information 'cascading' down through an organization. The difference between briefing and quality circles (see below) centres on their respective contents. Briefing sessions are likely to be more general and relate to the whole organization, whereas quality circles relate to the specific work activity of a particular group of employees. Any general points of satisfaction or dissatisfaction can be aired in briefings and then taken up in specific quality circles.

- Quality circles (QCs) are small groups of employees who meet together with a supervisor or group leader in an attempt to discuss their work in terms of production quality and service delivery. To be successful, the QC leader has to be willing to listen to and act upon issues raised by QC members. This is essential if the QC is to be sustained. Circle members must feel their participation is real and effective, therefore the communication process within the QC must be two-way. If quality circles appear to become only routinized listening sessions, members may consider them to be just another form of managerial control.

- The pattern of ownership of an organization can influence the level of consent and participation. Where the workforce owns a significant share of a business, there should in principle be less cause for 'us and them' attitudes to develop between management and workforce. For this reason, many labour-intensive service organizations have significant worker shareholders and there is evidence that such companies can out-perform more conventionally owned organizations.

- Mission statements are used by service organizations in an attempt to create a shared vision for all employees. A corporate **mission statement** is a means of reminding everyone within the organization of its essential purpose. In the service sector, where the interface between the consumer and production personnel is often critical, communication of the values contained within the mission statement assumes great importance. The statement is frequently repeated by organizations in staff newsletters and in notices at their place of work. An example of a mission statement which is widely communicated to the workforce – as well as to customers – is provided by Easy Group (see the vignette below). Is a mission statement a valuable guiding principle for all of a firm's employees, or just more management fudge? Too often, mission statements are ridiculed by employees (and customers) because of the vacuous nature of the language which is used, or because they are regarded as very unrealistic.

Easy Group mission statement

As the private holding company of Stelios, the serial entrepreneur, our mission is to extend the easy brand to more sectors ("paint the world orange') whilst creating real wealth for all stakeholders. We will build on our core brand values of being low cost, innovative, fun and always an 'underdog' fighting for the little guy. We will protect our brand from internal and external threats and manage appropriately the business and other risks inherent in venturing. We will develop our people and ensure their reward is aligned to realized shareholder returns.

We will create wealth by:

1. selling shares in incubated businesses which have become substantial and profitable enough to IPO

2. charging royalty fees for licensing our IP to reputable established entities or new ventures we control and franchise.

12.5 Leadership

Many of the most successful services companies, including Virgin Group, Federal Express and McDonald's attribute their success in part to the quality of leadership within their organizations. The results of poor leadership are evident in many failing service organizations, especially within the public sector.

The principles of human resource management need to be implemented with effective leadership. What is good leadership for one organization need not necessarily be so for another. Organizations operating in relatively stable environments may be best suited to a leadership style which places a lot of power in a hierarchical chain of command. In the UK, many banks until recently had leadership styles which have been drawn from models developed in the armed forces, evidenced by some managers having titles such as superintendent and inspector. Such rigid, hierarchical patterns of leadership may be less effective where the marketing environment is changing rapidly and a flexible response is called for (as has happened in the banking sector). The literature has developed two typologies of leadership – transactional and

453

Who's driving the bus?

Many service firms proudly promote the fact that they are owned by their employees. But do they deliver better service quality to customers? Research undertaken by Dolan and Brierley (1992) in the bus sector showed how two companies – People's Provincial of Fareham and Derbyshire-based Chesterfield Transport – had capitalized on their worker ownership to perform better than their more conventionally owned rivals.

To the employees, a financial investment in the two companies studied proved attractive. Over a period of five years, the value of employees' investments in People's Provincial more than doubled, while with Chesterfield Transport, it increased over four-fold within two years. Like many employee buy-outs of larger government-owned organizations, take-over bids were attracted from larger bus operators, boosting the value of employees' share holdings.

The research highlighted four important benefits which had resulted from worker ownership.

1. Traditional hierarchies were broken down, which gave much greater operational flexibility to the companies (for example, inspectors and management would accept it as normal to change their duties and drive buses when the need arose). This was particularly important as the uneven pattern of demand required great flexibility.

2. Costs were held down because staff recognized that they would benefit directly from the resulting increase in profits. Similarly, staff became more willing to pass on ideas about ways in which services could be improved or costs saved.

3. Absenteeism was reduced, as was the need for formal disciplinary measures to be taken. Employees could see the need for a high level of service performance and were able to share in the resulting benefits.

4. All workers had access to financial information, resulting in a more constructive approach to negotiations on work schedules and pay, for example.

The authors concluded that employee ownership – by increasing the level of participation – can give companies a competitive advantage in services industries where flexibility in production and commitment to high standards of service quality are important. But the question remains why so many employee-owned bus companies in the UK have sold out to larger organizations, such as Stagecoach and First Group. Is a one-off cash bonus to employee shareholders more important than involvement in the ownership of their company? Do customers notice any difference once a large company takes over?

transformational – which broadly correspond, respectively, with the control and empowerment approaches described above.

What makes a good leader of people? And are leaders born, or can individuals acquire the skills of leadership? On the latter point there is little doubt that development is possible, and successful companies have invested heavily in leadership development programmes. As for what makes a successful leader of people, there have been many suggestions of desirable traits, including:

- setting clear expectations of staff

- recognizing excellence appropriately and facilitating staff in overcoming their weaknesses

- leading by example

- being able to empathize with employees

- showing adaptability to changing circumstances.

Managers told to get packing their bags

Beginning with a small shop in Dundalk in 1960, the Irish grocery retailer SuperQuinn has grown to a successful chain of 12 shops and 7 shopping centres employing over 2000 people throughout Ireland. A large part of this success has been attributed to the leadership style of the company's founder, Feargal Quinn, and the emphasis on linking employees' activities to excellence in service quality. But what makes such leadership style distinctive?

An important principle is that managers should lead by example and never lose contact with the most important person in the organization – the customer. It is the task of a leader to set the tone for customer-focused excellence. To prevent managers losing sight of customers' needs, Quinn uses every opportunity to move them closer to customers, including locating their offices not in a comfortable room upstairs, but in the middle of the sales floor. Managers regularly take part in customer panels where customers talk about their expectations and perceptions of SuperQuinn. Subcontracting this task entirely to a market research agency is seen as alien to the leadership culture of the company. The company requires its managers to spend periods doing routine front-line jobs (such as packing customers' bags), a practice which has become commonplace in many successful service organizations. This keeps managers close to the customer and improves their ability to empathize with junior employees.

Does this leadership style work? Given the company's level of growth, profits and rate of repeat business, it must be doing something right, contradicting much of scientific management theory that management is a specialist task which can be separated from routine dealings with customers and employees.

In too many companies, bad leadership is characterized by:

- 'management by confusion', in which expectations of staff are ambiguously stated and management actions are guided by a secretive 'hidden agenda'
- reward systems which are not based on performance and are perceived as being unfair
- the deliberate or inadvertent creation of an 'us and them' attitude
- failing to understand the aspirations of employees
- failing to take the initiative where environmental change calls for adaptation.

12.6 Recruiting, training and rewarding employees

Attention is now given to the application of a number of the important principles of **human resource management (HRM)** referred to above. Emphasis is placed on the impact of such personnel practices on the marketing activities of service organizations through the methods of recruiting, selecting, training and rewarding staff.

12.6.1 Recruitment and selection

Recruitment is the process by which an organization secures its human resources. Traditionally the recruitment function has been performed by personnel specialists who as functional specialists are removed from line management. Current HRM practice favours the integration of the recruitment function into the line areas where a potential employee will be working.

The focus of recruitment activity is to attract and hopefully retain the right employee for the right job within the organization. Clearly, the recruitment process is closely linked to that of selection. The process of selection (described below) concerns how potential recruits are tested in terms of the job and person specifications.

In order to recruit the right personnel, service organizations must consider carefully just what they want from particular employees. As an example, tour operators seeking to recruit representatives to work in overseas resorts recognize that academic qualifications are not in themselves an important characteristic which should be possessed by new recruits. Instead, the ability to work under pressure, to empathize with clients, to work in groups and to be able to survive for long periods without sleep may, from previous experience, be identified as characteristics which allow representatives to perform their tasks in a manner which meets customers' expectations.

There are five key elements of the recruitment process:

1. development of recruitment policies
2. establishment of routine recruitment procedures
3. establishment of job descriptions
4. development of a person specification
5. advertising of job vacancies.

The process of selection is concerned with identifying and hopefully employing the most suitable candidate and involves six principal tasks:

1. examining candidates' CVs or application forms
2. shortlisting candidates
3. inviting candidates for interview
4. interviewing and testing candidates
5. choosing a candidate for employment
6. offering and confirming the employment.

Traditionally all of these areas have been considered to be the preserve of the personnel department. However, there are many examples of how customers' expectations have influenced the recruitment and selection process. One example is the use of a Service Predisposition Instrument (SPI) to identify attitudes of applicants and provide measures of service elements, cognitive expressions and a personal service outcome (Lee-Ross, 2000).

Timpsons makes *Times* Top 100 employers

For labour-intensive service industries, recruiting the best staff, training them and continually motivating them to achieve high standards is a vitally important task that calls for an integrated view between marketing and human resource management. During times of full employment and labour shortages, companies must sell themselves as good employers so that they can recruit the people who will ultimately deliver marketers' promises to customers. The *Sunday Times* conducts an annual survey of Britain's best companies to work for, and the shoe repair and key-cutting chain Timpson has scored highly for a number of years. Employee benefits include at least 16 weeks' maternity leave on full pay (compared to the statutory minimum of six weeks at 90% pay) and/or at least four weeks' leave above the statutory minimum of 40 weeks. One sign of the company's success is a low level of staff turnover – at least 40% of its staff have worked at the company for more than five years. Managers are given considerable discretion in how they run their branch, for example in terms of the prices that they charge. Customers have come to trust the chain and have rewarded it with sustainable long-term profits.

12.6.2 **Training and development**

Training refers to the acquisition of specific knowledge and skills which enable employees to perform their job effectively. The focus of staff training is the job. In contrast to this, staff development concerns activities which are directed to the future needs of the employee, which may themselves be derived from the future needs of the organization. For example, workers may need to become familiar with personal computers, electronic mail and other aspects of information technology which as yet may not be elements within their own specific job requirements.

If a service organization wishes to turn all of its employees who interface with the public into 'part-time marketers' it must include such an objective within its overall corporate plan and identify the required training and development needs. This is essential if any process of change is to be actively consented to by the workforce. Initially this may be merely an awareness training programme whereby the process of change is communicated to the workforce as a precursor to the actual changes. It may involve making employees aware of the competitive market pressures which the organization faces and how the organization proposes to address them. This initial process may also involve giving employees the opportunity to make their views known and to air any concerns they might have. This can help to generate some moral involvement in the process of change and could itself be the precursor to an effective participation forum.

If marketing is to become a function which is integrated into the jobs of all employees, marketing managers cannot merely state this need at strategic HRM meetings – it is also essential that programmes are developed by which such strategies can be operationalized. In many cases, it may be possible to specify these needs in terms of the levels of competence required in performing particular tasks. For example, in the case of bank counter staff, personnel might be required to be aware of a number of specific financial services offered by the bank and able to evaluate customers and make appropriate suggestions for service offers. Failure to develop general sales skills and to disseminate knowledge of specific services available could result in lost opportunities for the organization.

A practical problem facing many service organizations who allocate large budgets to staff training is that many other organizations in their sector may spend very little, relying on staff being poached from the company doing the training. This occurs for example within the banking sector where many building societies have set up cheque account operations using the skills of staff attracted from the 'big four' UK banks. The problem also occurs in many construction-related industries and in the car repair business.

While the ease with which an organization can lose trained staff may be one reason to explain UK companies' generally low level of spending on training and development, a number of policies can be adopted to maximize the benefits of such expenditure to the organization. Above all else, training and development should be linked to broader HRM policies which have the effect of generating longer-term loyalty by employees. Judged by narrow criteria, training can be seen as a short-term risky activity which adds relatively little to the long-term profitability of an organization.

Where involvement-generating HRM policies alone are insufficient to retain trained staff, an organization may seek to tie an individual to it by seeking reimbursement of any expenditure if the employee leaves the organization within a specified time period. Reimbursement is most likely to be sought in the case of expenditure aimed at developing the general abilities of an individual as opposed to his or her ability to perform a functional and organizational specific task. Thus an organization might seek to recover the cost of supporting an individual to undertake an Open

University degree, but not a product-specific sales training course. In some instances, government initiatives exist to support staff training and development.

Where an organization is a market leader, it may have no alternative but to accept a certain level of wastage in return for maintaining a constant competitive advantage over other organizations, and hence achieving higher levels of profitability. In this way, the travel agency chain Thomas Cook provides a level of training which is considered to be one of the best in the sector. A travel clerk who is Thomas Cook trained can readily find employment with one of its competitors. Against such potential loss – which itself is offset by the HRM policies adopted by the company – Thomas Cook enjoys an excellent reputation with the travel-buying public. This in turn has allowed it to position itself as a high-quality services provider, removing much of the need to take part in price discounting which has harmed many of its rivals.

12.6.3 Career development

Another mechanism which can assist an organization in its goals of recruiting and retaining staff is a clearly defined career progression pathway. Career progression refers to a mechanism which enables employees to visualize how their working life might develop within a particular organization. Clearly defined expectations of what an individual employee should be able to achieve within an organization and clear

---

Drive-it-yourself train service?

What does it take to be a guard on a busy rail commuter service? To those who have spent many years working in the industry, an intimate knowledge of operating procedures is essential if accidents are to be avoided. Trades union representatives not surprisingly expressed shock at the Great Eastern Railway Company's plans in 1997 to recruit part-time guards for its commuter services into London's Liverpool Street Station. For the company, the idea seemed to offer flexibility in meeting customers' needs efficiently and effectively, given the highly peaked demand for commuter services into London. The job would suit people who live in the Essex suburbs and work in Central London, providing a paid journey to work which would supplement the modest £5.25 an hour pay. After the equivalent of a week's training, given at weekends and in the evenings, new staff would be accompanied by a trained guard for three days before taking on responsibility for a train by themselves. Was this moving towards a 'do-it-yourself railway' in which safety considerations came second to profit objectives? Or had technology, such as the use of automatic train doors and closed-circuit television, simplified the task of being a guard to such an extent that it could sensibly be tackled by part-time staff? Was this one way of overcoming the high cost of operating commuter train services, which were becoming increasingly expensive to customers, and often loss-making for the train operator?

statements of promotion criteria can assist the employee in this regard. Additionally, the creation and use of an internal labour market, for instance, through counselling and the dissemination of job vacancy details are vital. An organization can introduce vertical job ladders or age- or tenure-based remuneration and promotion programmes to assist in the retention of core employees.

During periods of scarcity among the skilled labour force, offers of defined career paths may become essential if the right calibre of staff are to be recruited and retained. As an example, many retailers which had previously operated relatively casual employment policies introduced career structures for the first time during the tight labour market of the late 1980s. Conversely, during the following period of recession it became very difficult for employers to maintain their promises with a consequent demotivational effect on staff. In this way, the demise of profitability in UK branch banking in the 1990s brought about considerable disillusionment among core bank employees who saw their career-progression prospects made considerably more difficult than they had expected, despite good work performance on their part.

12.6.4 Rewarding staff

The process of staff recruitment and more crucially the retention of staff, is directly influenced by the quality of reward on offer. The central purpose of a reward system is to improve the standard of staff performance by giving employees something which they consider to be of value in return for good performance. What employees consider to be a good reward is influenced by the nature of the motivators which drive each individual. For this reason, one standardized reward system is unlikely to achieve maximum motivation among a large and diverse workforce.

Reward systems have been seen by many as an essential tool to link corporate goals, such as customer orientation, with individual and organizational performance (e.g. Milkovich and Newman, 2002). While some studies have demonstrated positive effects of incorporating non-financial measures into employees' reward schemes (e.g. Widmier, 2002), many companies have encountered problems in linking pay to customer satisfaction. Reasons for this can be attributed to the measurement of customer satisfaction as well as to the missing link between customer satisfaction and customer retention.

In principle, the Balanced Scorecard (BSC) approach (described in Chapter 6) should offer a way forward for linking performance measures with employees' rewards. It will be recalled that the BSC framework can be used for describing value-creating strategies that link tangible and intangible assets (Speckbacher *et al.*, 2003). This is done by formulating strategic objectives with respect to assets in four perspectives: financial, customer and internal business process, as well as learning and growth (see Kaplan and Norton, 2001; Malmi, 2001).

Although it is widely assumed that the great strength of the BSC concept is its link with an organization's reward system (Kaplan and Norton, 1996; Otley, 1999; Malmi, 2001), very few organizations appear to have actually made this link successfully.

Research by Speckbacher *et al.* (2003) showed that while 27 of a sample of 38 companies (that is, more than 70%) had linked incentives to the BSC – only half were actually able to formulate cause-and-effect relationships among the different objectives and measures. Of these, just under half had linked incentives to BSC measures.

Rewards to employees can be divided into two categories: non-monetary and monetary. Non-monetary rewards cover a wide range of benefits, some of which will be a formal part of the reward system, for example subsidized housing or sports facilities and public recognition for work achievement (as where staff are given diplomas signifying their level of achievement). At other times, non-monetary rewards could be informal and represent something of a hidden agenda for management. In this way, a loyal, long-standing restaurant waiter may be rewarded by being given a relatively easy schedule of work, allowing unpopular Saturday nights to be removed from his duty rota.

Many HRM people would not recognize these non-monetary benefits as being part of a narrowly defined reward system. Instead, they are seen as going to the root of the relationship between staff and employer. Subsidized sports facilities are not merely a reward, but part of the total work environment which encourages consent, moral involvement and participation by the workforce. In the case of the hidden agenda of informal non-monetary rewards, these would be seen as being potentially harmful to the employment relationship by reducing the level of consent from the workforce at large.

Monetary rewards are a more direct method of improving the performance of employees and form an important element of a traditional 'hard' HRM policy. In the absence of well-developed HRM policies to promote involvement, monetary rewards can form the principal motivator for employees. A number of methods are commonly used in the service sector to reward employees financially.

- Basic hourly wages are used to reward large numbers of secondary, or non-core employees. These are generally rewarded according to their inputs rather than outputs. Compared to the manufactured goods sector, it is generally more difficult to measure service outcomes and to use these as a basis for payment, but nevertheless, it sometimes occurs. Delivery drivers employed by a courier firm may, for instance, be paid a fixed amount for each parcel delivered. In many cases, strict payment by output could have potentially harmful effects on customers – the delivery driver may concentrate on delivering as many parcels as quickly as possible, but with little regard for courtesies when dealing with people.

- A fixed salary is more commonly paid to the core workers of an organization. Sometimes the fixed salary is related to length of service – for example, many public-sector service workers in the UK receive automatic annual increments not related to performance. As well as being administratively simple, a fixed salary avoids the problems of trying to assess individuals' eligibility for bonuses, which can be especially difficult where employees work in teams. A fixed salary can be useful to a firm where long-term development of relationships with customers is important and staff are evaluated qualitatively for their ability in this respect rather than quantitatively on the basis of short-term sales achievements. Many financial services companies have adopted fixed salaries to avoid possible unethical conduct by employees who may be tempted to sell commission-based services to customers whose needs have not been properly assessed.

■ A fixed annual salary plus a variable commission is commonly paid to service personnel who are actively involved in selling, as a direct reward for their efforts. A problem for organizations who use this approach is that a sales person who aims to maximize his or her commission earnings is often not involved in the service production/delivery process and therefore not in a position to maximize customer satisfaction and thereby secure repeat business. Where service production employees are in fact involved in selling (e.g. many restaurant waiting staff), this form of payment can be a motivator to good service delivery as well as increasing sales.

■ Performance-related pay (PRP) has assumed increasing importance within the services sector. PRP systems seek to link some percentage of an employee's pay directly to their work performance. In some ways PRP represents a movement towards the individualization of pay. It was noted above that rewarding employees according to their performance may sound fine in principle, but can be difficult to achieve in practice. For some workers, outputs can be quantified relatively easily – for example, the level of new accounts opened forms part of most bank managers' performance-related pay. More qualitative aspects of job performance are much more difficult to appraise – for example, the quality of advice given by doctors or dentists. The Balanced Scorecard approach is one way of trying to overcome this problem. Qualitative assessment raises problems about which dimensions of job performance are to be considered important in the exercise and who is to undertake the appraisal. If appraisal is not handled sensitively, it could be viewed by employees with suspicion as a means of rewarding some individuals according to a hidden agenda. There is also the problem in many services industries that service outcomes are the result of joint activity by a number of employees and therefore the team may be a more appropriate unit for appraisal than the individual employee. Of course, appraisals should be carried out for reasons other than just determining employees' pay. Well-managed service organizations routinely appraise staff to assess their career development and training needs. Without a transparent system of assessment, suspicions can be raised within an organization about perceived favouritism which is not linked to performance.

■ Profit-sharing schemes can operate as a supplement to the basic wage or salary and can assist in the generation of employee loyalty through greater commitment. Employees can be made members of a trust fund set up by their employer where a percentage of profits are held in trust on behalf of employees, subject to agreed eligibility criteria. Profit-sharing schemes have the advantage of encouraging staff involvement in their organization. Such schemes do, however, have a major disadvantage where, despite employees' most committed efforts, profits fall due to some external factor such as an economic recession. There is also debate about whether profit sharing really does act as a motivator to better performance in large companies, or merely becomes part of basic pay expectations. In the UK, examples of profit-sharing schemes have been set up by Tesco, British Gas and Sainsbury's.

- In many service organizations, an important element of the financial reward is derived from outside the formal contract of employment, especially from customers in the form of tipping in return for good service. The acknowledgement of tipping by employers puts greater pressure on front-line service staff to perform well and in principle puts the burden of appraisal on the consumer of a service directly. It also reduces the level of basic wage that may be expected by employees. Against this, reliance on tipping poses a number of problems. Support personnel may be important contributors to the quality of service received by customers but may receive none of the benefits of tipping received by front-line staff. A chef may be an important element of the benefit received by a restaurant customer, but tipping systems tend to emphasize the quality of the final delivery system. Attempts to institutionalize tipping by levying service charges and sharing proceeds among all staff may, on the other hand, reduce individual motivation. A fixed service charge also reduces the ability of consumers to make charges based on perceived quality. A further problem of relying on tipping is that customers might be put off by the prospect of feeling obliged to pay a tip, and for this reason many service providers prohibit their employees from receiving tips. While customers from some countries – such as the United States – readily accept the principle of tipping, others – including the British – are more ambivalent. In the public sector, attempts at tipping are often viewed as a form of bribery.

12.6.5 **Industrial relations**

The service sector spans organizations from small family businesses to large multi-national organizations, covering external environments which range from protected and regulated to highly competitive. In reflection of this diversity, there is great variety in the manner in which managements negotiate employment conditions with their workforces. For service organizations employing large numbers of staff, much of the employment relationship has traditionally been conducted collectively between the employer and groups of employees.

Collective bargaining formally recognizes the presence within the organization of an outside body – the trades union. This may emphasize a divergence of interests between the employer and employees. Where divergence is great, a result may be overtime bans, 'go slows' and strikes, which might be used in order to pursue employee interests. As an element in collective bargaining, actions only come about where negotiation has failed. Nevertheless, many service sectors such as railways and airlines

A check-up for doctors?

How do you measure the performance of doctors, either individually or in teams? The UK's National Health Service (NHS) has focused its efforts on quality-of-service issues. It routinely monitors a number of quality-of-service indicators – for example, the waiting time to see a consultant or to have elective surgery undertaken. But even such apparently simple indicators can hide a lot of problems. What does it mean when one consultant is shown to keep patients waiting for longer than another consultant? To many people, a long waiting list may be a sign of a top-rated consultant who is very popular with patients, rather than a failing professional who cannot keep up with the demands put on him or her. And then, of course, figures for waiting time can often be manipulated, scrupulously or unscrupulously. For example, accident and emergency departments use triage nurses to assess new patients upon arrival, thereby keeping within their Patients' Charter target for the time taken to initially see a new patient. However, the hospital may be slower to provide actual treatment. In 2003, a number of ambulance services were reprimanded for trying to make their response times appear better than they actually were, by measuring the response time from when an ambulance set out, rather than when a call for help was received.

Attempts to measure doctors' medical performance are much less developed, with debate about the most appropriate methodologies for assessing the efficacy of an operation or clinical diagnosis. Many medical outcomes cannot be assessed simply on the basis of success/failure, but require more subjective quality of life assessments to be taken into account. Nevertheless, in the UK's private healthcare sector, BUPA announced in 2004 that it would publish statistics showing patients' recovery rates for its named doctors (*Sunday Telegraph*, 2004). Meanwhile, the National Health Service (NHS) is keeping an eye on developments.

Some doctors have expressed a concern that merely publishing performance indicators pushes up users' expectations of service delivery, so that in the end they may become more dissatisfied even though actual performance has improved. Is there a case for treating doctors as professionals whose professional ethics lead them to do their very best for their patients? Or is this inward-looking approach to professional standards becoming increasingly untenable in an era of well-informed consumers who know their rights and have high expectations?

have periodically suffered bad disruption as a result of failures in collective bargaining. Because services cannot be stored, the effects of withdrawal of labour can be felt by customers immediately.

Service organizations which do not feel secure with trades unions are likely to attempt to marginalize their impact through their de-recognition and the creation of organization-specific employee relations policies, as described below. Within the services sector, many organizations have moved on from the traditional view of industrial relations to the situation where they speak of 'employee relations'. Employee relations focuses on that aspect of managerial activity which is concerned with fostering an identification with the employing organization and its business aims. It therefore concerns itself with direct relations between employees and management – that is, independently of any collective representation by trades unions.

12.7 Organizing the marketing department

So far, we have looked at the internal marketing environment of an organization from the perspective of employees and the encounters they have with customers. We turn our attention now to broader aspects of marketing management. Just as the quality and motivation of employees at the sharp end of the service encounter can impact on customers, so too can the way in which their managers are organized. Too many service organizations fail, not because of failings in front-line staff, but because of disorganized or poorly informed management structures and processes.

Should a service organization actually have a marketing department? The idea is becoming increasingly popular that the existence of a marketing department in an organization may in fact be a barrier to the development of a true customer-centred marketing orientation. By placing all marketing activity in a marketing department, non-marketing staff may consider themselves to be absolved of responsibility for the development of customer relationships. In services industries where production personnel are in frequent contact with the consumers of their service, a narrow definition of marketing responsibility can potentially be very harmful. On the other hand, a marketing department is usually required in order to co-ordinate and implement those functions which cannot sensibly be delegated to operational personnel – advertising, sales management and pricing decisions, for example. The importance that a marketing department assumes within any organization is a reflection of the nature of its operating environment. An organization operating in a fiercely competitive environment would typically attach great importance to its marketing department as a means of producing a focused marketing mix strategy by which it can gain competitive advantage over its competitors. By contrast, an organization operating in a relatively stable environment is more likely to allow strategic decisions to be taken by personnel who are not marketing strategists – for example, pricing decisions may be taken by accountants with less need to understand the marketing implications of price decisions.

Responsibilities given to marketing departments within service organizations vary from one organization to another, reflecting the competitive nature of their business environments and also their traditions and organizational inertia. Within marketing departments, four basic approaches to allocating these responsibilities are identified here, although, in practice, most marketing departments show more than one approach. The four approaches allocate marketing responsibilities by:

1. functions performed

2. geographical area covered

3. products or groups of products managed

4. market segments managed.

12.7.1 Organization based on functional responsibilities

A traditional and common basis of organizing a marketing department is to divide responsibilities into identifiable marketing functions. Typically, these functions may be advertising, sales, research and development, marketing research, customer services, etc. The precise division of the functional responsibilities will depend upon the nature of an organization. Buying and merchandising are likely to be an important feature in a retailing organization, while research and development will be important for technology-based services such as telecommunications.

The main advantage of a functional organization lies in its administrative simplicity. Against this, there can be a tendency for policy responsibility on specific services or markets to become lost between numerous functional specialists. There is also the possibility of destructive rivalry between functional specialists for their share of marketing budgets – for example, rivalry between an advertising manager and a sales manager for a larger share of the promotional budget.

12.7.2 Organization based on geographical responsibilities

Organizations providing a service nationwide frequently organize many marketing functions on a geographical basis. This particularly applies to the sales function, although it could also include geographically designated responsibilities for service development (e.g. opening new outlets) and some local responsibility for promotion. For service organizations operating at an international level, there is usually some geographical basis to organize in the manner in which marketing activities are organized in individual national markets.

12.7.3 Management by product type

Multi-output organizations frequently appoint a product manager to manage a particular service or group of services. This form of organization does not replace the functional organization, but provides an additional layer of management which co-ordinates the functions' activities. The product manager's role includes a number of key tasks:

■ developing a long-range and competitive strategy for a service or group of services

■ preparing a budgeted annual plan

■ working with internal and external functional specialists to develop and implement marketing programmes, for example in relation to advertising and sales promotion

- monitoring the service's performance and changes occurring in its business environment

- identifying new opportunities and initiating service improvements to meet changing market needs.

A product management organization structure offers a number of advantages for service providers.

- The product offering benefits from an integrated cost-effective approach to planning. This particularly benefits minor products which might otherwise be neglected.

- The product manager can in theory react more quickly to changes in the product's marketing environment than would be the case if no one had specific responsibility for the product. Within a bank, a mortgage manager is able to devote a lot of time and expertise to monitoring trends in the mortgage market and can become a focal point for initiating and seeing through change when this is required because of environmental change.

- Control within this type of organization can be exercised by linking divisional managers' salaries to performance.

Against this, product management structures are associated with a number of problems.

- The most serious problem occurs in the common situation where a product manager is given a lot of responsibility for ensuring that objectives are met, but relatively little control over the resource inputs they have at their disposal. Product managers typically must rely on persuasion to get the co-operation of advertising, sales and other functional specialist departments. Sometimes this can result in conflict, for example where a product manager seeks to position a service in one direction, while the advertising manager seeks to position it in another in order to meet broader promotional objectives.

- Confusion can arise in the minds of staff within an organization as to whom they are accountable to for their day-to-day actions. Staff involved in selling insurance policies in a branch bank may become confused at possibly conflicting messages from an operations manager and a product marketing manager.

- Product marketing management structures can lead to larger numbers of people being employed, resulting in a higher cost structure which may put the organization at a competitive disadvantage in price-sensitive markets.

- Research has suggested that the existence of the optimal product management form is rare and that it is typically associated with an unwillingness of senior management to delegate authority to product managers. Furthermore, research in the service industries suggests that the interdependencies within many service industries makes product management structures difficult to implement and control. Research by Ingham into the UK insurance industry found a high level of intra-organization transactions and a lack of profit centre status enjoyed by divisions, associated with inappropriate internal transfer pricing and poor incentive and control systems. While the product management form may be appropriate for a diversified conglomerate, it was shown to be inappropriate for insurance businesses where many functions are closely interdependent, allowing very little freedom of action for individual product managers. Within the insurance industry, a hybrid structure was observed which reflected the need for some degree of centralization (Ingham, 1991).

12.7.4 Market management organization

Many organizations provide services to a diverse range of customers who have widely varying needs. As an example, a cross-channel ferry operator provides the basically similar service of transport for private car drivers, coach operators and freight operators, among others. However, the specific needs of each group of users vary

---

Chinese walls prevent whispers between employees

The conventional wisdom is that product managers in service firms should work together to put their customers' needs above internal management demarcations. But could there sometimes be an ethical case against too much sharing of information by product managers?

Consider the case of merchant banks which offer investment management and capital-raising services. In a proposed take-over bid, it is often necessary for those involved in raising the capital required by a client to work very discreetly for fear of prematurely raising the share price of the target company. If this information was available to those staff working in investment management, it would give them an unfair advantage over the market generally, allowing them to build up a shareholding in the target company ahead of the announcement of a take-over bid. Merchant banks have sought to build 'Chinese walls' around their operations where this risk is present, and the adoption of a functional marketing management structure allows greater effective separation of functions. Numerous other services industries can be identified where similar ethical problems can be lessened by the adoption of a product management structure – accountants selling both auditing services and management consultancy services to a company may be tempted to gain business in the latter area at the expense of integrity in the former. The fallout from the accountant Arthur Andersen's involvement with the collapsed Enron company provided a warning to accountancy firms who had previously been diversifying on the assumption that bigger was better. How do large diversified service firms convince their customers that information given in confidence to one section of the organization will not be used against them in another?

significantly. A coach operator is likely to attach different importance to a road haulier to service attributes such as flexibility, ease of reservations, the type of accommodation provided, etc. In such situations, market managers can be appointed to oversee the development of particular markets, in much the same way as a product manager oversees particular products. Instead of being given specific financial targets for their products, market managers are usually given growth or market share targets. The main advantage of this form of organization is that it allows marketing activity to be focused on meeting the needs of distinct and identified groups of customers – something which should be at the heart of all truly marketing-oriented organizations. It is also likely that new innovative services are more likely to emerge within this structure than where an organization's response is confined within traditional product management boundaries – for example, a market manager specifically responsible for developing coach tour traffic might be in an advantageous position to develop innovative group package holidays aimed at coach operators. Market management structures are also arguably more conducive to the important task of developing relationships with customers, especially for business-to-business services. Where an organization has a number of very important customers, it is common to find the appointment of key account managers to handle relationships with those clients in order to exploit marketing opportunities which are of mutual benefit.

Many of the disadvantages of the product management organization are also shared by market-based structures. There can again be a conflict between responsibility and authority, and this form of structure can also become expensive to operate.

The differences in organizational structures described above, and their typical application to a vehicle ferry operator, are shown in Figure 12.4. The great diversity of organizational structures highlights the fact that there is not one unique structure which is appropriate to all firms, even within the same services sector. Overall, the organization of a marketing department must allow for a flexible and adaptable response to customers' needs within a changing environment, while aiming to reduce the level of confusion, ambiguity and cost inherent in some structures.

12.8 The relationship between marketing and other organizational functions

In a truly marketing-oriented service organization, marketing responsibilities cannot be confined to a group of people who belong to something called a marketing department. In the words of Drucker (1973): 'Marketing is so basic that it cannot be considered to be a separate function. It is the whole business seen from the point of view of its final result, that is, from the customer's point of view.'

In marketing-oriented organizations, the customer is at the centre of all of the organization's activities. The customer is not simply the concern of the marketing department, but also all of the production and administrative personnel whose

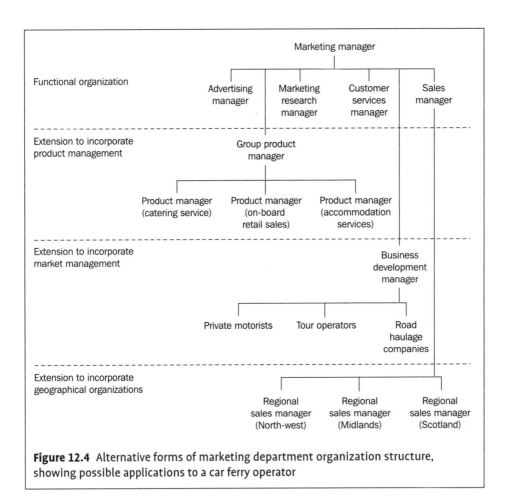

Figure 12.4 Alternative forms of marketing department organization structure, showing possible applications to a car ferry operator

actions may directly or indirectly impinge upon the customers' enjoyment of the service. In a typical service organization, the activities of a number of functional departments impinge on the service outcome received by customers.

- As we have seen earlier in this chapter, personnel plans can have a crucial bearing on marketing plans. The selection, training, motivation and control of staff cannot be considered in isolation from marketing objectives and strategies. Possible conflict between the personnel and marketing functions may arise where, for example, marketing demands highly trained and motivated front-line staff, but the personnel function pursues a policy which places cost reduction above all else.

- Operations managers may have a different outlook compared to marketing managers. A marketing manager may seek to respond as closely as possible to customers' needs, only to find opposition from operations managers who argue that a service of the required standard cannot be achieved. A marketing manager of a train-operating company may seek to segment markets with fares tailored to meet the needs of small groups of customers, only to encounter hostility from operations managers who are responsible for actually issuing and checking travel tickets on a day-to-day basis and who may have misgivings about the confusion which finely segmented fares might cause.

■ The actions of finance managers frequently have direct or indirect impact on marketing plans. Ultimately, finance managers assume responsibility for the allocation of funds which are needed to implement a marketing plan. At a more operational level, finance managers' actions in respect of the level of credit offered to customers, or towards stock-holdings where these are an important element of the service offering, can also significantly affect the quality of service and the volume of customers which the organization is able to serve.

Marketing requires all of these departments to 'think customer' and to work together to satisfy customer needs and expectations. There is argument as to what authority the traditional marketing department should have in bringing about this customer orientation. In a truly mature marketing-oriented service company, marketing is an implicit part of everyone's job. In such a scenario, marketing becomes responsible for a narrow range of specialist functions such as advertising and marketing research. Responsibility for the relationship between the organization and its customers is spread more diffusely throughout the organization. Gummesson (2001) has used the term 'part-time marketer' to describe staff working in service organizations who may not have any direct line management responsibility for marketing, but whose activities may indirectly impinge on the quality of service received by customers.

It can be argued that the introduction of a traditional marketing department – as described above – to a service organization can bring problems as well as benefits. In a survey of 219 executives representing public- and private-sector service organizations in Sweden, Grönroos (1982) tested the idea that a separate marketing department may widen the gap between marketing and operations staff. This idea was put to a sample drawn from marketing as well as other functional positions using a Likert-type scale with five points ranging from agreeing strongly to disagreeing strongly. The results indicated that respondents in a wide range of service organizations considered there to be dangers in the creation of a marketing department – an average of 66% agreed with the notion, with higher than average agreement being found among non-marketing executives, and those working in the hotel, restaurant, professional services and insurance sectors.

The problem of how to bring people together in an organization to act collectively, while also being able to place responsibility on an individual, is one which continues to generate considerable discussion. Organizations which produce many different products for many different markets may experience difficulties if they adopt a purely product or market-based structure. If a product management structure is adopted, product managers would require detailed knowledge of very diverse markets. Likewise, in a market management structure, market managers would require detailed knowledge of possibly very diverse product ranges. To avoid the problem of function managers acting and thinking with a 'silo' mentality, there has been a tendency for services organizations to develop clusters of individuals who focus on creating value for targeted groups of consumers and profits for their company.

Within such a cluster, product managers can concentrate on excellence in production, while market managers focus on meeting consumer needs without any preference for a particular product. An example of a 'matrix structure', as these are sometimes known (Figure 12.5), can be found in many vehicle distributors where market managers can be appointed to identify and formulate a market strategy in respect of the distinct needs of private customers, contract hire customers, etc., as well as being appointed to manage key customers. Market managers work alongside product managers who can develop and specialize activities such as servicing, bodywork repairs and vehicle hire which are made available to final customers through the market managers.

The most important advantages of such clusters are that they can, in principle, allow organizations to respond rapidly to environmental change. Short-term project teams can be assembled and disbanded at short notice to meet changed needs. Project teams can bring together a wide variety of disciplines and can be used to evaluate new services before full-scale development is undertaken. A bank exploring the possibility of developing a banking system linked to personal customers' home computers might establish a team drawn from staff involved in marketing to personal customers and staff responsible for technology-based research and development. The former may include market researchers and the latter computer development engineers.

The flexibility of such structures can be increased by bringing temporary workers into the structure on a contract basis as and when needed. During the past decade there has been a trend for many service organizations to lay off significant numbers of workers – including management – and to buy these back when needed. As well as

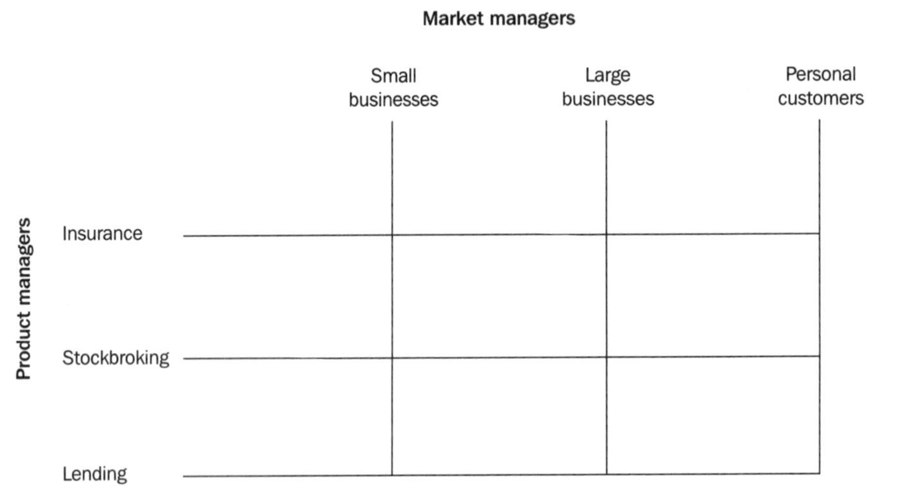

Figure 12.5 Matrix organization structure applied to a financial services organization

cutting fixed costs, such organizations have the potential to respond very rapidly to environmental change.

Where inter-functional clusters exist, great motivation can be present in effectively managed teams. Against this, matrix-type structures can have their problems. Most serious is the confused lines of authority which may result. Staff member may not be clear about the superior to whom they are responsible for a particular aspect of their duties, resulting in possible stress and demotivation. Where a matrix-type structure is introduced into an organization with a history and culture of functional specialization, it can be very difficult to implement effectively. Staff may be reluctant to act outside a role which they have traditionally defined narrowly and guarded jealously. Finally, such structures invariably result in more managers being employed within an organization. At best this can result in a costly addition to the salary bill. At worst, the existence of additional managers can also slow down decision-making processes where the managers show a reluctance to act outside a narrow functional role.

Having multi-functional clusters of individuals may represent a desirable structure for an organization, but getting there can be a slow and painful process. Most management change within organizations occurs incrementally. The result of this is often a compromised organization structure which is unduly influenced by historic factors which are of no continuing relevance. Vested interests within an organization frequently result in an organization which is production rather than customer focused. Some organizations have been more radical, started with a clean sheet of paper and asked, 'How would we design our structures and processes if we were starting out today?'

The underlying principle of business process re-engineering is to design an organization around key value-adding activities. Essentially, re-engineering is about *radically* redesigning the *processes* by which an organization does business in order that it can achieve major savings in cost, or improvements in service levels, or both. Seen as a model, the organization which is most effective is the one which adds most value (as defined by customers) for the least cost.

To be effective, re-engineering needs to be led by strong individuals who have authority to oversee implementation from beginning to end. They will need a lot of clout because fear, resistance and cynicism will inevitably slow the task down. Successful companies therefore seek to involve their employees in the detail of implementation, even if the radical nature of the agenda is not negotiable.

12.9 **Reducing dependency on human resources**

Employees represent an expensive and difficult asset to manage and, furthermore, the quality of employees' contribution to the total service offer can often be seen by final consumers as being highly variable. Service organizations therefore frequently pursue strategies to reduce the human element of their production process. The aim of employee replacement schemes can be to reduce service variability, to reduce costs, or both. Cost-cutting could be important where an organization is pursuing a cost leadership strategy, allowing it to gain a competitive advantage.

A number of strategies to reduce dependency on the organization's employees can be identified.

- At one extreme, the human element in a service production and delivery process can be completely replaced by automatic machinery. Examples include bank ATMs, vending machines and automatic car washes. Constraints on employee replacement come from the limitations of technology (for example, completely automatic car washes can seldom achieve such high standards of cleanliness as those where an operator is present to perform some operations inaccessible to machinery); the cost of replacement equipment (it is only within the past few years that the cost of servers and access to the Internet has fallen to a point where retailers can move from labour-intensive telephone sales to automated online sales); and the attitudes of consumers towards automated service delivery (many segments of the population are still reluctant to use Internet banking services, preferring the reassurance provided by human contact).

- Equipment can be used alongside employees to assist them in their task. This often has the effect of deskilling their task by reducing the scope they have for exercising discretion, thereby reducing the variability in quality perceived by customers. In this way computerized accounting systems in hotels reduce the risk of front-of-house staff incorrectly adding up a client's bill. Similarly, the computer systems used by many airline reservation staff include prompts which guide their interaction with clients.

- The inseparability of the service offer means that consumers of a service are usually involved in some way as co-producers of the service. The involvement of the service provider's personnel can be reduced by shifting a greater part of the production process to the consumer. In this way, most petrol service stations expect customers to fill their own car with fuel, rather than have this task undertaken by the station's own staff. Similarly, a television repair company may require customers to bring equipment to its premises for repair. In both cases, the customer has greater control over the quality of service by undertaking part of it themselves.

Case study

'Theory of business' used to evaluate employees' contribution at Direkt Anlage Bank AG

By Sven Tuzovic, Daniela Kudernatsch and Manfred Bruhn, University of Basel

This chapter has shown how there are many barriers in the service–profit chain preventing service organizations becoming truly customer-oriented, but key among these barriers are issues relating to human resource management. Trying to understand the process of value creation within an organization can be very difficult, involving many linkages between different elements of an internal value chain. Just how much is each individual employee, or group of employees, worth to a company? It is essential for organizations to establish effective and efficient management systems for encouraging their employees to perform at their maximum, and, in this sense, compensation systems are an essential tool to link corporate goals such as customer orientation with individual and organizational performance.

While some studies have shown positive effects of incorporating non-financial measures into employees' pay (e.g. Widmier, 2002), many companies have encountered problems after linking pay to customer satisfaction. Reasons for this can be attributed to the measurement of customer satisfaction as well as to the missing link between customer satisfaction and customer retention. (Is it actually profitable to provide a high level of customer satisfaction?) Hence, there is a strong need for the development of an holistic performance measurement model enabling an organization to identify cause-and-effect relationships when developing a customer-oriented compensation system.

The Balanced Scorecard approach was used by the German Direkt Anlage Bank AG (DAB) to give it a better estimate of the linkages within its service profit chain. DAB used the Balanced Scorecard to record information down to the lowest level of the command structure – that is, every employee had a personal BSC derived from divisional BSCs, which are in turn derived from the corporate BSC. In 1999 the management of DAB developed a 'theory of business', portrayed as a diagram of hypothesized cause-and-effect linkages among key performance indicators, including qualitative and quantitative indicators. To test the theory, DAB developed a monitoring system to collect the necessary data. Since January 2000, DAB had measured all the BSC indicators on a monthly basis. These indicators comprised the four perspectives of the BSC (see Kudernatsch, 2001):

1. *human resources* (global employee satisfaction, recommendation rate of DAB as employer, employee turnover, employee fluctuation, job performance such as number of failures and absence)

2. *customers* (global customer satisfaction, satisfaction with dimensions and items, intention to remain loyal, recommendation rate of DAB, market share, number of new customers, name recognition rate)

3. *processes* (cycle time, capacity, number of failures, service level, productivity), and

4. *finance* (profitability, revenue, cost, shareholder value).

DAB used longitudinal data to develop and estimate a structural equation model of its 'theory of business', enabling the estimation of the direction and strength of the hypothesized relationships (Figure 12.6). The model allowed DAB to simulate the effects of changes across linkages – for example, how an increase in employee satisfaction would lead to better processes, how this might influence customer satisfaction, and, ultimately, the effect on profitability. The development of such a model might seem a remarkable achievement, given the complexity of large organizations.

The first analysis at DAB showed a negative correlation between customer satisfaction and contribution margin (that is, the more dissatisfied the DAB customers, the better the financial results of the bank). At first sight, this might appear to have provided some evidence that a company can 'over-deliver' service quality to the point where it incurs a loss. However, the inclusion of more mediating variables such as positive word-of-mouth identified an indirect positive relationship between customer satisfaction and the contribution margin. Due to these empirical

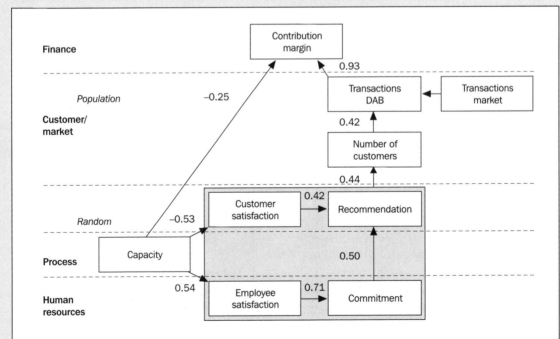

Figure 12.6 A model showing the hypothesized linkages between human resources and financial contribution; figures indicate the observed strength of linkages at Direkt Anlage Bank AG (Source: Bruhn, Kudernatsch and Tuzovic, 2004)

cause-and-effect relationships within the BSC it became evident that customer satisfaction is a relevant pre-economic performance indicator for DAB improving financial results in the long term. In consequence, the existence of such a BSC linkage model can facilitate the development of employee payment systems which reward good performance.

Case study review questions

1. What measurement problems are likely to occur in developing a model such as that shown in Figure 12.6?

2. Is the approach adopted by DAB particularly suited to some types of service organization? What types of service organization might it be unsuitable for?

3. Can quantitative models of employees' contribution to a business ever really hope to capture the more qualitative contributions that can make all the difference in the eyes of customers?

Chapter summary and links to other chapters

Human resource management (HRM) is not something which should be considered as separate from marketing management. For services which involve a high level of contact between employees and customers, high levels of service quality may only be achieved with appropriate HRM. There has been much debate about the nature of internal marketing and its relationship to HRM theories. Control and empowerment are two important issues which have a long history of debate within the HRM literature.

The close relationship between this chapter and **Chapter 3** on the service encounter and **Chapter 8** on service quality should be evident. Issues of HRM are central to many organizations' attempts to develop relationship marketing strategies (**Chapter 5**). Without appropriately trained staff, relationships can degenerate to little more than data stored on a computer.

Chapter review questions

1. What are the principal ways in which the management of personnel is likely to be different in a services organization, as compared with a manufacturer?

2. Discuss the ways in which a fast-food restaurant can increase the level of participation among its staff.

3. Using an industry with which you are familiar, identify methods by which the effects of variability of the personnel inputs can be minimized in order to produce a consistent standard of output.

4. What is the link between personnel and service quality?

5. What are the shortcomings of traditional personnel management for the effective marketing of services?

6. Using examples, show how human resource management policies can help to overcome the problems associated with peaked patterns of demand.

Activity

Consult the jobs section of your local newspaper and examine jobs which are advertised by local service organizations. To what extent is the organization's communication through its job advertisements consistent with its communication to customers? What do stated job requirements say about the service standards offered by the organization? Do you notice any difference in job requirements between staff required for front-line roles and those required for behind-the-scenes functions? Does the marketing environment of an organization influence the way it seeks new staff, for example is there a difference between private-sector, public-sector and not-for-profit organizations?

Key terms

Customization The deliberate and planned adaptation of a service to meet the special requirements of individual customers.

Empowerment Giving employees authority to act using their own initiative, without reference to senior management.

Human resource management (HRM) Strategies and practices to improve the effectiveness and efficiency of an organization's human resources.

Internal marketing The application of the principles and practices of marketing to an organization's dealings with its employees.

Mission statement A means of reminding everyone within an organization of the essential purpose of the organization.

Selected further reading

This chapter has discussed very briefly some of the basic principles of human resource management as they apply to service organizations. For a fuller discussion of these principles, the following texts are recommended.

Beardwell, I. and Holden, L. (2003) *Human Resource Management: A Contemporary Approach*, FT Prentice Hall.

Bratton, J. and Gold, J. (2003) *Human Resource Management: Theory and Practice*, Macmillan, Palgrave.

The following texts provide a further insight into the role of internal marketing.

Ballantyne, D. (2003) 'A relationship-mediated theory of internal marketing', *European Journal of Marketing*, 37 (9), 1242–60.

Ahmed, P. and Rafiq, M. (2003) 'Internal marketing issues and challenges', *European Journal of Marketing*, 37 (9), 1177–86.

Naudé, P., Desai, J. and Murphy, J. (2003) 'Identifying the determinants of internal marketing orientation', *European Journal of Marketing*, 37 (9), 1205–20.

Varey, R.J. and Lewis, B.R. (1999) 'A broadened conception of internal marketing', *European Journal of Marketing*, 33 (9/10), 926–44.

The marketing role of front-line employees is explored in the following articles.

Gummesson, E. (1991) 'Marketing-orientation revisited: The crucial role of the part-time marketer', *European Journal of Marketing*, 25 (2), 60–75.

Papasolomou-Doukakis, I. (2002) 'The role of employee development in customer relations: The case of UK retail banks', *Corporate Communications*, 7 (1), 62–76.

Hartline, M.D. and Ferrell, O.C. (1996) 'The management of customer contact service employees: An empirical investigation', *Journal of Marketing*, 60 (October), 52–70.

Leadership and empowerment in the context of services industries are discussed in the following texts.

Lashley, C. (2000) 'Empowerment through involvement: A case study of TGI Friday's restaurants', *Personnel Review*, 29 (6), 791–815.

Prabhu, V. and Robson, A. (2000) 'Achieving service excellence – Measuring the impact of leadership and senior management commitment', *Managing Service Quality*, 10 (5), 307–17.

Melhem, Y. (2003) 'The antecedents of customer–contact employees' empowerment', *Employee Relations*, 26 (1), 72–93.

Bowen, D.E. and Lawler, E.E. (1992) 'The empowerment of service workers: What, why, how and whom', *Sloan Management Review*, Spring, 31–9.

References

Ahmed, P. and Rafiq, M. (2003) 'Internal marketing issues and challenges', *European Journal of Marketing*, 37 (9), 1177–86.

Albrecht, K. (1990) *Service Within*, Dow Jones-Irwin, Homewood, IL.

Arnett, D.B., Laverie, D.A. and McLane, C. (2002) 'Using job satisfaction and pride as internal-marketing tools', *Cornell Hotel & Restaurant Administration Quarterly*, 43 (2), 9–17.

Bateson, J.E.G. (1989) *Managing Services Marketing – Text and Readings*, 2nd edn, Dryden Press, Forth Worth, USA.

Berry, L.L. (1980) 'Services marketing is different', *Business*, 30 (3), 24–9.

Berry, L.L. (1995) 'Relationship marketing of services: Growing interest, emerging perspectives', *Journal of the Academy of Marketing Science*, 23 (4), 236–45.

Bienstock, C.C., DeMoranville, C.W. and Smith, R.K. (2003) 'Organizational citizenship behaviour and service quality', *Journal of Services Marketing*, 17 (4), 357–78.

Bowen, D.E. and Lawler, E.E. (1992) 'The empowerment of service workers: What, why, when, and how', *Sloan Management Review*, Spring, 31–9.

Bruhn, M., Kudernatsch, D. and Tuzovic, S. (2004) 'Integrating the Balanced Scorecard approach with the concept of customer-oriented compensation systems: The need for causality', Proceedings of the 6th Australasian Services Marketing Workshop, Dunedin, University of Otago.

Buchanan, D.A. and Huczynski, A.A. (2003) *Organizational Behaviour: An Introductory Text*, 5th edn, FT Prentice Hall, Harlow.

Denton, D.K. (1990) 'Customer focused management", *HR Magazine*, August, Lexington, MA, 62–7.

Dolan, P. and Brierley, I. (1992) *A Tale of Two Bus Companies*, Partnership Research, London.

Donavan, D.T., Brown, T.J. and Mowen, J.C. (2004) 'Internal benefits of service-worker customer orientation: Job satisfaction, commitment, and organizational citizenship behaviours', *Journal of Marketing*, 68 (1), 128–46.

Drucker, P.F. (1973) *Management: Tasks, Responsibilities and Practices*, Harper & Row, New York.

Foreman, S. and Money, A. (1995) 'Internal marketing: Concepts, measurement and application', *Journal of Marketing Management*, 11 (8), 755–68.

Garvin, D.A. (1993) 'Building a learning organization', *Harvard Business Review*, July–August, 78–91.

Grönroos, C. (1982) *Strategic Management and Marketing in the Service Sector*, Swedish School of Economics and Business Administration, Helsingfors, Findland.

Gummesson, E. (2001) *Total Relationship Marketing*, Butterworth-Heinemann, London.

Hales, C. (1994) ' "Internal marketing" as an approach to human resource management: A new perspective or a metaphor too far?', *Human Resource Management Journal*, 5 (1), 50–71.

Hart, C.W.L., Sasser, W.E. Jr and Heskett, J.L. (1990) 'The profitable art of service recovery', *Harvard Business Review*, July–August, 148–56.

Hartline, M.D. and Ferrell, O.C. (1996) 'The management of customer contact service employees: An empirical investigation', *Journal of Marketing*, 60 (October), 52–70.

Ingham, H. (1991) 'Organizational structure and internal control in the UK insurance industry', *The Services Industries Journal*, 11 (4; October), 425–38.

Kaplan, R.S. and Norton, D.P. (1996) *The Balanced Scorecard: Translating Strategy into Action*, Harvard Business School Press, Boston.

Kaplan, R.S. and Norton, D.P. (2001) 'Transforming the Balanced Scorecard from performance measurement to strategic management', *Accounting Horizons*, 15 (1), 87–104.

Kelley, S.W. (1993) 'Discretion and the service employee', *Journal of Retailing*, 69 (1; Spring), 104–26.

Kudernatsch, D. (2000) 'Die Einführung der Balanced Scorecard im Customer Care Management der Direkt Anlage Bank AG', in W. Engelbach and R. Meier (eds), *Customer Care Management*, Munich, 161–75.

Lee-Ross, D. (2000) 'Development of the service predisposition instrument', *Journal of Managerial Psychology*, 15 (2), 148–57.

Lukas, B.A. and Maignan, I. (1996) 'Striving for quality: The key role of internal and external customers', *Journal of Market Focused Management*, 1, 175–97.

Malmi, T. (2001) 'Balanced Scorecards in Finnish companies: A research note', *Management Accounting Research*, 12 (2), 207–20.

Martin, C.L. (1996) 'How powerful is empowerment?', *The Journal of Services Marketing*, 10 (6), 4–5.

Maslow, A. (1943) 'A theory of human motivation', *Psychological Review*, 50 (4), 370–96.

McGregor, D. (1960) *The Human Side of Enterprise*, McGraw-Hill, New York.

Milkovich, G.T. and Newman, J.M. (2002) *Compensation*, 7th edn, McGraw-Hill, New York.

Otley, D. (1999) 'Performance management: A framework for management control systems research', *Management Accounting Research*, 10 (4), 363–82.

Porter, M.E. (1980) *Competitive Strategy: Techniques for Analyzing Industries and Competitors*, Free Press, New York.

Reynoso, J.F. and Moores, B. (1996) 'Internal relationships', in F. Buttle (ed.), *Relationship Marketing: Theory and Practice*, Paul Chapman Publishing, London, 55–73.

Silvestro, R. (2002) 'Dispelling the modern myth: Employee satisfaction and loyalty drive service profitability', *International Journal of Operations and Production Management*, 22 (1), 30–49.

Speckbacher, G., Bischof, J. and Pfeiffer, T. (2003) 'A descriptive analysis on the implementation of Balanced Scorecards in German-speaking countries', *Management Accounting Research*, 14, 361–87.

Sunday Telegraph (2004) 'BUPA to be first medical provider to show success rates of surgeons', *Sunday Telegraph*, London, 2.

Varey, R.J. (1995) 'Internal marketing: A review and some interdisciplinary research challenges', *International Journal of Service Industry Management*, 6 (1), 40–63.

Varey, R.J. and Lewis, B.R. (1999) 'A broadened conception of internal marketing', *European Journal of Marketing*, 33 (9/10), 926–44.

Widmier, S. (2002) 'The effects of incentives and personality on salesperson's customer orientation', *Industrial Marketing Management*, 31 (7), 609–15.

13

Managing capacity

Learning objectives

This chapter will explain:

- the effects of service perishability on a services organization's ability to supply a service at the time and place that customers require it

- the nature of variable customer demand.

- techniques used to match service supply with demand

- queuing and reservation systems

- Yield management techniques, which allow companies to maximize their returns from variable demand for fixed capacity.

13.1 Introduction

Imagine a restaurant in the centre of town which is popular with tourists in summer. During the quiet winter months, the restaurant could manage with a building which is half the size it currently occupies. But during the busy summer months, it faces a very high level of demand which keeps its facilities and staff fully employed. This situation is typical of many services industries whose output is perishable, but whose customers' preferred time for consuming the service might not coincide with the company's preferred time for producing it. Perishability is an important characteristic of services, and the possibility of producing output during the quiet period to sell in the busy period – common among manufacturing firms – is not generally possible with a service such as a restaurant. Strategic marketing planning for such seasonal service businesses raises a number of important questions.

- What level of demand should the business aim to cater for at its peak? It may not be viable for the company to simply invest in larger facilities if these are only going to be used for a few weeks, or even days, during the year.

- How should the business maximize the revenue it can earn during the busy periods without alienating the core business which will be needed to sustain it during the quieter periods?

- How can demand be stimulated to fill spare capacity during quiet periods?

- How are problems of congestion to be handled at times of peak demand?

Managing the relationship between supply and demand challenges the strategic and tactical skills of the services marketer. This chapter begins by gaining an understanding of the causes and consequences of fluctuating demand for services. It then looks at methods of changing patterns of demand on the one hand and changing the pattern of supply on the other. Reservation and queuing systems aim to reconcile differences between supply and demand at any one time. Yield management has emerged as a technique for turning fluctuating demand from a problem to an opportunity whereby service organizations can make the maximum revenue for the available level of demand.

13.2 The management of customer demand

Service providers face various patterns of demand, ranging from negative demand (e.g. where many people actually would have to be paid to receive dental services which are perceived as 'bad') to overfull and unwholesome demand (e.g. the queues which build up for some unique historic tourist sites during the peak tourism season).

Irregular patterns of demand can cause major problems for service organizations. Manufacturing companies also often face irregular patterns of demand, but they are generally better able to cope with such patterns. Because goods manufacturers are able to separate production from consumption, they have the ability to hold stocks of goods which can be built up in order to cater for any peaks in demand which occur. As an example, lawnmower manufacturers can work during the winter months making lawnmowers to store in order to meet the sudden surge in demand which occurs each spring. Those lawnmowers which are not sold in that spring can be sold later in the year at a lower clearance price, or put back into stock for the following year. By contrast, the perishability and inseparability of the service offer means that it is not sufficient to broadly match supply and demand over the longer term within a broadly defined geographical market. Instead, supply and demand must be matched temporally and spatially. An excess of production capacity in one time period cannot be transferred to another period when there is a shortage, nor can excess demand in one area normally be met by excess supply which is located in another area.

The fact that services cannot be stored does not generally cause a problem where demand levels are stable and predictable. However, most services experience demand which shows significant temporal variation. Peaks in demand can take a number of forms:

- daily variation (commuter train services in the morning and evening peaks, leisure centres during evenings)

- weekly variation (nightclubs on Saturday nights, trains on Friday evenings)

- seasonal variation (air services to the Mediterranean in summer, department stores in the run-up to Christmas)

- cyclical variation (the demand for mortgages and architectural services)

- unpredictable variation (the demand for building repairs following storm damage).

In practice, many services experience demand patterns which follow a number of these peaks – a restaurant, for example, may have a daily peak (at midday), a weekly peak (Fridays) and a seasonal peak (e.g. December).

Financial success for organizations in competitive markets facing uneven demand comes from being able to match supply with demand at a cost which is lower than its competitors, or with a standard of service which is higher, or both. In free markets, a service organization must take a strategic view as to what level of demand it seeks to cater for. In particular, it must decide to what extent it should even attempt to meet peak demands, rather than turn business away. The precise cut-off point is influenced by a number of factors, as described below.

- Infrequently occurring peaks in demand may be very expensive to provide for where they require the organization to provide a high level of equipment or personnel which cannot be laid off or found alternative uses during quiet periods. Commuter rail operators often do not stimulate peak period demand – or may even try to reduce it – because they would be required to purchase and maintain additional rolling stock whose entire overhead cost would be carried by those few journeys during the peak time which they operate. Similarly, enlarged platforms at terminals may be required in order to cater for just a few additional peak trains each day.

- Peaks in demand may bring in a high level of poor-quality custom. Restaurants in tourist areas may regard the once-only demand brought by bank holiday day-trippers to be of less long-term value than catering for the relatively stable all-year-round trade from local residents.

- Quality of service may suffer when a services organization expands its output beyond optimal levels – for example, waiting time in a restaurant may become unacceptable if it seeks to cater for additional customers in the peak period, without investing in additional kitchen facilities.

- On the other hand, some organizations may lose valuable core business if they do not cater for peaks. A bank which frequently suffers lunchtime queues for cash-handling transactions may risk losing an entire relationship with customers if it transfers not only its cheque facility to a competing bank, but also its mortgage and insurance business.

An indication of the financial implications for organizations of uneven patterns of demand is shown in Figure 13.1, where two levels of capacity are indicated. The *optimum* capacity is notionally defined as that for which a facility was designed – any additional demand is likely to result in queues or discomfort. The *maximum available* capacity is the upper technical limit of a service to handle customers (e.g. a 70-seat railway carriage can in practice carry up to 200 people in crush conditions). At the

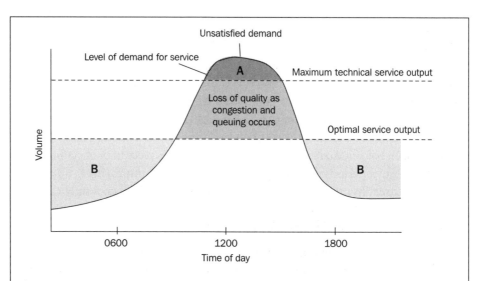

Figure 13.1 Implications of uneven service demand relative to capacity. The shaded area 'A' represents lost revenue opportunities, as the company is unable at this time of day to satisfy customers who are able and willing to pay. The shaded areas marked 'B' represent a waste of resources for the company. At these times, the company has capacity available, but no revenue is earned

peak, business is lost; when demand is satisfied above the optimum capacity level, customer service suffers; while in the slack period, resources are wasted.

Once a strategic decision has been made about the level of demand which it is desirable to meet, tactics must be developed to bring about a match between supply and demand for each time period. The task of marketing management can conceptually be broken down into two components:

1. managing the state of demand to even out peaks and troughs

2. managing the supply of service to match the pattern of customer demand.

13.2.1 Managing the pattern of customer demand

Where demand is highly peaked, an organization could simply do nothing and allow queues to develop for its service. This is bad strategy, which could harm the long-term development of relationships with customers, and may deny the short-term opportunities which peaks and troughs can present. A simple queuing strategy is most typical of services operating in non-competitive environments, for example some elective surgery undertaken by the National Health Service. In competitive markets, a more proactive market-oriented strategy is needed to manage the pattern of demand, and the methods most commonly used are described below.

- Demand is frequently stimulated during the off-peak periods using all of the elements of the marketing mix. Prices are often reduced during slack periods in a number of tactical forms (e.g. 'off-peak' train tickets, the 'happy hour' in pubs, and money-off vouchers valid only during slack periods). The product offering can itself be reformulated during the off-peak period by bundling with other services or goods (e.g. activity breaks offered at weekends in business hotels to fill spare room capacity). Distribution of a service could be made more favourable to customers during slack periods – for example, during quiet times of the day or season, a take-away restaurant may offer a free home delivery service. Promotion for many service companies is concentrated on stimulating demand during slack periods (Figure 13.2). For some services where consumption takes place in public, stimulating demand in quiet periods may be important as a means of improving the quality of the service itself. In the case of theatres, having more customers not only results in increased income, but also a greater ambience for all customers who come for the atmosphere which the interaction of a live performer and audience creates.

- Similarly, demand is suppressed during peak periods using a reformulation of the marketing mix. Prices are often increased tactically, either directly (e.g. surcharges for rail travel on Friday evenings, higher package holiday prices in August), or indirectly (e.g. removing discounting during peak periods). Promotion of services associated with peak demand is often reduced (e.g. train operators in the London area concentrate most of their advertising on leisure travel rather than the highly peaked journey to work). Distribution and the product offering are often simplified

Figure 13.2 This restaurant has a novel idea for stimulating demand during the quiet early-evening period. To encourage early diners (when there is surplus capacity), it charges customers individually according to the time that their order is taken. As the evening gets busier, the price goes up

at peak periods (e.g. restaurants and cafés frequently turn away low-value business during peak periods).

13.2.2 Effects of the Internet on demand management

The Internet has proved to be extremely valuable to service organizations seeking to maximize their yields, for a number of reasons. Use of the Internet can significantly reduce transaction costs by encouraging direct sales via the organization's own website. The Internet also allows the organization to collect large amounts of data regarding customer buying behaviour from third-party sites. Hence, price can be tailored to match customer value by using a high level of differential pricing according to individual customers' previous buying behaviour and their estimated willingness to pay. However, the Internet also poses challenges for yield management. The ability of service providers to operate differential pricing where only the price – and not service features – is altered, is lessening. The Internet has led to greater competition between service providers, while at the same time there is evidence of increasing levels of customer awareness (and convenience) in evaluating and comparing competitors' offers (Yelkur and Nêveda DaCosta, 2001). The opportunistic customer has ample scope to switch from one service provider to another, by quickly evaluating booking conditions and products via the Internet. Therefore a growing issue is not so much one of identifying market segments with different levels of willingness to pay, but of how to administer differential schemes without alienating customers who have become smarter with powerful new technology.

13.3 Managing service capacity

There is a limit to how far it is desirable or practical to change the pattern of demand that a company faces. Where this is so, a service provider must look to manage its capacity more effectively so that it more closely follows the pattern of demand which it faces.

The extent to which an organization is able to adjust its output to meet changes in demand is a reflection of the flexibility of its production processes. Capacity is said to be completely inflexible where it is impossible to produce additional capacity. It is not possible, for example, to enlarge a historic stately home to cater for a demand peak which occurs on summer Sunday afternoons. Capacity is said to be flexible where supply can be adjusted in response to demand. Highly flexible supply allows an organization to meet very short-term variations in demand by introducing additional capacity at short notice. Sometimes, capacity can be flexible up to a certain point, but inflexible beyond that. A railway operator can provide additional trains to meet morning commuter peaks until it runs out of spare rolling stock and terminal facilities, when supply becomes very inflexible. Any discussion of the concept of flexibility of supply requires a time frame to be defined – supply may be inflexible to very sudden changes in demand, but it may be possible to supply additional capacity with sufficient advance planning.

In the area of supply management, marketing management cannot be seen in isolation from operations management and human resource management. Typical strategies which are used within services industries for making supply more responsive to demand include the following.

- Equipment and personnel can be scheduled to switch between alternative uses to reflect differing patterns of demand for different services. A hotel complex can switch a large hall from meeting a peak demand for banquets and parties – which occurs in the evenings – to meeting a peak demand for conferences which occurs during the working day. Similarly, personnel can be trained to allow different jobs to be performed at different peak periods. Tour operators often train staff to be representatives in Mediterranean resorts during the summer peak for beach holidays, and skiing representatives in the Alps during the winter skiing peak.

- Efforts are often made to switch resources between alternative uses at very short notice. For example, a store assistant engaged in restocking shelves can be summoned at short notice to perform much more perishable and inseparable service functions, such as giving advice on products or reducing checkout queues.

- Capacity can be bought in on a part-time basis at periods of peak demand. This can involve both personnel resources (e.g. bar staff hired in the evenings only, tour guides hired for the summer only) and equipment (aircraft chartered for the summer season only, shops rented on short leases for the run-up to Christmas).

- Operations can be organized so that as much back-up work as possible is carried out during slack periods of demand. This particularly affects the tangible component of the service offering. In this way, equipment can be serviced during the quiet periods (e.g. winter overhaul programmes carried out on a holiday charter operator's fleet of aircraft) and personnel can do as much preparation as possible in the run-up to a peak (a theatre bar taking orders for interval drinks before a performance and preparing them ready to serve during the interval).

Although it is desirable that the supply of service components should be made as flexible as possible, these components must not be looked at in isolation. The benefits of flexibility in one component can be cancelled out if they are not matched by flexibility in other complementary components of a service. For example, a strategy which allows a holiday tour operator to increase the carrying capacity of its aircraft at short notice will be of only limited value if it cannot also increase the availability of additional hotel accommodation. A strategy to carry out routine aircraft maintenance work during the quieter winter season may simply create an additional peak problem for the airline's maintenance facility. Capacity management must therefore identify critical bottlenecks which prevent customers' demands being satisfied.

Can full buses lose money?

The accountants came into a large bus company and worked out the cost of running special school buses during the peak period. Sadly, although the buses were invariably full, the accountants calculated that they were not making any profit, as they were tying up assets with no alternative use during the day. The accountants decided that the school bus journeys should in future bear all of the fixed costs of assets used, with the result that, on paper, they then became loss making. So one morning and evening journey a day had to be able to cover all of the capital, depreciation and maintenance costs of the vehicle, as well as the direct operating costs of wages and fuel. The marketing people at the bus company were exhorted to choke off demand for the school buses and to encourage more use of buses during the off-peak period. The new costing base encouraged them to run more off-peak services which could make a profit with even small numbers of customers. The result? The engineers employed during the day to service the buses when they came into the depot between the morning and afternoon peaks found they had no buses to work on. Instead, they had to service the buses during the evening which involved higher overtime rates of pay. The marketing department had got rid of one peak, but had seemingly created a new maintenance peak for the engineers. This example emphasizes the importance of taking a broad view of demand management to avoid creating further bottlenecks.

13.3.1 **Flexible employees**

For many service organizations, employees are the biggest item of cost and potentially the biggest cause of bottlenecks in service delivery systems. Having the right staff in the right place at the right time can demand a lot of flexibility on the part of employees. Too often, customers are delayed because, although staff are available, they are not trained to perform the task which currently needs performing urgently. At other times, employees may go about a backroom task oblivious to the fact that delays are occurring elsewhere in the front-line delivery system. Worse still, employees could have a negative attitude towards their job which sees a customer's problem as nothing to do with them and take no interest in finding staff who may be able to help. Many service industries have been notorious in the past for rigid demarcation between jobs which were organization-focused rather than customer-focused. In Britain, train drivers and guards for a long time existed as two separate groups which were not able to stand in for each other.

To improve their flexibility, many service providers have sought to develop multiple skills among their employees so that they can be switched between tasks at short notice. Within the hotel sector, for example, it is quite usual to find staff multi-skilled in reception duties, food and beverage service, and room service. If staff shortages occur within one area, staff can be rapidly transferred from less urgent tasks where there may be sufficient staff coverage.

An effective multi-tasking strategy must be backed up by adequate training so that employees can effectively perform all the functions that are expected of them. Transferring poorly trained employees to tasks with which they are not familiar may actually make service delivery worse, not better. Multi-skilling is closely related to the development of empowerment discussed in the previous chapter. This implies that employees become problem-solvers on behalf of customers and use their initiative to resolve an issue, either by direct action themselves, or by referral to others who are capable of resolving the issue.

Flexibility in working also applies to the rostering of employees' duties. Where patterns of demand are unpredictable, it is useful to have a pool of suitably trained staff who can be called up at short notice. Many service providers therefore operate 'standby' or 'callout' rotas, where staff are expected to be available to go into work at short notice.

A flexible workforce sounds attractive in principle, but there are some drawbacks. Training in multiple skills would appear to be against the principles of scientific management (discussed in the previous chapter), wherein employees specialize in one task and perform this as efficiently as possible. Multiple skill training represents an investment for firms, and in service sectors with high turnover, such as the hospitality sector, the benefits of this training may be short-lived. Recruiting staff may become more expensive, with staff capable of performing numerous tasks able to command higher salaries than someone whose background only allows them to perform a narrower range of tasks. Finally, there is also the problem that requiring staff to work flexible hours may make their working conditions less attractive than a job where they had certainty over the days and times that they would be working. Expecting excessive flexibility may be contrary to the principles of internal marketing discussed in the previous chapter, exacerbating problems where there is a shortage of skilled staff. Service industries must compete with other sectors for good employees and if a job is perceived as offering too much uncertainty, staff may prefer to work elsewhere where working conditions are more predictable.

As well as being able to achieve short-term flexibility, service organizations must also have the flexibility over the longer term to shift their human resources from areas in decline to those where there is a prospect of future growth. For example, in order to retain its profitability, a bank must have the ability to move personnel away from relatively static activities such as cash handling and current account chequing towards the more profitable growth area of financial services.

Flexibility within a service organization can be achieved by segmenting the work-force into core and peripheral components. Core workers have greater job security and have defined career opportunities within an internal labour market. In return for this job security, core workers may have to accept what Atkinson (1984) described as 'functional flexibility', whereby they become responsible for a variety of job tasks. Peripheral employees, on the other hand, have lesser job security and limited career opportunities. In terms of Atkinson's prescription, they are 'numerically flexible', while financial flexibility is brought about through such processes as short-term employment contracts, subcontracting and outsourcing. The principal characteristics of the flexible firm are illustrated in Figure 13.3.

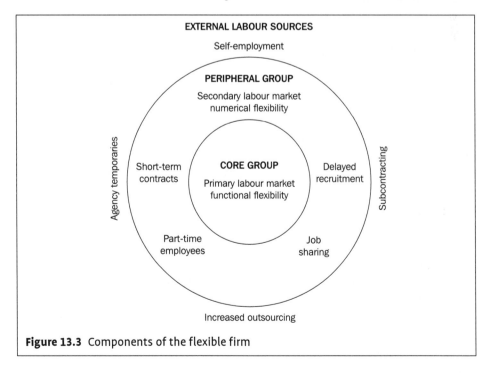

Figure 13.3 Components of the flexible firm

As a strategic tool, the model of the flexible firm has important implications for service organizations which experience fluctuating demand. However, critics of the concept have suggested that the strategic role attributed to the flexibility model is often illusory, with many organizations introducing 'flexibility' in very much an opportunistic manner. It has been suggested in one study of the hospitality sector that the distinction between core and peripheral employees is not as great as has commonly been portrayed (Deery and Jago, 2002).

Too much flexibility for staff?

The conventional wisdom is that service organizations need highly flexible employment practices so that they can effectively and efficiently meet customers' demands when and where they occur. But how far should a company go in pursuit of flexibility? Stories abound of services companies that pay young people the basic minimum wage level and provide very insecure employment. Some fast-food chains have been known to make a habit of laying staff off at short notice if they don't have the level of demand to keep them busy.

To some people, this may sound like exploitation but, to others, young people were at least being given an opportunity to work, and customers benefited by lower prices and service when they needed it. But apart from the ethics of such practices is the question of whether too much flexibility makes good business sense. If staff can be laid off at very short notice, will they show such concern to customers as an employee who has more secure employment? Or will the insecurity keep employees on their toes to perform well at all times? Can flexibility be applied to complex service processes, or is it realistically limited to jobs which have been highly industrialized and deskilled?

13.4 Queuing and reservation systems

Where demand exceeds the supply capacity of a service, and demand and supply management measures have failed to match the two, some form of queuing or reservation system is often desirable. A formal queuing or reservation system is preferable to a random free-for-all for a number of reasons.

- From an operational viewpoint, advance reservation systems allow an organization to identify when peaks in demand will occur. Where there is reasonable mid- to short-term supply flexibility, supply can be adjusted to meet demand, either by bringing in additional capacity to meet an unexpected surge in demand or by laying off capacity where demand looks like falling below the expected level. In this way, advance reservations for a charter airline can help it to schedule its fleet to accommodate as many potential passengers as possible. Similarly, a low level of advance reservations could lead to some unpromising-looking flights being cancelled, or 'consolidated'.

■ Queuing and reservation systems allow organizations to develop a relationship with their customers from an early stage. This relationship can be formed at the simplest level by using a telephone enquiry to gain some degree of commitment from a potential customer and to offer a service at a time when both customer and supplier can be assured of achieving their objectives. Or the relationship can be developed from the time when a potential customer walks into a service outlet and joins a queue.

Queues are an inevitable part of service delivery processes where it is not possible to manage supply or demand to bring them into line. Queues for some services which cannot easily be expanded have become legendary, for example during the summer months it is not uncommon to find queues of several hundred people waiting to get into the Tower of London. Long waits have been shown to be a major source of customer dissatisfaction (see Bitner *et al.*, 1990). There is also evidence indicating that customers' dissatisfaction with long waits affects both their overall satisfaction with the service and their future intentions to use those providers (Taylor, 1994). There are a number of approaches to dealing with queues where these are inevitable.

■ *Understand customers' expectations of waiting time.* Individuals differ in their expectations of waiting time and, even for a particular individual, expectations may be situation-specific. A rail passenger travelling on a business journey may regard a minor delay as a failure, but be more prepared to accept a longer delay for a leisure journey. An attempt should be made to understand the psychological world of the consumer when he or she enters the service process. With younger people expecting instant gratification in a wide range of goods and services, their expectations of delay may be quite different to an older consumer who has long memories of waiting for goods and services.

■ *Reduce actual waiting time.* The most direct approach to deal with queuing is to decrease actual waiting time. Operational methods to accomplish this goal include various forecasting techniques, and the use of staffing and resource allocations models to meet the demand. If demand can be forecast accurately, then in some instances resource allocation could be modified to deal with fluctuating demand patterns. However, it was noted above that capacity might not always be sufficiently flexible to avoid queuing situations.

■ *Don't over-promise on waiting time.* Organizations should be careful about the promises they make with regard to queuing time. Where expectations of a short wait are held out, any lengthening of the waiting time will be perceived as a service failure. This could have serious implications for customers' perception of subsequent stages in the service which they are about to receive. It may be better to warn customers to expect a long delay, then if the actual delay is subsequently shorter, customers will perceive this as exceeding their expectations. They will then enter the next stage of the service process in a more positive frame of mind. Many airline customers have felt relieved when their plane arrived 'only' 15 minutes late instead of the 30 minutes which was previously announced by the airline.

- *Reduce perceptions of waiting time.* If the actual waiting time cannot be reduced, customers' subjective perceptions of the length of the delay might be managed. This is especially important given evidence showing that customers tend to over-estimate the actual length of their wait time (Hornik, 1984; Katz *et al.,* 1991). By offering activities to fill up waiting time or by providing various distractions, service providers may reduce customers' perceptions of waiting time length. As an example, customers waiting to collect their car from servicing may have their mind taken off their wait by the provision of a comfortable television lounge. Waiting time will appear to pass by more quickly where the customer can perceive that progress is being made – for example, by seeing that a queue is moving steadily. Uncertainty about the length of waiting time left causes anxiety and makes perceived time longer. Customers should also be able to perceive that the queue is being processed fairly. Where a delay is of uncertain duration, regular communication to customers makes time appear to pass by more quickly – the hardship caused by delay in waiting for a train can be lessened with appropriate communication to customers, explaining the cause of the delay. Good communication skills by front-line employees can transform the impact of waiting time.

- *Manage the impact of waiting time.* Service providers should be able to recognize where excessive waiting time has amounted to a service failure, and take actions to bring about an equitable resolution to the consequences of failure. Employees' actions, such as apologizing for a delay, may provide some immediate help. Other actions, such as making compensation payments may also be considered.

It should not be forgotten that a queue represents opportunities for service providers as well as problems. During the waiting process, an organization can make

Can a queue be part of the treat?

Ask anyone who has visited a popular theme park about their worst experience and they will probably mention the queues for the popular rides. However, researchers at Alton Towers theme park in Staffordshire, UK, found that queuing could actually enhance the enjoyment of a visit. They noted that **queuing systems** seemed to be so successful that visitors could wait for up to an hour for the popular Nemesis ride and hardly seemed to notice the wait. A number of tricks were used to bring this about. Queues were designed to twist in multiple directions, making it difficult for visitors to estimate their length. By exposing those in the queue to those who have just come off a ride, the level of anticipation was raised. Astonishingly, Alton Towers' researchers found that on quiet days when there was very little queuing, visitors were scoring lower levels of enjoyment than on busy days. Why could this be? Could a queue actually heighten visitors' sense of anticipation and achievement? Are there other services for which queuing might actually improve customers' perceived level of satisfaction?

its customers more familiar with other services which may be of interest to them at some other time. Diners waiting for a meal may have the time and interest to read about a programme of special events which associated hotels within the chain are offering. Sometimes, the organization may be able to use a queue for one service to try to cross-sell a higher-value service. In this way, a potential customer for an economy-class air ticket may be persuaded to buy an upgraded class of ticket rather than wait for the next available economy-class seat. Having a queue can also make a company's operations more efficient, as there is no slack time between customers. These efficiency gains may be passed on in the form of lower prices, thereby strengthening an organization's competitive position in a price-sensitive market.

13.5 **Yield management**

Many service industries struggle to match a probabilistic demand pattern to a finite set of resources in order to optimize profits. It is quite intuitive that when demand is strong, a company should seek to charge the highest price achievable for the use of its finite resources, while at less busy times it will be prepared to accept a lower price. This is the basis of **yield management** (**YM**) – sometimes also referred to as revenue management – which has become an increasingly widespread management technique throughout the service sector.

Yield management has gained widespread acceptance within the airline and hotel industries. The term originated in the airline industry to mean yield per available seat mile, but has since been applied to other industries by altering it to yield per available inventory unit. Simply put, YM is the process of allocating the right type of capacity or inventory unit to the right kind of customer at the right price so as to maximize revenue, or yield. Highlighting its link with marketing, yield management has been defined as a 'revenue technique which aims to increase net yield through the predicted allocation of available capacity to predetermined market segments at optimum price' (McMahon-Beattie and Yeoman, 2004).

Yield management suits service organizations where the capacity is fixed, where the demand is unstable and where the market can be segmented (Kimes, 1989). Analysing these features further, Kimes identified a number of preconditions for the success of YM and suggested a number of factors or ingredients that are prerequisites for the effective operation of a YM system (Kimes, 1997). Preconditions include fixed capacity, high fixed and low variable costs, and variable demand through time. This means that organizations such as hotels can benefit from controlling capacity when demand is high and relaxing that control when demand is low. Utilization of reservation systems can assist in managing demand because such systems can log requests for inventory units in advance of consumption.

Managers who are familiar with their organization's booking and demand patterns will be more confident in their decision about which reservations to accept or deny. A detailed knowledge of sales and booking data is essential to help managers forecast peaks and troughs in demand, thereby allowing them to align demand with supply more effectively.

It has been noted by Kimes that, 'Yield management is essentially a form of price discrimination.' In reality, hotels and airlines operate YM systems that rely on opening and closing rate bands. During low periods of demand a service provider can offer discount prices. At high demand periods, discounts can be closed off. Also, by offering multiple rates, the service manager will, hopefully, profitably align price, product and buyer, and increase net yield. Service firms should have the ability to divide their customer base into distinct market segments, such as business and leisure, to which they can apply the principles of differential pricing. Airlines typically segment their passengers by their willingness to pay. Low fares are offered to passengers who are willing to accept restrictions on travel. Business people or time-sensitive travellers are usually willing to pay higher fares to travel at peak times with no restrictions.

Overbooking is a common feature of yield management. By overbooking, service firms risk not being able to accommodate customers who have made a reservation, thereby creating a service failure in the eyes of the customer. So why is deliberate overbooking a feature of yield management? In an ideal world, a company would achieve 100% utilization of its resources at all times. In some cases, the conditions of an advance booking by a customer result in the customers forfeiting payment for the service if they do not show up for the service at the allotted time. However, in many markets, competitive pressures mean that customers would be deterred from making a binding commitment in advance, and therefore the market works on the basis of verbal, no-commitment reservations. This is typical, for example, within the UK car rental sector, where rental companies must presume that a certain proportion of bookings will be 'no shows'. Where the scale of an operation is large and there is a lot of historical data to work from, a company should be able to predict the proportion of no-shows at any particular time and overbook on the assumption that this proportion of bookings will not materialize. Where there is a rapid turnaround in resources (typical of car rental businesses), the effects of an under-assumption of no shows (i.e. more customers turn up than there is capacity) may simply be a delay (e.g. a wait while returning cars are prepared for a new customer). Sometimes, a company can overcome an overbooking situation by offering customers a free upgrade to a higher grade of facility (e.g. an overbooked airline economy cabin may be overcome if selected economy passengers are upgraded to business class). At other times, the consequences of overbooking may be difficult to handle. An airline may have overbooked a flight on a route where the next flight may not be until the following day, or even week. Attempts are therefore made to 'buy back' a booking from customers who have turned up. Incentives such as free tickets for future use and cash bonuses are offered to try to tempt customers to wait for a later flight. Many customers are happy to accept these incentives in return for the inconvenience that has been caused. For the service provider, the cost of these incentives must be assessed against the benefits of getting closer to full utilization of resources. In the case of air travel within Europe, an EU directive requires airlines to pay compensation on a graduated scale if a passenger is denied boarding because of overbooking.

At times of extreme demand (for example, hotels located close to where a major sporting event is due to take place), service providers may seek non-refundable deposits. This is necessary because there may be no history of no shows for that specific event. Also, the service provider may be much more constrained in its options for resolving an overbooked situation. Offering an incentive for a customer to come back later may be irrelevant where the whole purpose of consuming the service is to take part in a specific event.

It should also be noted that the level of overbooking is also part of a company's marketing mix positioning. A service provider may undertake less overbooking than its rivals and thereby reduce inconvenience to its customers. This should be reflected in its pricing and promotional strategy.

Overbooking occurs not just with respect to individual customer bookings, but also with respect to the utilization of components of the total service offer. Assumptions must be made in a service blueprint about how long each stage of a sequential process should take. For many service processes there will be variability in actual process times, for example the number of repair calls undertaken by an electrician or the number of journeys completed by a taxi. Service organizations are often tempted to overbook these resources, with insufficient recovery time allowed between services. So if the engineer is delayed on one job, there may be insufficient time allowed for him or her prior to the next booked job. The result is that the quality of service perceived by customers will fall. Service providers must try to balance the needs for high levels of reliable service delivery (which may imply having spare capacity in reserve) and the need for keeping costs to a minimum (which may mean reducing any unutilized capacity). In many markets, these considerations form part of companies' marketing mix, with the result that different service levels are targeted at different market segments. Within the UK aircraft charter market, for example, Civil Aviation Authority statistics have shown a poor reliability performance by Monarch Airlines, which can be attributed to tight scheduling of its aircraft in order to achieve lowest unit costs for price-sensitive market segments. During 1999, one of the top charter operators in terms of reliability, Air 2000, was less reliant on low-cost budget travel.

13.5.1 The link between marketing and yield management

Using the Chartered Institute of Marketing's definition of marketing, the term 'yield management' could easily replace the word 'marketing' to define the core concept of YM. So the definition becomes 'Marketing [YM] is the management process responsible for identifying, anticipating and satisfying customer requirements profitably.' The effectiveness of a yield management system is dependent upon the implementation of a number of market-focused principles and techniques:

■ identification of a customer base using a detailed segmentation process

- developing an awareness among managers of the changing needs and expectations of customers

- estimating the price **elasticity of demand** per market segment

- making managers responsive to changing market conditions

- accurate historical demand analyses combined with a reliable forecasting method.

A close connection can also be seen between yield management and 'relationship marketing'. The guiding principle of relationship marketing is that each customer transaction should not be seen in isolation, but in the context of previous transactions and expected future transactions. Yield management in its most developed form uses extensive information on customers' purchase patterns, which can be additionally used to build up a customer history and to enter a dialogue with individual customers. Such a dialogue can assist a company in forming a view about what price/product offer can be sustained with individual customers and allows it to communicate special offers to existing customers in order to fill spare capacity.

There is nothing new in the principles of yield management. The process of maximizing returns on assets can be traced back to the routine bargaining for goods and services by traders in many less-developed economies. Industrialization of many service processes has often had the effect of simplifying pricing structures in order that they can be administered and implemented by relatively junior employees. However, recent developments in information technology have enabled computers to do what the trader in an eastern bazaar was able to do in his head – estimate the maximum value that could be extracted from each potential customer and sell to those customers who are prepared to offer the best price.

13.5.2 **Yield management or everyday low-cost pricing?**

Many service organizations have resorted to offering standardized prices, or 'everyday low prices', instead of finely segmented prices. This would appear to be contrary to the principles of marketing and of yield management, but does appear to have a number of advantages. Firstly, the process of setting prices is simplified, resulting in less administrative effort being required by staff and less potential for confusion among customers. Secondly, there may be communication advantages of offering a single price. A price position can be readily established in the minds of potential consumers. Simple price structures may help to develop trust among buyers who may otherwise feel deceived by not being able to obtain promotional prices, or by comparing the price they paid with a lower price paid by another customer for a basically similar product.

There are many recent examples of service organizations that appear to have gone against the philosophy of marketing by offering near-uniform prices for all customers. The hotel sector, for example, has been a leading adopter of yield management techniques, yet the Travel Inn chain has grown rapidly by offering basically standard prices for each similar unit of output sold. Is this position sustainable?

There is some evidence that organizations that have initially adopted uniform prices subsequently revert to more sophisticated pricing systems based on the price sensitivity of individual segments for a basically similar product. Even Travel Inn, which initially promoted one single price, has since made promotional voucher offers to fill spare capacity during off-peak times.

The co-existence of 'everyday low pricing' and yield management techniques raises a number of interesting questions. Are companies who offer uniform prices going against the fundamental philosophy of marketing by not taking account of individual customers' differing needs and expectations? Is uniform pricing a stable solution or is there always the opportunity for competitors to exploit sub-segments of a company's market with differentiated product offers and prices? And, finally, is it possible to define types of products and markets for which each approach (uniform pricing or yield management) is particularly appropriate?

Case study

Cultural change needed to manage hotel yields more effectively

By Una McMahon-Beattie, University of Ulster

Today, yield management (or revenue management) can be seen in a wide variety of industries such as airlines, conferencing, package holidays, cruising, football and movie theatres. Indeed in the hotel industry, it is now common practice for hotel guest rooms, but its introduction is often far from smooth. It has long been recognized that achieving success with yield management requires far more than having the right technology. There are a variety of managerial and organizational factors that have an enormous influence on the level of benefits obtained from such a system. One such critical success factor is effective management of the people behind the system. An analysis by Huyton and Peters of a large 180-bedroomed hotel in Warwick illustrated some of the problems that can occur in implementation.

Prior to introducing a yield management system, the hotel had used the Champs management information system, which provided a good method for providing occupancy reports and statistics, but had only limited use for forecasting, which is a fundamental part of yield management. It was essentially retrospective and was not able to provide meaningful forecasts about the future. Forecasting of demand is crucial to give rooms managers the confidence to 'hang out' for the highest possible rate. This idea of 'hanging out' for a higher rate, rather than taking the first available customer that comes along, is an essential part of yield management. One implication is that the volume of business for a hotel may remain constant, but through effective yield management, the amount of profit yielded by each customer may increase. Knowing when to 'hang out' for a higher rate is a management skill, helped by reliable

499

data and forecasting methods. In addition to the forecasting system, an effective yield management system calls for a computerized decision support system, such as Fidelio, which was used in the case study hotel, and effective communications within the hotel.

Perhaps the biggest challenge facing management was to change the attitudes of front-desk staff who had previously been happy to register anyone who came along. Now they had to learn to 'hang out' by saying no. As one of them commented following introduction of the new yield management system: 'The reservation staff sit there and say to prospective customers "we're terribly sorry, we are fully booked" but in actual fact we have got 15 to 20 rooms to sell (but because of the rate offered by the client we won't take it.' Sales staff had been used to a culture in which rewards are given according to the volume of sales, rather than the profit they yield. An early part of the training programme for reservation staff was to teach them to say no. In practice, this proved to be quite difficult, so the rooms manager resorted to going into the system and blocking off rooms so that reservations staff could see that there was no availability. Reservations staff had to learn not to be afraid of quoting the full 'rack rate' to an enquirer. It is much easier to subsequently offer a discounted price than to try to recover margin from a customer who has been sold a room at a low price. Management has the confidence to hold out for a higher rate because they know, on the basis of probability, that they will get someone else who will pay the full or second-highest rack rate. Staff incentives, which were previously based on the volume of sales made, were changed to reflect the number of sales made at higher rates.

Just as a conductor unifies the diverse talents and capabilities of the musicians in an orchestra, yield management plays a key role in co-ordinating the selling activities of a number of areas in the hotel. As such, the hotel formed a forecasting team that involved a number of departmental managers:

- general manager
- rooms manager
- food and beverage manager
- financial controller.

The authors were surprised to note that the sales manager was not included in this forecasting team, although the results of each meeting were communicated to them in the form of sales targets.

The forecasting team met once a month to discuss forecasts for the coming months. The yield management ethos helped to identify trends in demand, and in particular shifts in the balance between the main market segments of corporate, leisure and conferences.

Regular meetings, armed with appropriate information, allowed the hotel to see ahead. For example, during the previous year the hotel had found itself with a very quiet Friday and Saturday in June. There had just been two bank holidays and everyone that wanted to come to Warwick for the weekend had been and gone, so there was not much more that the rooms manager could do at the time to stimulate demand. But with a yield management system, the forecasting team could have been more proactive earlier in the year when it should have been able to spot, on the basis of previous experience, the potential quiet spot in June. Back in January or February, the hotel would have had enough time to book in a relatively low-yielding coach group for that weekend – some revenue would have been better than no revenue.

Another issue that arose was the need to manage the yield of the hotel as a whole, rather than of individual elements within it. As an example, food and beverage sales may suffer as a result of the hotel holding out for a higher proportion of corporate customers paying a high rate, because business people are more likely to eat out in the evening, thereby depriving the restaurant of revenue. On the other hand, a conference may yield less per room, but this could be made up by high spending on catering and beverages.

The hotel persevered with implementation of its yield management system. Was it all worth the effort? Within the first year of implementing the system, the hotel noticed an average improvement in yield per room of £5 per night, ahead of the general change in prices within the sector, and very credible given the competitive nature of the industry. Indeed, experts state that implementing yield or revenue management systems can generally increase revenue 3 to 7% or more and all this comes from using existing assets more effectively.

This case clearly shows that a yield or revenue management system is not just a piece of software that, once installed, should be left alone so that it can provide the benefits that it is capable of delivering. Such a system only operates with maximum efficiency when the people in the organization understand and capitalize on its strengths and weaknesses, and accept it as a normal part of their daily activities.

Source: adapted from J.H. Huyton and S.D. Peters (2000) 'Application of yield management to the hotel industry', in A. Ingold, U. McMahon-Beattie and I. Yeoman (eds), *Strategies for the Service Industries*, 2nd edn, Cassell.

Case study review questions

1. Summarize the issues which are likely to detract from an organization-wide pursuit of maximum yields.

2. What techniques can be used to improve a hotel's accuracy in forecasting demand?

3. To what extent do you think that fluctuating prices, which are associated with yield management systems, may undermine customers' trust in a hotel brand?

Chapter summary and links to other chapters

Marketing in the services sector is made more complex by the perishability and inseparability of the service offer, with the consequence that supply and demand must be closely matched by time and place. This demands close integration of marketing and operations management functions. Fluctuating patterns of demand are often seen as a problem within the service sector, but can also be seen as an opportunity, which yield management practices address.

Capacity management is closely related to the study of the service encounter (**Chapter 3**). This chapter has taken a broader management overview to supplement the previous discussion of service design. A critical aspect of making a service organization more flexible lies in the flexibility of its employees, discussed in **Chapter 12**. The need for appropriate information about demand patterns was raised in **Chapter 6**. Capacity management, and the way in which customers are processed, can contribute towards a service provider's positioning strategy (**Chapter 7**). The handling of customers during queuing processes can be a major contributor to customers' perceptions of service quality, discussed in **Chapter 8**.

Chapter review questions

1. Why is a fluctuating demand pattern much more of a problem in the services sector than it is for manufacturing firms?

2. What is the difference between short- and long-term inelasticity of supply? In what ways can an airline make its services more elastic in the short term?

3. Consider a queue for a service which you have been involved in recently. Critically assess the methods used for handling the queue. How could these have been improved?

4. To what extent can a city-centre sandwich bar change the pattern of demand it faces? What methods might it use to achieve this?

5. Choose a capacity-constrained service industry and identify the options which are available to increase its elasticity of supply.

6. To which service industries is the practice of yield management particularly appropriate? Can you identify sectors where its use may be inappropriate?

Activity

Search the websites of airlines such as easyJet (www.easyjet.com), Ryanair (www.ryanair.com) and British Airways (www.ba.com). Select a journey on a busy route, such as London to Paris, and check the price charged on different dates and at different times. How wide is the variation? What factors might explain this variation?

Key terms

Elasticity of demand The responsiveness of customer demand to changes in price or some other variable.

Queuing system A system for handling temporal excesses of demand relative to capacity.

Yield management (YM) Methods used to maximize revenue from each unit of finite and perishable capacity.

Selected further reading

Some of the basic principles of matching service capacity to demand through the techniques of yield management are discussed in the following texts.

McMahon-Beattie, U. and Yeoman, I. (2004) *Revenue Management and Pricing*, Thomson Learning.

Ingold, A., McMahon-Beattie, U. and Yeoman, I. (eds) (2001) *Yield Management: Strategies for the Service Industries*, Thomson Learning.

Methods of handling queuing situations are discussed in the following texts.

Sheu, C., McHaney, R. and Babbar, S. (2003) 'Service process design flexibility and customer waiting time', *International Journal of Operations and Production Management*, 23 (8), 901–17.

Taylor, S. (1994) 'Waiting for service: The relationship between delays and evaluation of service', *Journal of Marketing*, 58 (April), 56–69.

Katz, K.L., Larson, B.M. and Larson, R.C. (1991) 'Prescription for the waiting-in-blues: Entertain, enlighten, and engage', *Sloan Management Review*, 32 (Winter), 44–53.

The role of flexible employees can be critical to matching capacity with demand and is discussed further in the following texts.

Sarel, D. and Marmorstein, H. (1999) 'Managing the delayed service encounter: The role of employee action and customer prior experience', *The International Journal of Bank Marketing*, 17 (6), 286–94.

Bitner, M., Booms, B.H. and Mohr, L.A. (1994) 'Critical service encounters: The employee's viewpoint', *Journal of Marketing*, 58 (October), 95–106.

Hartline, M.D. and Ferrell, O.C. (1996) 'The management of customer contact service employees: An empirical investigation', *Journal of Marketing*, 60 (October), 52–70.

References

Atkinson, J. (1984) 'Manpower strategies for flexible organizations', *Personnel Management*, August, 15–26.

Bitner M.J., Booms, B.H. and Tetreault, M.S. (1990) 'The service encounter: Diagnosing favorable and unfavorable incidents', *Journal of Marketing*, 54 (January), 71–84.

Deery, M. and Jago, L.K. (2002) 'The core and the periphery: An examination of the flexible workforce model in the hotel industry', *International Journal of Hospitality Management*, 21 (4), 339–51.

Hornik, J. (1984) 'Subjective vs objective time measures: A note on the perception of time in consumer behavior', *Journal of Consumer Behavior*, 32, 44–53.

Katz, K.L., Larson, B.M. and Larson, R.C. (1991) 'Prescription for the waiting-in-blues: Entertain, enlighten, and engage', *Sloan Management Review*, 32 (Winter), 44–53.

Kimes, S. (1989) 'The basics of yield management', *Cornell Hotel and Restaurant Administration Quarterly*, 30 (3), 14–19.

Kimes, S. (1997) 'Yield management: An overview', in I. Yeoman, and A. Ingold (eds), *Yield Management, Strategies for the Service Industries*, Cassell, London, 3–11.

Taylor, S. (1994) 'Waiting for service: The relationship between delays and evaluation of service', *Journal of Marketing*, 58 (April), 56–69.

Yelkur, R., Nêveda DaCosta, M. (2001) 'Differential pricing and segmentation on the Internet: The case of hotels', *Management Decision*, 39 (4), 252–61.

14

International marketing of services

Learning objectives

This chapter will explain:

- the nature of international trade in services and reasons for its development

- methods used by service firms to assess the attractiveness of overseas opportunities

- the development of marketing plans which are sympathetic to local market needs

- market entry strategies, including the need to balance risk and control.

14.1 **Introduction**

At some point, many service organizations recognize that their growth can only continue if they exploit foreign markets. However, entering foreign markets can be an extremely risky business for services companies, as evidenced by examples of recent failures where companies failed to foresee all of the problems involved.

- British Airways failed in its attempts to enter the North American market through its investment in the ailing airline USAir. BA had difficulties in overcoming trades union objections to changes in working practices, among other things, which led the company to eventually pull out of its involvement with USAir.

- The mobile phone company mmO$_2$ invested over £1.5 billion in the Dutch mobile phone operator Telfort but failed to achieve higher than fifth ranking in the Dutch market. In April 2003 the company admitted defeat and sold the entire Dutch operation for just £16 million.

- The grocery retailer Sainsbury's pulled out of Egypt in 2001, only two years after investing in a chain of 100 supermarkets. Sainsbury's had gone out on a limb in Egypt, which had no tradition of supermarket shopping, and the company was not helped by persistent rumours of links with Jewish owners. Sainsbury's two years of involvement in the Egyptian market incurred a loss of over £100 million.

- Even the fast-food retailer McDonald's initially failed to make profits when it entered the UK market in the 1970s and had rapidly to adjust its service offer in order to achieve viability.

Nevertheless, a company which has successfully developed its marketing strategy should be well placed to extend this development into foreign markets. There are many examples of companies who have successfully developed foreign markets, including the following.

- The retailer Tesco has successfully reduced its dependence on the saturated UK grocery market by developing outlets in Ireland, the Far East and eastern Europe.

- The mobile phone company Vodafone has expanded from its UK base and now provides service in 30 countries, reducing the company's unit costs through economies of scale, and offering seamless, added-value services to international travellers.

- The Irish airline Ryanair started life with a route network which focused on Dublin. With successful expansion of this network, most of its services now do not call at its Irish base.

- Carphone Warehouse was the brainchild of entrepreneur Charles Dunstone, and after a small-scale start in London, it has successfully expanded to operate more than 1100 stores throughout Europe, operating under the Carphone Warehouse banner in the UK and The Phone House in France, Spain, Germany, Sweden and the Netherlands.

Many of the fundamental principles of marketing management which have been applied to a firm's domestic market will be of relevance in an international setting. The processes of identifying market opportunities, selecting strategies, implementing those strategies and monitoring performance involve fundamentally similar principles as those which apply within the domestic market. One study found that foreign operations in service firms are driven by a similar set of variables to those of manufacturing companies, but that the intensity and direction of some key relationships require modification and adaptation (Cicic et al., 1999). The major challenge to services companies seeking to expand overseas lies in sensitively adapting marketing strategies which have worked at home to the needs of foreign markets whose environments may be totally different to anything previously experienced.

New challenges face the international marketer. According to Naomi Klein, global services brands such as Shell, Wal-Mart and McDonald's have become metaphors for a global economic system gone awry, evidenced by growing concern about the pay and conditions of workers in the less developed world. She believes that brands and their multi-national owners, rather than governments, will increasingly become the target for activists (Klein, 2000).

The purpose of this chapter is to identify the main differences facing the task of marketing management when services are provided in an international rather than a purely domestic environment. Some of the key differences between trade in goods and trade in services are emphasized, in particular the diverse nature of buyer–seller interaction which causes international trade in services to take a number of forms.

In addition to extending knowledge of services marketing to the international context, this chapter provides useful integrative revision.

14.2 The importance of international trade in services

International trade in services is becoming increasingly important, representing not only opportunities for domestic service producers to earn revenue from overseas, but also threats to domestic producers from foreign competition. Some indication of the importance of international trade in services for Britain can be seen in the trade statistics. In 2003, the UK earned £88.306 billion from 'exporting' services overseas (£18.77 billion was earned from exporting goods). More importantly, the UK had a surplus (£13.847 billion) in services, compared with a deficit in goods (£46.249 billion). A closer examination of trade statistics indicates the relative importance of the main service sectors. The most important in terms of foreign sales continues to be financial services, with credits ('exports') exceeding debits ('imports'). Travel-related sectors were the next most significant group recorded by national statistics, although, here, the UK is a now a net importer of services as UK tourists' spending overseas exceeds that of foreigners visiting the UK.

Many national economies have come to rely heavily on foreign currency earnings generated by their services industries. Notable examples include the Bahamas and Malta, whose financial services and tourism sector earnings offset the countries' need to import many manufactured goods and agricultural products. Developing countries often find that they need to buy in specialist services in order to develop their economies further (e.g. banking and consulting engineering), but eventually aim to achieve self-sufficiency (or even export earnings) in these sectors. India is a good example of a developing economy which has deliberately sought to reduce its reliance on imported services and is now a net exporter of some types of service (e.g. call centres).

The EU as a whole has in recent years managed a small surplus in its trade in services with non-EU countries. Net earners included banking, air transport, tourism and business services. There has been a net deficit in insurance, sea transport and communications.

14.3 Defining international trade in services

Conceptual difficulties can occur in attempting to analyse international trade in services. While trade in manufactured goods can be represented by stocks of goods moving in one direction, and payment (in cash or in goods) in the other, the intangible nature of most services makes it difficult to measure a physical flow. Trade statistics, for example, cannot rely on records of goods passing through Customs. Any analysis of international trade in services is complicated by the diverse nature of producer–supplier interaction, stemming from the inseparability of service production/consumption processes.

International trade statistics for services hide the fact that trade can take a number of forms. Sometimes, credits are earned by customers from overseas travelling to an organization's domestic market in order to consume a service (for example, a foreign tourist visiting the UK). On other occasions, credits are earned by domestic producers taking their production processes to customers in foreign markets. A further category of services can be identified which allow production and consumption to be separated – for these services, producers and consumers do not need to meet in order for international trade to occur. The form that international trade takes is dependent on the mobility of both producer and consumer, and the separability of the production/consumption process (see Figure 14.1).

Immobility in service production processes occurs where it is either not possible or sensible to produce a service in a foreign market – customers in these markets must travel if they are to receive the service. This is typical of many tourism-related services which are based on a unique historic site. In other cases, it is customers who are inflexible, requiring the production process to be taken overseas to wherever customers are located (e.g. building contractors must travel to a building requiring renovation).

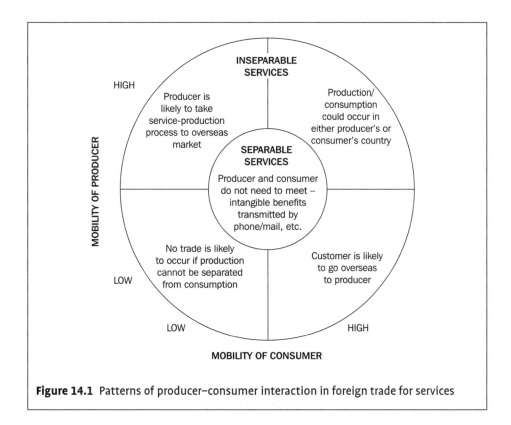

Figure 14.1 Patterns of producer–consumer interaction in foreign trade for services

Because of the diverse ways in which international trade takes place, estimates of the total value of international trade in services are much more unreliable than for manufactured goods, and frequently subject to subsequent revision.

From the diversity of producer–consumer interaction, three important patterns of trade can be identified, as described in the following sub-sections.

14.3.1 Production of a service in one country for consumption in another

While manufactured goods are commonly traded on this basis, this can only occur for services where production and consumption can be separated. This has often been achieved using postal and telephone communications. In this way, an insurance policy for a ship can be produced at Lloyds of London, but the benefits of the policy relayed to the policy-holder at the point of their choice. Falling costs of telecommunications have created new opportunities for call centres to provide a service to a customer who may be located thousands of miles from the call centre. The subject of global **e-commerce** is considered later, in a separate section of this chapter. It can be difficult for official statistics to accurately record both the outward flow of services and the inward flow of money for this type of trade.

14.3.2 **Production of a service by a domestic company in a foreign market for foreign consumption**

Where the problem of inseparability cannot be overcome, a domestic service producer may only be able to access a foreign market by setting up production facilities in that market. Examples of services in this category include catering and cleaning services, which must deliver a tangible outcome at a point of the customer's choice. The various methods by which a company can set up foreign service outlets are discussed later in this chapter. While this type of international trade can be of great importance to service organizations, it only appears in a country's balance of payments in the form of capital movements, remitted profits and trade in the tangible components of a service offer.

14.3.3 **Production of a service at home for sale to foreign customers for consumption in the domestic market**

It is often expensive or impossible to take a service production process to foreign customers, therefore customers must travel to consume the service. This can occur for a number of reasons.

- Demand for a highly specialized service may be very thinly dispersed, making it uneconomic to take highly specialized staff and equipment to the market. As an example, it is common for patients to travel long distances to visit specialist doctors in London's Harley Street.

- The laws of a foreign country may make the provision of a service in that market illegal, forcing those seeking the service to travel overseas. Countries which forbid abortion operations often do so to the benefit of abortion clinics in countries such as Britain where a more liberal regime applies.

- Production costs may be lower in an organization's own country, making it attractive for foreign customers to travel in order to obtain a service. As an example, the lower price of labour in many less developed countries makes it attractive for ship owners to send their ships away for major overhaul work to be undertaken.

- A country may possess unique geographical features which form an important element of a service offer and, in order to receive the benefits of related services, customers must travel to that country (Figure 14.2). This is particularly important in the case of tourism-related industries, where the benefits of services associated with heritage sites or climatic differences cannot be taken to consumers. If American citizens wish to visit the Tower of London, they must travel to London. Similarly, if British holidaymakers want to purchase a holiday with guaranteed sunshine, they must travel overseas.

Figure 14.2 The tourism sector presents many reasons why consumers must travel to the producer in order to benefit from a service offer. Many tourist attractions, such as London's Big Ben, are quite unique and very difficult or impossible to replicate at a location closer to consumers. Some attempts have been made at replication – for example, the former London Bridge was moved to Arizona in the USA, but the total service offer failed to match what many consumers sought. Consumers seeking this total service offer must therefore travel to the producer. Even theme parks, which do not rely so much on geographically specific features, have experienced difficulty in taking their service concept to consumers in their home market, as witnessed by the failure, in many people's minds, of Disney to replicate its American theme parks in France.

14.4 Reasons for international trade in services occurring

However it is measured, international trade in services has been increasing. Taking the UK as an example, while the value of GDP increased by 21% between 1995 and 2002, the value of exports increased by 31%. From the perspective of national economies, a number of reasons can be identified for the increasing importance of international trade in services.

■ Services are traded between economies in order to exploit the concept of comparative cost advantage. This holds that an economy will export those goods and services that it is particularly well suited to producing, and import those for which another country has an advantage. Although the concept of comparative cost advantage was developed to explain the benefits to total world wealth resulting from each country exploiting its comparative cost advantages with regard to access to raw materials and energy supplies, it can also have application to the service sector. In this way, a favourable climate or outstanding scenery can give a country an advantage in selling tourism services to foreign customers, a point which has not been lost to tourism operators in the Canary Islands and Switzerland respectively. Another basis for comparative cost advantage can be found in the availability of low-cost or highly trained personnel (cheap labour for the shipping industry and trained computer software experts for computer consultancy respectively). Sometimes the government of a country can itself directly create comparative cost advantages for a service sector, as where it reduces regulations and controls on an industry, allowing that industry to produce services for export at a lower cost than its more regulated competitors (for example, many 'offshore' financial services centres impose lower taxation and standards of regulation than their mainstream competitors).

■ The removal of many restrictions on international trade in services (such as the creation of the single European market) has allowed countries to exploit their comparative cost advantages. Nevertheless, restrictions on trade in services generally remain more significant than those on manufactured goods.

■ Increasing disposable household incomes result in greater consumption of those categories of services which can only be provided by foreign suppliers, especially foreign travel and tourism. Against this, economic development within an economy can result in many specialized services which were previously bought in from overseas being provided by local suppliers – many developing countries, for example, seek to reduce their dependence on foreign banking and insurance organizations.

■ Cultural convergence, which has resulted from improved communications and increasing levels of foreign travel, has led to a homogenization of international market segments. Combined with the decline in trade barriers, convergence of cultural attitudes towards services allows many services providers to regard parts of their foreign markets as though they are part of their domestic market.

For an individual company, development of foreign markets can be attractive for a number of reasons. These can be analysed in terms of 'pull' factors which derive from the attractiveness of a potential foreign market, and 'push' factors which make an organization's domestic market appear less attractive.

■ For firms seeking growth, foreign markets represent new market segments which they may be able to serve with their existing range of products. In this way, a company can stick to producing the services that it does well. Finding new foreign markets for existing or slightly modified services does not expose a company to the risks of expanding both its product range and its market coverage simultaneously.

■ Saturation of its domestic market can force a service organization to seek foreign markets. Saturation can come about where a service reaches the maturity stage of its life cycle in the domestic market, while being at a much earlier stage of the cycle in less developed foreign markets. While the markets for fast-food restaurants may be approaching saturation in a number of western markets – especially the USA – they represent a new service opportunity in the early stages of development in some eastern European countries.

■ Environmental factors may make it difficult for a company to fully exploit its service concept in its domestic market, forcing it to look overseas for opportunities. As an example, restrictions on new out-of-town retail developments in the UK during the 1990s led many retailers to seek expansion of their format in foreign markets such as Ireland and eastern Europe.

■ As part of its **portfolio management,** an organization may wish to reduce its dependence upon one geographical market. The attractiveness of individual national markets can change in a manner which is unrelated to other national markets – for example, costly competition can develop in one national market but not others, world economic cycles show lagged effects between different economies, and government policies – through specific regulation or general economic management – can have counterbalancing effects on market prospects.

■ The nature of a service may require an organization to become active in a foreign market. This particularly affects transport-related services such as scheduled airline services and courier services. A UK scheduled airline flying between London and Paris would most likely become involved in exploiting a foreign market at the Paris end of its route.

■ Industrial companies operating in a number of foreign countries may require their services suppliers to be able to cater for their needs across national boundaries. A company may wish to engage accountants who are able to provide auditing and management accounting services in its foreign subsidiaries. To achieve this, the firm of accountants would probably need to have created an operational base overseas. Similarly, firms selling in a number of foreign markets may wish to engage an advertising agency which can organize a global campaign in a number of foreign markets.

■ There are also many cases where private consumers demand a service that is internationally available. An example is the car hire business where customers frequently need to be able to book a hire car in one country for collection and use in another. To succeed in attracting these customers, car hire companies need to operate internationally.

■ Some services are highly specialized and the domestic market is too small to allow economies of scale to be exploited. Foreign markets must be exploited in order to achieve a critical mass which allows a competitive price to be reached. Specialized aircraft engineering services and oil exploration services fall into this category.

■ Economies of scale also result from extending the use of service brands in foreign markets. Expenditure by a fast-food company on promoting its brand image to UK residents is wasted when those citizens travel abroad and cannot find the brand which they have come to value. Newly created foreign outlets will thus enjoy the benefit of promotion to foreign visitors at little additional cost.

14.5 Analysing opportunities for overseas development of services

Foreign markets can represent very different opportunities and threats compared to those which an organization has been used to in its domestic market. Before a detailed market analysis is undertaken, an organization should consider in general terms whether the environment of a market is likely to be attractive. By considering in general terms such matters as political stability or cultural attitudes, an organization may screen out potential markets for which it considers further analysis cannot be justified by the likelihood of success. Where an exploratory analysis of a foreign marketing environment appears to indicate some opportunities, a more thorough analysis might suggest important modifications to a service format which would need to be made before the service could successfully be offered to the market.

The following section firstly identifies some general questions which need to be asked in assessing the marketing environment of foreign countries and then considers specific aspects of researching such markets.

Is the glass half full or half empty?

The story is told of a business development team from a tour operator which was sent abroad to investigate the possibilities for offering package holidays in the format which had worked well at home. The main finding was that very few people in that market bought package holidays. But what did this mean? One member of the team concluded that the current level of sales indicated a lack of interest in the product and the market should therefore be best avoided in favour of other possible markets. But to another member of the team, this was the sign of huge potential – 'Just wait until these people discover the advantages of buying package holidays!' This simple example emphasizes that any analysis of overseas market potential can only be based on a combination of factual analysis and judgement.

14.6 **The foreign marketing environment**

The combination of environmental factors that contributed to success within an organization's domestic market may be absent in a foreign market, resulting in the failure of attempts to export a service format. In this section, questions to be asked in analysing a foreign marketing environment are examined under the overlapping headings of the political, economic, social, demographic and technological environments.

14.6.1 **The political environment**

Government and quasi-government organizations influence the legislative and economic frameworks within which organizations operate. Although the most important political influences originate from national governments, inter-government agreements can also be important in shaping a national market.

National government framework

At a national level, individual governments can influence trade in services in a number of ways.

- At the most general level, the stability of the political system affects the attractiveness of a particular national market. While radical change rarely results from political upheaval in most western countries, the relative instability of some central and eastern European governments has led to uncertainty about the economic and legislative framework in which services will be provided.

- Licensing systems may be applied by governments in an attempt to protect domestic producers. Licences can be used to restrict individuals practising a particular profession (e.g. licensing requirements for accountants or solicitors may not recognize experience and licences obtained overseas) or licences can be used to restrict foreign owners setting up a service operation (e.g. the US government does not allow non-US investors to own more than 25% of the shares in its domestic scheduled airlines).

- Regulations governing service standards may require expensive reconfiguration of the service offer to meet local regulations, or may prohibit its provision completely – gambling-related and medical services often fall into this category.

- Import controls can be used to restrict the supply of goods which form an integral part of a service. A restaurant seeking foreign outlets may be forced to source its materials locally, leading to possible problems in maintaining consistent quality standards and also possibly losing economies of scale.

- Service production possibilities can be influenced by government policies. Minimum wage levels and conditions of service can be important in determining the viability of a service. For example, many countries restrict the manner in which temporary seasonal staff can be employed – this could make the operation of a seasonal holiday hotel inflexible and uneconomic.

- Restrictions on currency movements may make it difficult to repatriate profits earned from a foreign service operation.

- Governments are major procurers of services and may, formally or informally, give preference in awarding contracts to locally owned service organizations.

- Legislation protecting trademarks varies between countries – in some countries, such as Thailand, the owner may find it relatively hard to legally protect itself from imitators.

Beyond the nation state, international institutions can have important consequences for the international marketing of services. Some of the more important are described below.

The European Union

Although the EU was conceived as a vehicle for reducing trade barriers, this has so far benefited mainly trade in raw materials and manufactured goods. Many non-tariff barriers have existed to restrict the amount of services trade which takes place between EU member states. However, the Single European Act 1987 sought to remove many of these barriers. Most importantly, licensing arrangements are being harmonized so that a company seeking to set up in another member state does not need to go through a lengthy approval process in that country. Licences of one state are increasingly being accepted as valid for companies seeking to operate in other member states. This can potentially benefit a wide range of service organizations, such as insurance companies and banks, which are heavily regulated and can increasingly regard Europe as one large domestic market, free of national borders.

As an example, national licensing regulations have previously restricted the ability of airlines and road haulage companies located in one EU member state to offer domestic services within other member states. The result has been large differences in prices charged by these industries within different EU member states. The effective removal of trade barriers is creating a more competitive market in which prices for road haulage and airline services should become more harmonized throughout the EU. Already a number of low-cost airlines, such as Ryanair and easyJet, have exploited Europe-wide opportunities beyond their own domestic markets. Service organizations are also increasingly affected by the requirement that large public-service contracts should be put out to EU-wide tendering – this has resulted in cross-border competition for highway building and maintenance contracts.

Nevertheless, uncertainties still remain for UK firms seeking expansion within the EU. The UK's non-membership of the single European currency means that companies earning money overseas can never be sure how much this will translate to in sterling, a particular problem where income is in one currency and expenditure in another. The cost of exchanging money alone can put non-domestic companies at a competitive disadvantage. Despite talk of a single market in services, many ingrained differences in consumer behaviour and language barriers will continue to pose a challenge for UK marketers.

Other trading blocs

The EU is an example of a trading bloc which seeks to create favourable trading conditions for companies located within the bloc, regardless of the existence of national borders within the bloc. The development of the EU has been paralleled by the development of a number of other regional trading blocs, most notably the ASEAN group of South-East Asian countries and the NAFTA grouping of the USA, Canada and Mexico.

For service organizations seeking to develop within one of those countries, the trading blocs create problems and opportunities. The problems occasionally arise where tariffs or other restrictions are placed on goods and services imported from outside the bloc. The biggest opportunity is that once an exporter is inside one member country, the process of expansion to other bloc member countries can be made very much easier through the harmonization of standards and dismantling of internal borders.

The World Trade Organization

The World Trade Organization (WTO) has its origins in the post-war General Agreement on Tariffs and Trade. Members of the World Trade Organization seek greater international economic prosperity by exploiting fully the comparative cost advantages of nations by reducing the barriers which inhibit international trade. Members agree not to increase tariffs or quotas on imports, except in permitted circumstances.

The World Trade Organization has proceeded to reduce tariffs and quotas through several rounds of negotiations. However, success in respect of services has been relatively slow compared to goods. Because of the multilateral nature of WTO negotiations, attempts to liberalize trade in services can be impeded by arguments in completely unrelated areas of trade. For example, attempts to liberalize trade in financial services have been linked to demands for action to reduce agricultural subsidies given by some countries. The signing of the General Agreement on Trade in Services in 1995 by member countries occurred only after a lot of such bargaining, and there are signs that implementing it is a slower process than in the case of manufactured goods. Many critics of the WTO's attempts to liberalize trade in services claim that they will create disadvantages for developing countries (for example, it may be plausible for FedEx to run a privatized Indian Post Office, but could there really be much chance of the Indian Post Office challenging FedEx on its home ground?)

Other international agreements and institutions

A wide range of other agreements and institutions affect service organizations. At their simplest, these include bilateral agreements between two countries, while more complex multi-lateral agreements between governments can create policies and institutions which directly affect the marketing environment of firms – examples include the International Civil Aviation Organization and the Universal Postal Union.

14.6.2 **The economic environment**

A generally accepted measure of the economic attractiveness of a foreign market is the level of GDP per capita. The demand for most services increases as this figure increases. However, organizations seeking to sell services overseas should also consider the distribution of income within a country which may identify valuable niche markets. As an example, the relatively low GDP per head of South Korea still allows a small and relatively affluent group to create a market for high-value foreign holidays (see Figure 14.3).

An organization assessing a foreign market should place great emphasis on future economic performance and the stage which a country has reached in its economic development. While many western developed economies face saturated markets for a number of services, less developed economies may be just moving on to that part of their growth curve where services begin to appeal to large groups of people (Figure 14.4).

A crucial part of the analysis of a foreign market focuses on the level of competition within that market. This can be related to the level of economic development achieved within a country – in general, as an economy develops, its markets become more saturated. This is true of the market for household insurance which is mature and highly competitive in North America and most western European countries, but relatively new and less competitive in many developing economies where better margins may be achieved.

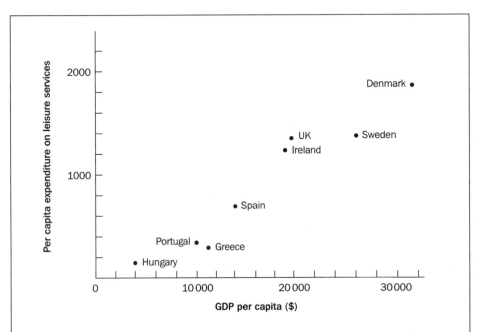

Figure 14.3 This graph shows, for selected European countries, the tendency for GDP per capita to be closely correlated with per capita expenditure on leisure services (based on National Statistical Offices/Keynote data for 1998 or the most recent year available)

Figure 14.4 For many developing countries, such as Indonesia, there is a long tradition of fast-food provided by hawkers' stalls, such as this one, which provide low-cost food. As economies develop, hawkers' stalls have tended to decline, but where will the growing number of wealthy consumers choose to spend their money? Will they patronize new western-style fast-food outlets? Or will they invest in home-cooking equipment which allows them to store food and prepare a wider selection of food quickly and efficiently? The introduction of fast-food restaurants has not always been an immediate success in developing countries, and even in the developed economy of Singapore, cultural traditions have led to a continuing role for organized 'hawkers' markets'.

The level of competitive pressure within a market is also a reflection of government policy towards the regulation of monopolies and the ease with which it allows new entrants to enter a market. The government of a country can significantly affect the competitive pressure within a market by legislation aimed at reducing anti-competitive practices.

14.6.3 **The social and cultural environment**

Together, the social and cultural environments represent the values of a society. An understanding of culture, and, in particular, an appreciation of cultural differences, is clearly important for marketers. Individuals from different cultures not only buy different services, but may also respond in different ways to the same services. Examples of differing cultural attitudes and their effects on international trade in services include the following.

■ Buying processes vary between different cultures – for example, the role of women in selecting a service may differ in a foreign market compared to the domestic market, thereby possibly requiring a different approach to service design and promotion.

■ Some categories of services may be rendered obsolete by certain types of social structure. As an example, extended family structures common in some countries have the ability to produce a wide range of services within the family unit, including caring for children and elderly family members. Extended families also often reduce the need for bought-in financial services by recirculating funds within a very close system.

■ A service which is taken for granted in the domestic market may be seen as socially unacceptable in a foreign market – interest charged on bank loans may be regarded as a form of usury in some Muslim cultures, for example.

■ Attitudes towards promotional programmes differ between cultures – the choice of colours in advertising or sales outlets needs to be made with care because of symbolic associations (e.g. the colour associated with mourning/bereavement varies across cultures).

■ What is deemed to be acceptable activity in procuring sales varies between cultures. In Middle Eastern markets, for example, a bribe to a public official may be considered essential, whereas it is unacceptable in most western countries.

In short, culture not only conditions an individual's response to products and influences the nature of the purchase process, but it also exercises considerable influence on the structure of consumption within a given society. It should also be remembered that no society is totally homogeneous. Every culture contains smaller sub-cultures, or groups of people with shared value systems, which are based on common experiences and situations. These identifiable sub-groups may be distinguished by race, nationality, religion, age, geographical location or some other factor, and share attitudes and behaviour which reflect sub-cultural influences.

It has been common to talk about cultural convergence, implying that individuals are becoming more alike in the way that they think and behave. Advocates of the concept of cultural convergence remind us that needs are universal and therefore there should be no reason why satisfaction of those needs should not also be universal. If a Big Mac satisfies a New Yorker's need for hygienic, fast and convenient food, why should it not satisfy those similar needs for someone in Cairo? Against this, many observers have noted individuals' growing need for *identity* in a world which is becoming increasingly homogenized. Support for regional breakaway governments (e.g. by the Kurdish and Basque people) may provide some evidence of this. During the build-up to the Iraq War in 2003, many consumers in Arab countries used purchases of Muslim products to identify themselves with an anti-American cause. Many western service brands have become despised by some groups as symbols of an alien identity. Banks in many Muslim countries have reported increased interest in Syariah-

---

Saturated burgers for less-saturated markets?

A saturated domestic market is often the spur for companies to seek new foreign markets. But is there a moral case against companies seeking to promote a western style of service consumption in countries with well-established and sustainable lifestyles? Fast-food companies have stepped up their efforts to develop new foreign markets as western markets for fast food become saturated. Is it responsible to promote burgers which are high in saturated fats to people whose diets are inherently healthier? Is it right that fast-food companies should develop low-fat burgers for the American market, partly out of fear of litigation, while selling higher-fat burgers to less developed countries where legislation and consumer awareness of health issues are more lax? Defenders of fast-food companies point to the fact that they are providing hygienic food prepared in conditions which may be far superior to the norm in many developing countries. They have offered jobs to individuals which can be the envy of peer groups. Should the solution be greater education of consumers in healthy eating, rather than more regulation? Is greater education a realistic prospect in a culture where fast food has become a cultural icon?

---

based banking services, based on the law of Islam, which covers every aspect of life (*Business Times*, 2002).

14.6.4 The demographic environment

It is also important to consider the demographic structure of a foreign market. Within the EU countries, the total population in recent times has increased at a natural rate of about 1.0 per 1000 population (that is, for every 1000 deaths, there are 1001 births). However, this hides a range of rates of increase, with, at each extreme, Ireland having a particularly high birth rate and Germany a particularly low one. This has major implications for future age structures and consumption patterns. By 2030, people over 65 in Germany will account for almost half the adult population, compared with one-fifth in 2000. And unless the country's birth rate recovers from its present low of 1.3 per woman, over the same period its population of under-35s will shrink about twice as fast as the older population will grow. The net result will be that the total population, now 82 million, will decline to 70–73 million, and the number of people of working age will fall by a quarter, from 40 million today to 30 million. In Japan, the population will peak in 2005, at around 125 million and by around 2030, the share of the over-65s in the adult population will have grown to about half (*Economist*, 2001). Much faster population growth is expected to occur in Africa and Latin America.

In addition, the geographical distribution of the population and structure of household units may be significantly different to that which had brought about success in the domestic market. For example, EU statistics show a number of interesting contrasts in geodemographic characteristics between member states which could have implications for the marketing of a service, as described below.

- Very significant differences occur in home ownership patterns, with implications for demand for a wide range of home-related services. The proportion of households living in rented accommodation ranges from 21% in Spain to 53% in western Germany, while the proportion with a mortgage ranges from 8% in Spain to 44% in the UK.

- The proportion of the population living within metropolitan areas varies from 13% in Italy to 44% in France. The resulting differences in lifestyle can have implications for services as diverse as car repair services, entertainment and retailing.

- The proportion of self-employed people ranges from 45% in the Netherlands to 17% in Italy, with implications for the sale of personal pension schemes, etc.

- Average household size ranges from a low of 2.26 in Denmark to a high of 4.16 people in Ireland, having implications for the types and quantities of services bought by household units.

14.6.5 **The technological environment**

An analysis of the technological environment is important for service organizations that require the use of a well-developed technical infrastructure and a workforce which is able to use technology. Communications are an important element of the technological infrastructure – poorly developed telephone and postal communications may inhibit attempts to make credit cards more widely available, for instance.

14.7 **Sources of information on foreign markets**

The methods used to research a potential foreign market are, in principle, similar to those which would be used to research a domestic market. Companies would normally begin by using secondary data about a potential foreign market which is available to them at home. Sources which are readily available through specialized libraries, online services, government organizations and specialist research organizations include Department of Trade and Industry information for exporters, reports of international agencies such as the Organization for Economic Co-operation and Development (OECD), Chambers of Commerce and private sources of information such as that provided by banks. Details of some specific sources are shown in Table 14.1.

Initial desk research at home will identify those markets which show the greatest potential for development. A company will then often follow this up with further desk research of materials available locally within the shortlisted markets, often carried out by appointing a local research agency. This may include a review of

A hotel for lunatics?

Hilton International, owner of many of the world's most prestigious hotels, has joined the race to build the first hotel on the Moon. It has developed a project called the Lunar Hilton, which would comprise a complex with 5000 rooms. Powered by two huge solar panels, the resort would have its own beach and sea as well as a working farm. Experts disagree on the practicalities of life on the Moon, but barriers seem to be diminishing as new discoveries are made.

'Space tourism' received a boost in April 2001 when the determined multimillionaire Dennis Tito paid $20 million for a round-trip ticket to the International Space Station. Such is the interest in exploiting the Moon for tourism that there is now a Space Tourism Association and a lot of national pride is at stake. The Russians put the first man in space and now the first tourist in space. In Japan, the Kinki Nippon Tourist (KNT) Company, the country's second largest wholesale tour operator, set up a space travel club in 2002. Back in 1998, KNT helped a Japanese Pepsi franchisee to launch a sweepstake for a sub-orbital flight. The company received 650 000 applications for five tickets, each valued at $98 000. The company is convinced that excursion-class spaceships will become a driving force for the travel industry in the 21st century.

Three Japanese companies have between them already spent £25 million on development work for their own Moon projects. Compared to this, Hilton's expenditure to date of £100 000 looks quite modest. Is the company mad in believing that people will want to visit the Moon? Or is this just the kind of longterm strategic thinking that so many businesses lack? With the world becoming smaller and increasingly saturated with goods and services, does the Moon offer a unique opportunity for expansion?

reports published by the target market's own government and specialist locally based market research agencies.

Just as in home markets, secondary data has limitations in assessing market attractiveness. Problems in foreign markets are compounded by the greater difficulty in gaining access to data, although the development of online information services has helped in this respect. There may also be language differences and problems of definition which may differ from those with which an organization is familiar. In the case of services which are a new concept in a foreign market, information on current usage and attitudes to the service may be completely lacking. For this reason, it would be difficult to use secondary data to try to assess the likely response from consumers to large out-of-town superstores in some eastern European countries. Despite these problems, the World Wide Web is allowing companies to undertake a lot of preliminary assessment of a foreign market from their office-based computers.

Primary research is used to overcome shortcomings in secondary data. Its most important use is to identify cultural factors which may require a service format to be modified or abandoned altogether. A company seeking to undertake primary research in a proposed foreign market would almost certainly use a local specialist research agency. Apart from overcoming possible language barriers, a local agency would better understand attitudes towards privacy and the level of literacy that might

---

Table 14.1 Sources of secondary information on foreign markets

Government agencies

    Department of Trade and Industry market reports

    Foreign governments – e.g. USA Department of Commerce

    Foreign national and local development agencies

International agencies

    European Union (Eurostat, etc.)

    Organization for Economic Co-operation & Development (OECD)

    World Trade Organization

    United Nations

    International Monetary Fund

    Universal Postal Union

    World Health Organization

Research organizations

    Economist Intelligence Unit

    Dun & Bradstreet International

    Mintel

    Market research firms

Publications

    Financial Times country surveys/ft.com

    Business International

    International Trade Reporter

    Banks' export reviews

Trade associations

    Chambers of Commerce

    Industry-specific associations – e.g. IATA

Online resources

    Eurostat

    Mintel Online

    FT Online

---

affect response rates for different forms of research. However, the problem of comparability between markets remains. For example, when a Japanese respondent claims to 'like' a product, the result may be comparable to a German consumer who claims to 'quite like' the product. It would be wrong to assume on the basis of this research that the product is better liked by Japanese consumers than German consumers.

Primary research is generally undertaken overseas when a company has become happy about the general potential of a market, but is unsure of a number of factors which would be critical for success – for example, whether intermediaries would be willing and able to handle their new service, or whether traditional cultural attitudes will present an insurmountable obstacle for a service not previously available in that market. Prior to commissioning its own specific research, a company may go for the lower cost but less specific route of undertaking research through an omnibus survey. These are surveys regularly undertaken among a panel of consumers in foreign markets (for example, the Gallup European Omnibus) which carry questions on behalf of a number of organizations.

14.8 **International services marketing management**

Having decided to enter a new foreign market, a company must consider the most effective way of managing its marketing effort in that market. The process of defining the organization's mission, analysing opportunities, setting quantifiable goals, implementing and monitoring results is just as important in foreign operations, if not more so.

Objectives must be clearly stated for each foreign market, preferably in a quantified form. Objectives must be set with due regard to local conditions by being achievable. A global return on investment objective may be inappropriate in locally competitive markets where a service firm wants a presence in order to secure international coverage and thereby develop wide-ranging relationships with its profitable customers. For this reason a hotel chain might develop in a popular area to satisfy the needs of its regular users and retain their international loyalty, even though the hotel will not be able to achieve its normal profit objective.

Like any new venture, objectives are essential if performance is to be monitored and any corrective action taken. Because foreign markets are generally much less certain than domestic markets, it is important that any variance from target is rapidly analysed and corrective action taken. There must be a clearly defined process by which failing services can be assessed for their prospects of long-term viability or withdrawn from a foreign market. It may be, for instance, that assumptions on which a market entry decision was based have proved to be false and that no amount of local reformulation of a service will allow it to break even.

A major issue in the international management of services marketing concerns the extent to which an organization's headquarters should intervene in the management of foreign subsidiaries. A commonly heard complaint from marketing managers of the latter is that they are given insufficient freedom to respond to local market conditions. Against this is the argument that intervention from headquarters is vital in order to secure the development of a consistent standard of service output in a planned way. Where a service is quite specialized to a national market and international brand-building relatively unimportant (e.g. municipal contract cleaning services), there is strong argument for delegation of management responsibilities on a geographical basis. On the other hand, where the service appeals to an international audience, there is a stronger case for introducing product or market management structures to which foreign managers are answerable.

14.9 Refining the marketing programme for foreign markets

A crucial task of foreign marketing management is the design of a marketing programme which is sensitive to local needs. The following sections examine the extent to which adaptation of the marketing mix to local needs is either desirable or possible. In particular, should a company seek to develop one globally uniform service offer, or make it different in each of the foreign markets which it serves?

The process of globalizing a service offer can be quite different than is the case with tangible goods, on account of the greater variability of services. In addition to being highly variable, services can be extremely flexible – they are more likely than goods to be designed around the specific requirements of small groups of consumers using a basically common formula. Whether service firms choose to standardize their products globally or to adapt them to the needs of local markets is dependent on the nature of the services they offer. Some fast-food restaurants have, for example, adapted their menus, architectural designs and staff training methods to suit local needs, while retaining a common process formula worldwide. Services can often enjoy the best of both worlds, retaining their competitive advantage by remaining true to their basic managerial approach, while changing their product to meet local needs.

One approach to globalizing services is the process of 'industrializing' the service through the replacement of people with machines and through a systems approach to management. Levitt (1976) found an explanation of the worldwide success of McDonald's restaurants in the 'same systematic modes of analysis, design, organization and control that are commonplace in manufacturing'. This process has occurred not just within the restaurant sector, but also in the construction, hotel, professional and technical service sectors. Standardization is often accompanied by a high degree of centralization, sometimes creating further management problems when local managers are instructed to sacrifice their local autonomy in order to benefit the organization globally.

14.9.1 **Product and promotion decisions**

At the heart of international marketing mix strategy are product and promotion decisions. Five generic strategies can be identified, based on the extent to which the configuration of the service offer and the promotional effort differ from a global norm.

1. Maintain a uniform product and promotion worldwide

This approach effectively develops a global marketing strategy as though the world was a single entity. The benefits of this approach are numerous. Customers travelling from one market to another can immediately recognize a service provider and the values which its global brand stands for. If, on the other hand, the service formulation was different in a foreign market, a traveller visiting a foreign outlet may come away confused about the qualities of the brand. As an example, a car rental company with an established position in its home market as the operator of a very modern fleet of cars, could harm its domestic image if it pursued a strategy of operating older cars in a foreign market. Standardization of the service offer can also yield benefits of economies of scale which include economies in market research and the design of buildings and uniforms, etc., although the greater adaptability of services often renders these benefits less than in the case of manufactured goods. The use of a common brand name in foreign markets for either the service provider or for specific services also benefits from economies of scale. Travellers to foreign markets will already be familiar with the brand's values as a result of promotion in the domestic market. However, care must be taken in selecting a brand name which will have no unfortunate connotations in foreign markets – the 'Big Mac' for example, translates in French as 'the big pimp'. There can also be problems where legislation prevents an international slogan being used. In Quebec, for example, companies have been fined for using standard Anglicized advertising material without changing it to French as required by the province's legislation.

In the case of transport services which operate between different markets, it may not be feasible to adapt the service offering to each of the local markets served, and either a compromise must be reached or the needs of the most important market given precedence. Airlines flying between two countries may find the pricing of in-flight services, the decor of the aircraft and catering having to satisfy very different market needs at either end of the route.

2. Retain a uniform service formulation, but adapt promotion

This strategy produces an essentially uniform global service, but adapts promotional effort to meet the sensitivities of local markets. The manner in which brand values are communicated in advertisements is a reflection of the cultural values of a society. For this reason, an airline may use a straightforward, brash hard-sell approach in its American market, a humorous approach in its British market and a seductive approach in its French market, even though the service offer is identical in each market. Similarly, certain objects and symbols used to promote a service might have the opposite effect to that which might be expected at home. Animals, which are often used in Britain to promote a range of home-based goods and services, present a caring and comfortable image, but in some markets such as Japan, animals are seen as unclean, disgusting objects.

3. Adapt the service offering only

This may be done in order to meet specific local needs or legislation, while retaining the benefits of a global image. For this reason, a car rental company may offer a range of predominantly compact cars in areas where average journeys are short (e.g. the Channel Islands), while offering jeeps and vans in areas such as the United States where motoring costs are lower and distances generally much greater.

4. Adapt both product and promotion

In practice, a combination of slight service and promotion modification is needed in order to meet both differing local needs and differences in local sensitivity to advertising.

5. Develop new services

Markets may emerge overseas for which a domestic company has no product offering that can easily be adapted. In the field of financial services, the absence in some foreign countries of state provision for certain key welfare services may create a market for

---

Ireland rocks

How do you promote the image of a tourist destination in foreign markets? The destination itself cannot be adapted to suit the needs of individual markets. The Tower of London will always be the same for tourists whether they are from Manchester, Madras or Melbourne. But the promotional message can be fine-tuned to stress the aspects on which different markets place high value. Take the case of the Brand Ireland campaign, a joint effort by the Northern Ireland Tourist Board and Bord Failte to increase the number of visitors to Ireland, north and south. Several hours of footage was filmed featuring tourist attractions around Ireland. This was reduced to a series of 15- and 30-second television commercials, but a different cut was made for each of the major markets targeted by the campaign. The German cut stressed the wild, rugged nature of the country, the Italian cut stressed the romance of the island, the American cut stressed Ireland's history, and the English cut stressed that Ireland is so close, but so different. The strap-line 'Live a different life' worked well in most markets, but had to be changed in the USA after focus groups identified unfortunate associations with cross-dressing.

> ### 'Less is more'
>
> How does a large American hotel chain adapt its service offer to the Japanese market? Hotels operated by Hilton International in the USA have bedrooms which, to many visitors from overseas, are surprisingly large. But what would an American think of a typical Japanese hotel? Land prices in America are generally fairly low outside of the main metropolitan areas, hence the relatively spacious facilities offered. But in Japan, space is at a premium and has given rise to all sorts of miniaturized hotel formats, aimed at keeping prices at an affordable level. How could Hilton International remain affordable yet retain its generic brand values? Following extensive research, the company developed a hotel format which was appropriate to the Japanese market. To avoid the problem of visitors from America being shocked by the relatively cramped hotels, Hilton International developed and applied a separate brand format 'Wa No Kutsurogi', providing comfort and service the Japanese way.

insurance-related products (e.g. dental health insurance cover) which is largely absent in the domestic UK market where the welfare state is relatively comprehensive. Similarly, the social and economic structure of a country can result in quite different products being required. For example, the pattern of property ownership in Malaysia has given rise to a novel two-generation property mortgage not generally found in west European markets.

14.9.2 Pricing decisions

The issue of whether to globalize or localize the service offer arises again in respect of pricing decisions. On the one hand, it might be attractive for an organization to be able to offer a standard charge for a service regardless of where in the world the service is consumed – consumers will immediately have an idea of how much a service will cost and this helps to develop a long-term relationship between client and company. However, the reality is that a variety of factors cause global service operators to charge different prices in the different markets in which they operate. There is usually no reason to assume that the pricing policies adopted in the domestic market will prove to be equally effective in a foreign market. Furthermore, for those overseas-produced services which are consumed mainly by the local population, it may be of no great importance that comparability between different markets is maintained.

There are a number of factors which affect price decisions overseas, as detailed below.

- Competitive pressure varies between markets, reflecting the stage of market development that a service has reached and the impact of regulations against anti-competitive practices.

- The cost of producing a service may be significantly different in foreign markets. For services which use labour-intensive production methods, variations in wage levels between countries will have a significant effect on total costs. Personnel costs may also be affected by differences in welfare provision which employers are required to pay for. Other significant cost elements which often vary between markets include the level of property prices or rental costs – the cost of acquiring space for a service outlet in Britain, for example, is usually significantly more than in southern or eastern Europe.

- Taxes vary between different markets – for example, the rate of value added tax (or its equivalent sales tax) can be as high as 38% in Italy compared to 17½% in the UK. There are also differences between markets in the manner in which sales taxes are expressed – in many markets, these are fully incorporated into price schedules, although on other occasions (such as in the USA) it is more usual to price a service exclusive of taxes.

- Local customs influence buyers' expectations of the way in which they are charged for a service. While customers in the domestic market might expect to pay for bundles of services, in a foreign market consumers might expect to pay a separate price for each component of the bundle, or vice versa. Also, in some countries, it is customary to expect customers to pay a tip to the front-line person providing a service, whereas other cultures expect to pay an all-inclusive price without the need to subsequently add a tip. Formal price lists for a service may be expected in some markets, but in others, the prevalence of bartering may put an operator which sticks to a fixed price list at a competitive disadvantage.

- Government regulations can limit price freedom in foreign markets. In addition to controls over prices charged by public utilities, many governments require 'fair' prices to be charged in a wide range of services – e.g. tourism-related services – and for the prices charged to be clearly publicized.

- The price charged for a service can reflect the stage of development in a market. For a category of service which is already established in a foreign market, a newcomer might only be able to gain market share by offering significant price incentives. In the early stages, discounting may have to be used to establish trial of the service until the brand is sufficiently strongly established that the company can charge a premium price. As an example of this, international airlines often charge premium prices at the domestic end of a route (where their brand is well known), compared to the overseas end (where the brand is relatively unknown).

Service organizations are generally much better able to sustain discriminatory pricing policies between countries compared to exporters of manufactured goods. If wide differences in the pre-tax price of goods emerge between countries, it is open to entrepreneurs to buy goods in the lower priced market and sell them in the higher priced market (evidenced by the large volumes of cigarettes and alcohol which are imported from the low-price French market to the high-price UK market). The inseparability of production and consumption generally prevents this happening with services – a low-priced hotel room cannot be taken from the relatively cheap Spanish market and offered for sale in the London market.

14.9.3 **Accessibility decisions**

Where a service organization is launching a service into a new foreign market, intermediaries can have a vital role in making the service available to consumers. The selection of intermediaries to facilitate the introduction of a service to a new foreign market is considered in more detail below. Consideration is given briefly here to the place and manner in which a service will be made available.

The analysis of location decisions presented in Chapter 9 can be applied equally to foreign markets. However, a service provider must avoid assuming that a locational strategy that has worked in one market will work just as effectively in a foreign market. A revised strategy may be required on account of differences in the geography of the foreign market, differences in consumer expectations, differences in current methods of making that type of service available and differences in legislative constraints.

- Geographical differences can be important where land use patterns differ greatly in the target foreign market. As an example, the extensive nature of many urban areas within the USA results in there being a series of suburban commercial areas rather than a clearly defined central business district. A European retail bank with a city-centre service format which had worked well in its domestic market may only be able to succeed by developing out-of-town formats of its branches for a proposed expansion in the USA.

- Consumer behaviour may differ significantly in foreign markets. What is a widely accepted outlet in one country may be regarded with suspicion in another. The idea of taking refreshments in a snack bar located within a bookshop may appear quite ordinary within the UK, but may encounter resistance in more traditional markets. Also, the extensiveness of outlet networks will be influenced by customers' expectations about ease of access, for example in relation to the availability of car-parking facilities or the distance that they are prepared to travel.

- Differences in the social, economic and technical environments of a market can be manifested in the existence of different patterns of intermediaries. As an example, the interrelatedness of wholesalers and retailers in Japan can make it much more difficult for a foreign retailer to get into that market compared to other foreign opportunities. In some markets, there may be no direct equivalent of a type of intermediary found in the domestic market – estate agents on the UK model are often not found in many markets where the work of transferring property is handled entirely by a solicitor. The technological environment can also affect accessibility decisions – the relatively limited and unreliable postal and telecommunications services of many less developed countries makes direct availability of services to consumers relatively difficult.

■ What is a legal method of distributing a service in the domestic market may be against the law of a foreign country. Countries may restrict the sale of financial services, holidays and gambling services – among others – to a much narrower set of possible intermediaries than is the case in the domestic market.

14.9.4 People decisions

It has already been noted that the people element of the marketing mix is more important for services than for goods, therefore it is important that this element is appropriately formulated for a foreign market. Where overseas service delivery involves direct producer–consumer interaction, a decision must be made on whether to employ local or expatriate staff. The latter may be preferable where a service is highly specialized and may be useful in adding to the global uniformity of the service offering. In some circumstances, the presence of front-line expatriate serving staff can add to the appeal of a service, for example a chain of traditional Irish pubs established in mainland Europe may add to their appeal by employing authentic Irish staff.

For relatively straightforward services, a large proportion of staff would be recruited locally, leaving just senior management posts filled by expatriates. Sometimes, an extensive staff development programme may be required to ensure that locally recruited staff perform in a manner which is consistent with the company's global image. This can in some circumstances be quite a difficult task – a fast-food operator may have difficulty developing values of speed and efficiency among its staff in countries where the pace of life is relatively slow.

Where staff are recruited locally, employment legislation can affect the short- and long-term flexibility of service provision. This can affect the ease with which staff can be laid off or dismissed should demand fall – for example, in Germany, the Dismissals Protection Law (*Kundigungsschutzgesetz*) gives considerable protection to salaried staff who have been in their job for more than six months, allowing dismissal only for a 'socially justified' reason. There are also differences between countries in the extent to which an employer can prevent an employee with valuable trade secrets leaving their employment to work for a competitor. In Germany, a 'non-competition' clause can be expressly agreed for a maximum of two years after termination of employment, but only under a number of conditions.

14.10 Market entry strategies

A new foreign market represents both a potential opportunity and a risk to an organization. A company's **market entry strategy** should aim to balance these two elements. The least risky method of developing a foreign service market is to supply that market from a domestic base, something which can be a possibility in the case of separable service offerings. A wide variety of financial and information services can be provided to foreign markets by post or telephone, avoiding the cost and risk of setting up local service outlets.

Where inseparability of service production and consumption occurs and the producer must go to the consumer, local outlets must be established. Risk can be minimized by gradually committing more resources to a market, based on experience to date. Temporary facilities could be established which have low start-up and close-down costs, and where the principal physical and human assets can be transferred to another location. A good example of risk reduction through the use of temporary facilities is found in the pattern of retail development in eastern Germany following reunification. West German retailers who initially entered east Germany in large numbers were reluctant to commit themselves to building stores in specific locations in a part of the country which was still economically unstable and where patterns of land use were changing rapidly. The solution adopted by many retailers was to offer branches of their chain in temporary marquees or from mobile vehicles. These could move in response to the changing pattern of demand. While the location of retail outlets remained risky, this did not prevent retailers from establishing their networks of distribution warehouses which were considered to be more flexible in the manner in which they could respond to changing consumer spending patterns.

Market entry risk reduction strategies also have a time dimension. While there may be long-term benefits arising from being the first company to develop a new category of service in a foreign market, there are also risks. If development is hurried and launched before service quality can be guaranteed to live up to an organization's international standards, the company's long-term image can be damaged, both in the new foreign market and in its wider world market. In the turbulent marketing environment of eastern Europe in the late 1980s, two of the world's principal fast-food retailers – McDonald's and Burger King – pursued quite different strategies. The former waited until political, economic, social and technological conditions were capable of allowing it to launch a restaurant which met its global standards. In the case of Burger King, its desire to be first in the market led it to offer a very substandard service giving it an image from which it subsequently struggled to recover.

Where the inseparability of a service offer makes it impossible for an organization to supply the service to a foreign market from its home base, an assessment of risk is required in deciding whether an organization should enter a foreign market on its own or in association with another organization. The former maximizes the strategic and operational control which the organization has over its foreign operations, but it exposes it to the greatest risk where the foreign market is relatively poorly understood. A range of entry possibilities are considered below.

14.10.1 Direct investment in foreign subsidiary

This option gives a service organization maximum control over its foreign operations, but can expose it to a high level of risk on account of the poor understanding it may have of the foreign market. A company can either set up its own foreign subsidiary from scratch (as many UK hotel companies have done to develop hotels in foreign markets), or it can acquire control of a company which is already trading (such as the acquisition by the German company Sixt of the UK Kenning vehicle rental business).

Where the nature of the service offer differs relatively little between national markets, or where it appeals to an international market (e.g. hotels), the risks from creating a new subsidiary are reduced. Where there are barriers to entry and the service is aimed at an essentially local market with a different culture to the domestic market, the acquisition of an established subsidiary may be the preferred course of action. Even the latter course of action is not risk free, as was illustrated by the problems encountered by the British bus operator Stagecoach following its acquisition of the US bus operator Coach USA, which it sold in 2004 for less than it had paid to acquire the company six years earlier. Stagecoach had failed to appreciate the difficulties of changing established employment practices, as it had successfully done in the UK, and consequently incurred heavy operating losses.

Direct investment in a foreign subsidiary may be made difficult by legislation restricting ownership of certain services by foreigners – civil aviation is an example where many countries prevent foreign companies owning a controlling interest in a domestic airline.

14.10.2 **Management contracting**

Rather than setting up its own service organization overseas, a company with a proven track record in a service area may pursue the option of running other companies' businesses for them. For a fee, a foreign organization which seeks to develop a new service would contract a team to set up and run the facility. In some cases, the intention may be that the management team should get the project started, and gradually hand over the running of the facility to a local management. This type of arrangement is useful for an expanding overseas organization where the required management and technical skills are difficult to obtain locally. In countries where the educational infrastructure offers less opportunity for management and technical training, a company (or in many cases, foreign governments) can buy in state-of-the-art management skills.

For the company supplying management skills under such contracts, the benefits are numerous. Risks are kept to a minimum as the company generally does not need to invest its own capital in the project. The company gathers overseas market knowledge which it may be able to use to its own advantage if it plans similar ventures of its own in other countries. For staff employed by the company, the challenge of working on an overseas project can offer career opportunities outside the mainstream domestic management route.

Management contracting has found many applications in the service sector. For UK companies, the demise of the British Empire resulted in most newly independent colonies seeking to establish their own service organizations, which they were ill-equipped to manage themselves. Most countries immediately set up their own airline, making use of management expertise bought in from BOAC – the forerunner of British Airways. More recently, economic development in eastern Europe resulted in many opportunities for UK-based service companies, including the management of hotels, airlines and educational establishments.

14.10.3 **Licensing/franchising**

While exporters of manufactured goods frequently license a foreign producer to manufacture and sell their products, a company developing a service overseas is more likely to establish a franchise relationship with its foreign producers. The inseparability of service offers makes service producers an integral part of a service, requiring greater control over the whole process by which an overseas business operates.

Franchising in a foreign market can take a number of forms. At one extreme, the organization seeking to develop overseas could enter into a direct franchising relationship with each individual franchisee. The problem with this approach is the difficulty in monitoring and controlling a possibly large number of franchisees in a country far from home. To alleviate some of these problems, the franchisor would normally establish its own subsidiary in the foreign territory which would negotiate and monitor franchisees locally or, alternatively, grant a master franchise for an area to a franchisee where the latter effectively becomes the franchisor in the foreign country. In between these options are a number of permutations of strategy – for example, a subsidiary could be set up as a **joint venture** with a local company in order to develop a franchise network.

As with the development of a domestic franchise service network, franchising can allow an organization to expand rapidly overseas with relatively low capital requirements. While a clearly defined business format and method of conducting business is critical to the success of a foreign franchise, things can still go wrong for a number of reasons. The service format could be poorly proven in the home market, making foreign expansion particularly difficult. Unrealistic expectations may be held about the amount of human and financial resources which need to be devoted to the operation of a foreign franchise. Problems in interpreting the spirit and letter of contractual agreements between the franchisor and franchiseer can result in acrimonious misunderstanding. These problems were evident in 1997 when the UK retailer The Body Shop decided to take back control of its French outlets from its French master franchisor, following the latter's alleged poor performance.

14.10.4 **Joint ventures**

An international joint venture is a partnership between a domestic company and a foreign company or government. Joint ventures can balance a company's desire for control with risk minimization and can be attractive in many situations.

■ A joint venture with an organization already based in the proposed foreign market makes the task of collecting information about the market, and responding to it sensitively, relatively easy.

■ A joint venture can spread risk where the initial capital requirement threshold is high.

■ Where foreign governments restrict the rights of foreign companies to set up business on their account, a partnership with a local company – possibly involving a minority shareholding – may be the only means of entering the market.

■ There may be significant barriers to entry which a company already based in the foreign market could help to overcome. A common barrier to entry is access to a comprehensive network of intermediaries.

■ There may be reluctance on the part of consumers to deal with what appears to be a foreign company. A joint venture can allow the operation to be fronted by a domestic producer with whom customers can be familiar, while allowing the foreign partner to provide capital and management expertise. As an example, the UK mortgage market is dominated by banks and building societies, largely selling their own mortgages, and a number of foreign banks have taken the view that their best market entry strategy would be to work in partnership with a smaller building society, providing them with funds and allowing them to sell the mortgages under their own name through their established network of branches.

■ Taxation of company profits may favour a joint venture rather than owning a foreign subsidiary outright.

A distinction can be made between equity and non-equity joint ventures. The former involve two or more organizations joining together to invest in a 'child' organization which has its own separate identity. A non-equity joint venture involves agreement between partners on such matters as marketing research, new service development, promotion and distribution, without any agreement to jointly provide capital for a new organization.

Joint ventures are an important feature of many service sectors where the benefits listed above can be achieved. They have assumed particular importance in the hotels, airline and financial service sectors – some recent examples in the latter are shown in Table 14.2.

Strategic alliances – whether or not involving joint equity – are becoming increasingly important within the services sector. These are agreements between two or more organizations where each partner seeks to add to its competencies by combining its resources with those of a partner. A strategic alliance generally involves co-operation between partners rather than joint ownership of a subsidiary set up for a specific purpose, although it may include agreement for collaborators to purchase shares in the businesses of other members of the alliance.

Strategic alliances can be very powerful within the service sector (Figure 14.5). They are frequently used to allow individual companies to build upon the relationship which they have developed with their clients by allowing them to sell on services which they do not produce themselves, but are produced by another member of the alliance. This arrangement is reciprocated between members of the alliance. Strategic

Table 14.2 **Examples of UK financial services organizations' involvement in foreign joint ventures**

Venture partners	% holding	Subsidiary/purpose
Equity joint ventures		
British Telecom	50%	Development of Telfort mobile telephone
NS Dutch Railways	50%	service in the Netherlands
Prudential	50%	Creation of Prudential Assicurazione to
Inholding (Italy)	50%	provide insurance services in Italy
GfK	40%	Creation of ORG-GfK Marketing Services,
ORG-Marg	60%	based in Bangalore, India, to monitor monthly retail sales in retail outlets for the consumer technology markets
International Power	20%	Operation of gas-powered electricity
Malakoff	80%	generation in Malaysia
Non-equity joint ventures		
Commercial Union		Agreement for CI to sell and distribute CU's
Credito Italiano (Italy)		life and non-life insurance policies in Italy
Hambros Merchant Bank		Co-operation agreement in cross-frontier
Bayerische Vereinsbank (West Germany)		merger and acquisition finance
Barclays Bank		Agreement gave Barclays Bank a banking
Tokyo Trust (Japan)		licence to operate in Japan to provide trust management and securities handling in collaboration with its partner

alliances have assumed great importance within the airline industry, where operators share their route networks through 'code-sharing', thereby increasing the range of origin–destination opportunities which can be provided with a through ticket.

International strategic alliances can involve a principal nominating a supplier in related service fields as a preferred supplier at its outlets worldwide. This strategy has been used by car rental companies to secure a tie-in with other transport principals, to offer what the latter see as a value-added service. An example is the agreement whereby Hertz Car Rental was appointed by British Airways as preferred supplier worldwide. Under the arrangement, passengers could reserve a Hertz car at the same time as their air ticket and, in some instances, Hertz guaranteed that a car would be waiting for passengers at their destination airport even if no prior reservation had been made. Hertz gained additional custom for its car rental business, while British Airways was able to add value to its service offer.

Figure 14.5 With the globalization of markets, strategic alliances are becoming increasingly important as a means of gaining competitive advantage. In the airline sector, an alliance such as the One World alliance allows one airline's services to be marketed by all other alliance members. For customers, British Airways is able to offer 'seamless' travel around the globe on services of fellow alliance members. For the company, there are opportunities to rationalize its operations in foreign countries. However, although global airline alliances are highly visible, it should not be forgotten that the fastest-growing sector of civil aviation in recent years has been based on a low-cost, 'no-frills' model, in which membership of a strategic alliance is seen as a costly burden, rather than a benefit which adds to competitive advantage. (Reproduced with permission of the One World alliance)

14.10.5 **Global e-commerce**

The development of the Internet has offered new opportunities for the providers of services which are essentially intangible and which can overcome the problems of inseparability. At the business-to-business level, a lot of backroom service processing, such as invoicing, data entry and software development can now be carried out in parts of the world where there is a plentiful supply of low-cost, skilled workers and the results sent back to the customer by a data link (see case study). At the consumer level, many service providers now promote themselves to global audiences through the Internet. A consumer in the UK, for example, could find a hotel in Australia and book a room online without the hotel needing to use an intermediary. The costs to service providers of reaching global audiences in this way can be low.

The service sector has been at the leading edge of developments in electronic commerce, helped by the fact that there is often very little, if any, tangible content which must physically be delivered to the customer. Travel-related services and financial services have seen major developments in electronic commerce. However, the limitations of the Internet in gaining access to foreign markets should be recognized. For many private consumers, purchasing through the Internet is perceived as being very risky, and this riskiness is likely to increase when the supplier is based overseas. In the case of Internet banking services offered in the UK from overseas, customers may find themselves not protected by legislation which protects customers of UK-based banks. Some service providers are careful about how they make their services available globally through the Internet in order to preserve price discrimination. It will be recalled that providers of inseparable services are able to charge different groups different prices, without the fear of a low price segment selling on the service to high price segments. For this reason, airlines often restrict sales of tickets through the Internet to local national markets, to prevent customers buying in the cheapest global market.

Finally, it should be remembered that the Internet is becoming increasingly cluttered with websites and it is not sufficient for a service 'exporter' simply to have a website. One of the biggest challenges is to get a potential customer to a company's site. In the case of many consumer services, the only sensible solution may be to pay one of the many information intermediaries who act as a cyber-exchange between often geographically separated buyers and sellers. Online service intermediaries such as expedia.com and ebookers.com have become important service sectors in their own right. For many service companies entering a foreign market, it may be safer and more cost-effective to work through these, rather than acting alone. The Internet is undoubtedly offering new opportunities for service firms to enter foreign markets, but basic rules of foreign market entry still apply and many of the successful uses of global e-commerce have involved more traditional approaches based on joint ventures and strategic alliances.

Case study

Call centres and data create hope for new service economy in less developed countries

Dial an 0800 customer helpline in the UK and your call may be answered not in Bradford or Birmingham, but quite likely in Banagalore or Bombay. Operating call centres on behalf of western clients has become big business for many suppliers based in less developed countries. In September 2004, over 250 call centre providers from around the world exhibited at Call Centre Expo to try to sell their services. Such an international service sector would have been almost unthinkable only 20 years ago.

Handling customer services enquiries and data emerged as a new international service sector in the 1990s. At first, organizations of all kinds found increasing need to enter information into computerized databases: records of customer sales, services performed, details of rolling stock movements, to name but a few. In the early days, most firms regarded this as a backroom function which they could perform most cost-effectively by using their own staff at their own premises. With time, an increasing volume of data to be processed and the growing sophistication of data analysis systems, many services companies emerged to take the burden of data processing off client companies.

At first, most data-processing companies operated close to their clients. However, by the late 1980s, large volumes of data began entering international trade to be processed by companies in foreign countries where costs were lower, working regulations more relaxed and trades unions often non-existent. An important factor accounting for this development in international trade was the rapid pace of technological development. Processed data could now be transmitted back to a client company very quickly and cheaply using satellites or fibre-optic links.

Data processing has established a firm foothold as an exportable service in areas such as India, the Caribbean and the Philippines. Each of these countries is characterized by relatively low wage rates with skills which are at least as good as those of workers in more developed countries.

In the USA, the development of the Kansas-based Saztec company illustrates the way in which international trade can be developed. Saztec has won data-processing contracts from major organizations throughout the world, including a number of UK government departments, such as the Home Office and the Treasury. Yet these services are generally produced far away from either the company's or the client's base. The company employs over 800 people in the Philippines, who earn an average of £75 per month – much less than the salary paid to its staff in Kansas. Staff turnover at less than 1% is much lower than the 35% annual rate in Kansas. Furthermore, the company is able to obtain a higher quality of output by the military-style organization and control of its staff – something which would not be accepted in the USA.

The Philippines has become an important exporter of data-processing services by exploiting its comparative cost advantage in labour inputs – something that is useful in capturing high-volume, basic data input where accuracy and cost are paramount. Another country which has developed this service sector in a big way is Jamaica, which in addition to exploiting its low labour costs offers the advantages of a sophisticated infrastructure – such as satellite links – and generous tax incentives. Ireland, by contrast, has exploited the fact that it has a relatively highly educated and English-speaking workforce who have earned less than their counterparts would earn in the UK or the USA. A number of computer companies, such as AOL and Dell, have set up customer telephone support services in Ireland to handle customer enquiries. For a caller from the UK, only the accent may indicate that their call is being answered overseas.

The Philippines, like most developing countries, has a long way to go before it becomes a predominantly service-based – rather than an agricultural- or manufacturing-based – economy. In the case of data processing, new communications technologies have allowed production to take place in a totally different location to the customer, thereby overcoming the problem of inseparability. The continuing fall in telecommunication costs has led to call centres located several thousands of miles away from a client becoming a financially attractive proposition. There are clearly limits on developing countries' abilities to export services, but marketers in these countries will be looking for new opportunities to separate production and consumption and export the benefits to relatively wealthy western clients. Meanwhile, the development of these countries' domestic economies will doubtless lead to growing demand for producer services from the growing business sector and for consumer services from the emerging middle classes.

Case study review questions

1. Why has data processing emerged as a major new service industry in world trade?
2. What are the advantages and disadvantages to a western European-based insurance company of outsourcing its call centre operation to a supplier in India?
3. What are the advantages to the Philippines economy of developing its data-processing industry? Are there any disadvantages?

Chapter summary and links to other chapters

This chapter has highlighted the increasingly competitive and global nature of services markets. The inseparable nature of services is reflected in quite different challenges for the development of foreign markets, compared to goods. Very often, a service organization can only develop an overseas market by locating there. Understanding a foreign market is crucial and firms have available to them a variety of techniques for assessing the cultural, economic and political acceptability of a service in a foreign market. Sensitive adaptation of a service formula is crucial to success and many services which have been successful at home have failed because of false assumptions about the needs of a proposed foreign market. The involvement of a joint venture partner can lessen the risk of entering an unknown market, but this has to be balanced against a loss of control.

All of the principles of services marketing which have been discussed in previous chapters in the context of the domestic market apply also to foreign markets. However, their application may differ. So the nature of the service offer and the processes involved in service encounters may need to be adapted (**Chapters 2 and 3**). Buyers may evaluate a service offer quite differently and be more or less amenable to the concept of relationship marketing (**Chapters 4 and 5**). Managing people in foreign operations can be quite different, and can inhibit the development of universal brands and standards of service (**Chapters 7 and 12**). Issues of accessibility, pricing and promotion need to be sensitively managed (**Chapters 9, 10 and 11**). Management processes and structures face new strains when stretched to foreign markets, and information for planning and control purposes becomes more difficult to obtain, analyse and disseminate (**Chapters 6, 12 and 13**).

Chapter review questions

1. Examine the reasons why a UK-based general insurance company should seek to expand into continental Europe.

2. What cultural differences might cause problems for a hotel chain developing a location in India?

3. How might a bank go about researching market potential for business development loans in a foreign country?

4. In what circumstances is a global, rather than a localized marketing strategy likely to be successful?

5. Suggest methods by which a firm of consulting engineers can minimize the risk of proposed foreign expansion.

6. What is meant by a strategic alliance and why are these of importance to the service sector? Give examples of strategic alliances.

Activity

Choose two or three international service providers from the following sectors: hotels, airlines, fast food, car rental, accountancy. Go to their websites and click through to a selection of their national sites in countries with a different socio-economic profile to your own. Analyse what is common between the service offer and the promotional messages between the different countries in which the company operates. Then try to identify ways in which the service offer has been adapted to meet local conditions.

Key terms

E-commerce Trading activities which are facilitated by computer-mediated exchange.

Joint venture Two or more organizations join together to exploit their respective strengths and develop new product or market opportunities.

Management contracting Selling an organization's management expertise to manage another organization's facility on its behalf.

Market entry strategy A plan by which an organization seeks to enter and establish itself in a new market.

Portfolio management Managing a range of services to ensure long-term stable profitability.

Selected further reading

The following texts offer a general review of the factors that influence firms' foreign expansion decisions.

Czinkota, M. and Ronkainen, I.A. (2003) *International Marketing*, 7th edn, South Western.

Doole, I. (2001) *International Marketing Strategy: Analysis, Development and Implementation*, Thomson Learning.

Keegan, W.J. and Green, M.C. (2001) *Global Marketing Management*, 7th edn, Prentice Hall, NJ.

There is a growing body of literature which specifically relates to services organizations' foreign market entry decisions.

Javalgi, R.G. and White, S.D. (2002) 'Strategic challenges for the marketing of services internationally', *International Marketing Review*, 19 (6), 563–81.

Burt, S.L., Dawson, J.A. and Sparks, L. (2003) *Failure in International Retailing: Research Propositions,* Institute of Retail Studies, University of Stirling, UK.

Mellahi, K., Jackson, T.P. and Sparks, L. (2002) 'An exploratory study into failure of successful organizations: The case of Marks & Spencer', *British Journal of Management*, 13, 15–19.

Cicic, M., Patterson, P.G. and Shoham, A, (1999) 'A conceptual model of the international-ization of service firms', *Journal of Global Marketing*, 12 (3), 81–106.

Kanso, A. and Kitchen, P.J. (2004) 'Marketing consumer services internationally: Localization and standardization revisited', *Marketing Intelligence and Planning*, 22 (2), 201–15.

Erramilli, M.K. and Rao, C.P. (1993) 'Service firms' international entry-mode choice: A modified transactional cost analysis approach', *Journal of Marketing*, 57 (July), 19–38.

For a general overview of trends in international business, consult the following texts.

Overseas Trade, a DTI–FCO magazine for exporters published 10 times per year by Brass Tacks Publishing Co., London.

World Trade Organization, Annual Report, published annually.

Trade Policy Review (serial).

Economic Trends, a monthly publication of the UK Office for National Statistics which includes statistics relating to international trade performance.

Overseas Direct Investment, detailed breakdown of UK overseas direct investment activity, outward and inward, by component, country and industry (Office for National Statistics).

References

Business Times (2002) 'More local banks now offer Islamic products, services', *Business Times* (February), 12.

Cicic, M., Patterson, P.G. and Shoham, A. (1999) 'A conceptual model of the international-ization of service firms', *Journal of Global Marketing*, 12 (3), 81–106.

Economist (2001) 'The new demographics', 361 (8246), Special Section, 5–8.

Klein, N. (2000) *No Logo*, Flamingo.

Levitt, T. (1976) 'Addendum on marketing and the post-industrial society', *The Public Interest*, 44 (Summer), 69–103.

15

Case study: CD Marketing Services

Business background

Some 50 years ago, few people would have imagined that large amounts of consumer profile data would be bought and sold by companies. But today the collection, analysis and dissemination of marketing information have led to the emergence of a whole new service sector. Service organizations have been both major consumers of information services and producers of ever more sophisticated services. Information has become increasingly crucial to firms in their attempts to target new customers and to track existing ones. Information technology and firms' desire to target customers individually rather than en masse has given rise to new opportunities for service suppliers. A seemingly bewildering array of organizations have developed a previously unimaginable range of information services which help client companies to get their message to customers more cost-effectively than their competitors.

One company that has ridden the crest of the information wave is Circular Distributors Ltd. It has been in business for over half a century as a supplier of targeted messages, acting on behalf of numerous goods and services suppliers. Like most companies in the service sector, it has found its marketing environment changing at an increasingly rapid rate. The company has been deeply affected by technological developments which affect the way it operates, the expectations of its customers, and the activities of its competitors. An analysis of its recent marketing activities shows how service organizations must constantly monitor their marketing environment and respond to change.

The company is essentially in the business of supplying direct marketing services. As a proportion of all firms' promotional expenditure, direct marketing has been increasing its share, giving rise to exciting opportunities for companies who had developed a sound knowledge of techniques for dealing with customers on a one-to-one basis. Some indication of the shift in promotional expenditure is shown in Figure 15.1. When the direct mail component of this expenditure is examined more closely, it is evident that the business-to-consumer element has been expanding more rapidly than the business-to-business element (Figure 15.2).

Circular Distributors was founded as a very low-tech distributor of leaflets from door to door. One of its early achievements was to deliver 10 million free samples of soap for Lever Brothers in the first-ever door-to-door distribution of its kind. From a scattergun approach to distribution, the company had gradually refined its techniques to deliver promotional leaflets and sample offers of products that typically included shampoo, tea bags and soap. Some 50 years ago, many manufacturers of fast-moving consumer goods (fmcg) would have been more than happy with the company's approach, which by today's standards would be considered quite simplistic. It was essentially putting a fairly generic product into the hands of a fairly homogeneous market to encourage trial, and hopefully a subsequent purchase. Over time, markets have become more fragmented, as distinctive lifestyle groups have emerged. In response to this, companies have sought to differentiate their products to appeal to ever smaller niche segments. The fairly generic, low value-added service that Circular Distributors was selling had become too blunt an instrument for fmcg companies, who now had an exciting range of value-added marketing services available to them

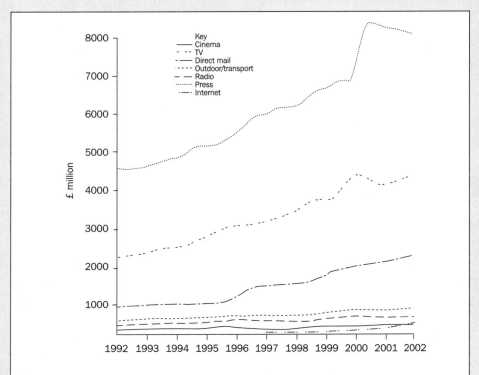

Figure 15.1 Advertising expenditure by medium (adapted from Advertising Association data)

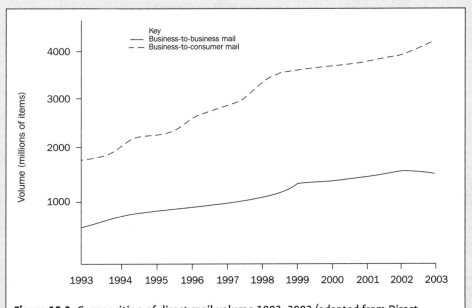

Figure 15.2 Composition of direct mail volume 1993–2003 (adapted from Direct Marketing Information Service (www.dmis.co.uk) data)

to target customers more cost-effectively. Nevertheless, door-to-door distribution remained big business and in 2002 the Direct Marketing Association estimated that over 8 billion items were delivered through consumers' letterboxes – an average of 304 items per household. Of that total, a substantial 31% consisted of unaddressed material, the result of door-drop marketing. Total turnover of the industry in the UK was estimated at over £576 million.

Management buyout

Circular Distributors' management team, headed by Nick Wells and three fellow directors had taken control of the company in 1991 in a £1.1 million management buyout. An important part of the new management's business development plan during the 1990s was to concentrate on services that were able to target smaller groups of consumers. Groups who were at transition points in their lives represented particularly promising opportunities, because such groups were likely to be very receptive to messages about types of purchase which were still new to them. Mothers-to-be – who faced many new types of purchase decision – were seen as a very promising target for the company's strategy. An important part of its strategy was subsequently based on a publication called *Emma's Diary*, launched in 1992 and produced in association with the Royal College of General Practitioners. The 132-page booklet is a week-by-week guide to pregnancy and is given out by GPs and midwives to women when their pregnancy is confirmed. The company's research has claimed that it is read by 78% of expectant mothers and 81% of first-time mothers-to-be. This gives *Emma's Diary* higher readership than all of the competing 13 parenting magazines combined.

Advertising in the bi-annual publication by producers of baby-related products has accounted for almost a third of *Emma's Diary*'s revenue. A further third of revenue comes from companies paying for the distribution of product samples in the mother's gift pack, which is distributed free to readers through selected shops. The mother's gift pack is an effective marketing medium, collected in 1999 by 400 000 of the total of 720 000 expectant mothers. The remaining one-third of revenue comes from sales of consumer information, which is gathered when expectant mothers register to qualify for the mother's pack.

Slow rate of growth

By 1999 the company appeared to be moving along at a very pedestrian pace. In the information age, too much of its energies still appeared to be directed at stuffing envelopes, and too little to the collection, analysis and sale of marketing information. The third of revenue for *Emma's Diary* which came from data sales had highlighted the possibilities for the company, but it seemed to be moving at a much slower pace than other companies such as Claritis and Experian, who were growing rapidly through the sale of consumer information. In June 1999 *The Sunday Times* ran an article on the company and the expert commentators consulted were not over-impressed. Ray Perry of the Chartered Institute of Marketing described Circular Distributors as 'a flat and stagnant company' that needed 'a new lease of life and a new identity'. John Eggleston of KPMG said its managers 'need to take action quickly, accept that growth demands some risk and develop firm and practical plans' to seize opportunities for growth.

Managers were criticized for focusing too much on internal issues and lacking the drive to respond to market changes. The article concluded:

If Circular Distributors is to maintain its profits, it needs to provide door-to-door services of a higher value. It must change its image from a letterbox-stuffing operation to a distributor of marketing materials and services. Ultimately it may need to change its name to attract the right clients.

The criticism implicit in the *Sunday Times* article goaded the company into a more adventurous approach to its business. For a start, the company changed its name from Circular Distributors to CD Marketing Services and developed Lifecycle Marketing as a brand in its own right to distinguish it from the relatively low-value letterbox distribution service. The Circular Distributors name was retained for the door-to-door distribution service. This part of the business was still very large and in 1999 delivered a total of more than one and a half billion items throughout the UK. However, within its portfolio of services, the sale of consumer information may have been the star or growth service, but door-to-door distribution was in danger of going from being a cash cow to a dog.

New technology

During 1999 the company invested heavily in new technologies aimed at giving it a competitive advantage in the growing field of data analysis. The immediate effect of this investment was to reduce profits by about £400 000, but this expenditure within two years contributed to an increase in annual sales to £33 million and profits to £2.4 million in 2002. CD invested heavily in developing more sophisticated services than stuffing promotional material and product samples through letterboxes.

Among the new services developed by CD were CD Microtargeting, which can pinpoint precisely where a target market lives in units of just 700 households; CD Newshare offering high-speed 'with-newspaper' distribution, providing delivery within just three days – CD itself delivered over 3 million free newspapers itself each week; and the Solus scheme to undertake targeted door-to-door mailshots. Virgin Holidays used the Solus scheme in 2002 to deliver more than half a million leaflets personalized by shop name to the catchment areas of Co-op Travel and Travelcare stores, which offer Virgin Holidays. The door-drop activity ran alongside an integrated media campaign including, radio, new media and point of sale.

In developing these more specifically targeted products, the company had subtly changed its core business. The emphasis was now as much on collecting information about consumers as on distributing product samples.

With regard to *Emma's Diary*, the focus of the company's service offer had shifted from distribution to information management. By 1999 CD already had a database of 3.5 million families. It was now collecting data on 600 000 families each year, with 100 000 being 'cleansed' to remove those that changed address. The aim was to build Britain's largest database of families with young children.

What was the nature of the service being offered by the company's Lifecycle Marketing division? Segmented lists of consumers created by the company could be rented by organizations for one-off use. The company also sold licences by which other organizations could include CD's data in their own databases. As a further service, CD offered its clients the chance to include specific questions in its publications, for which the client would have exclusive rights to use the data generated. Given the growing difficulty of getting consumers to respond to questionnaires, and the high response rates achieved by CD's targeted publications, this service was highly valuable in its own right.

Refining the target markets

Who were the customers for CD's life-cycle information services? The two most important groups of customers were financial services and home-shopping businesses, which each accounted for about 30% of data sales. Remaining sales were spread between suppliers of baby products, children's book clubs and various other types of business. All of these clients were attracted by the fact that readers of the company's publications were going through some form of life change, such as becoming a parent or getting married, or having a child starting at school. Each of these life changes is typically associated with new spending priorities and in the absence of previous knowledge about these new types of purchase, mailshots may be particularly welcomed by individuals. Client companies particularly valued the high coverage of the target segments, and the low wastage rate within the lists.

In 1999, the company expected that within three years the revenue of its Lifecycle Marketing division would grow almost three-fold, generating sales of £3 million from the publications and gift packs and, more significantly, £4 million from information sales. This was a much faster growth rate than that of the core door-to door distribution business, which had continued to show modest growth. But did a dash into information services spell dangers as well as opportunities for the company?

The company knew the door-to-door business inside out and had carved a valuable niche for itself where it could offer unrivalled coverage, flexibility and economies of scale. But now that it was moving into the supply of information services it was competing on territory already staked out by much larger competitors. Companies such as Claritas and Experian had already built up massive databases of consumer information, not just on new mothers. They could also offer services in many of the overseas markets in which their clients operated. It was not good enough for CD to claim that it had superior knowledge of a small number of niche market segments, because its larger competitors had been steadily building up ever more sophisticated databases of consumer niches. The company saw a major problem in convincing clients to defect from its larger competitors to use its own information services.

Would CD always be seen as a low-value letterbox stuffer? Or could it use its long-standing relationships with many fmcg companies to add information services to its service offer? The company needed to build trust and confidence among clients that had never used its services or only perceived the company as a provider of lower-value door-to-door distribution.

At the same time, the company was aware that it should not lose sight of its core letterbox market, which was still profitable. A number of initiatives to raise the value of services offered to clients were attempted, for example offering a weekend distribution service. The company had previously only operated a weekday distribution service, but had identified that clients' messages could be more effective if they were delivered to a target customer on the day when they had most time to read it. New types of clients appeared for the door-to-door service, such as Internet Service Providers, who sought distribution of free CD-ROMs to targeted households. The company also extended its gift pack concept by delivering it door to door, without the need to collect it from a designated retail outlet. During 2000, a trial took place to distribute children's school packs door to door. Each pack consisted of a plastic bag containing a back-to-school calendar (carrying advertising messages), a CD-ROM from an Internet Service Provider, and samples of products aimed at children aged between 5 and 14. A response card sought to increase the volume of information that the company could sell on to its clients.

European expansion

CD also sought to expand into mainland Europe. It formed strategic alliances with a number of companies who were members of the European Letterbox Marketing Association, so that it was now able to offer its UK clients a 'one-stop shop' distribution service to 140 million homes in France, Germany, Spain and Italy. As evidence that it was taking European expansion seriously, it recruited three multi-lingual sales staff to handle European sales. By having the ability to offer Europe-wide distribution, the company hoped that it would be able to cater for clients such as L'Oréal, Kimberly-Clark and Gillette, which have pan-European marketing operations.

The company had moved into areas of expertise which were previously unknown to it, and thereby taken big risks. But in the rapidly changing market for information services, it could not afford to stand still. New methods of distributing information to target customers are appearing all the time, with recent examples being the Internet, digital television and WAP mobile phones. How widely should CD spread its resources? Which new media are worth investing in, and which ones may disappear as quickly as they appeared? Could it afford to become involved in marketing through new 'third generation' mobile phones? How far can the company's brand be stretched? There is a great danger that any investment in emerging media may be too little to be effective. It could simply end up having some representation with all media, but being effective in none. The company has made steps into the Internet by setting up a website for *Emma's Diary*, and has gained some information about visitors to the site. It has also earned revenue from 'click throughs' to advertisers on the site. But to be in this business seriously, the company needs to devote serious amounts of time and resources to it. With an ever increasing number of Internet Service Providers offering portals which seek users and advertisers, CD is just one of many minnows in a crowded marketplace.

Circular Distributors has moved from providing a low-value service in a slowly growing market to providing higher-value services in rapidly expanding markets. Although the information age has produced many opportunities, it has also produced many casualties among companies that have expanded too fast and failed to deliver a credible value proposition to their customers. During early 2000 'dotcom' fever appeared to reach a peak, with large amounts of money being poured into new ventures seeking to gain more information about consumers. Should CD have taken a bolder approach, or was caution more appropriate? And what about door-to-door distribution, the bread and butter of CD's business – shouldn't the company focus on what it knows best? For the future, one of the main problems facing the company is knowing just where the next threat from its business would come. What, for instance, would be the effect of third-generation mobile phones on consumer information services? Which new technologies should the company invest in? What new services should it seek to offer? Where does the traditional service of door-to-door distribution fit into its portfolio?

Sell-out

With so many calls on the company's investment capital, and the opportunities of continental Europe beckoning, it seemed that some form of alliance, beyond membership of the European Letterbox Marketing Association, was needed to ensure a prosperous future. After looking at a number of alternative strategies, the company agreed in 2001 to a take-over by TNT Post Group (TPG), which includes the Dutch Post Office (Royal PTT Post) and TNT. The deal, which gave TNT a 90% stake, would strengthen TNT's position in the UK market and formed part of the group's strategy to become the leading European supplier for mail-related services. TNT set about applying to the UK postal regulator Postcomm for an interim UK postal service licence, something which would have been very difficult for CD Marketing Services to achieve on its own.

Sources: based on Circular Distributors Ltd website (http://www.cdltd.co.uk) and http://www.Emmasdiary.co.uk; Direct Mail Information Service (http://www.dmis/keystats/html); *Sunday Times* Enterprise Network, 21 May 2000, (3), 17.

Case study review questions

1. What business is CD Marketing Services in? What business should it be in?

2. Draw a product/market expansion matrix identifying the growth options for CD Marketing Services. How would you assess the riskiness of each identified growth option?

3. On what bases can CD position itself relative to its competitors? What position would you recommend that it adopts? What do you consider to be the most important sources of sustainable competitive advantage for CD?

4. What methods should the company use to scan its environment for new opportunities/threats? How should they be assessed?

5. There is a view that information technology will increasingly allow CD's clients to do much of the data analysis that they currently buy in from CD themselves. In such a scenario, how can CD add value to its service offer?

6. Critically assess CD's opportunities for overseas expansion. What factors should influence the company's overseas expansion strategy?

Index of companies and brands

Index of authors cited

Index of subjects

561